2025年用

共通テスト 実戦模試

❶ 英語リーディング

Z会編集部 編

スマホで自動採点！ **学習診断サイトのご案内**

スマホでマークシートを撮影して自動採点。ライバルとの点数の比較や，学習アドバイスももらえる！　本書のオリジナル模試を解いて，下記 URL・二次元コードにアクセス！

Z会共通テスト学習診断　検索

https://service.zkai.co.jp/books/k-test/

二次元コード →

詳しくは別冊解説の目次ページへ

目次

本書の効果的な利用法

本書の特長

本書は，共通テストで高得点をあげるために，**過去からの出題形式と内容，最新の情報を徹底分析して作成した実戦模試である**。本番では，限られた時間内で解答する力が要求される。本書では時間配分を意識しながら，出題傾向に沿った良質の実戦模試に複数回取り組める。

■ 共通テスト攻略法 ―― 情報収集で万全の準備を

以下を参考にして，共通テストの内容・難易度をしっかり把握し，本番までのスケジュールを立て，余裕をもって本番に臨んでもらいたい。

データクリップ ➡ 共通テストの出題教科や 2024 年度本試の得点状況を収録。

傾向と対策 ➡ 過去の出題や最新情報を徹底分析し，来年度に向けての対策を解説。

■ 共通テスト実戦模試の利用法

1．本番に備える

本番を想定して取り組むことが大切である。時間配分を意識して取り組み，自分の実力を確認しよう。巻末のマークシートを活用して，記入の仕方もしっかり練習しておきたい。

2．令和７年（2025 年）度の試作問題も踏まえた「最新傾向」に備える

今回，実戦力を養成するためのオリジナル模試の中に，大学入試センターから公開されている令和７年度に向けた試作問題の内容を加味した類問を掲載している。詳細の解説も用意しているので，合わせて参考にしてもらいたい。

3．「今」勉強している全国の受験生と高め合う

『学習診断サイト（左ページの二次元コードから利用可能）』では，得点を登録すれば学習アドバイスがもらえるほか，**現在勉強中の全国の受験生が登録した得点と「リアル」に自分の点数を比較し切磋琢磨ができる**。全国に仲間がいることを励みに，モチベーションを高めながら試験に向けて準備を進めてほしい。

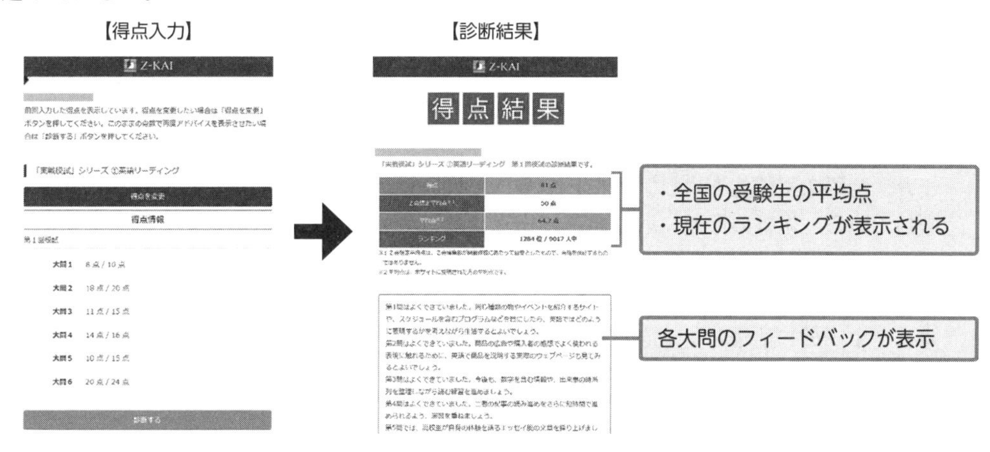

共通テストに向けて

■ 共通テストは決してやさしい試験ではない。

共通テストは，高校の教科書程度の内容を客観形式で問う試験である。科目によって，教科書等であまり見られないパターンの出題も見られるが，出題のほとんどは基本を問うものである。それでは，基本を問う試験だから共通テストはやさしい，といえるだろうか。

実際のところは，共通テストには，適切な対策をしておくべきいくつかの手ごわい点がある。まず，勉強するべき科目数が多い。国公立大学では共通テストで「6教科8科目」を必須とする大学・学部が主流なので，科目数の負担は決して軽くない。また，基本事項とはいっても，あらゆる分野から満遍なく出題される。これは，“山”を張るような短期間の学習では対処できないことを意味する。また，広範囲の出題分野全体を見通し，各分野の関連性を把握する必要もあるが，そうした視点が教科書の単元ごとの学習では容易に得られないのもやっかいである。さらに，制限時間内で多くの問題をこなさなければならない。しかもそれぞれが非常によく練られた良問だ。問題の設定や条件，出題意図を素早く読み解き，制限時間内に迅速に処理していく力が求められているのだ。こうした処理能力も，漫然とした学習では身につかない。

■ しかし，適切な対策をすれば，十分な結果を得られる試験でもある。

上記のように決してやさしいとはいえない共通テストではあるが，適切な対策をすれば結果を期待できる試験でもある。共通テスト対策は，できるだけ早い時期から始めるのが望ましい。長期間にわたって，**①教科書を中心に基本事項をもれなく押さえ，②共通テストの過去問で出題傾向を把握し，③出題形式・出題パターンを踏まえたオリジナル問題で実戦形式の演習を繰り返し行う**，という段階的な学習を少しずつ行っていけば，個別試験対策を本格化させる秋口からの学習にも無理がかからず，期待通りの成果をあげることができるだろう。

■ 本書を利用して，共通テストを突破しよう。

本書は主に上記③の段階での使用を想定して，Ｚ会のオリジナル問題を教科別に模試形式で収録している。巻末のマークシートを利用し，解答時間を意識して問題を解いてみよう。そしてポイントを押さえた解答･解説をじっくり読み，知識の定着･弱点分野の補強に役立ててほしい。早いスタートが肝心とはいえ，時間的な余裕がないのは明らかである。できるだけ無駄な学習を避けるためにも，学習効果の高い良質なオリジナル問題に取り組んで，徹底的に知識の定着と処理能力の増強に努めてもらいたい。

また，**全国の受験生を「リアルに」つなぎ，切磋琢磨を促す仕組みとして『学習診断サイト』も用意している**。本書の問題に取り組み，採点後にはその得点をシステムに登録し，全国の学生の中での順位を確認してみよう。そして同じ目標に向けて頑張る仲間たちを思い浮かべながら，受験をゴールまで走り抜ける原動力に変えてもらいたい。

本書を十二分に活用して，志望校合格を達成し，喜びの春を迎えることを願ってやまない。

Ｚ会編集部

共通テストの段階式対策

0. まずは教科書を中心に，基本事項をもれなく押さえる。

▼

1. さまざまな問題にあたり，上記の知識の定着をはかる。その中で，自分の弱点を把握する。

▼

2. 実戦形式の演習で，弱点を補強しながら，制限時間内に問題を処理する力を身につける。とくに，頻出事項や狙われやすいポイントについて重点的に学習する。

▼

3. 仕上げとして，予想問題に取り組む。

Z会の共通テスト関連教材

1.『ハイスコア！ 共通テスト攻略』シリーズ
オリジナル問題を解きながら，共通テストの狙われどころを集中して学習できる。

▼

2.『2025年用　共通テスト過去問英数国』
複数年の共通テストの過去問題に取り組み，出題の特徴をつかむ。

▼

3.『2025年用　共通テスト実戦模試』（本シリーズ）

▼

4.『2025年用　共通テスト予想問題パック』
本シリーズを終えて総仕上げを行うため，直前期に使用する本番形式の予想問題。

※『2025年用　共通テスト実戦模試』シリーズは，本番でどのような出題があっても対応できる力をつけられるように，最新年度および過去の共通テストも徹底分析し，さまざまなタイプの問題を掲載しています。そのため，『2024年用　共通テスト実戦模試』と掲載問題に一部重複があります。

共通テスト攻略法
データクリップ

1 出題教科・科目の出題方法

下の表の教科・科目で実施される。なお，受験教科・科目は各大学が個別に定めているため，各大学の要項にて確認が必要である。

※解答方法はすべてマーク式。以下の表は大学入試センター発表の『令和7年度大学入学者選抜に係る大学入学共通テスト出題教科・科目の出題方法等』を元に作成した。

※『　』は大学入学共通テストにおける出題科目を表し，「　」は高等学校学習指導要領上設定されている科目を表す。

教科	出題科目	出題方法（出題範囲，出題科目選択の方法等）	試験時間（配点）
国語	『国語』	・「現代の国語」及び「言語文化」を出題範囲とし，近代以降の文章及び古典（古文，漢文）を出題する。 分野別の大問数及び配点は，近代以降の文章が3問110点，古典が2問90点（古文・漢文各45点）とする。	90分（200点）
地理歴史 公民	『地理総合，地理探究』 『歴史総合，日本史探究』 『歴史総合，世界史探究』 『公共，倫理』 『公共，政治・経済』 →(b) 『地理総合／歴史総合／公共』 →(a) (a)：必履修科目を組み合わせた出題科目 (b)：必履修科目と選択科目を組み合わせた出題科目	・左記出題科目の6科目のうちから最大2科目を選択し，解答する。 ・(a)の『地理総合／歴史総合／公共』は，「地理総合」，「歴史総合」及び「公共」の3つを出題範囲とし，そのうち2つを選択解答する（配点は各50点）。 ・2科目を選択する場合、以下の組合せを選択することはできない。 (b)のうちから2科目を選択する場合 『公共，倫理』と『公共，政治・経済』の組合せを選択することはできない。 (b)のうちから1科目及び(a)を選択する場合 (b)については，(a)で選択解答するものと同一名称を含む科目を選択することはできない。	1科目選択 60分（100点） 2科目選択 130分 （うち解答時間120分） （200点）
数学①	『数学Ⅰ・数学A』 『数学Ⅰ』	・左記出題科目の2科目のうちから1科目を選択し，解答する。 ・「数学A」については，図形の性質，場合の数と確率の2項目に対応した出題とし，全てを解答する。	70分（100点）
数学②	『数学Ⅱ，数学B，数学C』	・「数学B」及び「数学C」については，数列（数学B），統計的な推測（数学B），ベクトル（数学C）及び平面上の曲線と複素数平面（数学C）の4項目に対応した出題とし，4項目のうち3項目の内容の問題を選択解答する。	70分（100点）
理科	『物理基礎／化学基礎／生物基礎／地学基礎』 『物理』『化学』『生物』『地学』	・左記出題科目の5科目のうちから最大2科目を選択し，解答する。 ・『物理基礎／化学基礎／生物基礎／地学基礎』は，「物理基礎」，「化学基礎」，「生物基礎」及び「地学基礎」の4つを出題範囲とし，そのうち2つを選択解答する（配点は各50点）。	1科目選択 60分（100点） 2科目選択 130分 （うち解答時間120分） （200点）
外国語	『英語』 『ドイツ語』『フランス語』 『中国語』『韓国語』	・左記出題科目の5科目のうちから1科目を選択し，解答する。 ・『英語』は「英語コミュニケーションⅠ」，「英語コミュニケーションⅡ」及び「論理・表現Ⅰ」を出題範囲とし，【リーディング】及び【リスニング】を出題する。受験者は，原則としてその両方を受験する。その他の科目については，『英語』に準じる出題範囲とし、【筆記】を出題する。 ・科目選択に当たり，『ドイツ語』，『フランス語』，『中国語』及び『韓国語』の問題冊子の配付を希望する場合は，出願時に申し出ること。	『英語』 【リーディング】 80分（100点） 【リスニング】 30分（100点） 『ドイツ語』『フランス語』『中国語』『韓国語』 【筆記】80分（200点）
情報	『情報Ⅰ』		60分（100点）

2 2024年度の得点状況

2024年度は，前年度に比べて，下記の平均点に★がついている科目が難化し，平均点が下がる結果となった。

特に英語リーディングは，前年より語数増や英文構成の複雑さも相まって，平均点が51.54点と，共通テスト開始以降では最低の結果となった。その他，数学と公民科目に平均点の低下傾向が見られた。また一部科目には，令和7年度共通テストに向けた試作問題で公開されている方向性に親和性のある出題も確認できた。なお，今年度については得点調整は行われなかった。

		本試験（1月13日・14日実施）		追試験（1月27日・28日実施）
教科名	科目名等	受験者数（人）	平均点（点）	受験者数（人）
国語（200点）	国語	433,173	116.50	1,106
地理歴史（100点）	世界史B	75,866	60.28	1,004（注1）
	日本史B	131,309	★56.27	
	地理B	136,948	65.74	
公民（100点）	現代社会	71,988	★55.94	
	倫理	18,199	★56.44	
	政治・経済	39,482	★44.35	
	倫理，政治・経済	43,839	61.26	
数学①（100点）	数学Ⅰ・数学A	339,152	★51.38	1,000（注1）
数学②（100点）	数学Ⅱ・数学B	312,255	★57.74	979（注1）
理科①（50点）	物理基礎	17,949	28.72	316
	化学基礎	92,894	★27.31	
	生物基礎	115,318	31.57	
	地学基礎	43,372	35.56	
理科②（100点）	物理	142,525	★62.97	672
	化学	180,779	54.77	
	生物	56,596	54.82	
	地学	1,792	56.62	
外国語（100点）	英語リーディング	449,328	★51.54	1,161
	英語リスニング	447,519	67.24	1,174

※2024年3月1日段階では，追試験の平均点が発表されていないため，上記の表では受験者数のみを示している。

（注1）国語，英語リーディング，英語リスニング以外では，科目ごとの追試験単独の受験者数は公表されていない。
このため，地理歴史，公民，数学①，数学②，理科①，理科②については，大学入試センターの発表どおり，教科ごとにまとめて提示しており，上記の表は載せていない科目も含まれた人数となっている。

共通テスト攻略法
傾向と対策

■2025年度の新課程でのテストについて

2022年11月の大学入試センター公表資料で，試作問題第A問・第B問が発表されています。

なお，試験時間と配点については，2023年6月の公表資料では，現行同様です。

●英語リーディング：　80分/100点

	試作問題　英語リーディング	
	第A問	第B問
配点	18点	12点
形式	情報の整理と意見論述の準備	文章の推敲

試作問題の詳しい解説は ☞ P. 10 へ

■過去3年間の出題内容

年度	大問		設問数	配点	本試・問題の概要
2024年度	第1問	A	2	4	語学学校のイベントの案内
		B	3	6	3つの観光ツアーの案内
	第2問	A	5	10	高校の戦略ゲームクラブへの勧誘チラシ
		B	5	10	留学生による旅行保険についてのレビュー
	第3問	A	2	6	フォトラリーのイベントに関するブログ記事
		B	3	9	南の島へのバーチャルツアーに関する学校新聞
	第4問		5	16	英語クラブ室の改善策について
	第5問		5	15	同級生3人が高校卒業後に再会するまでの物語
	第6問	A	4	12	時間の知覚
		B	5	12	トウガラシなどの香辛料が持つ特徴と人体への影響

※設問数は「問」の数でカウントしています。

年度	大問		設問数	配点	本試・問題の概要
2023年度	第1問	A	2	4	劇とミュージカルの案内
		B	3	6	夏の英語キャンプの案内
	第2問	A	5	10	新発売のシューズの広告
		B	5	10	効率的な時間の使い方の調査報告
	第3問	A	2	6	バックパックの詰め方と暖の工夫についてのニュースレター
		B	3	9	「アドベンチャー・ルーム」の創り方についてのブログ
	第4問		5	16	効果的な学習法についての2人の見解の記事
	第5問		5	15	卓球から得た教訓について高校生が書いた文章
	第6問	A	4	12	収集についての記事
		B	5	12	クマムシに関する論説文

※設問数は「問」の数でカウントしています。

年度	大問		設問数	配点	本試・問題の概要
2022年度	第1問	A	2	4	ブラジルの料理本
		B	3	6	キリンの赤ちゃんの名前コンテストの参加要項
	第2問	A	5	10	大学図書館の利用についてのお知らせ
		B	5	10	学校内新聞の記事
	第3問	A	2	6	日本文化体験イベントについてのブログ
		B	3	9	登山チャレンジについての雑誌記事
	第4問		5	16	家電購入のアドバイスについての大学新入生向けのブログ
	第5問		5	15	テレビ発明の特許を巡ってのFarnsworthの伝記
	第6問	A	4	12	朝型・夜型の生活スタイルについての記事
		B	3	12	プラスチックの分類とリサイクルについての記事

※設問数は「問」の数でカウントしています。

特記事項

・大問数・配点は2021年度以降，ほぼ同様です。
・難易度については2023年度に比べ，総語数が6300語近くまで200語弱増加したことと合わせて，平均点も過去最低だったため，難化したと言えます。
・今回，出題傾向や，形式の変更が見られましたが，これは新課程に対応する2025年度実施予定の共通テストに向けての変化とも考えられます。

2024年度の本試出題内容詳細

第1問A・B （解答目安時間：6分）

2023年度から大きな形式の変化はありません。

第2問A （解答目安時間：6分）

例年出題される事実と意見を分別する問題は，2023年度同様に「意見」を選ぶもの1問のみでした。また，本文で言及されていないものを選ぶ問題が新たに出題されました。

第2問B （解答目安時間：6分）

2023年度は本文が2つのエリアに明確に分かれていましたが，2024年度はエリア分けのない一続きの文章でした。

第3問A （解答目安時間：5分）

2023年度の設問は本文の直接的な記述から判断できるものだったのに対し，2024年度は本文の内容から推測し，応答の適切さを自分で判断する必要があるものでした。

第3問B （解答目安時間：5分）

2023年度と同様に，時系列に沿って選択肢を並べ換える問題が出題されました。ただし，昨年の選択肢は単なる出来事の記述だったのに対し，2024年度の選択肢はイベントに参加した生徒のコメント（感想）だったため，事実と意見を分別し，解答に必要な情報を的確に判断することが必要でした。

第4問 （解答目安時間：12分）

例年と同じく，2つの資料から情報を読み取る問題が出題されました。資料は，2023年度が記事2つだったのに対し，2024年度は記事とアンケート結果でした。客観的な記事と，主観的なアンケート結果を総合しながら解答する必要がありました。

第5問 （解答目安時間：14分）

物語文を読んでプレゼンテーション用のメモを完成させる問題で，設問形式は2023年度とほぼ同じであるものの，語数が増加しました。加えて，2024年度は3人の人物それぞれについて，約20年間の出来事が時を前後し，場面も頻繁に切り替わりながら話が進められています。英文構成が複雑になった上に語数が大幅に増加したため，情報を整理しながら素早く読み進める必要がありました。

第6問A （解答目安時間：12分）

2023年度と同様，英文の記事を読んでその内容に関するメモの空欄を埋める問題が出題されました。例年通りの出題のほかに，本文中で述べられている概念に当てはまる具体例を選ぶという新傾向の問題も出題され，本文の内容を正確に理解した上で思考・判断する力が問われました。

第6問B （解答目安時間：14分）

例年と同じく，本文を読み，アウトラインをまとめる力を問う問題でした。英文自体は2023年度より身近な題材でやや読みやすい印象ですが，難易度の高い語句・表現の理解を必要とする，解きにくい設問も含まれていました。

2025年度の新課程に向けた分析 は
次のページへ ▶▶▶

■令和７年(2025年)度大学入学共通テスト　試作問題の要点分析

試作問題から見える大きな変更の方針

「英語リーディング」で問われている力

- 第Ａ問：資料を活用して**文章のアウトライン**を作成する力
- 第Ｂ問：論理構成や展開に配慮して**文章を推敲する**力

⇒主にライティングにつながる力が問われているのが特徴

問題A Step1 → 2 → 3 と資料を読み進め，「自分」の発表を完成させるために思考する問題

Step1：まず，身近な内容に関する発表テーマについて情報源が５つ提示され，それらの内容を理解します

ポイント①　情報源は Author（筆者）Ａ～Ｅという形で提示されます。

ポイント②　設問では，複数の Author の主張に共通する点や，ある Author の主張から推論できることを解答するものが問われています。

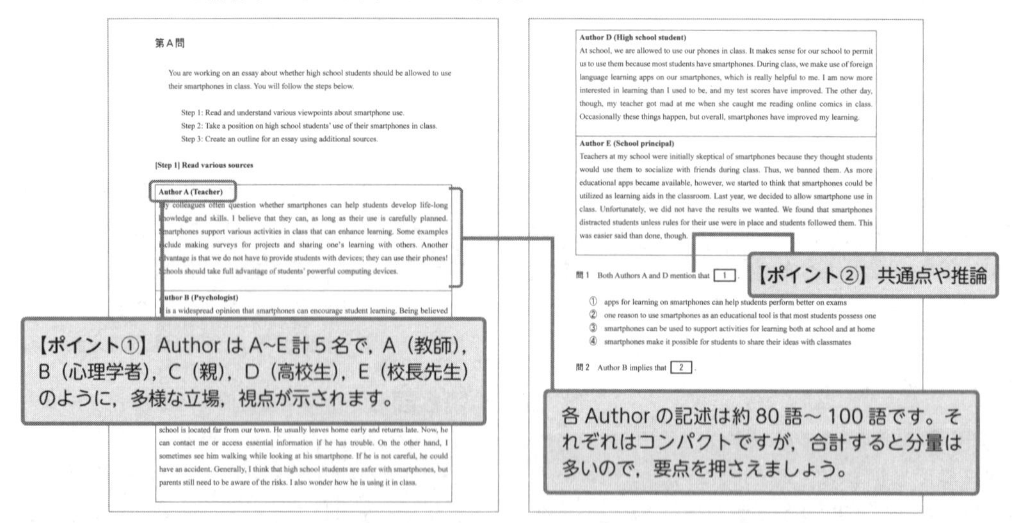

第Ａ問

You are working on an essay about whether high school students should be allowed to use their smartphones in class. You will follow the steps below.

Step 1: Read and understand various viewpoints about smartphone use.
Step 2: Take a position on high school students' use of their smartphones in class.
Step 3: Create an outline for an essay using additional sources.

[Step 1] Read various sources

Author A (Teacher)
y colleagues often question whether smartphones can help students develop life-long nowledge and skills. I believe that they can, as long as their use is carefully planned. martphones support various activities in class that can enhance learning. Some examples clude making surveys for projects and sharing one's learning with others. Another vantage is that we do not have to provide students with devices; they can use their phones! hools should take full advantage of students' powerful computing devices.

uthor B (Psychologist)
is a widespread opinion that smartphones can encourage student learning. Being believed …

… school is located far from our town. He usually leaves home early and returns late. Now, he can contact me or access essential information if he has trouble. On the other hand, I sometimes see him walking while looking at his smartphone. If he is not careful, he could have an accident. Generally, I think that high school students are safer with smartphones, but parents still need to be aware of the risks. I also wonder how he is using it in class.

Author D (High school student)
At school, we are allowed to use our phones in class. It makes sense for our school to permit us to use them because most students have smartphones. During class, we make use of foreign language learning apps on our smartphones, which is really helpful to me. I am now more interested in learning than I used to be, and my test scores have improved. The other day, though, my teacher got mad at me when she caught me reading online comics in class. Occasionally these things happen, but overall, smartphones have improved my learning.

Author E (School principal)
Teachers at my school were initially skeptical of smartphones because they thought students would use them to socialize with friends during class. Thus, we banned them. As more educational apps became available, however, we started to think that smartphones could be utilized as learning aids in the classroom. Last year, we decided to allow smartphone use in class. Unfortunately, we did not have the results we wanted. We found that smartphones distracted students unless rules for their use were in place and students followed them. This was easier said than done, though.

問１　Both Authors A and D mention that [1].

① apps for learning on smartphones can help students perform better on exams
② one reason to use smartphones as an educational tool is that most students possess one
③ smartphones can be used to support activities for learning both at school and at home
④ smartphones make it possible for students to share their ideas with classmates

問２　Author B implies that [2].

Step2：次に，「あなたの意見」をまとめます

ポイント　提示される Your Position（立場）をしっかり理解し，Authorの記述をまとめましょう。

> Step1～3までの総語数は「約1300語」で，現在までの共通テスト 英語リーディングで最長となる2024年度第5問の「約1200語」を超えます。
> 情報整理の速度が非常に重要になります。

[Step 2] Take a position

問３　Now that you understand the various viewpoints, you have taken a position on high school students' use of their smartphones in class, and have written it out as below. Choose the best options to complete [3], [4], and [5].

<u>Your position:</u> High school students should not be allowed to use their smartphones in class.

- Authors [3] and [4] support your position.
- The main argument of the two authors: [5].

Options for [3] and [4] (The order does not matter.)

① A
② B
③ C
④ D
⑤ E

Options for [5]

① Making practical rules for smartphone use in class is difficult for school teachers
② Smartphones may distract learning because the educational apps are difficult to use
③ Smartphones were designed for communication and not for classroom learning
④ Students cannot focus on studying as long as they have access to smartphones in class

Step3：最後に，発表資料を完成させます

ポイント　Source A（記事）とB（グラフと分析）の内容を踏まえてReason（理由）を完成させます。

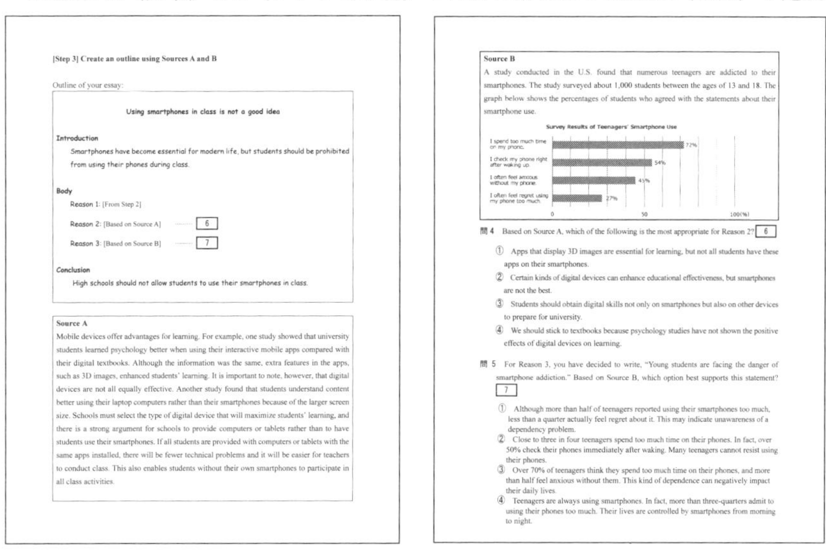

[Step 3] Create an outline using Sources A and B

Outline of your essay:

Using smartphones in class is not a good idea

Introduction

Smartphones have become essential for modern life, but students should be prohibited from using their phones during class.

Body

Reason 1: [From Step 2]

Reason 2: [Based on Source A] ……… 6

Reason 3: [Based on Source B] ……… 7

Conclusion

High schools should not allow students to use their smartphones in class.

Source A

Mobile devices offer advantages for learning. For example, one study showed that university students learned psychology better when using their interactive mobile apps compared with their digital textbooks. Although the information was the same, extra features in the apps, such as 3D images, enhanced students' learning. It is important to note, however, that digital devices are not all equally effective. Another study found that students understand content better using their laptop computers rather than their smartphones because of the larger screen size. Schools must select the type of digital device that will maximize students' learning, and there is a strong argument for schools to provide computers or tablets rather than to have students use their smartphones. If all students are provided with computers or tablets with the same apps installed, there will be fewer technical problems and it will be easier for teachers to conduct class. This also enables students without their own smartphones to participate in all class activities.

Source B

A study conducted in the U.S. found that numerous teenagers are addicted to their smartphones. The study surveyed about 1,000 students between the ages of 13 and 18. The graph below shows the percentages of students who agreed with the statements about their smartphone use.

Survey Results of Teenagers' Smartphone Use

Statement	%
I spend too much time on my phone.	72%
I check my phone right after waking up.	54%
I often feel anxious without my phone.	45%
I often feel regret using my phone too much.	27%

問 4　Based on Source A, which of the following is the most appropriate for Reason 2? 6

① Apps that display 3D images are essential for learning, but not all students have these apps on their smartphones.
② Certain kinds of digital devices can enhance educational effectiveness, but smartphones are not the best.
③ Students should obtain digital skills not only on smartphones but also on other devices to prepare for university.
④ We should stick to textbooks because psychology studies have not shown the positive effects of digital devices on learning.

問 5　For Reason 3, you have decided to write, "Young students are facing the danger of smartphone addiction." Based on Source B, which option best supports this statement? 7

① Although more than half of teenagers reported using their smartphones too much, less than a quarter actually feel regret about it. This may indicate unawareness of a dependency problem.
② Close to three in four teenagers spend too much time on their phones. In fact, over 50% check their phones immediately after waking. Many teenagers cannot resist using their phones.
③ Over 70% of teenagers think they spend too much time on their phones, and more than half feel anxious without them. This kind of dependence can negatively impact their daily lives.
④ Teenagers are always using smartphones. In fact, more than three-quarters admit to using their phones too much. Their lives are controlled by smartphones from morning to night.

問題B　「自分」の書いた作文を添削してもらい，アドバイスに沿って英文を修正する

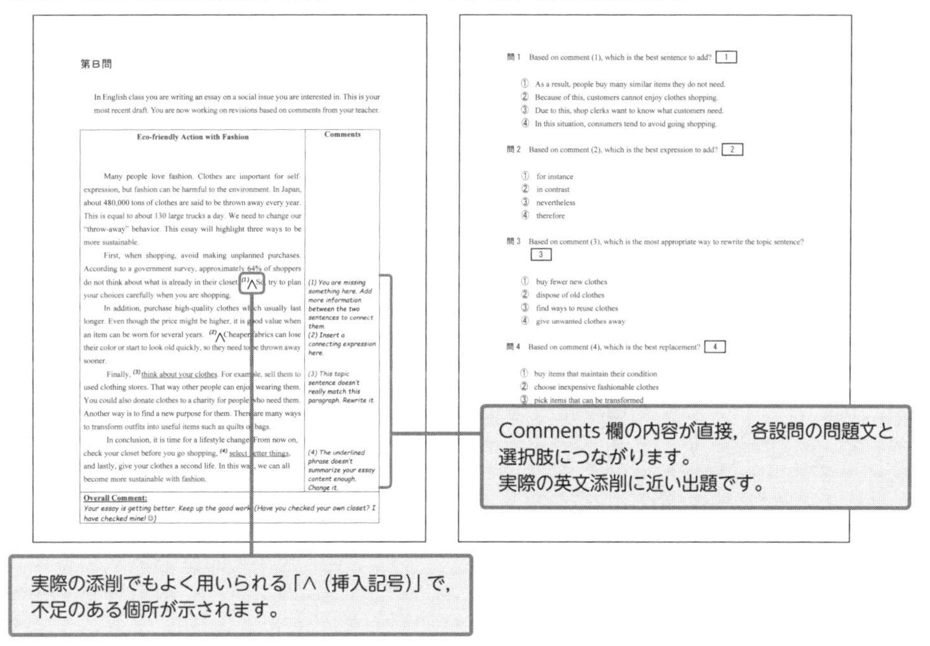

第B問

In English class you are writing an essay on a social issue you are interested in. This is your most recent draft. You are now working on revisions based on comments from your teacher.

Eco-friendly Action with Fashion	Comments
Many people love fashion. Clothes are important for self-expression, but fashion can be harmful to the environment. In Japan, about 480,000 tons of clothes are said to be thrown away every year. This is equal to about 130 large trucks a day. We need to change our "throw-away" behavior. This essay will highlight three ways to be more sustainable.	
First, when shopping, avoid making unplanned purchases. According to a government survey, approximately 64% of shoppers do not think about what is already in their closet. (1)∧ So, try to plan your choices carefully when you are shopping.	(1) You are missing something here. Add more information between the two sentences to connect them.
In addition, purchase high-quality clothes which usually last longer. Even though the price might be higher, it is good value when an item can be worn for several years. (2)∧ Cheaper fabrics can lose their color or start to look old quickly, so they need to be thrown away sooner.	(2) Insert a connecting expression here.
Finally, (3) think about your clothes. For example, sell them to used clothing stores. That way other people can enjoy wearing them. You could also donate clothes to a charity for people who need them. Another way is to find a new purpose for them. There are many ways to transform outfits into useful items such as quilts or bags.	(3) This topic sentence doesn't really match this paragraph. Rewrite it.
In conclusion, it is time for a lifestyle change. From now on, check your closet before you go shopping, (4) select better things, and lastly, give your clothes a second life. In this way, we can all become more sustainable with fashion.	(4) The underlined phrase doesn't summarize your essay content enough. Change it.

Overall Comment:
Your essay is getting better. Keep up the good work. (Have you checked your own closet? I have checked mine! ☺)

問 1　Based on comment (1), which is the best sentence to add? 1

① As a result, people buy many similar items they do not need.
② Because of this, customers cannot enjoy clothes shopping.
③ Due to this, shop clerks want to know what customers need.
④ In this situation, consumers tend to avoid going shopping.

問 2　Based on comment (2), which is the best expression to add? 2

① for instance
② in contrast
③ nevertheless
④ therefore

問 3　Based on comment (3), which is the most appropriate way to rewrite the topic sentence? 3

① buy fewer new clothes
② dispose of old clothes
③ find ways to reuse clothes
④ give unwanted clothes away

問 4　Based on comment (4), which is the best replacement? 4

① buy items that maintain their condition
② choose inexpensive fashionable clothes
③ pick items that can be transformed

新傾向への対策

試作問題を通して見える新しい形式は，見た目上は斬新に感じるかもしれませんが，その出題を通して問われる力の本質は，共通テスト開始時から大きくは変わっていません。英語についての知識の丸暗記ではなく，それをいかに活用して問題に取り組むかが重要である点は一貫しています。また次のページには，これを踏まえた対策法も紹介しています。当たり前に思う部分も多いかもしれませんが，ぜひ自身の学習の中に取り入れたり，意識するようにしてみてください。

■対策

●分野ごとに，足りない知識を補強しよう！

<単語>

単語そのものの意味を問うような設問は出題されませんが，読解の分量が増えた分，語彙力は重要な要素になります。『速読英単語 入門編』『同 必修編』（Z会）などを使って，**文章の中で単語を覚える**学習法がオススメです。また，これまでもanalyse（= analyze）やpractise（= practice）といったイギリス綴りの英単語やイギリス英語特有の表現が見られたので，読解問題の本文で登場した時には復習時に覚えるとよいでしょう。

<文法>

文法問題を解くための知識ではなく，文の意味を理解するための知識が必要になります。読解問題に取り組む際には，必ず文法書を手元に置いて，疑問に思った事項を都度確認していくとよいでしょう。

●いろいろな英文を数多く読もう！

総語数は6,000語程度であり，80分で解くには**精読よりはむしろ速読**の能力が求められていますので，日頃の読解量がものを言います。

また，共通テストでは，SNS，手紙文，ブログ，雑誌記事，説明文，ノンフィクションまでいろいろなタイプの英文が出題されています。**ジャンルを問わず，幅広い分野の英文に慣れておくこと**も大切です。

●問題意識をもって英文を読もう！

設問の中で特徴的な本文中の**「事実」と「意見」を見分ける**問題については，意見と事実の判別を意識しながら読み進めることで，内容理解が深まります。英文を読む時は，その情報が個人の意見なのか，実際に起こったり言われたりした事実なのかを意識しましょう。

また，複数の文章からの情報を読み，それらを整理して総合的に理解する力が求められる設問への対策として，内容をまとめながら読む習慣をつけておきましょう。

※この問題冊子の『注意事項』は，実際の共通テストを想定して掲載しました。

模試　第1回

(100点 80分)

〔英　　語（リーディング）〕

注　意　事　項

1　解答用紙に，正しく記入・マークされていない場合は，採点できないことがあります。

2　試験中に問題冊子の印刷不鮮明，ページの落丁・乱丁及び解答用紙の汚れ等に気付いた場合は，手を高く挙げて監督者に知らせなさい。

3　解答は，解答用紙の解答欄にマークしなさい。例えば，[10]と表示のある問いに対して③と解答する場合は，次の(例)のように**解答番号10の解答欄**の③に**マーク**しなさい。

(例)

解答番号	解答欄								
10	①	②	●(③)	④	⑤	⑥	⑦	⑧	⑨

4　問題冊子の余白等は適宜利用してよいが，どのページも切り離してはいけません。

5　**不正行為について**

①　不正行為に対しては厳正に対処します。

②　不正行為に見えるような行為が見受けられた場合は，監督者がカードを用いて注意します。

③　不正行為を行った場合は，その時点で受験を取りやめさせ退室させます。

6　試験終了後，問題冊子は持ち帰りなさい。

英　語（リーディング）

各大問の英文や図表を読み，解答番号 1 ～ 45 にあてはまるものとして最も適当な選択肢を選びなさい。

第１問 （配点　6）

You visited the website of a shop and found an interesting notice.

February Classes:

Sewing for Beginners

Come to Bonnie's Sewing Shop on Saturday, February 8, for a day of free workshops in basic sewing skills. If you attend any of the classes, you will receive 20% off the price of one item in the store. This discount is valid for February 8 and 9.

We encourage you to bring in items you would like to work on, but you do not have to. All the materials you will need for the classes will be provided by the store.

Schedule of Classes

9 a.m.	Try the basic straight stitch
10 a.m.	Mending a small hole
11 a.m.	Sewing on a button
1 p.m.	Putting on a patch
2 p.m.	Working with difficult materials Leather and silk
3 p.m.	Getting creative Use fun colors to add style to your clothes
4 p.m.	Sewing Social Hour Enjoy free snacks and hot chocolate with our teachers

- Children must be at least 10 to participate in a class, and children under 16 must come with an adult.
- The classes will be taught in English and Japanese, but our teachers are very good at demonstrating skills without the use of words. Everyone is welcome, no matter what language you speak.

Space is limited to 20 people in a class. You may reserve a spot by signing up below.

▶▶ Sign Up

問 1 The purpose of this notice is to let people know about [1].

① a big sale at a shop during February
② a discount on special sewing workshops
③ a session for new workers at a shop
④ sewing lessons they can take at no cost

問 2 At the event, participants can [2].

① buy clothes made by the owners of the shop
② eat and drink with their teachers
③ see a display of items made of silk
④ stitch together leather with other participants

問 3 People cannot participate in the event if they [3].

① are a group of thirty people
② are younger than sixteen years old
③ do not speak either English or Japanese
④ forget to sign up online before February 8

第2問 （配点　10）

A high school student named Tanaka Mayumi read the latest novel by a British novelist, Andrew Lawrence. She sent an email to his publisher, and received a reply from the novelist. You are reading their emails in a magazine.

Dear Andrew Lawrence,

Hello, my name is Tanaka Mayumi. I am a high school student in Japan. The other day, I read your latest novel *Carrying My Hope*, and I was really impressed with it. The story was full of surprises, so I could not guess how it was going to end. It was so interesting that I finished reading it in only a day! What's more, it dealt with the theme of great family love, and there were many nice people in the novel, so it warmed my heart.

In fact, I want to be a novelist like you in the future. I would appreciate it if you could answer a few questions. How do you come up with the ideas for your stories? How did you learn how to write novels? And how do you practice writing them? I am looking forward to reading your next novel.

Best regards,
Tanaka Mayumi

Dear Tanaka Mayumi,

Hello, Mayumi. Thank you for writing to me. I am really glad that you liked my novel so much.

Regarding your questions, my answers are as follows. First, I often observe people around me to get ideas for stories. I can learn a lot of things from other people. Regarding your second question, to tell the truth, I didn't learn how to write novels at school, but I try to read as many books, including novels, as possible. This helps me extend my range of expression. Third, I suggest you should summarise passages of about one thousand words in about one hundred words.

I hope I can read your novel someday!

Best wishes,
Andrew Lawrence

問 1　Mayumi wrote her email to Mr Lawrence to [4].

① ask him what novel he was going to write next
② inform him how many Japanese fans his novels have
③ learn when he decided to be a novelist
④ tell him her impression of his new novel

問 2　One **fact** written in Mayumi's email is that [5].

① *Carrying My Hope* will be published next week
② it took one day for Mayumi to read
③ she felt scared after reading *Carrying My Hope*
④ the story in *Carrying My Hope* was amazing

問 3　Why did Mayumi ask Mr Lawrence questions? [6]

① Because she wanted to know why he had become a novelist.
② Because she wanted to learn how to write novels.
③ Because she was interested in British life.
④ Because she was interested in his personal life.

問 4　In Mr Lawrence's reply to Mayumi, one **fact** is that he [7].

① found it embarrassing to watch people carefully
② improves his writing skills by himself
③ makes short passages as long as possible
④ rarely reads books other than novels

問 5　After reading the email from Mr Lawrence, what would Mayumi be most likely to do first? [8]

① She would ask her friends to read her novel.
② She would go and buy the second volume.
③ She would guess the ending of his latest novel.
④ She would try following some of his advice.

第3問 (配点　9)

You found the following story in an international student magazine.

Can You Keep a Secret?

Saya Iida

It can be hard to trust others, even when they are the people you know best.

My brother Daiki has two close friends, Junpei and Kenji. They have always done everything together since they were little.

When Daiki was going to turn sixteen, Kenji and Junpei decided to throw him a party at a restaurant. They let me in on the secret so I could help.

One day, Kenji and Junpei asked me to keep my brother busy after school so they could meet to plan the party. Unfortunately, I forgot they were going to meet in the school courtyard, and I took Daiki right past them on our way home.

"Wait —— isn't that Kenji and Junpei?" Daiki said. "They both said they couldn't hang out today because they had soccer practice."

He looked sad. Then Kenji and Junpei made things worse by running away when they saw Daiki had seen them.

"No, I don't think it was them. Now, come on, you said you would help me study for my English exam. I want to get a good grade," I said.

Daiki's expression grew darker. He said angrily, "If they don't want to be my friend anymore, I wish they would just say so."

"I'm sure that's not it," I said.

At home, Daiki's mind was not on homework. I asked him the same question three times before he said, "Sorry, what did you say, Saya?"

The party was two weeks away. I thought it would be bad if Daiki felt like this for two weeks. I asked my brother if he could keep a secret and he said yes. Then I told him about the party.

Daiki's mouth fell open. "Wow, really?"

"You must pretend you don't know," I said. "Junpei and Kenji will be disappointed if you don't."

"Don't worry. They're my best friends. I'd do anything for them," said Daiki happily. And he did.

問 1 Put the following feelings (①~④) in the order Daiki experienced them.

[9] → [10] → [11] → [12] → glad

① hurt
② mad
③ not focused
④ surprised

問 2 Junpei and Kenji wanted to celebrate Daiki's [13].

① birthday
② good grade
③ graduation
④ soccer victory

問 3 From this story, you learned that Daiki [14].

① could not concentrate on his English homework because he was excited that he knew his friend's secret
② had learned his friends' secret from Saya in advance and made them disappointed
③ promised to practice soccer with his friends but failed to carry out the promise
④ thought his friends no longer liked him until his sister told him what they were hiding from him

第4問 (配点 12)

In English class you are writing an essay on a health issue to prepare for a presentation. This is your most recent draft. You are now working on revisions based on comments from your teacher.

<table>
<tr><th>Treat Your Eyes Well</th><th>Comments</th></tr>
<tr><td>How many of your classmates wear glasses or contacts? With more screen time and less time spent outside, children have worse vision than they used to. Doctors do not all agree on what leads to bad vision. (1) ∧ There are some steps you can take for your eye health in general.</td><td>(1) Insert a connecting expression here.</td></tr>
<tr><td>First, when you look at something, try to hold it at least one foot away from your face. Whether you are looking at a book or a smartphone screen, your eyes have to work harder to focus on things that are very close. This makes them tired, and studies show a relationship between close work and bad vision.</td><td></td></tr>
<tr><td>Second, (2) <u>pay attention to numbers</u>. "20-20-20" is easy to remember. This means take a 20-second break every 20 minutes and look 20 feet away when you have to look at something close for a long time. This helps reduce eye strain and may help protect your vision as well. It can also give you a short mental break.</td><td>(2) This topic sentence doesn't really match this paragraph. Rewrite it.</td></tr>
<tr><td>Lastly, wear sunglasses with ultraviolet (UV) protection. You probably use sunscreen to protect your skin from UV damage. (3) ∧ UV damage does not cause bad vision, but it does lead to many diseases that are common in the elderly. If you want to have healthy eyes in fifty years' time, you should start protecting them now.</td><td>(3) You are missing something here. Add more information between the two sentences to connect them.</td></tr>
<tr><td>As we have seen, there are some easy things you can do to take care of your eyes. (4) <u>Rest your eyes when you read</u>, take a break to look into the distance, and wear sunglasses when you go outside. Having healthy habits will help keep your eyes happy.</td><td>(4) The underlined phrase doesn't summarize your essay content enough. Change it.</td></tr>
<tr><td colspan="2"><u>Overall Comment:</u>
This draft is much better. There's just a little more to improve before the presentation. (Do you wear sunglasses? I'm going to go buy a pair! ☺)</td></tr>
</table>

問 1　Based on comment (1), which is the best expression to add? 15

① indeed
② moreover
③ nevertheless
④ thus

問 2　Based on comment (2), which is the most appropriate way to rewrite the topic sentence? 16

① find something 20 feet away
② rest for 60 seconds every half hour
③ take an "eye break"
④ use a timer when you do close work

問 3　Based on comment (3), which is the best sentence to add? 17

① For this reason, your eyes need protection from UV rays.
② In the same way, you should use sunglasses to protect your eyes.
③ On the other hand, sunglasses are also a good idea.
④ Sunscreen is becoming better for your skin because of recent improvements.

問 4　Based on comment (4), which is the best replacement? 18

① Don't use your smartphone when you are tired
② Keep some distance between your eyes and hands
③ Look at things which are far away
④ Spend more time working outdoors

第5問 （配点　16）

You are doing research on science education. You found two articles.

Women in Physics

by Riva Singh

October, 2018

Women have been working as scientists for thousands of years, from the Mesopotamian princess Enheduanna to the 3rd-century Egyptian chemist Cleopatra the Alchemist. However, for most of history, women have made up only a small fraction of professional scientists. Today, only about 30% of scientific researchers worldwide are female.

The numbers are changing in the biological sciences. In the early 2000s, nearly half of advanced degrees in the biomedical sciences were earned by women. In the field of physics, however, the gender gap is still considerable. A study of girls and boys in the UK shows that this professional divide is connected to the choices girls make in high school.

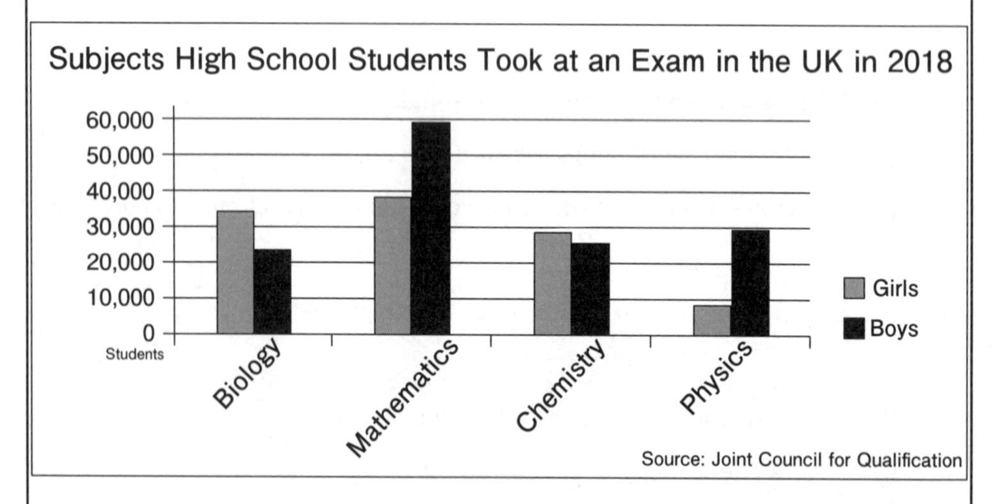

Nearly 1.5 times as many girls as boys chose to study biology in 2018. But while almost 30,000 boys studied physics, less than 10,000 girls did the same. In 2016, not one female student chose to study physics in 50% of British schools. It should come as no surprise that in the UK, only 17% of

physics lecturers are women.

Many say that girls just aren't interested in physics, so this isn't a problem. However, in my opinion, girls don't have enough female role models in physics, and because of this lack, they don't give serious consideration to the fact that physics is something they could or should pursue. This theory is supported by research in the United States. There, researchers at the University of Texas found that in schools in communities that had a higher percentage of female scientists, the number of girls and boys who studied physics was about the same.

Opinion on "Women in Physics"

by E.C.

November, 2018

As a female physicist, I can relate to this very well. Working in physics can sometimes get a little lonely for women. My husband has been a high school science teacher in the UK for the last five years, and he was surprised when I first told him that for most of my studies, I was the only girl in class. But after seeing this data, his reaction makes sense. According to Riva Singh's article, girls outnumber the boys who study my husband's subject in high school by about 10 percent.

We must work harder to get more women into physics careers. The girls who do study physics in the UK consistently score equally well —— and sometimes even a little better —— than boys do on their exams in that subject. As a scientific community, we are undoubtedly losing out on talent by not attracting an equal number of male and female students to the profession. Particularly in those communities where there are not a lot of female scientists, I think it would be effective for university physics departments to send female physicists to give talks at schools.

It would also be helpful to talk about this issue with parents of young children. If both boys and girls are given interesting toys that introduce them to the concepts of physics, they will be more likely to feel confident and excited about studying the subject at a higher level later.

問 1　Neither Riva Singh nor the physicist mentions [19].

① boys' and girls' physics test scores
② female scientists from history
③ high school girls who study natural science
④ reasons why boys prefer physics

問 2　The physicist's husband teaches [20].

① biology
② chemistry
③ mathematics
④ physics

問 3　According to the articles, in British high schools [21].

① all students are required to take advanced math
② more students study foreign languages than chemistry
③ there were science classes no women attend
④ women don't score as well as men on physics tests

問4 Riva Singh states that female students **[22]**, and the physicist states that they **[23]**. (Choose a different opinion for each box.)

① are more interested in biology than in physics
② choose careers similar to those of their parents
③ in Texas high schools are most likely to study chemistry
④ should be introduced to physics as small children
⑤ studied biomedical science at rates equal to male students

問5 Based on the information from both articles, you are going to write a report for homework. The best title for your report would be "**[24]**."

① Female Students' Test Scores Are Improving in Physics
② More Girls Want to Be Physicists than Ever Before
③ The Talent Pool in Physics Research Is Growing
④ Ways to Address the Gender Gap in Physics

第6問 （配点 18）

You are working on an essay about whether the legal driving age in Japan should be lowered to 16. You will follow the steps below.

Step 1: Read and understand various viewpoints about the legal driving age.

Step 2: Take a position on lowering the legal driving age to 16.

Step 3: Create an outline for an essay using additional sources.

[Step 1] Read various sources

Author A (Traffic officer)
Lowering the driving age to 16 needs to be thought about very carefully. Safety on the roads is the most important thing. Data in the United States, where 16-year-olds are allowed to drive, shows that young drivers are more likely to have an accident. In many cases, they don't have enough driving or life experience to make the best decisions. For example, they don't always concentrate on driving because they are often with their friends and talking, which is not safe. We need to be really careful before we let younger people drive. We have to think about whether teenagers are really ready for such a big responsibility.

Author B (High school student)
If we could drive at 16, it would make us more independent. It would mean that we can handle big responsibilities earlier. It would show that adults trust us with important things. Being able to drive would help us get around by ourselves and help our families too. Besides, we can already ride a motorcycle. A car would be even more convenient. Some older people think we're not ready, but we are good with technology. Also, cars are much safer now. They even help us drive safely. I think we can learn to drive well and be safe.

Author C (Driving instructor)
I teach teenagers to drive. I believe that age is less important than good teaching. If young people get good driving lessons, they can learn to drive safely. They need to understand how to be careful, see dangers, and always follow the road rules. If we let younger people drive, it's very important to give them these good lessons. Programs could also be introduced in high school, and families can help too. This will prepare them to drive safely. I think with the right education, teenagers could drive just as safely as adults.

Author D (Parent)
It would be useful if my 16-year-old son could drive. I wouldn't need to take him everywhere, and he could also drive me places. But I have worries. Driving isn't just about handling a car. Drivers need to think fast and make safe choices. Teenagers can be tempted to do risky things while driving, like using their smartphone to check their social media or watch videos. This makes me wonder if they really understand what it means to drive. Are they ready to keep their eyes on the road? This is a big concern for me.

Author E (Japanese car salesperson)
Many young people in the U.S. drive, and it's very helpful for their families. We should consider this for Japan too. It's true that young drivers can sometimes cause accidents. But we have good driving schools in Japan. We can teach young people to be more careful. Just because you are young, it doesn't mean you can't be safe. This could also be good for our economy. If more young people drive, we could sell more second-hand cars and young people might travel more. We should think seriously about this idea and its benefits to our society.

問1 Both Authors C and E mention that [25].

① changing the rules could lead to other benefits for the country
② how safe you are as a driver is related not only to how old you are
③ Japan's effective education system helps children mature quickly
④ lowering the driving age to 16 would help families

問2 Author B implies that [26].

① many parents trust their child's driving skills
② teenagers' technological skills make them ready for today's safer, more automated vehicles
③ the advanced car safety features in modern cars make young people more independent
④ young people find driving a car more challenging than riding a motorcycle

[Step 2] Take a position

問 3　Now that you understand the various viewpoints, you have taken a position on lowering the legal driving age to 16 and have written it out as below. Choose the best options to complete [27], [28], and [29].

Your position: The legal driving age in Japan should not be lowered to 16.

- Authors [27] and [28] support your position.
- The main argument of the two authors: [29].

Options for [27] and [28] (The order does not matter.)

① A

② B

③ C

④ D

⑤ E

Options for [29]

① Statistics provide the most important evidence against lowering the legal driving age

② The process of driving is too complicated for a 16-year-old to understand properly

③ Young people are more likely than adults to lose focus while driving a car

④ Young people need more life experience before they are able to take on responsibility

[Step 3] Create an outline using Sources A and B

Outline of your essay:

Lowering the legal driving age to 16 in Japan is not a good idea

Introduction

Although lowering the legal driving age would provide young people with more freedom, the driving age should not be changed.

Body

Reason 1: [From Step 2]

Reason 2: [Based on Source A] ········· **30**

Reason 3: [Based on Source B] ········· **31**

Conclusion

The legal driving age in Japan should remain the same.

Source A

There are several reasons why Japan shouldn't lower the legal driving age. It is generally agreed that teenagers, especially those under 18, are still undergoing important brain development. This is most noticeable in areas such as risk assessment and decision-making. This would explain why data shows that young people, especially new drivers, are more likely to have a car accident. This has a serious impact on the cost of car insurance. Of course, young people have to pay more. If Japan lets younger people drive, insurance companies will have to rethink how they decide these costs. It is certain that insurance prices will go up. As a result of the higher price of insurance, families and young people could find it harder to afford a car. This means that changing the law may only be acceptable to wealthy families. This also goes against the idea of letting younger people drive to give them more freedom. For these reasons, we need to be careful about this choice because it could make things harder for young people and their families and lead to more division in society.

Source B

A 2012 survey of over 1,700 teenagers carried out in the US by New Liberty Mutual Insurance and SADD (Students Against Destructive Decisions) found that while it is true that young people may not be the best decision makers, it might not be all their fault. Many teenagers may just be copying their parents' bad driving behaviors.

New Liberty Mutual Insurance/SADD 2012 Teen Driving Survey		
	Parental Driving Behavior (observed by teens)	Teen Driving Behavior (self-reported)
Talk on a cell phone while driving	91%	90%
Speed	88%	94%
Text messages	59%	78%
Drive without a seatbelt	47%	33%
Drive under the influence of alcohol	20%	15%
Drive under the influence of marijuana	7%	16%

問 4 Based on Source A, which of the following is the most appropriate for Reason 2? [30]

① An increase in insurance costs for young drivers will make it harder for them to afford the expense of brain development.

② Lowering the driving age will result in higher accident rates because young drivers are less capable of driving safely.

③ The increase in insurance costs could have a bigger effect on families that are poorer, which is not fair for everyone.

④ Young people's lack of experience makes them more likely to have an accident and is an issue for insurance companies.

問 5 For Reason 3, you have decided to write, "The poor driving habits of adults need to be considered before we change the law." Based on Source B, which option best supports this statement? [31]

① Close to 40% of parents drive under the influence of alcohol or marijuana, which is one of the most common bad habits among adults. This may be the result of alcohol or drug addiction.

② More than three-quarters of teens admit to texting while driving and more than 90% of them ignore speed limits. However, their poor driving habits generally follow a pattern similar to that of their parents.

③ Nine in ten teens talk on the phone while driving. Additionally, teens are 8% more likely to ignore speed limits than their parents. This may indicate that teens are more careless.

④ Parents behave worse than teens in more than half of the behaviors listed. They demonstrate bad habits, which creates a poor learning environment.

第7問 (配点 15)

Your group is preparing a poster presentation entitled "Roberto Clemente Walker: Athlete and Humanitarian," using information from the magazine article below.

The "Roberto Clemente Award" is given to Major League baseball players who exhibit sportsmanship and a dedication to helping others. One of the first Latin American players in the Major League, Roberto Clemente is remembered today not only for his athleticism but also for his empathy and his willingness to stand up for both himself and his community.

Roberto Clemente Walker was born on August 18, 1934 in Carolina, Puerto Rico, an island in the Caribbean that is a territory of the United States. He showed an early talent for athletics, and, by the age of 17, he was playing for the Santurce Crabbers in the Puerto Rican Baseball League.

Clemente caught the attention of the Brooklyn Dodgers, a celebrated team that in the previous season had advanced to the World Series. A Dodgers scout, Clyde Sukeforth, said of Clemente that he could throw and run as well as any man that ever lived. In 1954, Clemente was signed by the Dodgers with a $10,000 bonus, a large sum at that time. After playing for a year with the Dodgers' minor league team in Montreal, however, Clemente was up for grabs in a draft from other baseball clubs. He was taken from the Dodgers by the Pittsburgh Pirates, which in 1954 had come in last place in the National League.

On April 1, 1955, Clemente played his first game in major league baseball with the Pirates. Over the next five years, Clemente struggled with injuries as well as with a language barrier and an American press that often made fun of his accent. Reporters also tried to Americanize Clemente's name, calling him "Bob" or "Bobby." Clemente always politely asserted that he went by the Latin name "Roberto."

Soon the struggling Pirates began to improve. In 1960, with an impressive batting average, Clemente led his team to the World Series, where they beat the New York Yankees. Over the next seven years, Clemente won four National League batting titles, and in 1966, he received the National League Most Valuable Player Award. In his position in right field, Clemente's famously strong arm earned him twelve straight Gold Glove Awards. His quick and bold base running elevated the excitement of the game and made him a fan favorite.

Clemente played eighteen seasons with the Pirates. During the off-season, he played in the Puerto Rican League. He also sponsored baseball lessons in Puerto Rico for school-aged athletes who dreamed of following in his footsteps. In 1971, Clemente helped Pittsburgh win another World Series, and in 1972, he made his 3000th hit at bat, an accomplishment only ten players had achieved before him.

That year also brought tragedy. An earthquake in Nicaragua on December 23 prompted Clemente to raise money with his wife and other players to help. When he heard that some supplies were being stolen rather than getting to the people who needed them, Clemente decided to bring his aid to the country directly. On the 31st, he rented a supply plane and boarded it to accompany it to Nicaragua. At only 38 years old, Clemente died when the plane crashed just off the Puerto Rican coast.

The Baseball Hall of Fame made an exception to its typical five-year waiting period to honor a player after retirement or death. In July of 1973, Clemente was the first player born in Latin America to be admitted.

Roberto Clemente Walker: Athlete and Humanitarian

■ The Life of Roberto Clemente

Period	Events
1934–1954	Clemente grew up playing sports in Puerto Rico ↓ 32 ↓ 33 ↓ 34
1955–1973	35 ↓ 36 ↓ Clemente died in a plane crash

Roberto Clemente Walker

■ A Remarkable Talent in Baseball

▸ Clemente's skills in baseball were recognized in a number of ways: 37 38

■ **Clemente's Volunteer Work**

▶ During the part of the year that he did not play in the major leagues, Clemente could often be found [39].

▶ His last humanitarian act: [40]

問1 Members of your group listed important events in Clemente's life. Put the events into the boxes [32]～[36] in the order that they happened.

① Clemente became the 11th player to reach 3000 hits

② Clemente helped the Pirates win the World Series

③ Clemente signed a contract with the Brooklyn Dodgers

④ Clemente was drafted by Pittsburg's major league team

⑤ Clemente was on the Santurce Crabbers team

問2 Choose the best two options for [37] and [38] to complete the poster. (The order does not matter.)

① An American reporter called Clemente the best player of all time.

② Clemente ended up in the Baseball Hall of Fame.

③ Clemente was given a big bonus to play for the Pirates.

④ Clemente won a dozen awards for throwing.

⑤ Clemente won seven National League batting titles.

問 3　During the part of the year that he did not play in the major leagues, Clemente could often be found [39].

① helping his wife at his house in Puerto Rico
② meeting with the Pittsburgh fans who loved him
③ organizing baseball training sessions for children
④ working with youth teams near his Montreal hometown

問 4　Choose the best option for [40] to complete the poster.

① Clemente gathered money to help people after an airplane crash.
② Clemente helped clean up Nicaragua after an earthquake in 1972.
③ Clemente paid the medical expenses of victims of an airplane crash.
④ Clemente played a charity game for schools in Nicaragua.
⑤ Clemente tried to bring aid to people himself to prevent it from being stolen.

第 8 問 (配点 14)

You are studying the influence of social media on us. You are going to read the following online article to learn more about this theme.

Social media offer us a kind of space where we can enjoy sharing information, like photos or videos. In this way, we can express ourselves and easily interact with others online. Companies and VIPs, such as presidents of nations and well-known celebrities, are advertising themselves and getting opportunities to see the public's reaction on social media. Needless to say, social media are one of the most handy and influential means of communication used across the globe.

While social media are enjoyable and useful, some people are distressed by them. Some feel annoyed when they know their messages have been ignored even though they have been read. Others are ruled by a strong desire to seek more attention and distinguish themselves from others on social media. Such people expect too much from the reactions of others, and this makes them constantly feel stressed. All of these conditions are symptoms of what we call "social media fatigue."

There was a survey in 2019 about the social media fatigue felt by Japanese people who browse or post on social media once or more a week. It shows that women are more likely to feel this fatigue than men. About two out of every three women in their 20s have experienced social media fatigue. More than half of women in their 40s suffer from social media fatigue, which is not as many as women in their 20s. More women in their 50s experience social media fatigue than do women in their 30s. Women in their 60s are the least likely to feel stressed about social media.

How can we get along with social media without feeling unnecessary fatigue? Basically, limiting access to social media is effective. For example, you should try to use social media for no more than an hour a day. Moreover, it is good to find goals or hobbies other than social media. In addition, you should value your real friends more than people you know only on social media.

Apart from distancing yourself from social media, the ability to observe yourself objectively can be helpful in reducing social media fatigue. Those who get stressed about social media find it difficult to realize that they are addicted to them. So, if you grasp the situation you are in, you will be better able to deal with your problems. This ability is true for every situation in your life and will help you whenever you face some difficulty.

For some people, social media are fantastic platforms full of things that attract their interest. However, you need to realize the fact that they are just entertainment on a screen and nothing more than complementary tools in your life. It is true that it is important for you to build relationships with others and express yourself on the Internet, but you should not go too far. If you still want to enjoy social media, do it in a positive and appropriate way. Then, if you realize they can threaten your daily life or future, what should you do? A wise user would do something about that.

問 1　Some people don't enjoy social media anymore because they get stressed by **41**.

① caring too much about how others react
② getting too much attention from others
③ reading all the messages they receive
④ taking photos or videos to share online

問 2　You are summarizing the information about women on the survey in the passage. Which is the most appropriate combination to fill in blanks (A) to (D) in the graph? **42**

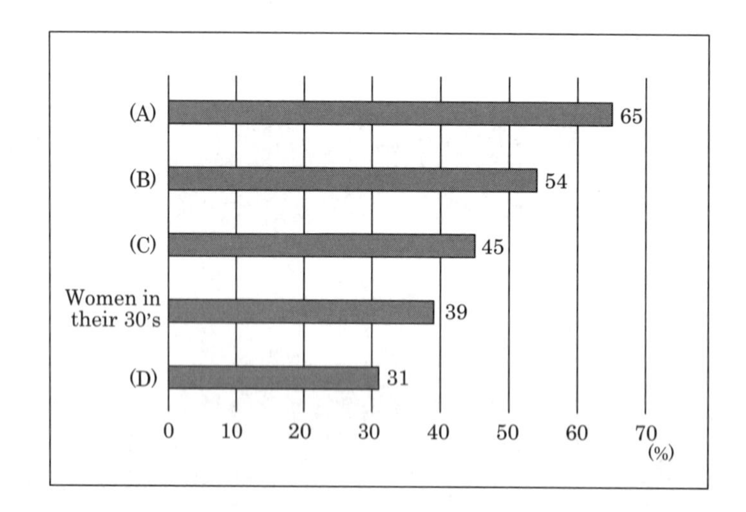

① (A) Women in their 20's　(B) Women in their 40's
(C) Women in their 50's　(D) Women in their 60's
② (A) Women in their 20's　(B) Women in their 40's
(C) Women in their 60's　(D) Women in their 50's
③ (A) Women in their 40's　(B) Women in their 20's
(C) Women in their 50's　(D) Women in their 60's
④ (A) Women in their 40's　(B) Women in their 20's
(C) Women in their 60's　(D) Women in their 50's

問 3 According to the article you read, which of the following are true? (Choose two options. The order does not matter.) [43] · [44]

① Celebrities are the least likely to experience social media fatigue.

② Limiting the use of social media can worsen social media fatigue.

③ Not devoting yourself to social media is a good way to reduce social media fatigue.

④ Seeing yourself from a distance helps you deal with everyday problems.

⑤ Women tend to value their real friends more than men do.

問 4 To describe the author's position, which of the following is most appropriate? [45]

① The author believes that balance is the key to healthy social media use.

② The author emphasizes that social media play an essential role in building friendships.

③ The author recommends that people make better use of social media to express themselves.

④ The author wonders if social media will continue to offer interesting content in the future.

※この問題冊子の『注意事項』は，実際の共通テストを想定して掲載しました。

模試　第2回

（100点 80分）

〔英　　語（リーディング）〕

注　意　事　項

1　解答用紙に，正しく記入・マークされていない場合は，採点できないことがあります。

2　試験中に問題冊子の印刷不鮮明，ページの落丁・乱丁及び解答用紙の汚れ等に気付いた場合は，手を高く挙げて監督者に知らせなさい。

3　解答は，解答用紙の解答欄にマークしなさい。例えば，[10] と表示のある問いに対して ③ と解答する場合は，次の（例）のように**解答番号10の解答欄**の ③ に**マーク**しなさい。

（例）

解答番号	解　答　欄
10	①　②　●(③)　④　⑤　⑥　⑦　⑧　⑨

4　問題冊子の余白等は適宜利用してよいが，どのページも切り離してはいけません。

5　**不正行為について**

①　不正行為に対しては厳正に対処します。

②　不正行為に見えるような行為が見受けられた場合は，監督者がカードを用いて注意します。

③　不正行為を行った場合は，その時点で受験を取りやめさせ退室させます。

6　試験終了後，問題冊子は持ち帰りなさい。

英　　語(リーディング)

各大問の英文や図表を読み，解答番号 1 ～ 45 にあてはまるものとして最も適当な選択肢を選びなさい。

第1問 (配点　6)

You visited the website of your city's public library and found the following notice.

School Vacation Week Programs for Teens
At Conway Public Library

Conway Public Library will have special programs for teens during the school vacation week. No prior experience or background knowledge is required. Join the programs that most fit your interests.

All programs are free of charge. Just bring your library card!

Dates	Program	Time
February 18	***Mystery Book club*** We will discuss our favorite mystery books or authors.	11am-1pm
	Programming Studio* A professional programmer will teach you computer programming through games.	12pm-2pm
February 19	***Let's move!*** A modern dancer Nikki Tajima will show you some easy and cool dance moves.	10am-12pm
February 20	***Origami time**** Learn Origami with our Japanese librarian Kanako.	1pm-2pm
	Meet an astronaut Astronaut Bruce Wang spent 5 years on the International Space Station. Listen to his amazing stories and ask questions!	1pm-3pm

February 21	***Learn ASL*** Learn to communicate by using American Sign Language.	10am-12pm
February 22	***Movie night*** We will watch some short silent movies.	5pm-7pm

*These programs require you to sign up in advance. Please call 501-333-XXXX.

To learn more about each program, click on the name of the program.

問 1 The purpose of this notice is to [1].

① announce upcoming special events
② ask what teens are interested in
③ remind people of weekly activities
④ tell people to sign up for a library card

問 2 During the week, the teens can [2].

① join activities mainly in the morning
② join multiple programs in a day
③ meet experts from different fields
④ volunteer at a local library

問 3 If you want to participate in the "Programming Studio," you will have to [3].

① call the library to register
② have studied programming
③ pay a special fee
④ visit the library at 3pm

第2問 （配点　10）

You are the editor of a school English newspaper. Tim, an exchange student from the UK, has written an article for the paper.

Do you want to learn another foreign language aside from English? According to a survey done at a university in Japan, about a quarter of the students there are learning Korean. This is higher than the proportion learning German, which is 20%. However, the language with the most learners is Chinese.

Why do they choose to learn these languages? Some reasons are mentioned in the survey:

・Have an interest in the language or culture
・Feel a necessity to learn another foreign language
・Hope to gain more job opportunities

There are various purposes and goals in learning a second foreign language. Some people learn Korean because they are big fans of Korean pop or dramas. Some study Chinese hard in order to have an advantage when job hunting, and others may just want to communicate with people in the local language when traveling abroad.

As for me, I was interested in the literature of the Heian era and decided to learn Japanese. Generally speaking, Japanese is one of the most difficult languages for Westerners to learn because it's very hard to learn all the Chinese characters as well as Japanese *kana*. In any case, it takes a lot of time and effort to master a language, but it's worth trying. Learning a foreign language opens a door to a new world. If you learn more than one, you can experience an even broader world. When you see things from different angles, you will understand them more deeply.

問 1　In terms of the popularity of second foreign languages among the students surveyed, which shows the languages' ranking from **highest to lowest**? [4]

① Chinese — German — Korean
② Chinese — Korean — German
③ German — Chinese — Korean
④ German — Korean — Chinese
⑤ Korean — Chinese — German
⑥ Korean — German — Chinese

問 2　According to Tim's report, some students learn a second foreign language because [5].

① they can learn the language with ease
② they must take an exam at university
③ they need to learn the difficulties in other countries
④ they want to understand the culture

問 3　The statement that best reflects one finding from the survey is [6]

① 'Chinese is thought to be quite important in business.'
② 'English has always been the most popular language.'
③ 'Western languages are difficult for Asians to learn.'
④ 'You'll be respected if you speak many languages.'

問 4　Which best summarises Tim's opinions about learning multiple languages? [7]

① It costs too much money and effort.
② It helps you gain other points of view.
③ It is necessary to work in the Western world.
④ It is not very difficult for Japanese people.

問 5　Which is the most suitable title for the article? [8]

① How Can You Get a Good Job?
② What Should You Do to Master English?
③ Which Language Should You Learn?
④ Why Learn a Second Foreign Language?

（下 書 き 用 紙）

英語（リーディング）の試験問題は次に続く。

第3問 (配点 9)

You found the following story in a study-abroad magazine.

The Art of Receiving Gifts

Andy Wei (International Student Advisor)

Gifts play an important role in Chinese culture. Receiving gifts may seem like a simple act, but without knowing the proper etiquette, you might end up offending the person giving you the gift.

Isabel was an exchange student from Australia. She was shy at first and did not know how to make friends in a foreign country. I decided to match her up with a Chinese student Ming so they could teach their own languages to each other. Isabel and Ming quickly became close friends, and Isabel got used to life in Guanxi. Isabel's Chinese improved so much she joined student organizations and even started her own at our university.

A few weeks before Isabel had to go back to Australia, Ming invited Isabel to her house for dinner. Isabel couldn't wait to meet her best friend's family. She enjoyed dinner and a nice conversation. When it was time for Isabel to leave, Ming's father handed Isabel a box wrapped with a ribbon. Pleasantly surprised, Isabel took it and immediately opened the box. It was a traditional Chinese comb. Ming's mother said, "It's very small." Isabel smiled and said, "Yes, and very light."

A few days later, Ming told Isabel that her parents were upset about that night. Ming explained that Isabel shouldn't have opened the gift right away because it made her seem more interested in the gift itself rather than the thought behind it. Also, when the gift giver makes a humble comment about the gift, the receiver is expected to deny it, saying how wonderful it is. Isabel felt terrible and ignorant. However, that experience made Isabel want to learn more about Chinese culture. She told me she is now taking a course on Chinese history and culture at her university in Australia.

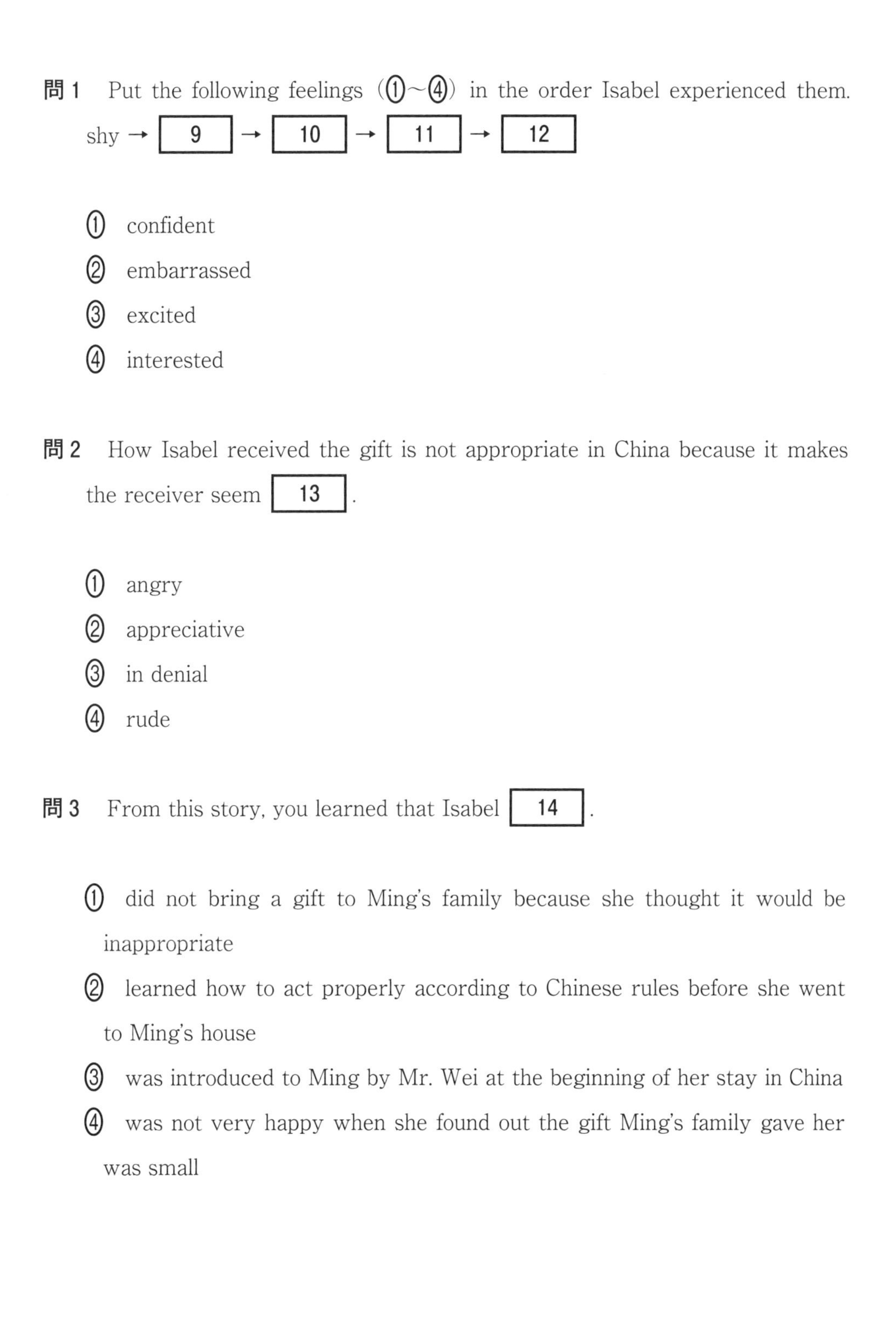

問1 Put the following feelings (①～④) in the order Isabel experienced them.

shy → [9] → [10] → [11] → [12]

① confident
② embarrassed
③ excited
④ interested

問2 How Isabel received the gift is not appropriate in China because it makes the receiver seem [13].

① angry
② appreciative
③ in denial
④ rude

問3 From this story, you learned that Isabel [14].

① did not bring a gift to Ming's family because she thought it would be inappropriate
② learned how to act properly according to Chinese rules before she went to Ming's house
③ was introduced to Ming by Mr. Wei at the beginning of her stay in China
④ was not very happy when she found out the gift Ming's family gave her was small

第4問 （配点　12）

In your English class, you are writing an essay about the suggestions to improve this school. This is your most recent draft. You are now working on revisions after reading your teacher's advice.

How to Improve Classes for Future Students	**Comments**
I think our school is well run and offers a safe and healthy learning environment where most students are happy. Even so, I believe learning would be more effective if some changes were made to classes and lesson structure.	
First, I would like the school to offer more individual learning plans. For example, several students go to cram schools after school for the sole purpose of preparing for university entrance exams. (1) ∧ If there were intensive classes to meet individual needs here at school, it would benefit all students.	*(1) You need more explanation. Could you add something here to clarify what you mean?*
Second, we should be able to learn in classes (2) <u>for ourselves</u>. Currently, we have classes based on ability only for math. However, if we could have discussions or do group work with students of around the same level, maybe in English, social studies and Japanese, we would feel more confident to speak up and be active in class.	*(2) It is not clear what you mean. Could you write a better expression here?*
My final point is that assignments should be tailored to suit the ability of the individual. In other words, I want teachers to plan lessons with easier or more difficult content, depending on individual academic achievement. (3) ∧ Everybody could feel more progress and motivation if the tasks were not too easy or too difficult.	*(3) Please insert a connecting expression here.*
Our school is already a good school in terms of academic level. However, we are all individuals with strong points and weak points. I feel that if there were more optional classes and (4) <u>students were more equal</u>, it would be a more efficient and positive experience for all students.	*(4) This doesn't summarize your point well. Change it.*
<u>Overall comment:</u> *You have some very interesting ideas. I like that you have thought clearly and carefully about how to improve life for all students.*	

問 1　Based on comment (1), which is the best sentence to add? [15]

① Meanwhile, other students are having a hard time with self-study.
② On the contrary, there are students of poor level here.
③ On the other hand, teachers are not helping average students.
④ Yet learning can be more effective through self-study.

問 2　Based on comment (2), which would be a clearer expression? [16]

① that are made for each of us
② where we can study on our own
③ with fewer students
④ with students suited to our academic level

問 3　Based on comment (3), which would be the best expression to use? [17]

① For a start,
② Furthermore,
③ In this way,
④ On the other hand,

問 4　Based on comment (4), which is the best replacement? [18]

① students were allowed to choose classes
② students were given the same assignments
③ students were helped in difficult classes
④ students were taught according to their level

第5問 (配点 16)

You are doing research on young people's sleep patterns. You found two articles.

Sleep Patterns among Teens **by Sharon Jones**

While sleep is important for everyone, it is particularly important for teens, whose brains go through rapid and dramatic developmental changes. During sleep, neural connections are strengthened, and information is transferred from short-term memory to long-term memory. Therefore, insufficient sleep not only makes students feel tired during the day, but it also leads to poor school performance. Moreover, a good night's sleep activates cells in a part of the brain which is responsible for higher-level thinking such as reasoning and decision making.

Despite a set of research proving the benefits of sleep, most school-aged children and teenagers are not getting enough of it. According to a study in 2015, only 15 percent of teenagers get the eight and a half hours of sleep a night recommended by experts. The gap between the recommended sleep time and the actual sleep time on average shown in the graph reveals an alarming reality.

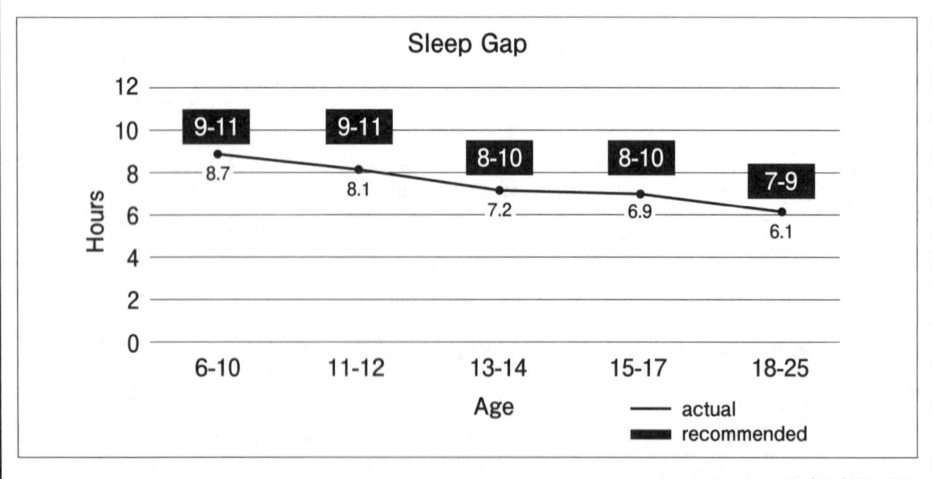

SleepFoundation.org の記事を参考に作成

A large-scale survey found that the amount of sleep teens have been getting has been consistently decreasing. In the early 1990s, about 52 percent of 15-year-olds and 36 percent of 18-year-olds reported sleeping seven hours or more per night. However, in the survey done in 2011-2012, the figures decreased to only 43 percent and 33 percent, respectively.

What makes the situation worse is teens' improper attitudes towards sleep. Many seem to think that it is cool to pull an all-nighter or stay up late. Young people need to know it is not a healthy habit and learn how to break the negative cycle.

Response to "Sleep Patterns among Teens" **by Ethan B.**

Working as a school doctor, I have seen more and more students develop sleep-related issues over the last decade. Students nowadays are busier with homework, extracurricular activities, and other responsibilities. Besides, they now have social media, which has them on their computer screens and smartphones late into the night.

Lack of sleep has countless negative consequences. The decline in learning abilities, as mentioned by Ms. Sharon Jones, is a serious problem. When students report having difficulties in class or getting lower grades, they often have sleep issues. But I have seen even more behavioral and psychological problems. When students do not get enough sleep, they seem to become more aggressive and have trouble getting along with their friends. They also get easily stressed and anxious.

Ms. Jones' article showed that while those in my students' age group need at least eight hours of sleep every night, their average night sleep is over an hour less than the recommendation. Parents and teachers must do a better job educating teens about the importance of sleep. At the same time, we need to help our youngsters establish healthy sleep habits. Setting a consistent bed time and wake-up time is the first step. They should also create a relaxing sleep environment: dark, cool, and quiet.

問 1　Neither Sharon Jones nor the school doctor mentions [19].

① reduced safety due to a lack of sleep
② the change in the amount of sleep teens get
③ the effects of social media on teens' sleep
④ what happens in the brain during sleep

問 2　The school doctor mainly sees people aged [20].

① 6 to 10
② 11 to 12
③ 13 to 14
④ 15 to 17

問 3　According to the articles, sleep has good effects on young people's [21].
(Choose the best combination of options.)

a　complex thinking
b　food choices
c　mental health
d　relationship with their parents

Combinations:

① a, b
② a, c
③ b, c
④ b, d

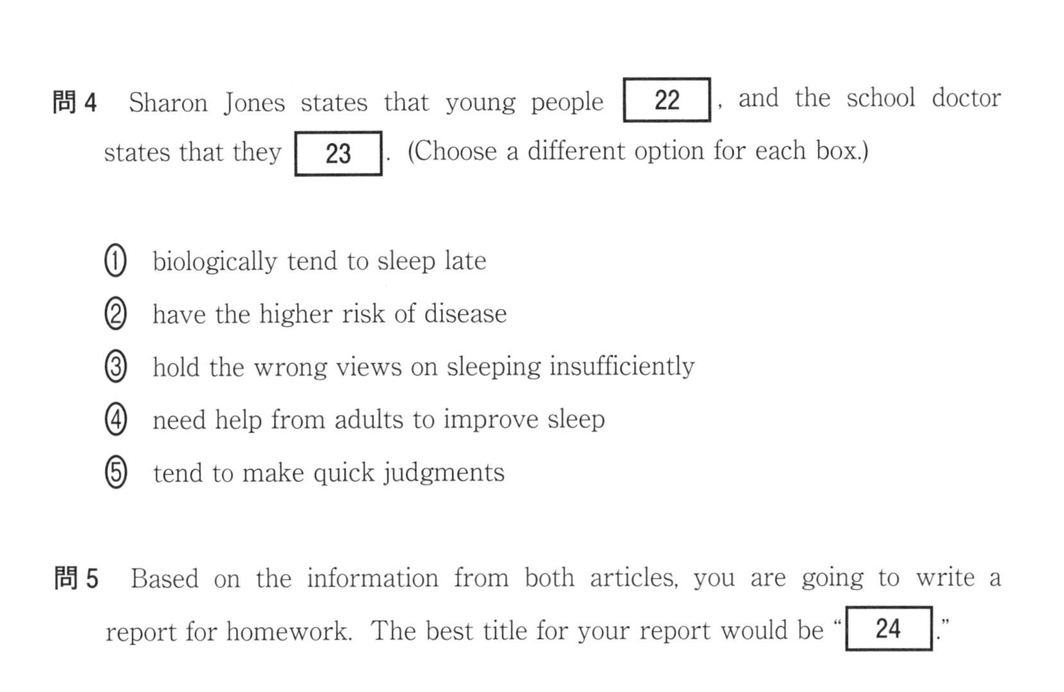

問 4 Sharon Jones states that young people [22], and the school doctor states that they [23]. (Choose a different option for each box.)

① biologically tend to sleep late
② have the higher risk of disease
③ hold the wrong views on sleeping insufficiently
④ need help from adults to improve sleep
⑤ tend to make quick judgments

問 5 Based on the information from both articles, you are going to write a report for homework. The best title for your report would be "[24]."

① How Poor Sleep Patterns Affect Teens
② Sleep Patterns Differ with Age
③ Teens' Lifestyle Change and Reasons to Stay Up at Night
④ Teens' Mysterious Brains Explained from the Viewpoint of Sleep

第6問 (配点 18)

You are working on an essay about whether the government should put a higher tax on unhealthy food. You will follow the steps below.

Step 1: Read and understand various viewpoints about tax on unhealthy food.

Step 2: Take a position on putting a higher tax on unhealthy food.

Step 3: Create an outline for an essay using additional sources.

[Step 1] Read various sources

Author A (Parent)
As a parent, I'm trying to encourage my children to make the right choices as they grow up. Of course, I worry about their health, and I try to provide healthy food for them. However, now they are teenagers, they spend time with their friends and buy their own snacks and school lunches. I hope that through health education at school and my positive influence, not by the effect of high taxes on the cost of food, they will learn to make good choices. We should educate them, not try to force their decision. That's why I disagree with these taxes — children should make good decisions themselves.

Author B (Doctor)
The scientific evidence shows that eating too many calories leads to poor health and shorter lives. This puts a cost on society as well as individuals as health care costs go up. I believe that putting taxes on unhealthy food will help people to make better choices about their food. Currently, junk food is often cheaper than healthy food, and this is one reason most people buy junk food. It is time to bring in these taxes to improve the health of the whole country and to enable us to better target diseases not caused by obesity.

Author C (Supermarket manager)
As a major supermarket chain, we stock a wide range of foods for people to choose from. We try to keep our prices low, but many families must shop carefully to match their food budget. Unhealthy foods are often sold at relatively low prices, and raising the price of such foods by taxing has a larger impact on poorer people. We provide advice and recipes for families to choose healthy options, but it should be the choice of those families. Sometimes, people want to eat sweet or high-calorie food as a treat. They should have the freedom to do this.

Author D (PE teacher)
The amount of physical activity that children do goes down every year and the number of overweight children increases. This is due to many factors. One reason is that children spend more time playing indoors on digital devices. However, the main factor is that children take in more sugar than in the past, especially in soda. In fact, boys between fourteen and eighteen take in more sugar than any other group. Sugar taxes are used in over fifty countries around the world, and these have had a positive effect on the health of children.

Author E (Student)
We recently studied this, and we found that taxes on unhealthy food can have a positive effect. It is difficult to just raise taxes on "unhealthy food," but taxes on sugar in some countries have been effective. One reason was that people started buying low-sugar options (for example, diet sodas, or low sugar snacks). However, the biggest effect was on the manufacturers. Many food producers in these countries changed the recipes of their original products. This helped them to sell a product that was healthier for customers.

問 1 Both Authors B and C mention that **25**.

① poorer people are usually too busy to try to cook healthier food recipes
② raising prices of unhealthy food will mean that poorer people can be healthier
③ reducing the calories people consume will lead to a reduction in the cost to society
④ unhealthy food is generally bought at a lower cost than healthy alternatives

問 2 Author E implies that **26**.

① companies reduce the cost of producing their low-calorie products in order to make more profit
② manufacturers in high-tax countries try to move from their original locations
③ putting a tax on junk food has had a positive effect in nearly every case that was tested
④ putting taxes on the sugar content of drinks leads the manufacturers to produce healthier products

[Step 2] Take a position

問 3 Now that you understand the various viewpoints, you have taken a position on putting a higher tax on unhealthy food, and have written it out as below. Choose the best options to complete **27**, **28**, and **29**.

Your position: The government should not put a higher tax on unhealthy food.

- Authors **27** and **28** support your position.
- The main argument of the two authors: **29**.

Options for **27** and **28** (The order does not matter.)

① A

② B

③ C

④ D

⑤ E

Options for **29**

① Choosing a diet that is healthy through education is the strongest way to make changes

② Discussing healthy food in class helps to make a balance between healthy and unhealthy menus

③ People should be able to choose what to eat according to their own decisions

④ Parents should be educated so that they provide healthy food for their children

[Step 3] Create an outline using Sources A and B

Outline of your essay:

Putting a higher tax on unhealthy food is not a good idea

Introduction

While a number of countries have increased taxes on unhealthy food or food with a high sugar content, this is not the best way to encourage healthy eating.

Body

Reason 1: [From Step 2]

Reason 2: [Based on Source A] ········· **30**

Reason 3: [Based on Source B] ········· **31**

Conclusion

The government should not put a higher tax on unhealthy food.

Source A

While increasing the cost of unhealthy foods through taxes can force customers to change their shopping and eating habits, it is not the only way. Rather than charging more for junk food, it is better to motivate people to change through reducing the cost of healthy options and by giving rewards. Governments could help to lower the cost of fruits and vegetables by paying some of the cost themselves. At first, this seems expensive, but it is not so. As the population eats healthier food, fewer people become sick because of bad diet. As a result, the government may even save money. Another method of encouraging healthy eating is by giving rewards. Supermarkets in some countries give a free piece of fruit to children who come shopping with their parents. It is fun for the child to choose different fruit rewards, and a survey showed that this helped to motivate children to eat more fruit instead of chocolates and cookies.

Source B

A US survey showed the percentages of adults in different income groups who responded that they consume sugary drinks more than 2 times daily. The survey clearly shows that there is a relation between the percentages of people who take in sweetened drinks and their income levels.

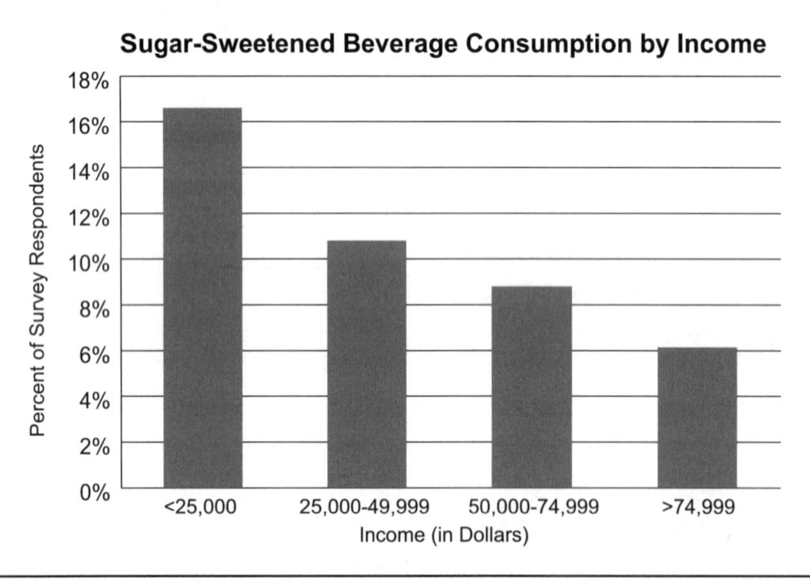

問4 Based on Source A, which of the following is the most appropriate for Reason 2? **30**

① Allowing children to choose the food that the family will eat can motivate parents to make better choices.
② Focusing on reducing health costs is an effective way of motivating people to change their unhealthy diets.
③ Giving people free choice while at the same time offering a positive reason to choose healthy food is the best strategy.
④ If some healthy food is given for free and unhealthy food is made more expensive, people will choose a healthier diet.

問5 For Reason 3, you have decided to write, "Putting higher taxes on unhealthy food has a negative influence on the poorer people in society." Based on Source B, which option best supports this statement? **31**

① Higher taxes on sugar-sweetened drinks will lead to fewer people drinking them. This will in the end require another way for the government to earn money.
② More than 90% of the people in the highest income group don't consume sweetened drinks more than twice a day. This shows that richer people don't pay more tax.
③ The percentage of those in the highest income group who drink sugary drinks more than twice a day is less than half that of the lowest income group. It could be said that poorer people tend to have more health problems.
④ The percentage of people who consume sugary drinks more than twice a day is the largest in the lowest income group. The proportion of income spent on these drinks will increase more for this group than for other groups.

第7問 (配点　15)

Your group is preparing a poster presentation entitled "A Pioneer in Children's Educational TV Programming," using the information from the magazine article below.

Anyone who grew up in the United States or Canada between 1968 and 2001 will recall Fred Rogers' TV show *Mister Rogers' Neighborhood* with warm feelings. A beloved television personality, producer, composer, writer, and minister, Rogers dedicated his life to children and touched millions of lives.

Fred McFeely Rogers was born on March 20, 1928, in Latrobe, Pennsylvania, near Pittsburgh. He graduated from Rollins College, Florida, in 1951, with a degree in music composition. He got his first job at the leading national television channel NBC, in New York, but quit because he thought commercial TV channels were harming young viewers. In 1953, Rogers moved back to Pittsburgh to work for WQED, the nation's first community-supported television station. He produced a program called *The Children's Corner*. In the early 1960s, Rogers was invited to Toronto, Canada, to create a children's program called *Misterogers*, which provided the foundation for Rogers' later productions. He returned to Pittsburgh and launched *Mister Rogers' Neighborhood* in 1966. It started to be aired nationwide on Public Broadcasting Service (PBS) two years later and continued to air for the next four decades.

Mister Rogers' Neighborhood was different from any other children's television programs at that time. Rogers could not stand how children's programs were often loud, fast-paced, and violent. In *Mister Rogers' Neighborhood*, Rogers' mission was to enrich children's lives by treating them with respect and accepting them for who they were. He directly talked to the viewers, sang the songs he wrote, and used hand puppets to talk about feelings. It was slow, inexpensive, and low-tech. Moreover, the show dealt with serious issues such as divorce, war, and death. Rogers believed that it was adults' responsibility to help children understand the negative parts of life. Another unusual and important aspect of the show is how he included minorities. In the 1960s, many white people were openly opposed to sharing a swimming pool with black people. Rogers thought it was ridiculous and wrote a script where he washed his feet in a little pool with one of the regular characters on the show, Officer Clemmons, who was played by an African American singer.

Rogers was also an advocate for children and families outside the world of television. In 1969, President Richard Nixon decided to cut funding for public broadcasting, of which *Mister Rogers' Neighborhood* was a part. Rogers went to Washington D.C. and gave a passionate speech about why children needed shows like his. His genuine and powerful words won PBS $20 million, saving the network. Rogers also wrote more than thirty books for both children and adults. Rogers received every major award, including the Presidential Medal of Freedom.

Despite the success of *Mister Rogers' Neighborhood*, there has not been another show like it. Most children's shows still prefer action over silence and rarely touch on the sensitive subjects that Rogers tackled in every episode of his program. However, his true legacy is how he used mass media to provide children with a safe place to be themselves and educate the public how best to relate to children. The tremendous level of kindness, honesty, and love he spread throughout his lifetime continues to live on.

A Pioneer in Children's Educational TV Programming

■ The Life of Fred Rogers

Period	Events
1928 -1940s	Rogers grew up in Latrobe, Pennsylvania.
1950s	Rogers graduated from university. ↓ 32 ↓ 33
1960s	Rogers created a children's program in Toronto. ↓ 34 ↓ 35

Fred Rogers

About *Mister Rogers' Neighborhood*

- Aired nationally in 1968.
- The show was unusual yet compelling for the following reasons:
  - Rogers directly talked to and sang to his viewers through television.
  - [36]
  - [37]

Fred Rogers' Legacy

- Rogers' philosophy is reflected in the songs he wrote, including, "Won't You Be My Neighbor?" "It's Such a Good Feeling," and "[38]."
- Fred Rogers is considered a pioneer in children's TV programming due to the following contributions:
  - [39]
  - [40]

問1 Members of your group listed important events in Rogers' life. Choose **four** out of the five events (①～⑤) in the order they happened to complete **The Life of Fred Rogers**.

[32] → [33] → [34] → [35]

① *Mister Rogers' Neighborhood* was first aired.

② Rogers fought to regain funding for public broadcasting.

③ Rogers got a job at a commercial TV station.

④ Rogers started working for a community TV station.

⑤ Rogers wrote as many as fifty books for children.

問 2　Choose the best two options for [36] and [37] to complete **About *Mister Rogers' Neighborhood***. (The order does not matter.)

① Rogers addressed unpleasant topics in life that children needed help to understand.
② Rogers believed in the effectiveness of early education, so he taught children reading and math skills.
③ Rogers featured people from ethnic minorities on the show to demonstrate acceptance.
④ Rogers identified the best time to air his show to attract more audience.
⑤ Rogers used a lot of animation to appeal to children.

問 3　Which of the following is most likely one of Rogers' songs? [38]

① It's You I Like
② Let's Not Talk About It
③ Might Is Right
④ Nothing Is Going to Change

問 4　Choose the best two options for [39] and [40] to complete **Fred Rogers' Legacy**. (The order does not matter.)

① Children moved away from spending too much time in front of television.
② Rogers established a standard for children's educational TV programming.
③ Rogers succeeded by doing the opposite of the mainstream.
④ Rogers used TV as a medium to do good for children.
⑤ School teachers started using educational TV shows in classroom.

第8問 （配点 14）

You are in a student group preparing a poster for a scientific presentation contest with the theme "Modern inventions that have changed the world." You have been using the following passage to create the poster.

Barcodes

A Universal Product Code (UPC), the most familiar type of barcode, is a small black and white image found on most products worldwide. Companies use these barcodes to quickly identify at checkout items being sold. They have practical uses for both businesses and customers alike. From the customers' point of view, barcodes provide a faster and more convenient shopping experience, and companies use the barcodes to track and manage inventory in their stores. Although they are now common, barcodes are a relatively modern invention. Research shows they were first used at checkout on a packet of chewing gum on June 26, 1974. It didn't take long for other companies to see the benefits. Their success is due to their convenience and the fact that they provide the same information from country to country. A nonprofit international organization called GS1 is responsible for managing this operation. They accept the applications from companies that want a barcode for their product.

The Universal Product Code has two distinct sections: The black and white "bars" read by laser scanners in stores, and a series of numbers below. Essentially, these two parts do a similar job, but the numbers are mainly for reading, whereas the bars are for computers.

Figure 1. Example barcode

When a laser scanner reads a barcode, it scans evenly spaced columns, otherwise called "bars." The scanner registers whether each bar reflects light or not. White bars, which reflect light, are registered as a 0 in the computer system, while black bars, which do not, are read as a 1. After the scan, the computer has a list of 95 0s or 1s. These are then grouped into 15 different sections. Twelve of these sections represent the numbers you see at the bottom of the barcode, and the remaining three sections are called "guards." One on the far left, one on the far right, and one in the center. The end-guards tell the computer where the barcode begins and ends, while the central guard tells the computer where the numbers are divided. This is important because it tells the computer whether it is reading the code left to right or upside-down. It knows this because the bars on the left of the central guard will have an odd number of 1s, and bars on the right have an even number of 1s.

Now that we know how a computer can read a barcode let's look at the numbers. You will see from *Figure 1* that the first number is on the left, sitting outside the barcode; this is called the "number system character." This number tells us what type of barcode we are looking at: "0", "1", "6", "7", "9" represent a standard barcode that can be used for any product; a "2" is a weighed item, like fruit or rice; a "3" is a pharmaceutical item, like medicine; a "4" is reserved for local use in stores; a "5" is a coupon, and so on. The following five numbers are the company's (or manufacturer's) code. A company must register with the GS1 to get a code, and as such, each code is unique to a specific company. The second set of five digits is the product code. The manufacturer selects and manages this code independently and does not need to register it. Finally, there is the check digit. This number, found on the far right, is the only information not found in the bars. It allows the computer to double-check that it has read the barcode correctly by checking the number against the rest of the barcode.

It's important to note that what we have described above is just the most popular type of barcode. This type (the Universal Product Code) is generally used with items that are sold; however, there are many other types of barcodes these days. Some are used to open websites, others to register people, and others for security checks. Each of these uses has a different barcode type and uses a slightly different system. Still, all these barcode types are essentially based on the basic invention, first used in 1974.

Your presentation poster draft:

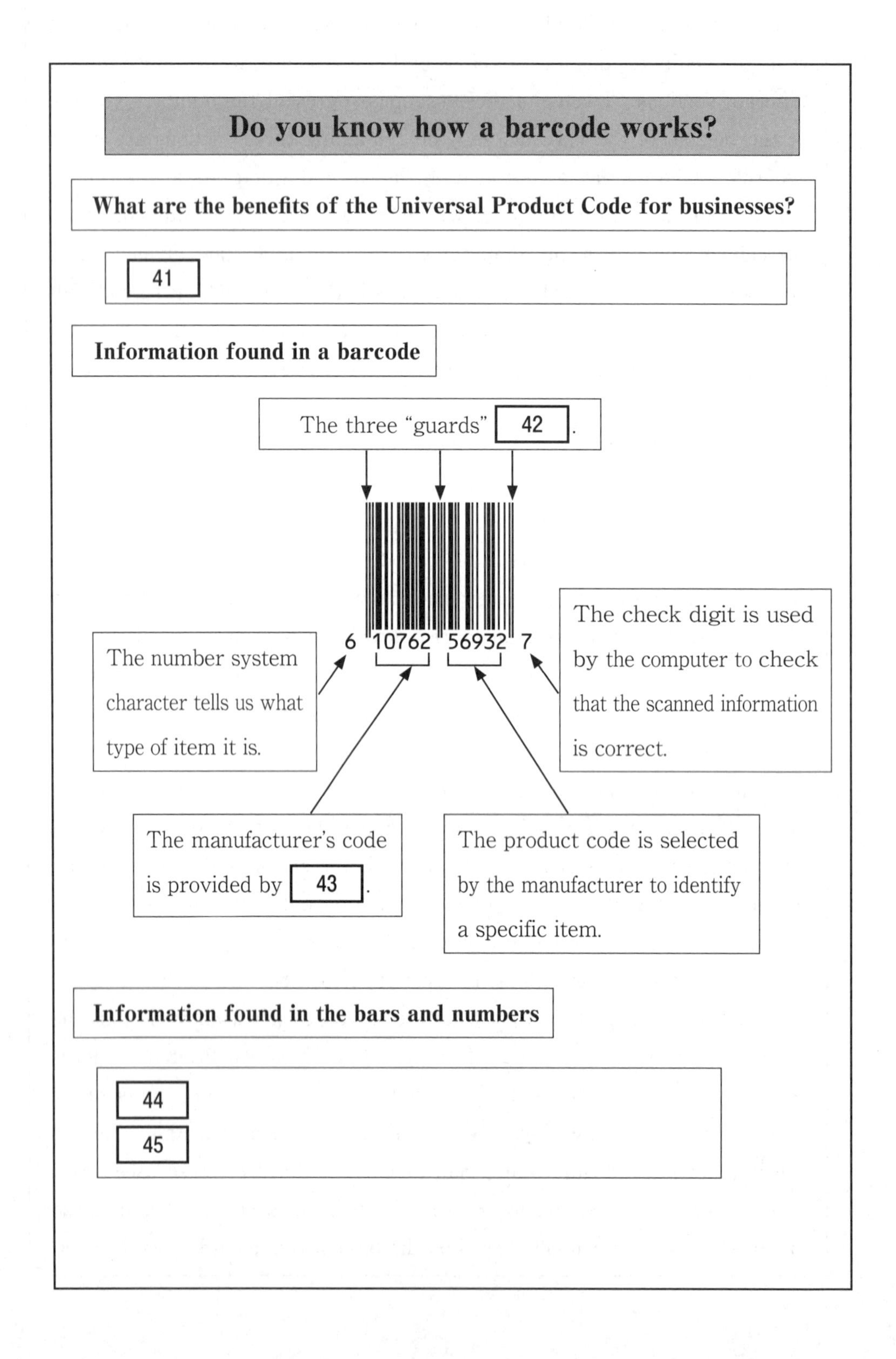

問 1 Under the first poster heading, your group wants to set out why Universal Product Codes are commonly used. As explained in the article, which of the following is most appropriate? **[41]**

① They are a cheaper alternative to traditional methods of tracking items.
② They can be used to understand how a product is manufactured.
③ They give companies data that enables them to trace and manage products in their inventory.
④ They provide a more reliable way for customers to see what they have purchased.

問 2 You have been asked to write descriptions of the guards and manufacturer's code. Choose the best options for **[42]** and **[43]**.

The three "guards" **[42]**
① limit the time the data is available
② stop criminals from using the barcode's information
③ tell the computer about the product
④ tell the computer the direction of the barcode

The manufacturer's code **[43]**
① a nonprofit organization in charge of regulating barcodes
② the company selling the item
③ the country's government
④ the organization which made the product

問 3 You are making statements about what kinds of information are found in a barcode. According to the article, which two of the following are correct? (The order does not matter.) **44** · **45**

① Both the bars and the numbers include information on the three guards.

② Some companies will share the same manufacturer's code.

③ The second set of five digits represents the type of business.

④ The number used to check the accuracy of the information is not found in the bars.

⑤ The second number tells us the weight of the item.

⑥ The type of product is the first piece of information provided.

※この問題冊子の『注意事項』は，実際の共通テストを想定して掲載しました。

模試　第3回

（100点
80分）

〔英　　語（リーディング）〕

注　意　事　項

1　解答用紙に，正しく記入・マークされていない場合は，採点できないことがあります。

2　試験中に問題冊子の印刷不鮮明，ページの落丁・乱丁及び解答用紙の汚れ等に気付いた場合は，手を高く挙げて監督者に知らせなさい。

3　解答は，解答用紙の解答欄にマークしなさい。例えば，[10] と表示のある問いに対して ③ と解答する場合は，次の（例）のように**解答番号10の解答欄**の ③ に**マーク**しなさい。

（例）

解答番号	解　　答　　欄
10	① ② ● ④ ⑤ ⑥ ⑦ ⑧ ⑨

4　問題冊子の余白等は適宜利用してよいが，どのページも切り離してはいけません。

5　**不正行為について**

①　不正行為に対しては厳正に対処します。

②　不正行為に見えるような行為が見受けられた場合は，監督者がカードを用いて注意します。

③　不正行為を行った場合は，その時点で受験を取りやめさせ退室させます。

6　試験終了後，問題冊子は持ち帰りなさい。

英　語(リーディング)

各大問の英文や図表を読み，解答番号 1 ～ 46 にあてはまるものとして最も適当な選択肢を選びなさい。

第1問 (配点　6)

You found the following article on an English information website for your town.

Restaurant Spotlight: Italiana Fresca

We are pleased to announce that Rocco Giuseppe selected our town for his second Italiana Fresca. The award-winning chef decided to build the new restaurant here to take advantage of our famous vegetables. Italiana Fresca will be celebrating its opening by hosting several events, including cooking classes taught by chef Giuseppe himself. Although the events will be held in English, cooking classes will be clear enough for anyone to follow by example. If you have never visited Italy and enjoyed real Italian cooking, this is a great opportunity.

Schedule

May 1	Grand opening party
May 3	Lecture I: Essential Italian for travel through Italy
May 4	Cooking class I: (1) How to make homemade pasta (2) Pesto, a vegetable sauce
May 15	Lecture II: How to gesture like an Italian
May 17	Cooking class II: (1) How to make Italian chicken (2) Italian breadsticks

May 21	Lecture III: Japan-Italy relations
May 23	Neapolitan pizza tasting event

- All events will be held from 3:00 - 5:00 PM at the restaurant. Children under thirteen years of age cannot participate alone in the cooking classes, but they are welcome to accompany their parents.
- Those attending any of the events will receive a 50% discount on a dinner ordered the same day.

To register to participate in any event, click **here**.

▶▶ Italiana Fresca: Official Site

問 1 The purpose of this notice is to inform people about [1].

① Italian classes taught by Rocco Giuseppe
② the new chef at a popular Italian restaurant
③ the sale of city's famous vegetables at a new Italian restaurant
④ the schedule for the first month of a new Italian restaurant

問 2 At one of the events, the participants will learn [2].

① how certain kinds of pizzas are made
② how Italian food and culture are changing
③ how to communicate better in Italy
④ how to find good deals on travel

問 3 People who participate in the events will be able to [3].

① eat pasta made by other participants at home
② have a meal at a lower price than usual
③ meet people who plan to visit Italy
④ teach table manners to elementary school children

第2問 (配点 10)

You are a member of the environmental club. The members are making plans for a new volunteer event and you have been asked to come up with suggestions. To get ideas, you are reading a blog about a community service project a student introduced at her school.

Ten-Minute Community Challenge

Arriving at school used to make me sad. There are several convenience stores and cafes in the area and people often drop litter on the ground —— cans, bottles, sweet wrappers, plastic bags, etc. Last year, I decided to do something. I put up posters asking students to come to school ten minutes earlier than usual for one week and use the extra time to pick up a few pieces of litter. It worked! An average of 150 students (10% of the school) took part each day. Nearly a third of that number participated the whole week. There were even a few teachers. Within three days, the area around the school was already much nicer. By the end, it was perfect. Surprisingly, since this event the area has stayed litter-free. Why is this? Feedback from the event seems to give the answer:

Feedback from the students and the local community

BT: I hadn't realised how unhappy this problem was making me. I can finally walk to school with a big smile on my face.

AK: Great project! As an adult living near the school, I was so happy to see school students helping the community. I joined in and got some neighbours involved, too. We still do it twice a week.

RN: We appreciate the difference it has made. My friends and I would have joined in but we didn't see the poster.

CF: This project helped me understand how action by a high school student can have a big impact.

WL: I am so thankful. I've lived here for 15 years and I feel I can be proud of this town again.

問 1　The aim of the activity was to [4].

① get students to support the community
② help locals to know each other
③ improve the school playground
④ make the environment look nicer

問 2　One **fact** about the Ten-Minute Community Challenge is that [5].

① it only lasted for three days
② only students picked up litter
③ the number of students who worked the whole week was around 50
④ the teachers were happy that the town looked cleaner

問 3　From the blog, we know that it is most likely true that [6].

A：more people may have wanted to take part
B：students encouraged the locals to join in
C：students like picking up garbage
D：the author didn't expect teachers to join in

① **A** and **B**
② **A** and **C**
③ **A** and **D**
④ **B** and **C**
⑤ **B** and **D**
⑥ **C** and **D**

問4 One of the participants' opinions about the Ten-Minute Community Challenge is that [7].

① everyone should take part in the challenge
② locals have always been happy to live in the area
③ one person can make a difference to the community
④ the challenge should have started 15 years ago

問5 The author's question is answered by [8].

① AK
② BT
③ CF
④ RN
⑤ WL

（下 書 き 用 紙）

英語（リーディング）の試験問題は次に続く。

第3問 (配点 9)

After a morning assembly about setting a New Year goal, your homeroom teacher shares a blog about how a British student was able to break a bad habit.

Break the Habit

As a student, it is easy to pick up bad habits, like leaving your homework until the last minute or playing video games a little too often. I managed to overcome some of my bad habits, and this is how I did it.

First, I needed to identify the problem. I fell asleep in the middle of a maths test and failed. The teacher called me into his office and asked about my routine. Then I realised I had a problem with my eating habits. Eating snacks was always a big issue for me. For an energy boost, I would usually grab a chocolate bar, some sweets, or a sugary drink. I didn't notice how much the extra calories were making me overweight and sleepy. Usually, 30 minutes after eating, my energy levels would crash.

I set myself a goal. I hated apples, bananas, and healthy options like that. Still, I replaced all my regular unhealthy snacks with fruit, nuts, and granola bars. I challenged myself to keep up the new diet for three months. To support me, my friends stopped eating snacks around me, and my brother promised to give me his watch that I wanted if I succeeded. I did!

Changing my diet has had a huge impact on my life. I have lost 12kg. I actually desire healthy food. I also have more energy, feel more awake, and I do better at school, which is a great joy. A few months ago, I used the same method to cut down on my screen time. I identified the issue, removed my triggers (putting my smartphone in my bag instead of my pocket), started new activities like playing board games, and rewarded myself with a trip to Disneyland. If you follow similar steps, you'll be on your way to breaking your bad habits and reaching your full potential.

問 1 Put the following events (①～④) into the order in which they happened.

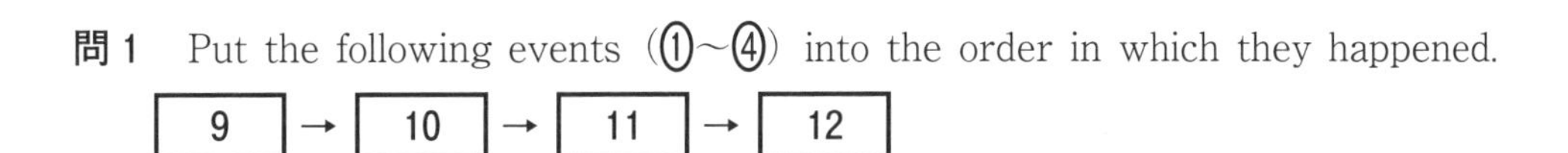

① People close to the author helped him.
② The author failed a test.
③ The author made poor food choices.
④ The author received something he wanted.

問 2 If you follow the author's advice, you should [13].

① ask your friends to change their habits for you
② find a better balance of study and fun
③ follow a system to make improvements in your life
④ trust what your teachers tell you

問 3 From this story, you understand that the author [14].

① found that his tastes have changed
② preferred going to Disneyland to playing board games
③ struggles to make effective plans
④ tried the method out only once

第4問 （配点　12）

In English class you are writing an essay on a social issue you are interested in. This is your most recent draft. You are now working on revisions based on comments from your teacher.

<table>
<tr><th>Gardening and Community Building</th><th>Comments</th></tr>
<tr><td>
Community gardens are pieces of land owned by local government where community members are allowed to grow vegetable or flower gardens in cooperation with their neighbors. To ensure that these gardens continue to exist in the future, it is important that we understand their value and their potential. This essay will discuss some benefits of community gardens.

First, at a time when urban isolation is increasingly common, community gardens offer opportunities for friendly interaction, particularly among the elderly. Nowadays there are few locations where residents can interact, especially in big cities. (1) ∧ So, community gardens may serve as rare community hubs where residents of different generations get to know each other.

Second, community gardens provide practical skills and knowledge for gardening and farming that residents can make use of. (2) ∧ Working on gardens requires teamwork; this will help improve communication skills and the individual's sense of responsibility.

Finally, (3) <u>we are responsible for what we eat.</u> Community ownership makes nutritious fruits, vegetables, and herbs more affordable. This leads to healthier eating habits, especially in areas where fresh produce may be limited or expensive.

In conclusion, community gardens (4) <u>help the elderly,</u> provide valuable lessons, and lastly, enrich our diet. We should do all we can to support them, as they will become more and more important to us in later life.
</td><td>
(1) You're missing something here. Add more information to connect the two sentences.
(2) Insert a connecting expression here.
(3) This topic sentence doesn't really match this paragraph. Rewrite it.
(4) The underlined phrase doesn't summarize your essay content enough. Change it.
</td></tr>
<tr><td colspan="2"><u>Overall Comment:</u>
I think this topic is something that will be increasingly important in our aging society. There's a community garden in my neighborhood too!</td></tr>
</table>

問 1　Based on comment (1), which is the best sentence to add? 15

① Besides, gardening is a popular activity that can be enjoyed regardless of age.
② For instance, they teach valuable lessons about how our food is produced.
③ Furthermore, community gardens provide people with a chance to be alone.
④ Similarly, community gardens promote sport in urban environments.

問 2　Based on comment (2), which is the best expression to add? 16

① additionally
② however
③ in contrast
④ therefore

問 3　Based on comment (3), which is the most appropriate way to rewrite the topic sentence? 17

① we can benefit from the harvest
② we can enjoy visiting the area
③ we can feel closer to nature
④ we can save shipping costs

問 4　Based on comment (4), which is the best replacement? 18

① are popular locations for holding events
② can create collaboration among local schools
③ have the potential to revitalize unwanted land
④ help build deeper relationships within the community

第5問 (配点　16)

Your teacher has asked you to read two articles about the theory of evolution. You will discuss what you learned in your next class.

Understanding Evolution

Scarlet Aguilar

Biology Teacher, Fletterville Senior High School

As a high school teacher, one trend I have noticed recently is students with some strange ideas about evolution. For instance, one student recently wrote, "Neanderthals, the ancestors of human beings, lived 5,000 years ago." There are two problems here. While Neanderthals appear to be somehow related to humans, it is too simple to call them our direct ancestors. In reality, it is more likely that there has been some crossbreeding between Neanderthals and Homo sapiens, that is modern human beings. It is commonly believed that Neanderthals and Homo sapiens share an ancestor called Homo heidelbergensis, although this theory is still being questioned by some researchers. Also, while it is difficult to date when Neanderthals lived, evidence says it's at least 50,000 years ago, not 5,000! Remember, evolution is no overnight process. It happens slowly, over hundreds of thousands of years.

Let's consider the case of Homo heidelbergensis. Homo heidelbergensis had much larger jawbones and larger brow ridges than Homo sapiens. However, modern humans have neither of these characteristics.

Species	Homo heidelbergensis
Jawbone(*) size * the bone that forms the shape of the lower part of the face	large and strong
Brow ridge	very large
Picture	

By providing my students with side-by-side comparisons of the two, I was able to help them appreciate how much we have evolved over time. In fact, explaining there were other human species in the past gives them a better appreciation of the wonders of gradual evolution.

Overnight Evolution

Estelle Kramer
Professor, Fletterville University

As a university professor, I really appreciate the work high school teachers do. I agree with Ms. Aguilar that students need to learn the facts about evolution. However, I must comment on Ms. Aguilar's recent article. She says evolution is "no overnight process," but I cannot completely agree. In recent years, the scientific community has come to believe that sudden bursts of evolution are more likely than gradual evolution.

In Ms. Aguilar's example of Homo heidelbergensis, she suggests slow evolution occurs over very long periods of time. However, if evolution were always a gradual process as she claims, then the changes between human ancestors and modern humans could be evenly observed over time. Evolution is actually much more uneven. Certain fossil remains show that sudden changes have had big impacts on how our ancestors evolved. Think of this as fast evolution. The idea behind fast evolution is that animals actually stay the same for long periods of time. After these long intervals, they undergo sudden evolutionary changes in only one or two generations.

One case that supports fast evolution is that of a species of bird called kingfishers in New Guinea. Mainland kingfishers in New Guinea show little difference between various species. However, on nearby islands, kingfishers appear to have experienced sudden periods of change. The short length of these changes has been proven by scientists who study the genetic code. They found the island birds have greater variety in their DNA. As a result, these island kingfishers may look and act very differently from their cousins on the mainland. These studies of island kingfishers support the theory of fast evolution.

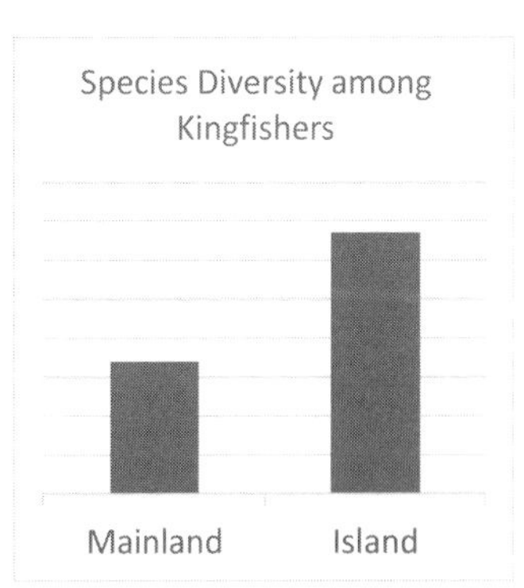

I hope that this explanation helps everyone better understand how quickly evolution can occur.

問 1　Aguilar thought that [19].

① evolution can happen in one day
② evolution has become unimportant in school
③ her students are strange in character
④ her student's comment was surprising

問 2　In the study discussed by Kramer, kingfishers found on islands off New Guinea are [20] than those on the mainland.

① larger in number
② larger in size
③ more likely to live longer
④ more varied

問 3　Aguilar explains gradual evolution, in which animals [21] slowly over an incredibly long time, and Kramer tries to [22] it with her argument. (Choose the best one for each box from options ①～⑥.)

① change
② deny
③ emphasize
④ grow
⑤ promote
⑥ prove

問 4　Both writers agree that [23].

① DNA affects evolution
② evolution is a gradual process
③ Neanderthals lived 5,000 years ago
④ students should learn about evolution

問 5　Which additional information would be the best to further support Kramer's argument for fast evolution? [24]

① Comparisons between kingfishers and Homo heidelbergensis
② Detailed data showing the greater variety in the DNA of island kingfishers compared to that of mainland kingfishers
③ Detailed information about the geography of New Guinea
④ Studies of the climate of ancient Earth

第6問 (配点 18)

You are working on an essay about whether medical companies should test their products on animals. You will follow the steps below.

Step 1: Read and understand various viewpoints on animal testing.

Step 2: Take a position on medical testing on animals.

Step 3: Create an outline for an essay using additional sources.

[Step 1] Read various sources

Author A (Hospital patient) I am recovering from a very dangerous disease. I heard that the medicine the doctors gave me to save my life was developed through animal testing. I am deeply thankful for the medicine, but it troubles me to think that it was developed through the suffering of innocent animals. I have heard that often animal testing is chosen because it is less expensive than other methods, such as those using state-of-the-art technology. I believe that animal testing should be replaced by other methods.
Author B (Animal rights expert) Some people argue that animal testing is acceptable because animals also benefit from medicine created for humans. I think that is a poor argument. We only use medicine to save animals that are of use to humans, such as companion animals or farm animals, not wild animals. Furthermore, the procedures are often cruel. For example, the animals are given diseases and then tested to see if the drugs or treatment work for the target diseases. I think that it is immoral.
Author C (Doctor) If it were not for animal testing, drugs and treatments would be too dangerous to recommend to my patients and so many people would die — many of them very young. Of course, I feel sad about the death and suffering of the animals, but a huge number of people are saved thanks to the whole procedure involved in developing medicine, which includes animal testing. In my opinion, that would compensate for the sacrifice. Also, much of the research for human medicine is also useful in making animal medicine.

Author D (High school student) My class discussed this topic at school in one of our biology lessons and I feel strongly against using animals in medical experiments. When it comes to testing new drugs or treatments, healthy animals are chosen as subjects and infected with disease. This is ethically wrong, I think. Our teacher told us that there are alternative methods for testing medicine. These include testing on human cells in test tubes, or predicting results using computer software rather than live animals. I hope that these methods will be more widely adopted.
Author E (Scientist) At my laboratory, we test medicines and treatments on animals every day. We test them on small animals like rats, but we also test them on dogs and chimpanzees. Sadly, many of the animals suffer a lot. I feel terrible when I see this every day. However, I wish people would understand that we are following very strict rules to keep the animals in decent conditions and that there are few really good alternatives. Actually, very few animals die and suffer in testing compared with the number of human lives we will save.

問1 Both Authors B and D mention that [25].

① human medicines should be tested on humans because animals are not similar enough

② nowadays we can verify the safety of new medicines without using animal testing

③ pets and farm animals also benefit from the medical research relying on animal testing

④ the animals used in medical testing are intentionally made sick by the researchers

問2 Author A implies that [26].

① he appreciates the chance to live that animals have given him

② he will dedicate his life to saving animals after he recovers

③ only medicine that is tested on animals can save the lives of humans

④ people should not have negative images of animal testing anymore

[Step 2] Take a position

問 3　Now that you understand the various viewpoints, you have taken a position on medical testing on animals, and have written it out as below. Choose the best options to complete [27], [28], and [29].

Your position: Testing medicine on animals is the right thing to do.

- Authors [27] and [28] support your position.
- The main argument of the two authors: [29].

Options for [27] and [28] (The order does not matter.)

① A
② B
③ C
④ D
⑤ E

Options for [29]

① Animals should only be used to find cures for diseases that affect people with healthy lifestyles.
② It is better to test medicines on small animals like rats because they may feel less pain than bigger animals.
③ The number of lives that will be saved by animal testing is large enough to make testing acceptable.
④ The number of medicines that can be made through animal testing is higher than if we only tested on humans.

[Step 3] Create an outline using Sources A and B

Outline of your essay:

Testing medicines on animals is an acceptable practice

Introduction

Testing medicines on animals has made it possible to produce many medicines. We should not stop researchers from using this important tool.

Body

Reason 1: [From Step 2]

Reason 2: [Based on Source A] ……… 30

Reason 3: [Based on Source B] ……… 31

Conclusion

Testing medicine on animals is the right thing to do.

Source A

Animal testing is often debated because of its cost in terms of animal lives. It is an emotional issue for most people. However, it's crucial to understand the strict rules that govern animal testing, aimed at ensuring humane treatment. Institutions conducting animal research are required to follow strict laws, which require testers to get approval for their research from special committees. Such committees are usually made up of experts in veterinary science, ethics, and research. They carefully check the proposed studies to ensure they are necessary and that every possible measure is taken to minimize animal suffering. Furthermore, researchers must follow comprehensive guidelines focusing on animal welfare. These include providing proper care, reducing the number of animals used, and refining procedures to reduce emotional stress. Regular inspections ensure these standards are maintained. While the loss of animal life in research is a sad reality, these regulations and observation systems help raise the level of ethical responsibility in scientific exploration.

Source B

The organizations that use animals in their medical research in the UK must record the number of experiments they do on live animals every year. The graph below shows how many horses, dogs, cats, and monkeys are used in medical research.

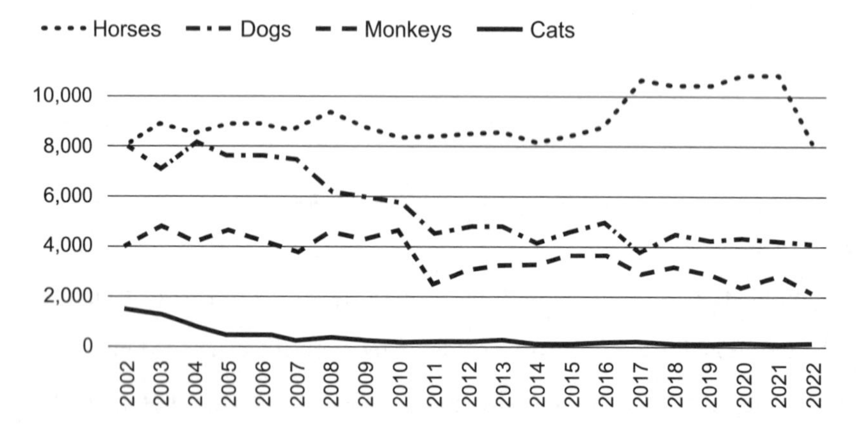

問4 Based on Source A, which of the following is the most appropriate for Reason 2? [30]

① Experts in veterinary science are advising researchers to use animals to find new medicines for humans.

② The government is encouraging animal testing by publishing guidelines for researchers to use.

③ The laws surrounding the use of animals for medical research are likely to become stricter in the future.

④ While it is unfortunate that some animals must die for research, there are rules in place to reduce their pain.

問5 For Reason 3, you have decided to write, "Researchers are using more caution in choosing whether or not to test medicines on certain animals." Based on Source B, which option best supports this statement? [31]

① About half as many dogs and monkeys were used in research in 2022 compared with 20 years before. This shows a growing concern for the welfare of these animals.

② Medical research using monkeys has dropped at nearly twice the rate of research involving dogs. This suggests that our relationship with dogs is being considered.

③ The number of cats and horses used for medical testing has remained fairly constant. These animals must have proven valuable to medical science.

④ The use of dogs and monkeys sharply decreased during the period 2012-2022. More and more researchers have come to respond to the demand for animal welfare.

第7問 （配点　15）

You are the president of your school's student council and plan to give an inspirational speech to other members, using notes. You have found a story written by a student in the UK who successfully campaigned for a change in her school.

Campaigning For Freedom of Expression

Kirstie Wood

I believe that everyone should have the freedom to express themselves in a way that makes them feel confident and comfortable. This is why my school's strict policy against students colouring their hair, always shocked me and made me sad. I felt that this rule was preventing me and my fellow students from expressing ourselves in a meaningful way.

I tried to ignore the rule and hoped that it would eventually change. As time went by, I realised that I couldn't just sit back and hope for change to happen. I needed to take action and fight for what I believed in. So, I decided to start a campaign to change the rule against students colouring their hair.

My first attempt to change the rule was met with opposition from the Student Services Director, Lucy Armstrong. She quoted concerns about the potential safety hazards of hair dye (the product used to colour hair) and the impact it could have on the school's image. Despite my best efforts to present research that showed that hair dye was safe when used properly and that it did not have a negative impact on a school's image, all appeals were ignored.

Not ready to give up, I decided to try again. This time, I reached out to my mum's hair stylist, Carol Smith, to see if she would give a workshop on colouring your hair safely. She spoke at our school assembly and the students and teachers were impressed. However, this attempt was also unsuccessful. Ms. Armstrong was not convinced that hair dye was safe and refused to change her mind.

Did I give up? Of course not. I decided to take a different approach.

Instead of focusing on the potential problems of students changing their hair colour, I decided to focus on the benefits. I researched the positive impact that self-expression can have on students. I found studies that showed that students who felt confident in their appearance were more likely to be engaged in the classroom and they believed in themselves more. I also found stories of students who had struggled with bullying but found that taking control of their hair colour provided a way for them to express themselves and feel more confident.

This time, I scheduled a meeting with the head teacher of the school, Ms. Jones. I presented the research and stories I had found and explained that by allowing students to express themselves by choosing their hair colour, we could create a more diverse and supportive school environment. To my surprise, she appeared very interested and genuinely moved. After the meeting, she agreed to check if the rule was reasonable and promised to take my arguments into consideration.

Several weeks went by and I had not heard anything. I was starting to feel a little worried, but then one day, Ms. Jones announced that there would no longer be any rules for students' hair, including colour or style. I was so delighted. This was more than I had asked for. All of my hard work had paid off.

The decision to change the rule was met with mixed reactions from students and parents. Some were extremely pleased with the change, while others were concerned about the potential consequences. However, I was confident that this was the right decision and that it would have a positive impact on the school community.

In the months that followed, I watched as students began to express themselves in new and creative ways. I saw students with brightly coloured hair, unique hairstyles, and newfound confidence. The school had become a place where students felt free to express themselves in a way that made them happy. A definite success.

Your notes:

Campaigning For Freedom of Expression

About the author (Kirstie Wood)

- Successfully changed a school policy.
- Started a campaign at school because she [32].

Important people in the story

- Lucy Armstrong : Director, who initially denied Kirstie's request.
- Carol Smith : Hair stylist, who [33].
- Ms. Jones : Head teacher, who changed the school rule.

Key steps in the process

First attempt was unsuccessful → [34] → [35] → [36] → [37] → Success

What Kirstie realised through this process

It can be important to [38].

What we can learn from this story

- [39]
- [40]

問 1　Choose the best option for 32.

① believed the school's policy kept students from expressing themselves
② didn't think her school had a good image in the local community
③ liked interacting with local business people
④ wanted more people to be like her

問 2　Choose the best option for 33.

① convinced the school that hair dye is safe
② gave advice on the best way to express yourself through hair colour
③ gave Kirstie the confidence to keep trying
④ lectured at the school about proper colouring techniques

問 3　Choose **four** out of the five options (①〜⑤) and rearrange them in the order they happened. 34 → 35 → 36 → 37

① Asked other students for advice
② Contacted a local professional for help
③ Had a meeting with the head teacher to explain her findings
④ Patiently waited but felt anxious
⑤ Researched stories of students' improved confidence

問4　Choose the best option for **38**.

① be patient and wait for things to change for the better
② focus on the positives rather than opposing the negatives
③ practice self-expression even if there are rules that go against it
④ speak to local professionals to get alternative points of view

問5　Choose the best two options for **39** and **40**. (The order does not matter.)

① Being yourself is more important than schoolwork.
② Follow your beliefs and be true to your values.
③ It is important to approach a problem from different perspectives.
④ We shouldn't worry about what other people think about us.
⑤ Your appearance has little influence on your confidence.

（下 書 き 用 紙）

英語（リーディング）の試験問題は次に続く。

第8問 （配点　14）

You are a student doing a group project for a biology class. You are using the following passage to create your presentation on the adaptability of microorganisms.

You can't talk about highly adaptive animals without bringing up creatures like Argentine ants, with their aggressive nature and huge colonies. Or perhaps tardigrades come to mind, with their ability to survive without food or water for decades. However, common worms known as nematodes are actually among the most adaptable little creatures in the world.

Nematodes, also known as roundworms, are tiny creatures. They are so small that they are often only visible through a microscope. They vary from 0.1 mm to 2.5 mm in length on average, although some species of nematodes grow to nearly a meter long. Their bodies are long and thin without arms and legs. Like the common worms found in your garden, they are tubular and shaped like a piece of soft spaghetti. Many nematodes are parasitic, meaning they live inside other creatures. Rare meter-long nematodes live inside whales, which are some of the largest mammals on Earth. However, most parasitic nematodes live inside smaller creatures, and they are very tiny. They can live almost anywhere: swamps, oceans, jungles, or even Antarctica.

Water is most important for nematodes' survival. They also need nutrition, which they usually get from eating other microorganisms in their environment. They consume food through their mouths located at one end of their bodies. The food passes through a body part that resembles a straw, called a stylet. Then the food goes through the intestine that breaks down the nutrients. Finally, the unused waste is pushed along by the rectal glands and sent out of the nematode's body through the anus.

Scientists struggle to research creatures that live in extreme environments on Earth such as toxic water masses or deep in the Earth's hard layer, neither of which provide much light or nutrition. That's where the nematode comes in. This incredible creature can adapt to just about any environment, so it offers researchers a unique chance to understand the ecology of extreme environments. Nematodes need very little oxygen to survive, can eat bacteria that live in tough conditions, and have very tough bodies. In fact, nematodes can even go into a kind of sleep called suspended animation when there is no food or water available. While in a state of suspended animation, they become completely inactive. Nematodes can survive in places like Antarctica in their inactive state for as long as 20-30 years. When conditions get better and food or water is nearby, the nematodes come alive as if by magic.

Naturally, scientists have done their best to explain the worm's magic with theories and data. In the 1970s, researchers began studying one species of nematode in particular, *C. elegans*. Its simple structure made *C. elegans* very appealing to researchers. These nematodes also grow into adults in only 3 days. By studying this species, scientists came to understand how their nervous systems work. The nervous system is the network of connections in an organism that allows it to understand sensory input, like taste and touch. For the *C. elegans*, it has a nerve ring that surrounds the pharynx (throat) and serves as the brain. This makes it similar to more advanced animals like snails or octopuses. In fact, nematodes are one of the simplest creatures ever discovered to have a nervous system. Their simple yet sophisticated bodies make them very tough to kill, even in extreme conditions.

One of the nematode's most unique features is how it reproduces. Normally, members of any animal species are considered either male or female. However, female nematodes can sometimes become what are called hermaphrodites. Basically, this means that they contain both male and female parts. A hermaphroditic female can fertilize the eggs it carries in its uterus. This amazing feature allows females to produce babies even when no males can be found in the area. In fact, males often make up only a tiny percentage of the worm population, less than one percent.

Your presentation slides:

Nematodes:
The Ultimate Adapters

1. Basic Information

- 0.1 mm to 2.5 mm in length
- long tubular bodies
-
- [41]
-
-

2. Habitats

- live almost everywhere
  - ✓ swamps ✓ jungles
  - ✓ oceans ✓ Antarctica
- can survive extreme environments, such as ...
  - ✓ toxic water masses
  - ✓ deep in the Earth's hard layer

3. Survival Strategy

- [42]
- [43]

4. Body Structure (Hermaphrodite)

[44]

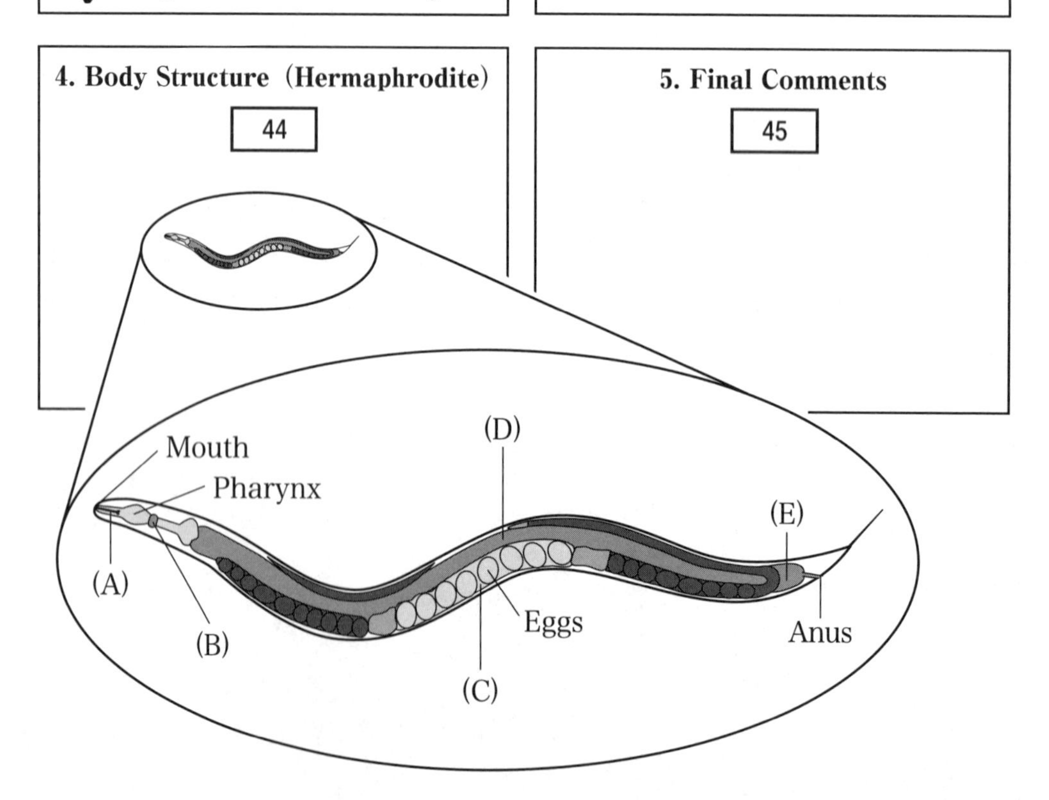

5. Final Comments

[45]

問 1　Which of the following should you **not** include for [41]?

① has a nerve ring
② has a straw-like stylet for ingesting food
③ lacks arms or legs
④ lacks male body parts
⑤ responds to touch and taste

問 2　For the **Survival Strategy** slide, select two features of the nematode which best help it survive. (The order does not matter.) [42] · [43]

① Their pharynx allows them to take in larger creatures.
② They do not need much oxygen.
③ They use their nervous system to avoid extreme environments.
④ Whenever they enter a toxic water mass, they immediately become inactive.
⑤ Without food or water, they can become inactive for a long time.

問 3　Complete the missing labels on the illustration of a nematode for the **Body Structure (Hermaphrodite)** slide. [44]

① (A) Rectal gland　(B) Stylet　(C) Intestine
　(D) Uterus　(E) Nerve ring
② (A) Nerve ring　(B) Intestine　(C) Uterus
　(D) Rectal gland　(E) Stylet
③ (A) Stylet　(B) Nerve ring　(C) Uterus
　(D) Intestine　(E) Rectal gland
④ (A) Uterus　(B) Intestine　(C) Nerve ring
　(D) Rectal gland　(E) Stylet
⑤ (A) Stylet　(B) Uterus　(C) Nerve ring
　(D) Intestine　(E) Rectal gland

問 4　Which is the best statement for the final slide?　**45**

① *C. elegans* is without a doubt the perfect worm for scientific study, as females manage to find partners to reproduce with despite the low number of males in the population.

② Clearly, nematodes have incredibly adaptive features to solve some of nature's biggest challenges: they have tough bodies, they can survive in extreme climates, and they don't need mating partners to reproduce.

③ In short, the nematode's hermaphroditic structure is responsible for its short life cycle and sophisticated body structure.

④ Nematodes have an amazing ability to survive almost anywhere on Earth. No one knows how this incredible creature will evolve in the future.

問 5　What can be inferred about nematodes?　**46**

① It is rare for a creature as simple as the nematode to have a nervous system.

② Scientists in the 1970s preferred *C. elegans*, but parasitic nematodes are becoming more popular because of their complicated nervous systems.

③ Their tubular body allows females more room to store eggs when they need to use their hermaphroditic abilities to reproduce.

④ They live inside sea creatures because there are fewer predators there.

※この問題冊子の『注意事項』は，実際の共通テストを想定して掲載しました。

模試　第4回

（100点 80分）

〔英　　語（リーディング）〕

注　意　事　項

1　解答用紙に，正しく記入・マークされていない場合は，採点できないことがあります。

2　試験中に問題冊子の印刷不鮮明，ページの落丁・乱丁及び解答用紙の汚れ等に気付いた場合は，手を高く挙げて監督者に知らせなさい。

3　解答は，解答用紙の解答欄にマークしなさい。例えば，［10］と表示のある問いに対して③と解答する場合は，次の（例）のように**解答番号10の解答欄**の③に**マーク**しなさい。

（例）

解答番号	解　答　欄
10	①　②　●　④　⑤　⑥　⑦　⑧　⑨

4　問題冊子の余白等は適宜利用してよいが，どのページも切り離してはいけません。

5　**不正行為について**

①　不正行為に対しては厳正に対処します。

②　不正行為に見えるような行為が見受けられた場合は，監督者がカードを用いて注意します。

③　不正行為を行った場合は，その時点で受験を取りやめさせ退室させます。

6　試験終了後，問題冊子は持ち帰りなさい。

英　語(リーディング)

各大問の英文や図表を読み，解答番号 1 ～ 45 にあてはまるものとして最も適当な選択肢を選びなさい。

第1問 (配点　6)

You visited a nearby public hall and found an interesting notice.

Trial Lesson Week

If you want to start something new, why not consider our trial lessons? We are offering the trial lessons listed as below for $5 each. They will be held in Barnaby Cultural Communication Center this month. Beginners can also attend, so please try them out if you are interested!

Lesson Information

Date / Time	Room Number	Details
April 11 2:00 p.m. ～ 3:30 p.m.	203	**Knitting** Learn the standard techniques in a simple way!
April 12 1:30 p.m. ～ 3:00 p.m.	204	**Jewelry Making** Learn the basics of how to make jewelry.
April 14 10:00 a.m. ～ 0:20 p.m.	205	**Illustration** Learn how to draw and use drawing materials. You can get our comments on your work.
April 17 1:30 p.m. ～ 3:30 p.m.	303	**Flower Arrangement** Choose and arrange flowers under the guidance of a professional flower designer.

Notes:

You need to make a reservation online to take part in these lessons. Click **here** and register by at least one day before the event that you wish to participate in. We are afraid that the number of participants in each lesson is limited. The lesson organizers will prepare what you need that day.

問 1　According to this notice, [1].

① all trial lessons start in the afternoon
② the flower arrangement class is the longest
③ those who aren't experienced cannot attend the lessons
④ you can choose which trial lessons you want to attend

問 2　During the trial lesson week, the participants can [2].

① learn advanced knitting skills
② learn flower arrangement from an amateur instructor
③ learn how to make accessories in room 203
④ receive feedbacks on your drawing

問 3　The participants in the trial lessons don't have to [3].

① pay a lesson fee
② prepare anything in advance
③ register online before the lesson
④ reserve the trial lessons

第２問 （配点　10）

Your English teacher gave you an article to help you prepare for the debate in the next class. A part of this article with one of the comments is shown below.

Will Telecommuting Change Our Way of Working?

By Nancy Garcia, Los Angeles
31 JULY 2018 • 5:17p.m.

The American Community Survey (ACS) updated their statistics on the telecommuting population in the USA. According to the data, the number of people who work at home for more than half of their working time using digital telecommunications was, as of 2016, 4.3 million; 3.2% of the total workforce. This did not include the self-employed.

David Howe, a business consultant, emphasizes the advantages of telecommuting, saying, "Telecommuting saves employees commuting time, which is useless and painful. For parents with small children, it gives them more time to spend with their children. For employers, it saves them transportation and utilities costs."

On the other hand, Mary Holden, who has experienced telecommuting, says, "Telecommuting has a lot of advantages, but some disadvantages, too. For example, telecommuters tend to have less opportunity to meet other people on business, and sometimes forget the meaning of their work. Additionally, if a teleworker is experienced, there is no problem, but if not, it might be difficult for them to communicate with other people about how to work. Furthermore, the increase in working hours and the large decrease in pay per hour are also problems."

15 Comments

Newest

Angela Jones 2 August 2018・7:20PM

I am also a telecommuter. Despite living in the countryside where I can enjoy the beauty of nature, I can earn enough money by telecommuting. If the number of telecommuters increases, there will be fewer cars on the road and the trains will be less crowded. We can save the environment by just changing the work style.

問 1 According to the article, the telecommuting population means the number of people who [4].

① are employed but work at home
② aren't employed and work at home using communication devices
③ work at home without using any communication device
④ work during commuting hours using communication devices

問 2 Your team will support the debate topic, "Telecommuting should be promoted." In the article, one **opinion** (not a fact) helpful for your team is that [5].

① it is a good way for parents raising children to earn more
② more than 5% of the total workforce work as telecommuters
③ the commuting time will be shortened
④ you can have more time with your children

問 3 The other team will oppose the debate topic. In the article, one **opinion** (not a fact) helpful for that team is that [6].

① companies have to pay money such as transportation fees for their workers
② telecommuting usually gives you a strong sense of achievement
③ you will have more opportunities to meet the people with whom you work
④ your level of experience can influence your attitude toward work

問 4 In the 3rd paragraph of the article, Mary Holden refers to the possibility of telecommuters [7].

① completely understanding why they work in the countryside
② decreasing their chance to have new experiences
③ earning less money despite having longer working hours
④ meeting a lot of people through their job

問 5 According to her comment, Angela Jones [8] promoting telecommuting.

① has no particular opinion about
② partly disagrees with
③ strongly agrees with
④ strongly disagrees with

（下 書 き 用 紙）

英語(リーディング)の試験問題は次に続く。

第3問 （配点　9）

You are reading a blog post of a Japanese friend who is on an exchange program in New York.

Taiko for the Drum Club!

Thank you for visiting my blog. As I've mentioned before, I am now an exchange student at the Bronx High School. There, my friends and I started a new drum club in February. My exchange program is almost over, but before I return to Japan, I want to leave something for the club: a new *taiko*.

Last December, two classmates, Greg Harris and Orion Favel, asked me to teach them the Japanese *taiko* drum. They had seen my performance at the city international festival the previous month. When I was nine, I started taking *taiko* lessons. Since then, I have been playing it, but I didn't have any teaching experience. Greg and Orion said they didn't mind. They had asked the school music teacher to teach them, but he didn't know how to play the *taiko*, so they came to me. For our first lesson, we met at Greg's house. It was very interesting to hear the difference between my *taiko* and their drums. Soon, other friends came to ask if they could join our *taiko* lessons. When we asked the school principal if we could meet at school, she explained the rules for making a new club. Now, fifteen members practice together once a week.

This April, we were asked to perform at the School Spring Concert. All the club members were nervous because we planned to perform original songs by mixing music from different cultures. However, the concert was a success! The audience really enjoyed our music.

Now, I want to thank my friends and school by giving a *taiko* drum to the club. That way, the club can continue to play Japanese *taiko* even after I return home. If you can make a donation for us to purchase a *taiko*, please put the money in the donation box near the teachers' room or contact Orion. Feel free to e-mail me if you have any questions.

Thanks so much for your support!

問 1 Put the following events (①～④) into the order they happened.

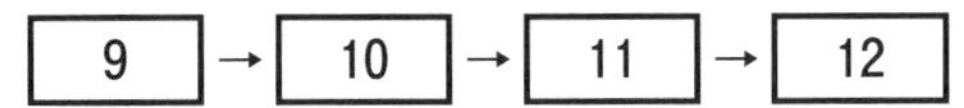

① Greg and Orion asked their music teacher to teach them *taiko*.
② The Bronx High School started a drum club.
③ The writer performed at the School Spring Concert.
④ Three students played *taiko* at Greg's house.

問 2 From this blog post, you learn that the Bronx High School drum club [13].

① can create new songs
② earns money by playing music
③ now meets at Greg's house
④ started with fifteen members

問 3 You have decided to support the club. What are you expected to do? [14]

① E-mail Greg for more details.
② Put money into the donation box.
③ Send a new *taiko* to the Bronx High School.
④ Talk to the school principal.

第 4 問 （配点　12）

In English class you are writing an essay on a social issue you are interested in. This is your most recent draft. You are now working on revisions based on comments from your teacher.

Under One Clean Sky

I saw a picture of Tokyo in the 1980s in my history class last week. I was shocked. The skyline was barely visible because of the air pollution. A lot has changed since then but I think we need to work harder to solve the problem on a global scale. The WHO estimates that almost 7 million people die each year due to air pollution! In this essay, I would like to consider what we can do.

First, there needs to be a bigger move towards electric cars and buses, since air pollution is mainly caused by gasoline-powered cars. (1) ∧ Take a look around and you will see the main reason. Because there are not enough charging stations, buying an electric vehicle (EV) is not practical for most people. I think the government needs to make EVs the cheaper and more convenient option.

Secondly, Japan needs to follow the lead of other environmentally advanced countries and introduce designed areas called LEZs, Low Emission Zones. Basically, drivers of vehicles that don't meet the low emission standards have to pay money to enter the LEZs. At present the Japanese policy seems to be to just hope that people buy eco-friendly cars. (2) ∧ European cities are taking positive action to encourage people to do more.

Finally, (3) <u>it's time to show that you care!</u> We need to plant more trees in city centers. As well as helping reduce air pollution by sucking up carbon dioxide, they would also provide shade for shoppers on hot summer days.

Comments

(1) You are missing something here. Add more information between the two sentences to connect them.

(2) Insert a connecting expression here.

(3) This topic sentence doesn't really match this paragraph. Rewrite it.

In conclusion, although Japan is a lot cleaner than it was in the past, we still must play our part as global citizens. We should promote the use of electric cars, (4) <u>know more about</u> controlling toxic gas, and work on further greening our cities. What we do here affects the entire global eco-system.	*(4) The underlined phrase doesn't summarize your essay content enough. Change it.*
Overall Comment: *Overall, it is well-written. It would be perfect with a few minor revisions. (I agree with your suggestion of creating LEZs in Japan! 😊)*	

問 1 Based on comment (1), which is the best sentence to add? 15

① As of 2023, electric cars were cheaper than gasoline cars.

② As of 2023, most people liked to drive electric cars.

③ As of 2023, taxi companies were already using electric cars.

④ As of 2023, only 3% of cars in Japan were electric.

問 2 Based on comment (2), which is the best expression to add? 16

① in contrast

② in particular

③ nevertheless

④ otherwise

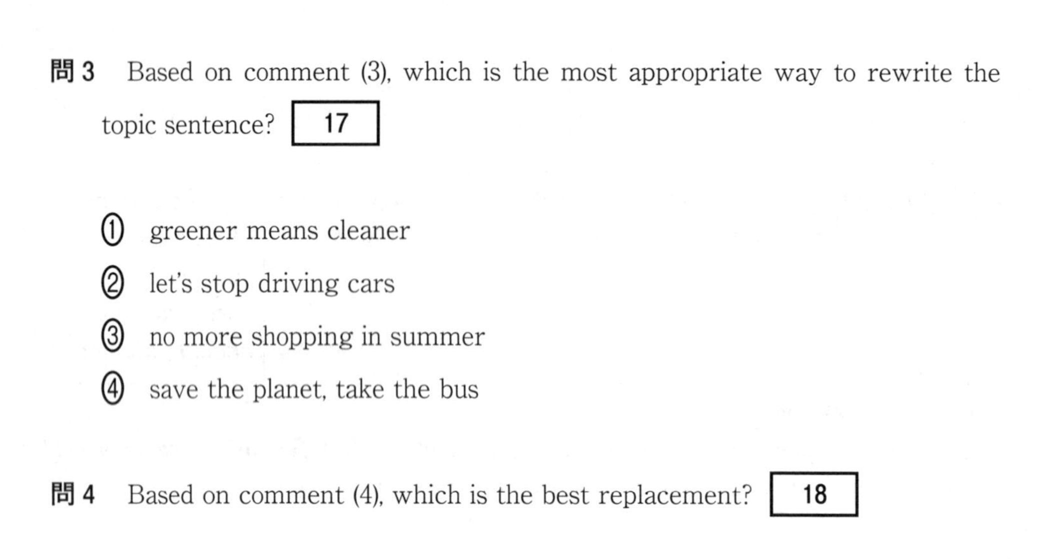

問 3 Based on comment (3), which is the most appropriate way to rewrite the topic sentence? **17**

① greener means cleaner
② let's stop driving cars
③ no more shopping in summer
④ save the planet, take the bus

問 4 Based on comment (4), which is the best replacement? **18**

① become more useful to the planet by
② create new vehicles which are suitable for
③ keep up with other environmentally advanced countries in
④ make more financial contributions for the purpose of

（下 書 き 用 紙）

英語（リーディング）の試験問題は次に続く。

第5問 （配点　16）

You are doing research on how happy people around the world feel. You found two articles.

Levels of Personal Happiness in Countries around the World

by Richard Kyle

November, 2018

The level of happiness people feel in their daily lives is different depending on the country they live in and what nationality they have. This is probably because there are differences in government policies, national character, and ways of thinking. Each person feels happy for different reasons. In some cases, for example, they have free health care and education. In countries which have high levels of personal happiness, people have a good work-life balance.

According to research done by the United Nations in 2018, people in countries which have good social services feel much happier. The graph below shows the national average score of those who answer the questions "Imagine a ladder, with steps numbered from 0 at the bottom to 10 at the top. Which step of the ladder would you say you personally feel you stand on at this time?"

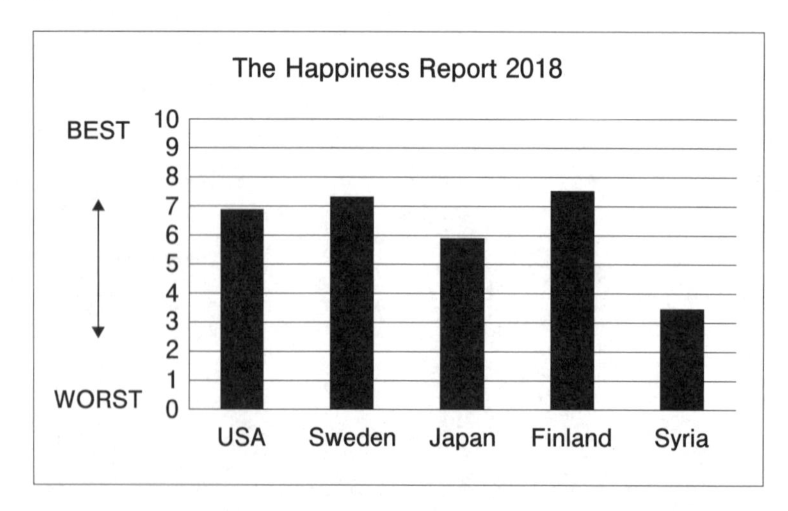

International Migration and World Happiness を元に作成

As mentioned above, two countries where social services are good have high levels of personal happiness. The level of happiness in the USA, where average incomes are high, is lower than that of similar people in Northern Europe on the graph. In the USA, people's mental and physical health is getting worse these days, and furthermore anxiety levels are increasing. It is common in Japan to work a lot of overtime and have less time to relax, which leads to the lower level of happiness. Syria has a very low level because it is in a state of civil war.

Happiness is not related to how much money people earn. In my opinion, private time to relax and physical condition are more important than expensive cars or large houses.

Opinion on "Levels of Personal Happiness in Countries around the World"

by A. O.

December, 2018

I study philosophy at university. My country's level of personal happiness is not the highest on the graph, but it is still high. This fact makes me really happy, and I am proud of it. According to Mr. Richard Kyle's article, in some countries like ours, which have high levels of personal happiness, we can receive free health care and education. However, it costs a lot of money to provide a good social welfare system. Our country stands as number one in Europe with the highest income tax rates.

Even though we have high tax rates, we feel relieved because we don't have to pay for health care. Thanks to this, we feel free to try whatever we like. It means that we have a good environment in which we can improve ourselves. Additionally, I think that it is good that everyone can get equal educational opportunities, because education is free. A lot of people will be able to contribute to society by gaining knowledge at school. Both of these factors increase their chances of having a good future, and they have a lot of options in their lives.

問 1　Neither Richard Kyle nor the university student mentions [19].

① educational opportunities
② free government services
③ happiness and living close to nature
④ the relationship between happiness and health

問 2　The university student is from [20].

① Finland
② Japan
③ Sweden
④ the USA

問 3　According to the articles, in countries which have high levels of personal happiness, government policies have a good effect on people's [21]. (Choose the best combination of statements.)

Statements:

a　education levels
b　employment status
c　income tax rate
d　mental well-being

Combinations:

① a, b
② a, c
③ a, d
④ b, c
⑤ b, d
⑥ c, d

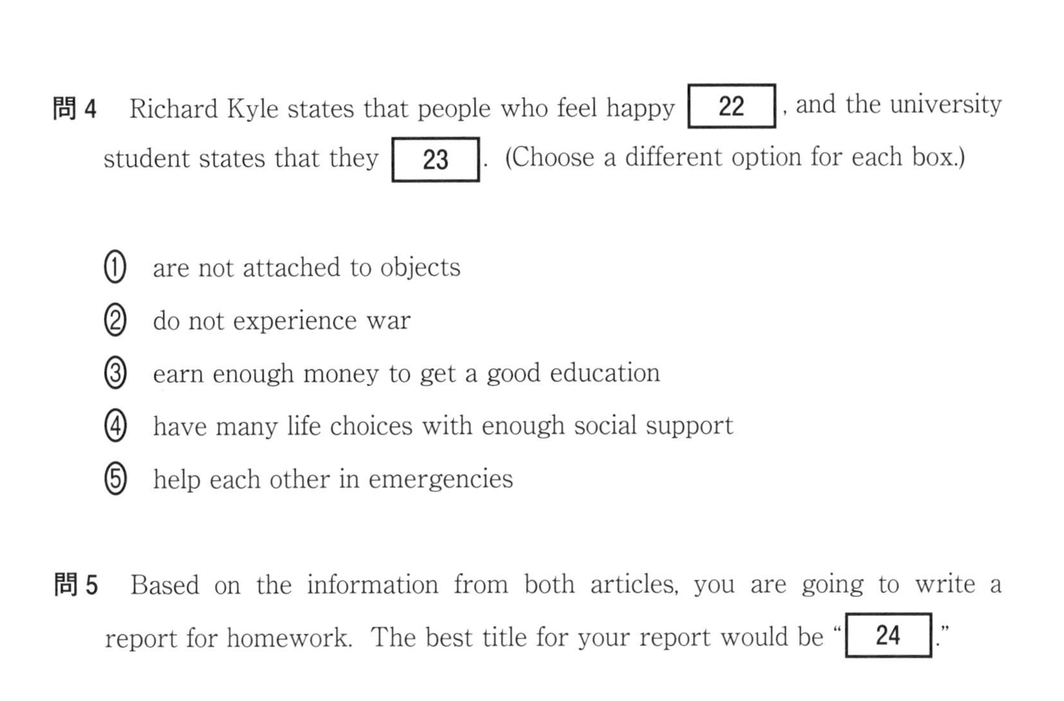

問 4 Richard Kyle states that people who feel happy [22], and the university student states that they [23]. (Choose a different option for each box.)

① are not attached to objects
② do not experience war
③ earn enough money to get a good education
④ have many life choices with enough social support
⑤ help each other in emergencies

問 5 Based on the information from both articles, you are going to write a report for homework. The best title for your report would be "[24]."

① How to Calculate Happiness
② The Levels of Happiness Are Changing with the Times
③ The Reason Why the Levels of Happiness in the 5 Countries Are So High
④ What Happiness Report Can Tell Us

第6問 (配点 18)

You are working on an essay about whether positive discrimination for gender should be used by companies in Japan. Hiring more women in jobs where there is low female participation, such as managerial roles, could be one solution. You will follow the steps below.

Step 1: Read and understand various viewpoints about positive discrimination and the use of gender quotas, for example, fixed allocation of women in employment.

Step 2: Take a position on companies introducing positive discrimination.

Step 3: Create an outline for an essay using additional sources.

[Step 1] Read various sources

Author A (University student)

I think that positive discrimination should be used by more companies. We often think that the word "discrimination" is a bad thing, but the problem is that many companies have more male than female managers. The average salary of women is also lower and people in the top jobs are usually men. This is clearly unfair. Half the population is made of women and half the people working in top jobs should also be female. I worry about my future as I study hard, and I want to have the same opportunities as men. A quota of 50% women would create more diverse and fairer workplaces.

Author B (Economics professor)

Around the world, various countries are introducing laws to tackle the gender gap in the workplace. Some of these include positive discrimination, such as Norway, which introduced a law back in 2008. This law obliges companies to employ women in at least 40% of managerial roles. However, it is not always necessary to introduce positive discrimination to achieve a fairer workplace. Many countries focus on just having equal pay for equal jobs, not on hiring more women. For example, companies in Iceland must prove that male and female workers earn the same salaries for the same jobs.

Author C (Company director)
Our company believes in giving equal opportunities to anybody, regardless of their gender, race or background. However, we are against what people term "positive discrimination." We feel that discrimination is discrimination. We need to hire the best person (male or female), but this view would prevent us from doing that. Let's say that a managerial position became open, but the most qualified candidates for this position were men, because a few decades ago we already hired more men than women. Nevertheless, should we have to promote a woman who was less qualified? This doesn't make sense in business.

Author D (Politician)
In the world of politics, over 130 countries have introduced quotas for women and this form of positive discrimination has had an enormous effect, increasing the number of female politicians and leaders worldwide. The effect of greater female participation in politics has led to a wider range of views and policies in a positive way. Also in the business world, when women receive the same opportunities as men, studies show companies achieve more stability and try to have more opportunity for development. More studies are needed, but I am fully in favor of obliging businesses to make sure that half their managers are female.

Author E (Mother of a high school boy)
As a woman, I'd like to support the idea of quotas. I feel I would have had more chances to get a better job when I was younger. On the other hand, I can't help thinking that this would affect my son's chances of getting the kind of job he is suited to. He studies hard at school and is aiming for a top university. What I worry about is that, despite gaining qualifications and experience, he may lose out on a job that he wants just because he is male. Women should try for positions based solely on their own talent.

問 1　Both Authors C and E mention that **25**.

① a qualified male candidate might lose a position to a female who is less qualified than him

② companies will always hire the best candidates for new jobs, regardless of the candidate's gender

③ it would be difficult for any man in the future to get a good job if he doesn't have a high level of education

④ women should be promoted based on their own ability, not by being given priority because of their sex

問 2　Author B implies that **26**.

① countries such as Norway have created a successful model that should be adopted around the globe

② it's far better for companies to introduce laws for equal pay rather than for positive discrimination

③ the positive discrimination model has not worked so well since 2008, so other countries are not following it

④ there may be a role for positive discrimination, but other methods may be equally or even more effective

[Step 2] Take a position.

問 3 Now that you understand the various viewpoints, you have taken a position on positive discrimination in favor of gender equality, and have written it out as below. Choose the best options to complete [27], [28], and [29].

Your position: The use of quotas and positive discrimination is an effective method for promoting gender equality in the workplace.

- Authors [27] and [28] support your position.
- The main argument of the two authors: [29].

Options for [27] and [28] (The order does not matter.)

① A
② B
③ C
④ D
⑤ E

Options for [29]

① Companies that have a 50% quota for women would be more competitive as they would save money on hiring and salaries
② Creating more chances for women to work in top jobs increases both fairness and the variety of ideas and views
③ Having a larger number of women in a company will also influence the political world and lead to more diverse governments
④ More than 50% of women would be able to gain higher salaries and help companies to arrange a better workplace

[Step 3] Create an outline using Sources A and B

Outline of your essay:

Companies should introduce positive gender discrimination for managerial positions

Introduction

The use of positive discrimination in the workplace by creating a quota for female managerial employees is a necessary step to improve gender equality and build stronger businesses in the future.

Body

Reason 1: [From Step 2]

Reason 2: [Based on Source A] ········· 30

Reason 3: [Based on Source B] ········· 31

Conclusion

Despite some opposition, studies support the creation of gender quotas in managerial positions, and companies should act on this quickly, for a better workplace and a fairer society.

Source A

In the US, there is criticism of quotas due to feelings of unfairness and the idea that unqualified candidates would take positions from qualified ones. But why do we assume that women or people from minority groups are unqualified? Is it really the case that there would be no qualified female candidates for a job?

People are quick to reject the idea of positive discrimination as something that "doesn't work" without ever showing evidence or proof. The fact is, quotas do work, and they work well. A recent study showed that positive discrimination in the workplace is effective for business. Companies with more diversity often perform better than their competitors. According to the *American Journal of Political Science*, companies with quotas for more women have better working conditions for everybody, including the men. These companies have a healthier working culture and keep employees for longer and are generally better places to work.

People may say quotas are undemocratic, but the numbers and results say otherwise.

Source B

Beginning in 2012, several European companies set quotas for the percentage of women on company boards (the highest positions in the company). Some companies set a strict fixed quota (the proportion which they had to achieve) of 40%, others set a soft quota (more of a target than a fixed rule) while a third group had no quota. The table shows the average rise in female representation in each of the three groups.

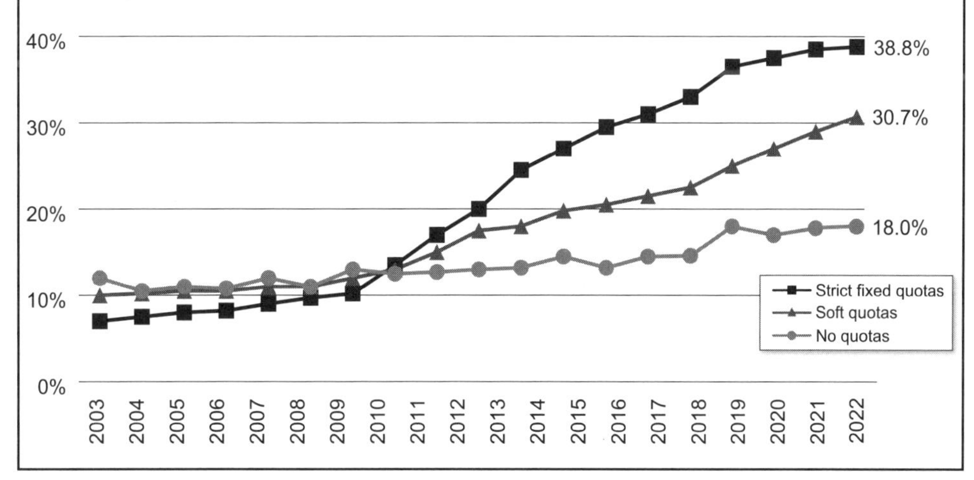

問 4 Based on Source A, which of the following is the most appropriate for Reason 2? **30**

① Although some women may be unqualified, they help to create a better atmosphere in the company through a healthy working culture.

② Evidence shows that introducing a quota not only improves the performance of a business but also motivates employees to remain in the company.

③ Having a quota helps minority groups and women to gain the right qualifications to work in better places that perform well.

④ Women have better working conditions than men due to the quotas, and so stay at the company for a long time.

問 5 For Reason 3, you have decided to write, "Setting a strict fixed percentage quota is effective and there are successful examples in other countries." Based on Source B, which option best supports this statement? **31**

① A strict fixed quota eventually leads to a higher number of women in senior positions. However, it takes a much longer time to increase these numbers than a relatively soft quota.

② Companies without a strict fixed quota mostly already had more female staff. The number of women rose more quickly in these companies as they already had a head start.

③ Setting a soft quota is most effective in helping companies to increase the number of women in managerial positions. It encourages women already working in the company to apply for higher level jobs.

④ Soft quotas work to some extent, producing a definite increase in the number of women in management. Nevertheless, a strict fixed quota shows a quicker increase, slowing only when the target is almost reached.

（下 書 き 用 紙）

英語（リーディング）の試験問題は次に続く。

第7問 (配点　15)

In your English class, your teacher has asked you to choose a woman in science to research and talk about in class. You found the following article and prepared notes for your presentation.

Rosalind E. Franklin

Most people have heard of DNA (the building blocks of all living things), and many could describe its structure (the double helix). However, do you know the full story of how this structure was discovered? You may be familiar with two of the scientists who won a Nobel Prize for this discovery, Watson and Crick. But what about Rosalind Franklin?

Rosalind Elsie Franklin was born on July 25, 1920, in London, to a family that believed strongly in education and public service. From an early age, Franklin was interested in science. At the time, this was not a common career path for girls, but Franklin was quickly recognized for her talents. At 18 years old, she received a scholarship to study chemistry and physics at Cambridge University. After Cambridge, she studied the structure of coal, which became the focus of her Ph.D. Her work with coal led to the development of better gas masks for the British during World War II, and allowed her to travel the world giving speeches about her work. In 1946, she moved to Paris where she developed X-ray techniques that allowed her to examine incredibly small structures in very fine detail. At that time, the scientist, J.T. Randall, had a lab at King's College in London which was working on the structure of DNA. Randall saw the importance of Franklin's work and invited her to work at his lab.

At King's College, Franklin started improving the lab's X-ray equipment. Unfortunately, the move did not go smoothly. Franklin was paired with another scientist, Maurice Wilkins, but Randall had not made their relationship clear. Wilkins had been working on the structure of DNA for several years and thought that Franklin had been hired as his assistant. This made it difficult for Wilkins and Franklin to work together. While Franklin worked on her research, Wilkins contacted his friend in Cambridge, Francis Crick. Crick was working with James Watson to build a model of DNA. Franklin knew Watson and Crick's work but thought that model building without data was not effective. She believed in science and mathematics and would not be satisfied with a result until it could be proven. In 1952,

Franklin and her Ph.D. student Ray Gosling took the now famous, Photo 51, which showed a clear X-ray image of DNA, and Franklin spent the next year working on her calculations.

Wilkins had seen Franklin's work, including Photo 51, and without telling her he took Photo 51 and showed it to Watson. Using the photo, Franklin's notes, and their own data, Watson and Crick were able to test several possible structures. They concluded that the structure must be a double helix and published their model in April 1953. Franklin had also finished her calculations and published her work in the same scientific journal. However, Watson and Crick's work was published first. This made it look like Franklin's work helped support Watson and Crick's conclusion, and led to their success. After leaving King's College in 1953, Franklin continued working with X-rays. She studied viruses and traveled the world talking about her findings. She died at age of 37, never knowing that Watson and Crick had seen her work.

In 1962, Watson, Crick, and Wilkins won a Nobel Prize for their work on DNA. At this time, Franklin's work was not appreciated. In 1968, in his book, "The Double Helix," Watson finally talked about the importance of Franklin's work. Unfortunately, Nobel Prizes are not given to people after they die so Franklin could not have shared the Nobel Prize even if her achievement had been recognized in 1962. However, it is clear that Rosalind Elsie Franklin deserves an important place in history and we should celebrate this great scientist and brave woman.

Your presentation notes:

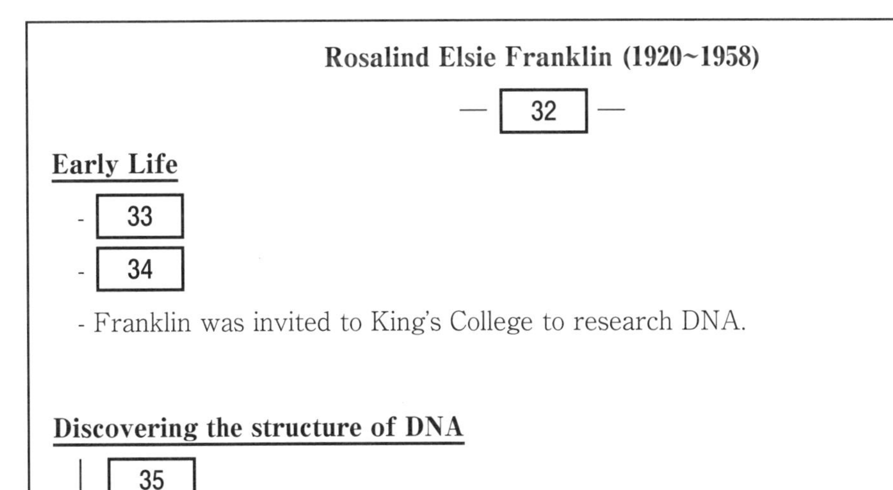

Rosalind Elsie Franklin (1920~1958)

— 32 —

Early Life

- 33
- 34
- Franklin was invited to King's College to research DNA.

Discovering the structure of DNA

35

Franklin joined the lab and updated its equipment.

36

Franklin continued her research and took Photo 51.

37

38

Watson and Crick's work was published in a scientific journal before Franklin's was.

After King's College

- Franklin 39 .
- Franklin died in 1957.
- Nobel prize was awarded to Watson, Crick, and Wilkins.
- Watson recognized Franklin for her role in discovering DNA.

Summary

- 40

問1 Which is the best subtitle for your presentation? 32

① A Brave Woman Making Advances in X-ray Techniques

② A Brilliant Woman Who Needs to Be Recognized

③ A Hard Person to Work With, but a Great Scientist

④ Mathematics Is Better Than Modeling

問2 Choose the best two options for 33 and 34 to complete **Early Life**. (The order does not matter.)

① Franklin attended lectures about coal's structure.

② Franklin created a new type of gas mask.

③ Franklin was interested in something that wasn't popular for girls.

④ Franklin worked on improving scientific methods in Paris.

⑤ Franklin's family moved to London to work in education.

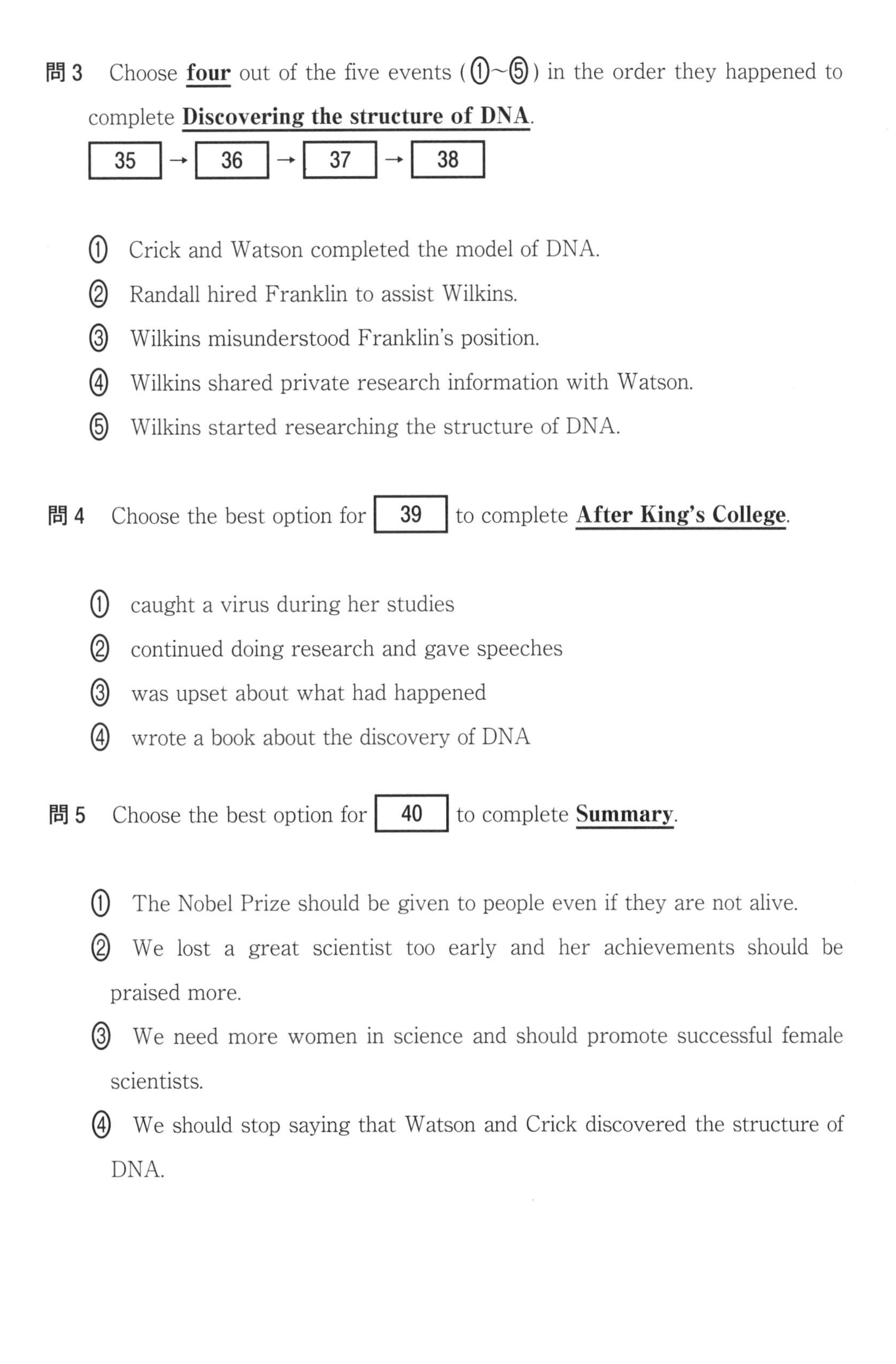

問3　Choose **four** out of the five events (①～⑤) in the order they happened to complete **Discovering the structure of DNA**.

[35] → [36] → [37] → [38]

① Crick and Watson completed the model of DNA.

② Randall hired Franklin to assist Wilkins.

③ Wilkins misunderstood Franklin's position.

④ Wilkins shared private research information with Watson.

⑤ Wilkins started researching the structure of DNA.

問4　Choose the best option for [39] to complete **After King's College**.

① caught a virus during her studies

② continued doing research and gave speeches

③ was upset about what had happened

④ wrote a book about the discovery of DNA

問5　Choose the best option for [40] to complete **Summary**.

① The Nobel Prize should be given to people even if they are not alive.

② We lost a great scientist too early and her achievements should be praised more.

③ We need more women in science and should promote successful female scientists.

④ We should stop saying that Watson and Crick discovered the structure of DNA.

第8問 （配点　14）

You are in a student group preparing a poster for a home economics presentation contest with the theme "Get to know dairy products better." You have been using the following passage to create the poster.

Fully Enjoying the World of Cheese

There are various kinds of cheese in the grocery store. We can get cheese easily, but can you explain the different types in detail? Knowing the classifications is incredibly helpful when choosing a cheese. First of all, cheese is largely divided into two groups, natural cheese and processed. To make natural cheese, milk is treated and solidified, that is, hardened, with a chemical change taking place to produce acid; and this type matures over time, like wine. This develops the flavor of the cheese. Processed cheese can be made by melting the natural cheese and cooling it until it solidifies. Processed cheese does not mature or change, as all of the microorganisms in it are dead. It can therefore also keep longer.

Second, it is said that there are over a thousand kinds of natural cheese. There is no globally-accepted classification, but in Japan natural cheese is classified into seven types. (Figure 1)

Figure 1. Natural cheese

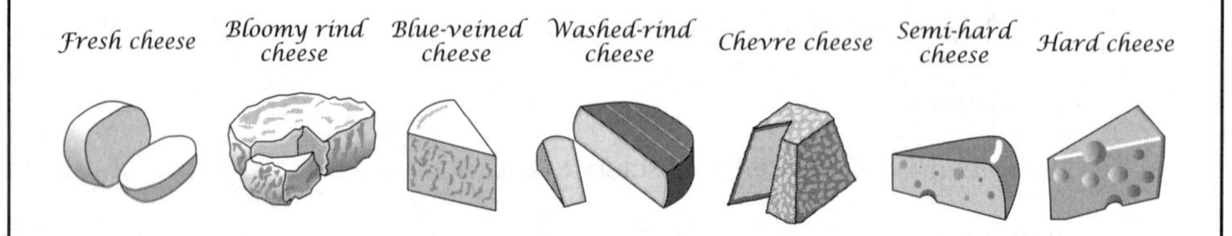

This is based on the French classification. Fresh cheese is unripened cheese which is soft in texture and just a little sour. It is also bright white in color. Examples of fresh cheese include Mozzarella, Cottage cheese, and Quark. Bloomy rind cheese contains white mold that matures and ripens the cheese from the outside. The surface of the cheese is covered in mold, and the inside is a creamy yellow color. Examples of bloomy rind cheese include Camembert and Brie. Blue-veined cheese is ripened with cultures of the mold *penicillium*. Needling is used to make many tiny holes in the cheese to create openings through which oxygen can enter, allowing the characteristic blue veins to form properly. These are ripened from the center outward. A well-ripened cheese has a strong flavor and rich taste. Examples of blue-veined cheese include Gorgonzola and Roquefort. Washed-rind cheese is washed with salt water or an alcohol like beer, wine or brandy during the maturing process. It has a strong smell. Examples of washed-rind cheese include Livarot, Munster, and Limburger. Chevre means goat in French, so chevre cheese is literally goat cheese. As the name suggests, these cheeses are made from goat's milk. They include a wide variety of styles, from soft fresh cheese to hard aged cheese. Examples of chevre cheese include Valencay, Banon, and Pyramide. Semi-hard cheese is relatively firm. There are various kinds depending on the maturing period, size, and amount of fat. Gouda, Maribo, and Raclette are examples of popular semi-hard cheeses. Hard cheese has a firm texture with rich flavors. As the maturing period is long, hard cheeses keep very well due to the lack of moisture. Examples of hard cheese include Cheddar, Emmental and Parmesan.

In Europe, where cheese production is a major industry, there is a system to protect excellent agricultural and dairy products, including cheese. The cheese is guaranteed to be of a certain quality and can be identified based on details such as its production area, shape, and maturing period. In France and Switzerland, this system is called A.O.C; in Italy and Spain, it is called D.O.P., and in the other EU countries, P.D.O.

There are numerous types of cheese, and it is not easy to describe them. Now you can see that the topic of cheese is actually quite deep. It is also interesting to consider how different types of cheese are named. For instance, Cheddar and Camembert are from place names, Mozzarella is from the production method, and Fromage blanc is named after its color. Learning these facts about cheese will likely give you more enjoyment in eating it.

Your presentation poster draft:

Let's learn about cheese in depth.

Do you know the differences between the two main cheese groups?

41

Types of natural cheese and their features

Type	Feature	Typical cheese
Fresh cheese	· Not left to age, these are cheeses that are soft in texture and bright white in color.	Mozzarella, Cottage, Quark
Blue-veined cheese	· Made with penicillium · Air holes are formed by needling 42 .	Gorgonzola, Roquefort
Chevre cheese	· Made from goat's milk · 43	Valencay, Banon, Pyramide

Cheeses with common features

· 44
· 45

問1 Under the first poster heading, you are going to add some basic facts about the cheeses as explained in the passage. Which of the following is the most appropriate? [41]

① Cheeses are categorized by how long they take to mature and how they taste.

② Cheeses are categorized by the place they are produced and the shape.

③ Cheeses are roughly divided into two groups, and both of them are heated.

④ Cheeses are roughly divided into two groups, and one is made from the other.

問2 You are going to fill in the table of cheese features. Choose the best options for [42] and [43].

Blue-veined cheese [42]

① and mold is poured into the holes

② but it is okay to skip this process

③ but with too many holes, it has the opposite result

④ to allow oxygen to get inside the cheese

Chevre cheese [43]

① France has the most varieties of cheese.

② It can be soft or hard depending on the aging period.

③ It can be strong in flavor and taste as it becomes soft.

④ It is easier to make soft cheese than hard cheese.

問 3　You are making statements about cheese which have common features. According to the article, which two of the following are correct? (The order does not matter.) [44] · [45]

① Both fresh cheese and bloomy rind cheese use mold and are made through aging.

② Chevre cheese and semi-hard cheese both have various aging periods.

③ European countries have systems that guarantee the quality of different kinds of cheese.

④ Hard cheese and blue-veined cheese keep longer because they lack moisture.

⑤ Most cheeses in Europe are named after places and people.

⑥ Washed-rind cheese and fresh cheese become soft due to being splashed with alcohol.

※この問題冊子の『注意事項』は，実際の共通テストを想定して掲載しました。

模試　第5回

(100点 80分)

〔英　　語（リーディング）〕

注　意　事　項

1　解答用紙に，正しく記入・マークされていない場合は，採点できないことがあります。

2　試験中に問題冊子の印刷不鮮明，ページの落丁・乱丁及び解答用紙の汚れ等に気付いた場合は，手を高く挙げて監督者に知らせなさい。

3　解答は，解答用紙の解答欄にマークしなさい。例えば，［10］と表示のある問いに対して③と解答する場合は，次の(例)のように**解答番号10の解答欄**の③に**マーク**しなさい。

(例)

解答番号	解　答　欄
10	① ② ●(3) ④ ⑤ ⑥ ⑦ ⑧ ⑨

4　問題冊子の余白等は適宜利用してよいが，どのページも切り離してはいけません。

5　**不正行為について**

①　不正行為に対しては厳正に対処します。

②　不正行為に見えるような行為が見受けられた場合は，監督者がカードを用いて注意します。

③　不正行為を行った場合は，その時点で受験を取りやめさせ退室させます。

6　試験終了後，問題冊子は持ち帰りなさい。

英　　語(リーディング)

各大問の英文や図表を読み，解答番号 **1** ～ **45** にあてはまるものとして最も適当な選択肢を選びなさい。

第1問 (配点　6)

You visited a local film school's website and saw an announcement about an upcoming movie festival.

Annual Student Film Festival

The students at our school create short films using the skills they learn in class for their final projects. Then, at the end of the year, we host a movie festival for the public to come and watch those films. Through this event, we hope to inspire more people to learn to make movies.

We will be showing four student films this year. At the end of the festival, the students will answer questions about their films at a celebration dinner. This year's films, along with a brief description, are listed on the schedule below.

Film Festival Schedule

April 7	**Film**: *United We Stand* A man searches the world for his missing brother.
April 8	**Film**: *The Kitchen* A daughter learns how to operate her family's 20-year-old restaurant from her father and aunts.
April 9	**Film**: *Lost and Found* Two twins spend ten years apart after a fight, only to meet again by chance at a friend's party.
April 10	**Film**: *Beyond Foster Hill* A young woman, finding out her grandfather's secret, learns how much he has loved his son.

April 11	**Event**: Celebration Dinner
	● Young people up to the age of 18 can attend for free by registering for a ticket on our website before March 15. ● Before each film, there will be a free class about recording and editing movies using a camera along with a computer or smartphone.

To register for a ticket, click **here** any time after February 1.

問 1 The main goal of the film festival is to [1].

① encourage more people to begin creating films
② give an award to the best film
③ invite local people to dinner with movie actors
④ show students films from different countries

問 2 The topic of all four films is most likely to be [2].

① difficulty of keeping secrets for long periods
② hope and fear in making important decisions
③ how to run a small business
④ relationships between family members

問 3 This film festival may be helpful for someone interested in becoming a filmmaker because [3].

① famous film producers will come to the event
② the films use some of the most advanced filmmaking techniques
③ they can learn about making movies throughout the event
④ they can make films for the following year

第2問 (配点 10)

You are the editor of your school English newspaper. Alfred, an exchange student from the UK, has written an article for the paper.

Which hand is your dominant one? In the Netherlands, the rate of being left-handed is estimated at 13%, and this is the highest among the selected countries. It is also around 12% in the US and the UK. In contrast, Japan and some other Asian countries have less than half as many people as North America and Western European countries.

Why is this so? A magazine about Japanese customs shows the reasons. The article mentions the following reasons for forcing people to be right-handed in Japan:

- They had a rule once in Japan that samurai must carry their swords at their left hips and draw their swords with their right hands, so being left-handed was shameful.
- It was considered hard to do actions in groups if some in the group were left-handed.
- Japanese set meals are basically arranged for right-handed people.

However, the advantages to being left-handed are now becoming more widely known. One of them is that they are good at paying attention to the space around them. It was found that right-handedness develops the language function controlled by the left side of one's brain, while being left-handed develops the recognition of images and space controlled by the right side of one's brain.

Left-handed people also have chances to use the left side of their brain in right-handed societies, so they can train both sides of brain in a well-balanced manner. This may help them generate more original and interesting ideas.

問 1　In terms of rates for left-handed people, which shows the rankings from **highest to lowest**? [4]

① Japan — The Netherlands — The UK
② Japan — The UK — The Netherlands
③ The Netherlands — Japan — The UK
④ The Netherlands — The UK — Japan
⑤ The UK — Japan — The Netherlands
⑥ The UK — The Netherlands — Japan

問 2　According to Alfred's report, one advantage of being left-handed is that [5].

① you can understand many languages
② you have a better sense of space
③ you will be called a genius
④ your life will have more value

問 3　The statement that best reflects one of the findings from the magazine is [6].

① 'How one's brain works and one's dominant hand are unrelated.'
② 'Left-handed people cannot take part in group behavior.'
③ 'Left-handed people were opposed to using their right hands.'
④ 'There was a cultural reason in Japan for forcing right-handedness.'

問 4　Which best summarises Alfred's opinions about being left-handed? **7**

① It is best to use both sides of our brains.
② It is hard to live in a right-handed society.
③ Some people try to use the hand that is not dominant.
④ There should be more left-handed people in Japan.

問 5　Which is the most suitable title for the article? **8**

① How Have Values about Being Left-handed Changed?
② What Are the Best Ways to Train Your Brain?
③ What Jobs Are a Good Fit for Left-handed People?
④ Why Does Being Right-handed Have Many Advantages?

（下 書 き 用 紙）

英語（リーディング）の試験問題は次に続く。

第３問 （配点　9）

You found the following story in a magazine about students studying abroad.

Starting a New Life Abroad

Samantha Waterson

I recently joined a study abroad program that sends students to live with families in Albania, a small country in Eastern Europe.

When the plane to Albania took off, the person sitting next to me asked me if I was alright. She must have seen my leg bouncing up and down because I was so anxious. I told her that I had never left my country before and didn't know what to expect. She was Albanian and told me a lot of things I wish I had studied before I left. For example, in Albania people nod their heads to say no and shake their heads to say yes. By the end of the flight, I couldn't wait to start exploring the country. I had already made a friend and learned so much.

I arrived at my new host family's house, and a young boy let me in. I gave him a kiss on the cheek because the woman on the plane told me it was good manners. The boy began repeating two words to me. I couldn't understand what he meant and thought he might be angry. I said, "Calm down, calm down," in English, but he only spoke louder and started to point at my mouth.

His mother walked into the room and saw us both repeating different words. She burst out laughing. "Stomach empty?" she said in a thick Albanian accent, as she pointed to the kitchen. He wasn't mad at me after all! I finally felt relaxed.

We all sat down at the kitchen table and had a delicious meal. Though we were barely able to communicate, we smiled and laughed as we started to get to know each other. I was glad to be staying with such a warm family.

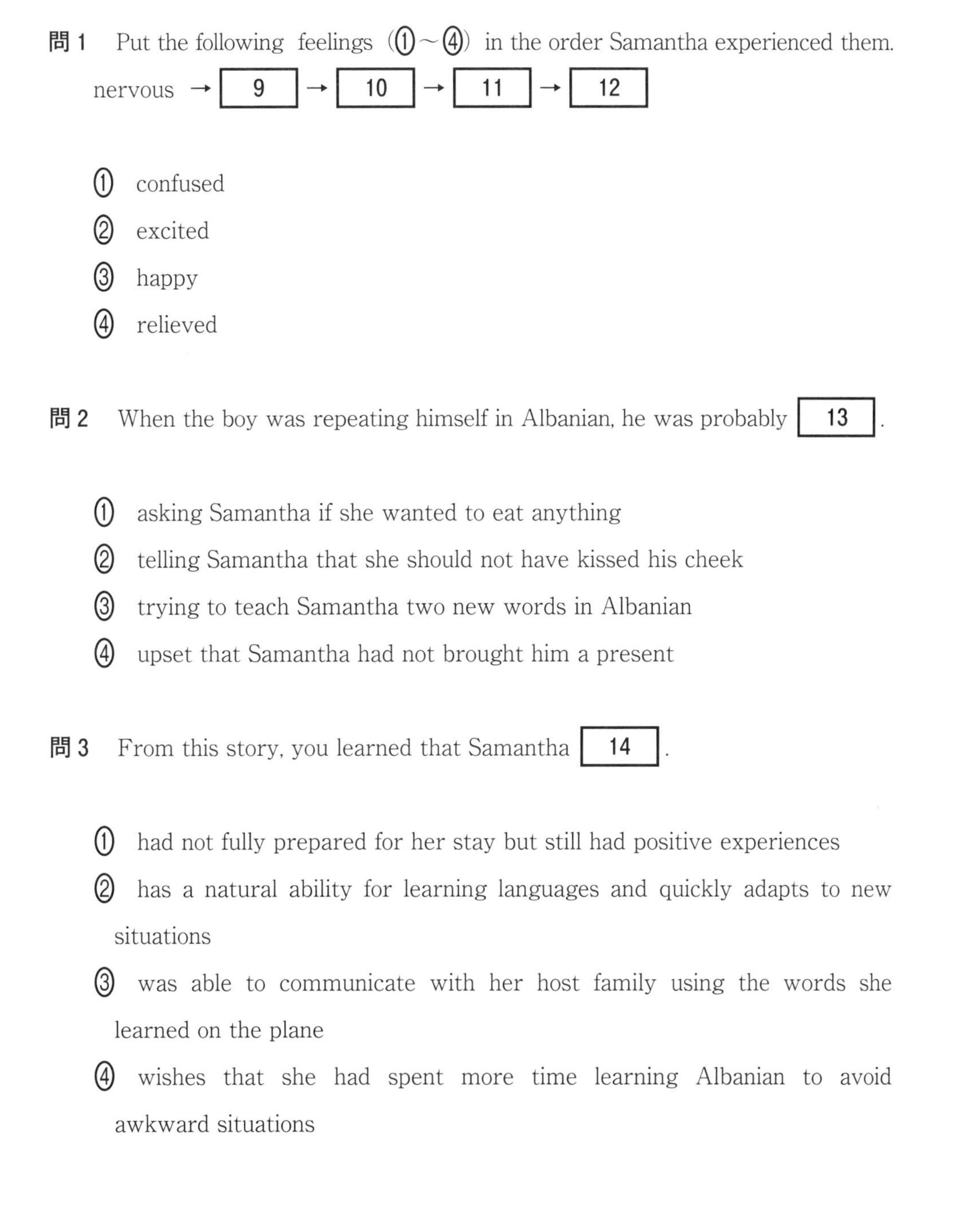

問 1 Put the following feelings (①～④) in the order Samantha experienced them.

nervous → [9] → [10] → [11] → [12]

① confused
② excited
③ happy
④ relieved

問 2 When the boy was repeating himself in Albanian, he was probably [13].

① asking Samantha if she wanted to eat anything
② telling Samantha that she should not have kissed his cheek
③ trying to teach Samantha two new words in Albanian
④ upset that Samantha had not brought him a present

問 3 From this story, you learned that Samantha [14].

① had not fully prepared for her stay but still had positive experiences
② has a natural ability for learning languages and quickly adapts to new situations
③ was able to communicate with her host family using the words she learned on the plane
④ wishes that she had spent more time learning Albanian to avoid awkward situations

第4問 （配点　12）

In English class you are writing an essay on a social issue you are interested in. This is your most recent draft. You are now working on revisions based on comments from your teacher.

How We Can All Enjoy Kyoto	Comments
When foreign tourists started to return to Japan in 2022, my city, Kyoto, was high on the list of 'must-see' places. After nearly three years of empty hotels, restaurants and shops, we were happy to see people coming back. (1)∧ The city is now struggling from 'over-tourism.' This essay will highlight the problems and ways to solve it.	*(1) You are missing something here. Add more information between the two sentences to connect them.*
First, crowding on buses. This is a serious problem that the city has discussed dealing with in a number of ways including charging higher fares for tourists. This will just cause more problems! Let's think of more practical solutions; (2)∧ how about introducing double-decker buses like in London? This would enable twice as many passengers to tour around the city.	*(2) Insert a connecting expression here.*
Second, (3) <u>we all hate trash</u>. Visitors often complain about the lack of trash cans. It would be effective to have more places where people can dispose of their trash. Furthermore, having QR codes on the trash cans would make it possible for visitors to scan them and tell the city if they need emptying outside regular collection hours.	*(3) This topic sentence doesn't really match this paragraph. Rewrite it.*
Finally, Kyoto has started a campaign to get tourists to visit the rural parts of Kyoto Prefecture. They are taking some measures to attract tourists to the Sea of Japan coast, 'Kyoto by the Sea.' It may be great to encourage locals to offer home-stay style hotels so people can experience not only beautiful scenery but also real Japanese lifestyles.	
In conclusion, we need to think of more ways in which people can enjoy Kyoto. Let's introduce high-capacity transportation, help keep Kyoto clean, and (4) <u>gather people in certain areas</u>.	*(4) The underlined phrase doesn't summarize your essay content enough. Change it.*

<u>Overall Comment:</u>
Your essay is well thought out. I especially like your idea of double-decker buses.

問 1　Based on comment (1), which is the best sentence to add? [15]

① After all, some people are interested in other areas.
② As a result, a lot of hotels still have available rooms.
③ Because of this, however, some places now have too many tourists.
④ Still, the number of tourists hasn't reached the number we expected.

問 2　Based on comment (2), which is the best expression to add? [16]

① for instance
② in contrast
③ moreover
④ nevertheless

問 3　Based on comment (3), which is the most appropriate way to rewrite the topic sentence? [17]

① Kyoto City should ask people to buy trash bags
② more people should recycle their trash
③ the problem of trash must be dealt with
④ visitors must take their trash back to their hotels

問 4　Based on comment (4), which is the best replacement? [18]

① act as representatives of our city
② avoid the concentration of people in the city center
③ entertain local people
④ teach tourists about Japan

第5問 （配点　16）

You are doing research on access to education around the world. You found two articles.

Global Crisis in Access to Education **by Matt Brown**

November 5, 2017

School attendance is a significant factor in improving family stability, reducing crime, and increasing job prospects. However, there are still places where some children never get the chance to step into a classroom. What's more, researchers have found that young girls do not have as much access to education as boys.

According to a UN study, there are 8.2 million boys and 16 million girls of primary school age who never get the chance to learn at school. The graph shows the number of children not enrolled in primary school in six countries. The gender gap varies by location, and in some countries in Africa, around twice as many girls as boys never go to school. While some children leave school temporarily and others plan to go to school eventually, more often than not, it's the boys who will go.

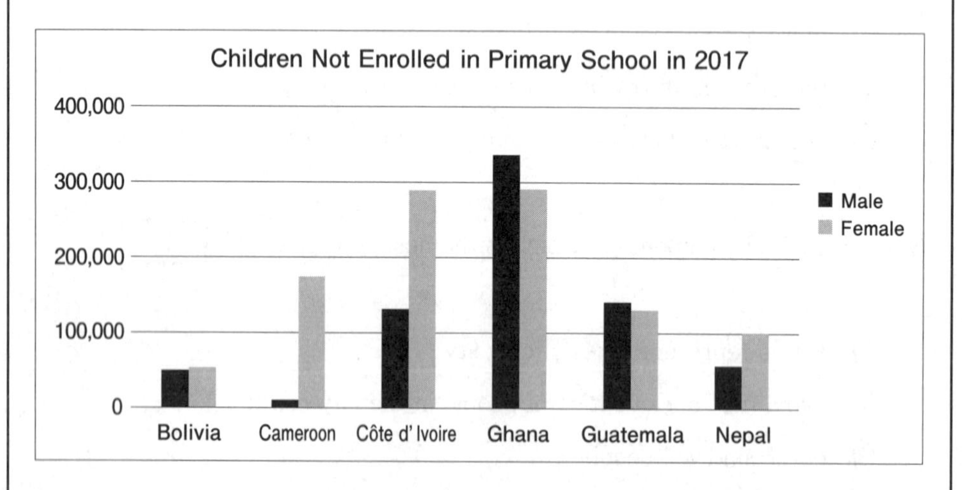

http://www.worldbank.org/ の資料を元に作成

There are several reasons for gender inequality in education. In many cultures, girls stay home to care for the young, sick, or elderly. They also spend more time cooking and cleaning. Low-income families with little to spend on essential supplies like school uniforms and textbooks may also choose to send a son rather than a daughter to school because the son is likely to earn more money in the future.

In my opinion, governments must make primary school completely free. Removing the financial burden of education will be extremely helpful to those living in poverty. In fact, countries that have already applied such policies have seen both more children and more girls attend primary school.

Opinion on "Global Crisis in Access to Education" **by Frances Nagura**

November 12, 2017

I work at a school where many children are absent because they must do things like collect firewood or cook meals for their families. Some leave school for a short time, sometimes helping their families work before returning. I always see more boys than girls in school. The country where I was born faces a similar problem. According to the article by Matt Brown, almost 300,000 girls in my country are not in school compared to only half as many boys.

One of the biggest problems I see is the lack of easy access to clean drinking water, and it is often the girls' job to fetch water for their families to use. In the village where I live, women and girls bring nearly 20 kg of water from more than 6 km away. This leaves no time for school. And even when there is water nearby, it may not be safe to drink. If families get sick, girls are the ones who must bear the burden.

Speaking of long distances, more schools need to be built in rural areas. Many children outside of major cities have to travel a long way to school, which can be both difficult and dangerous, especially for girls. One added benefit of more accessible schools is that children still have time to take care of household tasks at the end of the school day.

問 1　Neither Matt Brown nor Frances Nagura mentions [19].

① gender differences in specific regions of the world
② the lack of teachers in primary schools
③ the relationship between education and crime
④ why school uniforms might be an obstacle

問 2　The teacher is from [20].

① Cameroon
② Côte d'Ivoire
③ Ghana
④ Guatemala

問 3　According to the articles, girls often miss school [21]. (Choose the best combination of options.)

a　to do housework for their families
b　to sell the crops their families grow
c　to take care of family members
d　to teach their younger siblings how to study

Combinations:
① a, b
② a, c
③ b, d
④ c, d

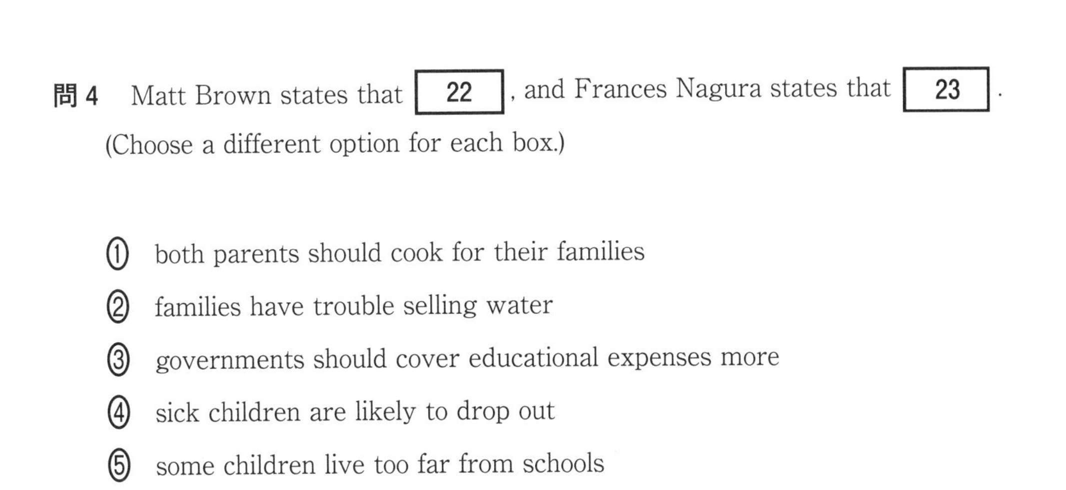

問4 Matt Brown states that **22**, and Frances Nagura states that **23**.
(Choose a different option for each box.)

① both parents should cook for their families
② families have trouble selling water
③ governments should cover educational expenses more
④ sick children are likely to drop out
⑤ some children live too far from schools

問5 Based on the information from both articles, you are going to write a report for homework. The best title for your report would be "**24**."

① Closing the Gender Gap in Primary School Education
② Girls Are Taking Responsibility for Their Own Education
③ How Private Schools Are Changing the Face of Education
④ Why Girls Are Less Happy Than Boys in Primary School

第6問 (配点 18)

You are working on an essay about whether or not AI should be used more in our society. You will follow the steps below.

Step 1: Read and understand various viewpoints about the impact of AI on society.

Step 2: Take a position on whether or not AI should be used more in our society.

Step 3: Create an outline for an essay using additional sources.

[Step 1] Read various sources

Author A (Student) I love gaming, and AI makes games even cooler. For example, I can meet an endless number of unique characters in my favorite online role-playing video game, and they are all created by AI. I don't even have to waste my time searching for new games to play anymore since my AI-powered software can accurately recommend the next great game I will enjoy. But some people do worry about the negative impact of AI, for example the fear that AI will completely take over game designers' jobs. Nevertheless, in my opinion human designers will still be required to complete AI designs and ensure quality.
Author B (Parent) As a parent, AI on social media scares me the most. It seems like AI just shows kids whatever keeps them online longer, not what's true or good for them. They end up seeing lots of fake news and getting some really weird ideas. Personally, instead of restricting my kids from accessing social media, I'm trying to teach them to be smart online. Still, it's hard when AI is programmed to grab their attention in any way it can. We need to think more deeply about our relationship with technology in order to be able to deal with the new era of AI-created content.

Author C (Business person)
There's no denying that AI in phones and other devices is pretty handy. I love how my phone's AI helps me organize my day and keep track of my health goals. It's like having a personal assistant in my pocket. AI suggestions for shopping and entertainment are highly accurate, which saves me tons of time. Sure, some of my friends complain about the devices knowing a bit too much about their users, but I think the convenience is well worth it. I can leave the boring tasks to my devices and instead focus my thoughts on more complex and meaningful ideas.

Author D (Journalist)
AI's role in the job market is a topic of intense debate. Supporters talk a lot about how it will create new technology industries with all sorts of new jobs, replacing the ones it destroys. The unfortunate truth, however, is that workers whose skills will be of no value because of technological advancements like AI are often middle-aged or older. If AI is not carefully controlled, these older workers may be forced to adapt to entirely different job industries with little support. Workers could face unemployment, leading to financial and emotional stress. Let's think twice before allowing new technology to completely change people's lives.

Author E (Programming teacher)
As a teacher of programming, I have always had to deal with adapting to technological changes every few years. However, I'm concerned that the rapid pace of AI advancements is more quickly than ever before reducing the importance of the skills I teach students. Moreover, the job market is always changing. These concerns make it hard for me to encourage students to study coding in order to be programmers in the future. Not to mention, there are some real moral dilemmas surrounding AI. I'm particularly concerned about how it might handle our private information in the future.

問 1 Both Authors D and E mention [25].

① the challenge of updating school education to keep up with AI advancements

② the change in the working world and the usefulness of current skills

③ the convenience of AI in daily life and the potential for privacy invasion

④ the potential for AI to create ethical dilemmas in the workplace

問 2　Author C implies that [26].

① AI will be able to come up with more complex ideas in the future
② every person should hire a personal assistant in order to lead a convenient life
③ the problem is that AI learns the personal information of its users
④ using AI in daily life has far more advantages than disadvantages

[Step 2] Take a position

問 3　Now that you understand the various viewpoints, you have taken a position on whether or not AI should be used more in our society, and have written it out as below. Choose the best options to complete [27], [28], and [29].

Your position: AI enhances our lives by providing us with various new opportunities.

- Authors [27] and [28] support your position.
- The main argument of the two authors: [29].

Options for [27] and [28] (The order does not matter.)

① A
② B
③ C
④ D
⑤ E

Options for 29

① AI is a useful technology in general, making our daily lives more efficient

② AI on social media can solve misinformation problems and has a positive influence on children

③ AI will overcome some moral dilemmas that have been challenging to solve

④ AI's rapid development in the technology industry promises more job opportunities and economic growth

[Step 3] Create an outline using Sources A and B

Outline of your essay:

AI should be used more in our society

Introduction

While the AI revolution comes with various challenges, it mainly improves our lives by providing us with exciting new opportunities.

Body

Reason 1: [From Step 2]

Reason 2: [Based on Source A] ········· 30

Reason 3: [Based on Source B] ········· 31

Conclusion

AI development and use should be encouraged in our society.

Source A

The influence of AI on everyday life can be seen in various popular applications. One type of AI, known as a virtual assistant, uses voice recognition and language processing technology to understand human speech and respond to it logically. Unlike previous virtual assistants that had a very limited capacity, these newer AI virtual assistants can provide detailed responses to a user's questions or commands. They are also capable of performing advanced tasks like automatically preparing people's schedules. The result has been a revolution in time management, greatly increasing personal efficiency. Moreover, apps with AI features can make it easier to balance diet and exercise by providing unique diet and exercise plans. They specialize in analyzing individual preferences and fitness levels to create a healthy lifestyle that matches the user's needs. These advances show off AI's role in making daily activities easier to accomplish, which will only change society for the better.

Source B

According to recent studies, the public's view on AI is largely positive. Many who were asked about the topic expressed their belief that it will help workers do their jobs more effectively. While some are worried about issues like job loss, most seem to support AI's potential to improve society as a whole.

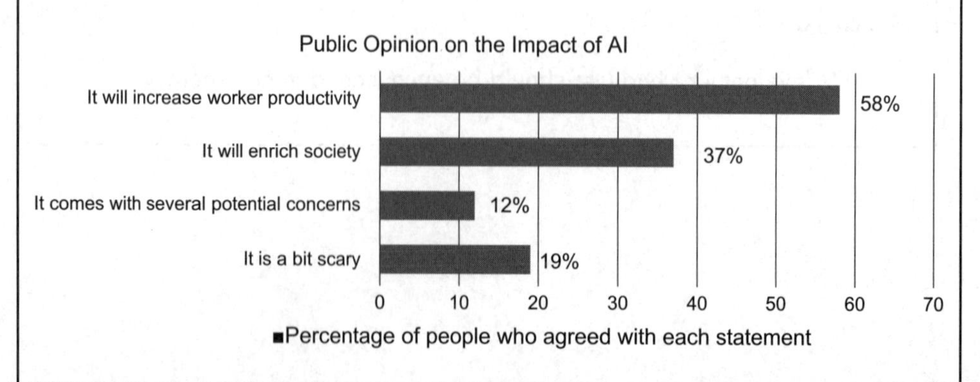

問 4 Based on Source A, which of the following is the most appropriate for Reason 2? **30**

① AI technology has led to an increase in personal efficiency, as it improves our physical ability.

② Although virtual assistants are only useful for performing tasks with a limited capacity, this is enough for most people.

③ The main benefit of AI in our lives is detailed responses to commands that make entertainment easier to access.

④ Virtual assistants can understand and respond to complex human speech, which has greatly improved personal task management.

問 5 For Reason 3, you have decided to write, "AI is being welcomed by many people." Based on Source B, which option best supports this statement? **31**

① A majority of people believe AI will have a positive effect on workstyles and society, while a comparatively small number express concern.

② Although a significant percentage of people recognize AI's problems, exactly half think such negative impacts are so small that they can ignore them.

③ Over 50% of those surveyed agree that AI has no demerits, with huge public support for its ability to improve society and the workplace.

④ While there are some negative opinions about AI, the majority welcome it, with just under 10% of people having a fear of AI.

第7問 (配点 15)

Your group is preparing a poster presentation entitled "Leaping from Great Heights," using information from the magazine article below.

André-Jacques Garnerin was born in Paris in 1769. Though he studied physics as a young man, his professional career took him in another direction. He began working as an inspector in the French army at the start of the French Revolution in the early 1790s. Although Garnerin was quickly captured by British forces and sent to a Hungarian prison, it proved to be an extremely important experience for him. The tall prison walls inspired him to consider how to escape. He believed that he could leap from the walls and land safely outside the prison if he could construct a primitive parachute to slow his fall. At the time, the only parachutes that had been successfully tested were shaped like umbrellas with wooden frames, and the highest parachute jump was from the top of a building.

In the end, Garnerin did not attempt his escape, and after two years he was released. Hot air balloons had recently been invented, and for the first time, humans were able to float thousands of feet up into the sky. Garnerin, who had never given up his parachuting ambitions, believed that he could create a frameless parachute that would allow him to safely descend from a balloon high in the air. But in order to test this theory, he would first need to become a more experienced balloonist.

Garnerin spent much of the following years planning his innovative parachute jump. His design for the parachute was simple. While most modern parachutes are opened up from a backpack that connects to a parachutist's body, the original designs were much less safe. Garnerin's parachute included a basket that he could stand inside —— the same basket that would be connected to the hot air balloon. Attached to the basket was a large, round piece of silk.

In 1797, Garnerin announced that he would go up to 1,000 meters in a hot air balloon before releasing the balloon and descending to the ground in his parachute. His first attempt was scheduled to take place in June, but high winds tore his balloon to pieces before it could take off. Nevertheless, Garnerin made a successful attempt in October of that year. With a crowd watching, he climbed into his balloon and rose steadily into the air. Just as planned, he released the balloon after rising to one kilometer and began falling back to the earth.

As he descended, he discovered a problem with his design. Newer parachutes have a hole at the top to allow the air to escape, but his parachute didn't. Consequently, he swung about violently during his drop. When he finally landed, he was uninjured, but the fall made him feel terribly sick. On his return, he was received as a hero.

Garnerin gained national fame for his scientific achievement. Through his efforts, he proved that the parachute designs he had made actually worked, and for this achievement, France named him its official Aeronaut. However, the importance of his work would not be widely known for more than a century. Until the 1900s, flight simply was not a regular part of life. But as planes and helicopters became common in the 20th century, Garnerin's bold efforts offered a foundation that generations of pilots and parachutists could build on. With improved designs and better materials, such as nylon, each new parachutist's jump owes its success to this great accomplishment more than two hundred years ago.

Leaping from Great Heights

■ The Life of André-Jacques Garnerin

Period	Events
Early Life	Garnerin began studying physics
Adult Life	32
	33
	34
	Garnerin used his parachute for the first time
	35

André-Jacques Garnerin

■ An Imperfect Design

▸ Though Garnerin's original design was successful, newer parachute designs have been improved by [36] and [37].

■ A Fall to the Earth Causes a Rise to Fame

▸ Garnerin was the first man to [38].

▸ Garnerin's achievement became known in the 20th century [39][40].

問 1　Members of your group listed important events in Garnerin's life. Choose **four** out of the five events (①～⑤) in the order they happened to complete sequence of Adult Life. [32] ～ [35]

① Garnerin began working on a parachute without frames
② Garnerin joined the army
③ Garnerin was named national Aeronaut
④ Garnerin was sent to prison
⑤ Garnerin's work benefited future generations

問 2　Choose the best two options for [36] and [37] to complete the poster. (The order does not matter.)

① giving the parachute an umbrella-like frame
② including a hole at the top of the parachute
③ introducing ropes to hold the cloth in place
④ making the corners of the parachute round to improve airflow
⑤ replacing the basket with a backpack design
⑥ using materials other than nylon

問 3　Choose the best statement to complete the poster. **38**

① design a parachute capable of supporting a person
② invent a hot air balloon
③ successfully land with a frameless parachute
④ survive a jump using a parachute

問 4　Choose the best two options for **39** and **40** to complete the poster. (The order does not matter.)

① after it was featured in magazines
② and it inspired generations of pilots and parachutists
③ as the French public came to think of Garnerin as a hero
④ in response to an increasing demand for parachutists
⑤ with a decrease in the number of parachutists
⑥ with the development of planes and helicopters

第8問 （配点 14）

You are in a student group preparing a poster for a visual presentation for the next science class. The theme is “Various types of rocks and their characteristics.” You have been using the following passage to create the poster.

Types of Rock

── Basic Facts ──

The earth's outer layer, known as the crust, is composed of many different types of rock, which can be broadly grouped into the following three major types: igneous, sedimentary, and metamorphic rocks. This broad classification tells us how they have formed over a long period of time ── millions of years, sometimes. To take igneous rocks as an example, they are formed from magma. They result from a natural phenomenon in which magma cools and hardens, whether the location where it happens is deep underground, at or near the surface. As for sedimentary rocks, a large number of them form at the bottom of lakes or oceans through the buildup of particles, such as sand and dead plants and animals, although this process happens on the surface as well. In any case, layer after layer of particles pile up over the course of time, and sedimentary rocks are “ready.” The other type is formed when rock that already exists, that is to say, either igneous or sedimentary rock, is transformed by heat, pressure, or some other force. That is why this type is given the name “metamorphic” rock.

Each major type contains subgroups, and we humans have used rock since ancient times, especially for building purposes. The figure below shows six specific types of rock. Different types of rock are suited for different uses. Let us first take a look at igneous rocks.

Figure 1. Six types of rock

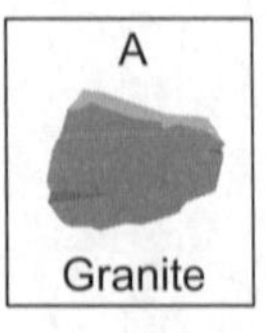

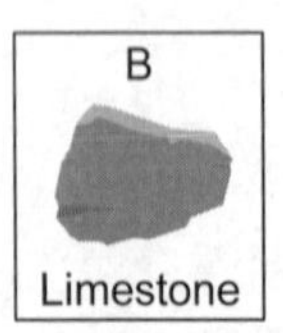

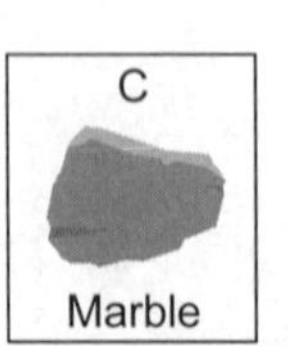

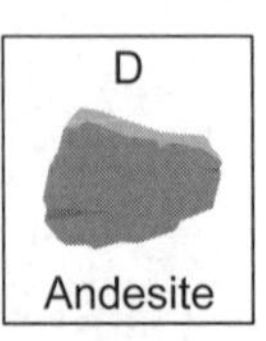

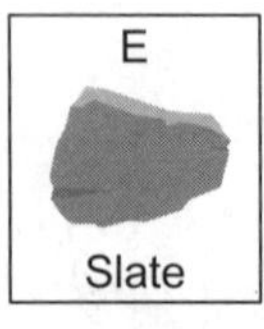

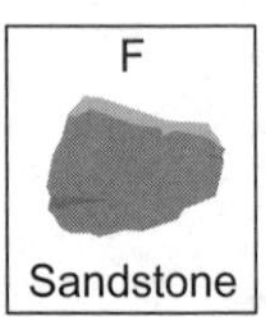

Type A and D rocks are called granite and andesite, respectively. As Type A is noted for its durability, it has been used extensively for external walls, columns, and monuments, to name a few things. In Japan, this coarse-grained rock is also called "*mikageishi*," and is commonly used for tombstones. However, uses of Type A are not limited to outdoor structures. It is also featured in interior decoration, and it can be found in bathrooms or kitchens as well. Andesite, Type D, whose name is derived from the Andes in South America, is also hard. Like granite, it is often used for building exteriors, and is featured in landscaping projects. Compared to Type A, Type D is much more resistant to fire. But still, it should be noted that even the former can withstand heat of over 500 degrees Celsius.

Types B (limestone) and F (sandstone) are both sedimentary rocks. The main component of Type B is calcium carbonate, while that of Type F is sand, as the name suggests. Although Type B is often considered neither as hard nor as durable as Type A, it has other advantages. One of them is that it can be processed relatively easily, and it has been used for roof work and flooring. Type F is also used for similar purposes, but has two remarkable properties. First, it is fire resistant. Second, it soaks up liquid well. Because of this property, Type F can be damaged by frost, and moss can easily grow on it. Therefore, it may not be the best option for constructing things like external walls.

The remaining two are metamorphic rocks, although Type E is sometimes categorized as a sedimentary rock. Marble, Type C, is considered excellent material for interior finishing, but it is used in many different ways, and marble has played an important part in adding to both the internal and external beauty of structures. This beautiful, shiny rock was featured in historical monuments like the Taj Mahal, the Parthenon, and many others. Interestingly enough, this rock is the result of the transformation of Type B. The other type is slate, and its main components include clay minerals. It is known that Type E is highly resistant to water. In addition, this type can be split quite easily into thin sheets, so it is especially useful for roofs and floors. But it also has other uses. One familiar example for Japanese will be an inkstone, an essential calligraphy tool.

Your presentation poster draft:

What do we learn from studying the many different types of rock?

By what standard are rocks classified into three types?

| 41 |

Examples of types of rock

Major type	Specific type	Description	Example of use
igneous	A (granite)	This type of rock is hard and durable, and is known as "*mikageishi*" in Japan.	external walls, columns
sedimentary	B (limestone)	This type of rock contains calcium carbonate, and 42 .	roof work
metamorphic	C (marble)	This type of rock is shiny, and 43 .	interior work

Rocks with common properties

| 44 |
| 45 |

問1　Under the first poster heading, you want to introduce what we can learn from studying the three major classifications described in the passage. Which of the following is the most appropriate? [41]

① How rapidly magma hardened to become rock, and which kind of rock is suitable for decorative purposes.
② How rocks underwent a process of becoming solid or changing over time.
③ What kind of particles piled up to become rocks over the course of time.
④ What part of the earth rocks originated in, and how fast the transformation took place.

問2　You have been asked to write descriptions of Type B and Type C rocks. Choose the best options for [42] and [43].

Type B [42]
① it is appropriate for landscaping work
② it was named after particular mountains
③ its durability equals that of Type A
④ processing it is not a demanding task

Type C [43]
① cannot withstand heat below 500℃
② is by far the most tolerant of heat
③ often contains clay minerals
④ was originally limestone

問3 You are making statements about some rocks which share common properties. According to the article, which two of the following are accurate? (The order does not matter.) [44] · [45]

① Buildings constructed using Type D and F are likely to be resistant to fire.

② Structures made of Type A and B would be equally weak against water.

③ Type A and F have contributed to shaping Japanese traditional culture since ancient times.

④ Type A, C, F are well suited for massive exterior walls.

⑤ Type B and F are igneous rocks, while Type C and E metamorphic.

⑥ Type B and Type E are both used to roof houses and for floors.

試作問題

〔英　　語（リーディング）〕

試作問題掲載の趣旨と注意点

この試作問題は，独立行政法人大学入試センターが公表している，大学入学共通テスト「令和７年度試験の問題作成の方向性、試作問題等」のウェブサイトに記載のある内容を再掲したものです。本書では，学習に取り組まれる皆様のために，これに詳細の解答解説を作成し，より学びを深めていただけるように工夫をしました。

本問題は，令和７年度大学入学共通テストについての具体的なイメージを共有することを目的として作成されていますが，過去の大学入試センター試験や大学入学共通テストと同様の問題作成や点検のプロセスは経ていないものとされています。本問題と同じような内容，形式，配点等の問題が必ず出題されることを保証するものではありませんので，その点につきましてご注意ください。

第A問

You are working on an essay about whether high school students should be allowed to use their smartphones in class. You will follow the steps below.

Step 1: Read and understand various viewpoints about smartphone use.
Step 2: Take a position on high school students' use of their smartphones in class.
Step 3: Create an outline for an essay using additional sources.

[Step 1] Read various sources

Author A (Teacher) My colleagues often question whether smartphones can help students develop life-long knowledge and skills. I believe that they can, as long as their use is carefully planned. Smartphones support various activities in class that can enhance learning. Some examples include making surveys for projects and sharing one's learning with others. Another advantage is that we do not have to provide students with devices; they can use their phones! Schools should take full advantage of students' powerful computing devices.
Author B (Psychologist) It is a widespread opinion that smartphones can encourage student learning. Being believed by many, though, does not make an opinion correct. A recent study found that when high school students were allowed to use their smartphones in class, it was impossible for them to concentrate on learning. In fact, even if students were not using their own smartphones, seeing their classmates using smartphones was a distraction. It is clear that schools should make the classroom a place that is free from the interference of smartphones.
Author C (Parent) I recently bought a smartphone for my son who is a high school student. This is because his school is located far from our town. He usually leaves home early and returns late. Now, he can contact me or access essential information if he has trouble. On the other hand, I sometimes see him walking while looking at his smartphone. If he is not careful, he could have an accident. Generally, I think that high school students are safer with smartphones, but parents still need to be aware of the risks. I also wonder how he is using it in class.

Author D (High school student)
At school, we are allowed to use our phones in class. It makes sense for our school to permit us to use them because most students have smartphones. During class, we make use of foreign language learning apps on our smartphones, which is really helpful to me. I am now more interested in learning than I used to be, and my test scores have improved. The other day, though, my teacher got mad at me when she caught me reading online comics in class. Occasionally these things happen, but overall, smartphones have improved my learning.
Author E (School principal)
Teachers at my school were initially skeptical of smartphones because they thought students would use them to socialize with friends during class. Thus, we banned them. As more educational apps became available, however, we started to think that smartphones could be utilized as learning aids in the classroom. Last year, we decided to allow smartphone use in class. Unfortunately, we did not have the results we wanted. We found that smartphones distracted students unless rules for their use were in place and students followed them. This was easier said than done, though.

問 1　Both Authors A and D mention that [1].

① apps for learning on smartphones can help students perform better on exams
② one reason to use smartphones as an educational tool is that most students possess one
③ smartphones can be used to support activities for learning both at school and at home
④ smartphones make it possible for students to share their ideas with classmates

問 2　Author B implies that [2].

① having time away from digital devices interferes with students' motivation to learn
② sometimes commonly held beliefs can be different from the facts that research reveals
③ students who do not have smartphones are likely to consider themselves better learners
④ the classroom should be a place where students can learn without the interference of teachers

[Step 2] Take a position

問 3　Now that you understand the various viewpoints, you have taken a position on high school students' use of their smartphones in class, and have written it out as below. Choose the best options to complete [3], [4], and [5].

Your position: High school students should not be allowed to use their smartphones in class.

- Authors [3] and [4] support your position.
- The main argument of the two authors: [5].

Options for [3] and [4] (The order does not matter.)

① A
② B
③ C
④ D
⑤ E

Options for [5]

① Making practical rules for smartphone use in class is difficult for school teachers
② Smartphones may distract learning because the educational apps are difficult to use
③ Smartphones were designed for communication and not for classroom learning
④ Students cannot focus on studying as long as they have access to smartphones in class

[Step 3] Create an outline using Sources A and B

Outline of your essay:

Using smartphones in class is not a good idea

Introduction

Smartphones have become essential for modern life, but students should be prohibited from using their phones during class.

Body

Reason 1: [From Step 2]

Reason 2: [Based on Source A] ········· 6

Reason 3: [Based on Source B] ········· 7

Conclusion

High schools should not allow students to use their smartphones in class.

Source A

Mobile devices offer advantages for learning. For example, one study showed that university students learned psychology better when using their interactive mobile apps compared with their digital textbooks. Although the information was the same, extra features in the apps, such as 3D images, enhanced students' learning. It is important to note, however, that digital devices are not all equally effective. Another study found that students understand content better using their laptop computers rather than their smartphones because of the larger screen size. Schools must select the type of digital device that will maximize students' learning, and there is a strong argument for schools to provide computers or tablets rather than to have students use their smartphones. If all students are provided with computers or tablets with the same apps installed, there will be fewer technical problems and it will be easier for teachers to conduct class. This also enables students without their own smartphones to participate in all class activities.

Source B

A study conducted in the U.S. found that numerous teenagers are addicted to their smartphones. The study surveyed about 1,000 students between the ages of 13 and 18. The graph below shows the percentages of students who agreed with the statements about their smartphone use.

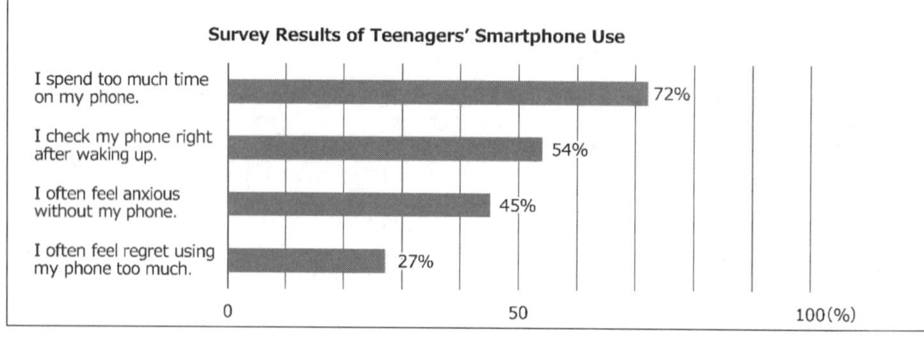

問 4 Based on Source A, which of the following is the most appropriate for Reason 2? [6]

① Apps that display 3D images are essential for learning, but not all students have these apps on their smartphones.

② Certain kinds of digital devices can enhance educational effectiveness, but smartphones are not the best.

③ Students should obtain digital skills not only on smartphones but also on other devices to prepare for university.

④ We should stick to textbooks because psychology studies have not shown the positive effects of digital devices on learning.

問 5 For Reason 3, you have decided to write, "Young students are facing the danger of smartphone addiction." Based on Source B, which option best supports this statement? [7]

① Although more than half of teenagers reported using their smartphones too much, less than a quarter actually feel regret about it. This may indicate unawareness of a dependency problem.

② Close to three in four teenagers spend too much time on their phones. In fact, over 50% check their phones immediately after waking. Many teenagers cannot resist using their phones.

③ Over 70% of teenagers think they spend too much time on their phones, and more than half feel anxious without them. This kind of dependence can negatively impact their daily lives.

④ Teenagers are always using smartphones. In fact, more than three-quarters admit to using their phones too much. Their lives are controlled by smartphones from morning to night.

（下 書 き 用 紙）

英語（リーディング）の問題は次に続く。

第B問

In English class you are writing an essay on a social issue you are interested in. This is your most recent draft. You are now working on revisions based on comments from your teacher.

Eco-friendly Action with Fashion	**Comments**
Many people love fashion. Clothes are important for self-expression, but fashion can be harmful to the environment. In Japan, about 480,000 tons of clothes are said to be thrown away every year. This is equal to about 130 large trucks a day. We need to change our "throw-away" behavior. This essay will highlight three ways to be more sustainable.	
First, when shopping, avoid making unplanned purchases. According to a government survey, approximately 64% of shoppers do not think about what is already in their closet. (1)∧So, try to plan your choices carefully when you are shopping.	*(1) You are missing something here. Add more information between the two sentences to connect them.*
In addition, purchase high-quality clothes which usually last longer. Even though the price might be higher, it is good value when an item can be worn for several years. (2)∧Cheaper fabrics can lose their color or start to look old quickly, so they need to be thrown away sooner.	*(2) Insert a connecting expression here.*
Finally, (3) <u>think about your clothes</u>. For example, sell them to used clothing stores. That way other people can enjoy wearing them. You could also donate clothes to a charity for people who need them. Another way is to find a new purpose for them. There are many ways to transform outfits into useful items such as quilts or bags.	*(3) This topic sentence doesn't really match this paragraph. Rewrite it.*
In conclusion, it is time for a lifestyle change. From now on, check your closet before you go shopping, (4) <u>select better things</u>, and lastly, give your clothes a second life. In this way, we can all become more sustainable with fashion.	*(4) The underlined phrase doesn't summarize your essay content enough. Change it.*

<u>Overall Comment:</u>
Your essay is getting better. Keep up the good work. (Have you checked your own closet? I have checked mine! ☺)

問 1　Based on comment (1), which is the best sentence to add? [1]

① As a result, people buy many similar items they do not need.
② Because of this, customers cannot enjoy clothes shopping.
③ Due to this, shop clerks want to know what customers need.
④ In this situation, consumers tend to avoid going shopping.

問 2　Based on comment (2), which is the best expression to add? [2]

① for instance
② in contrast
③ nevertheless
④ therefore

問 3　Based on comment (3), which is the most appropriate way to rewrite the topic sentence? [3]

① buy fewer new clothes
② dispose of old clothes
③ find ways to reuse clothes
④ give unwanted clothes away

問 4　Based on comment (4), which is the best replacement? [4]

① buy items that maintain their condition
② choose inexpensive fashionable clothes
③ pick items that can be transformed
④ purchase clothes that are second-hand

※この問題冊子の『注意事項』は，実際の共通テストを想定して掲載しました。

2024 本試

(100点 80分)

〔英　　語（リーディング）〕

注　意　事　項

1　解答用紙に，正しく記入・マークされていない場合は，採点できないことがあります。

2　試験中に問題冊子の印刷不鮮明，ページの落丁・乱丁及び解答用紙の汚れ等に気付いた場合は，手を高く挙げて監督者に知らせなさい。

3　解答は，解答用紙の解答欄にマークしなさい。例えば，[10]と表示のある問いに対して③と解答する場合は，次の(例)のように**解答番号10の解答欄**の③に**マーク**しなさい。

(例)

解答番号	解　答　欄
10	① ② ●(③) ④ ⑤ ⑥ ⑦ ⑧ ⑨

4　問題冊子の余白等は適宜利用してよいが，どのページも切り離してはいけません。

5　**不正行為について**

①　不正行為に対しては厳正に対処します。

②　不正行為に見えるような行為が見受けられた場合は，監督者がカードを用いて注意します。

③　不正行為を行った場合は，その時点で受験を取りやめさせ退室させます。

6　試験終了後，問題冊子は持ち帰りなさい。

英　　語(リーディング)

各大問の英文や図表を読み，解答番号 1 ～ 49 にあてはまるものとして最も適当な選択肢を選びなさい。

第1問　(配点　10)

A　You are studying English at a language school in the US. The school is planning an event. You want to attend, so you are reading the flyer.

The Thorpe English Language School

International Night

Friday, May 24, 5 p.m.-8 p.m.

Entrance Fee: $5

The Thorpe English Language School (TELS) is organizing an international exchange event. TELS students don't need to pay the entrance fee. Please present your student ID at the reception desk in the Student Lobby.

- **Enjoy foods from various parts of the world**
  Have you ever tasted hummus from the Middle East? How about tacos from Mexico? Couscous from North Africa? Try them all!
- **Experience different languages and new ways to communicate**
  Write basic expressions such as "hello" and "thank you" in Arabic, Italian, Japanese, and Spanish. Learn how people from these cultures use facial expressions and their hands to communicate.
- **Watch dance performances**
  From 7 p.m. watch flamenco, hula, and samba dance shows on the stage! After each dance, performers will teach some basic steps. Please join in.

Lots of pictures, flags, maps, textiles, crafts, and games will be displayed in the hall. If you have some pictures or items from your home country which can be displayed at the event, let a school staff member know by May 17!

問 1 To join the event free of charge, you must [1].

① bring pictures from your home country
② consult a staff member about the display
③ fill out a form in the Student Lobby
④ show proof that you are a TELS student

問 2 At the event, you can [2].

① learn about gestures in various cultures
② participate in a dance competition
③ read short stories in foreign languages
④ try cooking international dishes

B You are an exchange student in the US and next week your class will go on a day trip. The teacher has provided some information.

Tours of Yentonville

The Yentonville Tourist Office offers three city tours.

The History Tour

The day will begin with a visit to St. Patrick's Church, which was built when the city was established in the mid-1800s. Opposite the church is the early-20th-century Mayor's House. There will be a tour of the house and its beautiful garden. Finally, cross the city by public bus and visit the Peace Park. Opened soon after World War II, it was the site of many demonstrations in the 1960s.

The Arts Tour

The morning will be spent in the Yentonville Arts District. We will begin in the Art Gallery where there are many paintings from Europe and the US. After lunch, enjoy a concert across the street at the Bruton Concert Hall before walking a short distance to the Artists' Avenue. This part of the district was developed several years ago when new artists' studios and the nearby Sculpture Park were created. Watch artists at work in their studios and afterwards wander around the park, finding sculptures among the trees.

The Sports Tour

First thing in the morning, you can watch the Yentonville Lions football team training at their open-air facility in the suburbs. In the afternoon, travel by subway to the Yentonville Hockey Arena, completed last fall. Spend some time in its exhibition hall to learn about the arena's unique design. Finally, enjoy a professional hockey game in the arena.

Yentonville Tourist Office, January, 2024

問 1　Yentonville has [3].

① a church built 250 years ago when the city was constructed
② a unique football training facility in the center of the town
③ an art studio where visitors can create original works of art
④ an arts area with both an art gallery and a concert hall

問 2　On all three tours, you will [4].

① learn about historic events in the city
② see people demonstrate their skills
③ spend time both indoors and outdoors
④ use public transportation to get around

問 3　Which is the newest place in Yentonville you can visit on the tours?
[5]

① The Hockey Arena
② The Mayor's House
③ The Peace Park
④ The Sculpture Park

第2問 (配点 20)

A You are an exchange student at a high school in the UK and find this flyer.

Invitation to the Strategy Game Club

Have you ever wanted to learn strategy games like chess, *shogi*, or *go*? They are actually more than just games. You can learn skills such as thinking logically and deeply without distractions. Plus, these games are really fun! This club is open to all students of our school. Regardless of skill level, you are welcome to join.

We play strategy games together and. . .

- learn basic moves from demonstrations by club members
- play online against club friends
- share tips on our club webpage
- learn the history and etiquette of each game
- analyse games using computer software
- participate in local and national tournaments

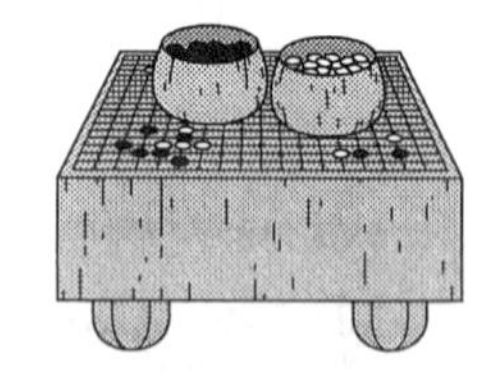

Regular meetings: Wednesday afternoons in Room 301, Student Centre

---

Member Comments

- My mind is clearer, calmer, and more focused in class.
- It's cool to learn how some games have certain similarities.
- At tournaments, I like discussing strategies with other participants.
- Members share Internet videos that explain practical strategies for chess.
- It's nice to have friends who give good advice about *go*.
- I was a complete beginner when I joined, and I had no problem!

問 1 According to the flyer, which is true about the club? [6]

① Absolute beginners are welcome.
② Members edit computer programs.
③ Professional players give formal demonstrations.
④ Students from other schools can join.

問 2 Which of the following is **not** mentioned as a club activity? [7]

① Having games with non-club members
② Playing matches against computers
③ Sharing game-playing ideas on the Internet
④ Studying the backgrounds of strategy games

問 3 One **opinion** stated by a member is that [8].

① comparing different games is interesting
② many videos about *go* are useful
③ members learn tips at competitions
④ regular meetings are held off campus

問 4 The club invitation and a member's comment both mention that [9].

① new members must demonstrate experience
② online support is necessary to be a good player
③ *shogi* is a logical and stimulating game
④ strategy games help improve one's concentration

問 5 This club is most likely suitable for students who want to [10].

① create their own computer strategy games
② improve their skill level of playing strategy games
③ learn proper British etiquette through playing strategy games
④ spend weekends playing strategy games in the club room

B You are a college student going to study in the US and need travel insurance. You find this review of an insurance plan written by a female international student who studied in the US for six months.

There are many things to consider before traveling abroad: pack appropriate clothes, prepare your travel expenses, and don't forget medication (if necessary). Also, you should purchase travel insurance.

When I studied at Fairville University in California, I bought travel insurance from TravSafer International. I signed up online in less than 15 minutes and was immediately covered. They accept any form of payment, usually on a monthly basis. There were three plans. All plans include a one-time health check-up.

The Premium Plan is $100/month. The plan provides 24-hour medical support through a smartphone app and telephone service. Immediate financial support will be authorized if you need to stay in a hospital.

The Standard Plan worked best for me. It had the 24-hour telephone assistance and included a weekly email with tips for staying healthy in a foreign country. It wasn't cheap: $75/month. However, it was nice to get the optional 15% discount because I paid for six months of coverage in advance.

If your budget is limited, you can choose the Economy Plan, which is $25/month. It has the 24-hour telephone support like the other plans but only covers emergency care. Also, they can arrange a taxi to a hospital at a reduced cost if considered necessary by the support center.

I never got sick or hurt, so I thought it was a waste of money to get insurance. Then my friend from Brazil broke his leg while playing soccer and had to spend a few days in a hospital. He had chosen the Premium Plan and it covered everything! I realized how important insurance is—you know that you will be supported when you are in trouble.

問 1 According to the review, which of the following is true? [11]

① Day and night medical assistance is available with the most expensive plan.
② The cheapest plan includes free hospitalization for any reason.
③ The mid-level plan does not include the one-time health check-up.
④ The writer's plan cost her over $100 every month.

問 2 Which is **not** included in the cheapest option? [12]

① Email support
② Emergency treatment
③ Telephone help desk
④ Transport assistance

問 3 Which is the best combination that describes TravSafer International? [13]

A : They allow monthly payments.

B : They design scholarship plans for students.

C : They help you remember your medication.

D : They offer an Internet-based registration system.

E : They require a few days to process the application form.

① **A** and **D**

② **A** and **E**

③ **B** and **D**

④ **B** and **E**

⑤ **C** and **D**

問 4 The writer's **opinion** of her chosen plan is that [14].

① it prevented her from being health conscious

② she was not satisfied with the telephone assistance

③ the option for cost reduction was attractive

④ the treatment for her broken leg was covered

問 5 Which of the following best describes the writer's attitude? [15]

① She believes the smartphone app is useful.

② She considers travel preparation to be important.

③ She feels the US medical system is unique in the world.

④ She thinks a different hospital would have been better for her friend.

第3問 (配点 15)

A Susan, your English ALT's sister, visited your class last month. Now back in the UK, she wrote on her blog about an event she took part in.

Hi!

I participated in a photo rally for foreign tourists with my friends: See the rules on the right. As photo rally beginners, we decided to aim for only five of the checkpoints. In three minutes, we arrived at our first target, the city museum. In quick succession, we made the second, third, and fourth targets. Things were going smoothly! But, on the way to the last target, the statue of a famous samurai from the city, we got lost. Time was running out and my feet were hurting from walking for over two hours. We stopped a man with a pet monkey for help, but neither our Japanese nor his English were good enough. After he'd explained the way using gestures, we realised we wouldn't have enough time to get there and would have to give up. We took a photo with him and said goodbye. When we got back to Sakura City Hall, we were surprised to hear that the winning team had completed 19 checkpoints. One of our photos was selected to be on the event website (click here). It reminds me of the man's warmth and kindness: our own "gold medal."

Sakura City Photo Rally Rules

- Each group can only use the **camera** and **paper map**, both provided by us
- Take as many photos of **25 checkpoints** (designated sightseeing spots) as possible
- **3-hour** time limit
- Photos must include **all 3 team members**
- All members must move **together**
- **No** mobile phones
- **No** transport

問 1　You click the link in the blog. Which picture appears? [16]

①

②

③

④

問 2　You are asked to comment on Susan's blog. Which would be an appropriate comment to her? [17]

① I want to see a picture of you wearing the gold medal!

② You did your best. Come back to Japan and try again!

③ You reached 19 checkpoints in three hours? Really? Wow!!

④ Your photo is great! Did you upgrade your phone?

B You are going to participate in an English Day. As preparation, you are reading an article in the school newspaper written by Yuzu, who took part in it last year.

Virtual Field Trip to a South Sea Island

This year, for our English Day, we participated in a virtual science tour. The winter weather had been terrible, so we were excited to see the tropical scenery of the volcanic island projected on the screen.

First, we "took a road trip" to learn about the geography of the island, using navigation software to view the route. We "got into the car," which our teacher, Mr Leach, sometimes stopped so we could look out of the window and get a better sense of the rainforest. Afterwards, we asked Mr Leach about what we'd seen.

Later, we "dived into the ocean" and learnt about the diversity of marine creatures. We observed a coral reef via a live camera. Mr Leach asked us if we could count the number of creatures, but there were too many! Then he showed us an image of the ocean 10 years ago. The reef we'd seen on camera was dynamic, but in the photo it was even more full of life. It looked so different after only 10 years! Mr Leach told us human activity was affecting the ocean and it could be totally ruined if we didn't act now.

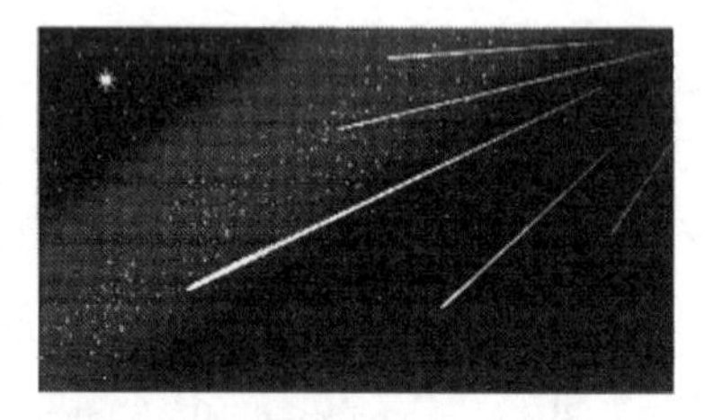

In the evening, we studied astronomy under a "perfect starry sky." We put up tents in the gymnasium and created a temporary planetarium on the ceiling using a projector. We were fascinated by the sky full of constellations, shooting stars, and the Milky Way. Someone pointed out one of the brightest lights and asked Mr Leach if it was Venus, a planet close to Earth. He nodded and explained that humans have created so much artificial light that hardly anything is visible in our city's night sky.

On my way home after school, the weather had improved and the sky was now cloudless. I looked up at the moonless sky and realised what Mr Leach had told us was true.

問 1 Yuzu's article also included student comments (①～④) describing the events in the virtual tour. Put the comments in the order in which the events happened.

①

I was wondering how dangerous the island was. I saw beautiful birds and a huge snake in the jungle.

②

It was really shocking that there had been many more creatures before. We should protect our beautiful oceans!

③

Setting up a camping site in the gymnasium was kind of weird, but great fun! Better than outside, because we weren't bitten by bugs!

④

We were lost for words during the space show and realised we often don't notice things even though they're there.

問 2 From the tour, Yuzu did **not** learn about the [22] of the south sea island.

① marine ecosystem
② night-time sky
③ seasonal weather
④ trees and plants

問 3 On the way home, Yuzu looked up and most likely saw [23] in the night sky.

① a shooting star
② just a few stars
③ the full moon
④ the Milky Way

（下 書 き 用 紙）

英語（リーディング）の試験問題は次に続く。

第4問 (配点 16)

Your college English club's room has several problems and you want to redesign it. Based on the following article and the results of a questionnaire given to members, you make a handout for a group discussion.

What Makes a Good Classroom?

Diana Bashworth, writer at *Trends in Education*

As many schools work to improve their classrooms, it is important to have some ideas for making design decisions. SIN, which stands for *Stimulation, Individualization*, and *Naturalness*, is a framework that might be helpful to consider when designing classrooms.

The first, Stimulation, has two aspects: color and complexity. This has to do with the ceiling, floor, walls, and interior furnishings. For example, a classroom that lacks colors might be uninteresting. On the other hand, a classroom should not be too colorful. A bright color could be used on one wall, on the floor, window coverings, or furniture. In addition, it can be visually distracting to have too many things displayed on walls. It is suggested that 20 to 30 percent of wall space remain free.

The next item in the framework is Individualization, which includes two considerations: ownership and flexibility. Ownership refers to whether the classroom feels personalized. Examples of this include having chairs and desks that are suitable for student sizes and ages, and providing storage space and areas for displaying student works or projects. Flexibility is about having a classroom that allows for different kinds of activities.

Naturalness relates to the quality and quantity of light, both natural and artificial, and the temperature of the classroom. Too much natural light may make screens and boards difficult to see; students may have difficulty reading or writing if there is a lack of light. In addition, hot summer classrooms do not promote effective study. Schools should install systems allowing for the adjustment of both light and temperature.

While Naturalness is more familiar to us, and therefore often considered the priority, the other components are equally important. Hopefully, these ideas can guide your project to a successful end.

Results of the Questionnaire

Q1: Choose any items that match your use of the English club's room.

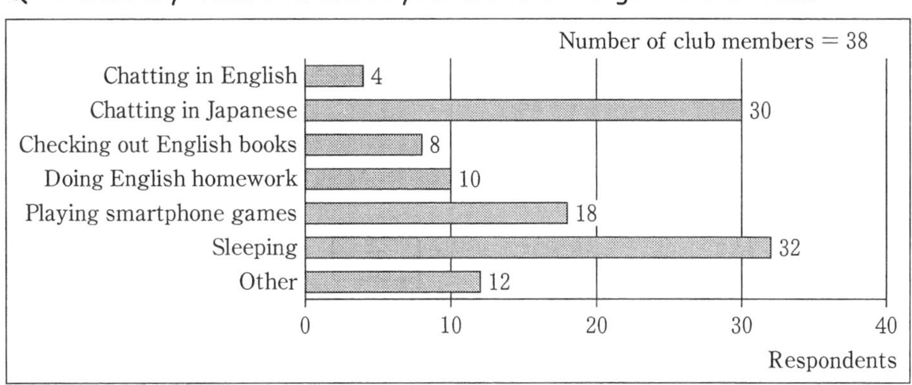

Q2: What do you think about the current English club's room?

Main comments:

Student 1 (S 1): I can't see the projector screen and whiteboard well on a sunny day. Also, there's no way to control the temperature.

S 2: By the windows, the sunlight makes it hard to read. The other side of the room doesn't get enough light. Also, the books are disorganized and the walls are covered with posters. It makes me feel uncomfortable.

S 3: The chairs don't really fit me and the desks are hard to move when we work in small groups. Also, lots of members speak Japanese, even though it's an English club.

S 4: The pictures of foreign countries on the walls make me want to speak English. Everyone likes the sofas — they are so comfortable that we often use the room for sleeping!

S 5: The room is so far away, so I hardly ever go there! Aren't there other rooms available?

S 6: There's so much gray in the room. I don't like it. But it's good that there are plenty of everyday English phrases on the walls!

Your discussion handout:

Room Improvement Project

■ **SIN Framework**

- What it is: [24]
- SIN = Stimulation, Individualization, Naturalness

■ **Design Recommendations Based on SIN and Questionnaire Results**

- Stimulation:
  Cover the floor with a colorful rug and [25].
- Individualization:
  Replace room furniture.
  (tables with wheels → easy to move around)
- Naturalness:
  [26]
  A. Install blinds on windows.
  B. Make temperature control possible.
  C. Move projector screen away from windows.
  D. Place sofas near walls.
  E. Put floor lamp in darker corner.

■ **Other Issues to Discuss**

- The majority of members [27] the room as [28]'s comment mentioned. How can we solve this?
- Based on both the graph and [29]'s comment, should we set a language rule in the room to motivate members to speak English more?
- S 5 doesn't like the location, but we can't change the room, so let's think about how to encourage members to visit more often.

問 1 Choose the best option for 24.

① A guide to show which colors are appropriate to use in classrooms
② A method to prioritize the needs of students and teachers in classrooms
③ A model to follow when planning classroom environments
④ A system to understand how classrooms influence students' performance

問 2 Choose the best option for 25.

① move the screen to a better place
② paint each wall a different color
③ put books on shelves
④ reduce displayed items

問 3 You are checking the handout. You notice an error in the recommendations under Naturalness. Which of the following should you **remove**? 26

① A
② B
③ C
④ D
⑤ E

問 4　Choose the best options for [27] and [28].

[27]

① borrow books from
② can't easily get to
③ don't use Japanese in
④ feel anxious in
⑤ take naps in

[28]

① S1
② S2
③ S3
④ S4
⑤ S5
⑥ S6

問 5　Choose the best option for [29].

① S1
② S2
③ S3
④ S4
⑤ S5
⑥ S6

（下 書 き 用 紙）

英語（リーディング）の試験問題は次に続く。

第5問 (配点 15)

You are in an English discussion group, and it is your turn to introduce a story. You have found a story in an English language magazine in Japan. You are preparing notes for your presentation.

Maki's Kitchen

"*Irasshai-mase*," said Maki as two customers entered her restaurant, Maki's Kitchen. Maki had joined her family business at the age of 19 when her father became ill. After he recovered, Maki decided to continue. Eventually, Maki's parents retired and she became the owner. Maki had many regular customers who came not only for the delicious food, but also to sit at the counter and talk to her. Although her business was doing very well, Maki occasionally daydreamed about doing something different.

"Can we sit at the counter?" she heard. It was her old friends, Takuya and Kasumi. A phone call a few weeks earlier from Kasumi to Takuya had given them the idea to visit Maki and surprise her.

Takuya's phone vibrated, and he saw a familiar name, Kasumi.

"Kasumi!"

"Hi Takuya, I saw you in the newspaper. Congratulations!"

"Thanks. Hey, you weren't at our 20th high school reunion last month."

"No, I couldn't make it. I can't believe it's been 20 years since we graduated. Actually, I was calling to ask if you've seen Maki recently."

Takuya's family had moved to Kawanaka Town shortly before he started high school. He joined the drama club, where he met Maki and Kasumi. The three became inseparable. After graduation, Takuya left Kawanaka to become an actor, while Maki and Kasumi remained. Maki had decided she wanted to study at university and enrolled in a preparatory school. Kasumi, on the other hand, started her career. Takuya tried out for various acting roles but was constantly rejected; eventually, he quit.

Exactly one year after graduation, Takuya returned to Kawanaka with his dreams destroyed. He called Maki, who offered her sympathy. He was surprised to learn that Maki had abandoned her plan to attend university because she had to manage her family's restaurant. Her first day of work had been the day he called. For some reason, Takuya could not resist giving Maki some advice.

"Maki, I've always thought your family's restaurant should change the coffee it serves. I think people in Kawanaka want a bolder flavor. I'd be happy to recommend a different brand," he said.

"Takuya, you really know your coffee. Hey, I was walking by Café Kawanaka and saw a help-wanted sign. You should apply!" Maki replied.

Takuya was hired by Café Kawanaka and became fascinated by the science of coffee making. On the one-year anniversary of his employment, Takuya was talking to Maki at her restaurant.

"Maki," he said, "do you know what my dream is?"

"It must have something to do with coffee."

"That's right! It's to have my own coffee business."

"I can't imagine a better person for it. What are you waiting for?"

Maki's encouragement inspired Takuya. He quit his job, purchased a coffee bean roaster, and began roasting beans. Maki had a sign in her restaurant saying, "We proudly serve Takuya's Coffee," and this publicity helped the coffee gain popularity in Kawanaka. Takuya started making good money selling his beans. Eventually, he opened his own café and became a successful business owner.

Kasumi was reading the newspaper when she saw the headline: *TAKUYA'S CAFÉ ATTRACTING TOURISTS TO KAWANAKA TOWN.* "Who would have thought that Takuya would be so successful?" Kasumi thought to herself as she reflected on her past.

In the high school drama club, Kasumi's duty was to put make-up on the actors. No one could do it better than her. Maki noticed this and saw that a cosmetics company called Beautella was advertising for salespeople. She encouraged Kasumi to apply, and, after graduation, she became an employee of Beautella.

The work was tough; Kasumi went door to door selling cosmetics. On bad days, she would call Maki, who would lift her spirits. One day, Maki had an idea, "Doesn't Beautella do make-up workshops? I think you are more suited for that. You can show people how to use the make-up. They'll love the way they look and buy lots of cosmetics!"

Kasumi's company agreed to let her do workshops, and they were a hit! Kasumi's sales were so good that eight months out of high school, she had been promoted, moving to the big city of Ishijima. Since then, she had steadily climbed her way up the company ladder until she had been named vice-president of Beautella this year.

"I wouldn't be vice-president now without Maki," she thought, "she helped me when I was struggling, but I was too absorbed with my work in Ishijima to give her support when she had to quit her preparatory school." Glancing back to the article, she decided to call Takuya.

"Maki wasn't at the reunion. I haven't seen her in ages," said Takuya.

"Same here. It's a pity. Where would we be without her?" asked Kasumi.

The conversation became silent, as they wordlessly communicated their guilt. Then, Kasumi had an idea.

The three friends were talking and laughing when Maki asked, "By the way, I'm really happy to see you two, but what brings you here?"

"Payback," said Takuya.

"Have I done something wrong?" asked Maki.

"No. The opposite. You understand people incredibly well. You can identify others' strengths and show them how to make use of them. We're proof of this. You made us aware of our gifts," said Takuya.

"The irony is that you couldn't do the same for yourself," added Kasumi.

"I think Ishijima University would be ideal for you. It offers a degree program in counseling that's designed for people with jobs," said Takuya.

"You'd have to go there a few times a month, but you could stay with me. Also, Takuya can help you find staff for your restaurant," said Kasumi.

Maki closed her eyes and imagined Kawanaka having both "Maki's Kitchen" and "Maki's Counseling." She liked that idea.

Your notes:

Maki's Kitchen

Story outline

Maki, Takuya, and Kasumi graduate from high school.

↓
[30]
[31]
[32]
[33]

Maki begins to think about a second career.

About Maki

- Age: [34]
- Occupation: restaurant owner
- How she supported her friends:

  Provided Takuya with encouragement and [35].

  〃 Kasumi 〃 〃 and [36].

Interpretation of key moments

- Kasumi and Takuya experience an uncomfortable silence on the phone because they [37].
- In the final scene, Kasumi uses the word "irony" with Maki. The irony is that Maki does not [38].

問 1　Choose **four** out of the five events (①～⑤) and rearrange them in the order they happened. [30] → [31] → [32] → [33]

① Kasumi becomes vice-president of her company.
② Kasumi gets in touch with Takuya.
③ Maki gets her university degree.
④ Maki starts working in her family business.
⑤ Takuya is inspired to start his own business.

問 2　Choose the best option for [34].

① early 30s
② late 30s
③ early 40s
④ late 40s

問 3　Choose the best options for [35] and [36].

① made the product known to people
② proposed a successful business idea
③ purchased equipment for the business
④ suggested moving to a bigger city
⑤ taught the necessary skills for success

問 4 Choose the best option for [37].

① do not want to discuss their success
② have not spoken in a long time
③ regret not appreciating their friend more
④ think Maki was envious of their achievements

問 5 Choose the best option for [38].

① like to try different things
② recognize her own talent
③ understand the ability she lacks
④ want to pursue her dreams

第6問 (配点　24)

A Your English teacher has assigned this article to you. You need to prepare notes to give a short talk.

Perceptions of Time

When you hear the word "time," it is probably hours, minutes, and seconds that immediately come to mind. In the late 19th century, however, philosopher Henri Bergson described how people usually do not experience time as it is measured by clocks (**clock time**). Humans do not have a known biological mechanism to measure clock time, so they use mental processes instead. This is called **psychological time**, which everyone perceives differently.

If you were asked how long it had taken to finish your homework, you probably would not know exactly. You would think back and make an estimate. In a 1975 experiment, participants were shown either simple or complex shapes for a fixed amount of time and asked to memorize them. Afterwards, they were asked how long they had looked at the shapes. To answer, they used a mental process called **retrospective timing**, which is estimating time based on the information retrieved from memory. Participants who were shown the complex shapes felt the time was longer, while the people who saw the simple shapes experienced the opposite.

Another process to measure psychological time is called **prospective timing**. It is used when you are actively keeping track of time while doing something. Instead of using the amount of information recalled, the level of attention given to time while doing the activity is used. In several studies, the participants performed tasks while estimating the time needed to complete them. Time seemed shorter for the people doing more challenging mental activities which required them to place more focus on the task than on time.

Time felt longer for the participants who did simpler tasks and the longest for those who were waiting or doing nothing.

Your emotional state can influence your awareness of time, too. For example, you can be enjoying a concert so much that you forget about time. Afterwards, you are shocked that hours have passed by in what seemed to be the blink of an eye. To explain this, we often say, "Time flies when you're having fun." The opposite occurs when you are bored. Instead of being focused on an activity, you notice the time. It seems to go very slowly as you cannot wait for your boredom to end. Fear also affects our perception of time. In a 2006 study, more than 60 people experienced skydiving for the first time. Participants with high levels of unpleasant emotions perceived the time spent skydiving to be much longer than it was in reality.

Psychological time also seems to move differently during life stages. Children constantly encounter new information and have new experiences, which makes each day memorable and seem longer when recalled. Also, time creeps by for them as they anticipate upcoming events such as birthdays and trips. For most adults, unknown information is rarely encountered and new experiences become less frequent, so less mental focus is required and each day becomes less memorable. However, this is not always the case. Daily routines are shaken up when drastic changes occur, such as changing jobs or relocating to a new city. In such cases, the passage of time for those people is similar to that for children. But generally speaking, time seems to accelerate as we mature.

Knowledge of psychological time can be helpful in our daily lives, as it may help us deal with boredom. Because time passes slowly when we are not mentally focused and thinking about time, changing to a more engaging activity, such as reading a book, will help ease our boredom and speed up the time. The next occasion that you hear "Time flies when you're having fun," you will be reminded of this.

Your notes:

Perceptions of Time

Outline by paragraph

1. [39]
2. Retrospective timing
3. Prospective timing
4. [40]
   - ➤ Skydiving
5. Effects of age
   - ➤ Time speeds up as we mature, but a [41].
6. Practical tips

My original examples to help the audience

A. Retrospective timing

Example: [42]

B. Prospective timing

Example: [43]

問 1 Choose the best options for [39] and [40].

① Biological mechanisms

② Effects of our feelings

③ Kinds of memory

④ Life stages

⑤ Ongoing research

⑥ Types of time

問 2 Choose the best option for [41].

① major lifestyle change at any age will likely make time slow down
② major lifestyle change regardless of age will likely make time speed up
③ minor lifestyle change for adults will likely make time slow down
④ minor lifestyle change for children will likely make time speed up

問 3 Choose the best option for [42].

① anticipating a message from a classmate
② memorizing your mother's cellphone number
③ reflecting on how many hours you worked today
④ remembering that you have a meeting tomorrow

問 4 Choose the best option for [43].

① guessing how long you've been jogging so far
② making a schedule for the basketball team summer camp
③ running into your tennis coach at the railway station
④ thinking about your last family vacation to a hot spring

B You are preparing a presentation for your science club, using the following passage from a science website.

Chili Peppers: The Spice of Life

Tiny pieces of red spice in chili chicken add a nice touch of color, but biting into even a small piece can make a person's mouth burn as if it were on fire. While some people love this, others want to avoid the painful sensation. At the same time, though, they can eat sashimi with wasabi. This might lead one to wonder what spiciness actually is and to ask where the difference between chili and wasabi comes from.

Unlike sweetness, saltiness, and sourness, spiciness is not a taste. In fact, we do not actually taste heat, or spiciness, when we eat spicy foods. The bite we feel from eating chili peppers and wasabi is derived from different types of compounds. Chili peppers get their heat from a heavier, oil-like element called capsaicin. Capsaicin leaves a lingering, fire-like sensation in our mouths because it triggers a receptor called TRPV1. TRPV1 induces stress and tells us when something is burning our mouths. Interestingly, there is a wide range of heat across the different varieties of chili peppers, and the level depends on the amount of capsaicin they contain. This is measured using the Scoville Scale, which is also called Scoville Heat Units (SHU). SHUs range from the sweet and mild *shishito* pepper at 50-200 SHUs to the Carolina Reaper pepper, which can reach up to 2. 2 million.

Wasabi is considered a root, not a pepper, and does not contain capsaicin. Thus, wasabi is not ranked on the Scoville Scale. However, people have compared the level of spice in it to chilis with around 1, 000 SHUs, which is on the lower end of the scale. The reason some people cannot tolerate chili spice but can eat foods flavored with wasabi is that the spice compounds in it are low in density. The compounds in wasabi vaporize easily, delivering a blast of spiciness to our nose when we eat it.

Consuming chili peppers can have positive effects on our health, and much research has been conducted into the benefits of capsaicin. When capsaicin activates the TRPV1 receptor in a person's body, it is similar to what happens when they experience stress or pain from an injury. Strangely, capsaicin can also make pain go away. Scientists found that TRPV1 ceases to be turned on after long-term exposure to chili peppers, temporarily easing painful sensations. Thus, skin creams containing capsaicin might be useful for people who experience muscle aches.

Another benefit of eating chili peppers is that they accelerate the metabolism. A group of researchers analyzed 90 studies on capsaicin and body weight and found that people had a reduced appetite when they ate spicy foods. This is because spicy foods increase the heart rate, send more energy to the muscles, and convert fat into energy. Recently, scientists at the University of Wyoming have created a weight-loss drug with capsaicin as a main ingredient.

It is also believed that chili peppers are connected with food safety, which might lead to a healthier life. When food is left outside of a refrigerated environment, microorganisms multiply on it, which may cause sickness if eaten. Studies have shown that capsaicin and other chemicals found in chili peppers have antibacterial properties that can slow down or even stop microorganism growth. As a result, food lasts longer and there are fewer food-borne illnesses. This may explain why people in hot climates have a tendency to use more chili peppers, and therefore, be more tolerant of spicier foods due to repeated exposure. Also, in the past, before there were refrigerators, they were less likely to have food poisoning than people in cooler climates.

Chili peppers seem to have health benefits, but can they also be bad for our health? Peppers that are high on the Scoville Scale can cause physical discomfort when eaten in large quantities. People who have eaten several of the world's hottest chilis in a short time have reported experiencing upset stomachs, diarrhea, numb hands, and symptoms similar to a heart attack. Ghost peppers, which contain one million SHUs, can even burn a person's skin if they are touched.

Luckily the discomfort some people feel after eating spicy foods tends to go away soon—usually within a few hours. Despite some negative side effects, spicy foods remain popular around the world and add a flavorful touch to the table. Remember, it is safe to consume spicy foods, but you might want to be careful about the amount of peppers you put in your dishes.

Presentation slides:

Characteristics (2)

chili peppers	wasabi
· oil-like elements	· [44]
· triggering TRPV1	· changing to vapor
· persistent feeling	· spicy rush

Positive Effects (3)

Capsaicin can... [45]

A. reduce pain.
B. give you more energy.
C. speed up your metabolism.
D. make you feel less stress.
E. decrease food poisoning.

Negative Effects (4)

When eating too many strong chili peppers in a short time,

· [46]
· [47]

Spice Tolerance (5)

[48]

Closing Remark (6)

[49]

問 1 What is the first characteristic of wasabi on Slide 2? [44]

① burning taste
② fire-like sensation
③ lasting feeling
④ light compounds

問 2 Which is an **error** you found on Slide 3? [45]

① A
② B
③ C
④ D
⑤ E

問 3 Choose two options for Slide 4. (The order does not matter.)
[46] · [47]

① you might activate harmful bacteria.
② you might experience stomach pain.
③ you might lose feeling in your hands.
④ your fingers might feel like they are on fire.
⑤ your nose might start hurting.

問 4 What can be inferred about tolerance for spices for Slide 5? 48

① People with a high tolerance to chili peppers pay attention to the spices used in their food.

② People with a high tolerance to wasabi are scared of chili peppers' negative effects.

③ People with a low tolerance to chili peppers can get used to their heat.

④ People with a low tolerance to wasabi cannot endure high SHU levels.

問 5 Choose the most appropriate remark for Slide 6. 49

① Don't be afraid. Eating spicy foods will boost your confidence.

② Next time you eat chili chicken, remember its punch only stays for a second.

③ Personality plays a big role in our spice preference, so don't worry.

④ Unfortunately, there are no cures for a low wasabi tolerance.

⑤ When someone offers you some spicy food, remember it has some benefits.

※この問題冊子の『注意事項』は，実際の共通テストを想定して掲載しました。

2023 本試

(100点
80分)

〔英　　語（リーディング）〕

注　意　事　項

1　解答用紙に，正しく記入・マークされていない場合は，採点できないことがあります。

2　試験中に問題冊子の印刷不鮮明，ページの落丁・乱丁及び解答用紙の汚れ等に気付いた場合は，手を高く挙げて監督者に知らせなさい。

3　解答は，解答用紙の解答欄にマークしなさい。例えば，［10］と表示のある問いに対して③と解答する場合は，次の（例）のように**解答番号10**の**解答欄**の③に**マーク**しなさい。

（例）

解答番号	解　答　欄
10	① ② ●(③) ④ ⑤ ⑥ ⑦ ⑧ ⑨

4　問題冊子の余白等は適宜利用してよいが，どのページも切り離してはいけません。

5　**不正行為について**

①　不正行為に対しては厳正に対処します。

②　不正行為に見えるような行為が見受けられた場合は，監督者がカードを用いて注意します。

③　不正行為を行った場合は，その時点で受験を取りやめさせ退室させます。

6　試験終了後，問題冊子は持ち帰りなさい。

英　語（リーディング）

各大問の英文や図表を読み，解答番号 [1] ～ [49] にあてはまるものとして最も適当な選択肢を選びなさい。

第１問 （配点　10）

A　You are studying in the US, and as an afternoon activity you need to choose one of two performances to go and see. Your teacher gives you this handout.

Performances for Friday

Palace Theater	**Grand Theater**
Together Wherever	***The Guitar Queen***
A romantic play that will make you laugh and cry	A rock musical featuring colorful costumes
▸ From 2:00 p.m. (no breaks and a running time of one hour and 45 minutes) ▸ Actors available to talk in the lobby after the performance ▸ No food or drinks available ▸ Free T-shirts for five lucky people	▸ Starts at 1:00 p.m. (three hours long including two 15-minute breaks) ▸ Opportunity to greet the cast in their costumes before the show starts ▸ Light refreshments (snacks & drinks), original T-shirts, and other goods sold in the lobby

Instructions: Which performance would you like to attend? Fill in the form below and hand it in to your teacher today.

✂- -

Choose (✔) one: *Together Wherever* ☐　　*The Guitar Queen* ☐

Name: ______________________________

問 1 What are you told to do after reading the handout? [1]

① Complete and hand in the bottom part.
② Find out more about the performances.
③ Talk to your teacher about your decision.
④ Write your name and explain your choice.

問 2 Which is true about both performances? [2]

① No drinks can be purchased before the show.
② Some T-shirts will be given as gifts.
③ They will finish at the same time.
④ You can meet performers at the theaters.

B You are a senior high school student interested in improving your English during the summer vacation. You find a website for an intensive English summer camp run by an international school.

Galley International School (GIS) has provided intensive English summer camps for senior high school students in Japan since 1989. Spend two weeks in an all-English environment!

Dates: August 1-14, 2023

Location: Lake Kawaguchi Youth Lodge, Yamanashi Prefecture

Cost: 120,000 yen, including food and accommodation (additional fees for optional activities such as kayaking and canoeing)

Courses Offered

◆**FOREST**: You'll master basic grammar structures, make short speeches on simple topics, and get pronunciation tips. Your instructors have taught English for over 20 years in several countries. On the final day of the camp, you'll take part in a speech contest while all the other campers listen.

◆**MOUNTAIN**: You'll work in a group to write and perform a skit in English. Instructors for this course have worked at theater schools in New York City, London, and Sydney. You'll perform your skit for all the campers to enjoy on August 14.

◆**SKY**: You'll learn debating skills and critical thinking in this course. Your instructors have been to many countries to coach debate teams and some have published best-selling textbooks on the subject. You'll do a short debate in front of all the other campers on the last day. (Note: Only those with an advanced level of English will be accepted.)

▲Application

Step 1: Fill in the online application **HERE** by May 20, 2023.

Step 2: We'll contact you to set up an interview to assess your English ability and ask about your course preference.

Step 3: You'll be assigned to a course.

問 1 All GIS instructors have [3].

① been in Japan since 1989
② won international competitions
③ worked in other countries
④ written some popular books

問 2 On the last day of the camp, campers will [4].

① assess each other's performances
② compete to receive the best prize
③ make presentations about the future
④ show what they learned at the camp

問 3 What will happen after submitting your camp application? [5]

① You will call the English instructors.
② You will take a written English test.
③ Your English level will be checked.
④ Your English speech topic will be sent.

第2問 (配点 20)

A You want to buy a good pair of shoes as you walk a long way to school and often get sore feet. You are searching on a UK website and find this advertisement.

Navi 55 presents the new *Smart Support* shoe line

Smart Support shoes are strong, long-lasting, and reasonably priced. They are available in three colours and styles.

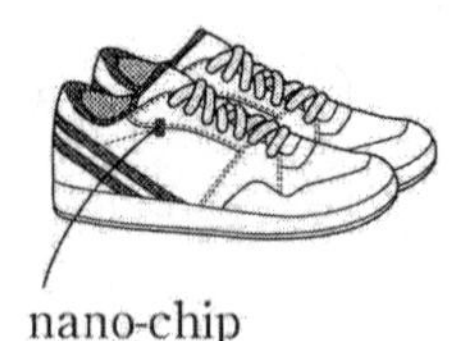

Special Features

Smart Support shoes have a nano-chip which analyses the shape of your feet when connected to the *iSupport* application. Download the app onto your smartphone, PC, tablet, and/or smartwatch. Then, while wearing the shoes, let the chip collect the data about your feet. The inside of the shoe will automatically adjust to give correct, personalised foot support. As with other Navi 55 products, the shoes have our popular Route Memory function.

Advantages

Better Balance: Adjusting how you stand, the personalised support helps keep feet, legs, and back free from pain.

Promotes Exercise: As they are so comfortable, you will be willing to walk regularly.

Route Memory: The chip records your daily route, distance, and pace as you walk.

Route Options: View your live location on your device, have the directions play automatically in your earphones, or use your smartwatch to read directions.

Customers' Comments

- I like the choices for getting directions, and prefer using audio guidance to visual guidance.
- I lost 2 kg in a month!
- I love my pair now, but it took me several days to get used to them.
- As they don't slip in the rain, I wear mine all year round.
- They are so light and comfortable I even wear them when cycling.
- Easy to get around! I don't need to worry about getting lost.
- They look great. The app's basic features are easy to use, but I wouldn't pay for the optional advanced ones.

問 1 According to the maker's statements, which best describes the new shoes? [6]

① Cheap summer shoes
② High-tech everyday shoes
③ Light comfortable sports shoes
④ Stylish colourful cycling shoes

問 2 Which benefit offered by the shoes is most likely to appeal to you? [7]

① Getting more regular exercise
② Having personalised foot support
③ Knowing how fast you walk
④ Looking cool wearing them

問 3 One **opinion** stated by a customer is that [8].

① the app encourages fast walking
② the app's free functions are user-friendly
③ the shoes are good value for money
④ the shoes increase your cycling speed

問 4 One customer's comment mentions using audio devices. Which benefit is this comment based on? [9]

① Better Balance
② Promotes Exercise
③ Route Memory
④ Route Options

問 5 According to one customer's opinion, [10] is recommended.

① allowing time to get accustomed to wearing the shoes
② buying a watch to help you lose weight
③ connecting to the app before putting the shoes on
④ paying for the *iSupport* advanced features

B You are a member of the student council. The members have been discussing a student project helping students to use their time efficiently. To get ideas, you are reading a report about a school challenge. It was written by an exchange student who studied in another school in Japan.

Commuting Challenge

Most students come to my school by bus or train. I often see a lot of students playing games on their phones or chatting. However, they could also use this time for reading or doing homework. We started this activity to help students use their commuting time more effectively. Students had to complete a commuting activity chart from January 17th to February 17th. A total of 300 students participated: More than two thirds of them were second-years; about a quarter were third-years; only 15 first-years participated. How come so few first-years participated? Based on the feedback (given below), there seems to be an answer to this question:

Feedback from participants

HS: Thanks to this project, I got the highest score ever in an English vocabulary test. It was easy to set small goals to complete on my way.

KF: My friend was sad because she couldn't participate. She lives nearby and walks to school. There should have been other ways to take part.

SS: My train is always crowded and I have to stand, so there is no space to open a book or a tablet. I only used audio materials, but there were not nearly enough.

JH: I kept a study log, which made me realise how I used my time. For some reason most of my first-year classmates didn't seem to know about this challenge.

MN: I spent most of the time on the bus watching videos, and it helped me to understand classes better. I felt the time went very fast.

問 1　The aim of the Commuting Challenge was to help students to [11].

① commute more quickly
② improve their test scores
③ manage English classes better
④ use their time better

問 2　One **fact** about the Commuting Challenge is that [12].

① fewer than 10% of the participants were first-years
② it was held for two months during the winter
③ students had to use portable devices on buses
④ the majority of participants travelled by train

問 3　From the feedback, [13] were activities reported by participants.

A：keeping study records
B：learning language
C：making notes on tablets
D：reading lesson notes on mobile phones

① A and B
② A and C
③ A and D
④ B and C
⑤ B and D
⑥ C and D

問 4 One of the participants' opinions about the Commuting Challenge is that [14].

① it could have included students who walk to school

② the train was a good place to read books

③ there were plenty of audio materials for studying

④ watching videos for fun helped time pass quickly

問 5 The author's question is answered by [15].

① HS

② JH

③ KF

④ MN

⑤ SS

第3問 (配点 15)

A You are studying at Camberford University, Sydney. You are going on a class camping trip and are reading the camping club's newsletter to prepare.

Going camping? Read me!!!

Hi, I'm Kaitlyn. I want to share two practical camping lessons from my recent club trip. The first thing is to divide your backpack into three main parts and put the heaviest items in the middle section to balance the backpack. Next, more frequently used daily necessities should be placed in the top section. That means putting your sleeping bag at the bottom; food, cookware and tent in the middle; and your clothes at the top. Most good backpacks come with a "brain" (an additional pouch) for small easy-to-reach items.

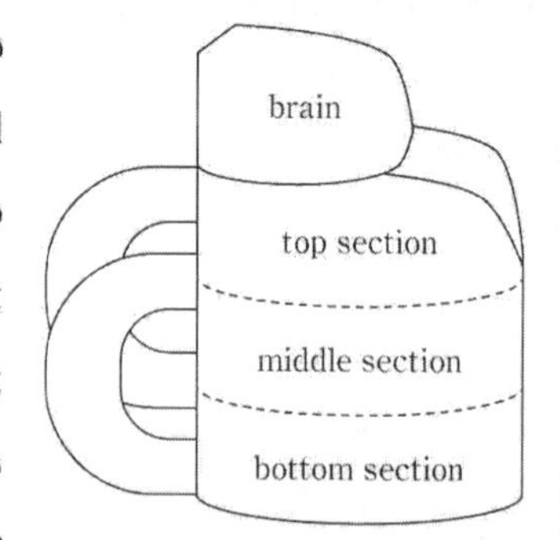

Last year, in the evening, we had fun cooking and eating outdoors. I had been sitting close to our campfire, but by the time I got back to the tent I was freezing. Although I put on extra layers of clothes before going to sleep, I was still cold. Then, my friend told me to take off my outer layers and stuff them into my sleeping bag to fill up some of the empty space. This stuffing method was new to me, and surprisingly kept me warm all night!

I hope my advice helps you stay warm and comfortable. Enjoy your camping trip!

問 1 If you take Kaitlyn's advice, how should you fill your backpack? [16]

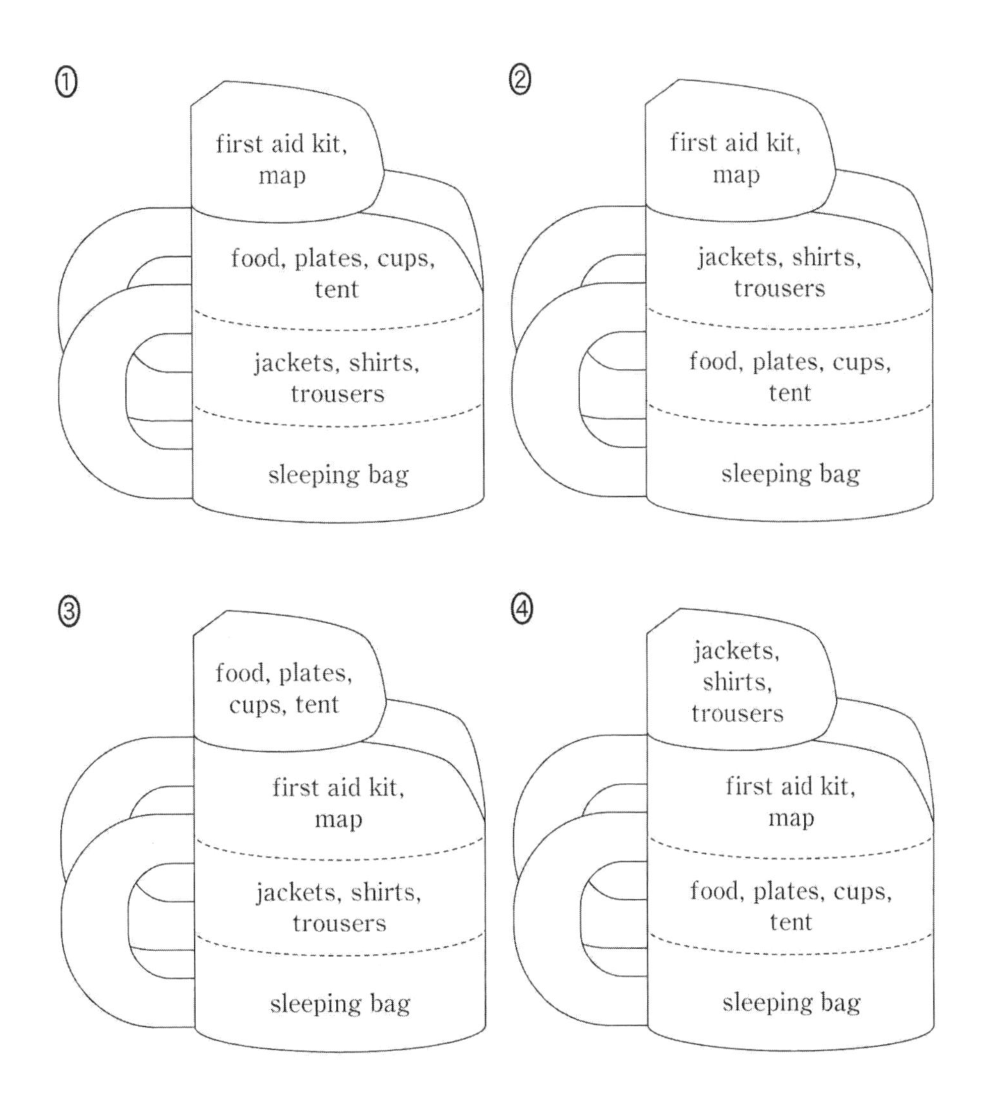

問 2 According to Kaitlyn, [17] is the best method to stay warm all night.

① avoiding going out of your tent
② eating hot meals beside your campfire
③ filling the gaps in your sleeping bag
④ wearing all of your extra clothes

B Your English club will make an "adventure room" for the school festival. To get some ideas, you are reading a blog about a room a British man created.

Create Your Own "Home Adventure"

Last year, I took part in an "adventure room" experience. I really enjoyed it, so I created one for my children. Here are some tips on making your own.

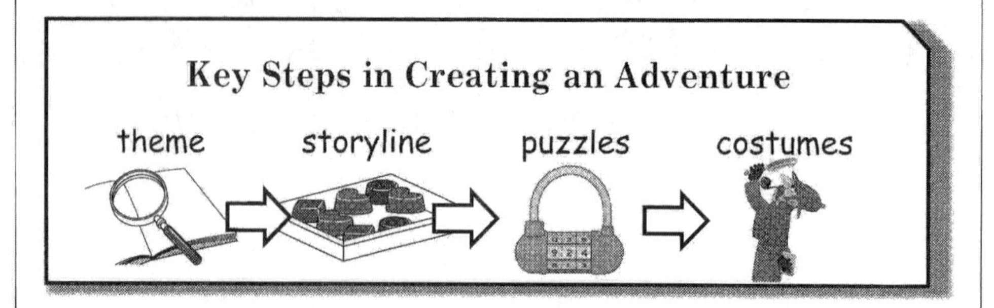

First, pick a theme. My sons are huge Sherlock Holmes fans, so I decided on a detective mystery. I rearranged the furniture in our family room, and added some old paintings and lamps I had to set the scene.

Next, create a storyline. Ours was *The Case of the Missing Chocolates*. My children would be "detectives" searching for clues to locate the missing sweets.

The third step is to design puzzles and challenges. A useful idea is to work backwards from the solution. If the task is to open a box locked with a three-digit padlock, think of ways to hide a three-digit code. Old books are fantastic for hiding messages in. I had tremendous fun underlining words on different pages to form mystery sentences. Remember that the puzzles should get progressively more difficult near the final goal. To get into the spirit, I then had the children wear costumes. My eldest son was excited when I handed him a magnifying glass, and immediately began acting like Sherlock Holmes. After that, the children started to search for the first clue.

This "adventure room" was designed specifically for my family, so I made some of the challenges personal. For the final task, I took a couple of small cups and put a plastic sticker in each one, then filled them with yogurt. The "detectives" had to eat their way to the bottom to reveal the clues. Neither of my kids would eat yogurt, so this truly was tough for them. During the adventure, my children were totally focused, and they enjoyed themselves so much that we will have another one next month.

問 1 Put the following events (①～④) into the order in which they happened.

[18] → [19] → [20] → [21]

① The children ate food they are not fond of.
② The children started the search for the sweets.
③ The father decorated the living room in the house.
④ The father gave his sons some clothes to wear.

問 2 If you follow the father's advice to create your own "adventure room," you should [22].

① concentrate on three-letter words
② leave secret messages under the lamps
③ make the challenges gradually harder
④ practise acting like Sherlock Holmes

問 3 From this story, you understand that the father [23].

① became focused on searching for the sweets

② created an experience especially for his children

③ had some trouble preparing the adventure game

④ spent a lot of money decorating the room

（下 書 き 用 紙）

英語（リーディング）の試験問題は次に続く。

第4問 (配点 16)

Your teacher has asked you to read two articles about effective ways to study. You will discuss what you learned in your next class.

How to Study Effectively: Contextual Learning!

Tim Oxford
Science Teacher, Stone City Junior High School

As a science teacher, I am always concerned about how to help students who struggle to learn. Recently, I found that their main way of learning was to study new information repeatedly until they could recall it all. For example, when they studied for a test, they would use a workbook like the example below and repeatedly say the terms that go in the blanks: "Obsidian is igneous, dark, and glassy. Obsidian is igneous, dark, and glassy. . . ." These students would feel as if they had learned the information, but would quickly forget it and get low scores on the test. Also, this sort of repetitive learning is dull and demotivating.

To help them learn, I tried applying "contextual learning." In this kind of learning, new knowledge is constructed through students' own experiences. For my science class, students learned the properties of different kinds of rocks. Rather than having them memorize the terms from a workbook, I brought a big box of various rocks to the class. Students examined the rocks and identified their names based on the characteristics they observed.

Rock name	Obsidian
Rock type	igneous
Coloring	dark
Texture	glassy
Picture	

Thanks to this experience, I think these students will always be able to describe the properties of the rocks they studied. One issue, however, is that we don't always have the time to do contextual learning, so students will still study by doing drills. I don't think this is the best way. I'm still searching for ways to improve their learning.

How to Make Repetitive Learning Effective

Cheng Lee

Professor, Stone City University

Mr. Oxford's thoughts on contextual learning were insightful. I agree that it can be beneficial. Repetition, though, can also work well. However, the repetitive learning strategy he discussed, which is called "massed learning," is not effective. There is another kind of repetitive learning called "spaced learning," in which students memorize new information and then review it over longer intervals.

The interval between studying is the key difference. In Mr. Oxford's example, his students probably used their workbooks to study over a short period of time. In this case, they might have paid less attention to the content as they continued to review it. The reason for this is that the content was no longer new and could easily be ignored. In contrast, when the intervals are longer, the students' memory of the content is weaker. Therefore, they pay more attention because they have to make a greater effort to recall what they had learned before. For example, if students study with their workbooks, wait three days, and then study again, they are likely to learn the material better.

Previous research has provided evidence for the advantages of spaced learning. In one experiment, students in Groups A and B tried to memorize the names of 50 animals. Both groups studied four times, but Group A studied at one-day intervals while Group B studied at one-week intervals. As the figure to the right shows, 28 days after the last learning session, the average ratio of recalled names on a test was higher for the spaced learning group.

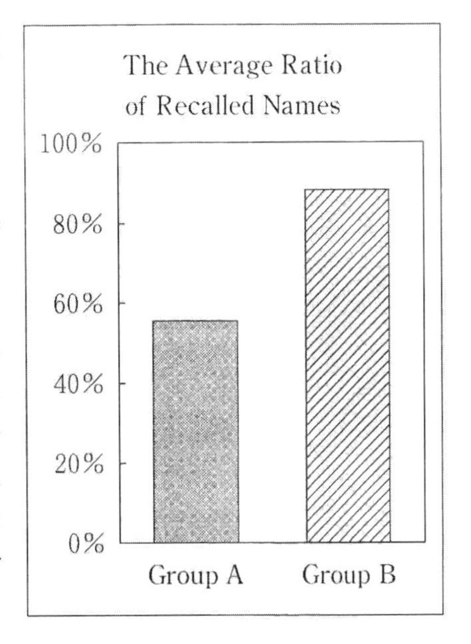

I understand that students often need to learn a lot of information in a short period of time, and long intervals between studying might not be practical. You should understand, though, that massed learning might not be good for long-term recall.

問 1 Oxford believes that [24].

① continuous drilling is boring
② reading an explanation of terms is helpful
③ students are not interested in science
④ studying with a workbook leads to success

問 2 In the study discussed by Lee, students took a test [25] after their final session.

① four weeks
② immediately
③ one day
④ one week

問 3 Lee introduces spaced learning, which involves studying at [26] intervals, in order to overcome the disadvantages of [27] learning that Oxford discussed. (Choose the best one for each box from options ①～⑥.)

① contextual
② extended
③ fixed
④ irregular
⑤ massed
⑥ practical

問 4 Both writers agree that [28] is helpful for remembering new information.

① experiential learning
② having proper rest
③ long-term attention
④ studying with workbooks

問 5 Which additional information would be the best to further support Lee's argument for spaced learning? [29]

① The main factor that makes a science class attractive
② The most effective length of intervals for spaced learning
③ Whether students' workbooks include visuals or not
④ Why Oxford's students could not memorize information well

第5問 （配点　15）

Your English teacher has told everyone in your class to find an inspirational story and present it to a discussion group, using notes. You have found a story written by a high school student in the UK.

Lessons from Table Tennis

Ben Carter

The ball flew at lightning speed to my backhand. It was completely unexpected and I had no time to react. I lost the point and the match. Defeat... Again! This is how it was in the first few months when I started playing table tennis. It was frustrating, but I now know that the sport taught me more than simply how to be a better athlete.

In middle school, I loved football. I was one of the top scorers, but I didn't get along with my teammates. The coach often said that I should be more of a team player. I knew I should work on the problem, but communication was just not my strong point.

I had to leave the football club when my family moved to a new town. I wasn't upset as I had decided to stop playing football anyway. My new school had a table tennis club, coached by the PE teacher, Mr Trent, and I joined that. To be honest, I chose table tennis because I thought it would be easier for me to play individually.

At first, I lost more games than I won. I was frustrated and often went straight home after practice, not speaking to anyone. One day, however, Mr Trent said to me, "You could be a good player, Ben, but you need to think more about your game. What do you think you need to do?" "I don't know," I replied, "focus on the ball more?" "Yes," Mr Trent continued, "but you also need to study your opponent's moves and adjust your play accordingly. Remember, your opponent is a person, not a ball." This made a deep impression on me.

I deliberately modified my style of play, paying closer attention to my opponent's moves. It was not easy, and took a lot of concentration. My efforts paid off, however, and my play improved. My confidence grew and I started staying behind more after practice. I was turning into a star player and my classmates tried to talk to me more than before. I thought that I was becoming popular, but our conversations seemed to end before they really got started. Although my play might have improved, my communication skills obviously hadn't.

My older brother Patrick was one of the few people I could communicate with well. One day, I tried to explain my problems with communication to him, but couldn't make him understand. We switched to talking about table tennis. "What do you actually enjoy about it?" he asked me curiously. I said I loved analysing my opponent's movements and making instant decisions about the next move. Patrick looked thoughtful. "That sounds like the kind of skill we use when we communicate," he said.

At that time, I didn't understand, but soon after our conversation, I won a silver medal in a table tennis tournament. My classmates seemed really pleased. One of them, George, came running over. "Hey, Ben!" he said, "Let's have a party to celebrate!" Without thinking, I replied, "I can't. I've got practice." He looked a bit hurt and walked off without saying anything else.

Why was he upset? I thought about this incident for a long time. Why did he suggest a party? Should I have said something different? A lot of questions came to my mind, but then I realised that he was just being kind. If I'd said, "Great idea. Thank you! Let me talk to Mr Trent and see if I can get some time off practice," then maybe the outcome would have been better. At that moment Patrick's words made sense. Without attempting to grasp someone's intention, I wouldn't know how to respond.

I'm still not the best communicator in the world, but I definitely feel more confident in my communication skills now than before. Next year, my friends and I are going to co-ordinate the table tennis league with other schools.

Your notes:

Lessons from Table Tennis

About the author (Ben Carter)

- Played football at middle school.
- Started playing table tennis at his new school because he [30].

Other important people

- Mr Trent: Ben's table tennis coach, who helped him improve his play.
- Patrick: Ben's brother, who [31].
- George: Ben's classmate, who wanted to celebrate his victory.

Influential events in Ben's journey to becoming a better communicator

Began playing table tennis → [32] → [33] → [34] → [35]

What Ben realised after the conversation with George

He should have [36].

What we can learn from this story

- [37]
- [38]

問 1 Choose the best option for [30].

① believed it would help him communicate
② hoped to become popular at school
③ thought he could win games easily
④ wanted to avoid playing a team sport

問 2 Choose the best option for [31].

① asked him what he enjoyed about communication
② encouraged him to be more confident
③ helped him learn the social skills he needed
④ told him what he should have said to his school friends

問 3 Choose **four** out of the five options (①～⑤) and rearrange them in the order they happened. [32] → [33] → [34] → [35]

① Became a table tennis champion
② Discussed with his teacher how to play well
③ Refused a party in his honour
④ Started to study his opponents
⑤ Talked to his brother about table tennis

問 4 Choose the best option for [36].

① asked his friend questions to find out more about his motivation
② invited Mr Trent and other classmates to the party to show appreciation
③ tried to understand his friend's point of view to act appropriately
④ worked hard to be a better team player for successful communication

問 5 Choose the best two options for [37] and [38]. (The order does not matter.)

① Advice from people around us can help us change.
② Confidence is important for being a good communicator.
③ It is important to make our intentions clear to our friends.
④ The support that teammates provide one another is helpful.
⑤ We can apply what we learn from one thing to another.

（下 書 き 用 紙）

英語（リーディング）の試験問題は次に続く。

第6問 （配点 24）

A You are in a discussion group in school. You have been asked to summarize the following article. You will speak about it, using only notes.

Collecting

Collecting has existed at all levels of society, across cultures and age groups since early times. Museums are proof that things have been collected, saved, and passed down for future generations. There are various reasons for starting a collection. For example, Ms. A enjoys going to yard sales every Saturday morning with her children. At yard sales, people sell unwanted things in front of their houses. One day, while looking for antique dishes, an unusual painting caught her eye and she bought it for only a few dollars. Over time, she found similar pieces that left an impression on her, and she now has a modest collection of artwork, some of which may be worth more than she paid. One person's trash can be another person's treasure. Regardless of how someone's collection was started, it is human nature to collect things.

In 1988, researchers Brenda Danet and Tamar Katriel analyzed 80 years of studies on children under the age of 10, and found that about 90% collected something. This shows us that people like to gather things from an early age. Even after becoming adults, people continue collecting stuff. Researchers in the field generally agree that approximately one third of adults maintain this behavior. Why is this? The primary explanation is related to emotions. Some save greeting cards from friends and family, dried flowers from special events, seashells from a day at the beach, old photos, and so on. For others, their collection is a connection to their youth. They may have baseball cards, comic books, dolls, or miniature cars that they have kept since they were small.

Others have an attachment to history; they seek and hold onto historical documents, signed letters and autographs from famous people, and so forth.

For some individuals there is a social reason. People collect things such as pins to share, show, and even trade, making new friends this way. Others, like some holders of Guinness World Records, appreciate the fame they achieve for their unique collection. Cards, stickers, stamps, coins, and toys have topped the "usual" collection list, but some collectors lean toward the more unexpected. In September 2014, Guinness World Records recognized Harry Sperl, of Germany, for having the largest hamburger-related collection in the world, with 3,724 items; from T-shirts to pillows to dog toys, Sperl's room is filled with all things "hamburger." Similarly, Liu Fuchang, of China, is a collector of playing cards. He has 11,087 different sets.

Perhaps the easiest motivation to understand is pleasure. Some people start collections for pure enjoyment. They may purchase and put up paintings just to gaze at frequently, or they may collect audio recordings and old-fashioned vinyl records to enjoy listening to their favorite music. This type of collector is unlikely to be very interested in the monetary value of their treasured music, while others collect objects specifically as an investment. While it is possible to download certain classic games for free, having the same game unopened in its original packaging, in "mint condition," can make the game worth a lot. Owning various valuable "collector's items" could ensure some financial security.

This behavior of collecting things will definitely continue into the distant future. Although the reasons why people keep things will likely remain the same, advances in technology will have an influence on collections. As technology can remove physical constraints, it is now possible for an individual to have vast digital libraries of music and art that would have been unimaginable 30 years ago. It is unclear, though, what other impacts technology will have on collections. Can you even imagine the form and scale that the next generation's collections will take?

Your notes:

Collecting

Introduction

- Collecting has long been part of the human experience.
- The yard sale story tells us that [39] .

Facts

- [40]
- Guinness World Records
  - Sperl: 3,724 hamburger-related items
  - Liu: 11,087 sets of playing cards

Reasons for collecting

- Motivation for collecting can be emotional or social.
- Various reasons mentioned: [41] , [42] , interest in history, childhood excitement, becoming famous, sharing, etc.

Collections in the future

- [43]

問 1 Choose the best option for [39].

① a great place for people to sell things to collectors at a high price is a yard sale
② people can evaluate items incorrectly and end up paying too much money for junk
③ something not important to one person may be of value to someone else
④ things once collected and thrown in another person's yard may be valuable to others

問 2 Choose the best option for [40].

① About two thirds of children do not collect ordinary things.
② Almost one third of adults start collecting things for pleasure.
③ Approximately 10% of kids have collections similar to their friends.
④ Roughly 30% of people keep collecting into adulthood.

問 3 Choose the best options for [41] and [42]. (The order does not matter.)

① desire to advance technology
② fear of missing unexpected opportunities
③ filling a sense of emptiness
④ reminder of precious events
⑤ reusing objects for the future
⑥ seeking some sort of profit

問 4 Choose the best option for [43].

① Collections will likely continue to change in size and shape.
② Collectors of mint-condition games will have more digital copies of them.
③ People who have lost their passion for collecting will start again.
④ Reasons for collecting will change because of advances in technology.

B You are in a student group preparing for an international science presentation contest. You are using the following passage to create your part of the presentation on extraordinary creatures.

Ask someone to name the world's toughest animal, and they might say the Bactrian camel as it can survive in temperatures as high as 50℃, or the Arctic fox which can survive in temperatures lower than −58℃. However, both answers would be wrong as it is widely believed that the tardigrade is the toughest creature on earth.

Tardigrades, also known as water bears, are microscopic creatures, which are between 0.1 mm to 1.5 mm in length. They live almost everywhere, from 6,000-meter-high mountains to 4,600 meters below the ocean's surface. They can even be found under thick ice and in hot springs. Most live in water, but some tardigrades can be found in some of the driest places on earth. One researcher reported finding tardigrades living under rocks in a desert without any recorded rainfall for 25 years. All they need are a few drops or a thin layer of water to live in. When the water dries up, so do they. They lose all but three percent of their body's water and their metabolism slows down to 0.01% of its normal speed. The dried-out tardigrade is now in a state called "tun," a kind of deep sleep. It will continue in this state until it is once again soaked in water. Then, like a sponge, it absorbs the water and springs back to life again as if nothing had happened. Whether the tardigrade is in tun for 1 week or 10 years does not really matter. The moment it is surrounded by water, it comes alive again. When tardigrades are in a state of tun, they are so tough that they can survive in temperatures as low as −272℃ and as high as 151℃. Exactly how they achieve this is still not fully understood.

Perhaps even more amazing than their ability to survive on earth — they have been on earth for some 540 million years — is their ability to survive in space. In 2007, a team of European researchers sent a number of living tardigrades into space on the outside of a rocket for 10 days. On their return to earth, the researchers were surprised to see that 68% were still alive. This means that for 10 days most were able to survive X-rays and ultraviolet radiation 1,000 times more intense than here on earth. Later, in 2019, an Israeli spacecraft crashed onto the moon and thousands of tardigrades in a state of tun were spilled onto its surface. Whether these are still alive or not is unknown as no one has gone to collect them — which is a pity.

Tardigrades are shaped like a short cucumber. They have four short legs on each side of their bodies. Some species have sticky pads at the end of each leg, while others have claws. There are 16 known claw variations, which help identify those species with claws. All tardigrades have a place for eyes, but not all species have eyes. Their eyes are primitive, only having five cells in total — just one of which is light sensitive.

Basically, tardigrades can be divided into those that eat plant matter, and those that eat other creatures. Those that eat vegetation have a ventral mouth — a mouth located in the lower part of the head, like a shark. The type that eats other creatures has a terminal mouth, which means the mouth is at the very front of the head, like a tuna. The mouths of tardigrades do not have teeth. They do, however, have two sharp needles, called stylets, that they use to pierce plant cells or the bodies of smaller creatures so the contents can be sucked out.

Both types of tardigrade have rather simple digestive systems. The mouth leads to the pharynx (throat), where digestive juices and food are mixed. Located above the pharynx is a salivary gland. This produces the juices that flow into the mouth and help with digestion. After the pharynx, there is a tube which transports food toward the gut. This tube is called the esophagus. The middle gut, a simple stomach/intestine type of organ, digests the food and absorbs the nutrients. The leftovers then eventually move through to the anus.

Your presentation slides:

Tardigrades:
Earth's Ultimate Survivors

1. Basic Information

- 0.1 mm to 1.5 mm in length
- shaped like a short cucumber
-
-
- [44]
-
-

2. Habitats

- live almost everywhere
- extreme environments such as...
  - ✓ 6 km above sea level
  - ✓ 4.6 km below sea level
  - ✓ in deserts
  - ✓ −272℃ to 151℃
  - ✓ in space (possibly)

3. Secrets to Survival

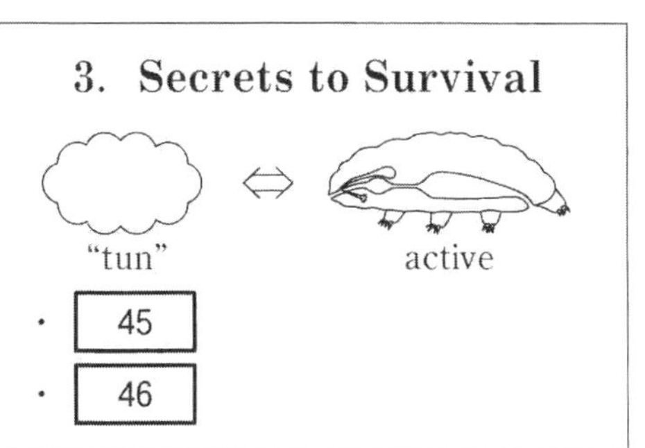

- [45]
- [46]

4. Digestive Systems [47]

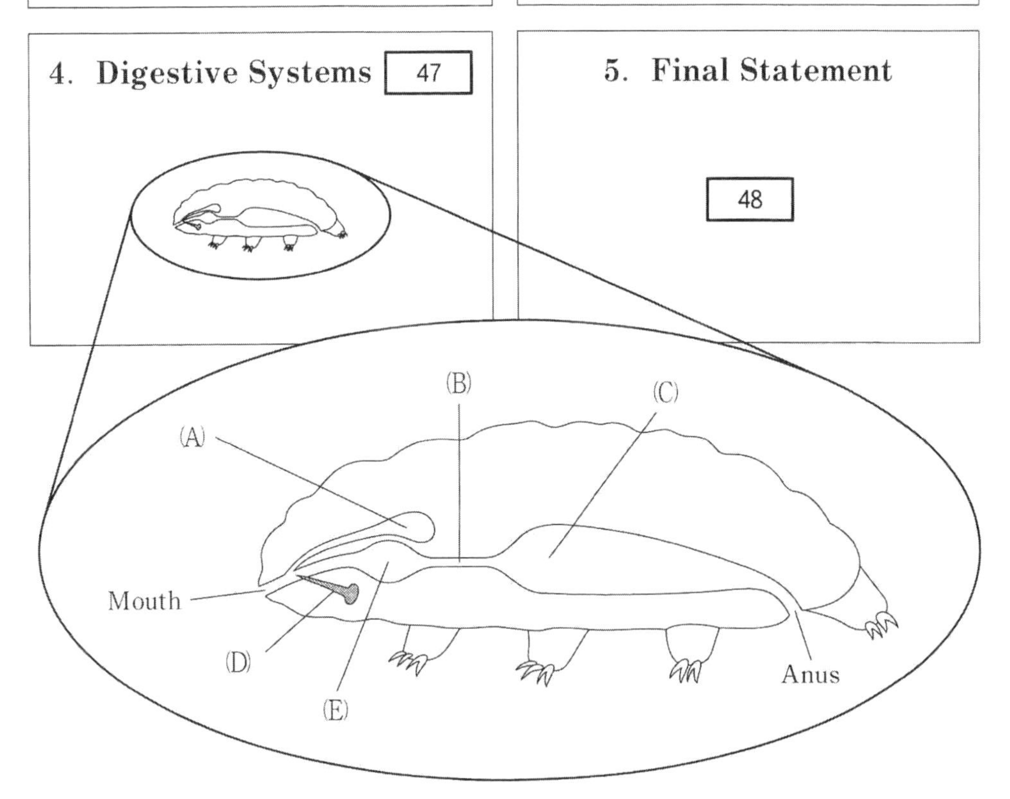

5. Final Statement

[48]

問 1 Which of the following should you **not** include for [44]?

① eight short legs
② either blind or sighted
③ plant-eating or creature-eating
④ sixteen different types of feet
⑤ two stylets rather than teeth

問 2 For the **Secrets to Survival** slide, select two features of the tardigrade which best help it survive. (The order does not matter.) [45]・[46]

① In dry conditions, their metabolism drops to less than one percent of normal.
② Tardigrades in a state of tun are able to survive in temperatures exceeding 151℃.
③ The state of tun will cease when the water in a tardigrade's body is above 0.01%.
④ Their shark-like mouths allow them to more easily eat other creatures.
⑤ They have an ability to withstand extreme levels of radiation.

問 3 Complete the missing labels on the illustration of a tardigrade for the **Digestive Systems** slide. [47]

①	(A) Esophagus	(B) Pharynx	(C) Middle gut
	(D) Stylets	(E) Salivary gland	
②	(A) Pharynx	(B) Stylets	(C) Salivary gland
	(D) Esophagus	(E) Middle gut	
③	(A) Salivary gland	(B) Esophagus	(C) Middle gut
	(D) Stylets	(E) Pharynx	
④	(A) Salivary gland	(B) Middle gut	(C) Stylets
	(D) Esophagus	(E) Pharynx	
⑤	(A) Stylets	(B) Salivary gland	(C) Pharynx
	(D) Middle gut	(E) Esophagus	

問 4 Which is the best statement for the final slide? [48]

① For thousands of years, tardigrades have survived some of the harshest conditions on earth and in space. They will live longer than humankind.

② Tardigrades are from space and can live in temperatures exceeding the limits of the Arctic fox and Bactrian camel, so they are surely stronger than human beings.

③ Tardigrades are, without a doubt, the toughest creatures on earth. They can survive on the top of mountains; at the bottom of the sea; in the waters of hot springs; and they can also thrive on the moon.

④ Tardigrades have survived some of the harshest conditions on earth, and at least one trip into space. This remarkable creature might outlive the human species.

問 5 What can be inferred about sending tardigrades into space? [49]

① Finding out whether the tardigrades can survive in space was never thought to be important.

② Tardigrades, along with other creatures that have been on earth for millions of years, can withstand X-rays and ultraviolet radiation.

③ The Israeli researchers did not expect so many tardigrades to survive the harsh environment of space.

④ The reason why no one has been to see if tardigrades can survive on the moon's surface attracted the author's attention.

毎月の効率的な実戦演習で本番までに共通テストを攻略できる！

専科 共通テスト攻略演習

7 教科 17 科目セット　教材を毎月1回お届け

セットで1カ月あたり **3,910**円（税込）※「12 カ月一括払い」の講座料金

セット内容

英語（リーディング）/ 英語（リスニング）/ 数学Ⅰ、数学 A / 数学Ⅱ、数学 B、数学 C / 国語 / 化学基礎 / 生物基礎 / 地学基礎 / 物理 / 化学 / 生物 / 歴史総合、世界史探究 / 歴史総合、日本史探究 / 地理総合、地理探究 / 公共、倫理 / 公共、政治・経済 / 情報Ⅰ

※答案の提出や添削指導はありません。
※学習には「Z 会学習アプリ」を使用するため、対応 OS のスマートフォンやタブレット、パソコンなどの端末が必要です。

※「共通テスト攻略演習」は 1 月までの講座です。

POINT 1 共通テストに即した問題に取り組み、万全の対策ができる！

2024年度の共通テストでは、英語・リーディングで読解量（語数）が増えるなど、これまで以上に速読即解力や情報処理力が必要とされました。新指導要領で学んだ高校生が受験する2025年度の試験は、この傾向がより強まることが予想されます。

本講座では、毎月お届けする教材で、共通テスト型の問題に取り組んでいきます。傾向の変化に対応できるようになるとともに、「自分で考え、答えを出す力」を伸ばし、万全の対策ができます。

新設「情報Ⅰ」にも対応！

国公立大志望者の多くは、共通テストで「情報Ⅰ」が必須となります。本講座では、「情報Ⅰ」の対応教材も用意しているため、万全な対策が可能です。

8月…基本問題　12月・1月…本番形式の問題

※3～7月、9～11月は、大学入試センターから公開された「試作問題」や、「情報Ⅰ」の内容とつながりの深い「情報関係基礎」の過去問の解説を、「Z 会学習アプリ」で提供します。
※「情報Ⅰ」の取り扱いについては各大学の要項をご確認ください。

POINT 2 月 60 分の実戦演習で、効率的な時短演習を！

全科目を毎月バランスよく継続的に取り組めるよう工夫された内容と分量で、本科の講座と併用しやすく、着実に得点力を伸ばせます。

1. 教材に取り組む

本講座の問題演習は、1 科目あたり月 60 分（英語のリスニングと理科基礎、情報Ⅰは月 30 分）。無理なく自分のペースで学習を進められます。

2. 自己採点する／復習する

問題を解いたらすぐに自己採点して結果を確認。わかりやすい解説で効率よく復習できます。

英語、数学、国語は、毎月の出題に即した「ポイント映像」を視聴できます。1 授業 10 分程度なので、スキマ時間を活用できます。共通テストならではの攻略ポイントや、各月に押さえておきたい内容を厳選した映像授業で、さらに理解を深められます。

POINT 3 戦略的なカリキュラムで、得点力アップ！

本講座は、本番での得意科目 9 割突破へ向けて、毎月着実にレベルアップできるカリキュラム。基礎固めから最終仕上げまで段階的な対策で、万全の態勢で本番に臨めます。

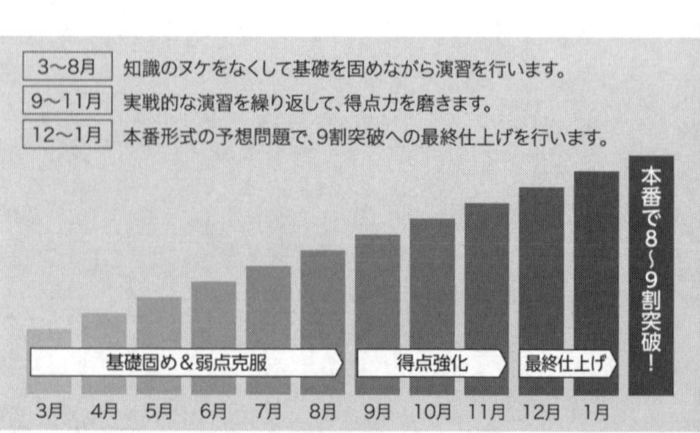

必要な科目を全部対策できる 7教科17科目セット

*12月・1月は、共通テスト本番に即した学習時間(解答時間)となります。
※2023年度の「共通テスト攻略演習」と一部同じ内容があります。

英語(リーディング)

学習時間(問題演習)	60分×月1回*
3月	情報の検索
4月	情報の整理
5月	情報の検索・整理
6月	概要・要点の把握①
7月	概要・要点の把握②
8月	テーマ・分野別演習のまとめ
9月	速読速解力を磨く①
10月	速読速解力を磨く②
11月	速読速解力を磨く③
12月	直前演習1
1月	直前演習2

英語(リスニング)

学習時間(問題演習)	30分×月1回*
3月	情報の聞き取り①
4月	情報の聞き取り②
5月	情報の比較・判断など
6月	概要・要点の把握①
7月	概要・要点の把握②
8月	テーマ・分野別演習のまとめ
9月	多めの語数で集中力を磨く
10月	速めの速度で聞き取る
11月	1回聞きで聞き取る
12月	直前演習1
1月	直前演習2

数学Ⅰ、数学A

学習時間(問題演習)	60分×月1回*
3月	2次関数
4月	数と式
5月	データの分析
6月	図形と計量, 図形の性質
7月	場合の数と確率
8月	テーマ・分野別演習のまとめ
9月	日常の事象~もとの事象の意味を考える~
10月	数学の事象~一般化と発展~
11月	数学の事象~批判的考察~
12月	直前演習1
1月	直前演習2

数学Ⅱ、数学B、数学C

学習時間(問題演習)	60分×月1回*
3月	三角関数, 指数・対数関数
4月	微分・積分, 図形と方程式
5月	数列
6月	ベクトル
7月	平面上の曲線・複素数平面, 統計的な推測
8月	テーマ・分野別演習のまとめ
9月	日常の事象~もとの事象の意味を考える~
10月	数学の事象~一般化と発展~
11月	数学の事象~批判的考察~
12月	直前演習1
1月	直前演習2

国語

学習時間(問題演習)	60分×月1回*
3月	評論
4月	文学的文章
5月	古文
6月	漢文
7月	テーマ・分野別演習のまとめ1
8月	テーマ・分野別演習のまとめ2
9月	図表から情報を読み取る
10月	複数の文章を対比する
11月	読み取った内容をまとめる
12月	直前演習1
1月	直前演習2

化学基礎

学習時間(問題演習)	30分×月1回*
3月	物質の構成(物質の構成, 原子の構造)
4月	物質の構成(化学結合, 結晶)
5月	物質量
6月	酸と塩基
7月	酸化還元反応
8月	テーマ・分野別演習のまとめ
9月	解法強化~計算~
10月	知識強化1~文章の正誤判断~
11月	知識強化2~組合せの正誤判断~
12月	直前演習1
1月	直前演習2

生物基礎

学習時間(問題演習)	30分×月1回*
3月	生物の特徴1
4月	生物の特徴2
5月	ヒトの体の調節1
6月	ヒトの体の調節2
7月	生物の多様性と生態系
8月	テーマ・分野別演習のまとめ
9月	知識強化
10月	実験強化
11月	考察力強化
12月	直前演習1
1月	直前演習2

地学基礎

学習時間(問題演習)	30分×月1回*
3月	地球のすがた
4月	活動する地球
5月	大気と海洋
6月	移り変わる地球
7月	宇宙の構成, 地球の環境
8月	テーマ・分野別演習のまとめ
9月	資料問題に強くなる1~図・グラフの理解~
10月	資料問題に強くなる2~図・グラフの活用~
11月	知識活用・考察問題に強くなる~探究活動~
12月	直前演習1
1月	直前演習2

物理

学習時間(問題演習)	60分×月1回*
3月	力学(放物運動, 剛体, 運動量と力積, 円運動)
4月	力学(単振動, 慣性力), 熱力学
5月	波動(波の伝わり方, レンズ)
6月	波動(干渉), 電磁気(静電場, コンデンサー)
7月	電磁気(回路, 電流と磁場, 電磁誘導), 原子
8月	テーマ・分野別演習のまとめ
9月	解法強化 ~図・グラフ, 小問対策~
10月	考察力強化1 ~実験・考察問題対策~
11月	考察力強化2~実験・考察問題対策~
12月	直前演習1
1月	直前演習2

化学

学習時間(問題演習)	60分×月1回*
3月	結晶, 気体, 熱
4月	溶液, 電気分解
5月	化学平衡
6月	無機物質
7月	有機化合物
8月	テーマ・分野別演習のまとめ
9月	解法強化~計算~
10月	知識強化~正誤判断~
11月	読解・考察力強化
12月	直前演習1
1月	直前演習2

生物

学習時間(問題演習)	60分×月1回*
3月	生物の進化
4月	生命現象と物質
5月	遺伝情報の発現と発生
6月	生物の環境応答
7月	生態と環境
8月	テーマ・分野別演習のまとめ
9月	考察力強化1~考察とその基礎知識~
10月	考察力強化2~データの読解・計算~
11月	分野融合問題対応力強化
12月	直前演習1
1月	直前演習2

歴史総合、世界史探究

学習時間(問題演習)	60分×月1回*
3月	古代の世界
4月	中世~近世初期の世界
5月	近世の世界
6月	近・現代の世界1
7月	近・現代の世界2
8月	テーマ・分野別演習のまとめ
9月	能力別強化1~諸地域の結びつきの理解~
10月	能力別強化2~情報処理・分析の演習~
11月	能力別強化3~史料読解の演習~
12月	直前演習1
1月	直前演習2

歴史総合、日本史探究

学習時間(問題演習)	60分×月1回*
3月	古代
4月	中世
5月	近世
6月	近代(江戸後期~明治期)
7月	近・現代(大正期~現代)
8月	テーマ・分野別演習のまとめ
9月	能力別強化1~事象の比較・関連~
10月	能力別強化2~事象の推移/資料読解~
11月	能力別強化3~多面的・多角的考察~
12月	直前演習1
1月	直前演習2

地理総合、地理探究

学習時間(問題演習)	60分×月1回*
3月	地図/地域調査/地形
4月	気候/農林水産業
5月	鉱工業/現代社会の諸課題
6月	グローバル化する世界/都市・村落
7月	民族・領土問題/地誌
8月	テーマ・分野別演習のまとめ
9月	能力別強化1~資料の読解~
10月	能力別強化2~地誌~
11月	能力別強化3~地形図の読図~
12月	直前演習1
1月	直前演習2

公共、倫理

学習時間(問題演習)	60分×月1回*
3月	青年期の課題/源流思想1
4月	源流思想2
5月	日本の思想
6月	近・現代の思想1
7月	近・現代の思想2/現代社会の諸課題
8月	テーマ・分野別演習のまとめ
9月	分野別強化1~源流思想・日本思想~
10月	分野別強化2~西洋思想・現代思想~
11月	分野別強化3~青年期・現代社会の諸課題~
12月	直前演習1
1月	直前演習2

公共、政治・経済

学習時間(問題演習)	60分×月1回*
3月	政治1
4月	政治2
5月	経済
6月	国際政治・国際経済
7月	現代社会の諸課題
8月	テーマ・分野別演習のまとめ
9月	分野別強化1~政治~
10月	分野別強化2~経済~
11月	分野別強化3~国際政治・国際経済~
12月	直前演習1
1月	直前演習2

情報Ⅰ

学習時間(問題演習)	30分×月1回*
3月~7月	※情報Ⅰの共通テスト対策に役立つコンテンツを「Z会学習アプリ」で提供。
8月	演習問題
9月~11月	※情報Ⅰの共通テスト対策に役立つコンテンツを「Z会学習アプリ」で提供。
12月	直前演習1
1月	直前演習2

書籍のアンケートにご協力ください

抽選で**図書カード**を

プレゼント！

2025年用　共通テスト実戦模試
①英語リーディング

初版第１刷発行…2024年７月１日
初版第３刷発行…2024年12月１日

編者…………Ｚ会編集部
発行人………藤井孝昭
発行…………Ｚ会
〒411-0033　静岡県三島市文教町1-9-11
【販売部門：書籍の乱丁・落丁・返品・交換・注文】
TEL 055-976-9095
【書籍の内容に関するお問い合わせ】
https://www.zkai.co.jp/books/contact/
【ホームページ】
https://www.zkai.co.jp/books/

装丁…………犬飼奈央
印刷・製本…日経印刷株式会社

ISBN978-4-86531-613-1 C7382

英語（リーディング） 模試 第1回 解答用紙

マーク例

良い例	悪い例
●	⊙ ⊗ ◐ O

513

解答科目欄				
英語（リーディング） ○	ドイツ語 ○	フランス語 ○	中国語 ○	韓国語 ○

受験番号欄					
千位	百位	十位	一位	英字	
—	⓪	⓪	⓪	Ⓐ	A
①	①	①	①	Ⓑ	B
②	②	②	②	Ⓒ	C
③	③	③	③	Ⓗ	H
④	④	④	④	Ⓚ	K
⑤	⑤	⑤	⑤	Ⓜ	M
⑥	⑥	⑥	⑥	Ⓡ	R
⑦	⑦	⑦	⑦	Ⓤ	U
⑧	⑧	⑧	⑧	Ⓧ	X
⑨	⑨	⑨	⑨	Ⓨ	Y
—	—	—	—	Ⓩ	Z

フリガナ	
氏名	

試験場コード	十万位	万位	千位	百位	十位	一位

解答番号	解答欄								
	1	2	3	4	5	6	7	8	9
1	①	②	③	④	⑤	⑥	⑦	⑧	⑨
2	①	②	③	④	⑤	⑥	⑦	⑧	⑨
3	①	②	③	④	⑤	⑥	⑦	⑧	⑨
4	①	②	③	④	⑤	⑥	⑦	⑧	⑨
5	①	②	③	④	⑤	⑥	⑦	⑧	⑨
6	①	②	③	④	⑤	⑥	⑦	⑧	⑨
7	①	②	③	④	⑤	⑥	⑦	⑧	⑨
8	①	②	③	④	⑤	⑥	⑦	⑧	⑨
9	①	②	③	④	⑤	⑥	⑦	⑧	⑨
10	①	②	③	④	⑤	⑥	⑦	⑧	⑨
11	①	②	③	④	⑤	⑥	⑦	⑧	⑨
12	①	②	③	④	⑤	⑥	⑦	⑧	⑨
13	①	②	③	④	⑤	⑥	⑦	⑧	⑨
14	①	②	③	④	⑤	⑥	⑦	⑧	⑨
15	①	②	③	④	⑤	⑥	⑦	⑧	⑨
16	①	②	③	④	⑤	⑥	⑦	⑧	⑨
17	①	②	③	④	⑤	⑥	⑦	⑧	⑨
18	①	②	③	④	⑤	⑥	⑦	⑧	⑨
19	①	②	③	④	⑤	⑥	⑦	⑧	⑨
20	①	②	③	④	⑤	⑥	⑦	⑧	⑨
21	①	②	③	④	⑤	⑥	⑦	⑧	⑨
22	①	②	③	④	⑤	⑥	⑦	⑧	⑨
23	①	②	③	④	⑤	⑥	⑦	⑧	⑨
24	①	②	③	④	⑤	⑥	⑦	⑧	⑨
25	①	②	③	④	⑤	⑥	⑦	⑧	⑨

解答番号	解答欄								
	1	2	3	4	5	6	7	8	9
26	①	②	③	④	⑤	⑥	⑦	⑧	⑨
27	①	②	③	④	⑤	⑥	⑦	⑧	⑨
28	①	②	③	④	⑤	⑥	⑦	⑧	⑨
29	①	②	③	④	⑤	⑥	⑦	⑧	⑨
30	①	②	③	④	⑤	⑥	⑦	⑧	⑨
31	①	②	③	④	⑤	⑥	⑦	⑧	⑨
32	①	②	③	④	⑤	⑥	⑦	⑧	⑨
33	①	②	③	④	⑤	⑥	⑦	⑧	⑨
34	①	②	③	④	⑤	⑥	⑦	⑧	⑨
35	①	②	③	④	⑤	⑥	⑦	⑧	⑨
36	①	②	③	④	⑤	⑥	⑦	⑧	⑨
37	①	②	③	④	⑤	⑥	⑦	⑧	⑨
38	①	②	③	④	⑤	⑥	⑦	⑧	⑨
39	①	②	③	④	⑤	⑥	⑦	⑧	⑨
40	①	②	③	④	⑤	⑥	⑦	⑧	⑨
41	①	②	③	④	⑤	⑥	⑦	⑧	⑨
42	①	②	③	④	⑤	⑥	⑦	⑧	⑨
43	①	②	③	④	⑤	⑥	⑦	⑧	⑨
44	①	②	③	④	⑤	⑥	⑦	⑧	⑨
45	①	②	③	④	⑤	⑥	⑦	⑧	⑨
46	①	②	③	④	⑤	⑥	⑦	⑧	⑨
47	①	②	③	④	⑤	⑥	⑦	⑧	⑨
48	①	②	③	④	⑤	⑥	⑦	⑧	⑨
49	①	②	③	④	⑤	⑥	⑦	⑧	⑨
50	①	②	③	④	⑤	⑥	⑦	⑧	⑨

キリトリ線

英語（リーディング） 模試 第2回 解答用紙

マーク例

良い例	悪い例
●	⊙ ⊗ ◔ O

514

解答科目欄

英語（リーディング）	ドイツ語	フランス語	中国語	韓国語
◯	◯	◯	◯	◯

受験番号欄

千位	百位	十位	一位	英字	
—	⓪	⓪	⓪	Ⓐ	A
①	①	①	①	Ⓑ	B
②	②	②	②	Ⓒ	C
③	③	③	③	Ⓗ	H
④	④	④	④	Ⓚ	K
⑤	⑤	⑤	⑤	Ⓜ	M
⑥	⑥	⑥	⑥	Ⓡ	R
⑦	⑦	⑦	⑦	Ⓤ	U
⑧	⑧	⑧	⑧	Ⓧ	X
⑨	⑨	⑨	⑨	Ⓨ	Y
—	—	—	—	Ⓩ	Z

フリガナ	
氏名	

試験場コード	十万位	万位	千位	百位	十位	一位

解答番号	解	答			欄				
	1	2	3	4	5	6	7	8	9
1	①	②	③	④	⑤	⑥	⑦	⑧	⑨
2	①	②	③	④	⑤	⑥	⑦	⑧	⑨
3	①	②	③	④	⑤	⑥	⑦	⑧	⑨
4	①	②	③	④	⑤	⑥	⑦	⑧	⑨
5	①	②	③	④	⑤	⑥	⑦	⑧	⑨
6	①	②	③	④	⑤	⑥	⑦	⑧	⑨
7	①	②	③	④	⑤	⑥	⑦	⑧	⑨
8	①	②	③	④	⑤	⑥	⑦	⑧	⑨
9	①	②	③	④	⑤	⑥	⑦	⑧	⑨
10	①	②	③	④	⑤	⑥	⑦	⑧	⑨
11	①	②	③	④	⑤	⑥	⑦	⑧	⑨
12	①	②	③	④	⑤	⑥	⑦	⑧	⑨
13	①	②	③	④	⑤	⑥	⑦	⑧	⑨
14	①	②	③	④	⑤	⑥	⑦	⑧	⑨
15	①	②	③	④	⑤	⑥	⑦	⑧	⑨
16	①	②	③	④	⑤	⑥	⑦	⑧	⑨
17	①	②	③	④	⑤	⑥	⑦	⑧	⑨
18	①	②	③	④	⑤	⑥	⑦	⑧	⑨
19	①	②	③	④	⑤	⑥	⑦	⑧	⑨
20	①	②	③	④	⑤	⑥	⑦	⑧	⑨
21	①	②	③	④	⑤	⑥	⑦	⑧	⑨
22	①	②	③	④	⑤	⑥	⑦	⑧	⑨
23	①	②	③	④	⑤	⑥	⑦	⑧	⑨
24	①	②	③	④	⑤	⑥	⑦	⑧	⑨
25	①	②	③	④	⑤	⑥	⑦	⑧	⑨

解答番号	解	答			欄				
	1	2	3	4	5	6	7	8	9
26	①	②	③	④	⑤	⑥	⑦	⑧	⑨
27	①	②	③	④	⑤	⑥	⑦	⑧	⑨
28	①	②	③	④	⑤	⑥	⑦	⑧	⑨
29	①	②	③	④	⑤	⑥	⑦	⑧	⑨
30	①	②	③	④	⑤	⑥	⑦	⑧	⑨
31	①	②	③	④	⑤	⑥	⑦	⑧	⑨
32	①	②	③	④	⑤	⑥	⑦	⑧	⑨
33	①	②	③	④	⑤	⑥	⑦	⑧	⑨
34	①	②	③	④	⑤	⑥	⑦	⑧	⑨
35	①	②	③	④	⑤	⑥	⑦	⑧	⑨
36	①	②	③	④	⑤	⑥	⑦	⑧	⑨
37	①	②	③	④	⑤	⑥	⑦	⑧	⑨
38	①	②	③	④	⑤	⑥	⑦	⑧	⑨
39	①	②	③	④	⑤	⑥	⑦	⑧	⑨
40	①	②	③	④	⑤	⑥	⑦	⑧	⑨
41	①	②	③	④	⑤	⑥	⑦	⑧	⑨
42	①	②	③	④	⑤	⑥	⑦	⑧	⑨
43	①	②	③	④	⑤	⑥	⑦	⑧	⑨
44	①	②	③	④	⑤	⑥	⑦	⑧	⑨
45	①	②	③	④	⑤	⑥	⑦	⑧	⑨
46	①	②	③	④	⑤	⑥	⑦	⑧	⑨
47	①	②	③	④	⑤	⑥	⑦	⑧	⑨
48	①	②	③	④	⑤	⑥	⑦	⑧	⑨
49	①	②	③	④	⑤	⑥	⑦	⑧	⑨
50	①	②	③	④	⑤	⑥	⑦	⑧	⑨

英語（リーディング）模試 第3回 解答用紙

マーク例

良い例	悪い例
●	◌ ⊗ ◔ O

515

解答科目欄

英語（リーディング）	ドイツ語	フランス語	中国語	韓国語
○	○	○	○	○

受験番号欄

千位	百位	十位	一位	英字	
—	0	0	0	A	A
1	1	1	1	B	B
2	2	2	2	C	C
3	3	3	3	H	H
4	4	4	4	K	K
5	5	5	5	M	M
6	6	6	6	R	R
7	7	7	7	U	U
8	8	8	8	X	X
9	9	9	9	Y	Y
—	—	—	—	Z	Z

フリガナ	
氏 名	

試験場コード	十万位	万位	千位	百位	十位	一位

解答番号	解答欄								
	1	2	3	4	5	6	7	8	9
1	1	2	3	4	5	6	7	8	9
2	1	2	3	4	5	6	7	8	9
3	1	2	3	4	5	6	7	8	9
4	1	2	3	4	5	6	7	8	9
5	1	2	3	4	5	6	7	8	9
6	1	2	3	4	5	6	7	8	9
7	1	2	3	4	5	6	7	8	9
8	1	2	3	4	5	6	7	8	9
9	1	2	3	4	5	6	7	8	9
10	1	2	3	4	5	6	7	8	9
11	1	2	3	4	5	6	7	8	9
12	1	2	3	4	5	6	7	8	9
13	1	2	3	4	5	6	7	8	9
14	1	2	3	4	5	6	7	8	9
15	1	2	3	4	5	6	7	8	9
16	1	2	3	4	5	6	7	8	9
17	1	2	3	4	5	6	7	8	9
18	1	2	3	4	5	6	7	8	9
19	1	2	3	4	5	6	7	8	9
20	1	2	3	4	5	6	7	8	9
21	1	2	3	4	5	6	7	8	9
22	1	2	3	4	5	6	7	8	9
23	1	2	3	4	5	6	7	8	9
24	1	2	3	4	5	6	7	8	9
25	1	2	3	4	5	6	7	8	9

解答番号	解答欄								
	1	2	3	4	5	6	7	8	9
26	1	2	3	4	5	6	7	8	9
27	1	2	3	4	5	6	7	8	9
28	1	2	3	4	5	6	7	8	9
29	1	2	3	4	5	6	7	8	9
30	1	2	3	4	5	6	7	8	9
31	1	2	3	4	5	6	7	8	9
32	1	2	3	4	5	6	7	8	9
33	1	2	3	4	5	6	7	8	9
34	1	2	3	4	5	6	7	8	9
35	1	2	3	4	5	6	7	8	9
36	1	2	3	4	5	6	7	8	9
37	1	2	3	4	5	6	7	8	9
38	1	2	3	4	5	6	7	8	9
39	1	2	3	4	5	6	7	8	9
40	1	2	3	4	5	6	7	8	9
41	1	2	3	4	5	6	7	8	9
42	1	2	3	4	5	6	7	8	9
43	1	2	3	4	5	6	7	8	9
44	1	2	3	4	5	6	7	8	9
45	1	2	3	4	5	6	7	8	9
46	1	2	3	4	5	6	7	8	9
47	1	2	3	4	5	6	7	8	9
48	1	2	3	4	5	6	7	8	9
49	1	2	3	4	5	6	7	8	9
50	1	2	3	4	5	6	7	8	9

英語（リーディング）模試 第4回 解答用紙

マーク例

良い例	悪い例
●	⊙ ⊗ ◔ O

516

解答科目欄				
英語（リーディング）	ドイツ語	フランス語	中国語	韓国語
○	○	○	○	○

受験番号欄					
千位	百位	十位	一位	英字	
—	⓪	⓪	⓪	Ⓐ	A
①	①	①	①	Ⓑ	B
②	②	②	②	Ⓒ	C
③	③	③	③	Ⓗ	H
④	④	④	④	Ⓚ	K
⑤	⑤	⑤	⑤	Ⓜ	M
⑥	⑥	⑥	⑥	Ⓡ	R
⑦	⑦	⑦	⑦	Ⓤ	U
⑧	⑧	⑧	⑧	Ⓧ	X
⑨	⑨	⑨	⑨	Ⓨ	Y
—	—	—	—	Ⓩ	Z

フリガナ	
氏名	

試験場コード	十万位	万位	千位	百位	十位	一位

解答番号	解答欄 1	2	3	4	5	6	7	8	9
1	①	②	③	④	⑤	⑥	⑦	⑧	⑨
2	①	②	③	④	⑤	⑥	⑦	⑧	⑨
3	①	②	③	④	⑤	⑥	⑦	⑧	⑨
4	①	②	③	④	⑤	⑥	⑦	⑧	⑨
5	①	②	③	④	⑤	⑥	⑦	⑧	⑨
6	①	②	③	④	⑤	⑥	⑦	⑧	⑨
7	①	②	③	④	⑤	⑥	⑦	⑧	⑨
8	①	②	③	④	⑤	⑥	⑦	⑧	⑨
9	①	②	③	④	⑤	⑥	⑦	⑧	⑨
10	①	②	③	④	⑤	⑥	⑦	⑧	⑨
11	①	②	③	④	⑤	⑥	⑦	⑧	⑨
12	①	②	③	④	⑤	⑥	⑦	⑧	⑨
13	①	②	③	④	⑤	⑥	⑦	⑧	⑨
14	①	②	③	④	⑤	⑥	⑦	⑧	⑨
15	①	②	③	④	⑤	⑥	⑦	⑧	⑨
16	①	②	③	④	⑤	⑥	⑦	⑧	⑨
17	①	②	③	④	⑤	⑥	⑦	⑧	⑨
18	①	②	③	④	⑤	⑥	⑦	⑧	⑨
19	①	②	③	④	⑤	⑥	⑦	⑧	⑨
20	①	②	③	④	⑤	⑥	⑦	⑧	⑨
21	①	②	③	④	⑤	⑥	⑦	⑧	⑨
22	①	②	③	④	⑤	⑥	⑦	⑧	⑨
23	①	②	③	④	⑤	⑥	⑦	⑧	⑨
24	①	②	③	④	⑤	⑥	⑦	⑧	⑨
25	①	②	③	④	⑤	⑥	⑦	⑧	⑨

解答番号	解答欄 1	2	3	4	5	6	7	8	9
26	①	②	③	④	⑤	⑥	⑦	⑧	⑨
27	①	②	③	④	⑤	⑥	⑦	⑧	⑨
28	①	②	③	④	⑤	⑥	⑦	⑧	⑨
29	①	②	③	④	⑤	⑥	⑦	⑧	⑨
30	①	②	③	④	⑤	⑥	⑦	⑧	⑨
31	①	②	③	④	⑤	⑥	⑦	⑧	⑨
32	①	②	③	④	⑤	⑥	⑦	⑧	⑨
33	①	②	③	④	⑤	⑥	⑦	⑧	⑨
34	①	②	③	④	⑤	⑥	⑦	⑧	⑨
35	①	②	③	④	⑤	⑥	⑦	⑧	⑨
36	①	②	③	④	⑤	⑥	⑦	⑧	⑨
37	①	②	③	④	⑤	⑥	⑦	⑧	⑨
38	①	②	③	④	⑤	⑥	⑦	⑧	⑨
39	①	②	③	④	⑤	⑥	⑦	⑧	⑨
40	①	②	③	④	⑤	⑥	⑦	⑧	⑨
41	①	②	③	④	⑤	⑥	⑦	⑧	⑨
42	①	②	③	④	⑤	⑥	⑦	⑧	⑨
43	①	②	③	④	⑤	⑥	⑦	⑧	⑨
44	①	②	③	④	⑤	⑥	⑦	⑧	⑨
45	①	②	③	④	⑤	⑥	⑦	⑧	⑨
46	①	②	③	④	⑤	⑥	⑦	⑧	⑨
47	①	②	③	④	⑤	⑥	⑦	⑧	⑨
48	①	②	③	④	⑤	⑥	⑦	⑧	⑨
49	①	②	③	④	⑤	⑥	⑦	⑧	⑨
50	①	②	③	④	⑤	⑥	⑦	⑧	⑨

キリトリ線

英語（リーディング） 模試 第5回 解答用紙

マーク例

良い例	悪い例
●	⊙ ⊗ ◐ O

517

解答科目欄

英語（リーディング）	ドイツ語	フランス語	中国語	韓国語
◯	◯	◯	◯	◯

受験番号欄

千位	百位	十位	一位	英字
—	⓪	⓪	⓪	Ⓐ A
①	①	①	①	Ⓑ B
②	②	②	②	Ⓒ C
③	③	③	③	Ⓗ H
④	④	④	④	Ⓚ K
⑤	⑤	⑤	⑤	Ⓜ M
⑥	⑥	⑥	⑥	Ⓡ R
⑦	⑦	⑦	⑦	Ⓤ U
⑧	⑧	⑧	⑧	Ⓧ X
⑨	⑨	⑨	⑨	Ⓨ Y
—	—	—	—	Ⓩ Z

フリガナ	
氏名	

試験場コード	十万位	万位	千位	百位	十位	一位

解答番号	解答欄 1	2	3	4	5	6	7	8	9
1	①	②	③	④	⑤	⑥	⑦	⑧	⑨
2	①	②	③	④	⑤	⑥	⑦	⑧	⑨
3	①	②	③	④	⑤	⑥	⑦	⑧	⑨
4	①	②	③	④	⑤	⑥	⑦	⑧	⑨
5	①	②	③	④	⑤	⑥	⑦	⑧	⑨
6	①	②	③	④	⑤	⑥	⑦	⑧	⑨
7	①	②	③	④	⑤	⑥	⑦	⑧	⑨
8	①	②	③	④	⑤	⑥	⑦	⑧	⑨
9	①	②	③	④	⑤	⑥	⑦	⑧	⑨
10	①	②	③	④	⑤	⑥	⑦	⑧	⑨
11	①	②	③	④	⑤	⑥	⑦	⑧	⑨
12	①	②	③	④	⑤	⑥	⑦	⑧	⑨
13	①	②	③	④	⑤	⑥	⑦	⑧	⑨
14	①	②	③	④	⑤	⑥	⑦	⑧	⑨
15	①	②	③	④	⑤	⑥	⑦	⑧	⑨
16	①	②	③	④	⑤	⑥	⑦	⑧	⑨
17	①	②	③	④	⑤	⑥	⑦	⑧	⑨
18	①	②	③	④	⑤	⑥	⑦	⑧	⑨
19	①	②	③	④	⑤	⑥	⑦	⑧	⑨
20	①	②	③	④	⑤	⑥	⑦	⑧	⑨
21	①	②	③	④	⑤	⑥	⑦	⑧	⑨
22	①	②	③	④	⑤	⑥	⑦	⑧	⑨
23	①	②	③	④	⑤	⑥	⑦	⑧	⑨
24	①	②	③	④	⑤	⑥	⑦	⑧	⑨
25	①	②	③	④	⑤	⑥	⑦	⑧	⑨

解答番号	解答欄 1	2	3	4	5	6	7	8	9
26	①	②	③	④	⑤	⑥	⑦	⑧	⑨
27	①	②	③	④	⑤	⑥	⑦	⑧	⑨
28	①	②	③	④	⑤	⑥	⑦	⑧	⑨
29	①	②	③	④	⑤	⑥	⑦	⑧	⑨
30	①	②	③	④	⑤	⑥	⑦	⑧	⑨
31	①	②	③	④	⑤	⑥	⑦	⑧	⑨
32	①	②	③	④	⑤	⑥	⑦	⑧	⑨
33	①	②	③	④	⑤	⑥	⑦	⑧	⑨
34	①	②	③	④	⑤	⑥	⑦	⑧	⑨
35	①	②	③	④	⑤	⑥	⑦	⑧	⑨
36	①	②	③	④	⑤	⑥	⑦	⑧	⑨
37	①	②	③	④	⑤	⑥	⑦	⑧	⑨
38	①	②	③	④	⑤	⑥	⑦	⑧	⑨
39	①	②	③	④	⑤	⑥	⑦	⑧	⑨
40	①	②	③	④	⑤	⑥	⑦	⑧	⑨
41	①	②	③	④	⑤	⑥	⑦	⑧	⑨
42	①	②	③	④	⑤	⑥	⑦	⑧	⑨
43	①	②	③	④	⑤	⑥	⑦	⑧	⑨
44	①	②	③	④	⑤	⑥	⑦	⑧	⑨
45	①	②	③	④	⑤	⑥	⑦	⑧	⑨
46	①	②	③	④	⑤	⑥	⑦	⑧	⑨
47	①	②	③	④	⑤	⑥	⑦	⑧	⑨
48	①	②	③	④	⑤	⑥	⑦	⑧	⑨
49	①	②	③	④	⑤	⑥	⑦	⑧	⑨
50	①	②	③	④	⑤	⑥	⑦	⑧	⑨

キリトリ線

英語（リーディング） 試作問題 解答用紙

※試作問題は自動採点に対応していません。

マーク例

良い例	悪い例
●	⊙ ⊗ ◐ 〇

解答科目欄

英語（リーディング）	ドイツ語	フランス語	中国語	韓国語
○	○	○	○	○

受験番号欄

千位	百位	十位	一位	英字	
—	⓪	⓪	⓪	Ⓐ	A
①	①	①	①	Ⓑ	B
②	②	②	②	Ⓒ	C
③	③	③	③	Ⓗ	H
④	④	④	④	Ⓚ	K
⑤	⑤	⑤	⑤	Ⓜ	M
⑥	⑥	⑥	⑥	Ⓡ	R
⑦	⑦	⑦	⑦	Ⓤ	U
⑧	⑧	⑧	⑧	Ⓧ	X
⑨	⑨	⑨	⑨	Ⓨ	Y
—	—	—	—	Ⓩ	Z

フリガナ	
氏名	

試験場コード	十万位	万位	千位	百位	十位	一位

第A問

解答番号	解答欄 1	2	3	4	5	6	7	8	9
1	①	②	③	④	⑤	⑥	⑦	⑧	⑨
2	①	②	③	④	⑤	⑥	⑦	⑧	⑨
3	①	②	③	④	⑤	⑥	⑦	⑧	⑨
4	①	②	③	④	⑤	⑥	⑦	⑧	⑨
5	①	②	③	④	⑤	⑥	⑦	⑧	⑨
6	①	②	③	④	⑤	⑥	⑦	⑧	⑨
7	①	②	③	④	⑤	⑥	⑦	⑧	⑨
8	①	②	③	④	⑤	⑥	⑦	⑧	⑨
9	①	②	③	④	⑤	⑥	⑦	⑧	⑨
10	①	②	③	④	⑤	⑥	⑦	⑧	⑨
11	①	②	③	④	⑤	⑥	⑦	⑧	⑨
12	①	②	③	④	⑤	⑥	⑦	⑧	⑨
13	①	②	③	④	⑤	⑥	⑦	⑧	⑨
14	①	②	③	④	⑤	⑥	⑦	⑧	⑨
15	①	②	③	④	⑤	⑥	⑦	⑧	⑨
16	①	②	③	④	⑤	⑥	⑦	⑧	⑨
17	①	②	③	④	⑤	⑥	⑦	⑧	⑨
18	①	②	③	④	⑤	⑥	⑦	⑧	⑨
19	①	②	③	④	⑤	⑥	⑦	⑧	⑨
20	①	②	③	④	⑤	⑥	⑦	⑧	⑨
21	①	②	③	④	⑤	⑥	⑦	⑧	⑨
22	①	②	③	④	⑤	⑥	⑦	⑧	⑨
23	①	②	③	④	⑤	⑥	⑦	⑧	⑨
24	①	②	③	④	⑤	⑥	⑦	⑧	⑨
25	①	②	③	④	⑤	⑥	⑦	⑧	⑨

第B問

解答番号	解答欄 1	2	3	4	5	6	7	8	9
1	①	②	③	④	⑤	⑥	⑦	⑧	⑨
2	①	②	③	④	⑤	⑥	⑦	⑧	⑨
3	①	②	③	④	⑤	⑥	⑦	⑧	⑨
4	①	②	③	④	⑤	⑥	⑦	⑧	⑨
5	①	②	③	④	⑤	⑥	⑦	⑧	⑨
6	①	②	③	④	⑤	⑥	⑦	⑧	⑨
7	①	②	③	④	⑤	⑥	⑦	⑧	⑨
8	①	②	③	④	⑤	⑥	⑦	⑧	⑨
9	①	②	③	④	⑤	⑥	⑦	⑧	⑨
10	①	②	③	④	⑤	⑥	⑦	⑧	⑨
11	①	②	③	④	⑤	⑥	⑦	⑧	⑨
12	①	②	③	④	⑤	⑥	⑦	⑧	⑨
13	①	②	③	④	⑤	⑥	⑦	⑧	⑨
14	①	②	③	④	⑤	⑥	⑦	⑧	⑨
15	①	②	③	④	⑤	⑥	⑦	⑧	⑨
16	①	②	③	④	⑤	⑥	⑦	⑧	⑨
17	①	②	③	④	⑤	⑥	⑦	⑧	⑨
18	①	②	③	④	⑤	⑥	⑦	⑧	⑨
19	①	②	③	④	⑤	⑥	⑦	⑧	⑨
20	①	②	③	④	⑤	⑥	⑦	⑧	⑨
21	①	②	③	④	⑤	⑥	⑦	⑧	⑨
22	①	②	③	④	⑤	⑥	⑦	⑧	⑨
23	①	②	③	④	⑤	⑥	⑦	⑧	⑨
24	①	②	③	④	⑤	⑥	⑦	⑧	⑨
25	①	②	③	④	⑤	⑥	⑦	⑧	⑨

英語（リーディング） 2024 本試 解答用紙

※過去問は自動採点に対応していません。

マーク例

良い例	悪い例
●	⊙ ⊗ ◔ 0

解答科目欄

英語（リーディング）	ドイツ語	フランス語	中国語	韓国語
○	○	○	○	○

受験番号欄

千位	百位	十位	一位	英字	
—	⓪	⓪	⓪	Ⓐ	A
①	①	①	①	Ⓑ	B
②	②	②	②	Ⓒ	C
③	③	③	③	Ⓗ	H
④	④	④	④	Ⓚ	K
⑤	⑤	⑤	⑤	Ⓜ	M
⑥	⑥	⑥	⑥	Ⓡ	R
⑦	⑦	⑦	⑦	Ⓤ	U
⑧	⑧	⑧	⑧	Ⓧ	X
⑨	⑨	⑨	⑨	Ⓨ	Y
—	—	—	—	Ⓩ	Z

フリガナ	
氏名	

試験場コード	十万位	万位	千位	百位	十位	一位

解答番号	解答欄 1	2	3	4	5	6	7	8	9
1	①	②	③	④	⑤	⑥	⑦	⑧	⑨
2	①	②	③	④	⑤	⑥	⑦	⑧	⑨
3	①	②	③	④	⑤	⑥	⑦	⑧	⑨
4	①	②	③	④	⑤	⑥	⑦	⑧	⑨
5	①	②	③	④	⑤	⑥	⑦	⑧	⑨
6	①	②	③	④	⑤	⑥	⑦	⑧	⑨
7	①	②	③	④	⑤	⑥	⑦	⑧	⑨
8	①	②	③	④	⑤	⑥	⑦	⑧	⑨
9	①	②	③	④	⑤	⑥	⑦	⑧	⑨
10	①	②	③	④	⑤	⑥	⑦	⑧	⑨
11	①	②	③	④	⑤	⑥	⑦	⑧	⑨
12	①	②	③	④	⑤	⑥	⑦	⑧	⑨
13	①	②	③	④	⑤	⑥	⑦	⑧	⑨
14	①	②	③	④	⑤	⑥	⑦	⑧	⑨
15	①	②	③	④	⑤	⑥	⑦	⑧	⑨
16	①	②	③	④	⑤	⑥	⑦	⑧	⑨
17	①	②	③	④	⑤	⑥	⑦	⑧	⑨
18	①	②	③	④	⑤	⑥	⑦	⑧	⑨
19	①	②	③	④	⑤	⑥	⑦	⑧	⑨
20	①	②	③	④	⑤	⑥	⑦	⑧	⑨
21	①	②	③	④	⑤	⑥	⑦	⑧	⑨
22	①	②	③	④	⑤	⑥	⑦	⑧	⑨
23	①	②	③	④	⑤	⑥	⑦	⑧	⑨
24	①	②	③	④	⑤	⑥	⑦	⑧	⑨
25	①	②	③	④	⑤	⑥	⑦	⑧	⑨

解答番号	解答欄 1	2	3	4	5	6	7	8	9
26	①	②	③	④	⑤	⑥	⑦	⑧	⑨
27	①	②	③	④	⑤	⑥	⑦	⑧	⑨
28	①	②	③	④	⑤	⑥	⑦	⑧	⑨
29	①	②	③	④	⑤	⑥	⑦	⑧	⑨
30	①	②	③	④	⑤	⑥	⑦	⑧	⑨
31	①	②	③	④	⑤	⑥	⑦	⑧	⑨
32	①	②	③	④	⑤	⑥	⑦	⑧	⑨
33	①	②	③	④	⑤	⑥	⑦	⑧	⑨
34	①	②	③	④	⑤	⑥	⑦	⑧	⑨
35	①	②	③	④	⑤	⑥	⑦	⑧	⑨
36	①	②	③	④	⑤	⑥	⑦	⑧	⑨
37	①	②	③	④	⑤	⑥	⑦	⑧	⑨
38	①	②	③	④	⑤	⑥	⑦	⑧	⑨
39	①	②	③	④	⑤	⑥	⑦	⑧	⑨
40	①	②	③	④	⑤	⑥	⑦	⑧	⑨
41	①	②	③	④	⑤	⑥	⑦	⑧	⑨
42	①	②	③	④	⑤	⑥	⑦	⑧	⑨
43	①	②	③	④	⑤	⑥	⑦	⑧	⑨
44	①	②	③	④	⑤	⑥	⑦	⑧	⑨
45	①	②	③	④	⑤	⑥	⑦	⑧	⑨
46	①	②	③	④	⑤	⑥	⑦	⑧	⑨
47	①	②	③	④	⑤	⑥	⑦	⑧	⑨
48	①	②	③	④	⑤	⑥	⑦	⑧	⑨
49	①	②	③	④	⑤	⑥	⑦	⑧	⑨
50	①	②	③	④	⑤	⑥	⑦	⑧	⑨

英 語（リーディング） 2023 本 試 解 答 用 紙

※過去問は自動採点に対応していません。

マーク例

良い例	悪い例
●	⊙ ⊗ ◐ O

解 答 科 目 欄

英語（リーディング）	ドイツ語	フランス語	中国語	韓国語
○	○	○	○	○

受 験 番 号 欄

千位	百位	十位	一位	英字	
—	⓪	⓪	⓪	Ⓐ	A
①	①	①	①	Ⓑ	B
②	②	②	②	Ⓒ	C
③	③	③	③	Ⓗ	H
④	④	④	④	Ⓚ	K
⑤	⑤	⑤	⑤	Ⓜ	M
⑥	⑥	⑥	⑥	Ⓡ	R
⑦	⑦	⑦	⑦	Ⓤ	U
⑧	⑧	⑧	⑧	Ⓧ	X
⑨	⑨	⑨	⑨	Ⓨ	Y
—	—	—	—	Ⓩ	Z

フリガナ	
氏 名	

試験場コード	十万位	万位	千位	百位	十位	一位

解答番号	解	答	欄						
	1	2	3	4	5	6	7	8	9
1	①	②	③	④	⑤	⑥	⑦	⑧	⑨
2	①	②	③	④	⑤	⑥	⑦	⑧	⑨
3	①	②	③	④	⑤	⑥	⑦	⑧	⑨
4	①	②	③	④	⑤	⑥	⑦	⑧	⑨
5	①	②	③	④	⑤	⑥	⑦	⑧	⑨
6	①	②	③	④	⑤	⑥	⑦	⑧	⑨
7	①	②	③	④	⑤	⑥	⑦	⑧	⑨
8	①	②	③	④	⑤	⑥	⑦	⑧	⑨
9	①	②	③	④	⑤	⑥	⑦	⑧	⑨
10	①	②	③	④	⑤	⑥	⑦	⑧	⑨
11	①	②	③	④	⑤	⑥	⑦	⑧	⑨
12	①	②	③	④	⑤	⑥	⑦	⑧	⑨
13	①	②	③	④	⑤	⑥	⑦	⑧	⑨
14	①	②	③	④	⑤	⑥	⑦	⑧	⑨
15	①	②	③	④	⑤	⑥	⑦	⑧	⑨
16	①	②	③	④	⑤	⑥	⑦	⑧	⑨
17	①	②	③	④	⑤	⑥	⑦	⑧	⑨
18	①	②	③	④	⑤	⑥	⑦	⑧	⑨
19	①	②	③	④	⑤	⑥	⑦	⑧	⑨
20	①	②	③	④	⑤	⑥	⑦	⑧	⑨
21	①	②	③	④	⑤	⑥	⑦	⑧	⑨
22	①	②	③	④	⑤	⑥	⑦	⑧	⑨
23	①	②	③	④	⑤	⑥	⑦	⑧	⑨
24	①	②	③	④	⑤	⑥	⑦	⑧	⑨
25	①	②	③	④	⑤	⑥	⑦	⑧	⑨

解答番号	解	答	欄						
	1	2	3	4	5	6	7	8	9
26	①	②	③	④	⑤	⑥	⑦	⑧	⑨
27	①	②	③	④	⑤	⑥	⑦	⑧	⑨
28	①	②	③	④	⑤	⑥	⑦	⑧	⑨
29	①	②	③	④	⑤	⑥	⑦	⑧	⑨
30	①	②	③	④	⑤	⑥	⑦	⑧	⑨
31	①	②	③	④	⑤	⑥	⑦	⑧	⑨
32	①	②	③	④	⑤	⑥	⑦	⑧	⑨
33	①	②	③	④	⑤	⑥	⑦	⑧	⑨
34	①	②	③	④	⑤	⑥	⑦	⑧	⑨
35	①	②	③	④	⑤	⑥	⑦	⑧	⑨
36	①	②	③	④	⑤	⑥	⑦	⑧	⑨
37	①	②	③	④	⑤	⑥	⑦	⑧	⑨
38	①	②	③	④	⑤	⑥	⑦	⑧	⑨
39	①	②	③	④	⑤	⑥	⑦	⑧	⑨
40	①	②	③	④	⑤	⑥	⑦	⑧	⑨
41	①	②	③	④	⑤	⑥	⑦	⑧	⑨
42	①	②	③	④	⑤	⑥	⑦	⑧	⑨
43	①	②	③	④	⑤	⑥	⑦	⑧	⑨
44	①	②	③	④	⑤	⑥	⑦	⑧	⑨
45	①	②	③	④	⑤	⑥	⑦	⑧	⑨
46	①	②	③	④	⑤	⑥	⑦	⑧	⑨
47	①	②	③	④	⑤	⑥	⑦	⑧	⑨
48	①	②	③	④	⑤	⑥	⑦	⑧	⑨
49	①	②	③	④	⑤	⑥	⑦	⑧	⑨
50	①	②	③	④	⑤	⑥	⑦	⑧	⑨

Z-KAI

2025年用

共通テスト 実戦模試

❶ 英語リーディング

解答・解説編

Z会編集部 編

学習診断サイトのご案内※1

『実戦模試』シリーズ（試作問題・過去問を除く）では，以下のことができます。

- マークシートをスマホで撮影して自動採点
- 自分の得点と，本サイト登録者平均点との比較
- 登録者のランキング表示（総合・志望大別）
- Ｚ会編集部からの直前対策用アドバイス

手順

①本書を解いて，以下のサイトにアクセス（スマホ・PC 対応）

Z会共通テスト学習診断　検索

https://service.zkai.co.jp/books/k-test/

二次元コード→

②購入者パスワード **57784** を入力し，ログイン

③必要事項を入力（志望校・ニックネーム・ログインパスワード）※2

④スマホ・タブレットでマークシートを撮影　→**自動採点**※3，**アドバイス Get！**

※1　学習診断サイトは 2025 年 5 月 30 日まで利用できます。

※2　ID・パスワードは次回ログイン時に必要になりますので，必ず記録して保管してください。

※3　スマホ・タブレットをお持ちでない場合は事前に自己採点をお願いします。

目次

リーディング模試　第１回　解答

第1問小計	第2問小計	第3問小計	第4問小計	第5問小計	第6問小計	第7問小計	第8問小計

合計点	／100

問題番号(配点)	設問	解答番号	正解	配点	自己採点
第１問(6)	1	1	④	2	
	2	2	②	2	
	3	3	①	2	
第２問(10)	1	4	④	2	
	2	5	②	2	
	3	6	②	2	
	4	7	②	2	
	5	8	④	2	
第３問(9)	1	9	①	3※	
		10	②		
		11	③		
		12	④		
	2	13	①	3	
	3	14	④	3	
第４問(12)	1	15	③	3	
	2	16	③	3	
	3	17	②	3	
	4	18	②	3	
第５問(16)	1	19	④	3	
	2	20	②	3	
	3	21	③	4	
	4	22	⑤	3※	
		23	④		
	5	24	④	3	
第６問(18)	1	25	②	3	
	2	26	②	3	
	3	27 ～ 28	①-④	3※	
		29	③	3	
	4	30	③	3	
	5	31	②	3	
第７問(15)	1	32	⑤	4※	
		33	③		
		34	④		
		35	②		
		36	①		
	2	37 ～ 38	②-④	4※	
	3	39	③	3	
	4	40	⑤	4	
第８問(14)	1	41	①	3	
	2	42	①	3	
	3	43 ～ 44	③-④	4※	
	4	45	①	4	

（注）１　※は，全部正解の場合のみ点を与える。
　　　２　-(ハイフン)でつながれた正解は，順序を問わない。

第1問

全訳 あなたはある店のウェブサイトを訪れ，面白そうな告知を見つけました。

2月の教室：初心者向けの裁縫

2月8日(土)にボニーの裁縫店にいらして下さい。基本的な裁縫技術の無料ワークショップの日です。1つでも教室に来て下さった方は，店で1商品20%オフの価格になるサービスを受けられます。この割引は2月8日，9日に有効です。

作りたいものをお持ちいただくことをお勧めしますが，お持ちいただかなくてもかまいません。教室で必要となる材料はすべて当店でご提供します。

教室のスケジュール

午前9時　基本の直線縫いに挑戦しよう
午前10時　小さな穴のつくろい
午前11時　ボタン付け
午後1時　あて布をする
午後2時　難しい素材を使った実習 —— 革と絹
午後3時　創造力を発揮する —— あなたの服をスタイリッシュにする楽しい色を使いましょう
午後4時　裁縫交流会 —— 無料の軽食とホットチョコレートを講師たちと楽しみましょう

●お子様が参加されるには10歳以上である必要があります。また，16歳未満のお子様は大人の付き添いが必要です。
●授業は英語と日本語で行われますが，講師は言葉を使わずに実演する能力に非常に長けています。お話しになる言語にかかわらずどなたでも歓迎いたします。

1クラスの定員は20名までです。以下でお申し込みいただいてお席を予約することもできます。

▶▶申し込み

問1 1 ④

「この告知の目的は，人々に［1］について知ってもらうことである。」
①「店の2月の大売り出し」
②「特別な裁縫ワークショップの割引」
③「店の新しい従業員の研修」
④「無料で受講できる裁縫教室」

タイトルに注目しよう。February Classes: Sewing for Beginners（2月の教室：初心者向けの裁縫）とある。本文第1文では，free workshops in basic sewing skills（基本的な裁縫技術の無料ワークショップ）への参加を促しており，スケジュール表でも裁縫教室の日程が紹介されている。したがって④が正解。第2文に，教室の参加者はreceive 20% off the price of one item in the store（店で1商品20%オフの価格になるサービスを受けられる）とあるが，店の大売り出しではないし，ワークショップはそもそも無料なので，①，②は不正解。③の従業員の研修に関する言及はない。

問2 2 ②

「イベントでは参加者は［2］ことができる。」
①「その店のオーナーが作った服を買う」
②「講師たちと食べたり飲んだりする」
③「絹でできた品々の展示を見る」
④「他の参加者と一緒に革を縫い合わせる」

②の内容がスケジュールの午後4時のEnjoy free snacks and hot chocolate with our teachers（無料の軽食とホットチョコレートを講師たちと楽しむ）と一致する。②が正解。「オーナーが作った服」や「絹製品の展示」については言及がないので①，③は不正解。午後2時から革と絹のような難しい素材を使った実習はあるが，他の参加者と一緒に縫うという説明はないから④も不正解。

問3 3 ①

「もし［3］なら，人々はイベントに参加することはできない。」
①「30人の団体」
②「16歳未満」
③「英語も日本語も話すことができない」
④「2月8日までにオンライン申し込みを忘れた」

お知らせの最後にSpace is limited to 20 people in a class.（1クラスの定員は20名までです。）とあるので，「30人の団体」が参加することは不可能。①が正解。スケジュール下の注意書きの1つ目にchildren under 16 must come with an adult（16歳未満の子供は大人の付き添いが必要）とあるが，付き添いがあれば16歳未満でも参加できるということなので②は不正解。注意書きの2つ目の最後にEveryone is welcome, no matter what language you speak.（お話しになる言語にかかわらずどなたでも歓迎いたします。）とあり，英語も日本語も話すことができなくても参加できるから③も不正解。

お知らせの最後にyou may reserve（予約してもよい）とあり，予約は強制ではないし締め切り日も明記されていないので，④も不正解。

【語句】

◇encourage O to *do*「Oに…するよう勧める」

◇mend「～を繕う；～（＝壊れたもの）を直す」

第2問

全訳 タナカマユミという名前のある高校生が，イギリスの小説家アンドリュー・ローレンスの最新小説を読みました。彼女は彼の出版社にメールを送り，その小説家から返事を受け取りました。あなたは雑誌で彼らのメールを読んでいます。

親愛なるアンドリュー・ローレンスさま，

こんにちは，私の名前はタナカマユミです。私は日本の高校生です。先日，私はあなたの最新小説『Carrying My Hope』を読んで，本当に感動しました。驚きに満ちたストーリーだったので，それがどのような結末になるのか想像がつきませんでした。とてもおもしろかったので，たった1日で読み終えました！　しかも，素晴らしい家族愛をテーマとして扱っていて，たくさんのすてきな人物が登場していて，心が温まりました。

実は，私は将来，あなたのような小説家になりたいと思っています。いくつか質問にお答えいただければ幸いです。物語のアイデアはどのように思いつきますか？　小説の書き方をどのように学びましたか？　そしてどのようにそれらを書く練習をしていますか？　あなたの次の小説を読むのを楽しみにしています。

敬具

タナカマユミ

親愛なるタナカマユミさん，

こんにちは，マユミさん。メールを書いてくれてありがとう。あなたが私の小説をとても気に入ってくれて本当にうれしいです。

あなたの質問に関して，私の答えは次のとおりです。第一に，物語のアイデアを得るために，私は周囲の人々をよく観察します。他の人からたくさんのことが学べるのです。第二の質問に関しては，実を言うと，私は学校では小説の書き方を学びませんでしたが，小説を含むできるだけ多くの本を読むようにしています。このことが私の表現の幅を広げるのに役立っています。第三に，私はあなたに約1,000語の文章を約100語に要約することをお勧めします。

いつかあなたの小説を読めることを願っています！

ご多幸を祈って

アンドリュー・ローレンス

問1　4　④

「マユミは［ 4 ］ためにローレンス氏にメールを書いた。」

①「彼に次にどんな小説を書くつもりなのかをたずねる」

②「彼の小説に日本人ファンが何人いるのかを知らせる」

③「彼がいつ小説家になる決心をしたのかを知る」

④**「彼の新しい小説の感想を伝える」**

マユミのメールの第1段落第3文に，The other day, I read your latest novel *Carrying My Hope*, and I was really impressed with it（= *Carrying My Hope*）.（先日，あなたの最新小説『Carrying My Hope』を読み，本当にそれ（=『Carrying My Hope』）に感動しました。）とあり，続けて最新小説の感想を具体的に述べる文が続く。したがって，④が正解。

ローレンスの次回作については，マユミのメールの第2段落最終文に，I am looking forward to reading your next novel.（あなたの次の小説を読むのを楽しみにしています。）とあるのみで，内容に関する質問はないので①は不正解。マユミのメールには，日本人ファンが何人いるかや，ローレンス氏が小説家になる決心をした時期をたずねる質問は書かれていないので，②，③も不正解。

問2　5　②

「マユミのメールに書かれている1つの**事実**は［ 5 ］ということである。」

①「『Carrying My Hope』は来週刊行される」

②**「マユミが『Carrying My Hope』を読むのに1日かかった」**

③「彼女は『Carrying My Hope』を読んだあとに怖くなった」

④「『Carrying My Hope』の物語は素晴らしかった」

マユミのメールに書かれている，個人の主観的なopinion（意見）ではなく，客観的なfact（事実）を選ぶ。マユミのメールの第1段落第5文に，I finished reading it（= *Carrying My Hope*）in only a day!（私はそれ（=『Carrying My Hope』）をたった1日で読み終えました！）とあり，これは客観的な事実なので，②が正解。

マユミのメールの第1段落第3文に，The other day, I read your latest novel *Carrying My Hope*（先日，私はあなたの最新小説『Carrying My Hope』を読みました）とあり，『Carrying My Hope』はすでに刊行されていることが読み取れるので，①は不正解。『Carrying My Hope』読後の感想は，マユミのメールの第1段落第3文で，I was really impressed with it（= *Carrying My Hope*）（本当にそれ（=『Carrying My Hope』）に感動しました。），第1段落最終文で，it（= *Carrying My Hope*）warmed my heart（それ（=『Carrying My Hope』）は私の心を温かくしました）と述べている。これらを簡潔にまとめると，素晴らしかったということになるが，これは客観的な事実ではなく，マユミの主観的な意見なので，④も不正解。また怖くなったとは書かれていないので，③も不正解。

問3　6　②

「マユミがローレンス氏に質問したのはなぜか。」 6

①「なぜ彼が小説家になったのか知りたかったから。」

②「小説の書き方を学びたかったから。」

③「イギリスの生活に興味があったから。」

④「彼の私生活に興味があったから。」

マユミのローレンス氏への質問は，マユミのメールの第2段落に書かれている。まず第1文で，I want to be a novelist like you in the future（私は将来，あなたのような小説家になりたいのです）と質問したい理由を述べている。続けて第3～5文で，How do you come up with the ideas for your stories? How did you learn how to write novels? And how do you practice writing them（= novels）?（物語のアイデアはどのように思いつきますか？　小説の書き方をどのように学びましたか？　そしてどのようにそれら（=小説）を書く練習をしていますか？）と具体的な質問を3つしている。これらはすべて小説の書き方に関する質問なので，②が正解。ローレンス氏が小説家になった理由や彼の私生活，またイギリスの生活についての質問はしていないので，①，③，④は不正解。

問4　7　②

「ローレンス氏のマユミへの返事において，1つの**事実**は，彼は 7 ということである。」

①「人々を注意深く見るのが恥ずかしいとわかった」

②「自分自身で書く技術を向上させている」

③「短い文章をできるだけ長くしている」

④「小説以外の本はめったに読まない」

ローレンス氏のメールに書かれている，個人の主観的なopinion（意見）ではなく，客観的なfact（事実）を選ぶ。

ローレンス氏のメールの第2段落第4～5文に，I didn't learn how to write novels at school, but I try to read as many books, including novels, as possible. This helps me extend my range of expression.（私は学校では小説の書き方を学びませんでしたが，小説を含むできるだけ多くの本を読むようにしています。このことが私の表現の幅を広げるのに役立っています。）とあることから，学校で学んだのではなく，自身で書く技術を向上させているという客観的事実が読み取れるので，②が正解。小説以外の本も読んでいるのであるから，④は不正解。ローレンス氏のメールの第2段落第2～3文に，I often observe people around me to get ideas for stories. I can learn a lot of things from other people.（物語のアイデアを得るために，私は周囲の人々をよく観察します。他の人からたくさんのことが学べます。）とあり，ローレンス氏は人々を観察することを恥ずかしいとは考えていないことが読み取れるので，①も不正解。③のようなことは書かれていないので，これも不正解。

問5　8　④

「ローレンス氏からのメールを読んだあと，マユミは最初に何をする可能性が最も高いか。」 8

①「彼女は友達に自分の小説を読んでもらうだろう。」

②「彼女は第2巻を買いに行くだろう。」

③「彼女は彼の最新小説の結末を推測するだろう。」

④「彼女は彼のアドバイスに従ってみるだろう。」

ローレンス氏のメールの概要は以下のとおり。

・第1段落：マユミのメールに対するお礼。

・第２段落：小説の書き方についてのマユミからの質問への回答。

⑴　物語のアイデアを得るために，周囲の人々をよく観察している。

⑵　学校で小説の書き方を学ばなかったが，多くの本を読むことで表現の幅を広げている。

⑶　文章を短く要約することで書く練習をするのがお勧めである。

・第３段落：いつかマユミの小説を読めるとよいと思っている。

したがって，マユミは小説家になるために，ローレンス氏からのアドバイスに従ってみると思われるので，④が正解。

マユミのメールの第１段落第４文に，I could not guess how it（= *Carrying My Hope*）was going to end（それ（=『Carrying My Hope』）がどのような結末になるのか想像がつきませんでした）とあり，マユミがローレンス氏の最新小説の結末を推測したのは過去のことなので，③は不正解。①，②のようなことはまったく述べられていないので，これらも不正解。

【語句】

◇publisher「出版社」

◇*be* impressed with ～「～に感動する」

◇deal with ～「～を扱う」

◇appreciate「～に感謝する」

◇come up with ～「～を思いつく」

◇regarding「～に関して」

◇summarise「～を要約する」（イギリス英語。アメリカ英語では summarize。）

第３問

全訳　あなたは留学生用の雑誌で次の話を見つけました。

あなたは秘密を守れますか

イイダ　サヤ

他人を信用するのが難しいことがあります。最もよく知っている人たちの場合でさえも。

兄のダイキには２人の親友，ジュンペイとケンジがいます。彼らは幼い頃からいつも何でも一緒にやってきました。

ダイキがもうすぐ16歳になる時，ケンジとジュンペイはレストランでダイキにパーティーをしてあげようと決めました。彼らは私が手伝えるように，私にその秘密を教えてくれました。

ある日，ケンジとジュンペイは自分たちがパーティーの計画を立てるために集まれるよう，放課後，ダイキがずっと忙しくなるようにしてほしいと私に頼みました。あいにく私は彼らが学校の中庭で集まろうとしていることを忘れて，帰宅途中にダイキを連れて彼らのちょうど近くを通ってしまいました。

「待って。あれはケンジとジュンペイじゃないか？」とダイキは言いました。「２人ともサッカーの練習があるから今日は遊べないって言っていたのに。」

ダイキは悲しそうでした。さらに，ケンジとジュンペイはダイキが自分たちを見たのに気づくと走って逃げたので事態はますます悪くなりました。

「ううん，ケンジとジュンペイではないと思うよ。さあ行こう。私の英語の試験勉強を手伝ってくれるって言ったじゃない。いい成績をとりたいの。」と私は言いました。

ダイキの表情はさらに暗くなりました。彼は怒って言いました。「もしあいつらがもう僕の友達ではいたくないなら，そう言ってくれればいいのに。」

「そんなはずないよ。」と私は言いました。

家ではダイキは宿題に集中していませんでした。私がダイキに同じ質問を３回もしたあとに，「ごめん，なんて言った？ サヤ」と言いました。

パーティーは２週間後でした。ダイキが２週間もこんなふうに感じているのはよくないと思いました。私がダイキに秘密を守れるかたずねると，守れると言いました。そこで私はダイキにパーティーのことを話しました。

ダイキは口をあんぐりと開けました。「わあ，本当？」

「知らないふりをしなくちゃだめだよ。」と私は言いました。「そうしないとジュンペイとケンジががっかりするだろうから。」

「心配しないで。あいつらは僕の親友だ。あいつらのためなら何でもするよ。」ダイキはうれしそうに言いました。そしてその通りにしました。

問１　9　①　10　②　11　③　12　④

「次の感情（①～④）をダイキが経験した順番に並

べよ。」

9 → 10 → 11 → 12 → glad

①「傷ついた」

②「怒った」

③「集中していない」

④「驚いた」

ダイキの気持ちを表す表現を順に追えばよい。ダイキの気持ちが初めに述べられているのはジュンペイとヒロキがダイキに嘘をついて学校の中庭にいるのを見かけたあと。He looked sad.（彼（＝ダイキ）は悲しそうでした。）はhurt（傷ついた）と言い換えられる。さらに2人が走り去ったのを見て，He said angrily（彼（＝ダイキ）は怒って言いました）と続くので2番目の感情はmad（怒った）。家でサヤの宿題を手伝っている時はDaiki's mind was not on homework（ダイキは宿題に集中していませんでした）とあるので，not focused（集中していない）が3番目。秘密を隠しきれなくなったサヤがパーティーのことをこっそり知らせると，ダイキは口を大きく開けてWow, really?（わあ，本当？）と言っている。これはsurprised（驚いた）の気持ちを表している。事情がわかったダイキは最後にsaid Daiki happily（ダイキはうれしそうに言いました）とあるからglad（うれしい）が5番目に来る。したがって，「傷ついた」→「怒った」→「集中していない」→「驚いた」となる① → ② → ③ → ④ が正解。

問2 13 ①

「ジュンペイとケンジはダイキの 13 を祝いたいと思った。」

①「誕生日」

②「よい成績」

③「卒業」

④「サッカーの勝利」

本文前半にWhen Daiki was going to turn sixteen, Kenji and Junpei decided to throw him a party at a restaurant.（ダイキがもうすぐ16歳になる時，ケンジとジュンペイはレストランでダイキにパーティーをしてあげようと決めました。）とあるから，①が正解。

問3 14 ④

「この話から，あなたはダイキが 14 ことを知った。」

①「友人の秘密を知ってわくわくしたために，自分の英語の宿題に集中できなかった」

②「サヤから友達の秘密をあらかじめ教えてもらい，彼らをがっかりさせた」

③「友達とサッカーの練習をすると約束したが，その約束を実現できなかった」

④「友達が何を隠しているかを妹が教えてくれるまで，友達がもう自分のことは好きではないと思った」

自分に内緒でジュンペイとケンジが会っていることを知ったダイキは中盤でIf they don't want … would just say so.（もしあいつらがもう僕の友達ではいたくないなら，そう言ってくれればいいのに。）と言っているが，見かねた妹がその後本当のことを話し，誤解は解けた。④の内容と一致する。友達の秘密が何かを知ったのは宿題に集中できなかったあとであり，宿題も妹のものなので①は不正解。ダイキは友達をがっかりさせないよう秘密について知らないふりをするようサヤに言われ，最後にAnd he did.（そしてその通りにしました。（＝知らないふりをした））とあるから，友達をがっかりさせてはいないと考えられる。②も不正解。③の記述はない。

【語句】

◇let A in on B「AにBを打ち明ける〔知らせる〕」

◇courtyard「中庭」

◇hang out「ぶらぶらと時を過ごす」

◇expression「表情」

第4問

全訳 英語の授業で，あなたは発表の準備のためにある健康問題に関するエッセイを書いています。これはあなたの最新の草稿です。今は先生からのコメントをもとに，推敲に取り組んでいるところです。

目を大切にしよう

眼鏡やコンタクトを着用しているクラスメートは何人いるだろうか。スクリーンタイムが増え，外で過ごす時間が減る中，子供たちの視力は以前と比べて悪化している。何が視力の悪化につながっているか，医師たちの見解は必ずしも一致していない。*(1)* 15 目の健康のためにできる一般的な対策がいくつかある。

まず，何かを見る時は，自分の顔から少なくとも1フィート（約30cm）は離して持つようにしよう。見ているものが本であれスマートフォンの画面であれ，非常に近いものに焦点を合わせるのは目にとって負担が大きくなる。これは目を疲れさせ，近距離作業と視力悪化の関連性を示す研究もある。

第二に，*(2)*数字に注目しよう。「20-20-20（ルール）」は覚えやすい。これは，近くのものを長時間見なければならない時は，20分ごとに20秒休憩をとり，20フィート先のものを見るようにする，というものだ。これは目の緊張をほぐす助けとなり，視力低下を防ぐ効果もあるかもしれない。ちょっとした頭の休息にもなりえる。

最後に，紫外線（UV）保護機能をもつサングラスをかけよう。たぶんあなたも，UVによるダメージから皮膚を守るために日焼け止めを使っているだろう。*(3)* 17 UVダメージは視力低下を引き起こすわけではないが，高齢になるとよくみられる多数の疾患にはつながる。50年後も健康な目でいたいなら，今から目を守ることを始めるべきだ。

このように，目を大切にするために簡単にできることはある。*(4)*ものを読む時は目を休め，休憩をとって遠くを見るようにし，外出時にはサングラスをかけよう。健康的な習慣を心掛ければ，あなたの目がずっとハッピーでいる助けとなるだろう。

コメント

(1) ここに接続表現を挿入しなさい。
(2) この主題文はこの段落にあまり合っていません。書き直しなさい。
(3) ここに何か足りません。2つの文をつなぐために，間にさらに情報を追加しなさい。
(4) 下線部の表現はあなたのエッセイの内容を十分に要約していません。変更しなさい。

総合的なコメント

原稿はかなりよくなりましたね。発表前にあと少し手直ししておきましょう。（あなたはサングラスをかけますか。私は1つ買いに行くつもりです！😊）

問1 15 ③

「コメント(1)に基づいて，付け加えるのに最も適当な表現はどれか。」 15

① 「本当に」
② 「そのうえ」
③ 「とはいえ」
④ 「したがって」

まず，(1)の直前の文を見てみると，Doctors do not all agree on what leads to bad vision.（何が視力の悪化につながっているか，医師たちの見解は必ずしも一致していない。）とある。一方，(1)が追加される文は There are some steps you can take for your eye health in general.（目の健康のためにできる一般的な対策がいくつかある。）とある。論の展開として，「視力悪化の原因は特定されていない」⇒とはいえ，「一般的な対策はある」とするのが自然なので，‘逆接’の接続表現である③の nevertheless が正解。その他の選択肢は，この2文を論理的につなぐことができない。

問2 16 ③

「コメント(2)に基づいて，この主題文を書き直すのに最適な方法はどれか。」 16

① 「20フィート先にあるものを見つけよう」
② 「30分ごとに60秒休もう」
③ 「『目の休憩』をとろう」
④ 「近距離作業をする時はタイマーを使おう」

下線部(2)がこの段落の主題文として適切でないというのが先生の指摘。この段落では，「20-20-20（ルール）」という眼精疲労を抑えるための具体策とその効果について述べている。したがって，この段落を要約する主題文としては，③「『目の休憩』をとろう」が最適である。①は「20-20-20（ルール）」の1つに近い（実際には「見つける」のではなく「見る」ことが目的）が，主題文になるには不十分。②は本文の内容と相違があり，④のタイマーの使用については言及がないので不正解。

問3 17 ②

「コメント(3)に基づいて，付け加えるのに最も適当な文はどれか。」 17

① 「このことから，目は紫外線から保護する必要がある。」
② 「同じように，目を守るためにサングラスを使うべきだ。」
③ 「一方，サングラスもまた名案である。」
④ 「日焼け止め剤は近年の改良により，皮膚によりよいものとなっている。」

(3)を含む第4段落の主題文で筆者は，UV保護機能のあるサングラスを着用すべきと主張している。

この段落内で筆者はその目的について明確に示していないから，(3)でそれを説明する必要がある。論の展開として，「UVから皮膚を守るのに日焼け止めを使うことはすでに普及している」⇒「同じように，目を守るためにサングラスを使うべきだ」とするのが自然だから，②が正解。①は，For this reason に相当するものが(3)の前に書かれていないからここには挿入できない。UVから目を保護する必要性については(3)の後で説明されている。③，④はサングラスの着用の目的を述べていないため不正解。

問4 18 ②

「コメント(4)に基づいて，置き換えるものとして最適なのはどれか。」 18

① 「疲れている時にスマートフォンを使うのはやめよう」

② 「目と手の間には多少の距離をとるようにしよう」

③ 「遠くにあるものを見よう」

④ 「野外での活動時間を増やそう」

最終段落は，それまでの段落で述べてきたことをまとめる役割を担っている。先生に「置き換えるべき」と指摘された下線部(4)に続く部分では，take a break to look into the distance と wear sunglasses when you go outside という2つの具体策が述べられ，これらはそれぞれ第3段落，第4段落で紹介されたものと対応している。下線部(4)はこの前者と重複しており，このままでは第2段落との対応が欠落している。したがって下線部(4)では，第2段落で紹介した対策を要約するのが自然だから，②が正解。本文に①，④のような記述はなく，③は第2，3段落の内容と重なるが漠然としており，要約として不十分である。

【語句】

◇screen time「（パソコン・スマートフォンなどの）画面を眺めて過ごす時間；スクリーンタイム」
◇vision「視力；視覚」
◇take a step for ～「～のために措置を講じる」
◇focus on ～「～に焦点を合わせる」
◇strain「過労；無理な負担」
◇sunscreen「日焼け止め剤」
◇look into the distance「遠くを見る」
◇問3 ④ improvement「改善；改良」

第5問

全訳 あなたは科学教育に関する調査をしています。あなたは2つの記事を見つけました。

物理学における女性 **リヴァ・シン**

2018年10月

メソポタミアの王女エンヘドゥアンナから3世紀エジプトの化学者である錬金術師クレオパトラまで，何千年もの間，女性は科学者として働いてきた。けれども歴史のほとんどの期間，女性は職業的な科学者としてはわずかな割合しか占めていない。今日では世界の科学研究者の約30％のみが女性である。

生物科学ではその数は変化しつつある。2000年代初頭には，生物医科学では上級学位の半数近くを女性が取得した。けれども物理学の分野では男女格差はまだ大きい。イギリスにおける女子と男子の研究は，この専門上の分断が高校で女子がする選択と関連していることを示している。

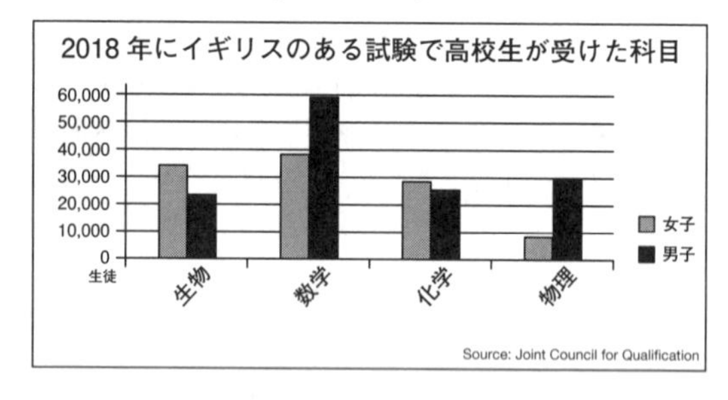

2018年には男子の1.5倍近くの女子が生物を学習することを選択した。しかし，ほぼ3万人の男子が物理を学習したのに対し，物理を学習した女子は1万人に満たない。2016年にはイギリスの学校の50％では物理を学ぶことを選択した女子が1人もいなかった。イギリスでは物理の講師のうち女性はわずか17％しかいないのは驚くべきことではない。

女子は物理学に興味がないだけだから，これは問題ではないという意見も多い。けれども私の考えでは，女子には物理学では女性のロールモデル（お手本）が十分ではなく，ロールモデルが足りないために，女子は物理学が自分たちにも追究できるもの，追究すべきものであるという事実を真剣に考えていないのだ。この理論はアメリカの研究に裏打ちされている。その研究では，テキサス大学の研究者が，女性研究者の割合が高い地域の学校では，物理を学ぶ男女の数はほぼ同じであることを発見したのだ。

「物理学における女性」についての意見

E. C.

2018年11月

女性物理学者として，私はこの問題にとても共感できます。物理学の世界で働くことは女性には少し心細いことがあります。私の夫はこの５年間イギリスで高校の理科の教師をしていますが，私が学校生活のほとんどにおいてクラスに１人だけの女子であることが多かったと初めて夫に話した時は驚いていました。でもこのデータを見たあとは，彼の反応の意味がわかりました。リヴァ・シンの記事によると，高校で夫の科目を学習する女子は男子より約10%多いのです。

我々はもっと多くの女性が物理の仕事に就けるようにさらに努力しなければなりません。イギリスで物理を実際に学んでいる女子は，常に物理の試験で男子と同等か時には少し上回る好成績すら収めています。科学界としては専門職に男女同数の学生を引き付けられないことにより，間違いなく才能を見逃しています。特に女性科学者が多くないこれらの業界では，大学の物理学科が女性物理学者を学校で講義するよう送り出すことは効果があるだろうと思います。

この問題について幼い子供の親御さんと話をするのも役立つでしょう。男の子と女の子のどちらにも，物理の概念を紹介する面白いおもちゃを与えたら，のちに彼らは自信を持ってわくわくしてその教科を高いレベルで学習するようになるでしょう。

問１　19　④

「リヴァ・シンも物理学者も両者とも 19 には言及していない。」

①「男女の物理のテストの点数」

②「歴史上の女性科学者」

③「自然科学を学ぶ女子高生」

④「男子が物理を好む理由」

２番目の記事を書いたE.C.は記事の冒頭でAs a female physicist（女性物理学者として）と述べているから設問のthe physicistはE.C.のことである。物理のテストの点数については，E.C.の記事第２段落第２文に，イギリスの学生の男女の点数の比較が紹介されている。歴史上の女性科学者についてはリヴァ・シンの記事の導入部分でふれられている。自然科学（生物・物理・化学など）を学ぶ女子高生については両者が話題に挙げており，リヴァ・シンはグラフを用いて理系科目とそれを学ぶ男女別の人数を，E.C.は夫が教えている科目と女子高生の人数について言及している。以上より①，②，③はいずれかが言及しているので不正解。④についてはどちらの記事でもふれられていないから④が正解。

問２　20　②

「物理学者の夫は 20 を教えている。」

①「生物」

②「化学」

③「数学」

④「物理」

物理学者は２つ目の記事の筆者。第１段落最終文にAccording to Riva Singh's article, … by about 10 percent.（リヴァ・シンの記事によると，高校で夫の科目を学習する女子は男子より約10%多い。）とある。リヴァ・シンの記事内にあるグラフを見ると，女子が男子より約10%多い科目はchemistryなので，②が正解。

問３　21　③

「記事によると，イギリスの高校では 21 。」

①「すべての学生が高等数学を受講することを求められる」

②「化学より外国語を学ぶ学生が多い」

③「女性が出席しない理科の授業があった」

④「物理のテストで女性は男性ほどには得点しない」

高等数学や外国語の授業については記述がないので①，②は不正解。１つ目の記事の第３段落第３文にnot one female student ... in 50% of British schools（イギリスの学校の50%では物理を学ぶことを選択した女子が１人もいなかった）とあるので③は正解。２つ目の記事第２段落第２文にThe girls who do study physics ... exams in that subject.（イギリスで物理を実際に学んでいる女子は，常に物理の試験で男子と同等か時には少し上回る好成績すら収めている。）とあるから④は不正解。

問４　22　⑤　23　④

「リヴァ・シンは女子学生は 22 と述べ，物理学者は女子学生は 23 と述べている。」（それぞれの空欄には異なる選択肢を選ぶこと。）

①「物理よりも生物に興味がある」

②「両親の職業と同じような職業を選ぶ」

③「テキサスの高校では化学を学習する可能性が最

も高い」

④「小さな子供の頃に物理を紹介されるべきである」 22

⑤「男子学生と同じくらいの割合で生物医科学を学んでいた」 23

リヴァ・シンは第2段落第2文でIn the early 2000s, ... were earned by women.（2000年代初頭には，生物医科学では上級学位の半数近くを女性が取得した。）と述べている。これは⑤の内容と一致する。物理学者は2つ目の記事の最後でIf both boys and girls are ... at a higher level later.（男の子と女の子のどちらにも，物理の概念を紹介する面白いおもちゃを与えたら，のちに彼らは自信を持ってわくわくしてその教科を高いレベルで学習するようになるだろう。）と述べており，これは④の内容と一致する。グラフでは生物を選択する女子は物理を選択する女子よりも多いが，1つ目の記事最終段落で「女子は物理に興味がない」という意見をリヴァ・シンは否定している。2つ目の記事にも生物と物理の興味の差についての言及はないから①は不正解。②，③についても両方の記事に記述がないので不正解。

問5 24 ④

「両方の記事の情報に基づいて，あなたは宿題でレポートを書く予定である。あなたのレポートに最適なタイトルは『 24 』であろう。」

①「女子学生の物理のテストの成績は伸びている」

②「以前よりも物理学者になりたい女子が増えている」

③「物理学研究における人材は増えつつある」

④「物理学における男女格差に対処する方法」

1つ目の記事のタイトルはWomen in Physics（物理学における女性）である。第2段落第3文から物理学におけるgender gap（男女格差）に言及している。教科ごとに試験を受けた男女それぞれの人数を比較したグラフを掲げ，物理を学習する女性が少ないことを説明している。第4段落では女性が少ない理由として，物理界に女性のロールモデルがいないことを挙げている。2つ目の記事の筆者は物理学者で，自分の経験から物理学は確かに女性が少ない分野であることを述べている。第2，3段落では，物理を学習する女子を増やすために，女性の物理学者を学校へ派遣して話をしてもらったり，子どもの頃から物理の概念を紹介するようなおもちゃを男女両方に与えたりすることを提案している。以上より，両方の記事で述べられているのは，物理学における男女格差についてと，それを解消する方法なので，適切なのは④である。1つ目の記事の第2段落に生物分野では女性科学者の数に変化があり増えていることが述べられているが，物理分野についての変化はふれられていないので②は不正解。①と③については，どちらの記事でもふれられていないので，不正解。

【語句】

◇alchemist「錬金術師」

◇a small fraction of ～「～の（全体に対して）ほんの一部」

◇advanced degree「上級学位」（修士号など）

◇outnumber「～より数が多い」

◇lose out on ～「～（＝好機など）を見逃す」

◇問5 ④ address「～に取り組む〔対処する〕」

第6問

全訳 あなたは，日本の法定運転年齢を16歳に下げるべきかどうかについてのエッセイに取り組んでいます。あなたは以下のステップに従います。

ステップ1：法定運転年齢に関するさまざまな見解を読み，理解する。

ステップ2：法定運転年齢を16歳に下げることに対しての立場を明確にする。

ステップ3：追加の資料を用いてエッセイの概要を作成する。

［ステップ1］さまざまな資料を読む

筆者A（交通警察官）

運転年齢を16歳に下げることは，とても慎重に考える必要があります。道路での安全が最も重要なことです。16歳で運転が許される米国のデータによると，若いドライバーの方が事故を起こしやすいです。多くの場合，彼らは最善の判断をするのに十分な運転経験や人生経験を積んでいません。例えば，友だちと一緒にいておしゃべりしていることが多いので，いつも運転に集中しているとは限らず，これは安全ではありません。若い人たちに運転をさせる前に，私たちは本当に注意深くなる必要があります。ティーンエイジャーが本当にそのような大きな責任を負う準備ができているのかどうか考えなければなりません。

筆者B（高校生）
もし16歳で運転できれば，もっと自立できるでしょう。つまり，より早く大きな責任を負えるようになります。それは，大人が重要なことに関して私たちを信頼していると示すことになるでしょう。運転できるようになれば，自分であちこち移動できるようになるし，家族にも役立ちます。それに，私たちはすでにバイクに乗れます。車があればもっと便利になるでしょう。私たちにはまだ早いと思っている年配の人もいるけれど，私たちは科学技術に強いです。また，今は自動車はずっと安全になっています。自動車は私たちが安全に運転することさえ助けてくれます。私たちは上手に運転して，安全でいられるようになると思います。

筆者C（自動車学校の教官）
私はティーンエイジャーに運転を教えています。年齢は，良い教え方をすることほど重要ではないと考えています。若者が良い運転教習を受ければ，安全に運転できるようになります。彼らは注意深く，危険を察知し，常に交通ルールを守る方法を理解する必要があります。より若い人たちに運転をさせるのであれば，これらの良い教習を受けさせることが非常に重要です。高校でもプログラムを導入することができますし，家族も手助けできます。そうすることで，彼らが安全に運転できる準備ができるのです。正しい教育を受ければ，ティーンエイジャーも大人と同じように安全に運転できると思います。

筆者D（保護者）
私の16歳の息子が運転できたら便利だと思います。いろいろな場所に連れて行く必要がなくなるし，彼が運転して私をあちこち連れて行くことができるでしょう。でも不安があります。運転は単に車を操るだけではありません。ドライバーは素早く考え，安全な選択をする必要があります。ティーンエイジャーは運転中，スマートフォンを使ってソーシャルメディアをチェックしたり，動画を見たりと，危険なことをしたくなることがあります。そのため，彼らが運転することの意味を本当に理解しているのか疑問に思います。彼らは道路に目を向け続ける覚悟ができているのでしょうか。これは私にとって大きな懸念です。

筆者E（日本の自動車販売員）
米国では多くの若者が車を運転し，大いに家族の役に立っています。日本においてもこのことを検討すべきです。確かに若いドライバーが事故を起こすこともあります。しかし，日本には良い自動車学校があります。若い人たちにもっと注意深くなるよう教えることができます。若いからといって安全を守れないわけではありません。これは経済にとっても良いことでしょう。若者の運転が増えれば中古車がもっと売れるし，若者はもっと旅行に行くかもしれません。私たちは，この考えと社会にとっての利点について真剣に考えるべきです。

［ステップ２］立場を決める
あなたの立場：日本での法定運転年齢を16歳に下げるべきではない。
●筆者［27］と［28］はあなたの立場をサポートする。
●２人の筆者の主な論拠：［29］。

［ステップ３］資料ＡとＢを用いて概要を作成する
あなたのエッセイの概要：

日本の法定運転年齢を16歳に下げるのは良い案ではない

導入
法定運転年齢の引き下げは若者により多くの自由を与えるだろうが，運転年齢は変更すべきではない。

本論
理由１：[ステップ２より]
理由２：[資料Ａに基づいて]……… ［30］
理由３：[資料Ｂに基づいて]……… ［31］

結論
日本の法定運転年齢は現行のままであるべきだ。

資料A
日本が法定運転年齢を下げるべきではない理由がいくつかある。ティーンエイジャー，特に18歳未満の若者がまだ脳の重要な発達段階にあることは一般的に認められている。これは，危険性の評価や意思決定などの分野で最も顕著で，若者，特に新人ドライバーが交通事故を起こしやすいというデータの説明になるだろう。これは自動車保険料に深刻な影響を与える。もちろん，若者はより多く支払わなければならない。日本がより若い人たちに自動車を運転させるようになれば，保険会社はその費用の決め方を再検討しなければならなくなるだろう。保険料が上がるのは確実である。保険料が高くなった結果，家族や若者は車を持つことが難しくなるかもしれない。つまり，法律を変えることは裕福な家庭にしか受け入れられない可能性があるのだ。これはまた，若い人たちにもっと自由を与えるために運転させるという考えにも反する。このような理由から，この選択をするには注意が必要だ。なぜなら，それが若者やその家族にとって物事を難しくし，さらなる社会の分断につながる可能性があるからである。

資料B

ニューリバティ相互保険とSADD（破壊的な決断に反対する学生たち）によるアメリカの1,700人以上のティーンを対象に実施された2012年の調査によると，若者が最良の意思決定者ではないかもしれないのは事実だが，それがすべて彼らの責任ではないかもしれない。多くのティーンエイジャーは，保護者の悪い運転態度を真似しているだけかもしれないのである。

ニューリバティ相互保険 / SADD 2012年ティーン運転調査		
	保護者の運転態度（ティーンの観察による）	ティーンの運転態度（自己申告）
運転中に携帯電話で話す	91%	90%
スピード違反をする	88%	94%
メールのやりとり	59%	78%
シートベルトなしでの運転	47%	33%
アルコールの影響下での運転	20%	15%
マリファナの影響下での運転	7％	16%

問1　**25**　②

「筆者CとEはともに［25］と言及している。」

①「規則を変えることは，国にとって他の利益にもつながる可能性がある」

②「ドライバーとしていかに安全であるかは，年齢だけに関係するわけではない」

③「日本の効果的な教育制度は，子供たちが早く成熟するのに役立っている」

④「運転年齢を16歳に下げることは，家族の助けになる」

筆者Cの意見の第2～3文にI believe that age is less important than good teaching. If young people get good driving lessons, they can learn to drive safely.（年齢は，良い教え方をすることほど重要ではないと考えています。若者が良い運転教習を受ければ，安全に運転できるようになります。）と書いてある。また，筆者Eの意見の第6文にJust because you are young, it doesn't mean you can't be safe.（若いからといって安全を守れないわけではありません。）とある。共通しているのは「安全運転は年齢だけに関係するわけではない」ということで，②に一致する。筆者Eは運転年齢引き下げの経済効果に言及しているが，筆者Cは書いていないので①は不正解。安全運転についての教育効果は両者とも言及しているが，子供の成熟については書かれていないので③も不正解。④に言及しているのは筆者Eだけなので不正解。

問2　**26**　②

「筆者Bは［26］と示唆している。」

①「多くの保護者は子供の運転技術を信頼している」

②「ティーンエイジャーの科学技術を扱う力は，今日のより安全でより自動化された自動車に対応する能力を備えている」

③「現代の車に搭載されている進化した安全機能が，若者の自立心を高めている」

④「若者はバイクに乗るよりも車の運転にやりがいを感じている」

ティーンエイジャーである筆者Bは，第7文後半でwe are good with technology（私たちは科学技術に強い）と書いている。さらに現代の自動車についてAlso, cars are much safer now. They even help us drive safely.（また，今は自動車がずっと安全になっています。自動車は私たちが安全に運転することさえ助けてくれます。）と続けている。最終文でI think we can learn to drive well and be safe.（私たちは上手に運転して，安全でいられるようになると思います。）とまとめているが，これは「科学技術を扱う力があり，安全運転を助けてくれる自動車を上手に運転できるからだ」と考えられる。この内容を簡潔にまとめた②が正解。筆者Bの意見に①の内容は書かれていない。安全機能と自立心の関係についてもふれていないので③も不正解。また，バイクと自動車の運転のやりがいについて比較はしていないので④も不正解。

問3 27 ① 28 ④ （順不同）
29 ③

「さて，あなたはさまざまな見解を理解した上で，法定運転年齢を16歳に下げることについての立場を決め，以下のように書いた。[27]，[28]，[29]を完成させるのに最も適当な選択肢を選びなさい。」

「[27]と[28]の選択肢（順不同）」

①「A」
②「B」
③「C」
④「D」
⑤「E」

「日本での法定運転年齢を16歳に下げるべきではない。」という立場をサポートする意見を選ぶ。5人の運転年齢引き下げについての意見を見ていこう。

筆者A：第1文にLowering the driving age to 16 needs to be thought about very carefully.（運転年齢を16歳に下げることは，とても慎重に考える必要があります。）と書き，運転年齢引き下げに賛成できない理由を挙げている。

筆者B：16歳から運転することのメリットを挙げたあと，若者が科学技術に長けていることを理由に，最終文でI think we can learn to drive well and be safe.（私たちは上手に運転して，安全でいられるようになると思います。）と書いている。

筆者C：最終文でI think with the right education, teenagers could drive just as safely as adults.（正しい教育を受ければ，ティーンエイジャーも大人と同じように安全に運転できると思います。）と書いている。

筆者D：前半で運転年齢引き下げのメリットを挙げているが，最後の部分でThis makes me wonder if they really understand what it means to drive. Are they ready to keep their eyes on the road? This is a big concern for me.（そのため，彼らが運転することの意味を本当に理解しているのか疑問に思います。彼らは道路に目を向け続ける覚悟ができているのでしょうか。これは私にとって大きな懸念です。）と，運転年齢引き下げに懸念を示している。

筆者E：第1文で米国の若者による運転の普及について書き，第2文でWe should consider this for Japan too.（日本においてもこのことを検討すべきです。）と続けている。また，若者が運転することによる社会への利点を挙げている。

以上から，運転年齢引き下げに賛成していないのはAとDなので，①と④が正解。

「[29]の選択肢」

①「統計が，法定運転年齢の引き下げに反対する最も重要な証拠を提供している」
②「運転の過程は，16歳が適切に理解するには複雑すぎる」
③「若者は車の運転中に集中力を失う可能性が大人より高い」
④「若者が責任を負うことができるようになるまでに，もっと人生経験が必要である」

筆者Aと筆者Dに共通する意見を選択する問題。

筆者Aは，若いドライバーが事故を起こしやすい理由として，第5文でthey don't always concentrate on driving ..., which is not safe（…いつも運転に集中しているとは限らず，これは安全ではありません）と書いている。筆者Dは第5～6文でDrivers need to think fast and make safe choices. Teenagers can be tempted to do risky things while driving, like ....（ドライバーは素早く考え，安全な選択をする必要があります。ティーンエイジャーは運転中，…など危険なことをしたくなることがあります。）と書いている。両者に共通するのは「集中力の欠如の可能性」なので③が正解。①②については書かれておらず，④は筆者Aだけが言及しているので不正解。

問4 30 ③

「資料Aに基づき，理由2として最も適当なものは次のうちどれか。」[30]

①「若いドライバーの保険料が上がれば，彼らが脳を発達させる費用を支払うことが難しくなる。」
②「運転年齢を下げると，若いドライバーは安全運

転する能力が低いので，結果として事故率が高くなるだろう。」

③ **「保険料の増加は，より貧しい家庭により大きな影響を与える可能性があり，それはすべての人にとって公平ではない。」**

④「若者の経験不足は事故を引き起こしやすく，保険会社にとって問題である。」

資料Aの前半では「若者の方が事故を起こす可能性が高いので，運転年齢が下がれば自動車保険料が上がるだろう」と書かれている。保険料値上げの影響が第9～10文にAs a result of the higher price of insurance, families and young people could find it harder to afford a car. This means that changing the law may only be acceptable to wealthy families.（保険料が高くなった結果，家族や若者は車を持つことが難しくなるかもしれない。つまり，法律を変えることは裕福な家庭にしか受け入れられない可能性がある。），第12文後半にit could make things harder for young people and their families and lead to more division in society（それが若者やその家族にとって物事を難しくし，さらなる社会の分断につながる可能性がある）と書かれている。この内容を簡潔にまとめた③が正解。

脳の発達にかかる費用については書かれていないので①は不正解。②と④は資料Aの内容の一部だが，「法律を変えるべきでない理由」として挙げているのは，「保険料の値上げが不公平につながる」ことであるので不正解。

問5 31 ②

「理由3として，あなたは『法律を変える前に，大人の悪い運転習慣が考慮されるべきだ。』と書くことにした。資料Bに基づき，この意見を最もよくサポートする選択肢はどれか。」 31

①「保護者の40％近くがアルコールやマリファナの影響下で運転しており，これは大人の間で最もよく見られる悪い習慣の1つである。これはアルコール中毒や薬物中毒の結果かもしれない。」

② **「ティーンの4分の3より多くが運転中にメールをしたことを認め，90％より多くが制限速度を無視している。しかし，彼らの悪い運転習慣は，一般的に保護者の運転習慣と類似したパターンをたどっている。」**

③「ティーンの10人に9人が運転中に電話で話している。さらに，速度制限を無視する割合が保護者より8％高い。これは，ティーンの方がより不注意であることを示しているかもしれない。」

④「挙げられた行動の半数を超えるものにおいて，保護者はティーンより悪い行動をとっている。保護者は悪い習慣を示しており，それが良くない学習環境を作り出している。」

②の「ティーンの4分の3より多くが運転中にメールをしたことを認め，90％より多くが制限速度を無視している。」は，資料Bの表にあるSpeed（スピード違反をする）とText messages（メールのやりとり）の数値に一致する。また，資料Bの第2文にMany teenagers may just be copying their parents' bad driving behaviors.（多くのティーンエイジャーは，保護者の悪い運転態度を真似しているだけかもしれないのである。）とある。表を見ると，ティーンが見た親の行動の中でこの2つの行動の割合も高く，筆者の考察を裏付けている。したがってこの内容と一致する②が正解。保護者のアルコール・マリファナ影響下での運転は30％以下なので①は不正解。③の「ティーンが速度制限を無視する割合が保護者より8％高い」は表のSpeedの数値に一致しないので不正解。また，表を見ると保護者の方がティーンより態度が悪いのは6項目中3項目で「半数を超えて」いない。④も不正解。

【語句】

◇legal「法律の，法定の」
◇viewpoint「見解，観点」
◇outline「概要」
◇additional「追加の」
◇source「出典，情報源，資料」
◇safety「安全性」
◇responsibility「責任」
◇get around「あちこち移動する」
◇*be* tempted to *do*「…したくなる」
◇risky「危険な」
◇economy「経済」
◇freedom「自由」
◇undergo「～を経験する」
◇noticeable「顕著な」
◇risk assessment「危険性の評価」
◇have an impact on ～「～に影響を与える」
◇wealthy「裕福な」
◇go against ～「～に反する」
◇division「分断」

◇destructive「破壊的な」
◇fault「責任，欠点」
◇behavior「態度，行動」
◇parental「保護者の」
◇observe「～を観察する」
◇問１　②　*be* related to ～「～に関係する」
◇問１　③　effective「効果的な」
◇問１　③　mature「成長する」
◇問２　②　technological skill「科学技術を扱う力」
◇問２　③　safety feature「安全機能」
◇問３　①　statistics「統計（データ）」
◇問３　①　evidence「証拠」
◇問３　②　process「過程」
◇問３　③　lose focus「集中力を失う」
◇問４　appropriate「適切な」
◇問４　①　expense「費用」
◇問４　②　result in ～「（結果的に）～につながる」
◇問４　②　*be* capable of ～「～の能力がある」
◇問５　①　drug addiction「薬物中毒」
◇問５　②　ignore「～を無視する」
◇問５　③　additionally「その上，さらに」
◇問５　③　indicate that ...「…ということを示す」
◇問５　④　demonstrate「～を示す」

第７問

全訳　あなたのグループは，下記の雑誌記事の情報を使って，「ロベルト・クレメンテ・ウォーカー：アスリートそして人道主義者」というタイトルでポスター発表の準備をしています。

「ロベルト・クレメンテ賞」はスポーツマンシップと他人を助ける献身を見せたメジャーリーガーに贈られる。メジャーリーグの最初のラテンアメリカ選手の１人であるロベルト・クレメンテは，今日その運動能力だけでなく共感力および彼自身と地域社会の両方に寄り添おうとする彼の意欲でも記憶されている。

ロベルト・クレメンテ・ウォーカーは1934年８月18日にカリブ海にあるアメリカ領の島，プエルトリコのカロライナに生まれた。彼は早くから運動の才を見せ，17歳までにはプエルトリコの野球リーグのサントゥルセ・クラバースでプレーしていた。

クレメンテは前のシーズンでワールドシリーズまで進んだ著名なチーム，ブルックリン・ドジャースの目に留まった。ドジャースのスカウト，クライド・スークフォースはクレメンテについて，これまでの誰よりもうまく投げたり走ったりできると言った。1954年にクレメンテは当時としては多額の１万ドルのボーナスでドジャースと契約した。けれども，モントリオールにあるドジャースのマイナーリーグで１年間プレーしたあと，クレメンテはドラフトで他の球団も獲得できるようになった。彼はドジャースからピッツバーグ・パイレーツに移籍した。パイレーツは1954年ナショナルリーグで最下位だった。

1955年４月１日にクレメンテはパイレーツでメジャーリーグの試合に初出場した。それから５年間，クレメンテは言葉の壁や，彼のアクセントをしばしばからかうアメリカのマスコミに加えて，怪我とも戦った。記者はクレメンテの名前をアメリカっぽくしようと「ボブ」や「ボビー」と呼んだ。クレメンテはいつも，自分はラテンの名前「ロベルト」という名で通っていると礼儀正しく主張した。

やがて不調だったパイレーツは上向き始めた。1960年，素晴らしい打率でクレメンテはチームをワールドシリーズへ導き，ワールドシリーズではニューヨーク・ヤンキースを破った。続く７年間で，クレメンテは４回ナショナルリーグの首位打者になり，1966年にはナショナルリーグのMVPにも輝いた。ライトという彼のポジションで，有名な強肩のおかげでクレメンテは12年連続でゴールドグラブ賞を獲得した。彼の機敏で大胆な走塁は試合を面白くし，そのおかげでクレメンテはファンに好かれた。

クレメンテは18シーズンをパイレーツでプレーした。オフシーズンには，彼はプエルトリコ・リーグでプレーした。彼に続くことを夢見る学齢期の選手のために，彼はプエルトリコで野球教室のスポンサーもした。1971年，クレメンテはピッツバーグ（パイレーツ）が再びワールドシリーズで勝つのに貢献し，1972年には彼の前には10選手しか達成していなかった偉業である3000本安打を達成した。

その年は悲劇ももたらした。12月23日にニカラグアで地震があり，そのためクレメンテは妻や他の選手とともに援助のための資金集めを行った。物資の一部がそれを必要とする人々に渡らずに盗まれたことを聞いて，クレメンテは自分の援助物資をニカラグアに直接届けることにした。12月31日に物資用の飛行機を借り，ニカラグアへと同行するためにその飛行機に搭乗した。プエルトリコの海岸沖にその飛行機が墜落し，クレメンテはわずか38歳で亡くなった。

野球の殿堂は，通常は選手をたたえるのは引退または死亡後5年待つが，特例を認めた。1973年7月にクレメンテは（殿堂入りが）認められた最初のラテンアメリカ生まれの選手となった。

ロベルト・クレメンテ・ウォーカー：アスリートそして人道主義者

■ロベルト・クレメンテの生涯

年代	出来事
1934－1954	クレメンテはプエルトリコでスポーツをして育った ↓ 32 ↓ 33 ↓ 34
1955－1973	35 ↓ 36 ↓ クレメンテは飛行機の墜落で死亡した

■野球の素晴らしい才能

▶野球におけるクレメンテの技術はさまざまな方法で認められた。 37 38

■クレメンテのボランティア活動

▶1年のうちメジャーリーグでプレーしない時期は，クレメンテはよく 39 のが見られた。
▶彼の最後の人道的な活動： 40

問1 32 ⑤ 33 ③ 34 ④ 35 ② 36 ①

「あなたのグループのメンバーはクレメンテの生涯における重要な出来事を挙げた。空欄 32 ～ 36 にそれらが起こった順に出来事を入れよ。」

①「クレメンテは3000本安打に達した11番目の選手となった」

②「クレメンテはパイレーツがワールドシリーズで優勝するのを助けた」

③「クレメンテはブルックリン・ドジャースとの契約書にサインをした」

④「クレメンテはピッツバーグのメジャーリーグチームにドラフトで獲得された」

⑤「クレメンテはサントゥルセ・クラバースの一員だった」

記事の第2段落最終文by the age of 17, ... the Santurce Crabbers（17歳までには…サントゥルセ・クラバースでプレーしていた）（⑤）→第3段落第3文In 1954, Clemente was signed by the Dodgers（1954年にクレメンテはドジャースと契約した）（③）→第3段落最終文He was taken from the Dodgers by the Pittsburgh Pirates（彼はドジャースからピッツバーグ・パイレーツに移籍した）（④）→第5段落第2文In 1960, with ... the New York Yankees.（1960年，素晴らしい打率でクレメンテはチーム（＝パイレーツ）をワールドシリーズへ導き，ワールドシリーズではニューヨーク・ヤンキースを破った。）（②）→第6段落最終文in 1972, he made ... achieved before him（1972年には彼の前には10選手しか達成していなかった偉業である3000本安打を達成した）（①）という順番。したがって，⑤，③，④，②，①の順が正解。

問2 37 38 ②，④

「 37 と 38 に入れてポスターを完成させるのに最も適切な選択肢を2つ選べ。（順不同）」

①「あるアメリカの記者はクレメンテを史上最高の選手と呼んだ。」

②「クレメンテは最後には野球殿堂入りした。」

③「クレメンテはパイレーツでプレーするための多額のボーナスをもらった。」

④「クレメンテは送球で12回も受賞した。」

⑤「クレメンテはナショナルリーグで7回首位打者になった。」

クレメンテの野球に関する正しい逸話を表すものを選ぶ。①は第4段落第3文に記者がクレメンテをボブ，ボビーと呼んだという記述はあるが，史上最高の選手と呼んだという記述はない。②は最終段落最終文にClemente was the first player born in Latin America to be admitted（クレメンテは（殿堂入りが）認められた最初のラテンアメリカ生まれの選手となった）とあるから正しい。③は多額のボーナスで契約したのはパイレーツではなくドジャース（第3段落第3文）。④は第5段落第4文にClemente's famously strong arm earned him twelve straight Gold Glove Awards（有名な強肩のおかげでクレメンテは12回連続でゴールドグラブ賞を獲得した）とあるから正しい。⑤は第5段落第3文にOver the next seven years, Clemente won four National League batting titles（続く7年間で，クレメンテは4回ナショナルリーグの首位打者になった）とあるが，7回首位打者になったわけではない。以上より，正解は②と④。

問3 39 ③

「1年のうちメジャーリーグでプレーしない時期には，クレメンテはよく［39］のが見られた。」

①「プエルトリコの自宅で妻を手伝う」

②「彼を愛するピッツバーグのファンと会う」

③「子供たちのために野球の練習会を開く」

④「地元モントリオール近くの若手チームと活動する」

設問の「1年のうちメジャーリーグでプレーしない時期」は記事の第6段落第2文のDuring the off-season（オフシーズンの間）に当たる。第3文にHe also sponsored baseball lessons in Puerto Rico for school-aged athletes（学齢期の選手のために，彼はプエルトリコで野球教室のスポンサーもした）とあるので③が正解。妻を手伝う，ファンと会うなどの記述はないので①，②は不正解。モントリオールは1954年に入団したドジャースのマイナーリーグがある場所であり，オフシーズンにそこでプレーしたという記述はないから④も不正解。

問4 40 ⑤

「［40］に入れてポスターを完成させるのに最も適切な選択肢を選べ。」

①「クレメンテは飛行機墜落のあとで人々を助けるためのお金を集めた。」

②「クレメンテは1972年の地震のあとでニカラグアの清掃を手伝った。」

③「クレメンテは飛行機墜落の犠牲者の医療費を支払った。」

④「クレメンテはニカラグアで学校支援のチャリティの試合をした。」

⑤「クレメンテは援助物資が盗まれるのを防ぐため，自分で援助物資を人々に運ぼうとした。」

クレメンテの最後の人道的活動が問われている。最後の活動は第7段落で紹介されている。12月23日にニカラグアで地震があり，クレメンテは妻や仲間とともに援助のお金を集めた。支援物資が盗まれると聞き，自分が直接届けることにした。物資用の飛行機を借り（rentは使用料を払って借りることを表す），ニカラグアへ向かった。その飛行機が墜落し彼は亡くなった，とあるので，⑤が正しい。クレメンテ自身が飛行機墜落で亡くなり，ニカラグアには到着していないから①，②，③，④は正しくない。よって，正解は⑤。

【語句】

◇dedication「献身」

◇athleticism「運動能力」

◇stand up for ～「～に味方する」

◇celebrated「有名な」

◇be up for grabs「手に入る」

◇assert that ...「…と主張する」

◇straight「連続して」

◇follow in *one*'s footsteps「～の足跡をたどる〔跡を継ぐ〕」

第8問

全訳 あなたは，ソーシャルメディアの私たちへの影響を勉強しています。あなたはこのテーマについてもっと知るために，次のオンライン記事を読むつもりです。

ソーシャルメディアは写真や動画のような情報を共有することを楽しめる，ある種のスペースを提供してくれる。このようなやり方で，私たちはオンラインで自分自身を表現し，他人と簡単に関わり合うことができる。企業や，国の大統領やよく知られた有名人などのVIPは，ソーシャルメディアで自分たちを宣伝したり，世間の反応を見る機会を得たりしている。言うまでもなく，ソーシャルメディアは世界中で使用されている最も便利で影響力のあるコミュニケーション手段の1つである。

ソーシャルメディアは楽しくて便利な一方で，一部の人々はそれらに悩まされている。メッセージが読まれたのに無視されたことがわかった時に，いらいらする人もいる。ソーシャルメディアでもっと注目を集め，他人と差をつけることを求める強い願望に支配されている人々もいる。そのような人は他人の反応に期待しすぎていて，このことが彼らに常にストレスを感じさせている。これらの状態はすべて，いわゆる「ソーシャルメディア疲れ」と呼ばれる症状である。

2019年に，週に1回以上ソーシャルメディアを閲覧または投稿する日本人が感じるソーシャルメディア疲れについての調査があった。それは女性が男性よりもこの疲労を感じやすいことを示している。20代の女性の約3人に2人がソーシャルメディア疲れを経験したことがある。40代の女性の半数以上がソーシャルメディア疲れを感じているが，それは20代の女性ほど多くはない。30代の女性よりも50代の女性の方がより多くソーシャルメディア疲れを経験している。60代の女性はソーシャルメディアについてストレスを感じる可能性が最も低い。

どうすれば不必要な疲労を感じることなくソーシャルメディアとうまく付き合うことができるのだろうか？　基本的に，ソーシャルメディアへのアクセスを制限することが効果的である。例えば，ソーシャルメディアの使用は1日1時間以内にするようにすべきだろう。さらに，ソーシャルメディア以外の目標や趣味を見つけるのがよい。加えて，ソーシャルメディアでしか知らない人々よりも，現実の友達を大切にすべきだ。

ソーシャルメディアから自分を遠ざけることとは別に，自分自身を客観的に観察する能力はソーシャルメディア疲れを軽減するのに役立つ。ソーシャルメディアにストレスを感じる人々は，自分がそれらに夢中になっていることに気づくのが難しいと思っている。だから，自分が置かれている状況を把握すれば，問題により上手に対処できるようになる。この能力は人生のあらゆる状況に当てはまり，何らかの困難に直面した時にはいつでも自分自身を助けてくれるであろう。

一部の人々にとって，ソーシャルメディアは興味を引くものであふれる素晴らしいプラットフォームである。しかし，それらは単なる画面上の娯楽であり，人生における補完的なツールにすぎないという事実を認識する必要がある。確かに他人との関係を築き，インターネットで自分を表現することは重要だが，やり過ぎてはいけない。それでもソーシャルメディアを楽しみたい場合は，前向きで適切な方法でそれをすることだ。そしてそれらが日常生活や将来を脅かすかもしれないことに気づいた場合，どうすべきか？　賢明なユーザーならばそれについて何かをするであろう。

問1　41　①

「 41 によってストレスを感じるため，ソーシャルメディアを楽しめなくなっている人々もいる。」

① **「他人がどう反応するかを気にしすぎること」**

②「他人からの注目を集めすぎること」

③「受信したすべてのメッセージを読むこと」

④「オンラインで共有するための写真や動画を撮影すること」

ソーシャルメディアにストレスを感じる人々については第2段落で述べられている。第2段落第4文に，Such people expect too much from the reactions of others, and this makes them constantly feel stressed.（そのような人は他人の反応に期待しすぎていて，このことが彼らに常にストレスを感じさせている。）とある。これを短く言い換えた①が正解。

第2段落第2文に，Some feel annoyed when they know their messages have been ignored even though they have been read.（メッセージが読まれたのに無視されたことがわかった時に，いらいらする人もいる。）とあり，自分が受信したメッセージをすべて読むことではなく，相手に自分のメッセージを無視された時にストレスを感じる人もいるということなので，③は不正解。第2段落第3文に，Others are ruled by a strong desire to seek more attention and distinguish themselves from others on social media.（ソーシャルメディアでもっと注目を集め，他人と差をつけることを求める強い願望に支配されている人々もいる。）とあり，他人に注目されることではなく，他人にもっと注目してもらいたいと思うことでストレスを感じる人もいるということなので，②も不正解。④のようなことは書かれていないので不正解。

問2　42　①

「あなたはこの文章の中の調査にある女性についての情報を要約している。グラフの空欄(A)～(D)に入れるのに最も適切な組み合わせはどれか。」

42

(A) (B) (C) 30代の女性 (D)

① **「(A)　20代の女性　(B)　40代の女性　(C)　50代の女性 (D)　60代の女性」**

②「(A)　20代の女性　(B)　40代の女性　(C)　60代の女性　(D)　50代の女性」

③「(A)　40代の女性　(B)　20代の女性　(C)　50代の女性　(D)　60代の女性」

④「(A)　40代の女性　(B)　20代の女性　(C)　60代

の女性　(D)　50代の女性」

第3段落第1文によると，調査は「週に1回以上ソーシャルメディアを閲覧または投稿する日本人が感じるソーシャルメディア疲れ」についてのものである。第3文以降に女性の年代別の割合が説明されているので，グラフに当てはめていけばよい。ヒントとなる箇所は以下のとおり。

・第3段落第3文：About two out of every three women in their 20s have experienced social media fatigue.（20代の女性の約3人に2人がソーシャルメディア疲れを経験したことがある。）→(A)は「20代の女性」。

・第3段落第4文：More than half of women in their 40s suffer from social media fatigue, which is not as many as women in their 20s.（40代の女性の半数以上がソーシャルメディア疲れに苦しんでいるが，それは20代の女性ほど多くはない。）→(B)は「40代の女性」。

・第3段落第5文：More women in their 50s experience social media fatigue than do women in their 30s.（30代の女性よりも50代の女性の方がより多くソーシャルメディア疲れを経験している。）→(C)は「50代の女性」。

・第3段落第6文：Women in their 60s are the least likely to feel stressed about social media.（60代の女性はソーシャルメディアについてストレスを感じる可能性が最も低い。）→(D)は「60代の女性」。したがって①が正解。

問3　43 ・ 44　③，④

「あなたが読んだ記事によると，次のうち正しいものはどれか。（2つの選択肢を選べ。順序は問わない。）」 43 ・ 44

①「有名人はソーシャルメディア疲れを経験する可能性が最も低い。」

②「ソーシャルメディアの利用を制限することはソーシャルメディア疲れを悪化させる可能性がある。」

③「ソーシャルメディアに没頭しないことがソーシャルメディア疲れを軽減するよい方法だ。」

④「距離を置いて自分を見ることが日常の問題への対処に役立つ。」

⑤「女性は男性よりも現実の友達を大切にする傾向がある。」

第4段落第1～2文に，How can we get along with social media without feeling unnecessary fatigue? Basically, limiting access to social media is effective.（どうすれば不必要な疲労を感じることなくソーシャルメディアとうまく付き合うことができるのだろうか？　基本的に，ソーシャルメディアへのアクセスを制限することが効果的である。）とある。これを短く言い換えた③が正解。これと反対のことを述べている②は不正解。

第5段落最終文に，This ability is true for every situation in your life and will help you whenever you face some difficulty.（この能力は人生のあらゆる状況に当てはまり，何らかの困難に直面した時にはいつでも自分自身を助けてくれるであろう。）とある。「この能力」とは同段落の第1文にある the ability to observe yourself objectively（自分自身を客観的に観察する能力）のこと。これらを短く言い換えた④も正解。

第1段落第3文に，Companies and VIPs, such as presidents of nations and well-known celebrities, are advertising themselves and getting opportunities to see the public's reaction on social media.（企業や，国の大統領やよく知られた有名人などのVIPは，ソーシャルメディアで自分たちを宣伝したり，世間の反応を見る機会を得たりしている。）とあるが，有名人とソーシャルメディア疲れの関連性は述べられていないので，①は不正解。第4段落最終文に，you should value your real friends more than people you know only on social media（ソーシャルメディアでしか知らない人々よりも，現実の友達を大切にすべきだ）とあるだけで，現実の友達を大切にする率の男女比については述べられていないので，⑤も不正解。

問4　45　①

「筆者の立場を述べるには，次のうちどれが最も適切か。」 45

①「筆者は，バランスがソーシャルメディアの健全な使用の秘訣であると信じている。」

②「筆者は，ソーシャルメディアが友情を築く上で重要な役割を果たすことを強調している。」

③「筆者は，自分を表現するためにソーシャルメディアをより上手に使用することを推奨している。」

④「筆者は，ソーシャルメディアが将来も興味深いコンテンツを提供し続けるのだろうかと疑問に思っている。」

段落ごとの概要は以下のとおり。
・第1段落：我々はソーシャルメディアで，自分自身を表現し，他人とやり取りできる。それは最も便利で影響力のあるコミュニケーション手段の1つである。
・第2段落：ソーシャルメディアは楽しくて便利な一方，「ソーシャルメディア疲れ」を感じる人もいる。
・第3段落：週に1回以上ソーシャルメディアを閲覧または投稿する日本人が感じるソーシャルメディア疲れについての調査結果。
・第4段落：アクセスを制限することが，ソーシャルメディア疲れをなくす効果的な手段である。またソーシャルメディアでしか知らない人々よりも，現実の友達を大切にすべきだ。
・第5段落：自分自身を客観的に観察する能力はソーシャルメディア疲れを軽減するのに役立つだけでなく，人生のあらゆる場面でも役立つ。
・第6段落：ソーシャルメディアは素晴らしいが，やり過ぎてはいけない。前向きで適切な方法で付き合い，それらが日常生活や将来を脅かすかもしれないことに気づいた場合，何かすべきである。

以上から，全体を通して，ソーシャルメディアは便利なツールだが行き過ぎるとストレスの原因になり得ることを指摘し，ソーシャルメディア疲れに注意してそれをバランスよく使用することを推奨しているので，①が正解。

第4段落で，ソーシャルメディアでしか知らない人々よりも，現実の友達を大切にすべきであると述べているので，②は不正解。自分を表現するためにソーシャルメディアを使用することは第1段落で少しふれているのみなので，③は不正解。④のような内容は述べられていない。

【語句】

◇interact with ～「～と関わり合う」
◇celebrity「有名人」
◇handy「便利な」
◇distressed「苦しんでいる」
◇annoyed「いらいらした」
◇ignore「～を無視する」
◇distinguish O from ～「Oを～と区別する」
◇fatigue「疲れ；疲労」
◇apart from ～「～は別として；～とは別に」
◇grasp「～を把握する」
◇nothing more than ～「～にすぎない」
◇complementary「補完的な」
◇threaten「～を脅かす」
◇問4 ② essential「不可欠な」

リーディング模試　第２回　解答

第1問小計	第2問小計	第3問小計	第4問小計	第5問小計	第6問小計	第7問小計	第8問小計

合計点	/100

問題番号(配点)	設問	解答番号	正解	配点	自己採点
第１問(6)	1	1	①	2	
	2	2	③	2	
	3	3	①	2	
第２問(10)	1	4	②	2	
	2	5	④	2	
	3	6	①	2	
	4	7	②	2	
	5	8	④	2	
第３問(9)	1	9	①	3※	
		10	③		
		11	②		
		12	④		
	2	13	④	3	
	3	14	③	3	
第４問(12)	1	15	①	3	
	2	16	④	3	
	3	17	③	3	
	4	18	④	3	

問題番号(配点)	設問	解答番号	正解	配点	自己採点
第５問(16)	1	19	①	3	
	2	20	④	3	
	3	21	②	4	
	4	22	③	3※	
		23	④		
	5	24	①	3	
第６問(18)	1	25	④	3	
	2	26	④	3	
	3	27 ～ 28	①-③	3※	
		29	③	3	
	4	30	③	3	
	5	31	④	3	
第７問(15)	1	32	③	4※	
		33	④		
		34	①		
		35	②		
	2	36 ～ 37	①-③	4※	
	3	38	①	3	
	4	39 ～ 40	③-④	4※	
第８問(14)	1	41	③	4	
	2	42	④	3	
		43	①	3	
	3	44 ～ 45	④-⑥	4※	

（注）　1　※は，全部正解の場合のみ点を与える。
　　　　2　-(ハイフン)でつながれた正解は，順序を問わない。

第1問

全訳　あなたは市立図書館のウェブサイトを閲覧して，次のお知らせを見つけました。

コンウェイ市立図書館が提供する，ティーンエイジャーのための学校休暇週間のプログラム

コンウェイ市立図書館は，学校の休暇週間に，ティーンエイジャーのための特別プログラムを開設します。これまでの経験や背景知識は必要ありません。あなたの関心に最も沿うプログラムに参加してください。

全プログラムが無料です。図書館カードだけをお持ちください！

日付	プログラム	時間
2月18日	**ミステリーブック・クラブ** お気に入りのミステリー作品や作家について論じます。	午前11時－午後1時
	プログラミング工房* プロのプログラマーが，ゲームを通じてプログラミングを教えてくれます。	正午－午後2時
2月19日	**体を動かそう！** モダンダンサーのニキ・タジマが簡単でかっこいいダンスの動きを教えてくれます。	午前10時－正午
2月20日	**折り紙の時間*** 日本人の図書館司書カナコと一緒に折り紙を学びます。	午後1時－午後2時
	宇宙飛行士に会おう 宇宙飛行士ブルース・ワンは，国際宇宙ステーションで5年間を過ごしました。彼の驚くべき話を聞いて，質問しましょう！	午後1時－午後3時
2月21日	**ASLを学ぶ** アメリカ式手話を使ってのコミュニケーションを学びます。	午前10時－正午
2月22日	**映画の夕べ** 短い無声映画を何作か見ます。	午後5時－午後7時

*これらのプログラムには，事前の申し込みが必要です。501-333-XXXXまでお電話ください。各プログラムについてより詳しく知るには，プログラム名をクリックしてください。

問1　1　①

「このお知らせの目的は［ 1 ］ことだ。」

①「近く開催される特別イベントについて告知する」

②「ティーンエイジャーが何に興味を持っているのかたずねる」

③「人々に毎週の活動を思い出させる」

④「図書館カードの発行を申請するよう人々に告げる」

お知らせはSchool Vacation Week Programsの開催の告知で，5日間に行われる7つのプログラムを表にして紹介している。①はこのプログラムをupcoming special eventsと言い換えており，これが正解。ティーンエイジャー向けのプログラムで，「各自の関心に最も沿うプログラムに参加するように」と述べられているが，彼らの関心をたずねてはいないので，②は不正解。学校の休みに合わせた特別プログラムの告知であり，定例の活動の周知が目的ではないので，③も誤り。「持参するのは図書館カードだけでよい」という旨の説明はあるが，その発行申請については何も述べられていないので，④も不可。

問2　2　③

「その1週間，ティーンエイジャーは［ 2 ］ことができる。」

①「主に午前中の活動に参加する」

②「1日に複数のプログラムに参加する」

③「いろいろな分野の専門家に会う」

④「地元の図書館でボランティア活動をする」

18日午後のプログラムではコンピュータープログラミングのプロ，19日にはモダンダンサー，20日午後には宇宙飛行士に会うことができる。21日の手話の講習でも，手話の専門家が指導してくれると期待できる。これらのことから，③が正解と判断するのが妥当である。7つのプログラム中，午前から行われるのは3つで半数以下なので，①は正解とはならない。18日と20日には2つのプログラムが行われるが，いずれも時間帯が重なっているので，両方に参加することはできない。よって②も誤り。図書館でのボランティア活動についてはふれられていないので，④も不可。

問3 3 ①

「『プログラミング工房』に参加したい場合は，3 必要がある。」

①「図書館に電話をして登録する」
②「プログラミングを学んだ経験がある」
③「特別料金を支払う」
④「午後3時に図書館を訪ねる」

表を見ると，Programming StudioとOrigami timeの2つのプログラム名に*印が付いている。表の下には，*印とともに，These programs require you to sign up in advance.（これらのプログラムには，事前の申し込みが必要です。）とあり，電話番号が併記されている。したがって，①が正解。告知の第2文にNo prior experience or background knowledge is required.（これまでの経験や背景知識は必要ありません。）とあるので，②は誤り。表の上にAll programs are free of charge.（全プログラムが無料です。）とあるので，③は不正解。午後3時では，正午～午後2時のこのプログラムは終了しているので，④も誤り。

【語句】

◇prior「前もっての」
◇free of charge「無料で」
◇International Space Station「国際宇宙ステーション」（15ヵ国が共同運用する有人宇宙施設）
◇ASL (American Sign Language)「アメリカ式手話言語」
◇問1 ① upcoming「やがて起こる」

第2問

全訳 あなたは学校の英字新聞の編集者です。イギリスから来た留学生のティムが新聞に記事を書きました。

英語に加えて，もう1つ外国語を学びたいですか。日本のある大学で行われた調査によると，そこの学生の約4分の1が韓国語を学んでいます。これは，ドイツ語を学ぶ割合の20%よりも高いです。しかし，最も学習者の多い言語は中国語です。

なぜ彼らはこれらの言語を学ぶことを選択するのでしょうか。調査では，いくつかの理由が述べられています。
・その言語や文化に興味がある
・もう1つの外国語を学ぶ必要を感じている
・より多くの仕事の機会を得たい
第二外国語を学ぶ，さまざまな目的や目標があります。韓流のポピュラー音楽やドラマの大ファンだから韓国語を学ぶ人もいます。就職活動をする時に有利になるように中国語を熱心に学習する人もいれば，ただ海外旅行をする時に，現地の言葉で人とコミュニケーションを取りたいという人もいるかもしれません。

私はというと，平安時代の文学に興味を持ち，日本語を学ぶことにしました。概して，日本語は欧米人にとって最も学ぶのが難しい言語の1つです。なぜなら，漢字も日本語の仮名もすべて覚えるのは非常に難しいからです。いずれにせよ，言語を習得するには多くの時間と努力が必要ですが，やってみる価値があります。外国語を学ぶことは新しい世界への扉を開きます。2つ以上の言語を学べば，さらに広い世界を体験できます。物事を異なる角度から見ると，それをより深く理解することができるでしょう。

問1 4 ②

「調査を行った学生の間の，第二外国語の人気に関して，**最も高いものから最も低いもの**へ言語の順位を表したものはどれか。」 4

①「中国語—ドイツ語—韓国語」
②「中国語—韓国語—ドイツ語」
③「ドイツ語—中国語—韓国語」
④「ドイツ語—韓国語—中国語」
⑤「韓国語—中国語—ドイツ語」
⑥「韓国語—ドイツ語—中国語」

調査結果（3つの言語を学習する学生の割合）は，ティムの記事の第1段落に書かれている。第2文後半から第3文 about a quarter of the students there are learning Korean. This is higher than the proportion learning German（学生の約4分の1が韓国語を学んでいます。これは，ドイツ語を学ぶ割合よりも高いです）とあり，韓国語＞ドイツ語とわかる。次の文に the language with the most learners is Chinese（最も学習者の多い言語は中国語）とあるので，中国語＞韓国語と判断できる。したがって，中国語－韓国語－ドイツ語の順に並べた②が正解。

問2　5　④

「ティムの記事によると，［5］から第二外国語を学習している学生もいる。」

①「その言語を簡単に学ぶことができる」

②「大学で試験を受けなければならない」

③「他国の困難な状況を知る必要がある」

④**「文化を理解したい」**

ティムの記事の第2段落に，調査からわかった外国語を学ぶ理由が書かれている。1つ目の Have an interest in the language or culture（その言語や文化に興味がある）を「文化を理解したい」と言い換えた④が正解。「簡単に学ぶことができるから第二外国語を学習する」という記述はないので，①は不正解。また「大学で試験を受ける」「他国の困難な状況を知る必要がある」という目的も記事には書かれていないので，②③も不正解。

問3　6　①

「調査からわかったことを最もよく示している発言は［6］である。」

①**『ビジネスでは中国語がかなり重要だと考えられている。』**

②『英語は常に最も人気のある言語である。』

③『アジア人にとって欧米の言語は学ぶのが難しい。』

④『多くの言語を話すと尊敬されるだろう。』

ティムの記事の第1・2段落に調査結果が書かれている。第1段落最終文に the language with the most learners is Chinese（最も学習者の多い言語は中国語です）とあり，その理由の1つが第2段落第8文に Some study Chinese hard in order to have an advantage when job hunting（就職活動をする時に有利になるように中国語を熱心に学習する人もいる）と書かれている。ここから「仕事をする上で中国語が重要だと考えている人がいる」と判断できる。したがって，①が正解。英語の人気に関する記述はないので②は不正解。第3段落第2文に Japanese is one of the most difficult languages for Westerners to learn（日本語は欧米人にとって最も学ぶのが難しい言語の1つです）という内容はあるが，「アジア人に欧米の言語が難しい」という記述はないので，③も不正解。第3段落第5文でティムは If you learn more than one, you can experience an even broader world.（2つ以上の言語を学べば，さらに広い世界を体験できます。）と書いてあるが，「尊敬される」とは書いていないので，④も不正解。

問4　7　②

「多数の言語を学ぶことに関するティムの意見を最もよく要約しているのはどれか。」［7］

①「お金と労力がかかりすぎる。」

②**「他の視点を得ることに役立つ。」**

③「欧米諸国で働くのに必要である。」

④「日本人にとってあまり難しくない。」

問題文の learning multiple languages（多数の言語を学ぶこと）と同じ意味を表すのは，第3段落第5文の If you learn more than one（2つ以上の言語を学べば）である。言語を学ぶことによって，you see things from different angles（物事を異なる角度から見る）と続けているが，これを gain other points of view（他の視点を得る）と言い換えた②が正解。第3段落第3文に it takes a lot of time and effort to master a language（言語を習得するには多くの時間と努力が必要です）とあるが，「お金がかかる」ことについては言及していないので①は不正解。③④について，ティムは意見を述べていないので，不正解。

問5　8　④

「この記事に最もふさわしいタイトルはどれか。」［8］

①「どうしたらよい職業に就けるか。」

②「英語を習得するために何をするべきか。」

③「どの言語を学ぶべきか。」

④**「なぜ第二外国語を学ぶのか。」**

記事の段落ごとの概要は以下の通り。

・第1段落：ある日本の大学での，英語以外にどの言語を学習しているかの調査結果。

・第2段落：学生が，学習する外国語を選んだ理由（言語や文化への関心・必要性を感じたから・就職活動のため等）

・第3段落：ティムの意見

(1)自分が日本語を学習する理由

(2)言語の習得は時間と労力がかかってもする価値がある

(3) 2つ以上の言語を学ぶことでさらに世界が広がり，異なる視点が持てる

上記のようにまとめると，大学生の調査結果から「英語以外に第二外国語を学ぶ理由」がわかり，ティムの意見からティムが「2つ以上の言語を学ぶことは価値がある」と考えている理由がわかる。したがって，④「なぜ第二外国語を学ぶのか」がタイトルとして適切である。第2段落に学生が挙げた理由の1つとして「外国語を学習すれば就職活動に有利」とあるが，記事全体の主題ではないので①は不正解。英語学習に関する記述はないので②も不正解。記事にいくつかの言語名があげられているが，どの言語を学ぶべきかは話題にされていないので，③も不正解。

【語句】

◇editor「編集者」
◇aside from ～「～の他に；～に加えて」
◇according to ～「～によると」
◇survey「調査」
◇proportion「割合」
◇necessity「必要」
◇have an advantage「優位に立つ」
◇era「時代」
◇generally speaking「概して」
◇Chinese character「漢字」
◇A as well as B「AもBも」
◇*be* worth *doing*「…する価値がある」
◇angle「角度」
◇問1　in terms of ～「～に関して」
◇問1　popularity「人気」
◇問4　summarise　(= summarize)「～を要約する」
◇問4　multiple「多数の」
◇問4 ②　point of view「視点」

第3問

全訳　あなたは留学情報誌で，以下の話を見つけました。

贈り物を受け取る時のこつ

アンディ・ウェイ（国際学生アドバイザー）

贈り物は中国の文化の中で重要な役割を果たしている。贈り物を受け取るのは簡単なことのように思えるかもしれないが，適切な礼儀を知らないと，贈る側を傷つけることにもなり得る。

イザベルはオーストラリアからの交換留学生だった。彼女は初めのうちは内気で，異国の地でどうやって友人を作ったらよいかわからなかった。互いに自国の言葉を教え合うことができるように，私は彼女を中国人の学生ミンと引き合わせることにした。イザベルとミンはすぐに親友になり，イザベルは中国の縁故社会での生活に慣れた。イザベルの中国語はとても上達して，彼女はいくつかの学生団体に加入した上に，本学で自身の団体も設立した。

イザベルがオーストラリアに帰国する数週間前に，ミンは自宅での夕食にイザベルを招いた。イザベルは親友の家族と会うのを待ちきれなかった。彼女は夕食と楽しい会話を堪能した。イザベルが帰る時間になった時，ミンの父がイザベルに，リボンで飾られた箱を手渡した。うれしい驚きに，イザベルは受け取るとすぐに箱を開けた。それは，中国の昔ながらのくしだった。ミンの母は，「取るに足りないものですが。」と言った。イザベルは微笑んで「ええ，それにとても軽いわ。」と言った。

数日後，ミンがイザベルに両親はあの夜のことで気分を害していると伝えた。ミンは，贈り物の背後にある気持ちよりも贈り物そのものに関心があるように見えるので，イザベルはすぐに贈り物を開けるべきではなかったと説明した。それに，贈り主が贈り物について謙遜した言葉を言ったら，受け取った側はそれを否定して，どれほど素晴らしいかを述べるのが当然だというのである。イザベルは心苦しくなり，自分は無知だと思った。しかし，この経験によって，イザベルは中国文化をもっと学びたいと思った。彼女は今，オーストラリアの大学で，中国の歴史と文化の講座を履修していると知らせてくれた。

問1　9　①　10　③　11　②　12　④

「次の感情（①～④）をイザベルが経験した順番に並べなさい。」

①「自信に満ちた」
②「恥ずかしい」
③「興奮した」
④「興味を持った」

イザベルの様子を，順を追って見ていくと，第2段落第2文で，She was shy at first（彼女は初めの

うちは内気だった）とある。第4～5文では，ミンを紹介されてから，Isabel got used to life in Guanxi. Isabel's Chinese improved so much she joined student organizations and even started her own at our university.（イザベルは中国の縁故社会での生活に慣れ，中国語はとても上達して，いくつかの学生団体に加入した上に，本学で自身の団体も設立した）とある。選択肢の形容詞ではconfident（自信に満ちた）が当てはまる。第3段落ではミンの家に招かれ，第2～3文で，Isabel couldn't wait to meet her best friend's family. She enjoyed dinner and a nice conversation.（イザベルは親友の家族と会うのを待ちきれなかった。彼女は夕食と楽しい会話を堪能した。）とある。第5文では，帰り際に贈り物をもらうというPleasantly surprised（うれしい驚きの）な出来事もあり，選択肢にある形容詞ではexcited（興奮した；大喜びの）が当てはまる体験をしている。第4段落では，意図せず礼を欠いた振る舞いをしていたことを教えられ，第4文にあるように，felt terrible and ignorant（心苦しくなり，自分は無知だと思った）となる。選択肢にある形容詞ではembarrassed（恥ずかしい）が当てはまる。しかし第5文で，イザベルは気を取り直し，that experience made Isabel want to learn more about Chinese culture（この経験によって，イザベルは中国文化をもっと学びたいと思った）と前向きになって，大学で勉強をしている。interested（興味を持った）な状態だと言える。以上より，「(内気な→)自信に満ちた→興奮した→恥ずかしい→興味を持った」（①→③→②→④）が正解。

問2　13　④

「イザベルの贈り物の受け取り方が中国では適切でないのは，受け取る側が［13］ように見えるからだ。」

① 「怒っている」
② 「感謝している」
③ 「拒否している」
④ 「無作法な」

第4段落第2～3文が該当箇所。まずミンは，贈り物をその場で開けるべきでなかった理由として，because it made her seem more interested in the gift itself rather than the thought behind it（贈り物の背後にある気持ちよりも贈り物そのものに関心があるかのように見えるので）と述べている。また，贈り主が謙遜したらthe receiver is expected to deny it, saying how wonderful it is（受け取った側はそれを否定して，どれほど素晴らしいかを述べるのが当然だ）と説明している。これらを端的に言えば，イザベルのしたことが「礼を欠いていた」と言えるので，④が正解となる。②は「感謝している」という意味で，適切でない理由にはなり得ない。「怒っている」ようだったり「拒否している」ようだったりする振る舞いとは言えないので，①③はいずれも不適切。

問3　14　③

「この話から，あなたはイザベルが［14］ことを学んだ。」

① 「ミンの家族に贈り物を持っていくのは適切でないだろうと思ったので，持っていかなかった」
② 「中国でのルールに従った適切な振る舞いを，ミンの家に行く前に教わった」
③ 「中国滞在の初めの頃に，ウェイ氏からミンに紹介された」
④ 「ミンの家族からもらった贈り物が小さかったので，あまりうれしくなかった」

第2段落第2～3文に，She (=Isabel) was shy at first and did not know how to make friends in a foreign country. I (=Andy Wei) decided to match her up with a Chinese student Ming（彼女（＝イザベル）は初めのうちは内気で，異国の地でどうやって友人を作ったらよいかわからなかった。私（＝アンディ・ウェイ）は彼女を中国人の学生ミンと引き合わせることにした）とある。したがって，③が正解。イザベルがミンの家族に贈り物を持参することを検討したかどうかは不明なので，①は不適。第4段落第2～3文から，ミンの家に行ったあとに，中国での適切な贈り物の受け取り方を知ったので，②も不適。ミンの家族から贈り物をもらったことについて，第3段落第5文で，Pleasantly surprised（うれしい驚きに）とあることから，イザベルは喜んでいるとわかるので，④も不適。

【語句】

◇art「こつ；要領」
◇match ～ up with ...「～を…と組み合わせる」
◇get used to ～「～に慣れる」
◇Guanxi「グワンシィ」（中国社会に特徴的な人的ネットワーク・人間関係）
◇immediately「すぐに；ただちに」

◇upset「気分を害した；取り乱した」
◇shouldn't have *done*「…するべきではなかった」
◇humble「謙遜した；謙虚な」
◇deny「～を否定する」

第４問

全訳 英語の授業で，あなたはこの学校を良くするための提案についてエッセイを書いています。これはあなたの最新の草稿です。今は先生からの助言を読んだあと，推敲に取り組んでいるところです。

未来の生徒のために授業をいかに改善するか

私たちの学校は適切に運営されており，安全で健全な学習環境を提供し，そこで学ぶ大半の生徒が満足していると思う。とはいえ，クラス（編成）や授業の構成にいくつかの変化が加えられれば，学習は今以上に効果的になるだろう。

まず，学校には，もっと個々人に合った学習計画を提供してほしい。例えば，一部の生徒は放課後に塾に通っているが，これはもっぱら大学入試対策のためだ。*(1)* [15] もしこの学校に個々の生徒のニーズに合った集中コースがあれば，生徒全員に役立つものとなるだろう。

第二に，*(2)*私たち自身のためのクラスで学べるようにすべきだ。現在，習熟度別クラスがあるのは数学だけである。でももし，例えば英語や社会，国語などの科目でも，議論やグループワークを自分と同じくらいのレベルの生徒とできるとしたら，授業でもっと自信をもって発言したり，積極的になったりすることができるだろう。

私の最後の提案は，課題を各生徒の実力に合うように設計してほしいということだ。つまり私は先生たちに，生徒それぞれの学業成績に合わせて，中身の難易度がもっと調節された授業を用意してほしいのである。*(3)* [17] 課題が易しすぎたり難しすぎたりしなければ，全員がもっと進歩やモチベーションを感じられるだろう。

私たちの学校は，学力の面で言えば，今でも優れた学校だ。しかし，私たちにはそれぞれ得意もあれば不得意もある。私は，選択制の授業がもっとあれば，そして*(4)*生徒がもっと平等だったら，すべての生徒にとってより効果的で望ましい経験となるだろうと感じている。

コメント

(1) もっと説明が必要です。何を言いたいのか明確になるようにここに何か付け足しなさい。
(2) 何を言いたいのか不明瞭です。ここにもっと適切な表現を書きなさい。
(3) ここに接続表現を挿入しなさい。
(4) この部分はあなたの主張を十分に要約していません。変更しなさい。

総合的なコメント

非常に興味深い考えを持っていますね。全生徒の学校生活を改善する方法について，明確かつ慎重に考えている点が素晴らしい。

問１ 15 ①

「コメント(1)に基づいて，付け加えるのに最も適当な文はどれか。」[15]

①「その一方，自学自習に苦労している生徒もいる。」
②「反対に，ここにはレベルの低い生徒もいる。」
③「他方，先生たちは平均的な生徒の助けになっていない。」
④「それでも，自学自習によって学習はより効果的になるだろう。」

(1)を含む第２段落で筆者は，more individual learning plans（もっと個々人に合った学習計画）を求め，暗に現行の学習計画が画一的で，各生徒のニーズを満たしていないことを示唆している。続いて大学入試対策のために塾に通う一部の生徒の存在に触れ，(1)を挟んで，「集中コース」の創設が生徒全員に役立つものとなるだろうと段落を結んでいる。「生徒全員に役立つ」と主張するからには，(1)に「塾に通っている生徒とは別の生徒」への言及が必要である。受験対策とは別のニーズの存在を示す①を挿入して，各種「集中コース」の必要性を訴えるのが最も論理的。①が正解。②，③，④はいずれも，前後の文を論理的につなぐことができない。

問２ 16 ④

「コメント(2)に基づいて，より明瞭な表現はどれか。」[16]

①「生徒一人一人のために作られた」
②「自分たちで勉強できる」

③「もっと生徒の少ない」

④**「自分の学力レベルと合った生徒たちから成る」**

「私たち自身のための（クラス）」という表現では意味が不明瞭というのが先生の指摘。第3段落での筆者の主張は，現行では数学のみに導入されているclasses based on ability（習熟度別クラス）を他教科にも導入してほしい，ということ。習熟度別クラスを言い換えた④が正解。①は間違いとは言えないが，筆者が個人ごとにオーダーメイドを望んでいるのは次の段落のテーマである「課題」についてである。②は自学自習のことで筆者の主張に合わず，③のクラスの人数について筆者は話題にしていない。

問3 17 ③

「コメント(3)に基づいて，用いるのに最も適当な表現はどれか。」 17

①「手始めに」

②「さらに」

③**「このようにして」**

④「他方」

この段落で筆者は，まず第一文で，課題を各生徒に合ったものにしてほしいとの希望を述べ，In other words（つまり）とつないで要求の具体的内容を記している。そして(3)のあとでは，その要求が実現した場合の帰結について予想している。こうしてほしい⇒「このようにして」望ましい結果が得られるだろう，とするのが自然な論理展開なので，③が正解。もし①For a start（手始めに）を入れるなら，そのあとに具体的な提案が必要となる。また②Furthermore（さらに）でつなぐなら，前で述べた内容への補足や新しい追加情報が必要だが，(3)のあとにそれに該当するものはない。④は対比を示す接続表現で，ここでは不適であるから，①，②，④は不正解。

問4 18 ④

「コメント(4)に基づいて，置き換えるのに最も適当なのはどれか。」 18

①「生徒がクラスを選べた」

②「生徒に一律の課題が課された」

③「生徒が難しい授業で助けを得られた」

④**「生徒が自分のレベルに応じて授業を受けられた」**

最終段落はエッセイ全体の結論を述べる役割を果たしており，下線部(4)を含むこの一文は，筆者がここまでに述べてきた論の要約となっている。この文の従属節は，if there were more optional classes and (4),（選択制の授業がもっとあれば，そして(4)ならば，）となっている。つまり，このif節で，筆者は自分の要求・希望をまとめようとしている。(4)の直前で第2段落で述べた「集中コース」の話をしているから，(4)では第3・4段落で述べた，「習熟度別クラスの拡大」と「各生徒に合った課題の設定」をまとめればよい。④が正解。according to 〜は，「〜によると」と情報源を示す意味とは別に，ここでのように「〜に応じて，〜にしたがって」という意味もあることは押さえておこう。①や③は本文で述べられておらず，②は筆者とは反対の主張である。

【語句】

◇run「〜を運営する」
◇structure「構成；仕組み」
◇individual「個人の；各自の；個人」
◇cram school「塾，予備校」
◇for the sole purpose of 〜「もっぱら〜を目的として」
◇intensive「集中的な；徹底的な」
◇meet *someone's* needs「〜のニーズを満たす」
◇benefit「〜の役に立つ；〜に利する」
◇speak up「発言する」
◇assignment「課題；宿題」
◇tailor「〜を（要求・必要などに）合わせて作る」
◇suit「〜に合う，適合する」
◇depending on 〜「〜次第で；〜に応じて」
◇academic「学問の；学業の」
◇in terms of 〜「〜に関して言えば」
◇optional「選択制の」
◇問1 ① have a hard time with 〜「〜で苦労する」
◇問1 ③ average「普通の；平均的な」
◇問4 ④ according to 〜「〜に応じて；〜にしたがって」

第5問

全訳 あなたは若者の睡眠パターンについて研究しています。あなたは2つの記事を見つけました。

ティーンエイジャーの睡眠パターン

シャロン・ジョーンズ 記

睡眠は誰にとっても重要だが，とりわけティーンエイジャーにとっては重要である。というのは，彼らの脳は急速で劇的な発育変動を経るからである。睡眠中には，神経結合が強化され，情報が短期記憶から長期記憶に移される。したがって，睡眠不足は学生に，日中の疲労感をもたらすだけでなく，学業不振をも引き起こす。さらに，夜間によく眠ると，脳細胞の，論理的思考や意思決定といった高レベルの思考を司っている部分が活性化する。

一連の研究によって睡眠の恩恵が明らかになっているにもかかわらず，大部分の学齢期の子供やティーンエイジャーは十分な睡眠をとっていない。2015年のある研究によると，専門家が勧める一晩に８時間半の睡眠をとっているのは，ティーンエイジャーのうちわずか15パーセントにすぎない。グラフに示されている，推奨されている睡眠時間と実際の平均的な睡眠時間との隔たりは，憂慮すべき現実を明らかにしている。

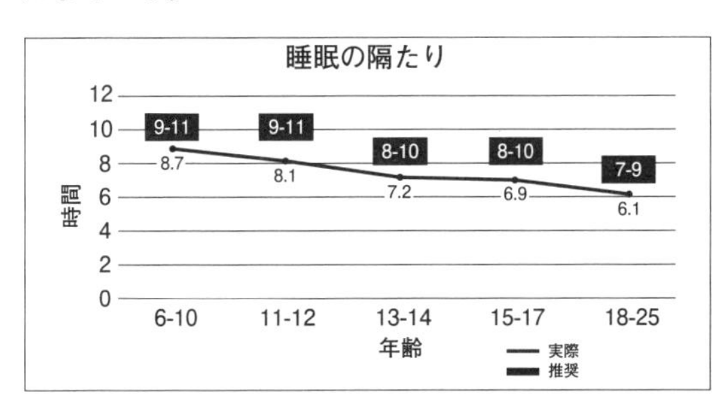

ある大規模な調査によると，ティーンエイジャーの睡眠時間は常に減り続けている。1990年代の初めには，15歳の約52パーセント，18歳の36パーセントが，一晩に7時間以上寝ているという調査結果だった。しかし，2011年～2012年の調査では，それぞれ43パーセント，33パーセントに減少した。

状況を悪化させているのは，ティーンエイジャーの睡眠に対する誤った考えである。彼らの多くが，徹夜をしたり夜更かしをしたりするのがかっこいいと思っているように見受けられる。若者たちは，それが健康的な習慣ではないということを知り，悪循環を断ち切る方法を学ぶ必要がある。

『ティーンエイジャーの睡眠パターン』への回答

イーサン・B記

私は校医として，過去10年間にわたって，ますます多くの学生が睡眠に関連する問題を抱えるのを見てきた。近頃の学生は，宿題，課外活動，その他のすべきことのために，以前より忙しくなっている。それに加えて，今はソーシャルメディアがあり，そのために彼らは，コンピューターのディスプレイやスマートフォンに夜遅くまで向かっている。

睡眠不足には数えきれない悪影響がある。学習能力の低下は，シャロン・ジョーンズ氏が述べた通り，深刻な問題だ。学生が，授業についていけない，成績が下がったといった報告をしてきた時，その学生はしばしば睡眠の問題を抱えている。しかし，私は，それ以上に行動と心理に関わる諸問題を見てきた。学生は睡眠が足りないと，より攻撃的になり，友人たちとの付き合いに問題を生じさせるようだ。また，ストレスや不安を感じやすくなる。

ジョーンズ氏の記事によれば，私の見ている年齢層の学生たちは毎晩，少なくとも８時間の睡眠が必要であるのに，平均の夜間睡眠時間はこの推奨値より１時間以上も少ないとのことだった。親と教師は，睡眠の重要性について，もっとよくティーンエイジャーを教育しなければならない。それと同時に，私たちは，若者たちが健康的な睡眠習慣を確立するのを手助けする必要がある。一定の就寝時刻と起床時刻をきちんと決めることが，その第一歩だ。リラックスできる睡眠環境，つまり暗く，涼しくて静かな環境を整えることもやるべきだ。

問１　19　①

「シャロン・ジョーンズも校医も言及していないのは，［19］である。」

① **「睡眠不足を原因とする安全性の低下」**

② 「ティーンエイジャーの睡眠時間の変化」

③ 「ティーンエイジャーの睡眠へのソーシャルメディアの影響」

④ 「睡眠中に脳内で起こること」

「述べられていないこと」を選ぶ問題。シャロン・ジョーンズの記事の第３段落で1990年代初めと2011～2012年の睡眠時間の比較がされているので，②は誤り。イーサン・Bの記事の第１段落第３文に Besides, they now have social media, which has ... late into the night.（それに加えて，今はソーシャルメディアがあり，…夜遅くまで向かっている。）とあるので，③も不可。睡眠中に脳内で起こることについては，シャロン・ジョーンズの記事の第１段落第２文で，「神経結合が強化され，情報が短期記憶から長期記憶に移される」と述べられており，④も不正解。睡眠不足により安全性が低下するという話は，ここでの２つの記事では述べられていないので，①が正解となる。

問２　20　④

「校医は主として年齢が 20 の人たちを見ている。」

①「６歳から10歳」

②「11歳から12歳」

③「13歳から14歳」

④「15歳から17歳」

校医は記事の第３段落冒頭で，Ms. Jones' article showed that while those in my students' age group need at least eight hours of sleep every night, their average night sleep is over an hour less than the recommendation.（ジョーンズ氏の記事によれば，私の見ている年齢層の学生たちは毎晩，少なくとも８時間の睡眠が必要であるのに，平均の夜間睡眠時間はこの推奨値より１時間以上も少ないとのことだった。）と述べている。これは，ジョーンズ氏の記事にあるグラフを見て述べられていることだと判断できる。グラフを見ると，「８～10時間の睡眠」を推奨されている年齢層が２つあるが，「13～14歳」は実睡眠時間が7.2時間で，その差が0.8時間。「15～17歳」では実睡眠時間が6.9時間で，その差は1.1時間。すなわち，④が正解となる。

問３　21　②

「記事によると，睡眠は若者の 21 によい影響を与える。（最も適切な選択肢の組み合わせを選びなさい。）」

a「複雑な思考」

b「食べ物の選択」

c「精神の健康」

d「親との関係」

シャロン・ジョーンズの記事の第１段落最後の文に，a good night's sleep activates cells in a part of the brain which is responsible for higher-level thinking such as reasoning and decision making（夜間によく眠ると，脳細胞の，論理的思考や意思決定といった高レベルの思考を司っている部分が活性化する）とあり，これがaに当てはまると考えられる。また，イーサン・Bの記事の第２段落の最後の２文にWhen students do not get enough sleep, they seem to become more aggressive and have trouble getting along with their friends. They also get easily stressed and anxious.（学生は睡眠が足りないと，より攻撃的になり，友人たちとの付き合いに問題を生じさせるようだ。また，ストレスや不安を感じやすくなる。）とある。これは「睡眠不足による精神面への悪影響」で，裏を返せばcに当てはまる。２つの記事ともに，睡眠と食べ物との関係には言及がないので，bは誤り。親の果たすべき役割について，イーサン・Bの記事の第３段落第２文に「親と教師が睡眠の重要性についてもっとティーンエイジャーを教育すべきだ。」とはあるが，睡眠が親子関係に及ぼす影響については述べられていないので，dも不可。したがって正解の組み合わせは，②。

問４　22　③　23　④

「シャロン・ジョーンズは若者たちが 22 と述べ，校医は若者たちが 23 と述べている。（それぞれの空欄には異なる選択肢を選ぶこと。）」

①「生物学的に，寝るのが遅くなりがちだ」

②「病気のリスクがより高い」

③「睡眠不足について誤った意見を持っている」　22

④「睡眠を改善するために，大人の助けが必要だ」　23

⑤「性急に判断を下しがちだ」

シャロン・ジョーンズは第４段落第１～２文でWhat makes the situation worse is teens' improper attitudes towards sleep. Many seem to think that it is cool to pull an all-nighter or stay up late.（状況を悪化させているのは，ティーンエイジャーの睡眠に対する誤った考えである。彼らの多くが，徹夜をしたり夜更かしをしたりするのがかっこいいと思っているように見受けられる。）と述べている。これを端的にまとめた③が 22 に当てはまる。 23 は，イーサン・Bの記事の第３段落第２～３文でParents and teachers must do a better job educating teens about the importance of sleep. At the same time, we need to help our youngsters establish healthy sleep habits.（親と教師は，睡眠の重要性について，もっとよくティーンエイジャーを教育しなければならない。それと同時に，私たちは，若者たちが健康的な睡眠習慣を確立するのを手助けする必要がある。）と述べており，④がこれに当てはまる。若者の夜更かしについて，生物学的な根拠があるとは述べられていないので，①は不可。健康によくないという指摘はあるが，具体的な疾病のリスクについてはふれられていないので，②も正解ではない。⑤は一般的な若者論に出てきそうな意見だが，ここでの話には関係ないので不可。

問5　24　①

「あなたは両方の記事の情報に基づいて，宿題のレポートを書く。レポートに最も ふさわしい題名は『24』であろう。」

① **「不十分な睡眠パターンはティーンエイジャーにどのような影響を与えるか」**

②「睡眠パターンは年齢によって異なる」

③「ティーンエイジャーの生活様式の変化と夜更かしをする理由」

④「睡眠の観点から解き明かすティーンエイジャーの不思議な脳」

どちらの記事も，ティーンエイジャーが概して睡眠不足であり，その状況が改善されなければならないことを訴えており，イーサン・Bの記事には，具体的な提言もある。したがって，選択肢の中では①が最も妥当。幼児や成年，中高年，老人の睡眠パターンについては言及がないので，②のタイトルでレポートを書くのは無理である。生活様式の変化と夜更かしの理由も付随的に述べられていることなので，③のタイトルもふさわしくない。脳の話は，あくまでも睡眠の必要性，睡眠不足の害の詳細としてふれられており，④のようなことは述べられていない。

【語句】

◇neural connection「神経結合」
◇strengthen「～を強くする」
◇transfer「～を移動させる」
◇short-term memory「短期記憶」
◇long-term memory「長期記憶」
◇insufficient「不十分な；不足している」
◇consistently「一貫して」
◇respectively「それぞれ；各々」
◇improper「間違った；不適切な」
◇extracurricular activity「課外活動」
◇social media「ソーシャルメディア」(インターネット上のSNS，ブログなど)
◇negative consequence「負の結果；よくない結果」
◇behavioral「行動に関する」
◇psychological「心の；精神的な」
◇aggressive「攻撃的な」
◇consistent「一貫した；着実な」
◇問4 ① biologically「生物学的に」
◇問4 ③ insufficiently「不十分に」

第6問

全訳　あなたは，政府が不健康な食品により高い税金を課すべきかどうかについてのエッセイに取り組んでいます。あなたは以下のステップに従います。

ステップ1：不健康な食品への税金に関するさまざまな観点を読み，理解する。

ステップ2：不健康な食品により高い税金をかけることに対する自分の立場を決める。

ステップ3：追加の資料を用いてエッセイの概要を作成する。

［ステップ1］さまざまな資料を読む

筆者A（親）

親として，私は子供たちが大きくなるまでは正しい選択をするよう働きかけようとしています。もちろん，子供たちの健康を心配し，健康的な食品を与えようとしています。しかし，今では子供たちはティーンエイジャーで，友だちと一緒に過ごし，軽食や学校の昼食は自分で買っています。私は，食費にかかる高い税金の影響ではなく，学校での健康教育や私からの良い影響によって，彼らが良い選択をできるようになることを願っています。私たちは彼らを教育すべきであり，彼らの決断を強要しようとするべきではありません。だから，私はこのような税金には反対です。子供たちは自分で正しい決断をするべきです。

筆者B（医師）

科学的な証拠によれば，カロリーの摂りすぎは不健康と寿命を縮めることにつながります。医療費が上がるので，このことは個人だけではなく社会にも負担をかけます。不健康な食品に税金をかけることは，人々が食品についてより良い選択をするのに役立つと思います。現在，ジャンクフードは健康的な食品よりも安いことが多く，これがほとんどの人がジャンクフードを買う理由の1つです。今こそ，国全体の健康を向上させ，肥満に起因しない病気をより的確に治療できるように，このような税金を導入する時なのです。

筆者C（スーパーマーケット経営者）

大手スーパーマーケット・チェーンとして，私たちは人々が選べるように幅広い食品を仕入れています。

私たちは値段を安く保とうと努力していますが，多くの家庭では食費の予算に合うように注意深く買い物をしなければなりません。不健康な食品はしばしば比較的低価格で販売されており，課税によってそのような食品の値段を上げることは，比較的貧しい人々により大きな影響を与えます。私たちは，家庭が健康的な選択肢を選べるようにアドバイスやレシピを提供していますが，それはその家庭の選択であるべきです。時には，人々はごほうびとしてスイーツや高カロリー食品を食べたいと考えます。人々にはそうする自由があるべきです。

筆者D（体育教師）

子供たちが行う身体活動の量は毎年減少し，太りすぎの子供の数が増えています。これは多くの要因によるものです。理由の1つは，子供たちがより多くの時間を室内でデジタル機器で遊んで過ごしていることです。しかし，主な要因は，子供たちが昔よりも砂糖を，特に炭酸飲料で摂取するようになったことです。実際，14歳から18歳の男子は，他のどのグループよりも多くの砂糖を摂取しています。砂糖税は世界の50カ国を超える国々で実施されており，これが子供たちの健康に良い影響を与えています。

筆者E（学生）

私たちは最近このことを研究し，不健康な食品に税金をかけると良い効果があることがわかりました。「不健康な食品」に対してだけ増税するのは難しいのですが，いくつかの国では砂糖に対する課税が効果を出しています。1つの理由は，人々が砂糖の少ない選択肢（例えば，ダイエット炭酸飲料や砂糖の少ない軽食）を買うようになったことです。しかし，最大の効果は製造業者にありました。これらの国の多くの食品製造業者は，自社製品のレシピを変更しました。これにより，顧客にとってより健康的な製品を販売する助けになりました。

［ステップ2］立場を決める

あなたの立場：政府は不健康な食品により高い税金をかけるべきではない。

●筆者 27 と 28 はあなたの立場をサポートする。

●2人の筆者の主な論拠： 29 。

［ステップ3］資料AとBを用いて概要を作成する

あなたのエッセイの概要：

不健康な食品により高い税金をかけるのは良い案ではない

導入

多くの国が不健康な食品や糖分を多く含む食品への税を引き上げているが，これは健康的な食生活を奨励する最善の方法ではない。

本論

理由1：［ステップ2から］

理由2：［資料Aに基づいて］……… 30

理由3：［資料Bに基づいて］……… 31

結論

政府は不健康な食品により高い税金をかけるべきではない。

資料A

税金をかけて不健康な食品の価格を上げることで，顧客に買い物や食生活の習慣を変えるように強いることはできるが，それが唯一の方法ではない。ジャンクフードの価格を高くするよりも，健康的な選択肢の価格を下げたり，ごほうびを与えたりすることで，人々に変わろうという気を起こさせる方がよい。果物や野菜のコストを政府が一部負担することで，その価格を下げる手助けをすることもできる。最初は経費がかかるように思えるが，そうでもない。国民がより健康的な食品を食べるようになれば，悪い食生活が原因で病気になる人が減る。その結果，政府はお金を節約することさえできるかもしれない。健康的な食事を奨励するもう1つの方法は，ごほうびを与えることである。いくつかの国のスーパーマーケットでは，保護者と一緒に買い物に来る子供たちに果物を一個無料で配っている。子供にとっては，さまざまな果物のごほうびを選ぶのは楽しいもので，ある調査では，チョコレートやクッキーの代わりに果物をもっと食べようと子供たちを動機付けるのに役立ったという結果が出た。

資料B

米国のある調査で，所得層別に，砂糖入り飲料を毎日3回以上飲むと答えた成人の割合が示された。この調査は，甘い飲み物を摂取する人の割合と所得水準との間に関係があることを明確に示している。

> （グラフ）
> **所得別の加糖飲料の消費量**
> 調査回答者のパーセント
> 所得（ドル）

問1 25 ④

「筆者BとCはともに 25 と言及している。」

① 「より貧しい人々はたいてい忙しすぎて，より健康的な料理のレシピを試してみることができない」

② 「不健康な食品の価格を上げることは，貧しい人々がより健康になりうることを意味するだろう」

③ 「人々が摂取するカロリーを減らすことは，社会的コストを減らすことになる」

④ 「一般的に，不健康な食品は健康的な選択肢よりも低価格で購入される」

筆者Bは第4文で junk food is often cheaper than healthy food（ジャンクフードは健康的な食品よりも安いことが多い）と書いている。筆者Cは第3文でUnhealthy foods are often sold at relatively low prices（不健康な食品はしばしば比較的低価格で販売されており）と書いている。2人に共通するこの内容に合う④が正解。①と②の内容は本文に書かれていないので不正解。③は筆者Bの内容から類推できるが直接言及されてはいない。

問2 26 ④

「筆者Eは 26 と示唆している。」

① 「企業はもっと利益を上げるために低カロリー製品の製造コストを削減する」

② 「税金が高い国の製造業者は，元の場所から移転しようとする」

③ 「ジャンクフードに税金をかけることは，試されたほぼすべての事例で好ましい効果をあげている」

④ 「飲料の糖分に課税することで，製造業者はより健康的な製品を製造するようになる」

筆者Eの意見の後半に，いくつかの国で砂糖に課税した効果が書かれている。その中で，第5～6文に Many food producers in these countries changed the recipes of their original products. This helped them to sell a product that was healthier for customers.（これらの国の多くの食品製造業者は，自社製品のレシピを変更しました。これにより，顧客にとってより健康的な製品を販売する助けになりました。）とあり，これに一致する④が正解。①と②の内容は，書かれていない。また，「いくつかの国では効果を出しています」とあり，ほぼすべての事例で効果があったとは言えないので，③も不正解。

問3 27 ，28 ①，③（順不同）
29 ③

「さて，あなたはさまざまな観点を理解した上で，不健康な食品により高い税金をかけることについての立場を決め，以下のように書いた。27，28，29 を完成させるのに最も適当な選択肢を選びなさい。」

「27 と 28 の選択肢（順不同。）」

① 「A」

② 「B」

③ 「C」

④ 「D」

⑤ 「E」

「政府は不健康な食品により高い税金をかけるべきではない。」という立場をサポートする意見を選ぶ。

5人が課税に賛成か反対か見ていこう。

筆者A：理由を挙げたあと，最終文でThat's why I disagree with these taxes（だから，私はこのような税金には反対です）と反対している。

筆者B：最終文でIt is time to bring in these taxes to ....（今こそ…するために，このような税金を導入する時なのです。）と賛成している。

筆者C：第3文でraising the price of such foods by taxing has a larger impact on poorer people（課税によってそのような（＝不健康な）食品の値段を上げることは，比較的貧しい人々により大きな影響を与えます），最終文で They should have the freedom to do this.（そうする（＝時にはスイーツや高カロリー食品を食べる）自由があるべきです。）と書いており，課税に反対している。

筆者D：最終文にSugar taxes are used in over fifty countries around the world, and these have had a positive effect on the health of children.（砂糖税は世界の50を超える国々で実施されており，これが子供たちの健康に良い影響を与えています。）と書いてあり，課税に賛成である。

筆者E：第1文でWe recently studied this, and we

found that taxes on unhealthy food can have a positive effect.（私たちは最近このことを研究し，不健康な食品に税金をかけると良い効果があることがわかりました。）と書き，具体例をあげている。反対の立場をとるのは筆者Aと筆者Cなので，①と③が正解。

「29の選択肢」

① 「教育を通じて健康的な食生活を選択することは，変化をもたらす最も有力な方法である」

② 「健康的な食品について授業で話し合うことが，健康的なメニューと不健康なメニューのバランスをとる助けになる」

③ 「人々は自分の決断で食べるものを選択できるべきである」

④ 「健康的な食事を子供に与えられるよう，保護者が教育されるべきである」

筆者Aと筆者Cに共通する意見を選択する問題。筆者Aは第5～6文で We should educate them, not try to force their decision .... —— children should make good decisions themselves.（私たちは彼らを教育すべきであり，彼らの決断を強要しようとするべきではありません。…子供たちは自分で正しい決断をするべきです。）と書いている。筆者Cは第4～6文で We provide advice and recipes for families to choose healthy options, but it should be the choice of those families. Sometimes, people want to eat sweet or high calorie food as a treat. They should have the freedom to do this.（私たちは家族が健康的な選択肢を選べるようにアドバイスやレシピを提供していますが，それはその家族の選択であるべきです。時には，人々はごほうびとしてスイーツや高カロリー食品を食べたいと考えます。人々にはそうする自由があるべきです。）と書いている。2人に共通するのは「人々は自分の決断で食べるものを選択するべき」という意見なので，③が正解。筆者Aは教育の大切さを述べているが，筆者Cは言及していないので，①と②は不正解。④については書かれていない。

問4　30　③

「資料Aに基づき，理由2として最も適当なものは次のうちどれか。」30

① 「子供に家族が食べる食品を選ばせることは，保護者がより良い選択をする動機付けになりうる。」

② 「医療費の削減に焦点をあてることは，人々に不健康な食生活を変えるよう動機付ける効果的な方法である。」

③ 「人々に自由な選択を与えると同時に，健康的な食品を選ぶ積極的な理由を提供することが最良の戦略である。」

④ 「健康的な食品が無料でいくらか提供され，不健康な食品がより高価になれば，人々はより健康的な食生活を選ぶだろう。」

資料Aから「不健康な食品への課税引き上げは，健康的な食生活を奨励する最善の方法ではない」理由を探す。資料Aの第2文にRather than charging more for junk food, it is better to motivate people to change through reducing the cost of healthy options and by giving rewards.（ジャンクフードの価格を高くするよりも，健康的な選択肢の価格を下げたり，ごほうびを与えたりすることで，人々に変わろうという気を起こさせる方がよい。）とあり，これを「健康的な食品を選ぶ積極的な理由を提供することが最良の戦略である」と言い換えた③が正解。「子供が健康的な食品を選ぶようになった」事例は書かれているが，「家族が食べる食品を選ぶ」とは書かれていないので，①は不正解。「健康的な食事が医療費の削減につながる」ことは書かれているが，人々への動機付けに用いるとは書かれていないので②は不正解。健康的な食品を値下げする案や子供に無料で果物が与えられる例はあるが，「不健康な食品がより高価になる」とは書かれていないので，④も不正解。

問5　31　④

「理由3として，あなたは『不健康な食品により高い税金をかけることは，社会の貧しい人々に悪影響を及ぼす。』と書くことにした。資料Bに基づき，この意見を最もよくサポートする選択肢はどれか。」31

① 「加糖飲料への税の引き上げは，加糖飲料を飲む人の減少につながる。これは結局，政府がお金を稼ぐ別の方法を必要とすることになる。」

② 「最高所得層の90%を超える人が，1日に3回以上は甘い飲料を飲まない。これは富裕層が税金をより多く払っていないことを示している。」

③ 「最高所得層で，1日3回以上砂糖入り飲料を飲む人の割合は，最低所得層の割合の半分より少ない。貧しい人々はより多くの健康問題を抱えている傾向があると言える。」

④「砂糖入り飲料を１日３回以上消費する人の割合は，最低所得層で最も多い。これらの飲料に費やす収入の割合は，他のグループよりもこのグループの方が増加するだろう。」

グラフを見ると，加糖飲料を１日３回以上飲む人の割合は，最低所得層で最も多い。収入が少ないのに他の所得層よりもたくさん飲んでいるのだから，もし加糖飲料により多く課税されれば，加糖飲料に費やす収入の割合の増加分が一番多くなると言えるので，④の内容と一致する。つまり，加糖飲料に増税すると，最低所得層の負担がさらに増えるので，『不健康な食品により高い税金をかけることは，社会の貧しい人々に悪影響を及ぼす』という論をサポートする根拠になる。したがって④が正解。政府が加糖飲料の税の引き上げをする目的は税収のためとは書かれていないし，税収減による貧しい人への影響も資料Bには書かれていないので，①は不正解。②の「最高所得層の90％を超える人が，１日に３回以上は加糖飲料を飲まない」はグラフに一致するが，飲料以外の納税額は資料Bから読み取れないので，②は正しくない。③の前半の内容はグラフと一致するが，「健康問題を抱えている傾向があると言える」とまではグラフからは言えない。

【語句】

◇evidence「証拠」
◇currently「現在」
◇junk food「ジャンクフード（高カロリー低栄養の食品）」
◇bring in ～「～を導入する」
◇obesity「肥満」
◇a wide range of ～「幅広い～；さまざまな～」
◇budget「予算」
◇relatively「比較的」
◇have an impact on ～「～に影響を与える」
◇treat「ごほうび」
◇physical activity「身体活動」
◇overweight「太りすぎの」
◇factor「要因」
◇device「機器」
◇manufacturer「製造業者」
◇sugar content「糖含量；糖度」
◇motivate ～ to *do*「～に…するよう動機付ける」
◇income「所得」
◇問１ ③　consume「～を消費する；摂取する」
◇問１ ④　alternative「代替品；選択肢」
◇問２ ①　profit「利益」
◇問４ ②　focus on ～「～に焦点をあてる」
◇問４ ③　strategy「戦略」
◇問５ ④　proportion「割合」

第７問

全訳 あなたのグループは，下の雑誌記事の情報を使って，『子供向けテレビ教育番組のパイオニア』と題したポスター発表を準備しています。

1968年から2001年の間にアメリカかカナダで育った人なら誰でも，フレッド・ロジャーズの「ミスター・ロジャーズ・ネイバーフッド」を温かい気持ちで思い出すだろう。皆に愛されたテレビ・パーソナリティ，プロデューサー，作曲家，作家，聖職者のロジャーズは，生涯を子供たちに捧げ，何百万もの人の人生に感動を与えた。

フレッド・マクフィーリー・ロジャーズは，1928年３月20日，ピッツバーグの近くのペンシルベニア州ラトローブで生まれた。彼はフロリダ州のロリンズ大学を1951年に卒業した。学位は作曲である。初めて就職したのは，ニューヨークにある全国ネットの一流テレビ局NBCだったが，商業テレビ局は幼い視聴者に害を及ぼしていると彼は考え，辞めてしまった。1953年，ロジャーズは，アメリカ初のコミュニティテレビ局WQEDで働くためにピッツバーグに戻った。彼は，「ザ・チルドレンズ・コーナー」という番組を制作した。1960年代初期，ロジャーズはカナダのトロントに招かれて「ミステロジャーズ」という子供向け番組を作り，これはロジャーズの後の制作の基礎を形成した。ロジャーズはピッツバーグに戻り，1966年に「ミスター・ロジャーズ・ネイバーフッド」を開始した。この番組は２年後に公共放送網（PBS）で全国放送が開始され，その後40年間続いた。

「ミスター・ロジャーズ・ネイバーフッド」は，当時のどんな子供向けテレビ番組とも違っていた。ロジャーズは，子供向け番組がたいてい騒々しく，テンポが速くて，暴力的であることが我慢ならなかった。「ミスター・ロジャーズ・ネイバーフッド」において，ロジャーズの使命は，子供たちを敬意を持って扱い，あるがままに受け入れることによって，彼らの人生を豊かにするすることだった。彼は気持ちを伝えるために，視聴者に直接話しかけ，自作の歌を歌い，指人形を使った。それは，ゆっくりしていて，費用がかからず，ローテクなやり方だった。さらに，この番組は離婚や戦争，死といった深刻な問題を扱った。ロジャーズは，子供たちが人生の負の側面を理解するのを助けることは，大人の責任だと信じていた。この番組の変わっていて重要なもう１つの特徴は，マイノリティのひき入れ方である。1960年代には，多くの白人が黒人と一緒に水泳プールに入ることを公然と拒否していた。ロジャーズはそれをばかげていると考え，番組で自分が番組のレギュラーキャラクターの１人と一緒に小さなプールで足を洗う台本を書いたが，そのキャラクターのクレモンズ警官を演じていたのは，アフリカ系アメリカ人の歌手だった。

ロジャーズは，テレビの外の世界にいる子供たちと家族の擁護者でもあった。1969年，リチャード・ニクソン大統領が公共放送の財源を削減することに決めた。「ミスター・ロジャーズ・ネイバーフッド」も公共放送の一番組であった。ロジャーズはワシントンDCに行き，なぜ彼の番組のような番組が子供たちにとって必要なのか，情熱的なスピーチを行った。彼の真摯で力強い言葉が2,000万ドルをもたらし，PBSは救われた。ロジャーズはまた，子供と大人両方のために30冊を超える本を書いた。ロジャーズは，大統領自由勲章をはじめ，あらゆる大きな賞を受けた。

「ミスター・ロジャーズ・ネイバーフッド」が成功したにもかかわらず，類似の番組は現れていない。大多数の子供向け番組は，沈黙よりもアクションを選び，ロジャーズが彼の番組で毎回取り組んだ微妙な話題にはめったにふれない。けれども，彼が残した真の遺産は，彼が子供たちに，自分自身でいられる安全な居場所を提供し，一般の人々に子供への最もよい関わり方を教えるためにマスメディアを使った，その使い方である。彼が生涯を通じて差し伸べてきた，とてつもないほどの優しさ，誠実さ，そして愛は，今も生き続けている。

子供向けテレビ教育番組のパイオニア

■フレッド・ロジャーズの生涯

時期	出来事
1928年－1940年代	ロジャーズはペンシルバニア州ラトローブで育った。
1950年代	ロジャーズは大学を卒業した。 ↓ 32 ↓ 33
1960年代	ロジャーズはトロントで子供向け番組を制作した。 ↓ 34 ↓ 35

■「ミスター・ロジャーズ・ネイバーフッド」について

- 1968年に全国放送を開始。
- 番組は普通ではなかったが，次の理由で説得力があった。
  - ・ロジャーズはテレビを通して，視聴者に直接話しかけ，歌を歌った。
  - ・36
  - ・37

■フレッド・ロジャーズの遺産

- ロジャーズの哲学は，彼の作った次のような歌に反映されている。「ウォント・ユー・ビー・マイ・ネイバー？」「イッツ・サッチ・ア・グッド・フィーリング」，そして「38」。
- フレッド・ロジャーズは，次のような貢献のために子供向けテレビ番組のパイオニアとみなされている。
  - ・39
  - ・40

問1　32　③　33　④　34　①
35　②

「あなたのグループのメンバーが，ロジャーズの人生における重要な出来事を挙げた。**『フレッド・ロジャーズの生涯』**を起こった順番に完成させるために，5つの出来事（①〜⑤）から4つを選びなさい。」

① **「『ミスター・ロジャーズ・ネイバーフッド』が初めて放映された。」**

② **「ロジャーズは公共放送の財源を復活させるために戦った。」**

③ **「ロジャーズは商業テレビ局に職を得た。」**

④ **「ロジャーズはコミュニティテレビ局で働き始めた。」**

⑤「ロジャーズは子供たちのために50冊もの本を書いた。」

選択肢で述べられている出来事の起こった時期を文中から確認すると，次のとおりだとわかる。③第2段落第2〜3文：「商業テレビ局に職を得る」→「1951年の大学卒業後。1953年までには辞めている」，④第2段落第4文：「コミュニティテレビ局で働き始める」→「1953年」，第2段落第6文：「トロントで子供向け番組を制作する」→「1960年代初め」，①第2段落第7文：「『ミスター・ロジャーズ・ネイバーフッド』が初めて放映される」→「1966年」，②第4段落第2〜4文：「公共放送の財源を復活させるために戦う」→「1969年」。

残る選択肢⑤は，第4段落第5文に Rogers also wrote more than thirty books for both children and adults.（ロジャーズはまた，子供と大人両方のために30冊を超える本を書いた。）とあるが，子供のために何冊書いたかには言及していないので本文と一致しない。

問2　36　37　①，③（順不同）

「36 と 37 に入れて**「『ミスター・ロジャーズ・ネイバーフッド』について」**を完成させるのに最も適切な選択肢を2つ選びなさい。（順不同。）」

① **「ロジャーズは，子供たちが理解するのに助けを必要とする，人生における不愉快な問題に取り組んだ。」**

②「ロジャーズは早期教育の効果を信じていたので，子供たちに読むことと数学の技能を教えた。」

③ **「ロジャーズは，受容の実例を示すために，番組で民族的マイノリティの人々を大きく扱った。」**

④「ロジャーズは，より多くの視聴者を引き付けるために，彼の番組の最適な放送時間をつきとめた。」

⑤「ロジャーズは，子供たちを引き付けるためにアニメーションを多用した。」

「ミスター・ロジャーズ・ネイバーフッド」が風変わりでありながら説得力があった理由を示すエピソードを選び出す。第3段落第6〜7文ではthe show dealt with serious issues such as divorce, war, and death. Rogers believed that it was adults' responsibility to help children understand the negative parts of life.（この番組は離婚や戦争，死といった深刻な問題を扱った。ロジャーズは，子供たちが人生の負の側面を理解するのを助けることは，大人の責任だと信じていた。）と述べられている。①がこれを指しているので正解。同じ段落の第8文には，Another unusual and important aspect of the show is how he included minorities.（この番組の変わっていて重要なもう1つの特徴は，マイノリティのひき入れ方である。）とあり，続いて，アフリカ系アメリカ人の歌手が演じているレギュラーの登場人物と一緒に足を洗う場面を放送したことが述べられている。これが③に当てはまるので正解。読むことや数学を教えたとも述べられていないので，②は誤り。放送の時間帯についてもふれられていないので，④も正しくない。アニメーションの使用についてはふれられていないので，⑤も不正解。したがって①③が正解。

問3　38　①

「ロジャーズの歌の中の1曲は，次のうちどれの可能性が最も高いか。」38

① **「イッツ・ユー・アイ・ライク」**

②「レッツ・ノット・トーク・アバウト・イット」

③「マイト・イズ・ライト」

④「ナッシング・イズ・ゴーイング・トゥ・チェンジ」

ポスター発表の「フレッド・ロジャーズの遺産」という項目の中で，ロジャーズの哲学を反映している歌の題名として，"Won't You Be My Neighbor?"（「僕のおとなりさんにならないかい？」），"It's Such a Good Feeling"（「とてもいい気分」）と並んで紹介されるのにふさわしい題名を選ぶ。ロジャーズの遺産と哲学は，記事の最終段落第3〜4文に provide children with a safe place to be themselves and educate the public how best to relate to children（子供たちに，自分自身でいられる安全な居場所を提供し，一般の人々に子供への最もよい関わり方を教える），The tremendous level of kindness, honesty, and love（とてつもないほどの優しさ，誠実さ，そして愛）とまとめられている。これらを考え合わせると，①のIt's You I Like（僕が好きなのは君）が最もふさわしいと考えられる。②のLet's Not Talk About It（そんなことを話すのはよそう），④のNothing Is Going to Change（何も変わりはしないだろう）では，後ろ向きで暗いイメージなので，ふさわしくないと判断できる。③のMight Is Right（力は正義だ）は，ことわざの1つだが，ロジャーズの哲学とは明らかに無関係なので不正解。

問4 39 40 ③，④（順不同）

「39 と 40 に入れて**『フレッド・ロジャーズの遺産』**を完成させるのに最も適切な選択肢を2つ選びなさい。（順不同。）」

①「子供たちは，テレビの前であまりにも長い時間を過ごすのをやめた。」

②「ロジャーズは，子供向け教育テレビ番組の標準を確立した。」

③「ロジャーズは，主流と正反対のことをすることによって成功した。」

④「ロジャーズはテレビを，子供たちのためになることをするための媒体として使った。」

⑤「学校の教師たちが，授業で教育的なテレビ番組を使い始めた。」

フレッド・ロジャーズが子供向けテレビ番組のパイオニアとみなされている理由となる貢献を選べばよい。第2段落第3文で，彼が商業テレビ局に就職したがすぐに辞めたことが紹介され，その理由としてhe thought commercial TV channels were harming young viewers（商業テレビ局は幼い視聴者に害を及ぼしていると彼は考えた）と述べられている。すなわち，その後の彼が公共放送で子供向けの番組を制作したことの根底には「子供たちに対してよいことをする」という考えがあったと考えるのが妥当なので，④は正解となる。また，第3段落第1～2文には *Mister Rogers' Neighborhood* was different from any other children's television programs at that time. Rogers could not stand how children's programs were often loud, fast-paced, and violent.（「ミスター・ロジャーズ・ネイバーフッド」は，当時のどんな子供向けテレビ番組とも違っていた。ロジャーズは，子供向け番組がたいてい騒々しく，テンポが速くて，暴力的であることが我慢ならなかった。）とある。これを短く言い換えた③も正解となる。子供のテレビ視聴時間については述べられていないので，①は正解ではない。「ミスター・ロジャーズ・ネイバーフッド」の成功にもかかわらず，there has not been another show like it（類似の番組は現れていない）と，最終段落の冒頭で述べられているので，②も誤り。学校の授業での使用についてはふれられていないので，⑤も不正解。したがって③④が正解。

【語句】

◇minister「聖職者；牧師」
◇community-supported「地域に支えられた；地域密着型の」
◇foundation「基礎；土台」
◇Public Broadcasting Service (PBS)「米国公共放送網」
◇enrich「～を豊かにする」
◇inexpensive「安価な」
◇divorce「離婚」
◇minority「（民族や宗教などの）少数集団；マイノリティ」
◇*be* opposed to ～「～に反対する」
◇ridiculous「ばかげた；とんでもない」
◇African American「アフリカ系アメリカ人」
◇advocate「擁護者；支持者；提唱者」
◇genuine「誠実な；本物の」
◇Presidential Medal of Freedom「大統領自由勲章」（アメリカの文民最高位の勲章）
◇tackle「～（＝手ごわい対象）に取り組む」
◇legacy「遺産」
◇tremendous「とてつもなく大きい」
◇compelling「説得力のある」
◇philosophy「哲学」
◇問2 ① address「～に（真剣に）取り組む」
◇問2 ② effectiveness「有効性」
◇問2 ④ identify「～をつきとめる；～を見分ける」

第8問

全訳 あなたは，『世界を変えた現代の発明』というテーマで，科学プレゼンテーションコンテストのためにポスターの準備をしている学生グループに所属している。ポスターを作るために以下の一節を使っている。

バーコード

最もよく知られているタイプのバーコードである「統一商品コード（UPC)」は，世界中でほとんどの製品に見られる小さな黒と白の画像だ。企業は，売られている商品をレジで素早く識別するためにこれらのバーコードを使用する。バーコードは企業にとっても顧客にとっても同様に実用性がある。顧客の視点からは，バーコードはより迅速で便利な買い物体験を提供してくれ，企業は店舗の全在庫品を追跡・管理するためにバーコードを使用している。現在では一般的になっているが，バーコードは比較的新しい発明品だ。調査によると，バーコードは1974年6月26日にパック入りのチューインガムに初めてレジで使用された。他の企業がその利点を理解するのにそれほど時間はかからなかった。バーコードの成功は，その利便性と，どこの国でも同じ情報を提供するという事実のおかげだ。GS1という非営利の国際組織がこの運用を管理する責任を担っている。その組織は，自社の製品にバーコードが欲しいという企業からの申請を受け付けている。

「統一商品コード」には，2つの明確に異なる部分がある。店のレーザースキャナで読み取られる黒と白の「バー（棒)」と，その下にある一連の「数字」である。基本的に，この2つの部分は同じような働きをするが，バーがコンピューター用であるのに対し，数字は主に読み取り用である。

図1． バーコードの例

レーザースキャナがバーコードを読み取る時，等間隔が開けられた縦の列，言い換えれば「バー」と呼ばれるものをスキャンする。スキャナは，それぞれのバーが光を反射しているかどうかを記録する。白いバーは光を反射し，0としてコンピューターシステムに登録される。一方，黒いバーは光を反射せず，1として読み取られる。スキャンのあとで，コンピューターには95個の0か1のリストがあり，それから15の異なる区画に分類される。これらの区画のうち12の区画は，バーコードの下に見える数字を表し，残りの3つの区画は「ガード」と呼ばれている。左端に1区画，右端に1区画，そして中央に1区画だ。両端のガードは，バーコードの始点と終点をコンピューターに教え，一方中央のガードは数字が分割される位置をコンピューターに伝える。これは，コードを左から右へ読んでいるのか，それとも逆さまに読んでいるのかをコンピューターに教えるので，重要だ。中央のガードより左側のバーには奇数個の1が，右側のバーには偶数個の1があるため，このことがわかるのだ。

コンピューターがバーコードを読み取る仕組みがわかったところで，数字を見よう。*図1*を見ると，最初の数字が左側にあり，バーコードの外側に位置していることがわかる。これは「ナンバーシステムキャラクター」と呼ばれる。この数字は，どのような種類のバーコードを見ているか教えてくれる。『0』，『1』，『6』，『7』，『9』はどんな商品にも使える標準的なバーコード，『2』は果物や米のような計量品，『3』は薬のような薬品，『4』は店舗で使用するために確保されている，『5』はクーポン券などを表している。続く5つの数字が企業（製造業者）コードだ。コードを取得するために，企業はGS1に登録しなければならず，したがって，各コードは特定の企業に対して1つだけのものとなっている。2つ目の5桁の組は商品コードだ。製造業者がこのコードを独自に選定・管理し，登録する必要はない。最後に，チェックディジットがある。この数字は右端にあるが，バーにはない唯一の情報である。この数字をバーコードの残りの部分と照合することで，コンピューターがバーコードを正しく読み取ったかどうかをダブルチェックすることができる。

上記で述べてきたのは最もよく使われているタイプのバーコードにすぎないということに留意することが重要だ。このタイプ（統一商品コード）は，一般に販売されている商品で使われている。しかし，最近では多くの他の種類のバーコードがある。ウェブサイトを開くために使われるものもあれば，人を登録するために使われるもの，また，セキュリティチェックのために使われるものもある。これらの用途にはそれぞれ異なる種類のバーコードがあり，少し異なるシステムを使っている。それでも，これらのすべてのバーコードの種類は本質的に，1974年に最初に使用された基礎となる発明を基にしている。

あなたのプレゼンテーションのポスター原稿：

問1 41 ③

「ポスターの最初の見出しの下で，あなたのグループはなぜ統一商品コードが一般的に使われているのかを発表したい。記事の説明によると，以下のうちどれが最も適切か。」 41

① 「従来の商品追跡方法の，より安価な代替手段である。」

② 「製品がどのように製造されたかを理解するために使用することができる。」

③ 「企業に，在庫の商品を追跡・管理することを可能にするデータを提供する。」

④ 「顧客が何を購入したかわかる，より信頼できる方法を提供する。」

見出しの下には What are the benefits of the Universal Product Code for businesses?（統一商品コードの企業にとっての利益は何か。）と書いてある。統一商品コードの説明は第1段落にあり，「企業にとっての利益」は，第2文 Companies use these barcodes to quickly identify at checkout items being sold.（企業は，売られている商品をレジで素早く識別するためにこれらのバーコードを使用する。）と，第4文後半 companies use the barcodes to track and manage inventory in their stores（企業は店舗の全在庫品を追跡・管理するためにバーコードを使用している）と書かれている。第4文後半の内容を言い換えた③が正解。統一商品コードが「安価な代替手段である」「製造過程を理解するために使用できる」という記述はないので，①②は不正解。④は本文中に記述がなく，また企業ではなく顧客の利益であるから，ここでは不正解。

問2 42 ④ 43 ①

「あなたはガードと製造業者コードの説明を書くように頼まれた。 42 と 43 に最も適する選択肢を選びなさい。」

3本の『ガード』 42

① 「データが利用可能な時間を制限する」

② 「犯罪者がバーコードの情報を使用することを阻止する」

③ 「コンピューターに商品情報を教える」

④ 「コンピューターにバーコードの向きを教える」

ガードの説明は第3段落にあり，第7・8文で3本のガードの位置と役割が説明されている。次に，第9文に This is important because it tells the computer whether it is reading the code left to right or upside-down.（これは，コードを左から右へ読んでいるのか，それとも逆さまに読んでいるのかをコンピューターに教えるので，重要だ。）と書かれている。つまり，「ガードがコンピューターにバーコードの向きを教える」のだから，④が正解。データが利用可能な時間や，犯罪の阻止については書かれていないので，①②は不正解。また，商品情報を伝えるのは，バーコードの別の部分なので③も不正解。

製造業者コード 43

① 「バーコードの規制を担当する非営利組織」

② 「商品を売っている企業」

③「その国の政府」
④「商品を作った団体」

製造業者コードの説明は，第４段落第５～６文に The following five numbers are the company's (or manufacturer's) code. A company must register with the GS1 to get a code（続く５つの数字が企業（製造業者）コードだ。コードを取得するために，企業はGS1に登録しなければならない）とある。ここから，コードを提供するのはGS1だとわかる。GS1については第１段落の最後から２文目に A nonprofit international organization called GS1（GS1という非営利の国際組織）と説明されているので，①が正解。

問３ 44 45 ④，⑥（順不同）

「あなたは，バーコードでどのような情報が見つかるかについて説明している。記事によると，次のうち適切なもの２つはどれか。（順不同。）」 44 ・ 45

①「バーと数字の両方が３本のガードについての情報を含む。」
②「いくつかの企業が同じ製造業者コードを共有するだろう。」
③「２つ目の５桁の組は事業の種類を表している。」
④「情報の正確さを確認するために使われる数字は，バーには見つからない。」
⑤「２番目の数字は商品の重さを伝える。」
⑥「商品の種類は最初に提供される情報だ。」

選択肢の内容が本文に一致するか見ていこう。第４段落第10文 This number, found on the far right, is the only information not found in the bars.（この数字は右端にあるが，バーにはない唯一の情報である。）から，バーに見つからない数字があるとわかる。次の文に，この数字の役割が It allows the computer to double-check that it has read the barcode correctly by ....（この数字を…することで，コンピューターがバーコードを正しく読み取ったかどうかをダブルチェックすることができる）と書かれている。この２文の内容を簡潔にまとめた④は正解。第４段落第２・３文に the first number is ... this is called the "number system character." This number tells us what type of barcode we are looking at（最初の数字があり…これは「ナンバーシステムキャラクター」と呼ばれる。この数字は，どのような種類のバーコードを見ているか教えてくれる）とあり，続く文で具体例を挙げている。つまり，最初に書かれている情報（＝数字）が商品の種類を表すのだから，⑥も正解。数字とバーの関連について，第３段落第５・６文に These are then grouped into 15 different sections. Twelve of these sections represent the numbers you see at the bottom of the barcode, and the remaining three sections are called "guards."（それから15の異なる区画に分類される。これらの区画のうち12の区画は，バーコードの下に見える数字を表し，残りの３つの区画は「ガード」と呼ばれている。）とある。つまり，ガードの情報を表す数字は存在しないので，①は不正解。製造業者コードについて，第４段落第６文に A company must register with the GS1 to get a code, and as such, each code is unique to a specific company.（コードを取得するために，企業はGS1に登録しなければならず，したがって，各コードは特定の企業に対して１つだけのものとなっている。）とあるので，「企業が同じコードを共有する」という②も不正解。バーコードの後半の５桁については，第４段落第７文に The second set of five digits is the product code.（２つ目の５桁の組は商品コードだ）とあり，事業の種類ではなく，商品を示すものなので③も不正解。weight（重さ）については，第４段落第４文に a "2" is a weighed item（『２』は計量品である）とあるが，これは the first number の説明で，２つ目の数字のことではないため，重さと関係ないとわかることから，⑤も不正解。したがって④と⑥が正解。

【語句】

◇passage「抜粋；一節」
◇Universal Product Code「統一商品コード」
◇image「画像」
◇worldwide「世界中で」
◇identify「～を識別する」
◇checkout「（店の）レジ」
◇practical use「実際的な用途；実用」
◇point of view「視点」
◇inventory「在庫；全在庫品」
◇relatively「比較的」
◇convenience「利便性」
◇nonprofit「非営利の」
◇*be* responsible for ～「～の責任を負う」
◇distinct「はっきりと異なる」

◇essentially「基本的に」
◇whereas「～である一方で」
◇evenly spaced「等間隔が開けられた」
◇column「柱」
◇reflect「～を反射する」
◇represent「～を表す」
◇remaining「残りの」
◇odd「奇数の」
◇even「偶数の」
◇pharmaceutical「製薬の」
◇manufacturer「製造業者」
◇register「～を登録する」
◇as such「したがって」
◇unique「ただ１つだけの；固有の」
◇specific「特定の」
◇independently「単独で」
◇digit「（数字の）桁」
◇check ～ against ...「～を…と照合する」
◇essentially「本質的に；本来」
◇問１　heading「見出し」
◇問１　commonly「通常」
◇問１ ①　alternative「代替手段」
◇問３　make a statement「説明する」
◇問３ ④　accuracy「正確さ」

リーディング模試　第3回　解答

第1問 小計	第2問 小計	第3問 小計	第4問 小計	第5問 小計	第6問 小計	第7問 小計	第8問 小計

合計点	/100

問題番号(配点)	設問	解答番号	正解	配点	自己採点
第1問 (6)	1	1	④	2	
	2	2	③	2	
	3	3	②	2	
第2問 (10)	1	4	④	2	
	2	5	③	2	
	3	6	③	2	
	4	7	③	2	
	5	8	①	2	
第3問 (9)	1	9	③	3※	
		10	②		
		11	①		
		12	④		
	2	13	③	3	
	3	14	①	3	
第4問 (12)	1	15	①	3	
	2	16	①	3	
	3	17	①	3	
	4	18	④	3	

問題番号(配点)	設問	解答番号	正解	配点	自己採点
第5問 (16)	1	19	④	3	
	2	20	④	3	
	3	21	①	3※	
		22	②		
	4	23	④	4	
	5	24	②	3	
第6問 (18)	1	25	④	3	
	2	26	①	3	
	3	27 ～ 28	③-⑤	3※	
		29	③	3	
	4	30	④	3	
	5	31	①	3	
第7問 (15)	1	32	①	3	
	2	33	④	3	
	3	34	②	3※	
		35	⑤		
		36	③		
		37	④		
	4	38	②	3	
	5	39 ～ 40	②-③	3※	
第8問 (14)	1	41	④	3	
	2	42 ～ 43	②-⑤	4※	
	3	44	③	2	
	4	45	②	2	
	5	46	①	3	

（注） 1　※は，全部正解の場合のみ点を与える。
　　　2　-(ハイフン)でつながれた正解は，順序を問わない。

第1問

全訳 あなたは町の英語情報サイトで次の記事を見つけました。

注目のレストラン：イタリアーナ・フレスカ

うれしいお知らせです。ロッコ・ジュゼッペがイタリアーナ・フレスカ2号店のために我が町を選んでくれました。受賞歴のあるそのシェフは，我が町の有名な野菜を利用するために，この地に新しいレストランを開くことにしたのです。イタリアーナ・フレスカは，シェフのジュゼッペ自らが教える料理教室など，いくつかのイベントを主催して開店を祝う予定です。イベントは英語で行われますが，料理教室はお手本があるのでどなたにも十分わかりやすいものになるでしょう。イタリアを訪れたり，本物のイタリア料理を楽しんだりしたことがない方には，素晴らしい機会です。

スケジュール

5/1	グランド・オープニング・パーティー
5/3	講義1： イタリア旅行のための必須イタリア語
5/4	料理教室1： (1) 自家製パスタの作り方 (2) ペストゥ（野菜ソース）
5/15	講義2： イタリア人のようなジェスチャーの仕方
5/17	料理教室2： (1) イタリアンチキンの作り方 (2) イタリアのスティックパン
5/21	講義3：日本とイタリアの関係
5/23	ナポリピザの試食会

・すべてのイベントは午後3時から5時にレストランで開催されます。13歳未満のお子様のみでは料理教室にご参加いただくことはできませんが，親御様とご一緒にいらっしゃるのは歓迎致します。

・いずれかのイベントに参加された方は，当日ご注文されるディナーが50%オフになります。

イベントへの参加登録はこちらをクリック

▶▶イタリアーナ・フレスカ　公式サイト

問1　1　④

「この告知の目的は人々に 1 について知らせることである。」

①「ロッコ・ジュゼッペが教えるイタリア語教室」

②「人気イタリア料理店の新しいシェフ」

③「新しいイタリア料理店におけるその町の有名な野菜のセール」

④「新しいイタリア料理店の初めの1カ月のスケジュール」

告知文では，有名シェフのイタリア料理店の2号店が町にオープンすること（第1文），料理教室などのイベントで開店を祝うこと（第3文）が述べられている。告知文の下にはイベントのスケジュールが表で提示されており，最後には注意書きなどが載っている。スケジュールはオープニング・パーティーで始まり，5月中のほぼ1ヵ月の予定が記されている。以上より④がこの告知の目的であると考えるのが妥当。スケジュールにEssential Italian for travel through Italy（イタリア旅行のための必須イタリア語）とあるが，これは告知されているイベントの1つにすぎないから①は不正解。告知されているのは新しいシェフではなく，新しいイタリア料理店だから②も不正解。野菜のセールについては述べられていないので，③も不正解。

問2　2　③

「イベントの1つでは，参加者は 2 を習う予定である。」

①「ある種のピザの作り方」

②「イタリアの料理と文化がどのように変化しているか」

③「イタリアでよりよくコミュニケーションをとる方法」

④「旅行でお得な品を見つける方法」

イベントの具体的な内容は，告知文の下にあるスケジュールで確認できる。ピザについては5月23日に試食会があるが，作り方を学ぶ機会はなく，①は不正解。料理については作り方の教室が2回，文化については講義が3回あるが，料理や文化の変化について扱っているものはないから②も不正解。講義1のイタリア語，講義2のイタリア人のようなジェスチャーの仕方，講義3の日本とイタリアの関係を知ることはイタリアでうまくコミュニケーションをとるのに役立つと考えられる。したがって③が正解。④のお得な品を見つける方法については述べられていない。

問3 3 ②

「イベントに参加した人は 3 ことができる。」

①「他の参加者が家で作ったパスタを食べる」

②「通常より低価格で食事をする」

③「イタリアを訪れる予定の人々と出会う」

④「小学生にテーブルマナーを教える」

スケジュール下の注意書きの２つ目に，イベントに参加した人はwill receive a 50% discount on a dinner ordered the same day（当日注文するディナーが50%オフになる）とあるから，②が正解。５月４日の料理教室１では自家製パスタの作り方を習うが，他の参加者が作ったパスタを食べるわけではないから①は不正解。イタリア旅行を計画している人々については記述がないから③も不正解。スケジュールの下の注意書きの１つ目に13歳未満の子供も親についてくることはできると書かれているが，テーブルマナーに関する記述はないので④も不正解。

【語句】

◇take advantage of ～「～を利用する」

◇essential「不可欠の；必須の」

◇問２ ④ good deals「お買い得品」

第２問

全訳 あなたは環境クラブのメンバーです。メンバーが新しいボランティアイベントの計画を立てていて，あなたは提案を出すように言われています。アイデアを得るために，ある生徒が自分の学校に導入した社会奉仕プロジェクトに関するブログを読んでいます。

10分間地域チャレンジ

以前は，学校に着くと悲しくなったものです。地域にはいくつかのコンビニエンスストアやカフェがあり，缶やビン，お菓子の包装紙，ビニール袋などのゴミを人々がよく地面に落とします。昨年，私はあることをしようと決めました。１週間普段より10分早く登校して，この追加の時間をいくつかのゴミを拾うのに使うように生徒たちに頼むポスターを貼りました。これがうまくいきました！毎日平均150人の生徒（学校の10%）が参加しました。そのうちの３分の１近くが１週間を通して参加しました。先生も数人いました。３日以内で，学校の周辺の地域はすでにはるかにきれいになっていました。終わりの頃には完璧になりました。驚いたことに，このイベント以来，この地域にはゴミが落ちていない状態が続いています。なぜでしょう？イベントについての意見が答えを与えてくれそうです。

生徒と地域社会からの意見

BT：この問題が私をどんなに不幸にしていたかわかっていませんでした。ようやく満面の笑みで歩いて学校に行けます。

AK：素晴らしいプロジェクトです！学校の近くに住む大人として，学校の生徒が地域社会に役立っているのを見て，とてもうれしく思いました。私も参加して，近所の人たちも巻き込みました。今でも週に２回やっています。

RN：このプロジェクトが起こした変化に感謝しています。（もしポスターを見ていれば）私と友人も参加したはずですが，ポスターを見ていませんでした。

CF：このプロジェクトを通して，１人の高校生の行動がいかに大きな影響力を持てるかを理解することができました。

WL：とても感謝しています。ここに15年住んでいて，またこの町に誇りを持てるようになった気がします。

問1 4 ④

「この活動の目的は， 4 ことであった。」

①「生徒に地域を支援させる」

②「地元の人たちがお互いを知るのを助ける」

③「学校の運動場を改善する」

④「環境をよりよく見えるようにする」

筆者が行った活動内容は，第４文にI put up posters asking students to come to school ten minutes earlier than usual for one week and use the extra time to pick up a few pieces of litter.（１週間普段より10分早く登校して，この追加の時間をいくつかのゴミを拾うのに使うように頼むポスターを貼りました。）と書かれている。また，このポスターを貼ったきっかけは，学校周辺の地面にゴミが落ちていることである。ゴミ拾いをすることで学校周辺の美観をよくしようとしたのだから④が正解。この活動は①の「地域支援」につながるが，活動を始めた目的は④なので①は不正解。②については書かれていないので不正解。また，改善しようとしたのは運動場ではないので，③も不正解。

問2 5 ③

「『10分間地域チャレンジ』に関する1つの**事実**は[5]ということだ。」

①「3日間しか続かなかった」

②「生徒達だけがゴミ拾いをした」

③「1週間通して働いた生徒の数は約50人だった」

④「町がよりきれいに見えるようになって，先生たちが喜んだ」

本文第6～7文にAn average of 150 students ... took part each day. Nearly a third of that number participated the whole week.（毎日平均150人の生徒…が参加し，そのうちの3分の1近くが1週間を通して参加しました。）とある。150人の3分の1近く（50人近く）が1週間毎日参加したのだから，③が正解。3日できれいになったが，チャレンジは1週間続いたので①は不正解。生徒だけでなく地域の人や教師も参加したので，②も不正解。地域の人の喜びの声はFeedbackにあるが，教師の感想は述べられていないので，④も不正解。

問3 6 ③

「ブログから，[6]が最も正しいと思われる。」

A:「より多くの人々が参加したかっただろう」

B:「生徒たちは地元の人たちに参加を促した」

C:「生徒たちはゴミ拾いが好きだ」

D:「筆者は教師が参加するとは予期していなかった」

①「AとB」　②「AとC」

③「AとD」　④「BとC」

⑤「BとD」　⑥「CとD」

RNの意見にMy friends and I would have joined in but we didn't see the poster.（私と友人も参加したはずですが，ポスターを見ていませんでした。）とある。参加希望者がもっと多くいたので，Aが正しい。地域住民が参加したが，「生徒が促した」という記述はないのでBは不正解。「生徒たちがゴミ拾いが好き」という記述もないのでCも不正解。本文第4文によると，筆者が参加を呼びかけたのは生徒だが，第8文にThere were even a few teachers.（先生も数人いました。）とあり，even（～までも）から教師の参加を予期していなかったとわかるので，Dは正しい。したがって，正解は③。

問4 7 ③

「『10分間地域チャレンジ』についての参加者の意見の1つは[7]ということである。」

①「皆がチャレンジに参加するべきだ」

②「地元の人たちは，この地域に住んでいて幸せだとずっと思っている」

③「1人の人間が地域を変えることができる」

④「チャレンジは15年前に始まるべきだった」

CFの意見にThis project helped me understand how action by a high school student can have a big impact.（このプロジェクトを通して，1人の高校生の行動がいかに大きな影響力を持てるかを理解することができました。）と書かれている。「影響力」は具体的には筆者の発案によって地域がきれいになったこと，すなわち筆者の行動が地域を変えたことを指す。したがって，③が正解。

①・④の意見は書かれていないので不正解。また，地域の人の意見に「ずっと幸せだった」ともないので②も不正解。

問5 8 ①

「筆者の質問は[8]に答えられている。」

①「AK」　②「BT」　③「CF」　④「RN」

⑤「WL」

筆者の質問は第11～12文のSurprisingly, since this event the area has stayed litter-free. Why is this?（驚いたことに，このイベント以来，この地域にはゴミが落ちていない状態が続いています。なぜでしょう？）である。AKの意見にI joined in and got some neighbours involved, too. We still do it twice a week.（私も参加して，近所の人たちを巻き込みました。今でも週に2回やっています。）とある。AKと近所の人がゴミ拾いを継続しているから，きれいな状態が保たれているのである。したがって，正解は①。

【語句】

◇community service「社会奉仕」

◇litter「ゴミ」

◇participate「参加する」

◇appreciate「～に感謝する」

◇問1 ② local「（通例複数形）地元の人たち」

◇問2 ① last「続く」

第3問

全訳 新年の目標を立てることについての朝の集会のあと，ある英国の生徒がどのようにして悪い習慣を断ち切ることができたかについてのブログを，担任の先生が共有します。

習慣を断ち切る

学生時代には，宿題をぎりぎりまで放置したり，テレビゲームを少しやりすぎたりするような悪い習慣が付きやすいです。私はどうにかしていくつかの悪い習慣を克服しました。これがその方法です。

習慣を変える重要な段階
特定する→取り除く→置き換える→報酬を与える

まず，問題を特定する必要がありました。数学のテストの途中で寝てしまい，落第点を取りました。先生は私を職員室に呼び，私の日課についてたずねました。そこで私は，自分の食習慣に問題があることに気づきました。おやつを食べることは，私にとっていつも大きな問題でした。エネルギーを補給するために，いつもチョコレートバーやお菓子，甘い飲み物を素早くとっていました。余分なカロリーがどれだけ私を太らせ，眠くさせているかに気づいていませんでした。通常，食後30分もすると，私の気力はなくなっていました。

私は自分自身の目標を設定しました。リンゴやバナナ，そのような健康的な選択肢が大嫌いでした。それでも，通常食べているすべての不健康なおやつを，フルーツやナッツ，グラノーラバーに置き換えました。3カ月間新しい食生活を継続することに挑戦しました。私を応援するために，友人たちは私の周りでおやつを食べるのをやめ，兄は成功したら私が欲しがっている腕時計をくれると約束してくれました。私は成功しました！

食生活を変えたことは私の人生に大きな影響を与えました。体重が12kg減りました。実際に健康的な食事が欲しいと強く思うようになりました。活力も増し，以前よりしっかりと目が覚め，学校での成績も良くなり，そのことをとても嬉しく思っています。数カ月前，画面を見ている時間を減らすために同じ方法を使いました。問題を特定し，（スマートフォンをポケットではなくバッグに入れることで）誘因を取り除き，ボードゲームをするなど新しい活動を始め，自分へのご褒美としてディズニーランドへの旅行をしました。あなたも同じような段階を踏めば，悪習慣を断ち切り，自分の最大限の可能性を発揮することができるでしょう。

問1　9　③　10　②　11　①　12　④

「次の出来事（①～④）を起こった順に並べなさい。」 9 → 10 → 11 → 12

①「筆者の身近な人が手助けをした。」
②「筆者はテストで落第点を取った。」
③「筆者は質の悪い食事の選択をした。」
④「筆者は欲しいものを受けとった。」

第2段落第2文 I fell asleep in the middle of a maths test and failed.（数学のテストの途中で寝てしまい，落第点を取りました。）が②に一致する。その原因が第5～7文に「おやつを食べることは，私にとっていつも大きな問題で，私はいつもチョコやお菓子や甘い飲み物を食べていた。余分なカロリーが私を太らせ，眠くさせていた」と書かれている。したがって，③→②の順になる。筆者はこの問題を解決するために食生活を改善し，第3段落第5文前半に To support me, my friends stopped eating snacks around me（私を応援するために，友人たちは私の周りでおやつを食べるのをやめた）とある。これが①の「身近な人が手助けした」に一致する。さらに第5文後半に my brother promised to give me his watch that I wanted if I succeeded（兄は成功したら私が欲しがっている腕時計をあげると約束してくれました）と書かれている。次の文I did!（私は成功しました！）から，④「（成功して）欲しいものを受け取った」と判断する。したがって，③→②→①→④の順に並べる。

問2　13　③

「もしあなたが筆者のアドバイスに従うなら， 13 べきである。」

①「あなたのために習慣を変えるように友達に頼む」
②「勉強と楽しみのよりよいバランスを見つける」
③「生活を改善するためにシステムに従う」
④「先生が言うことを信頼する」

筆者は第1段落第2文に I managed to overcome some of my bad habits, and this is how I did it.（どうにかしていくつかの悪い習慣を克服しました。これがその方法です。）と書き，4つの段階を図示している。さらに，最終段落最終文で If you follow similar steps, you'll be on your way to breaking your bad habits and reaching your full potential.（あなたも同じような段階を踏めば，悪習慣を断ち

切り，自分の最大限の可能性を発揮することができるでしょう。）と勧めている。したがって，筆者のアドバイスは「生活改善のシステム通りに行動する」ことなので，③が正解。筆者の周囲の友人は助けてくれたが，頼むことを勧めてはいないので，①は不正解。②・④のアドバイスは本文に書かれていないので不正解。

問3 14 ①

「この話から筆者が 14 ことがわかる。」

① **「彼の好みが変わってきたとわかった」**

②「ボードゲームをするよりもディズニーランドに行くことを好んだ」

③「効果的な計画を立てようと努力している」

④「その方法を１度だけ試した」

筆者は第３段落第２文でI hated apples, bananas, and healthy options like that.（リンゴやバナナ，そしてそのような健康的な選択肢が大嫌いでした。），第４段落第３文ではI actually desire healthy food.（実際に健康的な食事が欲しいと強く思うようになりました。）と書いている。食べ物の好みが変わってきているので，①が正解。筆者はボードゲームとディズニーランドの優劣を付けていないので②は不正解。筆者が努力しているのは，計画を立てることではなく実行することなので，③は不正解。第４段落第５文によると，筆者は画面を見ている時間を減らすために同じ方法を用いたので，④も不正解。

【語句】

◇assembly「集会」
◇pick up a habit「習慣が付く」
◇overcome「～を克服する」
◇identify「～を特定する」
◇maths（＝math）「数学」
◇overweight「太り過ぎの」
◇keep up ～「～を継続する」
◇desire「～が欲しいと強く思う」
◇trigger「きっかけ，誘因」
◇reach *one*'s full potential「人が最大限の可能性を発揮する」
◇問３ ③ struggle to *do*「…しようと努力する」
◇問３ ③ effective「効果的な」

第４問

全訳 あなたは英語の授業で，興味のある社会問題に関するエッセイを書いています。これはあなたの最新の草稿です。今は先生からのコメントをもとに，推敲に取り組んでいるところです。

ガーデニングと地域づくり

コミュニティ・ガーデンは，地方自治体が所有する土地の一部で，地域住民が近所の人たちと協力して菜園や花畑を作ることを許可されている場所である。このようなガーデンが将来も存続するのを確実にするために，その価値と可能性を理解することが重要である。このエッセイで，コミュニティ・ガーデンのいくつかの利点について論じる。

第一に，都市部での孤立がますます一般的になっている時代に，コミュニティ・ガーデンは特に高齢者間の友好的な交流の機会を提供する。現在，特に大都市では，住民が交流できる場所がほとんどない。*(1)* 15 だから，コミュニティ・ガーデンは，さまざまな世代の住民が互いに知り合う，希少なコミュニティ拠点としての役割を果たすかもしれない。

第二に，コミュニティ・ガーデンは，住民が活用できるガーデニングや農業の実用的な技術や知識を提供する。*(2)* 16 ガーデンでの作業にはチームワークが求められ，これはコミュニケーション技術と個人の責任感の向上に役立つだろう。

最後に，*(3)*私たちは自分が食べるものに責任がある。コミュニティが所有することで，栄養価の高い果物や野菜，ハーブをより手頃な価格で入手できる。これは，特に新鮮な農産物が限られていたり高価だったりする地域で，より健康的な食生活をもたらしてくれる。

結論として，コミュニティ・ガーデンは*(4)*高齢者を助け，貴重な学びを与え，そして最後に，食生活を豊かにしてくれる。コミュニティ・ガーデンはこれからの人生で私たちにとってますます重要な存在となるだろうから，それを支援するためにできる限りのことをするべきだ。

コメント

(1) ここに何か足りません。２つの文をつなぐために，間にさらに情報を追加しなさい。

(2) ここに接続表現を挿入しなさい。
(3) この主題文はこの段落にあまり合っていません。書き直しなさい。
(4) 下線部の表現はあなたのエッセイの内容を十分に要約していません。変更しなさい。

総合的なコメント
この主題は，高齢化社会でますます重要になるものだと思います。私の近所にもコミュニティ・ガーデンがあります！

問1 15 ①
「コメント(1)に基づいて，付け加えるのに最も適当な文はどれか。」 15
①「その上，ガーデニングは年齢にかかわらず楽しめる人気のある活動である。」
②「例えば，それらは食料がどのように生産されるかについて，貴重な知識を与えてくれる。」
③「さらに，コミュニティ・ガーデンは人々に一人になる機会を与える。」
④「同様に，コミュニティ・ガーデンは都市環境におけるスポーツを促進する。」
(1)の前後の内容を確認する。直前に Nowadays there are few locations where residents can interact, especially in big cities.（現在，特に大都市では，住民が交流できる場所がほとんどない）と書かれている。直後には So, community gardens may serve as rare community hubs where residents of different generations get to know each other.（だから，コミュニティ・ガーデンは，さまざまな世代の住民が知り合う希少なコミュニティ拠点としての役割を果たすかもしれない。）と続く。「ガーデニングは年齢にかかわらず楽しめる」という①を入れれば「さまざまな世代の住民が知り合う」という内容につながる。したがって，①が正解。②④は後ろの文にうまくつながらない。③はこの段落の内容に矛盾するので不正解。

問2 16 ①
「コメント(2)に基づいて，付け加えるのに最も適当な表現はどれか。」 16
①「さらに」
②「しかし」
③「それに対して」
④「したがって」
(2)の前後の内容を確認する。直前に community gardens provide practical skills and knowledge for ...（コミュニティ・ガーデンは…実用的な技術や知識を提供する），直後に Working on gardens requires teamwork; this will help improve communication skills and the individual's sense of responsibility.（ガーデンでの作業にはチームワークが求められ，これはコミュニケーション技術と個人の責任感の向上に役立つだろう。）とある。どちらも「コミュニティ・ガーデンによって住民が身に付けるもの」という関連する内容である。追加の情報を加える時，間に入れる接続表現として適当なのは①である。

問3 17 ①
「コメント(3)に基づいて，主題文を書き換えるのに最も適当なものはどれか。」 17
①「私たちは収穫の恩恵を受けることができる」
②「私たちはその場所を訪ねるのを楽しむことができる」
③「私たちは自然をより身近に感じることができる」
④「私たちは輸送費が節約できる」
主題文（topic sentence）は，その段落の内容を端的に表した文で，主題文のあとに具体的な内容が続く。ここでは Community ownership makes nutritious fruits, vegetables, and herbs more affordable. This leads to healthier eating habits, especially in areas where fresh produce may be limited or expensive.（コミュニティが所有することで栄養価の高い果物や野菜，ハーブをより手頃な価格で入手できる。これは，特に新鮮な農産物が限られていたり高価だったりする地域で，より健康的な食生活をもたらしてくれる。）と書かれている。これを端的にまとめたのは①の「収穫の恩恵」である。②③④はこの段落の要旨に合わないので不正解。

問4 18 ④
「コメント(4)に基づいて，置き換えるのに最も適当なものはどれか。」 18
①「イベント開催地として人気がある」
②「地域の学校間の協力を生み出す」
③「不用地を活性化する可能性がある」
④「地域内でより深い人間関係を構築するのに役立つ」
下線部(4)を含む文は In conclusion, community gardens ...（結論として，コミュニティ・ガーデン

は…）と書き始めている。全体のまとめとして，コミュニティ・ガーデンの３つの利点を挙げていると考える。(4)のあとに続く provide valuable lessons（貴重な学びを与える）は第３段落の「技術や知識，コミュニケーション技術や責任感を身に付ける」，enrich our diet（私たちの食生活を豊かにする）は第４段落の「栄養価の高い野菜や果物を入手する」を言い換えたものである。(4)は第２段落の「さまざまな世代の住民が知り合い交流する場所」について書くべきなので，④がふさわしい。①②③については本文で書かれていない。

【語句】

◇in cooperation with～「～と協力して」
◇ensure「～を確実にする」
◇potential「可能性」
◇urban「都市の」
◇isolation「孤立」
◇increasingly「ますます」
◇interaction「交流」（動詞はinteract「交流する」。）
◇resident「住民」
◇serve as ～「～としての役割を果たす；～として役立つ」
◇hub「（活動などの）中心地；拠点」
◇get to know ～「～と知り合う」
◇practical「実用的な」
◇responsibility「責任」
◇ownership「所有者であること；所有していること」
◇nutritious「栄養価の高い」
◇affordable「手頃な価格の」
◇produce「農産物；生鮮食品」
◇enrich「～を豊かにする」
◇diet「食習慣；食生活」
◇問１ ① regardless of ～「～にかかわらず」
◇問１ ③ furthermore「さらに」
◇問１ ④ similarly「同様に」
◇問２ ① additionally「さらに」
◇問２ ③ in contrast「その一方」
◇問３ ① harvest「収穫（物）」
◇問３ ④ shipping「運搬の；輸送の」
◇問４ ② collaboration「協力」
◇問４ ③ revitalize「～を活性化する」
◇問４ ③ unwanted「要らない；不要な」

第５問

全訳 先生があなたに進化論に関する２つの記事を読むように言いました。次の授業では，学んだことについて話し合うことになっています。

進化論を理解すること

スカーレット・アギラー

フレッタービル高校 生物教師

高校教師として最近気づいたある傾向は，進化について奇妙な考えを持つ生徒がいることです。例えば，ある生徒は最近「人類の祖先であるネアンデルタール人は5,000年前に生きていた」と書きました。ここには２つの問題があります。ネアンデルタール人は人類と何らかの関係がありそうですが，彼らを我々の直接の祖先と呼ぶのは単純すぎるのです。実際には，ネアンデルタール人とホモ・サピエンス，つまり現代人との間で何らかの交雑はあったという可能性が高いです。一般に，ネアンデルタール人とホモ・サピエンスは，ホモ・ハイデルベルゲンシスと呼ばれる祖先を共有していると考えられていますが，この説は一部の研究者によってまだ疑問視されています。また，ネアンデルタール人がいつ生きていたかを特定するのは困難ですが，証拠によると5,000年前ではなく，少なくとも50,000年前なのです！進化は一夜にして起こるものではないと覚えていてください。何十万年もかけてゆっくりと生じるのです。

ホモ・ハイデルベルゲンシスの例を考えてみましょう。ホモ・ハイデルベルゲンシスはホモ・サピエンスよりもはるかに大きな顎の骨を有して，眉も大きく隆起していました。しかし現代人は，このどちらの特徴も有していません。

生徒に二者の対照比較を与えることで，私たちがどれだけ進化してきたかを生徒が理解する手助けができました。実際に，過去に他の人類がいたことを説明することで，漸進的進化の不思議をより理解させることができるのです。

種	ホモ・ハイデルベルゲンシス
顎骨（*）の大きさ	大きく，頑丈

*顔の下部の形状を形成する骨	
眉の隆起	非常に大きい
絵	（イラスト省略）

一夜での進化

エステル・クレイマー

フレッタービル大学教授

大学教授として，高校の先生がする仕事に本当に感謝しています。生徒が進化についての事実を学ぶ必要があるという点では，アギラーさんに賛成です。しかし，アギラーさんの最近の記事についてコメントしなければなりません。彼女は，進化は「一夜にして起こるものではない」と言いますが，私は完全に同意することはできません。近年，科学界は，漸進的な進化よりも突発的な進化の可能性が高いと考えるようになっています。

アギラーさんは，ホモ・ハイデルベルゲンシスの例で，非常に長い期間をかけてゆっくりとした進化が起こることを示唆しています。しかし，もし彼女が主張するように進化が常にゆるやかな過程であるならば，人類の祖先と現代人との間の変化は，時間の経過とともに均等に観察できるはずです。進化は実際にはずっと不均一です。ある種の化石は，突然の変化が私たちの祖先の進化の仕方に大きな影響を与えてきたことを示しています。これを高速進化と考えましょう。高速進化の背後にある考え方は，動物が実際に長い間同じ状態のままでいることです。このような長い期間のあとで，わずか1～2世代で突然の進化をするのです。

高速進化を裏付ける事例として，ニューギニアのカワセミという鳥の種の例があります。ニューギニアの本土のカワセミは，さまざまな種の間でほとんど違いがありません。しかし，近くの島々では，カワセミは突然の変動期を経験してきたように見えます。この変化の期間が短いことは，遺伝情報を研究する科学者によって証明されています。彼らは島の鳥の方がDNAが多様であることがわかりました。その結果，島のカワセミは親戚である本土のカワセミとは見た目も行動もまったく異なることがあるのです。このような島のカワセミの研究は，高速進化の説を裏付けています。

この説明を進化がいかにすばやく起こり得るかを皆さんにより理解してもらうのに役立ててほしいです。

（グラフ）カワセミの種の多様性 本土・島

問1　19　④

「アギラーは 19 と考えた。」

①「進化は1日で起こりうる 」

②「学校では進化が重要ではなくなった」

③「生徒たちは変わった性格をしている」

④「生徒のコメントは驚くべきものだ」

アギラーの記事第1段落第1文はAs a high school teacher, one trend I have noticed recently is students with some strange ideas about evolution.（高校教師として最近気づいたある傾向は，進化について奇妙な考えを持つ生徒がいることだ。）で始まり，第2文にFor instance, one student recently wrote, “Neanderthals, the ancestors of human beings, lived 5,000 years ago.”（例えば，ある生徒は最近「人類の祖先であるネアンデルタール人は5,000年前に生きていた」と書いた。）と具体例を挙げている。アギラーは生徒の誤ったコメントに驚いているので，④が正解。

アギラーは「進化は短期間で起こらない」という考えを持っているので①は不正解。②・③のような記述は記事にないのでこれらも不正解。

問2　20　④

「クレイマーが論じた研究では，ニューギニア沖の島々で見つかったカワセミは本土で見つかったカワセミよりも 20 。」

①「数が多い」

②「サイズが大きい」

③「長生きする可能性が高い」

④「変化に富んでいる」

カワセミの研究については，クレイマーの記事の第3段落に書かれている。『カワセミの種の多様性』のグラフを見ると，本土よりも島の方が種が多いとわかる。したがって④が正解。

「カワセミの見た目や行動が異なる」とあるが，その具体的な内容は書かれていないので，①・②・③は正解と言えない。

問3　21　①　22　②

「アギラーは，動物がとてつもなく長い時間をかけてゆっくりと 21 する漸進的進化を説明し，クレイマーはそれを自分の主張で 22 しようとする。（選択肢①～⑥の中からそれぞれに最適なものを選びなさい。）」

①「変化」

②「否定」

③「強調」

④「成長」

⑤「促進」

⑥「証明」

21

アギラーの漸進的進化の説明は第1段落の最後の2文にRemember, evolution is no overnight process. It happens slowly, over hundreds of thousands of years.（進化は一晩で起こるものではないと覚えていてほしい。何十万年もかけてゆっくりと生じるのだ。）と書かれている。「ゆっくりと変化していく」のだから①が正解。

22

クレイマーは記事の第1段落第4文にShe says evolution is "no overnight process," but I cannot completely agree.（彼女は，進化は「一晩で起こるものではない」と言うが，私は完全に同意することはできない。）と書き，次の文でIn recent years, the scientific community has come to believe that sudden bursts of evolution are more likely than gradual evolution.（近年，科学界は，漸進的進化よりも進化の突発性の可能性が高いと考えるようになっている。）と別の説を紹介している。つまり，アギラーの説を否定しているのだから，②が正解。

問4　23　④

「両方の筆者は 23 ということに賛成する。」

①「DNAは進化に影響を与える」

②「進化はゆるやかな経過をたどる」

③「ネアンデルタール人は5,000年前に生きていた」

④「生徒は進化について学ぶべきだ」

アギラーの記事第3段落では自分の教え方を書いたうえで，第2文にIn fact, explaining ... gives them a better appreciation of the wonders of gradual evolution.（実際に…を説明することで，漸進的進化の不思議をより理解させることができる。）と，進化を教えていることが書かれている。また，クレイマーの記事第1段落第2文にI agree with Ms. Aguilar that students need to learn the facts about evolution.（生徒が進化についての事実を学ぶ必要があるという点では，アギラーさんに賛成だ。）とある。両者とも生徒が進化について学ぶ必要があると考えているので，④が正解。

進化とDNAの関係はクレイマーしか述べていないので①は不正解。ゆるやかな進化について，アギラーは主張するがクレイマーは反論しているので②は不正解。③は生徒が述べたことなので不正解。

問5　24　②

「クレイマーの高速進化を支持する意見をさらに裏付けるには，どの追加情報が最適か。」 24

①「カワセミとホモ・ハイデルベルゲンシスの比較」

②「島のカワセミのDNAが本土のカワセミより多様であることを示す詳細なデータ」

③「ニューギニアの地理に関する詳細情報」

④「古代の地球の気候に関する研究」

クレイマーは高速進化を裏付ける例として，第3段落でニューギニア本土と島のカワセミの研究結果を挙げている。グラフから「島のカワセミの方が種が多様である」とわかる。さらに第4・5文にThe short length of these changes has been proven by scientists who study the genetic code. They found the island birds have greater variety in their DNA.（この変化の期間が短いことは，遺伝情報を研究する科学者によって証明されている。彼らは島の鳥の方がDNAが多様であることがわかった。）と書かれている。島のカワセミのDNAの多様さをより詳細に示すデータがあれば，クレイマーの説をさらに裏付けることができる。したがって②が正解。

クレイマーは同じ種のものを比較することで進化を裏付けることができるので，①は不正解。ニューギニアの地理に関する理解を深めてもDNAの種類と直接的な因果関係はないので，③は不適当。クレイマーは気候と進化の関係については述べていないので，④も不正解。

【語句】

◇evolution「進化」

◇ancestor「祖先」

◇*be* related to ～「～に関連している」

◇in reality「実際に」

◇crossbreeding「交雑，異種交配」

◇evidence「証拠」

◇overnight process「一晩で解決するような問題」

◇hundreds of thousands of「何十万もの」

◇brow ridge「眉の隆起」
◇neither (of ~)「(~の) どちらも…ない」
◇side-by-side comparison「対照比較」
◇appreciate「~を正しく理解する」
◇human species「人類」
◇appreciation「理解」
◇gradual evolution「漸進的進化」段階的な進化のこと。
◇community「社会，団体，…界」
◇occur「起こる」
◇claim「主張する」
◇evenly「均等に」
◇observe「~を観察する」
◇uneven「不均一な」
◇fossil remains「化石」
◇have an impact on ~「~に影響を与える」
◇evolve「進化する」
◇undergo「~を経験する」
◇kingfisher「カワセミ」
◇genetic code「遺伝情報」
◇問2 ④ varied「変化に富んだ」
◇問3 ② deny「~を否定する」
◇問3 ③ emphasize「~を強調する」
◇問4 ① affect「~に影響を与える」
◇問5 additional「追加の」
◇問5 ② detailed「詳細な」

第6問

全訳 あなたは，医療企業が自社製品を動物実験すべきかどうかについてのエッセイに取り組んでいます。あなたは以下のステップに従います。
ステップ1：動物実験に関するさまざまな観点を読み，理解する。
ステップ2：動物で医療実験をすることに対する自分の立場を決める。
ステップ3：追加の資料を用いてエッセイの概要を作成する。

[ステップ1] さまざまな資料を読む
筆者A (入院患者)
私はとても危険な病気から回復しつつあります。私の命を救うために医師が与えた薬が，動物実験を通して開発されたものだと聞きました。私はその薬に深く感謝していますが，その薬が罪のない動物たちの苦痛を通して開発されたものだと思うと悩みます。最先端技術を使ったものなどの他の方法よりも安価であるため，動物実験がしばしば選択されると聞いたことがあります。動物実験は他の方法に置き換えられるべきだと思います。

筆者B (動物の権利に関する専門家)
動物も人間のために作られた薬の恩恵を受けているのだから動物実験は容認されると主張する人がいます。それは稚拙な主張だと思います。私たちが薬を使うのは，コンパニオンアニマル (ペット) や家畜など，人間にとって有用な動物を救うためだけで，野生動物のためではありません。さらに，その手段はしばしば残酷です。例えば，動物を病気に感染させ，それから薬や治療法が対象となる病気に効くかどうかを検査します。道義に反すると思います。

筆者C (医師)
もし動物実験がなかったら，薬や治療法が危険すぎて患者に勧められず，あまりに多くの人が，その中の多くはとても若くして，死んでしまうでしょう。もちろん，動物の死や苦痛は悲しいことだと思いますが，膨大な数の人々が救われているのは，医薬品開発に伴うすべての手順のおかげであり，その中に動物実験も含まれます。私の意見では，このことは犠牲を埋め合わせるものになっていると思います。また，人間の薬を対象とする研究の多くは，動物の薬を作るのにも役立っています。

筆者D (高校生)
私のクラスは学校の生物の授業でこの話題について話し合い，私は医療実験に動物を使うことに強く反対しています。新しい薬や治療法を試す場合に，健康な動物が被験動物として選ばれ，病気に感染させられます。これは倫理的に間違っていると思います。先生は，医薬品の試験には代替の方法があると教えてくれました。試験管に入れた人間の細胞で実験したり，生きた動物ではなくコンピュータソフトを使って結果を予測したりする方法が含まれます。このような方法がもっと広く採用されることを願っています。

筆者E（科学者）
私の研究室では，毎日動物を使って薬や治療法を試験しています。ラットのような小動物で検査しますが，犬やチンパンジーでも検査しています。悲しいことに，多くの動物がとても苦しんでいます。このような状況を毎日見て，私はつらい気持ちになります。しかし，私たちが動物を適切な環境に置くために非常に厳しい規則に従っていること，そして本当に良い代替手段がほとんどないことを理解してほしいと思います。実際，私たちが救おうとする人間の命の数に比べれば，検査で死んだり苦しんだりする動物はごくわずかです。

［ステップ2］立場を決める
あなたの立場：動物を使っての医薬品の実験は正しい行為である。
●筆者 27 と 28 はあなたの立場をサポートする。
● 2人の筆者の主な論拠： 29

［ステップ3］資料AとBを用いて概要を作成する
あなたのエッセイの概要：

動物を使っての医薬品の実験は容認されるべき行為である

導入
動物を使っての医薬品の実験によって，多くの医薬品を製造することが可能になった。私たちは，研究者がこの重要な手段を使うのを止めるべきではない。

本論
理由1：［ステップ2から］
理由2：［資料Aに基づいて］ ……… 30
理由3：［資料Bに基づいて］ ……… 31

結論
動物を使っての医薬品の実験は正しい行為である。

資料A
動物実験がしばしば議論されるのは，動物の命に関わる犠牲のためです。これはほとんどの人にとって感情的な問題です。しかし，人道的な扱いを保証することを目的とした，動物実験に適用される厳格な規則を理解することは極めて重要です。動物実験を実施する機関は，厳格な法律に従うことが要求され，実験者は特別な委員会から研究の承認を得ることが求められます。通常このような委員会は獣医学，倫理学，研究の専門家で構成されています。彼らは，提案された研究が必要であり，動物の苦痛を最小限に抑えるためにあらゆる可能な手段が講じられていることを確実にするため，慎重にチェックします。さらに研究者は，動物福祉を重視した包括的指針に従わなければなりません。これには，適切な世話をすること，使用する動物の数を減らすこと，感情的ストレスを軽減するために手順を改善することなどが含まれます。定期的な検査により，確実にこれらの基準が維持されるようにします。研究において動物の命が失われるのは悲しい現実ですが，このような規制や監視システムが，科学的探求における倫理的責任のレベルを高めるのに役立っています。

資料B
英国で医学研究に動物を使用する組織は，毎年生きた動物に対して行った実験の数を記録しなければなりません。下のグラフは，医学研究に使用されるウマ，イヌ，ネコ，サルの数を示しています。

（グラフ）
医学研究に使用される動物の数
ウマ　イヌ　サル　ネコ

問1 25 ④
「筆者BとDはどちらも 25 と述べている。」
① 「動物は人間に十分類似していないので，人間の医薬品は人間で実験すべきだ」
② 「現在では動物実験を行わなくても新薬の安全性を確認することができる」
③ 「ペットや家畜も動物実験に頼った医学研究の恩恵を受けている」
④ **「医学実験に使用される動物は，研究者によって意図的に病気にされる」**

筆者Bの意見の第5文に the animals are given diseases and then tested to ... （動物を病気に感染させ，それから…検査します）と書いてある。また，筆者Dの意見の第2文に When it comes to testing new drugs or treatments, healthy animals are chosen as subjects and infected with disease.（新しい薬や治療法を試す場合に，健康な動物が被験動物として選ばれ，病気に感染させられます。）とある。

実験用動物が意図的に病気にされることに言及しているので，④が正解。①については2人とも言及していないので不正解。②は筆者Dのみ，③は筆者Bのみが言及しているので不正解。

問2 26 ①

「筆者Aは 26 と示唆している。」

①「動物が与えてくれた生きるチャンスに感謝している」

②「回復後は動物を救うことに人生を捧げる」

③「動物実験をした薬だけが人間の命を救うことができる」

④「人はもう動物実験に否定的なイメージを持つべきではない」

患者である筆者Aは第2文で the medicine the doctors gave me to save my life was developed through animal testing（私の命を救うために医師たちが私に与えた薬が動物実験を通して開発された）と書き，I am deeply thankful for the medicine（その薬に深く感謝しています）と続けている。ここから，筆者の気持ちを表す文として①が適切。②④については言及していない。③は筆者Aが最終文で書いた「動物実験は他の方法に置き換えられるべき」という内容に反する。

問3 27, 28 ③，⑤（順不同）
29 ③

「あなたはさまざまな観点を理解したので，動物実験について自分の立場を決め，以下のように書いた。 27, 28, 29 を完成させるのに最も適当な選択肢を選びなさい。」

「 27, 28 の選択肢（順不同。）」

①「A」

②「B」

③「C」

④「D」

⑤「E」

「動物を使っての医薬品の実験は正しい行為である」という立場をサポートする意見を選ぶ。5人の見解を見ていこう。

筆者A：動物実験によってできた医薬品に感謝しながらも，最終文で I believe that animal testing should be replaced by other methods.（動物実験は他の方法に置き換えられるべきだと思います。）と書いている。

筆者B：動物実験の残酷さについて述べ，最終文で I think that it is immoral.（道義に反すると思います。）と書いている。

筆者C：第1文で If it were not for animal testing, ... so many people would die（動物実験がなかったら…あまりに多くの人が死んでしまうでしょう）と書き，さらに第2文で a huge number of people are saved thanks to the whole procedure involved in developing medicine, which includes animal testing（膨大な数の人々が救われているのは，動物実験も含む医薬品開発に伴うすべての手順のおかげ）と，動物実験の意義を認めている。

筆者D：第2文で動物実験の問題点を書き，第3文で This is ethically wrong, I think.（これは倫理的に間違っていると思います。）と表明している。さらに後半では代替の方法を提案している。

筆者E：動物実験を行う立場からの意見。第5文で I wish people would understand ... that there are few really good alternatives.（私は皆さんに…本当に良い代替手段がほとんどないことを理解してほしいと思います。），第6文で Actually, very few animals die and suffer in testing compared with the number of human lives we will save.（実際，私たちが救おうとする人間の命の数に比べれば，検査で死んだり苦しんだりする動物はごくわずかです。）と，動物実験を容認する意見を述べている。

以上から，動物実験を支持するのはCとEで，③と⑤が正解。

「 29 の選択肢」

①「動物は，健康的な生活習慣を持つ人に影響を及ぼす病気の治療法を見つけるためにのみ使われるべきだ。」

②「大きな動物よりも感じる痛みが少ないかもしれないので，ラットのような小さな動物で医薬品の検査をする方がよい。」

③「動物実験によって救われる人命の数は，実験を容認するのに十分なくらい多い。」

④「動物実験を通して作ることができる薬の数は，人間だけで実験した場合よりも多い。」

筆者Cと筆者Eに共通する意見を選択する問題。筆者Cは，第2文で a huge number of people are saved thanks to the whole procedure involved in developing medicine, which includes animal testing（膨大な数の人々が救われているのは，動物実験も含む医薬品開発に伴うすべての手順のおかげ）と書き，それに対し that would compensate for the sacrifice（このことは犠牲を埋め合わせるものになっている）と続けている。
筆者Eは最終文でActually, very few animals die and suffer in testing compared with the number of human lives we will save.（実際，私たちが救おうとする人間の命の数に比べれば，検査で死んだり苦しんだりする動物はごくわずかです。）と書いている。2人とも「動物実験で開発された医薬品で救われた人命の数とその犠牲」に言及しているので，③が正解。①②④については言及していないので不正解。

問4 30 ④

「資料Aに基づき，理由2として最も適当なものは次のうちどれか。」 30

①「獣医学の専門家は，人間のための新薬を見つけるために動物を使うよう研究者に助言している。」
②「政府は，研究者が使用するための指針を発行することで，動物実験を奨励している。」
③「医学研究のための動物使用に関する法律が将来厳しくなる可能性が高い。」
④「研究のために死ななければならない動物がいるのは不幸なことだが，その苦痛を軽減するための規則が施行されている。」

資料Aの最終文では the loss of animal life in research is a sad reality（研究において動物の命が失われることは悲しい現実だ）と認めている。しかし，資料A全体を通して伝えているのは第3文に書かれた it's crucial to understand the strict rules that govern animal testing, aimed at ensuring humane treatment（人道的な扱いを保証することを目的とした，動物実験に適用される厳格な規則を理解することは極めて重要です）であり，その具体例がThey carefully check the proposed studies to ensure they are necessary and that every possible measure is taken to minimize animal suffering.（彼らは提案された研究が必要であり，動物の苦痛を最小限に抑えるためにあらゆる可能な手段が講じられていることを確実にするため，慎重にチェックします。）である。この内容を簡潔にまとめた④が正解。①については言及していない。また，指針は動物実験の奨励のためではないので②も不正解。法律が今後厳しくなるとも書かれていないので③も不正解。

問5 31 ①

「理由3として，あなたは『研究者は特定の動物で医薬品を試験するかどうかの選択に，より慎重になっている。』と書くことにした。資料Bに基づき，この意見を最もよくサポートする選択肢はどれか。」
31

①「2022年には，20年前に比べて約半数のイヌとサルが研究に使用された。これは，これらの動物の福祉に対する関心が高まっていることを示している。」
②「サルを使った医学研究は，イヌを使った研究の約2倍の割合で減少している。これは人間とイヌとの関係が考慮されていることを示唆している。」
③「医学実験に使われるネコとウマの数は，ほぼ一定で推移している。これらの動物が医学にとって価値があることが証明されたに違いない。」
④「2012年から2022年の期間に，イヌとサルの使用は急激に減少した。動物愛護の要請に応える研究者がますます増えてきた。」

資料Bで示されたグラフに一致するものを選ぶ。2002年と2022年のデータを比べると，イヌ・サルを使った研究の数が半減しているので，①が正解。イヌとサルを使った研究はどちらも同じ割合（50%）で減っているので②は不正解。実験に使われたネコの数は2005年以降ほぼ一定だが，ウマの数は増減の幅が大きいので③は不正解。2012年から2022年の期間については，イヌ・サルの実験数が急激に減ったとは言えないので，④も不正解。

【語句】

◇suffering「苦痛」
◇innocent「無実の；罪のない」
◇state-of-the-art「最先端の」
◇of use「役に立つ」
◇companion animal「コンパニオンアニマル（ペット）」
◇procedure「手段」
◇immoral「道徳に反する」
◇compensate for ～「～を補う」
◇sacrifice「犠牲」
◇when it comes to ～「～に関して言えば」
◇subject「被験者；実験動物」
◇infect A with B「AをBに感染させる」
◇ethically「倫理的に」（形容詞は ethical「倫理の」，名詞は ethic（倫理，道徳），ethics（倫理学）。）

◇alternative「代替の；(名詞で) 代替手段」
◇cell「細胞」
◇adopt「～を採用する」
◇decent「適切な」
◇debate「～を議論する」
◇crucial「極めて重要な」
◇govern「～を管理する；～を統制する」
◇ensure「～を保証する」
◇humane「思いやりのある；(不必要な) 苦痛を与えない」
◇institution「機関」
◇conduct「～を実施する」
◇approval「承認」
◇committee「委員会」
◇veterinary science「獣医学」
◇propose「～を提案する」
◇minimize「～を最小限にする」
◇comprehensive guideline「包括的指針」
◇welfare「福祉」
◇refine「～に改良を加える；～を改善する」
◇inspection「検査」
◇regulation「規則」
◇observation「監視」
◇問1 ② verify「～を検証する」
◇問1 ④ intentionally「意図的に」
◇問2 ② dedicate A to B「AをBに捧げる」
◇問3 ① cure「治療法」
◇問4 ④ unfortunate「不幸な」
◇問4 ④ in place「施行されて」
◇問5 use caution「注意する」
◇問5 ① concern「関心；懸念」
◇問5 ③ constant「一定の」

第7問

全訳 あなたは学校の生徒会長で，メモを使って他のメンバーの心を動かすスピーチをする予定です。あなたは，自分の学校を変えるための運動を成功させた英国の生徒が書いた話を見つけました。

表現の自由を求める運動

カースティ・ウッド

私は，誰もが自信を持って安心できる方法で自分を表現する自由を持つべきだと思う。だから，生徒が髪を染めることを禁止するという私の学校の厳しい方針に，いつもショックを受け，悲しく思っていた。この規則が，私や学友が有意義な方法で自分を表現することを妨げていると感じた。

私はこの規則を無視しようとし，いつか変わることを願っていた。時間が経つにつれて，ただ傍観して変化が起こるのを願っていることはできないと悟った。自分が信じるもののために行動を起こし闘う必要があった。そこで私は，学生の毛染めを禁止する規則を変えるための運動を始めることにした。

規則を変えるための私の最初の試みは，学生サービス部長のルーシー・アームストロング先生の反対にあった。彼女は，毛髪染料（髪を染めるために使われる製品）に安全上の問題がある可能性や，学校のイメージに与えるだろう影響への懸念を引き合いに出した。適切に使えば毛髪染料は安全で，学校のイメージに悪影響を与えないという調査結果を提示する私の最大限の努力にもかかわらず，すべての訴えは無視された。

あきらめる心境になれず，私は再挑戦する決心をした。今度は，母の美容師であるキャロル・スミスさんに連絡を取り，髪を安全に染めるためのワークショップを開いてもらえないか確かめた。彼女は全校集会で話し，生徒たちや先生たちは感銘を受けた。しかし，この試みもまた失敗に終わった。アームストロング先生は，毛髪染料が安全であることに納得せず，考えを変えることを拒否した。

私はあきらめたか？もちろん，そうではない。別のやり方を取ることにした。生徒が髪の色を変えることで起こりうる問題に焦点を当てるのではなく，メリットに焦点を当てることにしたのだ。自己表現が生徒に与えうる肯定的な影響について調べた。自分の外見に自信がある生徒は，より授業に参加する傾向があり，自分自身をより信じるようになるという研究を見つけた。また，いじめに苦しんでいたが，髪の色をコントロールすることが自己表現をし，もっと自信を持つ手段を与えてくれるとわかった，という生徒たちの話も見つけた。

今回，私は学校長のジョーンズ先生との面談の予定を組んだ。自分が見つけた調査結果と話を提示し，生徒が髪の色を選ぶことで自己表現ができるようにすることで，より多様で協力的な学校環境を作ることができることを説明した。驚いたことに，彼女はとても興味を示し，心から感動しているように見えた。面談のあとで，この規則が妥当かどうかを確認することに同意し，私の主張を考慮することを約束してくれた。

数週間経っても何の連絡もなかった。少し心配になり始めたが，ある日，ジョーンズ先生が生徒の髪について，色や髪型も含めて，もう一切の規則を設けないと発表した。私はとてもうれしかった。これは，私が求めた以上のことだった。あらゆる苦労が報われたのだ。

規則を変えるという決定は，生徒や保護者からさまざまな反応を得た。この変更を非常に喜んだ人もいれば，起こりうる結果を心配する人もいた。しかし，これが正しい決定であり，学校社会によい影響を与えるだろうという自信があった。

その後数カ月，生徒たちが新しい創造的な方法で自分を表現するようになったのを見た。明るい色に染めた髪，ユニークな髪型，そして新たに手に入れた自信を持った生徒たちを見た。学校は，生徒が自分が幸せになると感じる方法で生徒が自由に自分を表現できる場所になった。疑う余地のない成功だ。

あなたのメモ

表現の自由を求める運動

筆者（カースティ・ウッド）について

・学校の方針を変えることに成功した。
・［32］ので学校での運動を開始した。

話に登場する重要人物

・ルーシー・アームストロング：部長で，最初にカースティの要求を拒否した。
・キャロル・スミス：美容師で，［33］。
・ジョーンズ先生：校長で，校則を変更した。

一連の行動の重要な段階

最初の試みは失敗した→［34］→［35］→［36］→［37］→成功

この一連の行動を通じて，カースティが気づいたこと

［38］ことは重要になりうる。

この話から私たちが学べること

・［39］
・［40］

問1　［32］　①

「［32］に入れるのに最適な選択肢を選びなさい。」

① **「学校の方針のために生徒が自己表現をできないと考えていた」**
②「自分の学校が地域社会でよいイメージを持たれていないと思っていた」
③「地元の経営者と交流するのが好きだった」
④「もっと多くの人に自分のようになってほしかった」

筆者のカースティ・ウッドが運動を始めた理由は第1段落に書かれている。第2文で my school's strict policy against students colouring their hair（髪を染めることを禁止するという私の学校の厳しい方針）があると書き，第3文で I felt that this rule was preventing me and my fellow students from expressing ourselves（この規則が，私や学友が自分を表現することを妨げていると感じた）と続けている。この2文を簡潔にまとめた①が正解。

筆者は第3段落最終文に書かれているように，染髪が学校のイメージを損なわないという調査結果を提示しており，「地域社会でよいイメージを持たれていない」とは感じていないので，②は不正解。③と④のような記述はないので，いずれも不正解。

問2　［33］　④

「［33］に入れるのに最適な選択肢を選びなさい。」

①「毛髪染料が安全であることを学校に納得させた」
②「髪の色を通して自己表現をする最良の方法についてアドバイスした」
③「カースティに挑戦し続ける自信を与えた」
④ **「適切な毛染めの技術について学校で講義をした」**

美容師のスミスさんは，第4段落に出てくる。第2・3文に I reached out to ... at our school assembly（母の美容師のキャロル・スミスさんに連絡を取り，髪を安全に染めるためのワークショップを開いてもらえないか確かめた。彼女は全校集会で話した）とある。スミスさんは依頼を受けて「髪を安全に染める方法を学校で話した」のだから④が正解。

第5文に書かれているように，スミスさんが話しても安全性を納得してもらえなかったので，①は不正解。②，③のような行動をしたとは書かれていないので，いずれも不正解。

問3 34 ② 35 ⑤ 36 ③ 37 ④

「5つの選択肢（①～⑤）から4つを選び，起こった順に並べ換えなさい。」

34 → 35 → 36 → 37

①「他の学生にアドバイスを求めた」
②「助けを求めて地元の専門家と連絡を取った」
③「自分の調査結果を説明するために校長と面談した」
④「辛抱強く待ったが，不安に感じた」
⑤「学生が自信を高めた話を調査した」

34

最初の試みに失敗したことは，第3段落に書かれている。**問2**で見たように，第4段落では，プロの美容師に連絡を取り，学校で講義をしてもらったことが書かれている。したがって，②が適当。

35

第5段落には「髪の色を変えるメリットや自己表現の肯定的な影響を調べた」ことが書かれ，その具体例として第7文にI also found ... and feel more confident（また，いじめに苦しんでいたが，髪の色をコントロールすることが自己表現をし，もっと自信を持つ手段を与えてくれるとわかった，という生徒たちの話も見つけた）とある。この内容を簡潔にまとめた⑤が入る。

36

次の段階として，第6段落第1・2文にThis time, I scheduled a meeting with the head teacher of the school, Ms. Jones. I presented the research and stories I had found（今回，私は校長のジョーンズ先生との面談の予定を組み，自分が見つけた調査結果と話を提示した）とある。したがって，③が正解。

37

面談後の経過が，第7段落第1・2文にSeveral weeks went by and I had not heard anything. I was starting to feel a little worried（数週間経っても何の連絡もなかった。少し心配になり始めた）と書かれているので，④が正解。

①のような記述は本文にはない。

問4 38 ②

「38 に入れるのに最適な選択肢を選びなさい。」

①「物事がよりよい方向へ変化するのを辛抱強く待つ」
②「否定的な意見に反対するのではなく，肯定的な意見に注目する」
③「それに反する規則があっても，自己表現を実践する」
④「別の視点を得るために，地元の専門家と話す」

各段落の要旨は以下の通り。

第2段落：規則を無視し，規則がいつか変わるだろうと待つが，変化がなかった。→①と③は不適当。

第3・4段落：「毛髪染料に安全上の問題がある」という考えに反対するために，調査結果を提示したり，美容師に講義をしてもらったが，校則が変わらなかった。

第5段落：髪の毛の色を変えることのデメリットではなくメリットに着目して，肯定的な研究結果や学生の話を調べた。

第6段落：調べたことを校長に話した。

第7～9段落：生徒の髪の毛の色や髪型が自由になり，生徒が自己表現できるようになった。

全体を通して見ると，「否定的な意見に反対してもうまくいかなかった」（第3・4段落）が，肯定的な意見に注目したらうまくいった」（第5～9段落）ことがわかる。したがって，正解は②。

地元の専門家と話したのは，別の視点を得るためではないので，④も不正解。

問5 39 40 ②，③（順不同）

「39 と 40 に入れるのに最適な選択肢を2つ選びなさい。（順不同。）」

①「自分らしくいることは学校の勉強よりも大切である。」
②「自分の信念に従い，自分の価値観に忠実でいなさい。」
③「さまざまな見方から問題に取り組むことが重要である。」
④「他人が自分をどう思うかを気にする必要はない。」
⑤「外見は，あなたの自信にほとんど影響を与えない。」

第1段落第1文で筆者は I believe that ... feel confident and comfortable.（私は，誰もが自信を持って安心できる方法で自分を表現する自由を持つべきだと思う。）と自分の考えを述べている。さらに校則が自分の価値観に合わないとわかると，校則を変えるための運動を起こしている。この姿勢から，「自分の信念に従い，価値観に忠実でいなさい」という②がまず正解。

また，筆者は毛髪についての校則を変える運動の中で，**問2**や**問4**で見たように「否定的な意見に反論するために専門家に講義をしてもらう」「肯定的な研究結果を見つけ，校長に話す」などさまざまな方法を用いている。したがって，「さまざまな物の見方からアプローチする」という③も正解。

①と④に関する記述はないので，不正解。また，⑤は第5段落に書かれた「外見を変えて自己表現することで自信が持てる」という例と反対の内容であり，不正解。

【語句】

◇student council「生徒会」
◇successfully「成功させて，うまく」
◇campaign for ～「～を求めて運動する」
◇express *oneself*「自分（の考え）を表現する」
◇policy「方針」
◇fellow student「学友」
◇ignore「～を無視する」
◇eventually「いつかは」
◇as time goes by「時間が経つにつれて」
◇sit back「傍観する」
◇opposition「反対」
◇quote「～を引き合いに出す」
◇potential「可能性のある」
◇safety hazard「安全上の問題」
◇appeal「訴え」
◇not ready to *do*「…する心境になれない」
◇mum（＝mom）「お母さん」
◇school assembly「全校集会」
◇impressed「感銘を受けて」
◇focus on ～「～に焦点を当てる」
◇struggle with ～「～に苦しむ」
◇bullying「いじめ」
◇diverse「多様な」
◇supportive「協力的な」
◇genuinely「心から」
◇take ～ into consideration「～を考慮に入れる」
◇consequence「結果」
◇confidence「自信」
◇definite「疑う余地のない」
◇initially「当初は」
◇問1　③　interact with ～「～と交流する」
◇問3　rearrange「～を配列し直す」
◇問4　④　alternative「代替の」
◇問5　③　perspective「（ものの）見方」

第8問

全訳　あなたは，生物学の授業でグループプロジェクトを行っている学生です。微生物の適応力について発表をするためにあなたは次の文章を使っています。

適応力の高い生物について，攻撃的な性質と巨大なコロニーを持つアルゼンチンアリのような生物を話題にしないでは語れない。または，何十年も食物や水なしで生き延びる能力があるクマムシがおそらく思い浮かぶ。しかし，線虫として知られているありふれた虫は，実は世界で最も適応力のある小さな生物の1つだ。

線虫は，回虫としても知られているとても小さな生物だ。とても小さいので，顕微鏡を通さないと見えないこともしばしばだ。平均して体長は0.1ミリメートルから2.5ミリメートル程度とさまざまである。もっとも，線虫には1メートル近くに成長する種もいるが。体は細長く，手足がない。庭で見つかる一般的な虫と同じように，筒状で1本の柔らかいスパゲッティのような形をしている。線虫の多くは寄生性で，つまり他の生物の中にすんでいる。珍しい長さ1メートルほどの線虫は地球上で最も大きな哺乳類の部類であるクジラの体内に寄生している。しかし，ほとんどの寄生線虫はもっと小さな生物の中にすんでいて，とても小さい。線虫はほとんどどこにでも，沼地，海，ジャングル，南極大陸にさえ生息することができる。

水は線虫の生存に最も重要だ。また，栄養も必要で，通常は周囲の他の微生物を食べることで摂取する。線虫は，体の一方の端にある口から食物を摂取する。食物は，スタイレットと呼ばれるストローに似た体の部分を通過する。その後，栄養を分解する腸を通過する。最後に，使われなかった廃棄物は直腸腺によって押し流され，肛門を通って線虫の体外に送り出される。

科学者は，光や栄養がほとんど供給されない有毒な水塊や硬い地層の奥深くのような，地球上の極限環境に生息する生物を研究するのに苦労している。そこで，線虫の出番だ。この信じがたい生物は大体どんな環境にも適応することができるため，極限環境の生態系を理解するために，研究者にまたとないチャンスを与える。線虫は生きていくためにほとんど酸素を必要とせず，厳しい状態に生息するバクテリアを食べることができ，非常に丈夫な体を持っている。実は，線虫は食物や水が手に入らない時，休眠状態と呼ばれる一種の眠りにつくことさえできる。休眠状態になっている間は，完全に不活発になる。線虫は，南極のような場所では，20〜30年もの間不活発な状態で生存することができる。条件が良くなり，食物や水が近くにあると，まるで魔法のように線虫は生き返る。

当然ながら，科学者たちは，この虫の魔法を理論やデータで説明しようと最善を尽くしてきた。1970年代，研究者は特にある種の線虫，C.エレガンスを研究し始めた。その単純な構造のため，C.エレガンスは研究者にとってとても興味をそそるものだった。また，この線虫はわずか3日で成虫になる。この種を研究することで，科学者はそれらの神経系がどのように機能するかを理解するようになった。神経系とは，味覚や触覚などの感覚の情報を理解できるようにする，生命体の中にあるネットワーク回路である。C.エレガンスの場合，咽頭（のど）を取り囲むように神経環があり，これが脳の役割を果たしている。このことが，線虫をカタツムリやタコなど，より高度な動物に似させている。実は線虫は，これまで発見された生物の中で，神経系を持つ最も単純な生物の1つだ。その単純だが精巧な身体のおかげで，極限状態でさえも非常に強く死ににくい。

線虫の最もユニークな特徴の1つは，繁殖の仕方だ。通常，どのような動物種の仲間もオスかメスのどちらかだと考えられている。しかしメスの線虫は，時々いわゆる雌雄同体になることができる。基本的には，オスとメスの両方の部分を持つということだ。雌雄同体のメスは子宮の中に抱えた卵を受精させることができる。この驚くべき特徴のため，周囲にオスが見つからない時でさえも子を産むことができるのだ。実際，オスのこの虫の個体数に占める割合はごくわずかなことが多く，1％未満である。

発表用スライド

線虫
究極の適応者

1.基本情報
・体長0.1ミリメートル〜2.5ミリメートル
・長い管状の体
・
・［41］
・
・

2. 生息地
・ほとんどどこにでもいる
✔ 湿地帯　✔ジャングル
✔ 海洋　✔ 南極大陸
・以下のような過酷な環境下でも生き抜くことができる
✔有害な水塊
✔地球の硬い層の奥深く

3. 生存戦略
・［42］
・［43］

4. 体の構造（雌雄同体）
［44］
（イラスト中）
口・咽頭・卵・肛門

5. 最終コメント
［45］

問1 41 ④

「次のうちどれを［41］に含むべきでは**ない**か。」

①「神経環がある」

②「食物を取り込むためのストロー状のスタイレットがある」

③「手足がない」

④「オスの体の部分がない」

⑤「感触や味に反応する」

線虫の情報として誤っているものを選ぶ。第6段落第3〜4文に female nematodes can sometimes become what are called hermaphrodites ... contain both male and female parts（メスの線虫は，時々いわゆる雌雄同体になることができ，…オスとメスの両方の部分を持つ）と書かれている。また，第6

段落にオスの線虫が存在することも書かれている。したがって，④を選ぶ。

第５段落第７文にnerve ring（神経環）の存在が書かれているので①は不正解。ストロー状のスタイレットについて第３段落第４文に書かれているので②も不正解。第２段落第４文によると手足がないので③も不正解。第５段落第６文から感触や味に反応するとわかるので⑤も不正解。

問２　42　②　43　⑤（順不同）

「**『生存戦略』**のスライドに，線虫が生き残るのに最も役立つ特徴を２つ選びなさい。（順不同）」 42 ・ 43

① 「咽頭があるため，より大きな生物を飲み込むことができる。」

② 「酸素をあまり必要としない。」

③ 「極限環境を回避するために神経系を使う。」

④ 「有毒な水塊に入るといつでも，すぐに不活発になる。」

⑤ 「食物や水がないと，長期間不活発になることができる。」

線虫が過酷な環境で生き延びる方法が第４段落に書かれている。１つ目は第４文のNematodes need very little oxygen to survive（線虫は生きていくためにほとんど酸素を必要としない）で，これは②に一致する。もう１つは第５～６文のnematodes can even go into a kind of sleep called suspended animation when there is no food or water available. While in a state of suspended animation, they become completely inactive.（線虫は食物や水が手に入らない時，休眠状態と呼ばれる一種の眠りにつくことさえできる。休眠状態になっている間は，完全に不活発になる。）で，⑤に一致する。

①の記述は本文にない。また，神経系を使うのは極限環境を回避するためではないので③も不正解。「有毒な水塊の中で生きられる」と書いてあるが，「すぐに不活発になる」とは書かれていないので，④も不正解。

問３　44　③

「**『体の構造（雌雄同体）』**スライドの線虫のイラストに欠けているラベルを完成させなさい。」 44

①（A）直腸腺（B）スタイレット（C）腸（D）子宮（E）神経環

②（A）神経環（B）腸（C）子宮（D）直腸腺（E）スタイレット

③（A）スタイレット（B）神経環（C）子宮（D）腸（E）直腸腺

④（A）子宮（B）腸（C）神経環（D）直腸腺（E）スタイレット

⑤（A）スタイレット（B）子宮（C）神経環（D）腸（E）直腸腺

本文から体の構造について書かれた部分を探す。第３段落第３～６文に食物が消化され排泄されるまでの順が書かれている。mouth（口）で食べたものがストロー状のstylet（スタイレット）を通り，intestine（腸）で分解される。さらにrectal gland（直腸腺）から anus（肛門）へ排泄される。これをあてはめると，（A）Stylet，（D）Intestine，（E）Rectal glandになる。また，第５段落第７文にit has a nerve ring that surrounds the pharynx（咽頭を取り囲むように神経環がある）とあるので，（B）が Nerve ring である。さらに第６段落第５文にA hermaphroditic female can fertilize the eggs it carries in its uterus.（雌雄同体のメスは子宮の中に抱えた卵を受精させることができる。）とあり，卵が中に入っている（C）はUterusである。正解は③。

問４　45　②

「最後のスライドの説明に最適なものはどれか。」 45

①「C.エレガンスは，オスの個体数が少ないにもかかわらず，メスが繁殖するための交尾相手をどうにかして見つけるので，間違いなく科学的研究に最適な虫である。」

②「頑丈な体を持ち，極端な気候でも生き延びることができ，繁殖するために交尾相手を必要としないなど，線虫は自然界の最大課題のいくつかを解決するための驚くべき適応性を持っていることは疑いがない。」

③「つまり，線虫の雌雄同体の構造は，その短いライフサイクルと精巧な身体構造の理由なのだ。」

④「線虫は，地球上のほとんどどこでも生き延びることができる驚くべき能力を持っている。この驚くべき生物が将来どのように進化していくかは誰にもわからない。」

スライドの最終ページには，ここまで調べてきたことをまとめ，考察したものが入る。

第４段落には「線虫が極限環境でも生き延びる」方法が書かれている。第６段落では「雌雄同体により，交尾をしないで繁殖する」ことが書かれている。このような線虫の適応性について考察した②が正解。

線虫は交尾相手が少ない状態では，相手を探さず雌雄同体になるので，①は不正解。③は雌雄同体が短いライフサイクルと精巧な身体構造の理由ではないので不正解。④はどこでも生存できる能力について書かれているが，これは本文に書かれている「線虫の適応能力」の一部でしかない。したがって解答としては不十分である。

問5 **46** ①

「線虫について，どのようなことが推察されるか。」

46

① **「線虫と同じくらい単純な生物が神経系を持つのは珍しい。」**

② 「1970年代の科学者たちはC.エレガンスを好んだが，寄生虫である線虫は複雑な神経系を持つため，より人気が出てきている。」

③ 「繁殖するために雌雄同体の能力を使う必要がある時，メスが卵を蓄えるスペースが広くなるように，筒状の体をしている。」

④ 「捕食者が少ないので，海の生物の体の中で生活する。」

第5段落で線虫の神経系について説明し，第8文ではより高度な生物と同じような神経系の働きがあることが書かれている。また，第9文にnematodes are one of the simplest creatures ever discovered to have a nervous system（線虫は，これまで発見された生物の中で，神経系を持つ最も単純な生物の1つだ）と書かれている。つまり，同程度に単純な生物が神経系を持つのは珍しいことなので，①が正解。

寄生する線虫の人気が出たという記述はないので②は不正解。筒状の体と卵を蓄えるスペースの関係は書かれていないので③は不正解。また，海の生物に寄生することと捕食者の関係も書かれていないので④も不正解。

【語句】

◇adaptability「適応力」
◇microorganism「微生物」
◇adaptive「適応できる」
◇bring up ～「～を（話題に）持ち出す」
◇aggressive「攻撃的な」
◇survive「生き残る」
◇decade「10年間」
◇worm「虫」
◇nematode「線虫，回虫」
◇visible「目に見える」
◇vary「さまざまである」
◇tubular「管状の」
◇parasitic「寄生性の」
◇mammal「哺乳類」
◇survival「生存」
◇nutrition「栄養」
◇consume「～を摂取する」
◇*be* located at ～「～に位置する」
◇resemble「～に似ている」
◇intestine「腸」
◇break down ～「～を分解する」
◇rectal gland「直腸腺」
◇extreme「極端な」
◇toxic「有毒な」
◇water mass「水塊」
◇hard layer「硬い層」
◇adapt to ～「～に適応する」
◇just about「大体」
◇ecology「生態系」
◇oxygen「酸素」
◇tough「厳しい，丈夫な」
◇suspended animation「休眠状態」
◇state「状態」
◇naturally「当然ながら」
◇appealing「魅力的な，興味をそそる」
◇sensory input「感覚の情報」
◇nerve ring「神経環」
◇sophisticated「精巧な」
◇hermaphrodite「雌雄同体」
◇basically「基本的に」
◇uterus「子宮」
◇ultimate「究極の」
◇habitat「生息地」
◇strategy「戦略」
◇問5　infer「～を推察する」
◇問5 ④　predator「捕食者」

リーディング模試　第4回　解答

第1問小計	第2問小計	第3問小計	第4問小計	第5問小計	第6問小計	第7問小計	第8問小計

合計点	/100

問題番号(配点)	設問	解答番号	正解	配点	自己採点
第1問(6)	1	1	④	2	
	2	2	④	2	
	3	3	②	2	
第2問(10)	1	4	①	2	
	2	5	④	2	
	3	6	④	2	
	4	7	③	2	
	5	8	③	2	
第3問(9)	1	9	①	3※	
		10	④		
		11	②		
		12	③		
	2	13	①	3	
	3	14	②	3	
第4問(12)	1	15	④	3	
	2	16	①	3	
	3	17	①	3	
	4	18	③	3	

問題番号(配点)	設問	解答番号	正解	配点	自己採点
第5問(16)	1	19	③	3	
	2	20	③	3	
	3	21	③	4	
	4	22	①	3※	
		23	④		
	5	24	④	3	
第6問(18)	1	25	①	3	
	2	26	④	3	
	3	27〜28	①-④	3※	
		29	②	3	
	4	30	②	3	
	5	31	④	3	
第7問(15)	1	32	②	3	
	2	33〜34	③-④	3※	
	3	35	⑤	3※	
		36	③		
		37	④		
		38	①		
	4	39	②	3	
	5	40	②	3	
第8問(14)	1	41	④	4	
	2	42	④	3	
		43	②	3	
	3	44〜45	②-③	4※	

(注)　1　※は，全部正解の場合のみ点を与える。
　　　2　-(ハイフン)でつながれた正解は，順序を問わない。

第1問

全訳 あなたは近くの公会堂を訪れ，興味深い掲示を見つけました。

体験レッスン週間

もし新しく何かを始めたいとお思いでしたら，こちらの体験レッスンを考えてみてはいかがでしょうか？こちらでは，下記の体験レッスンをそれぞれ5ドルで提供しております。今月はバーナビー文化交流センターで開催されます。初心者の方もご参加いただけますので，興味がある方はどうぞお試しください！

レッスン情報

日付／時間	部屋番号	詳細
4月11日 午後2時～午後3時30分	203号室	**編み物** 簡単なやり方で標準的な技術を学ぶ！
4月12日 午後1時30分～午後3時	204号室	**ジュエリー制作** ジュエリーの作り方の基礎を学ぶ。
4月14日 午前10時～午後0時20分	205号室	**イラスト** 絵の描き方や画材の使い方を学ぶ。作品に講評をもらうことができる。
4月17日 午後1時30分～午後3時30分	303号室	**生け花** プロのフラワーデザイナーの指導のもとで花を選んで生ける。

注意

これらのレッスンへの参加にはオンラインで予約していただく必要があります。こちらをクリックして，遅くとも参加を希望するイベント前日までにご登録ください。恐れ入りますが各レッスンの参加人数には限りがございます。当日に必要となるものはレッスンの主催者が用意いたします。

問1 1 ④

「この掲示によると，［1］ということだ。」

①「すべての体験レッスンは午後に始まる」

②「生け花のクラスは最も長い」

③「未経験者はレッスンに参加できない」

④「どの体験レッスンに参加したいかを選べる」

掲示には，4月11日から17日にかけてバーナビー文化交流センターで行われる体験レッスンへの誘いと各レッスンの情報が載せられている。この掲示では，どのレッスンについても参加要件があるとは述べられていない。したがって，希望者は自分が受けたいレッスンをどれでも受けることができるので，④が正解。レッスンの開始時間を見ると，イラストは午前10時に始まるので，①は不正解。レッスンの長さを見ると，編み物とジュエリー制作が1時間半，イラストが2時間20分，生け花が2時間なので，②は不正解。第4文にBeginners can also attend「初心者の方もご参加いただけます」とあるので，③は不正解。

問2 2 ④

「体験レッスン週間の間，参加者は［2］ことができる。」

①「高度な編み物技術を学ぶ」

②「アマチュアの講師から生け花を学ぶ」

③「203号室でアクセサリーの作り方を学ぶ」

④「自分の絵の感想を受け取る」

掲示のLesson Informationを見ると，イラストのクラスの説明にYou can get our comments on your work.「作品に講評をもらうことができる。」とあるので，④が正解。編み物のクラスの説明にLearn the standard techniques「標準的な技術を学ぶ」とあるので，①は不正解。生け花のクラスの説明にunder the guidance of a professional flower designer「プロのフラワーデザイナーの指導のもとで」とあるので，②は不正解。ジュエリー制作のレッスンは204号室で行われるので，③は不正解。

問3 3 ②

「体験レッスンの参加者は［3］必要がない。」

①「レッスン料を支払う」

②「何かを事前に用意する」

③「レッスン前にオンラインで登録する」

④「体験レッスンを予約する」

体験レッスンの参加者がしなくてもよいことが正解となる。Notesの最終文にThe lesson organizers will prepare what you need that day.「当日に必要となるものはレッスンの主催者が用意いたします。」とあり，参加者は自分で何も用意する必要がないことがわかる。したがって，②が正解。第2文に，体験レッスンの料金についてWe are offering the trial lessons listed as below for $5 each.「こちらでは，下記の体験レッスンをそれぞれ5ドルで提供しております。」とあるので，参加者は料金を払わなければならず，①は不正解。Notesの第1文にYou need to make a reservation online to take part in these lessons.「これらのレッスンへの参加にはオンラインで予約していただく必要があります。」とあるので，④は不正解。また予約の期限について，その直後の文にregister by at least one day before the event that you wish to participate in「遅くとも参加を希望するイベント前日までにご登録ください」とあるので，③は不正解。

【語句】

◇try out ～「～を試してみる」

◇knitting「編み物」

◇organizer「主催者」

◇問2 ④ feedback「フィードバック；感想」

第2問

全訳 あなたの英語の先生は次の授業での討論の準備に役立つ記事をくれました。この記事の一部と意見の1つは下記の通りです。

在宅勤務は私たちの働き方を変えるか？

ロサンゼルス ナンシー・ガルシア 記

2018年7月31日 午後5:17

米国コミュニティー調査（ACS）はアメリカ合衆国での在宅勤務人口の統計を更新した。そのデータによると，デジタル遠距離電気通信を用いて仕事時間の半分より多い時間を自宅で仕事をする人々の数は，2016年の時点で430万人，労働人口全体の3.2%であった。これは個人事業主を含んでいない。

ビジネスコンサルタントのデイビッド・ハウは在宅勤務の利点について次のように力説している。「在宅勤務は，被雇用者の無駄で苦痛を伴う通勤時間を省きます。小さい子供がいる親にとっては，子供と一緒に過ごす時間が増えます。雇用主にとっては，交通費や光熱費を省きます。」

一方，在宅勤務を経験したメアリー・ホールデンは，「在宅勤務には多くの利点がありますが，いくつか欠点もあります。例えば，在宅勤務者は仕事で他の人と会う機会が少ない傾向があり，時として自分の仕事の意義を見失います。加えて，在宅勤務者が経験豊かであれば問題ないのですが，そうでなければ，仕事の仕方について他人とやり取りするのは難しいかもしれません。さらに，労働時間の増加と時給の大幅な減少も問題となります。」と話している。

15のコメント

最新

アンジェラ・ジョーンズ 2018年8月2日午後7:20

私も在宅勤務者です。私は自然豊かな田舎に住んでいますが，在宅勤務によって十分な収入を得られています。在宅勤務者の数が増えれば，道路上の車は少なくなり，電車の混雑は軽減されるでしょう。私たちはただ仕事の仕方を変えるだけで，環境を救うことができるのです。

問1 4 ①

「記事によると，在宅勤務人口とは 4 人々の数を意味している。」

① **「雇われているが家で働いている」**

②「雇われていないが通信機器を使って家で働いている」

③「通信機器を使わずに家で働いている」

④「通勤時間の間に通信機器を使って働いている」

第1段落第1文にThe American Community Survey (ACS) updated their statistics on the telecommuting population in the USA.「米国コミュニティー調査(ACS)はアメリカ合衆国でのtelecommuting populationの統計を更新した。」とあり，その直後にAccording to the data, the number of people who work at home for more than half of their working time using digital telecommunications was ...「そのデータによると，デジタル遠距離電気通信を用いて仕事時間の半分より多い時間を自宅で仕事をする人々の数は…」と続くことから，telecommuting populationとは「デジタル遠距離電気通信を用いて自宅で仕事をする人々の数」であることがわかる。また，その次の文This did not include the self-employed.「これは個人事業主（＝自営業者）を含んでいない。」から，この数は雇用されている人々の数であることがわかる。したがって，①が正解。②はaren't employed「雇われていない」が，③はwithout using any communication device「通信機器を使わずに」が，それぞれ本文の内容に反するので不正解。また，通勤時間中に仕事をするということは述べられていないので，④は不正解。

問2　5　④

「あなたのチームは『在宅勤務の仕事は奨励されるべきだ。』という討論のトピックを支持する。記事の中で，あなたたちのチームの手助けとなる（事実ではなく）**意見**の1つは［5］ということだ。」

①「在宅勤務は子供を育てる親たちにとってより多く稼ぐよい方法である」

②「労働人口全体の5％より多くの人が在宅勤務者として働いている」

③「通勤時間は短縮されるだろう」

④「自分の子供といる時間をより多く持つことができる」

設問文で提示された討論のトピックは，「在宅勤務の仕事は奨励されるべきだ。」という立場である。これを支持するために役立つ意見を選ぶ。第2，3段落で，在宅勤務についての識者と経験者の意見を紹介しているので，ここに注目する。第2段落第2文にit gives them more time to spend with their children「それ（＝在宅勤務）は子供と一緒に過ごす時間を増やします」とある。これは，親の立場から言えば，子供と過ごす時間が増えるということなので，④が正解。第3段落最終文に「時給の大幅な減少も問題となります」とあり，在宅勤務の方が多く稼げるとは述べられていないので，①は不正解。「労働人口全体の5％より多くの人が在宅勤務者として働いている」というのは意見ではなく，しかも第1段落第2文からその内容が誤りであることがわかるので，②は不正解。commuting time（通勤時間）については，そもそも在宅勤務は通勤が不要なので通勤時間が存在しない。したがって，③は不正解。第2段落第1文のTelecommuting saves employees commuting timeのsaveは，〈save＋間接目的語（人）＋直接目的語〉の形で「人に金銭・時間・労力などを省かせる」という意味を表す用法で，上の英文は「在宅勤務のおかげで被雇用者は通勤時間を省くことができる」という意味を表している。

問3　6　④

「もう一方のチームはその討論のトピックに反対する。記事の中で，そのチームの手助けとなる（事実ではなく）**意見**の1つは［6］ということだ。」

①「企業は交通費などの費用を自分たちの労働者に支払わなければならない」

②「在宅勤務はたいてい本人に強い達成感をもたらす」

③「一緒に働く人たちと会う機会が増えるだろう」

④「経験の度合いが仕事に対する姿勢に影響を及ぼす可能性がある」

問2とは逆に，「在宅勤務の仕事は奨励されるべきだ。」という立場に反対するために役立つ意見を選ぶ。第3段落のメアリー・ホールデンの意見の中に在宅勤務のデメリットが述べられているので，そこに注目する。第3文にif a teleworker is experienced, there is no problem, but if not, it might be difficult for them to communicate with other people about how to work「在宅勤務者が経験豊かであれば問題ないのですが，そうでなければ，仕事の仕方について他人とやり取りするのは難しいかもしれません」と，労働者の経験が浅い場合のデメリットを述べているので，④が正解。同段落第2文にtelecommuters tend to have less opportunity to meet other people on business「在宅勤務者は仕事で他の人と会う機会が少ない傾向があり」とあるので，③は不正解。続いてsometimes forget the meaning of their work「時として自分の仕事の意義を見失います」とあるので，②は不正解。transportation fees（交通費）については，第2段落最終文に，在宅勤務の企業側のメリットとしてit saves them transportation and utilities costs「交通費や光熱費を省きます」とあるので，①は不正解。

問4　7　③

「記事の第3段落において，メアリー・ホールデンは在宅勤務者が［7］可能性に言及している。」

①「自分たちが田舎で働いている理由を完全に理解している」

②「新しい経験を得る機会を減少させる」

③「より長い労働時間にもかかわらず賃金が少ない」

④「自分たちの仕事を通して多くの人々と会う」

第3段落でメアリー・ホールデンが述べている意見に合致するものを選ぶ。最終文にthe increase in working hours and the large decrease in pay per hour are also problems「労働時間の増加と時給の大幅な減少も問題となります」とあり，これに合致する③が正解。work in the countryside「田舎で働く」ことについては，第3段落では何も述べられていないので，①は不正解。chance to have new experiences「新しい経験を得る機会」についても述べられていないので，②は不正解。また，第2文にtelecommuters tend to have less opportunity to meet other people on business「在宅勤務者は仕事で他の人と会う機会が少ない傾向があり」とあるので，④は不正解。

問5 8 ③

「アンジェラ・ジョーンズの意見によると，彼女は在宅勤務の奨励に 8 。」

①「ついて特別な意見はない」

②「部分的に反対だ」

③「強く賛成だ」

④「強く反対だ」

アンジェラ・ジョーンズの意見はComments欄で述べられている。第2文では，在宅勤務では自然が豊かな田舎に住みながら仕事ができる，第3，4文では，在宅勤務者が増えることで交通渋滞が減り，環境を救うことができると述べており，在宅勤務のメリットだけを挙げている。したがって，③が正解。在宅勤務のデメリットは何も挙げていないので，②と④はいずれも不正解。

【語句】

◇telecommuting「在宅勤務」

◇update「～を更新する」

◇as of ～「～の時点で」

◇utility「公共設備」（しばしばutilities）

第3問

全訳 あなたはニューヨークで交換留学プログラムに参加している日本人の友人のブログ記事を読んでいます。

ドラム部のために太鼓を！

私のブログにアクセスしてくれてありがとう。以前にも言った通り，私は今，ブロンクス高校の交換留学生です。そこで友達と私は2月に新しくドラム部を始めました。私の交換留学プログラムはもうすぐ終わりますが，日本に戻る前に，部に何か残したいと思います。それは新しい太鼓です。

昨年の12月，クラスメートのグレッグ・ハリスとオリオン・ファベルが私に和太鼓を教えてほしいと頼みました。彼らはその前の月，市の国際フェスティバルで私の演奏を見たのです。9歳の時，私は太鼓の稽古を受け始めました。それ以来，私はずっと太鼓を演奏していますが，教えた経験はありませんでした。グレッグとオリオンは問題ないと言いました。彼らは学校の音楽の先生に教えてほしいと頼んだのですが，彼は太鼓の奏法がわからなかったので，彼らは私のところに来たのです。最初の稽古では，私たちはグレッグの家に集まりました。私の太鼓と彼らのドラムの違いを聞くのはとても面白かったです。すぐに，他の友人たちも私たちの太鼓の稽古に参加できるかたずねてきました。校長先生に，私たちが学校で集まることができるかどうかをたずねたところ，彼女は新しい部の設立ルールを説明してくれました。現在，15人の部員が週に1度，一緒に練習しています。

今年の4月，私たちはスクール・スプリング・コンサートでの演奏を頼まれました。異なる文化の音楽をミックスしたオリジナル曲を演奏する予定だったので，部員はみな緊張していました。しかし，コンサートは成功でした！聴衆は私たちの音楽を本当に楽しんだのです。

私は今，部に太鼓を贈ることで友達や学校に感謝を伝えたいと思っています。そうすれば，私が帰国したあとも，部は和太鼓を演奏し続けることができます。もし私たちの太鼓購入のために寄付ができるなら，職員室の近くにある募金箱にお金を入れるか，オリオンに連絡してください。質問があれば，私にお気軽にメールしてください。

あなたのご支援に感謝します！

問1 9 ① 10 ④ 11 ② 12 ③

「次の出来事（①～④）を起こった順に並べよ。」

①「グレッグとオリオンは音楽の先生に太鼓を教えてくれるよう頼んだ。」

②「ブロンクス高校がドラム部を始めた。」

③「筆者はスクール・スプリング・コンサートで演奏した。」

④「3人の生徒がグレッグの家で太鼓を演奏した。」

ブログでは出来事が時系列で述べられているので，順に追っていけばよい。

・「グレッグとオリオンは学校の音楽の先生に太鼓を教えてほしいと頼んだが，彼は太鼓の奏法がわからなかったので，2人は筆者に頼んだ」（第2段落第6文）→①

・「グレッグの家で，筆者はグレッグとオリオンに太鼓を教えた。」（第2段落第7文）→④

・「校長先生が筆者たちにブロンクス高校における

新しい部の設立ルールを説明し，現在は15人の部員がいる。」（第２段落第10～11文）→②

・「筆者たちはスクール・スプリング・コンサートでの演奏を頼まれ，オリジナル曲を演奏し，成功をおさめた。」（第３段落第１～４文）→③

以上より，①→④→②→③の順。

問２ 13 ①

「このブログ投稿から，ブロンクス高校のドラム部は 13 ということがわかる。」

① **「新しい曲を作り出すことができる」**

②「音楽を演奏することでお金を稼ぐ」

③「現在はグレッグの家に集まっている」

④「15人の部員で始まった」

第３段落第２文に，we planned to perform original songs by mixing music from different cultures（私たちは異なる文化の音楽をミックスしたオリジナル曲を演奏する予定だった）とあるので，①が正解。

第２段落第７文に，For our first lesson, we(=Greg, Orion and the writer) met at Greg's house.（最初の稽古では，私たち（＝グレッグ，オリオンと筆者）はグレッグの家に集まりました。）とあり，次に第２段落第10～11文に，When we asked the school principal if we could meet at school, she explained the rules for making a new club. Now, fifteen members practice together once a week.（校長先生に私たちが学校で集まることができるかどうかをたずねたところ，彼女は新しい部の設立ルールを説明してくれました。現在，15人の部員が週に１度，一緒に練習しています。）とある。最初はグレッグの家で３人で始め，現在は学校で15人の部員で活動していることが読み取れるので，③，④は不正解。音楽を演奏してお金を稼いだとは書かれていないので，②も不正解。

問３ 14 ②

「あなたはその部を支援することにした。あなたは何をすることを期待されているか。」 14

①「詳細を聞くためにグレッグにメールする。」

② **「募金箱にお金を入れる。」**

③「新しい太鼓をブロンクス高校に送る。」

④「校長先生と話す。」

寄付の方法については第４段落第３文に，If you can make a donation for us to purchase a *taiko*, please put the money in the donation box near the teachers' room or contact Orion.（もし私たちの太鼓購入のために寄付ができるなら，職員室の近くにある募金箱にお金を入れるか，オリオンに連絡してください。）とある。したがって，②が正解。

第４段落第４文に，Feel free to e-mail me if you have any questions.（質問があれば，私にお気軽にメールしてください。）とある。詳細を聞くにはグレッグではなく筆者に連絡すべきなので，①は不正解。③，④のような記述はないので不正解。

【語句】

◇previous「前の」

◇school principal「校長先生」

◇donation「寄付」

◇feel free to *do*「自由に…する」

◇問３　*be* expected to *do*「…することを期待される」

第４問

全訳　あなたは英語の授業で，興味のある社会問題に関するエッセイを書いています。これはあなたの最新の草稿です。今は先生からのコメントをもとに，推敲に取り組んでいるところです。

一つのきれいな空の下で

私は先週の歴史の授業で1980年代の東京の写真を見て，ショックを受けました。大気汚染のせいでスカイラインがほとんど見えませんでした。それ以来多くのことが変わりましたが，世界規模でこの問題を解決するために私たちはもっと努力する必要があると思います。WHOは，大気汚染が原因で毎年ほぼ700万人が亡くなっていると推定しています！このエッセイでは，私たちにできることを考えたいです。

第一に，大気汚染は主にガソリン車によって起こるので，電気自動車や電気バスへのより大きな転換が必要です。*(1)* 15 周りを見渡せば，その主な理由がわかるでしょう。充電ステーションが十分にないため，ほとんどの人にとって電気自動車（EV）を購入することは現実的ではありません。政府はEVをより安価で便利な選択肢にする必要があると思います。

第二に，日本も環境先進国の他国に倣って，LEZ（低排出ゾーン）と呼ばれる指定地域を導入する必要があります。基本的に，低排出ガス基準を満たさない車の運転者はLEZに入るためにお金を払わなければなりません。現在の日本の政策は，人々がエコカーを購入することを願うことだけのようです。*(2)* 16 ヨーロッパの都市は，人々がもっと行動するように，積極的な措置を講じています。

最後に，*(3)*今こそ，あなたが関心をもっていると示す時です！ 市街地に樹木をより多く植える必要があります。樹木は二酸化炭素を吸い上げて大気汚染を減らすのに役立つだけでなく，暑い夏の日に買い物客に木陰を提供してくれるでしょう。

結論として，日本は過去に比べればかなり汚染がなくなりましたが，それでも私たちは地球市民としての役割を果たさなければなりません。電気自動車の普及を促進し，有毒ガスの抑制*(4)*についてもっと知り，さらに都市の緑化に取り組むべきです。私たちがここで行うことは，地球の生態系全体に影響を及ぼすのです。

コメント

(1) ここに何か足りません。2つの文をつなぐために，間にさらに情報を追加しなさい。

(2) ここに接続表現を挿入しなさい。

(3) この主題文はこの段落にあまり合っていません。書き直しなさい。

(4) 下線部の表現はあなたのエッセイの内容を十分に要約していません。変更しなさい。

総合的なコメント

全体的によく書けています。いくつか小さな修正をすれば完璧でしょう。(日本にLEZを作るという提案には賛成です！ ☺)

問1 15 ④

「コメント(1)に基づいて，付け加えるのに最も適当な文はどれか。」 15

① 「2023年時点で，電気自動車はガソリン自動車より安価だった。」

② 「2023年時点で，ほとんどの人は電気自動車を運転したがった。」

③ 「2023年時点で，タクシー会社はすでに電気自動車を使っていた。」

④ **「2023年時点で，日本における電気自動車は3%しかなかった。」**

(1)の前後の内容を確認する。直前で there needs to be a bigger move towards electric cars and buses（電気自動車や電気バスへのより大きな転換が必要）と書いているが，直後の文では Take a look around and you will see the main reason.（周りを見渡せば，その主な理由がわかるだろう）に続けて，電気自動車が少ない理由を挙げている。ここから「電気自動車を増やすべきだが，実情は数が少ない」と判断できるので，そのことを具体的な数値を挙げて書いた④が正解。①は直後の「政府はEVをより安価な選択肢にする必要がある（つまり現在は高い）」という内容に反する。②③については書かれていないので不正解。

問2 16 ①

「コメント(2)に基づいて，付け加えるのに最も適当な表現はどれか。」 16

① **「その一方」**

② 「特に」

③ 「それにもかかわらず」

④ 「そうでなければ」

(2)の前後の内容を確認する。直前に At present the Japanese policy seems to be to just hope that people buy eco-friendly cars.（現在の日本の政策は，人々がエコカーを購入することを願うことだけのようだ。），直後に European cities are taking positive action to encourage people to do more.（ヨーロッパの都市は，人々がもっと行動するように積極的な措置を講じている）と，日本とヨーロッパの対応が対照的であることを示している。対照的な内容を比較する時，間に入れる接続表現として最も適当なのは①である。

問3 17 ①

「コメント(3)に基づいて，主題文を書き換えるのに最も適当なものはどれか。」 17

① **「緑化は汚染を減らす」**

② 「車の運転をやめよう」

③ 「夏の買い物をやめよう」

④ 「地球を守ろう，バスに乗ろう」

主題文（topic sentence）は，その段落の内容を端的に表した文で，主題文のあとに具体的な内容がくる。ここでは We need to plant more trees in city centers.（市街地に樹木をより多く植える必要がある。）が続き，樹木が helping reduce air pollution（大気汚染を減らすことに役立つ）とある。

つまり，緑化が大気汚染の減少につながるので，①が正解。②③④については前後関係が合わないので不正解。

問4 **18** ③

「コメント(4)に基づいて，置き換えるのに最も適当なものはどれか。」 18

①「～によって，もっと地球の役に立つ」

②「～に適した新しい車を作る」

③「～において他の環境先進国に遅れをとらないようにする」

④「～のためにさらなる財政貢献をする」

エッセイの結論にあたる最終段落の第1文には we still must play our part as global citizens（それでも私たちは地球市民としての役割を果たさなければならない）とある。続く文はその具体的な方法が書かれており，(4)の前にある We should promote the use of electric cars（電気自動車の普及を促進する）は第2段落の内容，(4)のあとの work on further greening our cities（都市の緑化に取り組む）は第4段落の内容をまとめたものなので，(4)は第3段落に関連する修正を入れることになるとわかる。controlling toxic gas（有毒ガスの抑制）について確認すると，Japan needs to follow the lead of other environmentally advanced countries and introduce designed areas called LEZs（日本も環境先進国の他国に倣って，LEZを導入する必要がある），また At present the Japanese policy seems to be to just hope that people buy eco-friendly cars. (In contrast) European cities are taking positive action to encourage people to do more.（現在の日本の政策は，人々がエコカーを購入することを願うことだけのようだ。(一方) ヨーロッパの都市は，人々がもっと行動するように，積極的な措置を講じている。）とあるので，有毒ガス規制において日本が他国から遅れていることが書かれている。したがって「他国に遅れをとらない」という③がふさわしい。①②④については本文で書かれていない。

【語句】

◇skyline「スカイライン（空を背景とした山や高層建築物などのシルエット）」
◇barely「ほとんど…ない」
◇visible「目に見える」
◇global scale「世界規模」
◇estimate that ...「…と推定する」
◇move towards ～「～への移行〔変化〕」
◇cause「～を引き起こす」
◇practical「現実的な」
◇emission「排出（量）」
◇basically「基本的に」
◇standard「基準」
◇policy「政策」
◇suck up ～「～を吸い上げる」
◇carbon dioxide「二酸化炭素」
◇global citizen「地球市民」
◇toxic「有毒な」
◇affect「～に影響する」
◇entire ～「～全体の」
◇minor「ささいな；ちょっとした」
◇問1 ① as of ～「～の時点で」
◇問2 ① in contrast「その一方」
◇問2 ② in particular「特に」
◇問2 ③ nevertheless「それにもかかわらず」
◇問4 ③ keep up with ～「～に遅れずについていく」
◇問4 ④ contribution「貢献」

第5問

全訳 あなたは世界の人々がどれくらい幸せを感じているかについての調査をしています。あなたは2つの記事を見つけました。

世界各国の個人の幸福度　リチャード・カイル　記

2018年11月

日常生活で人々が感じる幸福の度合いは，その人が住んでいる国やその人がどの国籍を持っているかによって異なる。これはおそらく政府の政策や国民性，考え方に違いがあるからだ。それぞれの人が違った理由で幸せを感じる。例えば，無料の医療や教育が受けられる場合がある。幸福度の高い国では，人々は仕事と生活のバランスをうまく取っている。

2018年に国連によって行われた調査によると，よい社会サービスを持つ国の人々がより幸せを感じている。下記のグラフは，「踏み段に最下部の0から最上部の10まで番号が付けられたはしごを想像してください。現時点で，あなたははしごのどの踏み段に立っていると個人的に感じるか教えてください。」という質問に答えた人について，国ごとの平均点を表している。

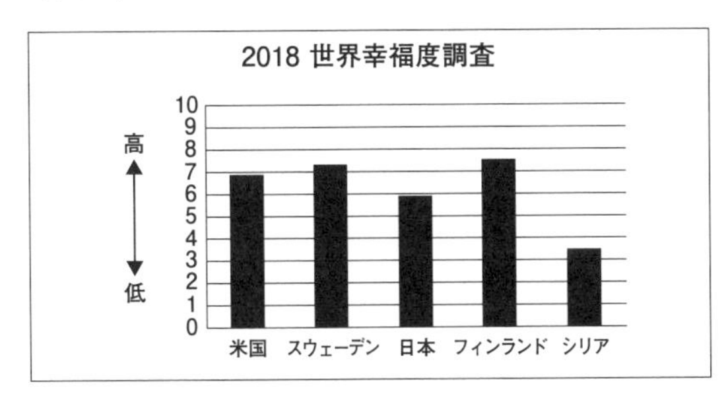

先に述べたように，社会サービスがよい2カ国は，個人の幸福度が高い。グラフ上で，平均所得が高い米国の幸福度は，北欧の同じような人々のそれよりも低い。米国では，近年人々の心身の健康が悪化しており，そしてさらに不安の度合いは増えつつある。多く残業してくつろぐ時間が少ないのは，日本ではよくあることで，それが幸福度の低さにつながっている。シリアは内戦状態にあるので，度合いはとても低い。

幸福は人々がどのくらいお金を稼ぐかに関連していない。私の意見としては，くつろぐための自分の時間や健康状態は高価な車や大きな家よりももっと重要なのである。

「世界各国の個人の幸福度」についての意見

A.O.　記

2018年12月

私は大学で哲学を勉強している。私の国の個人の幸福度は，グラフで一番ではないものの，それでも高い方だ。この事実は大変うれしく，誇りに思う。リチャード・カイルさんの記事によると，私たちの国のように個人の幸福度が高いいくつかの国では，無料の医療や教育を受けられる。しかし，よい社会福祉システムを提供するためには多くのお金がかかる。私たちの国は，所得税率の高さでヨーロッパの1位となっている。

高い税率ではあるが，医療に対して支払いをする必要がないので，私たちは安心している。このおかげで，自分たちは好きなことは何でも自由にチャレンジしている。これは自分自身を向上させるよい環境があることを意味する。加えて，教育が無料なので，誰もが平等な教育機会を得ることができるのはありがたいと思う。学校で知識を得ることによって，多くの人々が社会に貢献することができるだろう。これらの要因はいずれも明るい将来がある可能性を増やし，人々は人生においてたくさんの選択肢を持つ。

問1　19　③

「リチャード・カイルと大学生はどちらも 19 については述べていない。」

①「教育機会」

②「無料の政府のサービス」

③「幸福と自然の近くで生活すること」

④「幸福と健康の関係」

問題文のneither ～ nor ...は「～も…もない」という意味。どちらの記事でも述べられていない事柄はどれか，選択肢を順に検討しよう。

educational opportunities（教育機会）については，1つ目の記事の第1段落第4文にIn some cases, for example, they have free health care and education.「例えば，無料の医療や教育が受けられる場合がある。」と述べられており，また2つ目の記事の第2段落第4文でもit is good that everyone can get equal educational opportunities「誰もが平等な教育機会を得ることができるのはありがたい」と述べているので，①は不正解。free government services（無料の政府のサービス）については，1つ目の記事では上記第1段落第4文で述べられており，2つ目の記事では第1段落第4文にin some countries, ... we can receive free health care and education「…いくつかの国では，無料の医療や教育を受けられる」とあるので，②は不正解。living close to nature（自然の近くで生活すること）については両方の記事でまったく触れられていないので，③が正解。relationship between happiness and health（幸福と健康の関係）については，1つ目の記事の最終段落で幸福が何に関係するかを述べており，その中で筆者の意見としてprivate time to relax and physical condition are more important「くつろぐための自分の時間や健康状態はもっと重要だ」と述べられている。したがって，④は不正解。

問2　20　③

「大学生は 20 出身だ。」

①「フィンランド」

②「日本」

③「スウェーデン」

④「米国」

大学生による2つ目の記事の第1段落第2文にMy

country's level of personal happiness is not the highest on the graph, but it is still high.「私の国の個人の幸福度は，グラフで一番ではないものの，それでも高い方だ。」とある。また第6文にOur country stands as number one in Europe with the highest income tax rates.「私たちの国は，所得税率の高さではヨーロッパの1位となっている。」とあることより，筆者の国はヨーロッパにあることがわかる。グラフにあるヨーロッパの国はスウェーデンとフィンランドの2国。一方，グラフで幸福度が最も高いのはフィンランドだが，筆者の国は1位ではない。したがって，③が正解。

問3 21 ③

「記事によると，個人の幸福度の高い国では，政府の政策が国民の 21 へよい効果をもたらしている。」(最も適切な説明の組み合わせを選べ。)

a「教育レベル」

b「雇用状態」

c「所得税率」

d「精神面の健康」

2つの記事から，government policies(政府の政策)に関係のある箇所を探す。1つ目の記事の第1段落第4文にIn some cases, for example, they have free health care and education.「例えば，無料の医療や教育が受けられる場合がある。」と述べられているが，これは直前のEach person feels happy for different reasons.「それぞれの人が違った理由で幸せを感じる。」の「理由」の例である。したがって，政府の政策である，無料の医療と教育は人々の幸福度に寄与しているとわかる。このことは2つ目の記事の第1段落第4文でもin some countries like ours, which have high levels of personal happiness, we can receive free health care and education「私たちの国のように個人の幸福度が高いいくつかの国では，無料の医療や教育を受けられる」と述べられ，このあと第2段落第1文でwe feel relieved because we don't have to pay for health care「医療に対して支払いをする必要がないので，私たちは安心している」とある。これは，無料の医療が人々の精神面の安定を支えていると解釈できる。したがって，**d**のmental well-being は正解。さらに，第4文ではI think that it is good that everyone can get equal educational opportunities, because education is free.「教育が無料なので，誰もが平等な教育機会を得ることができるのはありがたいと思う。」とあるので，無料の教育という政策が人々の教育レベルにも好影響を与えていると考えられる。したがって，**a**のeducation levels も正解。employment status(雇用状態)についてはどちらの記事にも述べられていないので，**b**は不正解。income tax rate(所得税率)については，2つ目の記事の第1段落第5文でit costs a lot of money to provide a good social welfare system「よい社会福祉システムを提供するためには多くのお金がかかる」と述べられ，それに続いて筆者の国の所得税率がヨーロッパ最高であることが紹介されている。高い所得税率によって社会福祉が向上し，人々の幸福度が上がるわけだが，政府の政策が所得税率に好影響を与えるという関係ではない。したがって，**c**のincome tax rateは不正解。したがって正解の組み合わせは，③。

問4 22 ① 23 ④

「リチャード・カイルは幸福を感じる人々は 22 と述べ，大学生は幸福を感じる人々は 23 と述べている。」(それぞれの空欄には異なる選択肢を選ぶこと。)

①「物にこだわらない」 22

②「戦争を経験しない」

③「よい教育を受けるのに十分なお金を稼いでいる」

④「十分な社会サポートがあるので，たくさんの人生の選択肢がある」 23

⑤「緊急時にお互いに助け合っている」

22 は1つ目の記事で述べられていることを選ぶ。最終段落第2文にIn my opinion, private time to relax and physical condition are more important than expensive cars or large houses.「私の意見としては，くつろぐための自分の時間や健康状態は高価な車や大きな家よりももっと重要なのである。」とあるので，①を選べばよい。

23 は2つ目の記事で述べられていることを選ぶ。第2段落最終文にBoth of these factors increase their chances of having a good future, and they have a lot of options in their lives.「これらの要因はいずれも明るい将来がある可能性を増やし，人々は人生においてたくさんの選択肢を持つ。」とあり，このthese factorsはそこまでで紹介されたfree health care and education「無料の医療や教育」という社会的サポートを指す。したがって，④

を選べばよい。

戦争については，1つ目の記事の第3段落最終文で幸福度の低いシリアが内戦状態にあることに触れているが，幸福を感じる人々は戦争を経験しないとは述べられていない。また，2つ目の記事ではまったく述べられていないので，②はいずれにも入らない。お金を稼ぐことについては，1つ目の記事の最終段落第1文で，幸福とどれだけお金を稼ぐかは関係ないと述べられており，2つ目の記事では教育が無料だとあるので，③は不正解。互いに助け合うことについては，どちらの記事にも述べられていないので，⑤は不正解。

問5 24 ④

「両方の記事の情報に基づいて，あなたは宿題でレポートを書く予定である。あなたのレポートに最適なタイトルは『 24 』である。」

①「幸福を計算する方法」
②「幸福度は時代とともに変化している」
③「5カ国の幸福度がそれほど高い理由」
④「幸福の報告書が私たちに教えてくれること」

リチャード・カイルによる1つ目の記事では，2018年に国連によって行われた各国の幸福度の調査結果の紹介とそこから考察されることについて述べられている。2つ目の記事は，ヨーロッパの学生が1つ目の記事に触発されて，自国の状況を述べたものなので，④がレポートのタイトルとしては最適。1つ目の記事に，グラフの説明として幸福についての質問に対する回答方法が述べられているが，それが全体のテーマとは言えないので，①は不適。幸福度と時代の関係については，どちらの記事でも述べられていないので，②は不適。グラフにある5カ国のうち，シリアについては1つ目の記事の第3段落最終文で，幸福度が非常に低いと述べられているので，③の内容は記事と矛盾する。したがって，③は不適。

【語句】

◇the United Nations「国連」
◇ladder「はしご」
◇whatever「…するものは何でも」
◇問3 d well-being「健康」

第6問

全訳 あなたは，日本の企業で性別による積極的差別〔被差別者優遇〕が行われるべきかどうかについてのエッセイに取り組んでいます。管理職のような，女性の参画率が低い職種でより多くの女性を雇用することは，一つの解決策になり得ます。あなたは以下のステップに従います。

ステップ1：積極的差別や，雇用における女性の一定の割り当てのような性別定数制の活用に関するさまざまな見解を読み，理解する。
ステップ2：企業が積極的差別を導入することに対する自分の立場を決める。
ステップ3：追加の資料を用いてエッセイの概要を作成する。

［ステップ1］さまざまな資料を読む

筆者A（大学生）

積極的差別はもっと多くの企業で用いられるべきだと思います。「差別」という言葉は悪いことだと私たちはしばしば考えますが，問題は多くの企業で女性管理職よりも男性管理職の方が多いということです。女性の平均の給料も低く，幹部職の人はたいてい男性です。これは明らかに不公平です。人口の半分は女性が構成していて，幹部職に就いている人の半分も女性であるべきです。私は一生懸命勉強しつつも将来を心配していて，男性と同じ機会を得たいと思っています。50%の女性定数を設けることで，多様性が高まり，より公平な職場を作ることができるでしょう。

筆者B（経済学教授）

世界中で，さまざまな国が職場における性別格差に取り組むための法律を導入しています。（これらの中には，）さかのぼること2008年に法律を導入したノルウェーのように，積極的差別を含む法律もあります。この法律は，管理職のうち少なくとも40%に女性を雇用することを企業に義務付けています。しかし，より公平な職場を実現するためには，必ずしも積極的差別を導入する必要はありません。多くの国では，女性をより多く雇用することではなく，同一労働同一賃金を支払うことだけを重視しています。例えばアイスランドの企業は，男性労働者と女性労働者が同じ仕事をすると同じ給与を得ていると証明しなければなりません。

著者C（企業取締役）

私たちの会社は，性別，人種，経歴に関係なく，誰にでも平等に機会を与えることを信条としています。しかし，人々が「積極的差別」と呼ぶものには反対です。差別は差別だと考えています。私たちは最適な人材（男性でも女性でも）を雇う必要がありますが，この見解はそうすることを妨げるでしょう。例えば，管理職を開かれたものにしても，数十年前にすでに女性よりも男性の方を多く雇っていたから，最も適任の候補者たちは男性でした。それでも，適性の劣る女性を登用しなければならないのでしょうか。これはビジネスでは理にかなっていません。

著者D（政治家）

政治の世界では，130カ国以上が女性の定数制を導入しています。この種の積極的差別は非常に効果があり，おかげで世界中で女性の政治家や指導者の数が増えています。政治への女性の参画が拡大したことにより，より幅広い見解や政策がよい形で示されるようになりました。また，ビジネスの世界でも，女性が男性と同じ機会を得る場合，企業はより安定を実現し，発展の機会をより多く得ようとしている，という研究結果もあります。もっと研究が必要ですが，管理職の半数が確実に女性になるよう企業に義務付けることに，全面的に賛成です。

筆者E（男子高校生の母）

女性として，私は定数制の考えを支持したいです。私がもっと若かったら，もっとよい仕事に就くチャンスがあっただろうと思います。その一方で，息子に合う職種に就くチャンスに影響するのではないかと思わずにはいられません。息子は学校で一生懸命勉強し，一流大学を目指しています。心配なのは，資格や経験があるにもかかわらず，男性であるという理由だけで希望する仕事に就くチャンスを逃すかもしれないということです。女性は自分の才能だけで地位を得ようとするべきです。

［ステップ2］立場を決める

あなたの立場：定数制と積極的差別の使用は，職場におけるジェンダー平等を促進するための効果的な方法である。

●筆者 27 と 28 はあなたの立場を支持する。

●2人の筆者の主な論拠： 29 。

［ステップ3］資料AとBを用いて概要を作成する

あなたのエッセイの概要

企業は管理職に積極的性差別を導入すべきである

導入

女性管理職のための定数を設けることによる職場での積極的差別の活用は，ジェンダー平等を推進し，将来的により強い企業を構築するために必要な手段である。

本論

理由1：［ステップ2より］

理由2：［資料Aに基づいて］………… 30

理由3：［資料Bに基づいて］………… 31

結論

一部の反対はあるものの，管理職における性別定数の創設を支持する研究結果もあり，企業はよりよい職場とより公平な社会のために，早急にこの件に取り組むべきである。

資料A

アメリカでは，不公平感や，不適格な候補者が適格な候補者から地位を奪うことになるという考えから，定数制に対する批判があります。しかし，なぜ女性や少数グループの人々が不適格であると思い込むのでしょうか。本当に，ある仕事に対して適格な女性候補者がいないというのが事実でしょうか。

人々は積極的差別という考え方を，証拠も証明もまったく示さずに「うまくいかない」ものとしてすぐに拒絶します。実際には，定数制は有効であり，それもうまく機能しています。最近の研究では，職場における積極的差別はビジネスにとって効果的であることが示されました。より多様性のある企業は，競合他社よりも業績がよいことが多いのです。『アメリカン・ジャーナル・オブ・ポリティカルサイエンス』誌によれば，女性定数のより多い企業は，男性も含めた全員にとって労働条件がよりよいのです。このような企業は，さらに健全な労働文化をもち，従業員を長く雇用し，総じてより働きやすい職場です。

定数制は非民主的だと言われるかもしれませんが，数字と結果はそうでないことを示しています。

資料B

2012年以降，ヨーロッパのいくつかの企業は，取締役会（社内の最高の地位）に占める女性の割合に定数を設けました。40%という拘束力のある定数（達成しなければならない割合）を設定した企業もあれば，柔軟な定数（一定のルールというよりも目標）を設定した企業もあり，また定数を設定しなかった第3のグループもありました。表は，3つのグループそれぞれにおいて女性が占める割合の平均上昇率を示しています。

（グラフ）
EU諸国の取締役会における女性が占める割合
拘束力のある定数　柔軟な定数　定数なし

問1　25　①

「筆者CとEはともに[25]と言及している。」

① **「適格な男性候補者が，自分より適性の劣る女性に地位を奪われるかもしれない」**

②「企業は，候補者の性別に関係なく，新しい職に最適な候補者を常に採用するだろう」

③「高いレベルの教育を受けなければ，将来どのような男性もよい仕事に就くことは難しいだろう」

④「女性は，性別によって優先されるのではなく，その人自身の能力によって昇進されるべきである」

筆者Cの意見の第5～6文に Let's say that a managerial position became open, but the most qualified candidates for this position were men, because a few decades ago we already hired more men than women. Nevertheless, should we have to promote a woman who was less qualified?（例えば管理職を開かれたものにしても，数十年前に男性を多く雇っていたから，最も適任の候補者たちは男性だった。それでも，適性の劣る女性を登用しなければならないのか。）と書いてある。また，筆者Eの意見の第5文に What I worry about is that, despite gaining qualifications and experience, he may lose out on a job that he wants just because he is male.（心配なのは資格や経験があっても，男性であるという理由だけで希望する仕事に就くチャンスを逃すかもしれないこと。）とあり，これは「男性が資格や経験に劣る女性に職を奪われるかもしれない」ことを表す。2人に共通するのは①である。②については2人とも言及していない。③について筆者Eは「息子が一流大学を目指している」と書いているが，「そうしなければよい仕事に就くことが難しい」とは書いていないので不正解。④は筆者Eだけが最終文で述べていることで不正解。

問2　26　④

「筆者Bは[26]と示唆している。」

①「ノルウェーなどの国は，世界中で導入されるべき成功モデルを作り上げた」

②「企業にとっては，積極的差別よりも同一賃金のための法律を導入する方がはるかによい」

③「2008年以降，積極的差別のモデルケースがあまりうまく機能していないため，他の国々はそれに倣っていない」

④ **「積極的差別も一定の役割を果たしているかもしれないが，他の方法も同等かそれ以上に効果的かもしれない」**

筆者Bは，前半でノルウェーなどの国で積極的差別に関する法律があると述べ，第4文で it is not always necessary to introduce positive discrimination to achieve a fairer workplace（より公平な職場を実現するためには，必ずしも積極的差別を導入する必要はない）と続けている。さらに第5文で Many countries focus on just having equal pay for equal jobs, not on hiring more women.（多くの国では，女性をより多く雇用することではなく，同一労働同一賃金を支払うことだけを重視している）と書いてある。積極的差別を否定も肯定もせず，他の効果的な方法を紹介しているので，④が正解。積極的差別を成功とも失敗とも書いていないので，①と③は不正解。また，同一労働同一賃金を，積極的差別と比較して「はるかによい」という主旨のことは述べていないので②も不正解。

問3　27　①　28　④　（順不同）
29　②

「さて，あなたはさまざまな見解を理解したところで，ジェンダー平等を支持する積極的差別の側の立場をとり，以下のように書いた。[27]，[28]，[29]を完成させるのに最も適当な選択肢を選びなさい。」

「[27]と[28]の選択肢（順不同。）」

①「A」

②「B」

③「C」

④「D」

⑤「E」
「定数制と積極的差別の使用は，職場におけるジェンダー平等を促進するための効果的な方法である。」という立場を支持する意見を選ぶ。定数制に対する筆者5人の賛否を見ていこう。
筆者A：第1文に I think that positive discrimination should be used by more companies.（積極的差別はもっと多くの企業で使われるべき），最終文に A quota of 50% women would create more diverse and fairer workplaces.（50%の女性定数を設けることで，より多様性が高まり，より公平な職場を作ることができる。）と，賛成の意見を書いている。
筆者B：第4文で it is not always necessary to introduce positive discrimination to achieve a fairer workplace（公平な職場を実現するために必ずしも積極的差別を導入する必要はない）と書いている。筆者Bは導入に関して中立的立場である。
筆者C：第2文に we are against what people term "positive discrimination"（人々が「積極的差別」と呼ぶものには反対だ）と書き，その理由を続けている。
筆者D：第1文に In the world of politics, over 130 countries have introduced quotas for women and this form of positive discrimination has had an enormous effect（政治の世界では，130カ国以上が女性の定数制を導入しており，この種の積極的差別は非常に効果がある），最終文で I am fully in favor of obliging businesses to make sure that half their managers are female（管理職の半数が確実に女性になるよう企業に義務付けることに，全面的に賛成だ）と述べている。政治においても企業においても積極的差別の導入に賛成している。
筆者E：第1文では定数制を支持したい気持ちを述べながら，そのあとの部分では「息子を持つ母」の立場から女性が優遇されることに懸念を示している。
以上から，定数制と積極的差別を肯定しているのはAとDなので，①と④が正解。
「29の選択肢」
①「50%の女性定数を設けた企業は，採用費用や給料の節約になるので，競争力が高まるだろう」
②「女性が幹部職で働く機会を増やすことで，公平性が増し，発想や見解の多様性が増す」
③「企業における女性の数が増えれば，政界にも影響を与え，より多様性のある政府につながる」
④「50%より多くの女性がより高い給料を得ることができ，企業がよりよい職場を整えるのに役立つだろう」
筆者Aと筆者Dの主な論拠を選択する問題。筆者Aは，最終文で A quota of 50% women would create more diverse and fairer workplaces.（50%の女性定数を設けることで，より多様性が高まり，より公平な職場を作ることができる）と書いている。筆者Dは第2文で The effect of greater female participation in politics has led to a wider range of views and policies in a positive way.（政治への女性の参画が拡大したことにより，より幅広い見解や政策がよい形で示されるようになった）と書いている。2人の意見は「幹部職や政界に女性が増えることで，公平性が増し，多様性のある意見が出るようになる」ことなので，②の内容に一致する。
①の採用費用や給料の節約，③の企業から政界への影響ついては書かれていないので不正解。また女性の給料の不公平に言及しているのは筆者Aだけなので④も不正解。

問4 30 ②

「資料Aに基づき，理由2として最も適当なものは次のうちどれか。」30
①「女性の中には適性が不十分な者もいるかもしれないが，彼女たちは健全な職場環境を通じて社内のよりよい雰囲気作りに役立つ。」
②「定数制を導入することで，企業の業績が向上するだけでなく，従業員が会社に留まろうとする動機付けにもなるという証拠がある。」
③「定数制を設けることで，少数派のグループや女性が，業績の好調なよりよい職場で働くための適切な資格を得るのに役立つ。」
④「女性は，定数制のおかげで男性より労働条件がよいので，会社に長く勤める。」
資料Aから，定数制を支持する根拠を探す。第2段落第3～4文に A recent study showed that positive discrimination in the workplace is effective for business. Companies with more diversity often perform better than their competitors.（最近の研究では，職場における積極的差別はビジネスにとって効果的であり，より多様性のある企業は，競合他社よりも業績がよいことが多い。），第5～6文に companies with quotas for more women have better working conditions for everybody, including

the men. These companies ... keep employees for longer and are generally better places to work（女性定数のより多い企業は男性も含めたすべての人にとって労働条件がよりよく，…従業員を長く雇用し，総じてより働きやすい職場である）と書かれている。この２カ所の内容を簡潔にまとめた②が正解。

健全な職場環境と適性が不十分な女性の関連は書かれていないので①は不正解。③についての記述はないので不正解。また，女性が男性より労働条件がよいとは書かれていないので④も不正解。

問5 31 ④

「理由３として，あなたは『厳格な一定の割り当て比率の設定は効果的で，他国でも成功例がある。』と書くことにした。資料Ｂに基づき，この意見を最もよく支持する選択肢はどれか。」 31

①「拘束力のある定数制は，最終的に上級職に占める女性の数を増やすことにつながる。しかし，その数を増やすには，比較的柔軟な定数制よりもはるかに長い時間がかかる。」

②「拘束力のある定数制を設けない企業では，ほとんどの場合，すでにより多くの女性社員がいる。このような企業では，すでに有利なスタートを切ったことで，女性の数はより早く増加した。」

③「管理職に占める女性の数を増やすには，柔軟な定数を設定するのが最も効果的である。すでに会社で働いている女性がより高いレベルの仕事を志願することを促すからである。」

④**「柔軟な定数制はある程度効果があり，管理職の女性数は明確に増加する。しかしながら，拘束力のある定数制はより早い増加を示し，目標達成間近になって初めて鈍化する。」**

グラフは a strict fixed quota (the proportion which they had to achieve) of 40%（40%という拘束力のある定数（達成しなければならなかった割合）），a soft quota (more of a target than a fixed rule)（柔軟な定数（一定のルールというよりも目標）），no quota（定数なし）の３つを比較したものである。グラフを見ると，柔軟な定数制を導入した場合もある程度管理職に占める女性の割合が増えている。拘束力のある定数を設定した場合，女性の割合が急上昇するが，40%という目標達成目前に鈍化している。この状況を説明した④が正解。

柔軟な定数制よりも拘束力のある定数制の方が早く女性の割合が増えているので①は不正解。定数のない企業は，最初の数年は拘束力のある定数を設けた企業よりも女性の割合が多いが，2012年以降も微増のままなので②は不正解。最終的な女性の割合は，拘束力のある定数を設定した企業が柔軟な定数を導入した企業よりも多いので，③は不正解。

【語句】

◇positive discrimination「積極的差別（被差別者優遇）」
◇gender「ジェンダー（の）」
◇participation「参画；参加」
◇quota「定数；割り当て」
◇fixed「一定の」
◇allocation「割り当て」
◇additional「追加の」
◇diverse「多様な」
◇tackle「～に取り組む」
◇oblige ～ to *do*「～に…することを義務付ける」
◇focus on ～「～を重視する」
◇regardless of ～「～にかかわらず」
◇race「人種」
◇term A B「AをBと名付ける」
◇Let's say that ...「例えば…だとしよう」
◇decade「10年」
◇nevertheless「それにもかかわらず」
◇make sense「道理にかなう」
◇business「企業；ビジネス」
◇worldwide「世界中で」
◇policy「政策」
◇stability「安定性」
◇in favor of ～「～に賛成して」
◇can't help *doing*「…せざるを得ない」
◇affect「～に影響を与える」
◇be suited to ～「～にふさわしい」
◇lose out on ～「（チャンスを）逃す〔取り損なう〕」
◇solely「～だけに」
◇opposition「反対」
◇criticism「批判」
◇assume that ...「…だと思い込む；決めてかかる」
◇it is the case that ...「…というのは事実である」
◇reject「～を拒絶する」
◇working culture「職場環境」
◇undemocratic「非民主的な」
◇proportion「割合」
◇target「目標」

◇representation「代表（すること）」
◇問1 ④ give ～ priority「～を優先する」
◇問2 ① adopt「～を導入する」
◇問2 ④ effective「効果的な」
◇問3 ① competitive「競争力のある」
◇問3 ② fairness「公平性」
◇問4 ② motivate ～ to *do*「～に…する動機を与える」
◇問5 statement「意見」
◇問5 ① senior「上級の」
◇問5 ① relatively「比較的」
◇問5 ② head start「有利なスタート」
◇問5 ④ to some extent「ある程度」
◇問5 ④ definite「明確な」

第７問

全訳 先生が英語の授業で，科学界の女性を１人選び，調べて授業で話すように言いました。あなたは以下の記事を見つけ，発表のためのメモを準備しました。

（イラスト）ロザリンド・E・フランクリン

ほとんどの人がDNA（すべての生物の構成要素）のことを聞いたことがあり，多くの人がその構造（二重らせん）について説明できるだろう。しかし，この構造がどのようにして発見されたのか，その全貌をご存じだろうか。この発見でノーベル賞を受賞した２人の科学者，ワトソンとクリックについてはよく知っているかもしれない。しかし，ロザリンド・フランクリンについてはどうだろうか。

ロザリンド・エルシー・フランクリンは，1920年７月25日にロンドンで，教育と公共奉仕を非常に価値あるものとする家庭に生まれた。幼い頃からフランクリンは科学に興味を持っていた。当時，これは女子の一般的な進路ではなかったが，フランクリンはすぐにその才能を認められた。18歳の時，ケンブリッジ大学で化学と物理学を学ぶための奨学金を得た。ケンブリッジ大学を出た後，石炭の構造を研究し，それが博士号の中心テーマになった。石炭の研究は，第二次世界大戦中の英国のガスマスクの改良につながり，彼女は研究について講演するために世界中を旅することができた。1946年に彼女はパリに移り，非常に小さな構造をとても詳細に調べることを可能にするX線技術を開発した。当時，J. T. ランドールという科学者が，DNAの構造について研究する研究室をロンドンのキングス・カレッジに持っていた。ランドールはフランクリンの研究の重要性を見抜き，彼女を自分の研究室で働くよう招いた。

キングス・カレッジで，フランクリンは研究室のX線装置の改良を始めた。残念ながら，この移籍は順調に進まなかった。フランクリンは，もう１人の科学者モーリス・ウィルキンスとペアを組んだが，ランドールは２人の関係を明確にしていなかった。ウィルキンスは数年間DNAの構造を研究しており，フランクリンが自分の助手として雇われたのだと思っていた。そのため，ウィルキンスとフランクリンが一緒に研究することが困難になった。フランクリンが自分の研究に取り組んでいる間，ウィルキンスはケンブリッジ大学の友人であるフランシス・クリックに連絡を取った。クリックは，DNAのモデルを作るためにジェームズ・ワトソンと一緒に研究していた。フランクリンはワトソンとクリックの研究を知っていたが，データのないモデル構築は効果的でないと考えていた。彼女は科学と数学を信じ，証明ができるまで，その結果に満足することはなかった。1952年，フランクリンと博士課程の学生であるレイ・ゴズリングは，現在では有名な写真51を撮影し，それはDNAの鮮明なX線像を示していた。フランクリンは翌年を計算に取り組んで過ごした。

ウィルキンスは写真51を含むフランクリンの研究成果を見て，彼女に無断で写真51を入手し，ワトソンに見せた。その写真とフランクリンのメモ，自分たちのデータを使って，ワトソンとクリックはいくつかの可能性のある構造を検証することができた。彼らはその構造は二重らせんに違いないという結論を出し，1953年４月にモデルを発表した。フランクリンも計算を終えて，同じ科学ジャーナルに研究成果を発表した。しかし，ワトソンとクリックの研究が最初に掲載された。その結果，フランクリンの研究がワトソンとクリックの結論を裏付けるのに役立ったように見え，彼らの成功につながった。1953年にキングス・カレッジを去った後も，フランクリンはX線の研究を続けた。ウイルスを研究し，自分の発見について語りながら世界中を旅した。彼女はワトソンとクリックが自分の研究を見たことをついに知ることなく，37歳で亡くなった。

1962年にワトソンとクリックとウィルキンスは，

DNAの研究でノーベル賞を受賞した。当時，フランクリンの研究は評価されていなかった。1968年，ワトソンは自著『二重らせん』の中で，ようやくフランクリンの研究の重要性を述べた。残念ながら，ノーベル賞は死後に授与されるものではないので，1962年に彼女の業績が認められていたとしても，フランクリンはノーベル賞を共同受賞することはできなかっただろう。しかし，ロザリンド・エルシー・フランクリンが歴史上重要な位置を占めるに値することは明らかで，私たちはこの偉大な科学者であり勇敢な女性を称えるべきだ。

あなたの発表メモ

ロザリンド・エルシー・フランクリン
(1920～1958)
— 32 —

若年期
- 33
- 34
- フランクリンは，DNAを研究するためにキングス・カレッジに招かれた。

DNAの構造を発見

35
↓
フランクリンが研究室に加わり，機器を更新した。
↓
36
↓
フランクリンは研究を続け，写真51を撮影した。
↓
37
↓
38
↓
ワトソンとクリックの研究が，フランクリンの研究よりも前に科学ジャーナルに掲載された。

キングス・カレッジを去ったあと
- フランクリンは 39 。
- フランクリンは1957年に亡くなった。
- ワトソンとクリックとウィルキンスにノーベル賞が授与された。
- ワトソンは，DNAの発見でのフランクリンの役割を認めた。

要約
- 40

問1 32 ②

「あなたの発表に最適な副題はどれか。」 32

① 「X線技術を進歩させた勇気ある女性」

② 「認められるべき優秀な女性」

③ 「一緒に仕事をするのが難しい人物だが，偉大な科学者」

④ 「数学はモデリングより優れている」

副題はタイトルの『**ロザリンド・エルシー・フランクリン（1920～1958）**』の全生涯を表すものにする。フランクリンについて，第2段落では石炭の研究とX線技術の改良，第3・4段落ではDNAの研究に貢献したことが書かれている。ここからフランクリンは「優秀な科学者だった」と言える。しかし，最終段落第2文にFranklin's work was not appreciated（フランクリンの研究は評価されていなかった）とあり，最終文ではHowever, it is clear that ... and brave woman（しかし，フランクリンが歴史上重要な位置を占めるに値することは明らかで，私たちはこの偉大な科学者であり勇敢な女性を称えるべきだ）と締めくくっているので，筆者はフランクリンがもっと高く評価されるべきだと考えているとわかる。以上の2点を含む②が正解。

①は彼女の実績の一部しか表していないので副題には不十分。「フランクリンは一緒に仕事をするのが難しい」という記述はないので③も不正解。第3段落第8文にFranklin ... thought that model building ... effective（フランクリンは…データのないモデル構築は効果的ではないと考えていた）とあるが，数学の方がモデリングより優れているという記述はないので，④も副題としては不適当。

問2 33 34 ③，④（順不同）

「『**若年期**』を完成させるために， 33 と 34 に入れるのに最適な選択肢を2つ選びなさい。（順不同。）」

① 「フランクリンは石炭の構造に関する講義に出席した。」

② 「フランクリンは新型ガスマスクを開発した。」

③ 「フランクリンは女子に人気がないものに興味があった。」

④ 「フランクリンはパリで科学的手法の改良に取り組んだ。」

⑤ 「フランクリン一家は教育関係の仕事をするためにロンドンに移住した。」

キングス・カレッジに招かれるまでの，若年期の出来事は第2段落に書かれている。第2・3文From an early age, Franklin was interested in science. At the time, this was not a common career path for girls（幼い頃からフランクリンは科学に興味を持っていた。当時，これは女子の一般的な進路ではなかった）を簡潔にまとめた③が正解。第7文にIn 1946, she moved to Paris ... in very fine detail（パリに移住し，非常に小さな構造をとても詳細に調べることを可能にするX線技術を開発した）とある。「微小な構造を調べられるX線技術を開発した」を「科学的手法の改良に取り組んだ」と言い換えた④が正解。

「石炭の構造を研究した」とは書かれているが，「講義に出席した」という記述はないので①は不正解。「フランクリンの研究がガスマスクの開発につながった」とあるが，フランクリン自身が開発したとは書いていないので，②も不正解。フランクリンはロンドン生まれだが，「家族で移住した」という記述はないので⑤も不正解。

問3 35 ⑤ 36 ③ 37 ④ 38 ①

「**『DNAの構造を発見』**を完成させるために，5つの出来事（①～⑤）から**4つ**を選び，起こった順番に並べなさい。」

35 → 36 → 37 → 38

①「クリックとワトソンが DNA のモデルを完成させた。」

②「ランドールはウィルキンスを補佐するためにフランクリンを雇った。」

③「ウィルキンスはフランクリンの立場を誤解した。」

④「ウィルキンスはワトソンと個人的な研究情報を共有した。」

⑤「ウィルキンスはDNAの構造の研究を開始した。」

DNAの構造発見の過程は第3・4段落に書かれている。

35

第3段落第4文前半Wilkins had been working on the structure of DNA for several years（ウィルキンスは数年間DNAの構造を研究していた）から，フランクリンが実験室に参加する前にウィルキンスがDNAの構造の研究を始めたとわかるので，⑤を入れる。

36

第3段落第3文にFranklin was paired with ... their relationship clear（フランクリンはウィルキンスとペアを組んだが，ランドールは2人の関係を明確にしていなかった），第4文後半にWilkins ... thought that Franklin had been hired as his assistant（ウィルキンスはフランクリンが自分の助手として雇われたのだと思っていた）とある。ウィルキンスが誤解していたのだから③を入れる。

37

第4段落第1文にWilkins had seen Franklin's work, including Photo 51, and ... showed it to Watson（ウィルキンスは写真51を含むフランクリンの研究成果を見て…ワトソンに見せた）とあり，フランクリンに無断で彼女個人の研究情報を共有したとある。したがって④を入れる。

38

第4段落第3文They concluded that the structure must be a double helix and published their model in April 1953（彼らはその構造は二重らせんに違いないという結論を出し，1953年4月にモデルを発表した）から，「モデルを完成させた」という①を入れる。

選択肢②については，36の解説から，フランクリンはウィルキンスの補佐のために雇用されたわけではないとわかるのでどこにも当てはまらない。

問4 39 ②

「**『キングス・カレッジを去ったあと』**を完成させるために39に入れるのに最適な選択肢を選びなさい。」

①「研究中にウイルスに感染した」

②「研究を続け，講演を行った」

③「起きたことに動揺していた」

④「DNAの発見について本を書いた」

フランクリンがキングス・カレッジを去ってから亡くなるまでのことは，第4段落後半に書かれている。第7・8文のAfter leaving King's College ... about her findings（1953年にキングス・カレッジを去ったあとも，フランクリンはX線の研究を続けた。ウイルスを研究し，自分の発見について語りながら世界中を旅した）の内容を簡潔にまとめた②が正解。

ウイルスの研究はしたが，「感染した」という記述はないので①は不正解。「動揺した」とも書かれていないので③も不正解。本を書いたのはフランクリンではなくワトソンなので，④も不正解。

問5 40 ②

「**『要約』**を完成させるために40に入れるのに最

適な選択肢を選びなさい。」
①「ノーベル賞は，たとえ生存していなくても人々に与えられるべきである。」
②「偉大な科学者をあまりにも早く失ってしまい，彼女の功績はもっと賞賛されるべきだ。」
③「科学界にはもっと多くの女性が必要であり，成功した女性科学者を昇進させるべきである。」
④「ワトソンとクリックが DNA の構造を発見したと言うのをやめるべきだ。」

記事の段落ごとの要旨は以下の通り。

・第１段落：DNAの構造の発見に関連して，ロザリンド・フランクリンを知っているか。

・第２段落：フランクリンが科学者になり石炭の構造の研究やＸ線技術の開発を行った。DNAの構造を研究する研究室に招かれた。

・第３段落：フランクリンの同僚のウィルキンスはDNAの構造を研究していた。フランクリンがDNAの鮮明なＸ線画像を示した。

・第４段落：ウィルキンスはフランクリンが撮った写真をワトソンに見せた。フランクリンの画像や研究結果も参考にし，ワトソンとクリックがDNAの構造モデルを発表した。フランクリンの研究結果の方があとに掲載されたため，２人の成果を裏付けるものとされた。フランクリンが37歳で亡くなる。

・第５段落：ワトソンとクリックとウィルキンスがDNAの研究でノーベル賞を受賞。のちに，ワトソンがフランクリンの研究の重要性を自著に書いた。フランクリンの業績は称えられるべきだ。

記事の内容をまとめると，「フランクリンは偉大な科学者である」「37歳で早逝した」「フランクリンの業績は称えられるべきである」ということである。したがって②が正解。

①・③・④の考えは，本文に書かれていない。

【語句】

◇building block「構成要素」
◇structure「構造」
◇discovery「発見」
◇scholarship「奨学金」
◇coal「石炭」
◇X-ray「Ｘ線」
◇examine「～を分析する」
◇incredibly「非常に」
◇fine「細かい」
◇effective「効果的な」
◇image「画像」
◇calculation「計算」
◇conclude「～と結論を出す」
◇journal「ジャーナル」（専門分野の定期刊行物）
◇appreciate「～を正しく評価する」
◇deserve「～を受けるに値する」
◇問１　①　make advances in ～「～を進歩させる」
◇問３　③　misunderstand「～を誤解する」
◇問５　②　praise「～を賞賛する」

第８問

全訳　あなたは，『乳製品をもっとよく知ろう』というテーマで，家庭科のプレゼンテーションコンテストのためにポスターの準備をしている学生グループに所属している。ポスターを作るために以下の一節を使っている。

チーズの世界を満喫

食料品店にはさまざまな種類のチーズがある。手軽にチーズを手に入れることができるが，異なる種類を詳細に説明することができるだろうか。分類を知っておくと，チーズを選ぶ時に非常に役に立つ。

最初に，チーズは大きくナチュラルチーズとプロセスチーズの２つのグループに分けられる。ナチュラルチーズを作るために，牛乳が加工処理されて固められる，つまり酸を生成する化学変化が起こることで固まる。このタイプは時間の経過によってワインのように熟成し，これがチーズの風味を向上させる。ナチュラルチーズを溶かして堅くなるまで冷やすことでプロセスチーズを作ることができる。プロセスチーズは中の微生物が死滅しているため，熟成や変化をしない。そのためより長持ちもできる。

第二に，1000種類以上のナチュラルチーズがあると言われている。世界的に認められた分類はないが，日本ではナチュラルチーズは７種類に分類されている。（図１）

図１　ナチュラルチーズ
フレッシュチーズ　白カビチーズ　青カビチーズ
ウォッシュチーズ　シェーブルチーズ　セミハードチーズ　ハードチーズ

これはフランスの分類に基づいている。フレッシュチーズは，柔らかい食感でほんの少し酸味がある熟成していないチーズである。また，色は明るい白色をしている。フレッシュチーズの例としては，モッツァレラ，カッテージチーズ，クワルクがある。白カビチーズは，チーズを外側から熟成させる白カビを含む。チーズの表面はカビに覆われ，内部はクリームイエローをしている。白カビチーズの例としては，カマンベールやブリーがある。青カビチーズは，ペニシリウムという培養されたカビで熟成させられる。酸素が通り抜けて入れる隙間を作るように，たくさんの小さい穴をチーズに開けるために穿刺(せんし)がされ，それが特徴のある青いマーブル状の筋を適切に形成させる。このチーズは中心から外側に向かって熟成する。よく熟成したチーズは，風味が強く，濃厚な味がする。青カビチーズの例としては，ゴルゴンゾーラやロックフォールがある。ウォッシュチーズは，熟成の過程で塩水やビール，ワイン，ブランデーなどのアルコールで洗われる。匂いが強い。ウォッシュタイプチーズの例には，リヴァロ，マンステール，リンバーガーがある。シェーブルはフランス語でヤギを意味するので，シェーブルチーズは文字通りヤギ乳のチーズである。その名が示すように，このチーズはヤギの乳から作られる。柔らかいフレッシュチーズから硬い熟成チーズまで，さまざまな種類のものがある。シェーブルチーズの例としては，ヴァランセ，バノン，ピラミッドがある。セミハードチーズは，比較的硬い。熟成期間や大きさ，脂肪分の量によってさまざまな種類がある。ゴーダ，マリボー，ラクレットが代表的なセミハードチーズの例である。ハードチーズは，しっかりとした食感と豊かな風味を持つ。熟成期間が長いため，ハードチーズは水分がないのでとても長く保存できる。ハードチーズの例には，チェダー，エメンタール，パルメザンがある。

ヨーロッパでは，チーズの生産が主要な産業だが，チーズを含む優れた農産物や乳製品を保護する制度がある。チーズは一定の品質であると保証され，産地や形状，熟成期間などの詳細に基づいて認証される。フランスとスイスではこのシステムがA.O.Cと呼ばれ，イタリアとスペインではD.O.P，その他のEU諸国ではP.D.Oと呼ばれている。

非常に多くの種類のチーズがあり，それを説明するのは容易ではない。チーズの話題は実に奥が深いことが今はあなたにもわかるだろう。さまざまな種類のチーズがどのような名前がつけられているかを考えてみるのもおもしろい。例えば，チェダーとカマンベールは地名から，モッツァレラは製法から，フロマージュブランはその色にちなんで名づけられている。このようなチーズに関する事実を知ることは，あなたがチーズを食べる時にもっと楽しみを与えてくれるだろう。

あなたのプレゼンテーションのポスター原稿：

チーズについて深く学んでみよう

2つの主なチーズのグループの違いを知っていますか？

[41]

ナチュラルチーズの種類と特徴

種類	特徴	代表的なチーズ
フレッシュチーズ	・長期間熟成していないため，食感が柔らかく，色が鮮やかな白色のチーズ。	モッツァレラ，カッテージ，クワルク
青カビチーズ	・ペニシリウムを使って作る。 ・針で穴を開けることで空気穴が作られる[42]。	ゴルゴンゾーラ，ロックフォール
シェーブルチーズ	・ヤギの乳で作られる。 ・[43]	ヴァランセ，バノン，ピラミッド

共通の特徴を持つチーズ

[44]
[45]

問1 41 ④

「ポスターの最初の見出しの下に，あなたは引用文で説明されているように，チーズについていくつかの基本的な事実を加えるつもりだ。以下のうちどれが最も適切か。」[41]

① 「チーズは熟成するのにかかった期間と，どのような味がするかによって分類される。」
② 「チーズは生産地と，その形によって分類される。」
③ 「チーズは大きく2つのグループに分けられ，ど

ちらのグループも加熱される。」

④ **「チーズは大きく２つのグループに分けられ，一方のグループは他方のグループから作られる。」**

見出しの下には Do you know the differences between the two main cheese groups?「２つの主なチーズのグループの違いを知っていますか？」と書かれており，41 には２種類のグループの説明が入ると考える。第１段落第４文に cheese is largely divided into two groups, natural cheese and processed「チーズは大きくナチュラルチーズとプロセスチーズの２つのグループに分けられる」と書かれている。また，第５・６文でナチュラルチーズの作り方を説明したあと，第７文に Processed cheese can be made by melting the natural cheese and cooling it until it solidifies.「ナチュラルチーズを溶かして堅くなるまで冷やすことでプロセスチーズを作ることができる。」と書いてある。つまり，ナチュラルチーズを加工したものがプロセスチーズである。これを「一方のグループは他方のグループから作られる」と言い換えた④が正解。「熟成期間と味」または「生産地と形」は，２つのグループに分ける基準ではないので，①と②は不正解。プロセスチーズはmelting the natural cheese（ナチュラルチーズを溶かすこと）で作るが，ナチュラルチーズを作る時に加熱するとは書かれていないので，③も不正解。

問２　42　④　43　②

「あなたはチーズの特徴の表に記入するつもりだ。42 と 43 に最も適する選択肢を選びなさい。」

青カビチーズ　42

①「，そして穴の中にカビを流し込む」

②「が，この過程をとばしてもかまわない」

③「が，穴が多すぎると逆効果になる」

④ **「が，それはチーズ中に酸素を入らせるためだ」**

青カビチーズの作り方と特徴は，第３段落第７～11文に書かれている。空所 42 の前半にある「針で穴を開ける」という記述は，第９文にNeedling is used to make many tiny holes in the cheese to create openings through which oxygen can enter（酸素が通り抜けて入れる隙間を作るように，たくさんの小さい穴をチーズに開けるために穿刺がされる）とある。穴を開ける目的は「酸素が入るようにするため」だから，④が正解。「カビを流し込むため」とは書かれていないので①は不正解。また「この過程をとばしてもよい」「穴が多すぎると逆効果」という記述もないので，②③も不正解。

シェーブルチーズ　43

①「フランスはチーズの種類が最も多い。」

② **「熟成期間によって柔らかくなったり，硬くなったりする。」**

③「柔らかくなるにつれて，風味や味が強くなることがある。」

④「ハードチーズよりソフトチーズの方が作りやすい。」

シェーブルチーズの特徴は第３段落第16～18文に書かれている。第18文に They include a wide variety of styles, from soft fresh cheese to hard aged cheese.「柔らかいフレッシュチーズから硬い熟成チーズまで，さまざまな種類のものがある。」と書かれていることから，「熟成期間が硬さを左右する」と判断できる。したがって，②が正解。「フランスがチーズの種類が多い」という記述はないので①は不正解。シェーブルチーズの柔らかさと風味や味の関係や作りやすさは説明されていないので，③④も不正解。

問３　44　45　②，③（順不同）

「あなたは，共通の性質を持つチーズについて説明する。記事によると，次のうち適切なもの２つはどれか。（順不同。）」 44 ・ 45

①「フレッシュチーズも白カビチーズもカビを使い，熟成させることによって作られる。」

② **「シェーブルチーズもセミハードチーズもさまざまな熟成期間がある。」**

③ **「ヨーロッパの国々ではさまざまなチーズに対して品質を保証する制度がある。」**

④「ハードチーズと青カビチーズは水分がないため，比較的長期保存できる。」

⑤「ヨーロッパのチーズのほとんどは地名や人名にちなんで命名されている。」

⑥「ウォッシュチーズとフレッシュチーズは，アルコールをかけることで柔らかくなる。」

選択肢の内容が本文に一致するか見ていこう。第３段落第２文に Fresh cheese is unripened cheese「フレッシュチーズは熟成していないチーズである」とあるので，①は不正解。第３段落第18文のシェーブルチーズの説明 They include a wide variety of styles, from soft fresh cheese to hard aged cheese.（柔らかいフレッシュチーズから硬い熟成チーズまで，さまざまな種類のものがある。）と，第21文のセミハードチーズの説明 There are various kinds depending on the maturing period, size, and amount of fat.「熟成期間や大きさ，脂肪分の量によってさまざまな種類がある。」から，この２種類はさまざま熟成期間があるとわかる。したがって②は正解。第４段落第１・２文に In Europe, ..., there is a system to protect excellent agricultural and dairy products, including cheese. The cheese is guaranteed to be of a certain quality and can be identified based on details such as its production area, shape, and maturing period.「ヨーロッパでは…，チーズを含む優れた農産物や乳製品を保護する制度がある。チーズは一定の品質であると保証され，産地や形状，熟成期間などの詳細に基づいて認証される。」と書かれている。このような「品質を保証する制度がある」という事実に合致する③も正解。ハードチーズは第３段落第24文に「水分がないため長期保存できる」とあるが，青カビチーズの説明にはそのような記述がないので，④は不正解。チーズの命名については第５段落第４文に書かれているが，地名や人名以外から名付けられたものも多いので，⑤も不正解。ウォッシュチーズはアルコールで洗うことがあるという内容が第３段落第13文にあるが，フレッシュチーズにアルコールをかけるという記述はないので，⑥も不正解。したがって，②と③が正解。

【語句】

◇home economics「家庭科」
◇dairy product「乳製品」
◇grocery store「食料品店」
◇in detail「詳細に」
◇classification「分類」
◇incredibly「非常に」
◇processed「加工した」
◇treat「～を加工処理する」
◇solidify「～を凝固させる；凝固する」
◇harden「～を固くする」
◇chemical「化学的な」
◇acid「酸」
◇mature「熟成する」
◇flavor「（特有の）風味」
◇microorganism「微生物」
◇globally-accepted「世界的に認められている」
◇unripened「熟していない」
◇texture「食感」
◇mold「かび；菌」
◇ripen「～を成熟させる」
◇culture「培養された菌」
◇oxygen「酸素」
◇characteristic「特徴のある」
◇vein「筋；葉脈」
◇literally「文字通り」
◇relatively「比較的」
◇keep well「長く保存できる」
◇production「生産」
◇guarantee O to be ～「Oが確かに～だと保証する」
◇numerous「非常に多くの」
◇問３ ⑥ splash「～を（しぶきで）ぬらす」

リーディング模試　第5回　解答

第1問小計	第2問小計	第3問小計	第4問小計	第5問小計	第6問小計	第7問小計	第8問小計

合計点	/100

問題番号(配点)	設問	解答番号	正解	配点	自己採点
第1問(6)	1	1	①	2	
	2	2	④	2	
	3	3	③	2	
第2問(10)	1	4	④	2	
	2	5	②	2	
	3	6	④	2	
	4	7	①	2	
	5	8	①	2	
第3問(9)	1	9	②	3※	
		10	①		
		11	④		
		12	③		
	2	13	①	3	
	3	14	①	3	
第4問(12)	1	15	③	3	
	2	16	①	3	
	3	17	③	3	
	4	18	②	3	
第5問(16)	1	19	②	3	
	2	20	②	3	
	3	21	②	4	
	4	22	③	3※	
		23	⑤		
	5	24	①	3	
第6問(18)	1	25	②	3	
	2	26	④	3	
	3	27 ～ 28	①-③	3※	
		29	①	3	
	4	30	④	3	
	5	31	①	3	
第7問(15)	1	32	②	4※	
		33	④		
		34	①		
		35	③		
	2	36 ～ 37	②-⑤	4※	
	3	38	③	3	
	4	39 ～ 40	②-⑥	4※	
第8問(14)	1	41	②	4	
	2	42	④	3	
		43	④	3	
	3	44 ～ 45	①-⑥	4※	

(注)　1　※は，全部正解の場合のみ点を与える。
　　　2　-(ハイフン)でつながれた正解は，順序を問わない。

第１問

全訳 あなたは地元の映画学校のウェブサイトを訪れ，まもなく行われる映画祭についての告知を見つけました。

年に一度の学生映画祭

我が校の生徒たちは，授業で学んだ技術を使い，最終課題として短編映画を作ります。その後，年度末に，その映画を一般の方々に見に来ていただけるよう私たちは映画祭を主催します。このイベントを通じて，より多くの方々が映画作りを学ぶことに興味を持ってくだされば と望んでいます。

今年は４本の生徒の映画を披露します。映画祭の最後には祝賀夕食会にて，自分たちの映画に関する質問に生徒たちがお答えします。本年の映画は，短い解説付きで以下のスケジュール表に掲載されています。

映画祭スケジュール

4/7	映画：私たちは共にいる 男が行方不明の兄を求めて世界中を探す。
4/8	映画：キッチン 娘が20年続く家族経営のレストランの経営の仕方を父と叔母たちから学ぶ。
4/9	映画：なくしたもの，見つかったもの 双子の２人がけんか別れして10年が経ち，友達のパーティーで偶然再会することになる。
4/10	映画：フォスターヒルの向こう 若い女性が祖父の秘密を見つけ，彼が自分の息子をどれほど愛していたかを知る。
4/11	イベント：祝賀夕食会

・18歳以下の若者は3/15までにウェブサイトでチケットの申し込みをすれば無料で参加できます。
・各映画の上映前に，コンピューターやスマートフォンと連動したカメラを使った映画の録画や編集についての無料授業があります。

チケットの申し込みは，２/１以降のいつでもここをクリック。

問１ 1 ①

「映画祭の主な目的は［ 1 ］ことである。」

①「より多くの人が映画作りを始めるよう勧める」

②「最良の映画に賞を与える」

③「映画俳優との夕食会に地域の人々を招待する」

④「生徒にさまざまな国の映画を見せる」

映画祭の主な目的が問われている。第１段落最終文にThrough this event, we hope to inspire more people to learn to make movies.（このイベントを通じて，より多くの方々が映画作りを学ぶことに興味を持ってくだされば と望んでいます。）とあり，①がこの内容と一致する。inspire O to *do*は「Oを奮起させて…させる；Oに…するよう促す」という意味。選択肢ではこれをencourage O to *do*（Oが…するよう励ます，勧める）で表している。「賞を与える」，「映画俳優が夕食会に来る」，「さまざまな国の映画」といったことは本文ではふれられていないので，②，③，④は不適当。

問２ 2 ④

「４本の映画の主題はどれも［ 2 ］である可能性が最も高い。」

①「秘密を長期間守ることの難しさ」

②「重要な決断をする際の希望と恐怖」

③「小規模な商売をする方法」

④「家族間の関係」

４本の映画の内容については，スケジュール表の各映画のタイトル下にある短い紹介文を参照する。brother（兄），father and aunts（父と叔母たち），twins（双子），grandfather（祖父），son（息子）など家族を表す単語が４本とも含まれるので，④が適当である。①の「秘密」は4/10の映画に，③の「小規模な商売」は４/８の映画に関連する内容だが，その他の映画とは関係がない。②の「重要な決断」は，映画の紹介文には見当たらない。

問３ 3 ③

「この映画祭は映画製作者になりたい人にとって役立つかもしれない。なぜなら［ 3 ］からである。」

①「有名な映画プロデューサーがそのイベントに来る予定だ」

②「映画が，最先端の映画製作技術をいくつか使っている」

③「イベントの間中，映画作りについて学ぶことができる」

④「翌年用の映画を作ることができる」

第１段落最終文に映画祭を通じて来場者に映画作りを学ぶように促したいとあり，具体的な企画としては第２段落第２文the students will answer questions about their films（自分たちの映画に関する質問に生徒たちがお答えします），スケジュール表の下の２項目にはthere will be a free class about recording and editing movies（映画の録画や編集についての無料授業があります）などがある。以上から③が正解。①，②，④については本文に言及がない。

【語句】

◇ upcoming「まもなく起こる；近く公開の」
◇ host「～を主催する」
◇ inspire O to *do*「Oが…することを促す」
◇ by chance「偶然に」
◇ 問2 ③ run a business「事業を営む；経営する」

第2問

全訳 あなたは学校の英字新聞の編集者です。英国から来た交換留学生のアルフレッドが新聞に記事を書きました。

どちらの手があなたの利き手ですか。オランダでは左利きの割合は13%と推定されており，これは取り上げた国の中では最も高い割合です。米国と英国でも約12%です。対照的に，日本や他のいくつかのアジアの国々では，左利きの人は北米や西欧の国々の半分以下です。

これはなぜでしょうか。日本の習慣に関する雑誌がその理由を示しています。記事では日本で人々に右利きを強要する理由として以下のことを挙げています。

▶ かつての日本では，侍は刀を腰の左側に差し，右手で刀を抜かなければならないというしきたりがあったので，左利きは恥ずべきことでした。
▶ 集団内の誰かが左利きだと，集団行動が難しいと考えられていました。
▶ 日本の定食は基本的に右利きの人用に並べられています。

けれども，左利きであることの利点が今ではより広く知られるようになっています。そのうちの1つは，左利きの人は周囲の空間に注意を払うのが得意だということです。右利きは左脳に制御される言語機能を発達させ，左利きは右脳に制御される画像や空間の認識を発達させることがわかりました。左利きの人々は右利きの人の社会では左脳も使う機会があるため，バランスよく左右両方の脳を訓練することができます。このことが，左利きの人々がより独創的で面白いアイデアを生み出す助けとなるかもしれません。

問1 4 ④

「左利きの人々の割合に関して，**最も高い国から最も低い国**への順位を表したものはどれか。」 4

①「日本－オランダ－英国」
②「日本－英国－オランダ」
③「オランダ－日本－英国」
④ **「オランダ－英国－日本」**
⑤「英国－日本－オランダ」
⑥「英国－オランダ－日本」

日本，オランダ，英国の3か国の左利きの人の割合を比べればよい。左利きの人の割合は，本文第1段落に書かれている。第2文にIn the Netherlands, the rate of being left-handed is estimated at 13%, and this is the highest among the selected countries.（オランダでは左利きの割合は13%と推定されており，これは取り上げた国の中で最も高い割合です。）とあるから，オランダが1番目。第3文にIt is also around 12% in the US and the UK.（米国と英国でも約12%）とあり，オランダの13%に続く割合である。第4文に日本や他のアジアの国々ではless than half as many people（半分以下の人数）とある。以上より左利きの人の割合が高い順に「オランダ－英国－日本」の順である。④が正解。

問2 5 ②

「アルフレッドのレポートによると，左利きであることのメリットの1つは 5 ということである。」

①「多言語を理解することができる」
② **「空間感覚がすぐれている」**
③「天才と呼ばれるだろう」
④「人生がより価値あるものになるだろう」

箇条書きの次の段落の第2文にOne of them is that they are good at paying attention to the space around them.（そのうちの1つは，左利きの人は周囲の空間に注意を払うのが得意だということです。）とある。themは前の文にある「左利きであることの利点」を指すから，②の内容と一致する。その次の文に「右利きは左脳が制御する言語機能を発達させる」とあるので①は左利きの利点ではない。

③，④のような言及はレポート内にない。以上より②が正解。

問3 6 ④

「雑誌からわかったことの1つを最もよく示している記述は 6 である。」

① 『脳がどのように働くかと利き手は無関係だ。』

② 『左利きの人々は集団行動に参加できない。』

③ 『左利きの人々は右手を使うことに抵抗した。』

④ 『日本には右利きを強要する文化的理由があった。』

雑誌記事の前にThe article mentions the following reasons for forcing people to be right-handed in Japan（記事では日本で人々に右利きを強要する理由として以下のことを挙げています）とあり，このあとに侍のしきたりや定食の並べ方などの理由が述べられている。④はこれに当てはまる。雑誌記事の最後に，左利きと右利きの人それぞれが利き手と反対側の脳を発達させていることと，その脳が制御している機能が紹介されている。つまり利き手と脳の働きは関連しているから①は不適当。箇条書きの2つ目に「左利きの人は集団行動が難しいと考えられていた」とあるが，集団行動に参加できないわけではないので②も不適当。③のような内容は言及されていない。以上より④が正解。

問4 7 ①

「左利きであることに関するアルフレッドの意見を最もよく要約しているのはどれか。」 7

①「脳の左右両側を使うのに最適である。」

②「右利き社会で暮らすのは難しい。」

③「利き手ではない方の手を使おうとする人もいる。」

④「日本にはもっと左利きがいるはずだ。」

雑誌記事を踏まえたアルフレッドの意見は最終段落で述べられている。第1文でLeft-handed people also have chances to use the left side of their brain in right-handed societies, so they can train both sides of brain in a well-balanced manner.（左利きの人々は右利きの人の社会では左脳も使う機会があるため，バランスよく左右両方の脳を訓練することができます。）と述べており，①の内容と一致する。②は想像できる内容であるが「左利きの人も左脳を使う機会がある」ことをバランスがいいととらえているので不適当。③，④のような意見は述べていない。①が正解。

問5 8 ①

「この記事に最もふさわしいタイトルはどれか。」 8

①「左利きであることの価値はどのように変化してきたか。」

②「脳を鍛える最良の方法は何か。」

③「左利きの人々に向く職業は何か。」

④「右利きに多くの利点があるのはなぜか。」

記事の段落ごとの概要は以下の通り。

・第1段落：各国の左利きの人々の割合。日本やアジアでは北米や西欧の半分以下。

・第2段落：日本で右利きが多い理由を雑誌記事から探る。

・囲み記事：日本で右利きが強要される理由

→箇条書き：侍のしきたり，集団行動の困難さ，定食の配置の3例

・第3段落：左利きの利点も広く知られるようになってきた。利き手により働く脳の左右が異なり，発達する能力も異なる。

・最終段落：右利き社会では左利きの人は，左右両方の脳を訓練することができる。それが独創的で面白い発想を生み出す助けとなる。

全体を通して，かつては右利きが強要されていたが，現在では左利きの利点にも目が向けられるようになっているという流れだから，①がタイトルとして適当である。利き手によって脳の発達する部分が異なるという説明はあるが，脳を鍛える方法については述べていないので②は不適当。利き手による得意なことは囲み記事の考察部分でふれているが，職業については述べていないので③も不適当。囲み記事の箇条書きの部分が右利きが有利な理由となっているが，記事全体が右利きの利点について扱っているわけではない。以上より①が正解。

【語句】

◇editor「編集者；編集長」
◇dominant hand「利き手」
◇estimate O at ～「Oを～と見積もる」
◇in contrast「対照的に；それとは違って」
◇sword「刀；剣」
◇draw「(刀など) を抜く」
◇basically「基本的に」
◇language function「言語機能」
◇recognition「認識」
◇well-balanced「バランスのとれた」

◇manner「方法」
◇generate「生み出す」
◇問2 ③ genius「天才」
◇問3 statement「発言」
◇問3 reflect「～を示す」
◇問3 ① unrelated「無関係な」
◇問3 ③ *be* opposed to ～「～に反対する」

第3問

全訳 あなたは留学生に関する雑誌で次の話を見つけました。

海外での新生活開始

サマンサ・ウォーターソン

私は最近，東欧の小さな国アルバニアでホストファミリーと暮らすために学生を送り出す留学プログラムに参加しました。

アルバニア行きの飛行機が離陸した時，私の隣に座っていた人が，私に大丈夫かと聞いてきました。彼女は，私がとても不安だったため足を上下に揺すっていたのを見たに違いありません。私は彼女に，自分が今まで自分の国を出たことがないこと，この先どうなるかわからないことを話しました。彼女はアルバニア人で，私が出発前に勉強していればよかったと思うことをたくさん教えてくれました。例えば，アルバニアでは人々は「いいえ」と言う時にうなずき，「はい」と言う時に頭を横に振るのです。フライトが終わるまでには，私はアルバニアを探検し始めることが待ちきれなくなりました。もう友達ができて，たくさんのことを学んだのです。

初めて会うホストファミリーの家に到着すると，男の子が中へ入れてくれました。私は男の子の頬にキスをしました。飛行機の女性がそれがよい作法だと教えてくれたからです。男の子は私に2つの単語を繰り返し始めました。私は彼が言っていることがわからず，怒っているのかもしれないと思いました。私は「落ち着いて，落ち着いて」と英語で言いましたが，男の子はもっと大きな声で話すだけで，私の口を指さし始めました。

彼のお母さんが部屋に入ってきて，私たち2人が異なる単語を繰り返しているのを見ました。彼女は笑い出しました。「お腹，からっぽ？」と彼女は強いアルバニアなまりで台所を指さしながら言いました。男の子は私に怒ってなどいなかったのです！私はやっとくつろいだ気持ちになりました。

私たちはみんな台所のテーブルにつき，おいしいご飯を食べました。私たちはほとんどコミュニケーションをとることができませんでしたが，お互いのことがわかってくるにつれて，微笑んだり笑ったりしました。このように温かい家庭に滞在していることがうれしかったです。

問1 9 ② 10 ① 11 ④ 12 ③

「次の感情（①～④）をサマンサが経験した順番に並べなさい。」

①「困惑した」
②「興奮した」
③「うれしい」
④「安心した」

本文ではサマンサの行動や感情が時系列で述べられている。感情を表している表現を順に見ていこう。

・第2段落第2文の最後にI was so anxious（とても不安だった）とあるので，nervous から始まり，このあとの流れを完成させる。

・その後，飛行機の隣の席のアルバニア人女性と友達になり，第2段落最後から2文目に I couldn't wait to start exploring the country（その国を探検し始めることが待ちきれなかった）と気持ちが変わる。「待ちきれない」のだからexcited（興奮して）という気持ちである。

・第3段落では，到着したホストファミリーの家で男の子と言葉が通じない様子が述べられている。第4文にI couldn't understand what he meant and thought he might be angry.（私は彼が言っていることがわからず，怒っているのかもしれないと思いました。）とあり，その時の気持ちとして選択肢の中で当てはまる単語はconfused（困惑して）。

・第4段落ではホストマザーが登場し，男の子が怒っていたわけではないことがわかる。第4段落最後にI finally felt relaxed.（私はやっとくつろいだ気持ちになりました。）とある。選択肢にある単語ではrelieved（安心した；ほっとした）が近い。

・第5段落では楽しく食事をする様子が描かれている。最後にI was glad to ...（…してうれしかった）とある。選択肢の中で似た意味の単語はhappyである。

以上より，「(緊張→）興奮→困惑→安心→うれしい」②→①→④→③という順になる。

問2　13　①

「男の子がアルバニア語で同じ言葉を繰り返していた時，彼はおそらく［13］のだろう。」

①**「サマンサに何か食べたいかとたずねていた」**

②「サマンサに彼女は男の子の頬にキスをするべきではなかったと伝えていた」

③「サマンサにアルバニア語の新しい2語を教えようとしていた」

④「サマンサが彼にお土産を持ってこなかったことに腹を立てていた」

問われている場面は第3段落に出てくる。この段落の最後に，男の子は大きな声で話しながら started to point at my mouth（私の口を指さし始めた）とある。その後の第4段落では，状況を理解した彼の母親がStomach empty?と英語で言い直し，台所を指さしたことで，サマンサは男の子が腹を立てていたのではないことを理解した，とある。このことから，男の子がサマンサの口を指さして伝えようとしていたことは「何か食べたいかどうか」だと考えられる。このあと一緒に食事をとっていることからも，①が正解。第4段落以降の様子から，②，③，④の内容は読み取れない。

問3　14　①

「この話から，あなたはサマンサが［14］ことがわかった。」

①**「ホームステイの準備は万全ではなかったが，それでも有意義な体験をした」**

②「語学習得の天性の才能があり，新しい環境にすぐに順応する」

③「飛行機内で習った単語を使ってホストファミリーとコミュニケーションをとることができた」

④「気まずい状況を避けるため，アルバニア語を学ぶ時間をもっと取ればよかったのにと思っている」

話の第2段落では飛行機で隣の席のアルバニア人の女性が，「出発前に勉強していればよかったと思うことをたくさん教えてくれた」エピソードが，第3段落～第4段落ではホストファミリーの言葉がわからず，困惑したエピソードが書かれているが，最終段落ではThough we were barely able to communicate（私たちはほとんどコミュニケーションをとることができませんでしたが），we smiled and laughed（私たちは微笑んだり笑ったりしました），I was glad to be staying with such a warm family.（このように温かい家庭に滞在していることがうれしかったです。）と言葉は通じなくてもホームステイを楽しんでいる様子が書かれている。これは出発前の準備は万全ではなかったが楽しいホームステイ体験ができたということなので①が正解。最終段落に，コミュニケーションがほとんどとれなかったとあることから，「語学習得の天性の才能がある」，「飛行機内で習った単語を使った」という②，③は不適当。「気まずい状況を避ける」ことに関しては特に述べていないので④も正しくない。

【語句】

◇ bounce「(上下に）揺れる」

◇ nod「～（＝首）を縦に振る；うなずく」

◇ burst out *doing*「突然…し始める」

◇ 問2　repeat *oneself*「同じことを繰り返し言う〔行う〕」

◇ 問3　②　natural ability「生まれつきの才能；天賦の才」

◇ 問3　②　adapt to ～「～に順応する〔慣れる〕」

◇ 問3　④　awkward「落ち着かない；気まずい」

第4問

全訳　英語の授業で，あなたは興味のある社会問題に関するエッセイを書いています。これはあなたの最新の草稿です。今は先生からのコメントをもとに，推敲に取り組んでいるところです。

誰もが京都を楽しめるようにするには

2022年，外国人旅行客が日本に戻ってくるようになると，私の街，京都は「絶対訪れるべき」場所のリストの上位にあった。ほとんど3年間，ホテル，飲食店，商店がガラガラだったとあって，客足が戻ってきて私たちはうれしかった。*(1)*［15］京都は現在，「オーバーツーリズム」に悩まされている。このエッセイはその問題と解決法に焦点を当てる。

まず，バスの混雑だ。これは市がいくつかの形で対策を議論している深刻な問題で，中には旅行客に通常より高い料金を課すという案も含まれる。これは問題を増やすだけだ！　もっと現実的な解決策を考えよう。*(2)*［16］ロンドンを走っているような

２階建てバスを導入するのはどうだろう。これなら，京都を観て回る乗客の数を倍にできる。

第二に，(3)私たちは誰だってゴミが大嫌いだ。訪問者はよくゴミ箱の少なさに不満をこぼしている。ゴミを捨てられる場所を増やすことは効果的だろう。さらに，ゴミ箱にQRコードを貼付することで，訪問客がコードを読み取り，通常の収集時間外にゴミ箱を空にする必要があるかどうかを市当局に知らせることができるようになるだろう。

最後に，京都は，観光客に京都府の中心地から離れた地域を訪れてもらうキャンペーンを始めた。「海の京都」と銘打って，日本海沿岸に観光客を誘致するための策を打ち出しているのだ。地元住民がホームステイ型の宿泊施設を提供するのを奨励し，観光客が美しい景色だけでなく本物の日本の生活様式を体験できるようにするのは，すばらしいことだろう。

結論として，私たちは，人々が京都を楽しめるようになる方法をもっと考え出す必要がある。収容人数の多い交通機関を導入し，京都をきれいに保つ後押しをし，(4)特定の地域に人を集めよう。

コメント

(1) ここに何か足りません。2つの文をつなぐために，間にさらに情報を追加しなさい。
(2) ここに接続表現を挿入しなさい。
(3) この主題文はこの段落にあまり合っていません。書き直しなさい。
(4) 下線部の表現はあなたのエッセイの内容を十分に要約していません。変更しなさい。

総合的なコメント

あなたのエッセイはよく練られていますね。２階建てバスのアイデアは特に気に入りました。

問1　15　③

「コメント(1)に基づいて，付け加えるのに最も適当な文はどれか。」 15

① 「結局のところ，他の地域に興味がある人もいる。」
② 「結果として，多くのホテルがいまだに空室を抱えている。」
③ 「しかし，このために，今では観光客が多すぎるという場所もある。」
④ 「それでも，観光客の数はわれわれが期待していた数には達していない。」

(1)の直前は we were happy to see people coming back（客足が戻ってきて私たちはうれしかった）という肯定的な内容なのに対し，直後では The city is now struggling from ‘over-tourism.’（京都は現在，「オーバーツーリズム」に悩まされている。）という否定的な内容がきている。これらをつなぐには，‘逆接’の接続表現を含み，かつ「オーバーツーリズム」の様相を呈する現状を表す文を挿入したい。よって③が正解。①の他地域に興味を持つ人，②のホテルの空室，④の観光客の人数の伸び悩みはいずれも「オーバーツーリズム」につながらないので不正解。

問2　16　①

「コメント(2)に基づいて，付け加えるのに最も適当な表現はどれか。」 16

① 「例えば」
② 「対照的に」
③ 「そのうえ」
④ 「それにもかかわらず」

(2)に至るまでの流れと，その後に続く文の内容を確認しよう。筆者はこの段落の冒頭で「バスの混雑」を問題点として挙げ，その対策として市が検討している「観光客に通常より高額の料金を課す」という案を「問題を増やすだけだ」と一蹴し，Let's think of more practical solutions（もっと現実的な解決策を考えよう）と述べている。論の展開として，筆者はこのあとに，「もっと現実的な解決策」の具体案を自ら示さなくてはならない。実際，筆者は「２階建てバスの導入」という案を提示している。したがって，具体例の導入を示す①が正解。他の選択肢は，前後を自然につなぐことができない。

問3　17　③

「コメント(3)に基づいて，この主題文を書き直すのに最適な方法はどれか。」 17

① 「京都市は人々にゴミ袋を購入するよう求めるべきだ」
② 「自分のゴミをリサイクルする人が増えるべきだ」
③ 「ゴミの問題は対処されなければならない」
④ 「訪問客は自分のゴミを宿泊先まで持ち帰らなければならない」

下線部(3)は主題文として適切でない，というのが添削者である先生の指摘。主題文はその段落の要旨をわかりやすくまとめるものでなければならない。筆者はこの段落で，ゴミ箱の少なさが観光客の不満の種となっていることを挙げ，ゴミ捨て場の増設やQRコードの利用を対策案として掲げている。つまりこの段落の主題は，「ゴミ捨て場の少なさとその対策（の必要性）」であることがわかる。これと合い，かつ本文に記述があるのは③のみで，これが正解。①のゴミ袋の購入，②のリサイクル，④の宿泊先へのゴミの持ち帰りについては本文に言及がない。

問4 **18** ②

「コメント(4)に基づいて，置き換えるものとして最適なのはどれか。」 18

① 「私たちの街の代表として振る舞う」

② 「市の中心部に人が集中することを避ける」

③ 「地元の人たちを楽しませる」

④ 「観光客に日本のことを教える」

最終段落はエッセイ全体の結論を述べる役割を果たしており，下線部(4)を含むこの一文は，筆者がここまでに述べてきた論の要約となっている。introduce high-capacity transportation は第2段落で「2階建てバス」を例に提案したことで，help keep Kyoto clean は第3段落でふれたゴミ問題，それに続く(4)は第4段落の内容と合致させるのが自然。筆者が第4段落で挙げた，観光客を日本海沿岸地域へ誘致するキャンペーンの主眼は，日本海沿岸地域という特定地域に人を集める（gather people in certain areas）ことではなく，京都中心部の過度な混雑を緩和させることにあるから，②が正解。このエッセイが一貫して「オーバーツーリズム」を主題に据えていることを念頭に置いておけば，④と迷うこともないだろう。①，③のような記述は本文にない。

【語句】

◇must-see「必見の；ぜひ見るべき」
◇highlight「～を浮き彫りにする〔強調する〕」
◇crowding「混雑」
◇deal with ～「～に対処する」
◇a number of ～「いくつかの～」
◇charge「～（＝料金・値段）を請求する」
◇practical「現実的な；実際的な」
◇introduce「～を導入する」
◇double-decker bus「2階建てバス」
◇complain about ～「～について不平〔文句〕を言う」
◇trash can「（大型の）ゴミ箱」
◇dispose of ～「～を捨てる〔廃棄する〕」
◇scan「～をスキャンする」
◇need *doing*「…される必要がある」
◇empty「～を空にする」
◇outside regular collection hours「通常の収集時間外に」
◇take measures「手段を講じる；対策を取る」
◇encourage ～ to *do*「～に…するよう促す」
◇scenery「景色；景観」
◇high-capacity「収容人数の多い」
◇transportation「交通手段」
◇問1 ① after all「結局のところ」
◇問1 ② available「利用できる；（ホテルの部屋などが）空いている」
◇問4 ① act as ～「～の役割を務める」
◇問4 ① representative「代表者」
◇問4 ② concentration「（人・物の）集中」
◇問4 ② city center「街の中心；市街地」
◇問4 ③ entertain「～を楽しませる」

第5問

全訳 あなたは世界の教育の機会についての調査をしています。あなたは2つの記事を見つけました。

教育の機会における世界的な危機

マット・ブラウン記

2017年11月5日

学校へ通うことは，家庭の安定を促進し，犯罪を減少させ，就職の可能性を高める重要な要素である。しかし，子どもたちが教室に足を踏み入れる機会を決して得られない地域が依然としてある。さらに，女の子は男の子ほど教育を受ける機会が多くないことを，研究者たちは見出した。

国連の調査によると，学校で学べる機会を生涯得られないであろう小学校に通うべき年齢の男の子が820万人，女の子が1,600万人いる。グラフは，6ヵ国の小学校に入学していない子どもの数を示している。男女差は地域によって異なり，アフリカの一部の国では，男の子の約2倍の女の子が生涯学校に通うことがない。一時的に学校を離れる子どももいれば，いずれは学校に行く予定の子どももいるが，たいていの場合，学校へ通うことになるのは男の子である。

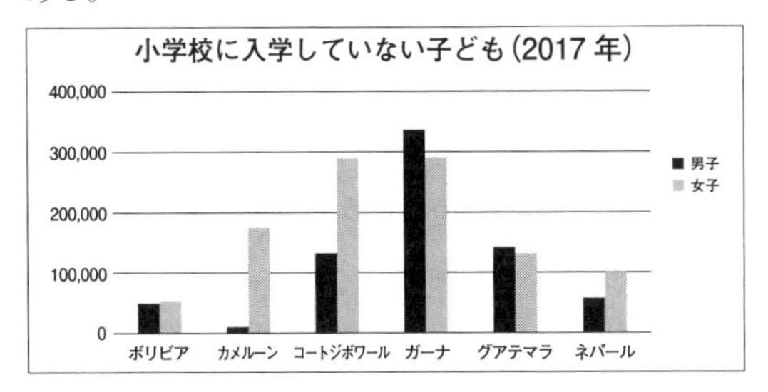

教育における男女の不平等にはいくつかの理由がある。多くの文化では，女の子は家にいて，小さな子ども，病気の人，または高齢者の世話をしている。また，料理や掃除により多くの時間を費やす。学校の制服や教科書などの必需品にほとんどお金が出せない低所得家庭も，将来息子の方がより多くのお金を稼ぐ可能性が高いため，娘よりも息子を学校に行かせる選択をしがちである。

私の意見としては，政府は小学校を完全に無料にしなければならない。教育の金銭的負担を取り除くことは，貧困層の人々にとっては大いに助けになるだろう。実際，このような政策をすでに適用している国では，小学校に通う子ども全体の数も女の子の数も増えている。

「教育の機会における世界的な危機」についての意見

フランシス・ナグラ記

2017年11月12日

家族のために薪を集めたり，食事を作ったりといったことをしなければならないため，欠席する子どもが多い学校で，私は働いている。短時間学校を離れ，学校に戻るまで家族の仕事を手伝う子どももいる。私はいつも学校で女の子よりも男の子を多く目にする。私が生まれた国も同様の問題に直面している。マット・ブラウンの記事によると，私の国では30万人近くの女の子が学校に通っておらず，対して，学校に通っていない男の子はその半数にとどまる。

私が思う最大の問題の1つは，きれいな飲料水がたやすく入手できないことで，多くの場合，家族が使用する水を汲んでくるのは女の子の仕事である。私が住んでいる村では，女性と女の子が6キロ以上離れたところから20キロほどの水を運ぶ。これでは学校に行く時間がない。また，近くに水がある場合でさえ，飲むのは安全ではないかもしれない。家族が病気になった場合，女の子が負担を負わなければならない。

長距離と言えば，より多くの学校を田舎に建設する必要がある。大都市外の多くの子どもたちは学校まで長い道のりを歩かなければならないが，これは特に女の子にとって困難で危険なことである。より通いやすい学校のもう1つの利点は，学校が終わってから，子どもがまだ家事をする時間があることだ。

問1　19　②

「マット・ブラウンもフランシス・ナグラも 19 については言及していない。」

①「世界の特定の地域における男女差」

②「小学校における教員の不足」

③「教育と犯罪の関連性」

④「制服が障害になるかもしれない理由」

どちらの記事でも述べられていない事柄は何かを考えよう。「世界の特定の地域における男女差」については，1つ目の記事では第2段落第3文で，The gender gap varies by location, and in some countries in Africa, around twice as many girls as boys will never go to school.「男女差は地域によって異なり，アフリカの一部の国では，男の子の約2倍の女の子が生涯学校に通うことがない。」とあるので，①は不正解。「教育と犯罪の関連性」については，1つ目の記事の第1段落第1文で，School attendance is a significant factor in improving family stability, reducing crime, and increasing job prospects.「学校へ通うことは，家庭の安定を促進し，犯罪を減少させ，就職の可能性を高める重要な要素である。」と述べているので，③も不正解。「制服が障害になるかもしれない理由」については，1つ目の記事の第3段落第4文で，Low-income families with little to spend on essential supplies like school uniforms and textbooks may also choose to send a son rather than a daughter to school because the son is likely to earn more money in the future.「学校の制服や教科書などの必需品にほとんどお金が出せない低所得家庭も，将来息子の方がより多くのお金を稼ぐ可能性が高いため，娘よりも息子を学校に行かせる選択をしがちである。」と述べているので，④も不正解。「小学校における教員の不足」については，どちらの記事でも述べられていない。したがって，②が正解。

問2 20 ②

「その教師は 20 出身だ。」

① 「カメルーン」

② 「コートジボワール」

③ 「ガーナ」

④ 「グアテマラ」

2つ目の記事の第1段落第4～5文に，The country where I was born faces a similar problem. According to the article by Matt Brown, almost 300,000 girls in my country are not in school compared to only half as many boys.「私が生まれた国も同様の問題に直面している。マット・ブラウンの記事によると，私の国では30万人近くの女の子が学校に通っておらず，対して，学校に通っていない男の子はそのわずか半数である。」とある。1つ目の記事のグラフから，30万人近くの女の子が学校に通っておらず，15万人近くの男の子が学校に通っていない国はコートジボワールなので，②が正解。

問3 21 ②

「記事によると，女の子は 21 しばしば学校を休む。（最も適切な選択肢の組み合わせを選びなさい。）」

a 「家族のために家事をするために」

b 「家族が育てた作物を売るために」

c 「家族の世話をするために」

d 「弟妹に勉強のやり方を教えるために」

すべての選択肢が副詞用法の不定詞で始まっているので，女の子が学校を休む理由を表している選択肢を選べばよい。1つ目の記事の第3段落第1～3文に，There are several reasons for gender inequality in education. In many cultures, girls stay home to care for the young, sick, or elderly. They also spend more time cooking and cleaning.「教育における男女の不平等にはいくつかの理由がある。多くの文化では，女の子は家にいて，小さな子ども，病気の人，または高齢者の世話をしている。また，料理や掃除により多くの時間を費やす。」とある。つまり，女の子は家事や家族の世話をするために学校を休むということなので，aとcが正しい。bとdについてはどちらの記事でも述べられていないので誤り。よって②が正解。

問4 22 ③ 23 ⑤

「マット・ブラウンは 22 と述べ，フランシス・ナグラは 23 と述べている。（それぞれの空欄には異なる選択肢を選ぶこと。）」

① 「両親は家族のために料理をすべきだ」

② 「家族が水を売るのに苦労している」

③ 「政府は教育費をもっと出すべきだ」 22

④ 「病気の子どもは辞めがちだ」

⑤ 「一部の子どもたちは学校からあまりに遠く離れて暮らしている」 23

22 は1つ目の記事で述べられていることを選ぶ。第4段落第1文に，In my opinion, governments must make primary school completely free.「私の意見としては，政府は小学校を完全に無料にしなければならない。」とある。政府がもっと教育費を出せば，小学校が無料化できるということになるので，③を選べばよい。

23 は2つ目の記事で述べられていることを選ぶ。第3段落第2文に，Many children outside of major cities have to travel a long way to school, which can be both difficult and dangerous, especially for girls.「大都市外の多くの子どもたちは学校まで長い道のりを歩かなければならないが，これは特に女の子にとって困難で危険なことである。」とあるので，⑤を選べばよい。

2つ目の記事の第2段落第1文に，One of the biggest problems I see is the lack of easy access to clean drinking water「私が思う最大の問題の1つは，きれいな飲料水がたやすく入手できないことだ」とあり，苦労しているのは飲料水を確保することであって水を売ることではないので，②は不正解。①と④についてはどちらの記事でも述べられていないので，いずれも不適。

問5 24 ①

「両方の記事の情報に基づいて，あなたは宿題でレポートを書く。レポートに最もふさわしい題名は『 24 』であろう。」

① 「小学校教育における男女差の解消」

② 「女の子は自分自身の教育に責任を負っている」

③ 「私立学校がいかに教育の様相を変化させているか」

④ 「小学校で女の子が男の子よりも幸せでない理由」

1つ目の記事の段落ごとの要旨は以下のとおり。

・第1段落：「学校へ通うことは重要だが，世界には子どもたちが学校へ行けない地域があり，また女の子は男の子ほど教育を受ける機会が多くはない。」

・第２段落：「国連の調査によると，学校に通っていない子どもたちの男女差は地域によって異なり，アフリカの一部の国では，学校に通うことのない女の子は男の子の約２倍いる。」

・第３段落：「女の子は家族の世話や家事をするという文化や，男の子の方が将来お金を稼ぐ可能性が高いということが，教育の機会の男女不平等の原因となっている。」

・第４段落：「政府が小学校を完全無料化にすれば，貧しい家庭は助かり，女の子が学校へ行く機会も増えるはずだ。」

２つ目の記事の段落ごとの要旨は以下のとおり。

第１段落：「筆者の出身国では，女の子は男の子ほど学校へ行く機会が得られていない。」

第２段落：「筆者の村では，女の子が６キロ以上離れた場所から20キロほどの水を汲んでこなければならず，このことが女の子の学校へ行く機会を失わせている。」

第３段落：「学校をもっと田舎に建設すれば，学校まで長距離を歩く必要がなくなって，女の子にとって安全で通いやすくなる。また，学校が終わってから家事をする時間もできる。」

つまり両方の記事ともに，女の子の方が男の子よりも教育を受ける機会に恵まれていないという現状を述べ，その男女差の解消のための提言を行っている。したがって，①が適切。

【語句】

◇crisis「危機」
◇attendance「出席」
◇stability「安定」
◇UN「国際連合」（United Nationsの略語）
◇vary「変わる」
◇eventually「最終的に」
◇inequality「不平等」
◇burden「負担」
◇fetch「～を取りに行く」
◇speaking of ～「～と言えば」
◇accessible「行きやすい」
◇問１　neither A nor B「AもBも…ない」
◇問３ d　sibling「きょうだい」

第６問

全訳　あなたは，私たちの社会でAIがもっと活用されるべきかどうかについてのエッセイに取り組んでいます。あなたは以下のステップに従います。

ステップ１：AIが社会に与える影響に関するさまざまな見解を読み，理解する。

ステップ２：私たちの社会でAIがもっと活用されるべきかについての立場を明確にする。

ステップ３：追加の資料を用いてエッセイの概要を作成する。

［ステップ１］さまざまな資料を読む

筆者A（生徒）

私はゲームが大好きで，AIはゲームをさらに刺激的なものにしてくれます。例えば，私のお気に入りのオンラインRPGでは無数のユニークなキャラクターに出会えるのですが，これは全部AIが作ったものです。新しくプレーしたいゲームを探して時間を無駄にする必要ももはやありません。私の使っているAI搭載ソフトが，私が楽しめそうな次のすばらしいゲームを正確に勧めてくれるからです。でも，AIの悪影響について実際に心配している人もいますね。例えば，AIがゲームデザイナーの仕事を完全に奪ってしまう，という懸念とか。しかし，私が思うに，AIが考えたデザインを完成させ，品質を確保するのに，まだ人間のデザイナーは必要とされるでしょう。

筆者B（親）

親として，一番怖いのはソーシャルメディア上のAIですね。AIは，ただ子供をオンライン上により長くとどまらせるものなら何でも見せているように思えます。正しいものとか，子供にとってよいものではなく。結果として子供たちはフェイクニュースをたくさん目にしたり，非常に奇妙な考えを持つようになったりしています。個人的には，子供がソーシャルメディアにアクセスするのを制限するのではなく，ネットを賢く使うよう教えているつもりです。それでも，AIがあらゆる手立てを使って子供たちの気を引くようプログラムされていると，それも難しくなります。私たちは，AIが生み出すコンテンツに満ちたこの新時代に対処すべく，テクノロジーとの関係についてもっと深く考える必要があるでしょう。

筆者C（ビジネスパーソン）
携帯電話などのデバイスに搭載されているAIがかなり便利だということは否定しようがありません。自分の携帯電話のAIが，私の一日のスケジュール管理をし，健康面の目標に関して記録を付けてくれるのを大変気に入っています。ポケットに個人アシスタントを入れているようなものです。買い物や娯楽に関するAIのおすすめは非常に正確で，おかげでかなり時間の節約になっています。確かに，デバイスがそのユーザーについてちょっと知りすぎていると不満を漏らす友人も中にはいますが，その利便性はそれを補って余りあると思います。退屈なタスクはデバイスに任せ，代わりにもっと複雑で意義のあるアイデアに私の思考力を使えるわけです。

筆者D（ジャーナリスト）
労働市場においてAIが果たす役割は，大いに議論されているテーマです。支持者がよく言うのは，AIはさまざまな新しい職を含む新しいテクノロジー産業を生み出し，AIが破壊する産業に取って代わるだろう，ということです。しかし，あいにく，AIなどの技術革新によってその人の持っているスキルが無用のものとなる働き手というのは，多くの場合，中高年なのです。AIが慎重にコントロールされなければ，こうした比較的年齢層の高い労働者が，ほとんど支援を受けられないまま，それまでとはまったく異なる産業での仕事に適応することを強いられることになるかもしれません。労働者たちは職を失い，結果として経済的・精神的ストレスに直面することもありえます。新たなテクノロジーが人々の生活を完全に変えてしまう前に，よく考えようではありませんか。

筆者E（プログラミング教員）
プログラミングを教える教員として，私はずっと技術的変化への適応ということを数年おきにやってこなければなりませんでした。しかし，AIが進化するその急速なペースはかつてないほど速くなっており，私が生徒に教えているスキルの重要性を損なっている，というのが私の懸念です。そのうえ，雇用市場も常に変化しています。こうした懸念から私は，将来プログラマーになるためにコーディングを学ぶよう生徒に勧めにくくなっています。言うまでもなく，AIをめぐっては深刻な倫理的ジレンマもあります。私たちのプライベートな情報をAIが今後どのように扱うかということについては特に心配です。

［ステップ2］立場を決める
あなたの立場：AIは私たちにさまざまな新しい機会をもたらし，生活をより豊かなものにする。
●筆者 27 と 28 はあなたの立場をサポートする。
●２人の筆者の主な論拠： 29 。

［ステップ3］資料AとBを用いて概要を作成する
あなたのエッセイの概要：

AIは私たちの社会でもっと活用されるべきだ

導入
AI革命はさまざまな困難を伴うが，基本的には，刺激的な新たな機会をもたらすことで，私たちの生活を向上させる。

本論
理由１：［ステップ２より］
理由２：［資料Ａに基づいて］……… 30
理由３：［資料Ｂに基づいて］……… 31

結論
私たちの社会においてAIの開発・利用は促進されるべきだ。

資料A
AIが日常生活に与える影響は，幅広く使われているさまざまなアプリケーションに見て取れる。バーチャルアシスタントとして知られるタイプのAIは，音声認識・言語処理技術を用いて人間の言葉を理解し，それに論理的に返答する。能力にかなり制約のあった以前のバーチャルアシスタントとは異なり，こうした最近のAIバーチャルアシスタントは，ユーザーの質問や指示に対して具体的な応答をすることができる。ユーザーのスケジュール設定を自動的に行うなど，高度なタスクを遂行する能力もある。それによってもたらされたのは時間管理革命とも言えるもので，個人の効率性を大幅に向上させている。

さらに，個々人にとって最適な運動・食事プランを提供することで，食事と運動のバランスを取りやすくするようなAI搭載アプリもある。そうしたアプリは，ユーザーのニーズに合った健康的なライフスタイルを確立するために，個々人の好みや健康水準を分析することに特化している。こうした進歩は，日常的な活動を達成しやすくするというAIの役割を引き立たせるもので，このことは社会を改善することにのみつながるだろう。

資料B

最近の調査によれば，AIに対する一般的な見解はおおむね肯定的なものである。この話題について問われた大勢の人が，AIは労働者がより効率的に仕事をするのを後押しするという考えを示した。職を失うなどの問題を懸念する向きもあるものの，大半の人は社会全体をよくするであろうAIの可能性を支持しているようだ。

（グラフ）
AIの影響に関する市民の意見

AIは労働者の生産性を向上させる	58%
AIは社会を豊かにするだろう	37%
AIにはいくつかの潜在的な懸念が付いて回る	12%
AIは少し恐ろしい	19%

■各項目に賛成した人の割合

問1 25 ②

「筆者DもEも 25 について述べている。」

①「AIの進化についていくために学校教育をアップデートさせることの難しさ」

②「仕事の世界における変化と今あるスキルの有用性」

③「日常生活におけるAIの便利さとプライバシー侵害の可能性」

④「AIが職場で倫理的ジレンマを生み出す可能性」

筆者Dは一貫して，労働市場においてAIが果たすであろう役割について語っている。筆者Eも the job market is always changing（雇用市場も常に変化しています）と述べている。

また，筆者Dは The unfortunate truth, however, is that workers whose skills will be of no value because of technological advancements like AI are often middle-aged or older.（しかし，あいにく，AIなどの技術革新によってその人の持っているスキルが無用のものとなる働き手というのは，多くの場合，中高年なのです。）と，現在の中高年の労働者が持っているスキルに言及している。筆者Eも，the rapid pace of AI advancements is ... reducing the importance of the skills I teach students（AIが進化するその急速なペースは…私が生徒に教えているスキルの重要性を損なっている）と，筆者自身が生徒に教えているスキルについてふれている。

これらから，筆者D，Eはともにthe change in the working world（仕事の世界における変化）と the usefulness of current skills（今あるスキルの有用性）について言及しているため，②が正解。

①は筆者Eが提示しているテーマだが，筆者Dはそのことにふれていない。③の the potential for privacy invasion については筆者Eがふれているものの，筆者Dは言及がなく，選択肢の前半部分はどちらも話題にしていない。筆者Eは moral dilemmasに言及しているが，あくまで一般的な文脈においてであり，ethical dilemmas in the workplace（職場における倫理的ジレンマ）には限定されないし，筆者Dはそれにふれていないから④は不正解。

問2 26 ④

「筆者Cは 26 ということを示唆している。」

①「いずれAIはより複雑なアイデアを出せるようになる」

②「便利な生活を送るために誰もが個人アシスタントを雇うべきだ」

③「AIはそのユーザーの個人情報を学んでしまうということが問題だ」

④「AIを日常生活で使うことには，短所をはるかに上回る長所がある」

筆者Cは第5文で I think the convenience is well worth it（その利便性はそれ（＝AIがもたらす問題）を補って余りあると思う）と述べている。これと一致する④が正解。退屈なタスクをAIに任せ，浮いた時間で自分が more complex and meaningful ideas（もっと複雑で意義のあるアイデア）について考えたい，というのが筆者Cの考えであり，①のようなことは述べていない。また，It's like having a personal assistant in my pocket.（ポケットに個人アシスタントを入れているようなものです。）では，AIの利用を比喩的に表現しているにすぎず，②のような主張はしていない。③は筆者Cの友人の見解であり，筆者Cはそのことを問題視していない。

問3 27 ① 28 ③ （順不同）
29 ①

「さて，あなたはさまざまな見解を理解した上で，AIが私たちの社会でもっと活用されるべきかどうかについての立場を決め，以下のように書いた。27，28，29を完成させるのに最も適当な選択肢を選びなさい。」

「27と28の選択肢（順不同。）」

① **「A」**
② 「B」
③ **「C」**
④ 「D」
⑤ 「E」

「AIは私たちにさまざまな新しい機会をもたらし，生活をより豊かなものにする」という立場を裏付ける意見を選ぶ。5人の意見を見ていこう。

筆者A：ゲーム愛好者の観点から，第1～3文でAIへの好感を述べ，その例として，多数の魅力的なキャラクターを生成できる，ユーザーの好みにあったゲームをおすすめできることを挙げている。これらは今までにはなかった「新しい機会」と言える。

筆者B：冒頭からソーシャルメディア上のAIに対する懸念を表明し，その後も一貫してAIを憂慮する見解を続けている。

筆者C：第2文の I love how my phone's AI helps me organize my day and keep track of my health goals.（自分の携帯電話のAIが，私の一日のスケジュール管理をし，健康面の目標に関して記録を付けてくれるのを大変気に入っています。）と，第4文の AI suggestions for shopping and entertainment are highly accurate, which saves me tons of time.（買い物や娯楽に関するAIのおすすめは非常に正確で，おかげでかなり時間の節約になっています。）から，この筆者がAIを多様な用途で活用し，それに満足していることがわかる。

筆者D：AIによる労働市場の変化を具体的に予測し，それに対する熟慮や対策の必要性を述べることに終始しているから，ここでの「あなたの立場」を裏付ける意見にはなり得ない。

筆者E：プログラミング教員として教育現場で日に日に増す困難や自信喪失に言及し，その懸念は，AIがもたらす倫理的ジレンマ，個人情報の取り扱いにも及んでいる。急速に進化するAIに苦慮しているというのが筆者Eのスタンスである。

以上から，AIの肯定的な可能性・利便性を支持しているのはAとCなので，①と③が正解。

「29の選択肢」

① **「AIはおおむね便利なテクノロジーで，私たちの日常生活の効率性を高めてくれる」**
② 「ソーシャルメディア上のAIは誤情報の問題を解決でき，子供たちに好ましい影響を与える」
③ 「AIは，これまで解決するのが困難だった倫理的ジレンマの一部を克服するだろう」
④ 「テクノロジー産業におけるAIの急速な発展は，雇用機会の増加とさらなる経済成長を約束するものだ」

筆者A，Cに共通する意見を選択する問題。前問で確認した通り，この二人は日々AIの利便性を享受している。筆者Aは第3文で I don't even have to waste my time searching for new games to play anymore（新しくプレーしたいゲームを探して時間を無駄にする必要ももはやない）と述べ，同様に筆者Cも ..., which saves me tons of time（…，おかげでかなり時間の節約になっている）と述べている。両者の見解を要約した①が正解。②，③，④について筆者A，Cはふれていないので不正解。

問4 30 ④

「資料Aに基づいて，理由2として最も適当なものは次のうちどれか。」30

① 「AI技術は，人の身体的能力を高めるので，個人の効率性の向上をもたらしてきた。」
② 「バーチャルアシスタントは限られた能力でタスクを遂行することのみに役立つものだが，大半の人にとってはそれで十分である。」
③ 「私たちの生活におけるAIの主な利点は，娯楽へのアクセスを向上させるような指示に対する具体的な応答である。」
④ **「バーチャルアシスタントは人間の複雑な言葉を理解し，応答することができ，それにより個人のタスク管理を大幅に改善している。」**

資料Aは，大きく3つの部分に分けることができる。まず第1～5文でAIのバーチャルアシスタントの有用性を述べ，第6～7文で食事や運動を管理するAI搭載アプリの有用性を述べ，AIを全面的に肯定する最終文で締めくくっている。

バーチャルアシスタントの能力を uses voice recognition and language processing technology to understand human speech and respond to it logically（音声認識・言語処理技術を用いて人間の言葉を理解し，それに論理的に返答する）と説明し，それがもたらす効果を a revolution in time management, greatly increasing personal efficiency（時間管理革命とも言えるもので，個人の効率性を大幅に向上させている）と言い切っている。これらをほぼそのまま言い換えた④が正解。

AIが our physical ability（人の身体的能力）を高めるという記述はないので，①は不正解。資料Aで a very limited capacity（かなり制約のある能力）と形容されているのは旧来のものなので，②も不正解。③の make entertainment easier to access に該当する記述はないので，これも不正解。

問5 31 ①

「理由3として，あなたは『AIは多くの人に歓迎されている』と書くことにした。資料Bに基づいて，この意見を裏付けるのに最も ふさわしい選択肢は次のうちどれか。」 31

① **「大半の人が，AIは働き方や社会に好ましい影響を与えるだろうと考えており，懸念を示す人は比較的少数にとどまっている。」**

②「かなりの割合の人がAIの問題について認識しているものの，ちょうど半数の人が，そのような悪影響は非常に些末なので無視できると考えている。」

③「アンケートに答えた人のうち50％以上がAIには欠点が一切なく，社会や職場を改善する能力を持っていることで広く一般から支持されている，ということに同意している。」

④「AIに関して否定的な意見がある一方，大半の人はAIを歓迎し，AIを恐れる人の数は10％を下回るものでしかない。」

まず，グラフを読み取ろう。上の2つの項目（＝「AIは労働者の生産性を向上させるだろう」「AIは社会を豊かにするだろう」）がAIの影響を肯定する項目で，下の2つの項目（＝「AIにはいくつかの潜在的な懸念が付いて回る」「AIは少し恐ろしい」）が否定的なものである。一番上は58％で，これが唯一半数を超える賛同を得ている。上から2つ目の項目は37％で，2番目に多い。上から3つ目は賛同者が最も少なく，わずかに10％を超えるにとどまり，一番下の項目も20％に満たない。

選択肢を見ていくと，①の前半はグラフの一番上の項目と一致し，後半も下2つの項目と一致する。①が正解。②は，選択肢後半の主語 exactly half（＝50％）に一致するデータ値がグラフ上に存在しないので，不正解。③の「AIには欠点が一切ないことに同意している」ことを占めすデータはそもそもグラフ上になく，正否を判断できないため，不正解。④は，前半は正しいが，AIに対する恐怖心，すなわちグラフにおける一番下の項目の割合の数値が間違っている。選択肢では「10％未満」とあるが，グラフでは20％近くあるから不正解。

【語句】

◇AI-powered「AIで稼働する；AI搭載の」
◇take over ～「～を乗っ取る」
◇ensure「～を確保する〔保証する〕」
◇end up *doing*「結局…することになる」
◇weird「奇妙な；異様な」
◇restrict ～ from *doing*「～が…するのを制限する」
◇grab *one's* attention「～の注目を引く」
◇there is no denying that ...「…ということは否定できない」
◇keep track of ～「～の記録をつける；～を把握する」
◇save A B「AにBを省かせる〔節約させる〕」
◇tons of ～「大量の～」
◇worth it「それだけの価値がある」
◇leave A to B「AをBに任せる」
◇focus A on B「Aの焦点をBに合わせる」
◇of intense debate「大いに議論されている」
◇all sorts of ～「あらゆる～；さまざまな～」
◇replace「～に取って代わる」
◇of no value「価値がない」
◇adapt to ～「～に適応する」
◇entirely「完全に；まったく」
◇think twice「よく考える；考え直す」
◇surrounding ～「～をめぐる」
◇handle「～を取り扱う」
◇come with ～「～が付いてくる〔～を伴う〕」
◇application「アプリケーション」くだけて app ともいう。
◇voice recognition「音声認識」
◇language processing「言語処理」

◇human speech「人間の言葉」
◇detailed「詳細な」
◇command「命令；指示」
◇balance A and B「AとBのバランスをとる」
◇diet「食事；食生活」
◇specialize in ～「～に特化する」
◇preference「好み」
◇fitness「体の健康」
◇match *one's* needs「～のニーズに合致する」
◇show off ～「～を誇示する」
◇enrich「～を豊かにする」
◇問1 ⓪ keep up with ～「～に遅れずについていく〔対処する〕」
◇問1 ② usefulness「有用性」
◇問1 ③ invasion「侵害」
◇問1 ④ ethical「倫理的な」
◇問2 ⓪ come up with ～「～を考え出す」
◇問3 enhance「～の質を高める」
◇問3 ⓪ in general「一般的に；概して」
◇問3 ② misinformation「誤情報」
◇問3 ③ challenging「困難な；厄介な」
◇問5 ⓪ comparatively「比較的；かなり」
◇問5 ② significant「かなりの；相当の」
◇問5 ③ survey「～を（アンケート）調査する」

第7問

全訳 あなたのグループは，下記の雑誌記事の情報を使って「すごい高さから跳び降りる」という題名でポスター発表の準備をしています。

アンドレ＝ジャック・ガルヌランは1769年にパリで生まれた。若い頃は物理学を学んだが，彼の専門的なキャリアは彼を別の方向へ導いた。1790年代初期にフランス革命が始まった時，彼はフランス陸軍の監察官として働き始めた。すぐにガルヌランはイギリス軍に捕らえられ，ハンガリーの牢獄に送られたが，それは彼にとって極めて重要な体験になった。高い牢獄の塀は，どうやって逃げるかを彼が考えるきっかけとなったのである。彼は落下の速度を落とす原始的なパラシュートを作ることができれば，自分は塀から跳び降りて牢獄の外に安全に着地できると考えた。当時，無事に試行できた唯一のパラシュートは木の骨組みのついた傘のような形のもので，パラシュートで最も高い位置から跳び降りた例は建物のてっぺんからのものであった。

結局，ガルヌランは逃亡を企てず，2年後に解放された。同じ頃，熱気球が発明されていて，初めて人類は何千フィートも空高く浮かぶことができるようになっていた。ガルヌランはパラシュートへの野望をあきらめてはおらず，空高くにある気球から安全に降りることができる骨組みなしのパラシュートを作ることができると信じていた。しかし，この理論を試すためには，まず，もっと経験を積んだ気球乗りになる必要があった。

ガルヌランはその後数年間，多くの時間を革新的なパラシュート降下の計画に費やした。彼のパラシュートのデザインはシンプルだった。現代のパラシュートのほとんどは，使用者の体につながったバックパックから広げられるが，最初のデザインは安全性がずっと低いものであった。ガルヌランのパラシュートには彼が中に立つことができるかごが付いていて，そのかごは熱気球に結び付けるようになっていた。かごには絹製の大きく丸い布が取り付けられていた。

1797年，ガルヌランは熱気球で1,000メートルの高さまで上昇し，気球を外してパラシュートで地上まで降下すると発表した。彼の最初の試みは6月に実施が予定されていたが，強風のため，彼の気球はバラバラに破けて離陸することができなかった。それにもかかわらず，ガルヌランはその年の10月に試みて成功した。大勢の人々が見守る中，ガルヌランは気球に乗り込み，着実に上昇した。計画通り，彼は1キロメートル上昇したのちに気球を外し，地面に向かって降下し始めた。

降下しながら，彼は自分のデザインの問題に気づいた。より新しいパラシュートには，てっぺんに空気を逃す穴が開いているが，ガルヌランのパラシュートにはそれがなかった。その結果，降下する間中，彼は激しく揺れた。ついに着陸した時，けがはなかったが，降下によってひどく気分が悪くなっていた。帰還した時，彼はヒーローとして迎えられた。

ガルヌランは科学的業績により，全国的な名声を得た。努力を通して，ガルヌランはそのパラシュートのデザインが実際に可能であることを証明し，この業績に対し，フランスは彼に公式飛行船操縦者の称号を与えた。けれども，彼の仕事の重要性は1世紀以上も知れ渡ることはなかった。1900年代まで，飛ぶことは生活において普通ではなかったからである。しかし，20世紀になり，飛行機やヘリコプターが一般的になるにつれて，ガルヌランの勇気ある取り組みが，何世代にもわたるパイロットやパラシュート降下員たちが足場とする基礎になった。デザインが改良され，ナイロンなど素材がよくなっても，新たなパラシュート降下1つ1つの成功は，200年以上前の偉業のおかげである。

すごい高さから跳び降りる

■アンドレ＝ジャック・ガルヌランの人生

期間	出来事
初期	ガルヌランが物理学の勉強を始めた
成年後	32
	33
	34
	ガルヌランが初めて自分のパラシュートを使った
	35

■不完全なデザイン

▶ガルヌランの初めのデザインは成功だったが，それより新しいパラシュートのデザインは 36 ことと 37 ことで改良されている。

■地上への降下が名声を高める

▶ガルヌランは 38 最初の人物であった。

▶ガルヌランの業績は 39 40 20世紀に知られるようになった。

問1 32 ② 33 ④ 34 ① 35 ③

「あなたのグループのメンバーは，ガルヌランの生涯における重要な出来事を一覧にした。『成年後』を起こった順番に完成させるために，5つの出来事（①～⑤）から4つを選びなさい。」

① **「ガルヌランが骨組みのないパラシュートに取り組み始めた」**

② **「ガルヌランが陸軍に入った」**

③ **「ガルヌランが公式飛行船操縦者の称号を得た」**

④ **「ガルヌランが牢獄に送られた」**

⑤「ガルヌランの業績はのちの世代のためになった」

記事では，ガルヌランの生涯における出来事が時系列に沿って述べられている。物理学を学んだあとの出来事を年代順に並べ替えればよい。

第1段落第3文のHe began working as an inspector in the French army ... in the early 1790s.（1790年代初期に…彼はフランス陸軍の監察官として働き始めた。）から，まず陸軍に入隊したことがわかる。②がこれに当たる。

次に，第1段落第4文にAlthough Garnerin was quickly captured by British forces and sent to a Hungarian prison（すぐにガルヌランはイギリス軍に捕らえられ，ハンガリーの牢獄に送られた）とあるので④の「牢獄に送られた」がこれに当たる。

2年後に牢獄から解放されてからの出来事は，第2段落第3文にGarnerin ... believed that he could create a frameless parachute（ガルヌランは…骨組みなしのパラシュートを作ることができると信じていた）とあり，さらに第3段落第1文にGarnerin spent much of the following years planning his innovative parachute jump.（ガルヌランはその後数年間，多くの時間を革新的なパラシュート降下の計画に費やした。）とあることから，①がこれに当たる。記事中のa frameless parachute（骨組みなしのパラシュート）が，①では a parachute without frames（骨組みのないパラシュート）と言い換えられている。

次の大きな出来事として，1797年6月のパラシュート降下の試みは強風のため離陸できずに終わるが，第4段落第3文にGarnerin made a successful attempt in October of that year（ガルヌランはその年の10月に試みて成功した）とあり，これに続く部分で1キロメートルの高さからパラシュートを使って跳び降り，着地したことが書かれている。表に示されているのは，この場面に当たる。

選択肢③は，第6段落第2文後半にFrance named him its official Aeronaut（フランスは彼に公式飛行船操縦者の称号を与えた）とあるので最後に入る。残る選択肢⑤は，さらにそのあとのことなので，起こった順に入れると入る余地がない。

以上より，32 ～ 35 には②→④→①→③の順に選択肢が入る。

問2 36 37 ②，⑤（順不同）

「36 と 37 に入れてポスターを完成させるのに最も適切な選択肢を2つ選びなさい。（順不同。）」

①「傘のような形の骨組みをパラシュートに付ける」

②「パラシュートのてっぺんに穴がある」
③「布を適正な位置に保つためにロープを取り入れる」
④「空気の流れをよくするために，パラシュートの角を丸くする」
⑤「かごをバックパックのデザインに変更する」
⑥「ナイロン以外の素材を使う」

新しいパラシュートについて，ガルヌランのパラシュートよりも改良されている点を選ぶ。

②のパラシュートのてっぺんの穴については，第5段落第2文にNewer parachutes have a hole at the top to allow the air to escape, but his parachute didn't.（より新しいパラシュートには，てっぺんに空気を逃がす穴が開いているが，ガルヌランのパラシュートにはそれがなかった。）とあるから，②は正解。文末の didn't の後ろには文の前半の have a hole ... to escapeが省略されている。

第3段落第3文にWhile most modern parachutes are opened up from a backpack（現代のパラシュートのほとんどはバックパックから広げられる）とあり，ガルヌランのパラシュートについては第4文にGarnerin's parachute included a basket（ガルヌランのパラシュートにはかごが付いていた）とある。新しいものはかごからバックパック型に変わっているので⑤は正解。

パラシュートの生地については，記事の第3段落の最終文にAttached to the basket was a large, round piece of silk（かごには絹製の大きく丸い布が取り付けられていた）とある。これがガルヌランのパラシュートの生地である。最終段落最後の文ではデザインや素材が改良されて，better materials, such as nylon（ナイロンのようなよりよい素材）と絹以外のものが紹介されているので⑥は不正解。

①のようなパラシュートの形は，ガルヌランの時代のものなので，改良されたものではない。③のropesは記事ではふれられていない。④のパラシュートの形状については，第3段落最終文からガルヌランのパラシュートがa large, round piece of silk（絹製の大きく丸い布）でできていたことがわかるが，新しいものの形状についての記述はない。したがって，正解は②と⑤。

問3 38 ③

「ポスターを完成させるのに最適な説明を選びなさい。」 38

①「人を支えることができるパラシュートをデザインした」
②「熱気球を発明した」
③「骨組みなしのパラシュートで着地に成功した」
④「パラシュートを使って無事跳び降りた」

ガルヌランが何を最初にした人なのかが問われている。第2段落第3文にGarnerin ... believed that he could create a frameless parachute（ガルヌランは…骨組みなしのパラシュートを作ることができると信じていた）とある。このパラシュートを使った2回目の挑戦について，第4段落最終文にJust as planned, he released the balloon after rising to one kilometer and began falling back to the earth.（計画通り，彼は1キロメートル上昇したのちに気球を外し，地面に向かって降下し始めた。）とあり，着陸の様子は第5段落第4文にWhen he finally landed, he was uninjured（ついに着陸した時，けがはなかった）とある。人が骨組みなしのパラシュートで無事に着地したのは，これが初めての例であるから，③が正解。第1段落最終文At the time, the only parachutes that had been successfully tested were shaped like umbrellas with wooden frames（当時，無事に試行できた唯一のパラシュートは木の骨組みのついた傘のような形のものだった）から，ガルヌラン以前に，人を支えることができるパラシュートがデザインされ，降下に成功していることがわかるので①と④は不適当。熱気球については記事の第2段落第2文にHot air balloons had recently been invented（同じ頃，熱気球が発明されていて）とあり，これもガルヌランによる発明ではないので②も不適当。

問4 39 40 ②，⑥（順不同）

「 39 と 40 に入れてポスターを完成させるのに最も適切な選択肢を2つ選びなさい。（順不同。）」

①「雑誌で特集されたあと」
②「そしてそれは何世代ものパイロットやパラシュート降下員を触発することになる」
③「フランスの大衆がガルヌランをヒーローとして考えるようになるにつれて」
④「ますます増えるパラシュート降下員の需要に応えて」
⑤「パラシュート降下員の減少にともなって」
⑥「飛行機やヘリコプターの発達にともなって」

ガルヌランの業績が20世紀になって知られるよう

になったことに関連する内容を選ぶ。

20世紀になってからのことは，最終段落第５文 But as planes and helicopters became common in the 20th century, Garnerin's bold efforts offered a foundation that generations of pilots and parachutists could build on.（しかし，20世紀になり，飛行機やヘリコプターが一般的になるにつれて，ガルヌランの勇気ある取り組みが，何世代にもわたるパイロットやパラシュート降下員たちが足場とする基礎となった。）とある。この内容の前半が⑥，後半が②に一致する。①，④，⑤に関連する記述は記事の中にはない。ガルヌランがヒーローとして迎えられたのは，彼が最初にパラシュートの降下に成功した直後のことで，20世紀になってから彼の業績が知れ渡るようになったこととは関係がないので③も不適当。したがって，正解は②と⑥。

【語句】

◇ entitled 〜「〜と題名を付けられた」
◇ inspector「監察官；視察官」
◇ capture「〜を捕らえる〔捕虜にする〕」
◇ prove to be 〜「〜であることがわかる」
◇ inspire O to *do*「Oを促して…させる」
◇ leap「跳ぶ」
◇ primitive「原始的な；素朴な，単純な」
◇ parachute「パラシュート」
◇ release「〜を解放する；〜を外す」
◇ descend「下る，降りる」
◇ innovative「刷新的な，革新的な」
◇ tear O to pieces「Oをばらばらに引き裂く」（toreはtearの過去形）
◇ steadily「しっかりと；着々と」
◇ consequently「その結果；必然的に」
◇ fame「名声」
◇ aeronaut「気球〔飛行船〕の操縦者」
◇ bold「大胆な，勇気ある」
◇ foundation「基礎；土台」
◇ owe O to 〜「Oに関して〜のおかげをこうむる」
◇ accomplishment「業績；成果」
◇ imperfect「不完全な」
◇ 問２　③　hold O in place「Oを適切な位置で支える」
◇ 問２　⑥　other than 〜「〜以外の」
◇ 問３　①　capable of 〜「〜の能力がある」
◇ 問３　④　survive「〜を生きのびる；〜（＝危機など）を切り抜ける」
◇ 問４　①　feature「〜を特集する」
◇ 問４　④　in response to 〜「〜に応じて」

第８問

全訳　あなたは，次の理科の授業での視覚的なプレゼンテーション用ポスターを準備している学生グループに所属しています。テーマは『様々な種類の岩石とその特徴』です。ポスターを制作するために次の文章を使っています。

岩石の種類
—基本的事実—

地殻として知られる地球の表層は様々なタイプの岩石で構成されており，それらは大きく分けて次の主要な３つ，火成岩，堆積岩，変成岩に分類される。この大まかな分類は，これらが長い期間，時には何百万年もかけて，どのように形成されてきたかを我々に教えてくれる。火成岩を例にとると，それらはマグマから形成される。火成岩はマグマが冷えて固まるという自然現象の結果で，それが起こる場所は地中深くの場合もあるし地表や地表近くの場合もある。堆積岩について言えば，多くの堆積岩は砂や死んだ動植物のような粒子が堆積して湖や海の底で形成されるが，この過程は地表でも起こる。いずれにせよ，時間の経過とともに粒子の層がどんどん重なっていき，堆積岩が「準備ができた」状態になる。最後のタイプは，すでに存在する岩石，すなわち火成岩あるいは堆積岩のどちらかが熱や圧力あるいは他の力によって変形したものである。そんなわけでこのタイプは「変成岩」という名前を与えられているのだ。

主なタイプのそれぞれには下位の分類があり，我々人類は古代から，特に建築の目的で岩石を使ってきた。下の図は岩石の具体的な６タイプを示している。それぞれの岩石にはそれぞれふさわしい用途がある。火成岩から見ていこう。

（図１　６タイプの岩：図省略）

タイプＡとＤの岩石はそれぞれ「花崗岩」と「安山岩」と呼ばれる。タイプＡは耐久性で知られているので，いくつか例を挙げると外壁や石柱，記念碑などに広く使われてきた。日本ではこの粒子が荒い岩石を「御影石」とも呼び，墓石によく使われる。けれども，タイプAの使用は屋外の建造物にとどまらない。室内の装飾物にも使われ，風呂場や台所で見かけることもある。タイプDの安山岩は南アメリカのアンデスにその名の由来があり，これも硬い。花崗岩同様，建物の外面によく使われ，造園事業でも使用される。タイプAと比べると，タイプDははるかに耐火性がある。しかしそれでも前者ですら摂氏500度以上にも耐えられることに注意すべきだろう。

タイプB（石灰岩）とF（砂岩）はどちらも堆積岩である。タイプBの主成分は炭酸カルシウムで，タイプFの主成分は名前が示している通り砂である。タイプBはタイプAほど硬くもなく耐久性もないとみなされることが多いが，ほかの利点がある。そのうちの1つは比較的簡単に加工できることで，屋根材や床材として使われてきた。タイプFも似た目的で使われるが，2つの際立つ特徴がある。1つ目は耐火性だ。2つ目は液体をよく吸収することだ。この性質のために，タイプFは霜の悪影響を受けることがあり，コケが生えやすい。したがってタイプFは外壁のような建築物には最良の選択肢ではないかもしれない。

残りの2つは変成岩だが，タイプEは時に堆積岩として分類されることもある。タイプCの大理石は内装仕上げとして優れた素材だとみなされているが，多くの様々な用途で使われており，建造物の内装と外装両方の美しさを増す重要な役割を果たしている。この美しくて光沢のある岩石は，タージマハルやパルテノン神殿，その他多くの歴史的記念建造物に用いられた。興味深いことに，この岩石はタイプBが変成した結果なのだ。もう1つのタイプは粘板岩で，その主成分は粘土鉱物を含んでいる。タイプEは高い耐水性があると知られている。加えて，このタイプは薄い板状にかなり容易に割くことができるので，屋根や床として特に役立つ。しかし，他の使い方もある。日本人になじみのある例の1つは，書道に欠かせない道具のすずりだろう。

プレゼンテーションポスターの下書き：

様々なタイプの岩石の研究からわかることは何か

どんな基準によって岩石を3つのタイプに分類するのか？

41

岩石のタイプの例

大まかなタイプ	具体的タイプ	説明	使用例
火成岩	A 花崗岩	このタイプの岩石は硬く耐久性があり，日本では「御影石」として知られている。	外壁，石柱
堆積岩	B 石灰岩	このタイプの岩石は炭酸カルシウムを含み，42。	屋根工事
変成岩	C 大理石	このタイプの岩石は光沢があり43。	室内工事

共通の性質を持つ岩石

44

45

問1 41 ②

「最初のポスターの見出しの下で，あなたは本文で説明されている3つの主な分類の研究から学べることを紹介したいと考えている。以下のうちどれが最も適切か。」41

①「マグマはいかに速く固まって岩石になったかと，どんな種類の岩石が装飾的な目的にふさわしいか。」

②「どのように岩石が時を経て固まったり変化したりする過程をたどったか。」

③「どんな種類の粒子が時間の経過とともに堆積して岩石になったか。」

④「地球のどの部分に岩石の起源があったか，またどれほど速く変成が起こったか。」

41には「どんな基準によって岩石を3つのタイプに分類するのか？」の答えとなる記述が入る。第1段落第1文に岩石は大きく3つのタイプに分けられるという説明があり，第2文にThis broad classification tells us how they have formed over a long period of time —— millions of years, sometimes.

(この大まかな分類はこれらが長い期間，時には何百万年もかけてどのように形成されてきたかを我々に教えてくれる。）とある。そのあと3タイプの岩石がそれぞれどのような過程を経て形成されたかの個々の説明が続くから，最初の見出しの下に適切なのは②。マグマが固まって岩石になるのは3つのうちの火成岩だけの説明である上に，装飾的な目的を基準に分類するわけではないので①は不適当。③は3タイプのうちの堆積岩だけの説明だから不適当。岩石のできる場所は石のタイプによって異なるが，変化の速さについては言及がない。④も不適当。

問2 42 ④ 43 ④

「あなたはタイプBとタイプCの岩石の説明を書くように頼まれている。42 と 43 に最も適する選択肢を選びなさい。」

タイプB 42

① 「造園工事に適している」
② 「特定の山脈にちなんで名づけられた」
③ 「耐久性はタイプAと同等である」
④ **「それを加工するのは骨の折れる仕事ではない」**

タイプBの説明は第4段落にある。第4文にOne of them (= other advantages) is that it can be processed relatively easily, and it has been used for roof work and flooring.（その（利点の）うちの1つは比較的簡単に加工できることで，屋根工事や床を貼る際に使われてきた。）とあり，これは④の内容と一致する。④が正解。①：造園工事について言及しているのは，タイプDの説明の中（第3段落第7文）。なのでタイプBとは関係がない。①は不正解。②：山脈にちなんで名づけられたのもタイプD。第3段落第6文に「アンデスにその名の由来があり」とある。②も不適当。③：タイプAは第3段落第2文にType A is noted for its durability（耐久性で知られている）とあるが，タイプBは第4段落第3文にType B is often considered neither as hard nor as durable as Type A（タイプBはタイプAほど硬くもなく耐久性もないとみなされることが多い）とあり，耐久性は同等ではない。③も不正解。

タイプC 43

① 「摂氏500度より低い熱に耐えられない」
② 「ずばぬけて熱に耐性がある」
③ 「粘土鉱物を含んでいることが多い」
④ **「元々は石灰岩だった」**

タイプCの説明は第5段落第2文から。第4文にthis rock (=Type C) is the result of the transformation of Type B（この岩はタイプBが変成した結果なのだ）とあり，Type Bは第4段落冒頭にあるようにlimestone（石灰岩）だから④が正解。耐火性についての説明があるのはタイプAとD（第3段落第8文）。タイプFも2つの目立つ特徴のうちの1つ目が耐火性だと述べられているが（第4段落第6文），タイプCには耐火性についての説明はない。①，②は不適当。粘土鉱物を含んでいるという説明があるのは粘板岩であるタイプE（第5段落第5文）だから③も不適当。

問3 44 45 ①，⑥（順不同）

「あなたは，共通の性質を持ついくつかの岩石についての説明文を作っている。記事によると，次のうち適切なもの2つはどれか。（順不同。）」 44 ・ 45

① **「タイプDとFを使って建設された建物は耐火性があると思われる。」**
② 「タイプAとBで作られた建造物は等しく水に弱いだろう。」
③ 「タイプAとFは古代から日本の伝統的な文化を形作るのに貢献してきた。」
④ 「タイプA，C，Fは巨大な外壁に非常に適している。」
⑤ 「タイプBとFは火成岩で，タイプCとEは変成岩である。」
⑥ **「タイプBとEはどちらも屋根を葺いたり床材として使われる。」**

選択肢の内容が本文に一致するか順に見ていこう。

① 問2の岩石Cの解説で見た通り，耐火性があるのはタイプA，D（第3段落第8文）とタイプF（第4段落第6文）だから①は正しい。

② タイプAとタイプBのどちらについても水に弱いとは述べられていないので正しくない。

③ 本文で「日本の伝統的な文化」が紹介されているのは第5段落最後の書写用の「すずり」である。ここで解説されているのはタイプE。タイプAには墓石に使われているとあるがFには日本文化とのつながりは紹介されていない。③は不正解。

④ タイプAは外壁に広く使われている（第3段落第2文）。タイプCは歴史的記念建造物に用いられているとあるが（第5段落第2～3文），外壁についての記載はない。タイプFは第4段落最後にit may not be the best option for constructing things like external walls.（外壁のような建築物には最良の選択肢ではないかもしれない）とある。タイプA以外は外壁に適しているとは言えないので④は不正解。

⑤ 第4段落第1文にTypes B (limestone) and F (sandstone) are both sedimentary rocks.（タイプB（石灰岩）とF（砂岩）は堆積岩である。）とある。どちらも火成岩ではないから⑤は正しくない。第5段落第1文にThe remaining two are metamorphic rocks（残りの2つは変成岩だ）とあり，「残りの2つ」はタイプCとEのことだから，⑤は後半部分のみ正しい。

⑥ タイプBは第4段落第4文で it has been used for roof work and flooring（屋根工事や床を貼る際に使われてきた）とある。タイプEは第5段落第7文にit is especially useful for roofs and floors（屋根や床として特に役立つ）とある。どちらも屋根材や床材として使われているから⑥は正しい。

以上より①と⑥が正解。

【語句】

◇ visual「視覚的な」
◇ theme「テーマ」
◇ passage「抜粋；一節」
◇ outer「外側の」
◇ layer「層；地層」
◇ crust「地殻」
◇ *be* composed of ～「～から構成されている」
◇ broadly「大雑把に；だいたい」
◇ igneous rock「火成岩」
◇ sedimentary rock「堆積岩」
◇ metamorphic rock「変成岩」
◇ classification「分類」
◇ magma「マグマ」
◇ phenomenon「現象」
◇ harden「固まる；固くなる」
◇ surface「表面」
◇ buildup「蓄積；増大」
◇ particle「小さな粒」
◇ over the course of time「時の経過と共に」
◇ that is to say「すなわち；つまり」
◇ transform「～を変形させる」
◇ pressure「圧力」
◇ force「力」
◇ specific「特定の」
◇ granite「花崗（かこう）岩」
◇ andesite「安山岩」
◇ respectively「それぞれ」
◇ durability「耐久性」
◇ extensively「広く；広範囲に」
◇ external「外の；外側の」
◇ column「柱；円柱」
◇ coarse-grained「粒子の荒い」
◇ tombstone「墓石」
◇ structure「建造物；構造」
◇ interior「室内の」
◇ decoration「装飾物；飾りつけ」
◇ *be* derived from「～に由来する」
◇ exterior「（建物などの）外面；外観」
◇ landscaping「造園」
◇ resistant「（熱などを）通さない；耐～」
◇ withstand「～に耐える；持ちこたえる」
◇ limestone「石灰岩」
◇ sandstone「砂岩」
◇ component「構成要素；成分」
◇ calcium carbonate「炭酸カルシウム」
◇ neither A nor B「AでもBでもない」
◇ durable「耐久性のある」
◇ remarkable「注目すべき；驚くべき」
◇ soak up「（液体）を吸収する，吸い取る」
◇ frost「霜」
◇ moss「コケ」
◇ marble「大理石」
◇ split「～を分ける；割く」
◇ inkstone「すずり」
◇ calligraphy「書道；カリグラフィー」
◇ 問1 heading「見出し」
◇ 問1 ① decorative「装飾的な」
◇ 問1 ④ transformation「変化」
◇ 問2 B② particular「特定の」
◇ 問2 B④ demanding「骨の折れる；きつい」
◇ 問2 C② tolerant「耐性がある」
◇ 問3 ④ suited「適した」
◇ 問3 ⑥ roof「屋根を葺く」

試作問題　解答

合計点	／30

問題番号(配点)	設問	解答番号	正解	配点	自己採点
第A問 (18)	1	1	②	3	
	2	2	②	3	
	3	3 - 4	②-⑤	3※	
		5	④	3	
	4	6	②	3	
	5	7	②	3	

問題番号(配点)	設問	解答番号	正解	配点	自己採点
第B問 (12)	1	1	①	3	
	2	2	②	3	
	3	3	③	3	
	4	4	①	3	

(注)　1　※は，全部正解の場合のみ点を与える。
　　　2　-(ハイフン)でつながれた正解は，順序を問わない。

英　語（リーディング）

問○と囲み枠内…正解の根拠となる箇所

第A問

You are working on an essay about whether high school students should be allowed to use their smartphones in class. You will follow the steps below.

Step 1: Read and understand various viewpoints about smartphone use.
Step 2: Take a position on high school students' use of their smartphones in class.
Step 3: Create an outline for an essay using additional sources.

[Step 1] Read various sources

Author A (Teacher)
My colleagues often question whether smartphones can help students develop life-long knowledge and skills. I believe that they can, as long as their use is carefully planned. 5 Smartphones support various activities in class that can enhance learning. Some examples include making surveys for projects and sharing one's learning with others. 問1(A) Another advantage is that we do not have to provide students with devices; they can use their phones! Schools should take full advantage of students' powerful computing devices.

Author B (Psychologist)
10 It is a widespread opinion that smartphones can encourage student learning. 問2 Being believed by many, though, does not make an opinion correct. A recent study found that 問3(B2) when high school students were allowed to use their smartphones in class, it was impossible for them to concentrate on learning. In fact, even if students were not using their own smartphones, seeing their classmates using smartphones was a distraction. It is clear that 問3(B1) schools should 15 make the classroom a place that is free from the interference of smartphones.

Author C (Parent)
I recently bought a smartphone for my son who is a high school student. This is because his school is located far from our town. He usually leaves home early and returns late. Now, he can contact me or access essential information if he has trouble. On the other hand, I 20 sometimes see him walking while looking at his smartphone. If he is not careful, he could have an accident. Generally, I think that high school students are safer with smartphones, but parents still need to be aware of the risks. I also wonder how he is using it in class.

Author D (High school student)
At school, we are allowed to use our phones in class. 問1(D) It makes sense for our school to permit 25 us to use them because most students have smartphones. During class, we make use of foreign language learning apps on our smartphones, which is really helpful to me. I am now more interested in learning than I used to be, and my test scores have improved. The other day, though, my teacher got mad at me when she caught me reading online comics in class. Occasionally these things happen, but overall, smartphones have improved my learning.

【語句・表現】

[Step 1]

l. 4 as long as... …する限りは
l. 5 enhance 他 ～を高める，向上させる
l. 9 psychologist 名 心理学者
l.14 distraction 名 気を散らすもの，こと
l.15 interference 名 じゃま；干渉
l.18 be located　位置する
l.29 occasionally 副 時折
l.29 overall 副 概して

30 **Author E (School principal)**
Teachers at my school were initially skeptical of smartphones because they thought students would use them to socialize with friends during class. Thus, we banned them. As more educational apps became available, however, we started to think that smartphones could be utilized as learning aids in the classroom. Last year, we decided to allow smartphone use in

問3(E) 35 class. Unfortunately, we did not have the results we wanted. We found that smartphones distracted students unless rules for their use were in place and students followed them. This was easier said than done, though.

l.31 skeptical 形 懐疑的な

l.34 utilize 他 ～を利用する

l.36 in place （法律などが）整って

[Step 2] Take a position

Your position: High school students should not be allowed to use their smartphones in class.

- Authors 3 and 4 support your position.
- The main argument of the two authors: 5 .

[Step 3] Create an outline using Sources A and B

Outline of your essay:

Using smartphones in class is not a good idea

Introduction

5 Smartphones have become essential for modern life, but students should be prohibited from using their phones during class.

Body

Reason 1: [From Step 2]

Reason 2: [Based on Source A] ……… 6

10 Reason 3: [Based on Source B] ……… 7

Conclusion

High schools should not allow students to use their smartphones in class.

[Step 3]
l. 5 prohibit 他 ～を禁止する

Source A
Mobile devices offer advantages for learning. For example, one study showed that university

15 students learned psychology better when using their interactive mobile apps compared with their digital textbooks. Although the information was the same, extra features in the apps, such as 3D images, enhanced students' learning. It is important to note, however, that digital devices are not all equally effective. Another study found that students understand content better using their laptop computers rather than their smartphones because of the larger screen

問4 20 size. Schools must select the type of digital device that will maximize students' learning, and there is a strong argument for schools to provide computers or tablets rather than to have students use their smartphones. If all students are provided with computers or tablets with the same apps installed, there will be fewer technical problems and it will be easier for teachers to conduct class. This also enables students without their own smartphones to participate in

25 all class activities.

l.15 interactive 形 相互に作用する

l.24 conduct class 授業を行う

l.24 participate in ～ ～に参加する

Source B

A study conducted in the U.S. found that numerous teenagers are addicted to their smartphones. The study surveyed about 1,000 students between the ages of 13 and 18. The graph below shows the percentages of students who agreed with the statements about their smartphone use. 30

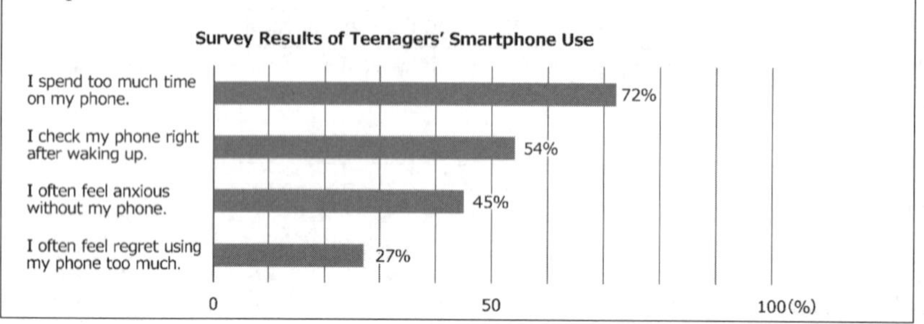

*l.*27 addicted 形 依存している；中毒な

◆全訳◆

あなたは，高校生が授業中にスマートフォンを使用することを許されるべきかどうかに関するエッセイに取り組んでいます。以下の手順に従います。

ステップ１：スマートフォン使用に関するさまざまな見解を読んで理解する。

ステップ２：授業中における高校生のスマートフォン使用に対しての立場を明確にする。

ステップ３：追加の資料を用いてエッセイの概要を作成する。

［ステップ１］さまざまな資料を読む

筆者A（教師）

私の同僚はよく，スマートフォンは生徒が生涯に渡る知識や技能を身に付けるのに役立つだろうかと疑問視しています。私はスマートフォンの使用が慎重に練られたものなら，それは可能だと信じています。スマートフォンは学習を向上させるさまざまな授業中の活動を支えてくれます。例えばプロジェクトのための調査を行ったり，学んだことを他の人たちと共有したりといったことなどです。問１(A) 他にも生徒に機器を提供する必要がないのも利点です。生徒は自分のスマートフォンを使えばいいのですから！ 学校は生徒が持つ強力なコンピューター機器を最大限に活用するべきです。

筆者B（心理学者）

スマートフォンが生徒の学習を促すことは，広く受け入れられている意見です。問２ しかし多くの人に信じられているからといって，意見が正しいということにはなりません。最近の研究では，問３(B2) 高校生が授業中にスマートフォンの使用を認められていると，生徒が学習に集中できないということがわかりました。実際，生徒は自分のスマートフォンを使っていない場合でも，クラスメートがスマートフォンを使うのを見ると気が散っていました。問３(B1) 学校は，教室をスマートフォンに邪魔されない場所にするべきだということは明らかです。

筆者C（親）

最近，私は高校生の息子にスマートフォンを買ってやりました。息子の学校は私たちの町から遠くにあるからです。息子は普段，早く家を出て遅くに帰ってきます。今は困ったことがあれば，私に連絡したり必要な情報にアクセスしたりすることができます。一方で，彼がスマートフォンを見ながら歩いているのを見ることがあります。油断すると事故に遭うかもしれません。全般的に，高校生はスマートフォンがあるほうが安全だと思いますが，親はリスクにも配慮する必要があります。授業でどのように使っているかも気になります。

筆者D（高校生）

学校で，私たちは授業中のスマートフォンの使用を許されています。問１(D) ほとんどの生徒がスマートフォンを持っているので，学校が私たちに使用を認めるのは理にかなっています。授業中に私たちはスマートフォンで外国語学習アプリを使い，それは本当に私の役に立っています。以前より学習への興味が強くなりテストの成績も上がりました。でも，先日私が授業中にオンライン漫画を読んでいるのを見つけて，先生が激怒しました。たまにこういうことが起こりますが，概ねスマートフォンは私の学習を向上させてくれています。

筆者E（学校長）
我が校の教師たちは当初はスマートフォンに懐疑的でした。生徒が授業中にスマートフォンを友達と連絡を取り合うために使うだろうと考えたからです。そのため私たちはスマートフォンを禁止しました。けれども，入手できる教育的アプリが増えるにつれ，スマートフォンを教室で学習を補助するものとして利用できると思い始めました。昨年，私たちは授業中のスマートフォン使用を許すことにしました。残念なことに，望んだ結果にはなりませんでした。**問3(E)** スマートフォン使用に関するルールを整え，それを生徒が守らない限り，スマートフォンは生徒の気を散らせることがわかったのです。しかし，これは言うは易し行うは難しです。

［ステップ2］：立場を決める
あなたの立場：高校生は授業中にスマートフォンを使用することを許されるべきではない。
・筆者［3］と［4］があなたの立場をサポートする。
・筆者2人の主な論拠：［5］。

［ステップ3］：資料AとBを用いて概要を作成する

あなたのエッセイの概要：

授業中のスマートフォン使用は得策ではない

導入
スマートフォンは現代の生活では欠かせないものになっているが，生徒は授業中にスマートフォンを使うことを禁じられるべきだ。

本論
理由1：［ステップ2より］
理由2：［資料Aに基づいて］……［6］
理由3：［資料Bに基づいて］……［7］

結論
高校は生徒に授業中のスマートフォン使用を許すべきではない。

資料A
モバイル機器は学習に有利である。例えばある研究では，大学生はデジタル教科書と比べると双方向のモバイルアプリを使った時のほうが心理学をよく学べることが明らかになった。情報が同じでも，アプリの3D画像のような追加機能が学生の学習を向上させたのだ。しかし，デジタル機器がすべて同じように効果的なわけではないと注意することが大切だ。別の研究では，学生はスマートフォンよりノートパソコンを使うほうが，大きい画面サイズのおかげでよりしっかりと内容を理解することがわかった。**問4** 学校は生徒の学習の成果を最大化するデジタル機器の種類を選ぶべきで，学校は生徒に個人のスマートフォンを使わせるのではなく，パソコンかタブレットを提供するべきだという強い主張がある。もし同じアプリがインストールされたパソコンかタブレットがすべての生徒に提供されたら，技術的な問題は少なくなり，教師が授業を行うのも楽になるだろう。これによりスマートフォンを持っていない生徒もすべての授業活動に参加できるようになる。

資料B
アメリカで行われた研究で，非常に多くの10代がスマートフォン中毒になっていることがわかった。その研究では13歳から18歳の約1,000人の生徒について調査した。下のグラフはスマートフォン使用に関する記述に当てはまると答えた生徒の割合を示している。

（グラフタイトル：10代のスマートフォン使用の調査結果）
（グラフ項目：私はスマートフォンに時間を使い過ぎる。／私は起きてすぐにスマートフォンをチェックする。／私はスマートフォンがないと不安になることがよくある。／私はスマートフォンを使い過ぎて後悔することがよくある。）

◆解説◆

問1 1 ❷

「筆者AとDはどちらも[1]と述べている。」

①「スマートフォンの学習用アプリは試験で生徒がよい成績をとるのに役立つことがある」≫**筆者Dのみ該当。Aは試験についてはふれていない。**

❷「教育ツールとしてスマートフォンを使用する理由の1つは，ほとんどの生徒が所有しているということである」

③「スマートフォンは学校と家庭の両方で学習活動を支援するのに使うことができる」≫**家庭での学習についてはA，D共に言及なし。**

④「スマートフォンは生徒が自分の考えをクラスメートと共有することを可能にする」≫**筆者Aのみ該当。**

本文・全訳の**問1(A)**，**問1(D)**にあるように，両者とも生徒が自分のスマートフォンを使用できることを利点として挙げている。正解は❷。

問2 2 ❷

「筆者Bは[2]と暗示している。」

①「デジタル機器から離れる時間を持つことは，生徒の学習意欲の妨げとなる」≫**逆。スマートフォンを使用することで学習に集中できなくなると言っている。**

❷「広く信じられていることが，研究が明らかにする事実とは異なることが時にある」

③「スマートフォンを持っていない生徒は自分たちのほうがいい学習者だと思いがちである」≫**本文にない。**

④「教室は生徒が教師の干渉を受けずに学習できる場であるべきだ」≫**スマートフォンの干渉については言及があるが，教師の干渉については本文にない。**

本文・全訳の**問2**と❷はほぼ同じことを言っている。**問2**の前で，広く受け入れられている意見にふれ，後ろでは研究の結果がそれとは異なることが紹介されている。❷が正解。

問3 3，4 ❷，❺（順不同） 5 ❹

「あなたはさまざまな見解を理解したので，高校生が授業中にスマートフォンを使うことへの立場を決め，以下のように書いた。[3]，[4]，[5]を完成させるのに最も適当な選択肢を選びなさい。」

「[3]，[4]の選択肢（順不同）」

①「A」≫**慎重に計画されれば授業中のスマートフォン使用は役立つ。デバイスとして生徒自身のスマートフォンを利用できるのも利点。**

❷「B」≫**スマートフォンを使うと生徒は学習に集中できない。**

③「C」≫**スマートフォンがあるとより安全だがリスクに配慮も必要。**

④「D」≫**多くの生徒がスマートフォンを持っている。学習アプリは効果がある。**

❺「E」≫**有用なアプリが増えたので使用を許可したが，望んだ結果になっていない。ルールによる管理が必要。**

授業中のスマートフォン使用に反対する立場の意見を選ぶ。筆者Bは本文・全訳の**問3(B1)**で教室でのスマートフォンの使用に強く反対している。筆者Eはスマートフォン使用を認めたところ，望んだような結果にはなっておらず，**問3(E)**でルールが必要だと述べている。現在はスマートフォン使用に反対の立場だと考えられる。筆者A，Dは授業中のスマートフォン使用に賛成の立場，筆者Cは授業中の使用については賛否を述べていない。正解は❷と❺。

「[5]の選択肢」

①「授業中のスマートフォン使用についての実践的なルールを作ることは教師には難しい」≫**Eのみの意見。ルールについてBは言及していない。**

②「教育アプリは使うのが難しいので，スマートフォンは学習の妨げになるかもしれない」≫**どちらもアプリを使うのが難しいとは述べていない。**

③「スマートフォンは，教室での学習用ではなくコミュニケーションのために設計された」≫**本文にない。**

❹「生徒は授業中スマートフォンにアクセスできる限り，勉強に集中することができない」

筆者B，Eに共通する主張を選択する。本文・全訳の**問3(B2)**，**問3(E)**ではどちらも生徒が学習に集中できないことを問題にしている。❹が正解である。

問4 6 ❷

「資料Aに基づき，理由2として最も適当なものは次のうちどれか。」[6]

①「3D画像を表示するアプリは学習には欠かせないが，すべての学生が自分のスマートフォンにそのアプリを入れているわけではない。」≫**3D画像アプリが欠かせないとは書かれていない。**

❷**「ある種のデジタル機器は教育的効果を向上させることができるが，スマートフォンは最良ではない。」**

③「生徒は大学に備えて，スマートフォンだけでなく他の機器でもデジタル技能を獲得するべきだ。」≫**大学に備えるという話題は資料Aにない。**

④「心理学研究では学習におけるデジタル機器のよい効果は示していないので，教科書にこだわるべきだ。」≫**デジタル機器の効果が最初の3文で紹介されている。**

前半ではモバイル機器とアプリが学習に効果的である例を挙げ，後半ではスマートフォンよりノートパソコンやタブレットのほうがよい理由が挙げられている。本文・全訳の**問4**から，最適なデジタル機器を選ぶべきだと主張していることがわかる。❷が正解。

問5 7 ❷

「理由3として，あなたは『若い学生はスマートフォン中毒の危険に直面している』と書くことにした。資料Bに基づき，この意見を最もよくサポートする選択肢はどれか。」 7

①「半数より多くの10代がスマートフォンを使い過ぎると報告しているが，実際にそれを後悔しているのは4分の1未満である。これは依存症の問題に気づいていないことを示しているのかもしれない。」≫**72%は「半数より多く」と言うには多く，後悔しているのは27%で4分の1より多い。**

❷**「4分の3近くの10代がスマートフォンに時間を使い過ぎている。実際，50%より多くが起きてすぐスマートフォンをチェックしている。多くの10代がスマートフォン使用を我慢できない。」**

③「70%より多くの10代が自分はスマートフォンに時間を使い過ぎると考えており，半数より多くがスマートフォンがないと不安だと感じている。この種の依存は日常生活に悪影響を与えることがある。」≫**スマートフォンがないと不安な人は45%で「半数より多く」ではない。**

④「10代は常にスマートフォンを使っている。実際4分の3より多くがスマートフォンを使い過ぎていることを認めている。彼らの生活は朝から晩までスマートフォンに支配されている。」≫**スマートフォンを使い過ぎているのは72%で「4分の3より多く」はない。最後の「朝から晩まで」はグラフからも説明文からも読み取れない。**

選択肢❷の第1文はグラフの第1項目に一致し，第2文は第2項目に一致する。グラフの各項目及び説明の第1文より，多くの10代がスマートフォンに依存していることがわかる。❷が正解である。

【設問・選択肢の語句・表現】

- **問1** ② possess 他 ～を所有している
- **問3** now that ... （いまや）…だから
- **問5** addiction 名 中毒
- **問5** ② resist 他 ～を我慢する
- **問5** ③ dependence 名 依存（症）

第B問

In English class you are writing an essay on a social issue you are interested in. This is your most recent draft. You are now working on revisions based on comments from your teacher.

Eco-friendly Action with Fashion

Many people love fashion. Clothes are important for self-expression, but fashion can be harmful to the environment. In Japan, about 480,000 tons of clothes are said to be thrown away every year. This is equal to about 130 large trucks a day. We need to change our "throw-away" behavior. This essay will highlight three ways to be more sustainable.

First, when shopping, avoid making unplanned purchases. According to a government survey, approximately 64% of shoppers do not think about what is already in their closet. (1) ∧ So, try to plan your choices carefully when you are shopping.

In addition, purchase high-quality clothes which usually last longer. Even though the price might be higher, it is good value when an item can be worn for several years. (2) ∧ Cheaper fabrics can lose their color or start to look old quickly, so they need to be thrown away sooner.

Finally, (3) think about your clothes. For example, sell them to used clothing stores. That way other people can enjoy wearing them. You could also donate clothes to a charity for people who need them. Another way is to find a new purpose for them. There are many ways to transform outfits into useful items such as quilts or bags.

In conclusion, it is time for a lifestyle change. From now on, check your closet before you go shopping, (4) select better things, and lastly, give your clothes a second life. In this way, we can all become more sustainable with fashion.

問1(1) 問1(2) 問2(1) 問2(2) 問3(1) 問3(2) 問3(3) 問4(1) 問4(2)

Comments

(1) You are missing something here. Add more information between the two sentences to connect them.

(2) Insert a connecting expression here.

(3) This topic sentence doesn't really match this paragraph. Rewrite it.

(4) The underlined phrase doesn't summarize your essay content enough. Change it.

Overall Comment:

Your essay is getting better. Keep up the good work. (Have you checked your own closet? I have checked mine! ☺)

【語句・表現】

- *l*. 4 self-expression 图 自己表現
- *l*. 5 harmful 形 有害な
- *l*. 8 highlight 他 ～を強調する
- *l*. 9 sustainable 形 持続可能な
- *l*.10 purchase 图 購入　*l*.14は 他 ～を購入する
- *l*.16 fabric 图 布地
- *l*.21 donate 他 ～を寄付する
- *l*.23 outfit 图 衣装
- *l*.23 quilt 图 キルト

◆全訳◆

英語の授業で，あなたは興味のある社会問題に関するエッセイを書いています。これはあなたの最新の草稿です。今は先生からのコメントをもとに，推敲に取り組んでいるところです。

ファッションで環境に配慮した行動を

多くの人はファッションが大好きである。服は自己表現に大切だが，ファッションは環境に対して害となることがある。日本では毎年約48万トンの衣類が捨てられると言われている。これは1日あたり大型トラック約130台分に相当する。私たちは「捨てる」行動を変える必要がある。このエッセイではより持続可能であるための3つの方法に力点を置く。

第一に，買い物をする時は無計画な購入を避けよう。政府の調査によると，**問1(1)** おおよそ64%の買い物客は何がすでに自分のクローゼットにあるかについて考えない。(1) 1 **問1(2)** だから，買い物をする時は選択を慎重に計画しよう。

次に，より長持ちすることの多い **問2(1)** 高品質の服を買おう。値段は高いかもしれないが，何年間も着ることができる物なら価値がある。(2) 2 **問2(2)** 安めの生地は，すぐに色落ちしたり古びて見え始めたりするので，より早く捨てなければならなくなる。

最後に，(3) 自分の服について考えよう。例えば，**問3(1)** それらを古着屋に売ろう。そうすれば別の人たちがその服を着て楽しむことができる。衣類を必要とする人々のために **問3(2)** 慈善活動に服を寄付することもできるだろう。**問3(3)** 衣類の新しい使い道を見つけるというやり方もある。衣装をキルトやバッグのような役立つ品に変える多くの方法がある。

結論として，今，生活スタイルを変える時なのだ。これからは，**問4(1)** 買い物に行く前にクローゼットをチェックし，(4) より良いものを選び，最後は **問4(2)** 自分の服に第2の使い道を与えよう。このようにして，私たちはみなファッションでより持続可能になることができる。

コメント

(1) ここに何か足りません。2つの文をつなぐために，間にさらに情報を追加しなさい。
(2) ここに接続表現を挿入しなさい。
(3) この主題文はこの段落にあまり合っていません。書き直しなさい。
(4) 下線部の表現はあなたのエッセイの内容を十分に要約していません。変更しなさい。

総合的なコメント

あなたのエッセイは良くなってきました。この調子でがんばってください。(あなたは自分のクローゼットをチェックしましたか？ 私は自分のクローゼットをチェックしましたよ！ ☺)

◆解説◆

問1 1 ❶

「コメント(1)に基づいて，付け加えるのに最も適当な文はどれか。」 1

❶ **「結果として，人々は必要のない多くの似た品物を買う。」**
② 「このため，客は服の買い物を楽しむことができない。」 **≫後ろの文にうまくつながらない。**
③ 「このため，店員は客が必要とするものを知りたがる。」 **≫店員の話題は出ていない。**
④ 「この状況では，客は買い物に出かけるのを避けがちだ。」 **≫後ろの文にうまくつながらない。**

(1) の前後の内容を確認する。**問1(1)** では「何がすでにクローゼットにあるかについて考えない」，つまり自分の持っている服を考慮しないということが書かれており，**問1(2)** では「だから，買い物をする時は選択を慎重に計画しよう」と続く。So で始まる **問1(2)** は，挿入する文を受けた内容となるはずで，❶を入れれば前後がうまくつながる。❶が正解。

問2 2 ❷

「コメント(2)に基づいて，付け加えるのに最も適当な表現はどれか。」 2

① 「例えば」
❷ **「対照的に」**
③ 「それにもかかわらず」
④ 「したがって」

問2(1) では「高品質の服」について，**問2(2)**

では「安めの生地」について述べている。対照的な物を比較する時，間に入れる接続表現として最も適当なのは❷である。

問3　3　❸

「コメント(3)に基づいて，主題文を書き換えるのに最も適当なものはどれか。」 3

① 「新しい服を買うのを減らそう」≫**他の段落で「服を慎重に選ぶ」よう言及しているが，この段落の主題ではない。**

② 「古い服を処分しよう」≫**捨てずに有効活用する方法を提案している。**

❸ **「服を再利用する方法を見つけよう」**

④ 「いらない服をただであげよう」≫**あげる以外の方法も提案しているので主題とは言えない。**

主題文（topic sentence）は，その段落の内容を端的に表した文である。主題文のあとに具体例が3つ挙げられている。**問3(1)**「古着屋に売る」，**問3(2)**「寄付する」，**問3(3)**「衣類の新しい使い道を見つける」とあり，これらはすべて服の再利用の方法だから，❸が正解。

問4　4　❶

「コメント(4)に基づいて，どれが最も適当な代替文か。」 4

❶ **「元の状態を保つ〔長持ちする〕品を買おう」**

② 「高くないおしゃれな服を選ぼう」≫**高くても長持ちする服を勧めている。**

③ 「変えることができる品を選ぼう」≫**他の品に変えることは提案しているが，それを考慮して買うことには言及していない。**

④ 「古着を買おう」≫**古着屋に売ることは提案しているが，古着を買うことは書いていない。**

最後の段落は全体のまとめである。第1段落で提示された3つの案が第2，3，4段落で1つずつ説明されており，第2段落で述べている1つめのやり方は**問4(1)**，第4段落で述べている3つめは**問4(2)**にあたる。代替文には第3段落で述べている2つめの提案，高くても長く着られる「高品質の服を買おう」に関する内容を入れるのが適当。正解は❶。

【設問・選択肢の語句・表現】

問3 ② dispose of ～　～を処分する

問3 ④ give ～ away　～（物）をただでやる

問4 replacement 名 代わりとなるもの

2024 本試　解答

第1問小計	第2問小計	第3問小計	第4問小計	第5問小計	第6問小計	合計点
						／100

問題番号(配点)	設問		解答番号	正解	配点	自己採点
第1問 (10)	A	1	1	④	2	
		2	2	①	2	
	B	1	3	④	2	
		2	4	③	2	
		3	5	①	2	
第2問 (20)	A	1	6	①	2	
		2	7	②	2	
		3	8	①	2	
		4	9	④	2	
		5	10	②	2	
	B	1	11	①	2	
		2	12	①	2	
		3	13	①	2	
		4	14	③	2	
		5	15	②	2	
第3問 (15)	A	1	16	②	3	
		2	17	②	3	
	B	1	18	①	3※	
			19	②		
			20	③		
			21	④		
		2	22	③	3	
		3	23	②	3	

問題番号(配点)	設問		解答番号	正解	配点	自己採点
第4問 (16)	1		24	③	3	
	2		25	④	3	
	3		26	④	3	
	4		27	⑤	2	
			28	④	2	
	5		29	③	3	
第5問 (15)	1		30	④	3※	
			31	⑤		
			32	①		
			33	②		
	2		34	②	3	
	3		35	①	3※	
			36	②		
	4		37	③	3	
	5		38	②	3	
第6問 (24)	A	1	39	⑥	3※	
			40	②		
		2	41	①	3	
		3	42	③	3	
		4	43	①	3	
	B	1	44	④	2	
		2	45	④	2	
		3	46 ～ 47	②-③	3※	
		4	48	③	3	
		5	49	⑤	2	

(注)　1　※は，全部正解の場合のみ点を与える。
　　　2　-(ハイフン)でつながれた正解は，順序を問わない。

問●と囲み枠内…正解の根拠となる箇所

第1問A

第1問 (配点 10)

A You are studying English at a language school in the US. The school is planning an event. You want to attend, so you are reading the flyer.

The Thorpe English Language School

International Night

5 Friday, May 24, 5 p.m.-8 p.m.

Entrance Fee: $5

The Thorpe English Language School (TELS) is organizing an international exchange event. TELS students don't need to pay the entrance fee. 問1 Please present your student ID at the reception desk in the Student Lobby.

10 ● **Enjoy foods from various parts of the world**

Have you ever tasted hummus from the Middle East? How about tacos from Mexico? Couscous from North Africa? Try them all!

● **Experience different languages and new ways to communicate**

Write basic expressions such as "hello" and "thank you" in Arabic, Italian, 15 Japanese, and Spanish. 問2 Learn how people from these cultures use facial expressions and their hands to communicate.

● **Watch dance performances**

From 7 p.m. watch flamenco, hula, and samba dance shows on the stage! After each dance, performers will teach 20 some basic steps. Please join in.

Lots of pictures, flags, maps, textiles, crafts, and games will be displayed in the hall. If you have some pictures or items from your home country which can be displayed at the event, let a school staff member know by May 17!

【語句・表現】

l. 2 flyer 图 チラシ

l.14 expression 图 表現

l.15 facial expression 表情

l.21 craft 图 工芸品

◆全訳◆

A あなたはアメリカの語学学校で英語を勉強しています。学校はイベントを計画しています。あなたは参加したいので，チラシを読んでいます。

ソープ英語学校

インターナショナルナイト

5月24日（金）午後5時～8時

入場料：5ドル

ソープ英語学校（TELS）が国際交流イベントを企画しています。TELSの学生は入場料を支払う必要はありません。問1 学生ロビー内受付にて学生証を提示してください。

●世界のさまざまな地域の料理を楽しもう

中東のフムスを食べたことがありますか？　メキシコのタコスは？　北アフリカのクスクスは？　全部食べてみてください！

●いろいろな言語や新しいコミュニケーション方法を体験しよう

アラビア語，イタリア語，日本語，スペイン語の “hello” や “thank you” などの基本的な表現を書いてみよう。

問2 これらの文化を背景にする人々が，コミュニケーションをとるのに表情や手をどのように使うか知ろう。

●ダンス公演を見よう

午後7時からは，ステージでのフラメンコ，フラ，サンバのダンスショーをご覧ください！ 各ダンス終了後，出演者が基本的なステップを教えます。参加してください。

会場にはたくさんの写真，旗，地図，織物，工芸品，ゲームなどが展示されます。イベントで展示できる自国の写真や品物をお持ちの方は，5月17日までに学校スタッフにお知らせください！

◆解説◆

問1 1 ❹

「このイベントに無料で参加するには，1 なければならない。」

①「自国の写真を持参し」≫**無料参加の条件ではない。**

②「展示についてスタッフに相談し」≫**本文にない。**

③「学生ロビーで申し込み用紙に記入し」≫**本文にない。**

❹「**TELSの学生である証拠を見せ**」

本文・全訳の問1の present your student ID（学生証を提示する）は show proof that you are a TELS student（TELSの学生である証拠を見せる）と言い換えられるので，❹が正解。

問2 2 ❶

「イベントでは 2 することができる。」

❶「**さまざまな文化のジェスチャーを学ぶ**」

②「ダンス競技会に参加する」≫**ダンスの講習に参加することはできるが，競技会とは言っていない。**

③「外国語で短い物語を読む」≫**本文にない。**

④「国際色豊かな料理を作ってみる」≫**調理はしない。**

本文・全訳の問2から❶が正解。facial expressions and their hands to communicate（コミュニケーションをとるための表情や手振り）を gestures（ジェスチャー）と言い換えている。

【設問・選択肢の語句・表現】

問1 ❹ proof 名 証拠

問2 ❶ gesture 名 身ぶり，ジェスチャー

問2 ② participate in ～　～に参加する

第1問B

B　You are an exchange student in the US and next week your class will go on a day trip. The teacher has provided some information.

Tours of Yentonville

The Yentonville Tourist Office offers three city tours.

5 **The History Tour**

The day will begin with a visit to St. Patrick's Church, which was built when the city was established in the mid-1800s. Opposite the church is the early-20th-century Mayor's House. There will be a tour of the house and its beautiful garden. Finally, cross the city by public bus and visit the Peace Park. Opened soon after World War II, it was the site of many demonstrations in the 1960s.

（問3②　問2(1)　問3③ 10）

【語句・表現】

l.7 establish 他 ～を設立する

l.8 mayor 名 市長

l.11 demonstration 名 デモ

The Arts Tour

問1 The morning will be spent in the Yentonville Arts District. We will begin in the Art Gallery where there are many paintings from Europe and the US. After lunch, enjoy a concert across the street at the Bruton Concert Hall before walking a short distance to the Artists' Avenue. This part of the district was developed 問3④ several years ago when new artists' studios and the nearby Sculpture Park were created. 問2(2) Watch artists at work in their studios and afterwards wander around the park, finding sculptures among the trees.

The Sports Tour

First thing in the morning, 問2(3) you can watch the Yentonville Lions football team training at their open-air facility in the suburbs. In the afternoon, travel by subway to 問3① the Yentonville Hockey Arena, completed last fall. 問2(4) Spend some time in its exhibition hall to learn about the arena's unique design. Finally, enjoy a professional hockey game in the arena.

Yentonville Tourist Office, January, 2024

l.17 avenue 名 通り
l.20 wander 自 歩き回る
l.23 facility 名 施設
l.24 suburb 名 郊外
l.24 subway 名 地下鉄
l.27 unique 形 ユニークな

◆全訳◆

B　あなたはアメリカにいる交換留学生で，来週あなたのクラスは日帰り旅行に出かけます。先生がいくつかの情報を提供してくれました。

イェントンビルツアー

イェントンビル観光局は，３つの市内ツアーを提供しています。

歴史ツアー

この日は最初に聖パトリック教会を訪れます。この教会は1800年代半ばに市が制定された時に建てられました。教会の向かいには，問3② 20世紀初期の市長の家があります。問2(1) 邸宅とその美しい庭のツアーがあります。最後に，公共バスで市内を横断し，平和公園を訪れます。問3③ 第二次世界大戦直後に開園し，1960年代には多くのデモが行われた場所です。

芸術ツアー

問1 午前はイェントンビル芸術地区で過ごします。ヨーロッパやアメリカの絵画が多数あるアートギャラリーから始めます。昼食後，通りの向かいの，ブルトンコンサートホールでコンサートを楽しんだあと，短い距離を歩いてアーティスト通りへ移動します。地区のこの場所は，問3④ 数年前に新しい芸術家の工房と近くの彫刻公園が作られた時に開発されました。問2(2) 芸術家たちが工房で制作している様子を見学し，その後公園を散策して木々の間にある彫刻を見つけましょう。

スポーツツアー

朝いちばんに，問2(3) 郊外の屋外施設でイェントンビル・ライオンズ・フットボールチームが練習しているのを見ることができます。午後は，問3① 昨年秋に完成したイェントンビル・ホッケーアリーナへ地下鉄で移動します。問2(4) アリーナの展示ホールで，アリーナのユニークなデザインについて学ぶ時間を過ごしましょう。最後にアリーナでプロホッケーの試合を楽しみましょう。

イェントンビル観光局，2024年１月

◆解説◆

問1 3 ❹

「イェントンビルには 3 がある。」

① 「250年前に市が構築された時に建てられた教会」≫市と教会ができたのは250年前ではない。

② 「町の中心部にあるユニークなサッカー練習場」≫中心部ではなく郊外にある。

③ 「訪問者がオリジナル作品を制作できる芸術工房」≫訪問者が制作できるとは書かれていない。

❹ 「アートギャラリーとコンサートホールの両方がある芸術地区」

本文・全訳の**問1**に書かれているように，芸術地区にはアートギャラリーとコンサートホールがあるので，❹が正解。

問2 4 ❸

「3つすべてのツアーで 4 だろう。」

① 「市の歴史的な出来事について学ぶ」≫歴史ツアーのみ

② 「人々が自分の技術を実演しているのを見る」≫歴史ツアーにはない。

❸ 「屋内と屋外の両方で過ごす」

④ 「あちこち移動するのに公共交通機関を使う」≫芸術ツアーでは使わない。

本文・全訳の**問2(1)**，**問2(2)**，**問2(3)**，**問2(4)**に書かれているように，どのツアーにも屋内と屋外での見学が含まれるので❸が正解。

問3 5 ❶

「ツアーで訪ねることができる，イェントンビルの最新の場所はどこか。」 5

❶ 「ホッケーアリーナ」

② 「市長の家」≫20世紀初頭に建てられた。

③ 「平和公園」≫第二次世界大戦直後にできた。

④ 「彫刻公園」≫数年前にできた。

本文・全訳の**問3①**，**問3②**，**問3③**，**問3④**から，昨年秋にできたホッケーアリーナがいちばん新しいので❶が正解。

【設問・選択肢の語句・表現】

問1 ① construct 他 ～を構築する
問2 ② demonstrate 他 ～を実演する
問2 ④ public transportation　公共交通機関

第2問A

第2問 (配点　20)

A　You are an exchange student at a high school in the UK and find this flyer.

Invitation to the Strategy Game Club

Have you ever wanted to learn strategy games like chess, *shogi*, or *go*? They are actually more than just games. You can learn skills such as thinking logically and deeply without distractions. Plus, these games are really fun! This club is open to all students of our school. Regardless of skill level, you are welcome to join.

(問4(1): without distractions／問1(1): Regardless of skill level, you are welcome to join.)

We play strategy games together and. . .

- learn basic moves from demonstrations by club members
- play online against club friends

【語句・表現】

l. 1 flyer 名 チラシ
l. 2 strategy 名 戦略
l. 5 logically 副 論理的に
l. 5 distraction 名 注意散漫
l. 9 demonstration 名 実演

問2④ 問2①

- share tips on our club webpage 問2③ 問5(1)
- learn the history and etiquette of each game
- analyse games using computer software
- participate in local and national tournaments

15 Regular meetings: Wednesday afternoons in Room 301, Student Centre

Member Comments

問4(2) – My mind is clearer, calmer, and more focused in class.
問3 – It's cool to learn how some games have certain similarities.
問5(2) – At tournaments, I like discussing strategies with other participants. 問2③
20 – Members share Internet videos that explain practical strategies for chess.
– It's nice to have friends who give good advice about *go*.
問1(2) – I was a complete beginner when I joined, and I had no problem!

l.13 analyse〈英〉他 〜を分析する
l.17 focused 形 (精神的に) 集中した
l.19 participant 名 参加者
l.20 practical 形 実用的な

◆全訳◆

A　あなたは英国の高校の交換留学生で，このチラシを見つけました。

戦略ゲームクラブへのお誘い

チェスや将棋，囲碁などの戦略ゲームを習いたいと思ったことはありませんか？　実はこれらは単なるゲームを超えたものです。問4(1) 注意散漫にならず論理的に深く考えるような技術を学ぶことができます。さらに，これらのゲームは本当におもしろいです！　このクラブには本校の全生徒が参加できます。問1(1) 技術レベルに関係なく，参加を歓迎します。

一緒に戦略ゲームをして…

- 部員による実演で基本的な動きを学びます
- オンラインでクラブの友だちと対戦します
- 問2③ 問5(1) クラブのウェブページでコツを共有します
- 問2④ 各ゲームの歴史や礼儀作法を学びます
- コンピュータソフトを使ってゲームを分析します
- 問2① 地元や全国的なトーナメントに参加します

定例会：水曜日午後，学生センター301号室

部員のコメント

- 問4(2) 以前より頭が冴え，落ち着き，授業に一層集中できます。
- 問3 ゲームにどのような共通点があるのかを学ぶのが素晴らしい。

問5(2)
- トーナメントで，他の参加者と戦略を議論するのが好きです。
- 問2③ チェスの実践的な戦略を説明するインターネットの動画を部員が共有しています。
- 囲碁について良いアドバイスをしてくれる友人がいるのがよいです。

- 問1(2) 入会した時はまったくの初心者でしたが，何の問題もありませんでした！

◆解説◆

問1　6　❶

「チラシによると，このクラブについて正しいのはどれか。」 6

❶「まったくの初心者が歓迎される。」

②「部員はコンピュータのプログラムを編集する。」 ≫本文にない。

③「プロのプレイヤーが正式な実演をする。」 ≫実演するのは部員。

④「他校の生徒が参加できる。」 ≫本文にない。

本文・全訳の問1(1)，問1(2)に書かれているように，初心者も入部できるので❶が正解。

問2 7 ❷
「クラブの活動として言及されていないものは次のうちどれか。」 7

① 「部員以外の人とゲームをすること」≫本文に一致する。

❷ **「コンピュータを相手に対戦すること」**

③ 「ゲームをプレイするアイディアをインターネットで共有すること」≫本文に一致する。

④ 「戦略ゲームの背景を学習すること」≫本文に一致する。

①③④は本文・全訳の**問2①**，**問2③**，**問2④**に一致する。オンラインで部員と対戦することはあるが，コンピュータと対戦するとは書かれていないので❷が正解。

問3 8 ❶
「部員が言及した意見の1つは 8 ということである。」

❶ **「さまざまなゲームを比較するのがおもしろい」**

② 「囲碁についての多くの動画が役に立つ」≫共有しているのはチェスの動画。

③ 「部員は競技会でコツを学ぶ」≫戦略を議論するが，コツを学ぶとは書かれていない。

④ 「定例会は校外で開かれる」≫コメントに書かれていない。

本文・全訳の**問3**に書かれているように，共通点を学ぶとはゲームを比較することなので，❶が正解。

問4 9 ❹
「クラブへのお誘いと部員のコメントの両方が 9 と言及している。」

① 「新入部員は経験を証明しなければならない」
≫初心者も入部できる。

② 「上手なプレイヤーになるにはオンラインサポートが必要である」≫必要だとは書いていない。

③ 「将棋は論理的で刺激的なゲームだ」≫部員のコメントにない。

❹ **「戦略ゲームは集中力を高めるのに役立つ」**

本文・全訳の**問4(1)**，**問4(2)**に書かれているように，論理ゲームをすることで，注意散漫にならず集中できるようになるので，❹が正解。

問5 10 ❷
「このクラブは 10 たい学生に最も適していそうだ。」

① 「自分のコンピュータ戦略ゲームを作り」≫本文にない。

❷ **「戦略ゲームの技術レベルを上げ」**

③ 「戦略ゲームをすることを通じて，英国での正しい礼儀作法を学び」≫学ぶのはゲームの礼儀作法。

④ 「週末を部室で戦略ゲームをして過ごし」≫部室に集まるのは水曜日。

本文・全訳の**問5(1)**，**問5(2)**に書かれているように，さまざまな手段で技術レベルを上げることができるので，❷が正解。

【設問・選択肢の語句・表現】

問1 ❶ absolute 形 完全な
問1 ② edit 他 ～を編集する
問1 ③ formal 形 正式な
問4 ③ stimulating 形 刺激的な
問4 ❹ concentration 名 集中

第2問B

B　You are a college student going to study in the US and need travel insurance. You find this review of an insurance plan written by a female international student who studied in the US for six months.

問5 There are many things to consider before traveling abroad: pack appropriate
5 clothes, prepare your travel expenses, and don't forget medication (if necessary). Also, you should purchase travel insurance.

【語句・表現】
l. 1 insurance 名 保険
l. 4 appropriate 形 適当な
l. 5 expense 名 費用

問 3-D 問 3-A

When I studied at Fairville University in California, I bought travel insurance from TravSafer International. I signed up online in less than 15 minutes and was immediately covered. They accept any form of payment, usually on a monthly basis. There were three plans. All plans include a one-time health check-up.

問 1

The Premium Plan is $100/month. The plan provides 24-hour medical support through a smartphone app and telephone service. Immediate financial support will be authorized if you need to stay in a hospital.

問 4

The Standard Plan worked best for me. It had the 24-hour telephone assistance and included a weekly email with tips for staying healthy in a foreign country. It wasn't cheap: $75/month. However, it was nice to get the optional 15% discount because I paid for six months of coverage in advance.

問 2

If your budget is limited, you can choose the Economy Plan, which is $25/month. It has the 24-hour telephone support like the other plans but only covers emergency care. Also, they can arrange a taxi to a hospital at a reduced cost if considered necessary by the support center.

I never got sick or hurt, so I thought it was a waste of money to get insurance. Then my friend from Brazil broke his leg while playing soccer and had to spend a few days in a hospital. He had chosen the Premium Plan and it covered everything! I realized how important insurance is—you know that you will be supported when you are in trouble.

l. 8 sign up 契約する
l. 9 payment 名 支払い
l. 9 on a monthly basis 月額で
*l.*12 medical 形 医療の
*l.*13 immediate 形 即時の
*l.*14 authorize 他 ～を認可する
*l.*16 assistance 名 支援
*l.*18 coverage 名 補償
*l.*18 in advance 前もって
*l.*19 budget 名 予算

◆全訳◆

B あなたはアメリカに留学する大学生で，旅行保険が必要です。アメリカで６ヵ月間勉強した留学生の女性が書いたこの保険プランのレビューを見つけました。

問 5 海外旅行の前に考えなければならないことがたくさんあります：適切な服を荷物に入れること，旅行費用を準備すること，（必要であれば）医薬品を忘れないこと。また，旅行保険に加入しておくべきです。

私がカリフォルニアのフェアビル大学で学んだ時，トラブセーファーインターナショナルの旅行保険に加入しました。**問 3-D** オンラインで15分もかからずに契約でき，すぐに保険が適用されました。**問 3-A** どんな支払い方法でも受けつけてくれ，通常は月額制です。３つのプランがありました。すべてのプランに１回の健康診断が含まれています。

プレミアムプランは月額100ドルです。**問 1** このプランでは，スマートフォンのアプリと電話サービスを通じて24時間医療サポートを提供します。入院が必要になった場合は，即時の金銭的サポートが認められます。

標準プランが私にはいちばん都合がよかったです。24時間の電話支援と，外国で健康を維持するためのヒントが書かれた週１回のＥメールが含まれていました。安くはなく，月75ドルでした。**問 4** しかし，前もって６ヵ月分の補償費用を支払ったので，オプションで15％の割引を受けられたのがよかったです。

予算に限りがある場合はエコノミープランを選ぶこともでき，月25ドルです。**問 2** 他のプランと同様に24時間の電話サポートがありますが，緊急医療のみカバーされます。また，サポートセンターが必要とみなしたら，病院までのタクシーを割引料金で手配してくれます。

私は病気やケガをしたことがなかったので，保険に入るのはお金の無駄だと思っていました。そんな時，ブラジル出身の友人がサッカーをしていて足を骨折し，数日間の入院をしなければなりませんでした。彼はプレミアムプランを選んでいて，すべてがカバーされました！　保険がいかに重要かわかりました。困った時に支援してくれるという安心感です。

◆解説◆

問1　11　❶

「レビューによると，次のうち正しいのはどれか。」 11

❶ **「いちばん高額のプランでは，日中・夜間の医療支援が受けられる。」**

② 「最も安いプランでは，どんな理由でも無料入院が含まれる。」**≫本文にない。**

③ 「中間レベルのプランには，１回の健康診断が含まれていない。」**≫すべてのプランに含まれる。**

④「筆者のプランは毎月100ドルより多くかかった。」**≫筆者が選んだ標準プランは月額75ドル。**

本文・全訳の**問1**に書かれているように，いちばん高いプレミアムプランは24-hour medical support（24時間の医療サポート）がある。これをday and night medical assistance（日中・夜間の医療支援）と言い換えた❶が正解。

問2　12　❶

「最も安いオプションに含まれていないものはどれか。」 12

❶ **「メールサポート」**

② 「緊急時の治療」**≫本文に一致する。**

③ 「電話ヘルプデスク」**≫本文に一致する。**

④ 「移送支援」**≫本文に一致する。**

本文・全訳の**問2**より，最安値のプランは電話サポートのみでメールサポートがない。❶が正解。

問3　13　❶

「トラブセーファーインターナショナルを説明する組み合わせとして，最も適当なのはどれか。」 13

A：**「月額払いが認められている。」**

B：「学生のための奨学金プランを企画している。」**≫本文にない。**

C：「薬を飲むのを忘れないように助けてくれる。」**≫本文にない。**

D：**「インターネットを利用した登録システムを提供している。」**

E：「申請書の処理に数日要する。」**≫申請後すぐに適用されたと書かれている。**

❶ **「AとD」**

②「AとE」

③「BとD」

④「BとE」

⑤「CとD」

本文・全訳の**問3-A**がAの内容，**問3-D**がDの内容に一致するので，❶が正解。

問4　14　❸

「自分が選んだプランに対する筆者の意見は 14 である。」

①「彼女の健康志向を妨げた」**≫本文にない。**

②「電話支援に満足していなかった」**≫本文にない。**

❸ **「費用削減のオプションが魅力的だった」**

④「彼女の足の骨折の治療がカバーされた」**≫筆者ではなく友人のことである。**

本文・全訳の**問4**に書かれているように，筆者は６ヵ月前払いによる割引（＝費用削減）に魅力を感じているので，❸が正解。

問5　15　❷

「筆者の考え方を表すのに，最も適当なものは次のうちどれか。」 15

①「スマートフォンアプリは便利だと思う。」**≫本文にない。**

❷ **「旅行の準備は大切だと考えている。」**

③「アメリカの医療制度は世界でもユニークだと感じている。」**≫本文にない。**

④「友人にとっては別の病院の方がよかったと思っている。」**≫本文にない。**

本文・全訳の**問5**に書かれているように，旅行の前にさまざまな準備が必要だと考えているので，❷が正解。

【設問・選択肢の語句・表現】

問2 ② treatment 名 治療
問3 combination 名 組み合わせ
問3 B scholarship 名 奨学金
問3 E process 他 ～を処理する
問4 ① health conscious 健康意識の高い
問4 ③ reduction 名 削減

第3問A

第3問 (配点 15)

問2(1) **A** Susan, your English ALT's sister, visited your class last month. Now back in the UK, she wrote on her blog about an event she took part in.

Hi!

I participated in a photo rally for foreign tourists with my friends: See the rules on the right. As photo rally beginners, we decided to aim for only five of the checkpoints. In three minutes, we arrived at our first target, the city museum. In quick succession, we made the second, third, and fourth targets. Things were going smoothly! But, on the way to the last target, the statue of a famous samurai from the city, we got lost. Time was running out and my feet were hurting from walking for over two hours. (問1(2)) We stopped a man with a pet monkey for help, but neither our Japanese nor his English were good enough. After he'd explained the way using gestures, (問2(2)) we realised we wouldn't have enough time to get there and would have to give up. (問1(3)) We took a photo with him and said goodbye. When we got back to Sakura City Hall, we were surprised to hear that the winning team had completed 19 checkpoints. One of our photos was selected to be on the event website (click here). (問1(1)) It reminds me of the man's warmth and kindness: our own "gold medal."

Sakura City Photo Rally Rules

- Each group can only use the **camera** and **paper map**, both provided by us
- Take as many photos of **25 checkpoints** (designated sightseeing spots) as possible
- **3-hour** time limit
- Photos must include **all 3 team members**
- All members must move **together**
- **No** mobile phones
- **No** transport

【語句・表現】

l.10 target 名 目標(物)
l.10 in quick succession 続けざまに
l.13 smoothly 副 順調に
l.18 neither A nor B AもBも～ない
l.24 warmth 名 温かさ

◆全訳◆

A　先月，英語 ALT の妹であるスーザンが，あなたのクラスを訪問しました。**問2(1)** スーザンは今は英国に戻っていて，参加したイベントについてブログに書きました。

こんにちは！
外国人観光客向けのフォトラリーに友だちと参加しました：右のルールを見てください。フォトラリー初心者として，私たちはチェックポイントのうち5つだけを目指すことにしました。3分で，最初の目標である市立博物館に到着しました。続けざまに，2つ目，3つ目，4つ目の目標に到着しました。順調な展開でした！　しかし，最後の目標であるその市出身の有名な侍の像に向かう途中で道に迷いました。時間がなくなり，2時間以上歩いたので足が痛くなりました。**問1(2)** ペットのサルを連れた男性に助けを求めて呼び止めましたが，私たちの日本語も彼の英語も十分なものではありませんでした。彼が身振りで道を説明してくれたあと，**問2(2)** 私たちはそこに着くには時間が足りず，あきらめるしかないとわかりました。**問1(3)** 私たちは彼と写真を撮ってさよならを言いました。さくら市役所に戻って，優勝チームが19のチェックポイントを達成したと聞いて驚きました。私たちの写真の1枚がイベントのウェブサイト掲載用に選ばれました（ここをクリック）。**問1(1)** それは男性の温かさと優しさを思いださせるもので，私たち自身の「金メダル」です。

さくら市フォトラリールール
・各グループは**カメラ**と**紙の地図**のみ使用でき，両方とも支給される
・**25ヵ所のチェックポイント**（指定観光地）の写真をできるだけ多く撮影すること
・制限時間は**3時間**
・写真は**チームメンバー3名全員**が写っていること
・全メンバーが**一緒に**行動すること
・携帯電話**不可**
・交通機関**不可**

◆解説◆

問1　16　❷

「あなたはブログのリンクをクリックした。どの写真が現れるか。」 16

①「チームメンバー3人が侍の像の前にいる写真」
≫グループは侍の像には行けなかった。また，サルを連れた男性がいない。

❷「チームメンバー3人とサルを連れた男性がフォトラリー中のどこかにいる写真」

③「チームメンバー3人とサルを連れた男性がゴールの前にいる写真」≫男性に会った場所は，ゴールではない。

④「チームメンバー3人が博物館の前にいる写真」
≫サルを連れた男性がいない。

本文・全訳の**問1(1)**から，写真には親切な男性が写っていると考える。さらに**問1(2)**から男性はサルを連れているとわかる。**問1(3)**から，男性に会ったのはゴールではない。この条件を満たす❷が正解。

問2　17　❷

「あなたはスーザンのブログにコメントするよう頼まれた。彼女への適切なコメントはどれか。」 17

①「金メダルをかけているあなたの写真が見たい！」
≫実際には金メダルはとっていない。

❷「頑張ったね。日本に戻ってきて，もう一度挑戦してください！」

③「3時間で19のチェックポイントを通過？　本当に？　すごい！」≫19のチェックポイントを達成したのは他のチーム。

④「あなたの写真は素晴らしい！ 携帯電話をアップグレードしたの？」≫ラリー中は携帯電話の使用禁止。

本文・全訳の**問2(1)**から，スーザンが今は日本にいないとわかる。また，**問2(2)**から，目標が達成できなかったとわかる。したがって，❷がふさわしい。

第3問B

【語句・表現】

B You are going to participate in an English Day. As preparation, you are reading an article in the school newspaper written by Yuzu, who took part in it last year.

Virtual Field Trip to a South Sea Island

5 This year, for our English Day, we participated in a virtual science tour. The winter weather had been terrible, so we were excited to see the tropical scenery of the volcanic island projected on the screen.

First, we "took a road trip" to learn about the geography of the island, using navigation software to view the route. We "got into the car," which our teacher, Mr Leach, sometimes stopped so we could look out of the window and get a better sense of the rainforest. Afterwards, we asked Mr Leach about what we'd seen. (問1①, 問2④; line 10)

Later, we "dived into the ocean" and learnt about the diversity of marine creatures. We observed a coral reef via a live camera. Mr Leach asked us if we could count the number of creatures, but there were too many! Then he showed us an image of the ocean 10 years ago. The reef we'd seen on camera was dynamic, but in the photo it was even more full of life. It looked so different after only 10 years! Mr Leach told us human activity was affecting the ocean and it could be totally ruined if we didn't act now. (問1②, 問2①; line 15)

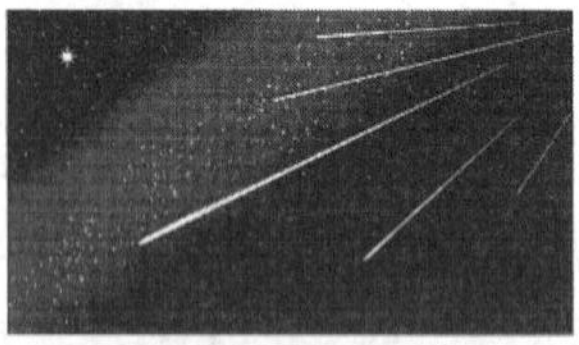

20 In the evening, we studied astronomy under a "perfect starry sky." We put up tents in the gymnasium and created a temporary planetarium on the ceiling using a projector. We were fascinated by the sky full of constellations, shooting stars, and the Milky Way. Someone pointed out one of the brightest lights and asked Mr Leach if it was Venus, a planet close to Earth. He nodded and explained that humans have created so much artificial light that hardly anything is visible in our city's night sky. (問1③, 問1④, 問2②, 問1④, 問3(2); line 25)

30 On my way home after school, the weather had improved and the sky was now cloudless. I looked up at the moonless sky and realised what Mr Leach had told us was true. (問3(1))

- *l.* 4 virtual 形 バーチャルな，仮想の
- *l.* 6 tropical 形 熱帯の
- *l.*13 diversity 名 多様性
- *l.*14 observe 他 ～を観察する
- *l.*14 coral reef サンゴ礁
- *l.*16 image 名 画像
- *l.*18 affect 他 ～に影響を与える
- *l.*19 ruin 他 ～を損なう
- *l.*20 astronomy 名 天文学
- *l.*22 gymnasium 名 体育館
- *l.*24 fascinate 他 ～を魅了する
- *l.*25 constellation 名 星座
- *l.*25 shooting star 流れ星
- *l.*26 point out ～を指す
- *l.*27 nod 自 うなずく
- *l.*28 artificial 形 人工の
- *l.*28 visible 形 目に見える

◆全訳◆

B あなたはイングリッシュ・デイに参加する予定です。準備のために，去年参加したユズが書いた学校新聞の記事を読んでいます。

南洋の島へのバーチャル遠足

今年，イングリッシュ・デイでバーチャルサイエンスツアーに参加しました。冬の天気が悪かったので，私たちはスクリーンに映し出される火山島の南国の風景を見て興奮しました。

最初に，島の地理について学ぶため，経路を見るためのナビゲーションソフトを使って『ドライブ旅行』をしました。私たちは『車に乗り』，講師のリーチ先生は時々車を止めて，**問1①** **問2④** 窓から外を見て熱帯雨林をよりよく感じることができるようにしてくれました。その後，私たちは見たものについてリーチ先生に質問しました。

問1② **問2①** その後，私たちは『海に潜り』，海洋生物の多様性について学びました。ライブカメラでサンゴ礁を観察しました。リーチ先生は生き物の数を数えられるかたずねましたが，多すぎました！ それから先生は，10年前の海の画像を見せてくれました。カメラで見たサンゴ礁はダイナミックでしたが，写真ではさらに多くの生き物であふれていました。たった10年でずいぶん変わったようでした！ リーチ先生は，人間の活動が海に影響を与えていて，今行動しなければ海が完全に損われてしまうかもしれないと教えてくれました。

夕方には，『完璧な星空』の下で天文学を学習しました。**問1③** 体育館にテントを張り，**問1④** **問2②** プロジェクターを使って天井に一時的なプラネタリウムを作りました。私たちは星座，流れ星，天の川で満天の空に魅了されました。誰かが最も明るい光の1つを指して，リーチ先生にそれは地球に近い惑星である金星かとたずねました。先生はうなずき，**問1④** **問3(2)** 人間が人工的な光をとてもたくさん作り出したため，私たちの街の夜空にはほとんど何も見えないのだと説明しました。

学校が終わったあとの帰り道，天気は回復し，今や空に雲ひとつありませんでした。**問3(1)** 私は月のない空を見上げて，リーチ先生が話してくれたことが本当だと実感しました。

◆解説◆

問1 18 ❶ 19 ❷ 20 ❸ 21 ❹

「ユズの記事には，バーチャルツアーでの出来事を描写した学生のコメント（①～④）も含まれている。コメントを出来事が起こった順に並べなさい。」

18 → 19 → 20 → 21

❶「島はどれくらい危険なのだろうかと思った。ジャングルで美しい鳥や大きなヘビを見た。」 18

❷「以前はもっとたくさんの生き物がいたということがとてもショックだった。私たちの美しい海を守るべきだ！」 19

❸「体育館でキャンプ場を設営したのは少し奇妙だったが，とても楽しかった！ 虫に刺されなかったから，外より良かった！」 20

❹「宇宙ショーの間は言葉を失った。そして，そこにあるにもかかわらず気づいてないものが多いことがわかった。」 21

各選択肢のキーワードと同じ内容の表現を本文中で探す。本文・全訳の**問1①**，**問1②**，**問1③**，**問1④**参照。本文の rainforest（熱帯雨林）を❶では jungle（ジャングル），put up tents（テントを張る）を❸では setting up a camping site（キャンプ場を設営する）と言い換えている。また，❹の「そこにあるにもかかわらず気づいてないもの」は**問1④**の「人工的な光のために見えなくなった星」を指す。

問2 22 ❸

「このツアーで，ユズは南洋の島の 22 について学ばなかった。」

① 「海の生態系」≫本文に一致する。

② 「夜空の星」≫本文に一致する。

❸「季節ごとの天気」

④ 「木と植物」≫本文に一致する。

①②④は本文・全訳の**問2①**，**問2②**，**問2④**に一致する。季節ごとの天気については学んでいないので❸が正解。

問3 23 ❷

「帰り道で，ユズは夜空を見上げて，おそらく 23 を見ただろう。」

① 「流れ星」≫プラネタリウムで見たが，帰り道では見ていない。

❷「ほんの少しの星」

③ 「満月」≫月がないと書かれている。

④ 「天の川」≫プラネタリウムで見たが，帰り道では見ていない。

ユズが見たものは具体的に書かれていない。本文・全訳の 問3(1) に「空を見上げて，リーチ先生が話してくれたことが本当だと実感しました」とある。問3(2) で，リーチ先生は「私たちの街の夜空にはほとんど何も見えない」と言っているので，これに一致する❷が正解。

【設問・選択肢の語句・表現】
問1 ❸ weird 形 奇妙な

第4問

第4問 (配点 16)

Your college English club's room has several problems and you want to redesign it. Based on the following article and the results of a questionnaire given to members, you make a handout for a group discussion.

What Makes a Good Classroom?

Diana Bashworth, writer at *Trends in Education*

As many schools work to improve their classrooms, it is important to have some ideas for making design decisions. SIN, which stands for *Stimulation, Individualization*, and *Naturalness*, is a framework that might be helpful to consider when designing classrooms. 問1

The first, Stimulation, has two aspects: color and complexity. This has to do with the ceiling, floor, walls, and interior furnishings. For example, a classroom that lacks colors might be uninteresting. On the other hand, a classroom should not be too colorful. A bright color could be used on one wall, on the floor, window coverings, or furniture. In addition, it can be visually distracting to have too many things displayed on walls. It is suggested that 20 to 30 percent of wall space remain free. 問2

The next item in the framework is Individualization, which includes two considerations: ownership and flexibility. Ownership refers to whether the classroom feels personalized. Examples of this include having chairs and desks that are suitable for student sizes and ages, and providing storage space and areas for displaying student works or projects. Flexibility is about having a classroom that allows for different kinds of activities.

Naturalness relates to the quality and quantity of light, both natural and artificial, and the temperature of the classroom. Too much natural light may make screens and boards difficult to see; students may have difficulty reading or writing if there is a lack of light. In addition, hot summer classrooms do not promote effective study. Schools should install systems allowing for the adjustment of both light and temperature. 問3-A・C 問3-E 問3-B

While Naturalness is more familiar to us, and therefore often considered the priority, the other components are equally important. Hopefully, these ideas can guide your project to a successful end.

【語句・表現】
- *l*. 3 handout 名 資料
- *l*. 7 stimulation 名 刺激
- *l*. 8 individualization 名 個別化
- *l*. 8 naturalness 名 自然さ
- *l*. 8 framework 名 枠組み
- *l*.10 aspect 名 側面
- *l*.10 complexity 名 複雑さ
- *l*.11 interior 形 室内の
- *l*.11 furnishings 備え付け家具
- *l*.14 visually 副 視覚的に
- *l*.15 distracting 形 気が散る
- *l*.18 consideration 名 検討事項
- *l*.18 ownership 名 所有権
- *l*.18 flexibility 名 柔軟性
- *l*.18 refer to ～ ～に言及する
- *l*.23 relate to ～ ～に関係する
- *l*.27 effective 形 効果的な
- *l*.28 adjustment 名 調節
- *l*.30 priority 名 優先事項
- *l*.30 component 名 要素

Results of the Questionnaire

Q1: Choose any items that match your use of the English club's room.

問5(1)

問4(1)

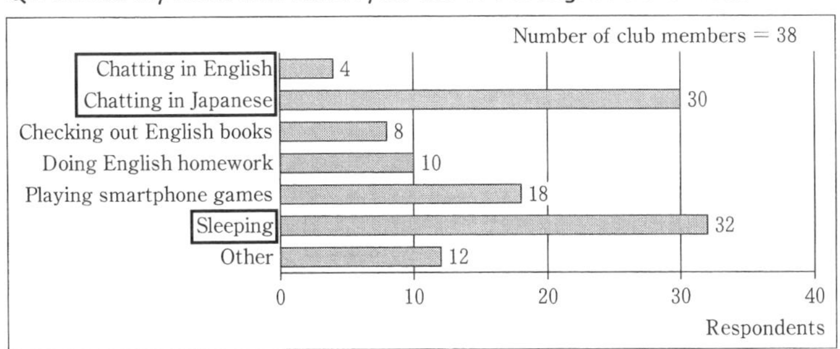

Q2: What do you think about the current English club's room?

Main comments:

Student 1 (S 1): I can't see the projector screen and whiteboard well on a sunny day. Also, there's no way to control the temperature.

S 2: By the windows, the sunlight makes it hard to read. The other side of the room doesn't get enough light. Also, the books are disorganized and the walls are covered with posters. It makes me feel uncomfortable.

問5(2)

S 3: The chairs don't really fit me and the desks are hard to move when we work in small groups. Also, lots of members speak Japanese, even though it's an English club.

問4(2)

S 4: The pictures of foreign countries on the walls make me want to speak English. Everyone likes the sofas — they are so comfortable that we often use the room for sleeping!

S 5: The room is so far away, so I hardly ever go there! Aren't there other rooms available?

S 6: There's so much gray in the room. I don't like it. But it's good that there are plenty of everyday English phrases on the walls!

グラフ中
respondent 名 回答者
l. 3 current 形 現在の

l. 8 disorganized 形 散らかった

Your discussion handout:

Room Improvement Project

■ **SIN Framework**

- What it is: [24]
- SIN = Stimulation, Individualization, Naturalness

■ **Design Recommendations Based on SIN and Questionnaire Results**

- Stimulation:

  Cover the floor with a colorful rug and [25].

資料内
recommendation 名 提案

– Individualization:
  Replace room furniture.
  (tables with wheels → easy to move around)

– Naturalness:
  [26]
  A. Install blinds on windows.
  B. Make temperature control possible.
  C. Move projector screen away from windows.
  D. Place sofas near walls.
  E. Put floor lamp in darker corner.

■ **Other Issues to Discuss**

– The majority of members [27] the room as [28]'s comment mentioned. How can we solve this?
– Based on both the graph and [29]'s comment, should we set a language rule in the room to motivate members to speak English more?
– S 5 doesn't like the location, but we can't change the room, so let's think about how to encourage members to visit more often.

資料内
majority 图 大多数

motivate ～ to *do*
～に…する意欲を起こさせる

◆全訳◆

あなたの大学の英語クラブの部室にはいくつかの問題があり，部室を改装したいと考えています。以下の記事と部員へのアンケートの結果に基づき，あなたはグループディスカッション用の資料を作成します。

何をしたら良い教室になるか？

ダイアナ・バシュワース，『教育のトレンド』誌の執筆者

多くの学校が教室の改善に取り組む中，デザインを決定するためのいくつかのアイディアを持つことは重要である。**問 1** SIN とは，Stimulation（刺激），Individualization（個別化），Naturalness（自然さ）を表すのだが，教室をデザインする際に考慮すると役立つであろう枠組みである。

最初の「刺激」には色と複雑さという２つの側面がある。これは天井，床，壁，室内の調度品に関係する。例えば，色のない教室はおもしろくないかもしれない。逆に，教室がカラフルすぎてもいけない。明るい色は壁の一面，床，窓の覆い，家具に使うことができるだろう。**問 2** さらに，壁にあまりにも多くのものが飾られていると，視覚的に気が散ってしまうこともある。壁面スペースの20～30％を空けておくことが推奨される。

枠組みの次の項目は「個別化」で，これは所有意識と柔軟性という２つの検討事項が含まれる。所有意識とは，教室が個人的なものになっていると感じられるかどうかを指す。例としては，学生の体格や年齢に合った椅子や机があること，収納スペースや学生の作品や研究課題を展示する場所を提供することなどがある。柔軟性とは，さまざまな活動ができる教室にすることである。

「自然さ」とは，自然なものと人工のもの両方の光の質と量，教室の温度に関するものである。**問 3-A・C** 自然光が強すぎると，スクリーンや黒板が見づらくなるかもしれない。**問 3-E** 光が不足すると，学生は読んだり書いたりするのが困難になるかもしれない。**問 3-B** さらに，夏の暑い教室では効果的な学習が促進されない。学校は光と温度の両方を調節できるシステムを導入すべきである。

「自然さ」は私たちにより身近なものであるため，優先事項だとみなされがちだが，その他の要素も等しく重要である。これらのアイディアが，あなたのプロジェクトを最終的に成功に導くことを願う。

アンケート結果

Q1：英語クラブの部室の使い方にあてはまるものを選んでください。

（グラフ内）

部員数＝38人

問5(1) 英語でおしゃべり　4人
日本語でおしゃべり　30人
英語の本を借りる　8人
英語の宿題をする　10人
スマホゲームをする　18人
問4(1) 睡眠　32人
その他　12人

回答者

Q2：現在の英語クラブの部室についてどう思いますか。

主なコメント

学生1(S1)：晴れた日にはプロジェクターのスクリーンやホワイトボードがよく見えない。また，温度調節をする方法がない。

S2：窓際では日差しが強くて読みにくい。部屋の反対側は光が十分に入らない。また，本が散らかり，壁はポスターで覆われている。そのため居心地が悪く感じる。

S3：椅子があまり自分に合わないし，小グループで作業する時に机が動かしにくい。問5(2) また，英語クラブなのに部員の多くが日本語を話している。

S4：壁に貼ってある外国の写真を見ると，英語を話したくなる。みんなソファが好きで，とても快適なので 問4(2) よく部室を寝るために使っています！

S5：部室がとても遠いので，めったに行かない！他に使える部屋はないのですか。

S6：室内に灰色がとても多く，好きでない。しかし，壁に日常的な英語のフレーズがたくさんあるのが良い。

あなたのディスカッション資料：

部室改善プロジェクト

■ SINの枠組み
- それは何か：［24］
- SIN＝刺激，個別化，自然さ

■ SINとアンケート結果に基づくデザイン提案
- 刺激：
床をカラフルなラグで覆い，［25］。
- 個別化：
部室の家具を入れ替える。
(キャスター付きテーブル→移動させやすい)
- 自然さ：
［26］
A. 窓にブラインドをつける。
B. 温度調節を可能にする。
C. プロジェクターのスクリーンを窓から離れた場所に移す。
D. ソファを壁際に置く。
E. 暗いコーナーに床置き電気スタンドを置く。

■その他の議論する問題点
- ［28］のコメントが言及しているように，大多数の部員が部室［27］。これをどう解決するか。
- グラフと［29］のコメントの両方に基づいて，部員にもっと英語を話す意欲を持たせるために，部室での言語ルールを設けるべきだろうか。
- S5は場所が気に入らないようだが，部屋を変えることはできない。だから部員がもっと頻繁に来るように励ます方法を考えよう。

◆解説◆

問1　24　❸

「［24］に入れるのに最も適当な選択肢を選びなさい。」

① 「どの色が教室で使うのに適切かを示すガイド」
≫色はSINの一部でしかない。

② 「教室における学生と教師のニーズに優先順位をつける方法」≫本文にない。

❸「教室の環境を計画する時に従うべき模範」

④ 「教室が学生の成果にどのような影響を与えるかを理解するためのシステム」≫成果をあげるための

システムで，理解するものではない。

本文・全訳の**問1**にSINが何か書かれている。「教室をデザインする際に考慮すると役立つであろう枠組み」だから，❸が正解。

問2 25 ❹

「25 に入れるのに最も適当な選択肢を選びなさい。」

① 「スクリーンをより良い場所に動かす」≫「自然さ」に対応する内容。

② 「それぞれの壁を異なる色で塗る」≫一面だけ明るい色にすることが推奨されている。

③ 「本を棚に並べる」≫本文のSINの説明にない。

❹ **「展示物を減らす」**

本文・全訳の**問2**で「壁面スペースの20～30%を空けておく」ことが推奨されているので，❹が正解。

問3 26 ❹

「あなたは資料をチェックしていて，『自然さ』の提案の誤りに気づいた。次のうちどれを取り除くべきか。」 26

① 「A」≫本文に一致する。

② 「B」≫本文に一致する。

③ 「C」≫本文に一致する。

❹ **「D」**

⑤ 「E」≫本文に一致する。

A・B・C・Eは，それぞれ本文・全訳の**問3-A**，**問3-B**，**問3-C**，**問3-E**に書かれている問題点の対処方法である。本文中では，ソファの位置と明るさや室温の関係に言及していないので，❹が正解。

問4 27 ❺ 28 ❹

「27 と 28 に入れるのに最も適当な選択肢を選びなさい。」

27

① 「で本を借りる」≫アンケートによると，本を借りるのは8人。

② 「に簡単に行けない」≫簡単に行けないとコメントしたのは1人。

③ 「で日本語を使わない」≫アンケートによると，多くの部員が日本語を使っている。

④ 「で不安を感じる」≫アンケートにない。

❺ **「で仮眠をとる」**

アンケート結果のグラフの**問4(1)**からわかるように，多くの部員が部室で睡眠をとっているので，❺が正解。

28

① 「S1」

② 「S2」

③ 「S3」

❹ **「S4」**

⑤ 「S5」

⑥ 「S6」

本文・全訳の**問4(2)**に書かれているように，部室での睡眠に言及しているのはS4で，❹が正解。

問5 29 ❸

「29 に入れるのに最も適当な選択肢を選びなさい。」

① 「S1」

② 「S2」

❸ **「S3」**

④ 「S4」

⑤ 「S5」

⑥ 「S6」

言語に関する項目をグラフで探すと，**問5(1)**から，英語を話す部員は少なく，日本語を話す部員が多いことがわかる。部員のコメントでこの点に言及しているのは，**問5(2)**のS3である。したがって❸が正解。

【設問・選択肢の語句・表現】

問1 ② prioritize 他 ～に優先順位をつける

問4 ❺ take a nap　仮眠をとる

第５問

第５問 （配点　15）

You are in an English discussion group, and it is your turn to introduce a story. You have found a story in an English language magazine in Japan. You are preparing notes for your presentation.

Maki's Kitchen

5 "*Irasshai-mase*," said Maki as two customers entered her restaurant, Maki's Kitchen. Maki had joined her family business at the age of 19 when her father became ill. After he recovered, Maki decided to continue. Eventually, Maki's parents retired and she became the owner. Maki had many regular customers who came not only for the delicious food, but also to sit at 10 the counter and talk to her. Although her business was doing very well, Maki occasionally daydreamed about doing something different.

問１④

"Can we sit at the counter?" she heard. It was her old friends, Takuya and Kasumi. A phone call a few weeks earlier from Kasumi to Takuya had given them the idea to visit Maki and surprise her.

問１②

◆◆◆◆◆

15 Takuya's phone vibrated, and he saw a familiar name, Kasumi.

"Kasumi!"

"Hi Takuya, I saw you in the newspaper. Congratulations!"

問２

"Thanks. Hey, you weren't at our 20th high school reunion last month."

"No, I couldn't make it. I can't believe it's been 20 years since we 20 graduated. Actually, I was calling to ask if you've seen Maki recently."

◆◆◆◆◆

Takuya's family had moved to Kawanaka Town shortly before he started high school. He joined the drama club, where he met Maki and Kasumi. The three became inseparable. After graduation, Takuya left Kawanaka to become an actor, while Maki and Kasumi remained. Maki had decided she wanted to 25 study at university and enrolled in a preparatory school. Kasumi, on the other hand, started her career. Takuya tried out for various acting roles but was constantly rejected; eventually, he quit.

問１④

Exactly one year after graduation, Takuya returned to Kawanaka with his dreams destroyed. He called Maki, who offered her sympathy. He was 30 surprised to learn that Maki had abandoned her plan to attend university because she had to manage her family's restaurant. Her first day of work had been the day he called. For some reason, Takuya could not resist giving Maki some advice.

"Maki, I've always thought your family's restaurant should change the

【語句・表現】

l. 8 eventually 副 最終的には

l.11 occasionally 副 時々

l.15 vibrate 自 振動する

l.18 reunion 名 同窓会

l.23 inseparable 形 切っても切れない

l.25 enroll in ～ ～に入る

l.25 preparatory school 予備校

l.27 constantly 副 いつも

l.27 reject 他 ～を不合格にする

l.29 sympathy 名 同情

l.30 abandon 他 ～をあきらめる

l.32 resist *doing* …するのを我慢する

coffee it serves. I think people in Kawanaka want a bolder flavor. I'd be happy to recommend a different brand," he said.

"Takuya, you really know your coffee. Hey, I was walking by Café Kawanaka and saw a help-wanted sign. You should apply!" Maki replied.

問1⑤ Takuya was hired by Café Kawanaka and became fascinated by the science of coffee making. On the one-year anniversary of his employment, Takuya was talking to Maki at her restaurant.

"Maki," he said, "do you know what my dream is?"

"It must have something to do with coffee."

"That's right! It's to have my own coffee business."

"I can't imagine a better person for it. What are you waiting for?"

Maki's encouragement inspired Takuya. He quit his job, purchased a coffee bean roaster, and began roasting beans. 問3① Maki had a sign in her restaurant saying, "We proudly serve Takuya's Coffee," and this publicity helped the coffee gain popularity in Kawanaka. Takuya started making good money selling his beans. Eventually, he opened his own café and became a successful business owner.

Kasumi was reading the newspaper when she saw the headline: *TAKUYA'S CAFÉ ATTRACTING TOURISTS TO KAWANAKA TOWN.* "Who would have thought that Takuya would be so successful?" Kasumi thought to herself as she reflected on her past.

In the high school drama club, Kasumi's duty was to put make-up on the actors. No one could do it better than her. Maki noticed this and saw that a cosmetics company called Beautella was advertising for salespeople. She encouraged Kasumi to apply, and, after graduation, she became an employee of Beautella.

The work was tough; Kasumi went door to door selling cosmetics. On bad days, she would call Maki, who would lift her spirits. 問3② One day, Maki had an idea, "Doesn't Beautella do make-up workshops? I think you are more suited for that. You can show people how to use the make-up. They'll love the way they look and buy lots of cosmetics!"

Kasumi's company agreed to let her do workshops, and they were a hit! Kasumi's sales were so good that eight months out of high school, she had been promoted, moving to the big city of Ishijima. Since then, she had steadily climbed her way up the company ladder until 問1① she had been named vice-president of Beautella this year.

問4(2) "I wouldn't be vice-president now without Maki," she thought, "she helped me when I was struggling, but I was too absorbed with my work in Ishijima to give her support when she had to quit her preparatory school." 問1② Glancing back to the article, she decided to call Takuya.

◆◆◆◆◆

"Maki wasn't at the reunion. I haven't seen her in ages," said Takuya.

"Same here. It's a pity. Where would we be without her?" asked Kasumi.

問4(1) The conversation became silent, as they wordlessly communicated their guilt. Then, Kasumi had an idea.

◆◆◆◆◆

l.35 flavor 名 風味
l.39 fascinate 他 ～を魅了する
l.46 encouragement 名 励まし
l.46 inspire 他 ～を奮い立たせる
l.46 purchase 他 ～を購入する
l.48 proudly 副 自信を持って
l.48 publicity 名 宣伝
l.49 popularity 名 人気
l.55 reflect on ～ ～を回顧する
l.58 advertise for ～ ～を募集する
l.61 cosmetics 化粧品
l.62 lift one's spirit ～を元気づける
l.68 steadily 副 着実に
l.71 vice-president 名 副社長
l.72 struggle 自 悪戦苦闘する
l.72 be absorbed with ～ ～に没頭する
l.73 glance back 見返す
l.76 It's a pity. 残念だ。
l.78 guilt 名 罪悪感

80 The three friends were talking and laughing when Maki asked, "By the way, I'm really happy to see you two, but what brings you here?"

"Payback," said Takuya.

"Have I done something wrong?" asked Maki.

問5(2) "No. The opposite. You understand people incredibly well. You can identify others' strengths and show them how to make use of them. We're proof of this. You made us aware of our gifts," said Takuya. 85

問5(1) "The irony is that you couldn't do the same for yourself," added Kasumi.

"I think Ishijima University would be ideal for you. It offers a degree program in counseling that's designed for people with jobs," said Takuya.

"You'd have to go there a few times a month, but you could stay with me. Also, Takuya can help you find staff for your restaurant," said Kasumi. 90

Maki closed her eyes and imagined Kawanaka having both "Maki's Kitchen" and "Maki's Counseling." She liked that idea.

l.81 payback 名 お返し，報復
l.83 incredibly 副 信じられないほど
l.84 identify 他 ～を明らかにする
l.86 irony 名 皮肉
l.87 ideal 形 理想的な

Your notes:

Maki's Kitchen

Story outline

Maki, Takuya, and Kasumi graduate from high school.

↓
30
31
32
33

Maki begins to think about a second career.

About Maki

- Age: 34
- Occupation: restaurant owner
- How she supported her friends:

  Provided Takuya with encouragement and 35.
  〃 Kasumi 〃 〃 and 36.

Interpretation of key moments

- Kasumi and Takuya experience an uncomfortable silence on the phone because they 37.
- In the final scene, Kasumi uses the word "irony" with Maki. The irony is that Maki does not 38.

メモ内 outline 名 あらすじ
メモ内 interpretation 名 解釈

◆全訳◆

あなたは英語のディスカッショングループにいて，物語を紹介する番です。あなたは日本の英語雑誌にある物語を見つけました。あなたは発表のためのメモを準備しています。

マキのキッチン

「いらっしゃいませ」，マキは２人の客が彼女のレストランであるマキのキッチンに入ると言いました。**問１④**マキは19歳の時に，父親が病気になった際に家業に加わりました。父親が回復したあと，マキは続けることを決心しました。最終的に，マキの両親は引退し，彼女がオーナーになりました。マキには，おいしい料理のためだけではなく，カウンターに座ってマキと話をするために来ている常連客がたくさんいました。商売はとてもうまくいっていたけれど，マキは時々，何か違うことをしたいと夢想しました。

「カウンターに座ってもいいですか？」と聞こえました。それは旧友のタクヤとカスミでした。**問１②**数週間前のカスミからタクヤへの電話がきっかけで，２人はマキを訪ねて驚かせようと考えたのでした。

タクヤの携帯電話が振動し，カスミというよく知っている名前が目に入りました。

「カスミ！」

「こんにちは，タクヤ。あなたを新聞で見たよ。おめでとう！」

問２「ありがとう。そういえば，先月の20回目の高校同窓会には来ていなかったね。」

「うん，行けなかった。卒業してから20年も経つなんて信じられない。実は，最近マキに会ったかどうか聞きたくて電話したんだ。」

タクヤの家族は，タクヤが高校に入学する少し前にカワナカ町に引っ越してきました。彼は演劇部に入り，そこでマキとカスミに出会いました。３人は切っても切れない仲になりました。卒業後，タクヤは俳優になるためにカワナカを離れ，マキとカスミは残りました。マキは大学で勉強したいと決心し，予備校に入りました。一方，カスミは就職しました。タクヤはさまざまな役柄を目指してオーディションを受けましたが，いつも不合格になり，ついに辞めました。

問１④卒業からちょうど１年後，タクヤは夢破れてカワナカに戻ってきました。彼はマキに電話をかけ，マキは同情の意を示しました。タクヤは，マキが家族のレストランを経営しなければならないので大学に入る計画をあきらめたことを知り，驚きました。彼女の初出勤の日が，彼が電話をした日でした。どういうわけか，タクヤはマキにアドバイスをせずにいられませんでした。

「マキ，僕はいつも思っていたんだけど，君の家族のレストランは出すコーヒーを変えるべきだ。カワナカの人はもっと強い風味を求めていると思うよ。喜んで別のブランドを推薦するよ。」と言いました。

「タクヤ，あなたは本当にコーヒーに詳しいね。ねえ，私はカフェ・カワナカのそばを歩いていて，求人広告の張り紙を見たんだ。あなたが応募するべきだよ！」とマキは答えました。

問１⑤タクヤはカフェ・カワナカに雇われ，コーヒー作りの科学に魅了されました。雇用されて１周年の日に，タクヤはマキのレストランでマキに話しかけていました。

「マキ，僕の夢が何かわかる？」と言いました。

「何かコーヒーと関係があることに違いないね。」

「そうだよ！　独立してコーヒービジネスをすることなんだ。」

「これ以上の適任者は想像できないよ。何を躊躇して待っているの？」

マキの励ましがタクヤを奮い立たせました。タクヤは仕事を辞め，コーヒー豆の焙煎機を購入し，豆の焙煎を始めました。**問３①**マキは自分のレストランに「当店では，自信を持ってタクヤのコーヒーを提供します」という看板を掲げ，この宣伝がカワナカでそのコーヒーが人気を得るのに役立ちました。タクヤはコーヒー豆の販売で高収入を得始めて，やがて自分のカフェを開業し，事業主として成功しました。

カスミは新聞を読んでいて，見出しを見ました：*『タクヤのカフェがカワナカ町に観光客を引き寄せている』*「タクヤがこんなに成功するなんて誰が思っていた？」カスミは自分の過去を思い出しながら心の中で思いました。

高校の演劇部では，カスミの役目は俳優にメイクを施すことでした。彼女ほど上手な人は他にはいませんでした。マキはそのことに気づき，ビューテラという化粧品会社が販売員を募集しているのを見つけました。マキはカスミに応募するよう促し，卒業後カスミはビューテラの社員になりました。

仕事はきつく，カスミは化粧品を一軒一軒売り歩きました。嫌なことがあった日は，カスミはマキに電話をして，マキは彼女を元気づけたものでした。**問3②** ある日，マキは思いつきました。「ビューテラは化粧品のワークショップをやらないの？　あなたはその方がもっと適任だと思う。人々に化粧品の使い方を教えることができる。みんな自分の見た目を気に入って，化粧品をたくさん買ってくれるよ！」

カスミの会社は彼女がワークショップをすることに同意し，大成功でした！カスミの売り上げはとても好調なので，高校を卒業して８ヵ月後には昇進し，大都市のイシジマに引っ越しました。それ以来，カスミは着実に昇進の階段を上り，**問1①** ついに今年ビューテラの副社長に任命されました。

「マキがいなければ，私は今，副社長になっていなかった」と彼女は思いました。**問4 (2)**「私が悪戦苦闘している時にマキは私を助けてくれた。でも私はイシジマでの自分の仕事にとても没頭していたから，彼女が予備校をやめなければならない時に支援ができなかった。」**問1②** ちらっと記事を見返し，彼女はタクヤに電話しようと決心しました。

◆◆◆◆◆

「マキは同窓会にいなかった。何年も会っていないよ。」とタクヤは言いました。

「こちらも同じよ。残念ね。マキがいなかったら，私たちはどうなっていたんだろう？」とカスミがたずねました。

問4 (1) 2人は沈黙しました。それはお互いの罪悪感を伝え合う沈黙でした。それから，カスミがあることを思いつきました。

◆◆◆◆◆

マキは友人と３人で談笑している時にたずねました。「ところで，あなたたち２人に会えてとてもうれしいけど，どうしてここに来たの？」

「お返しだよ。」とタクヤが言いました。

「私，何か間違ったことをした？」とマキがたずねました。

「いや，その反対だよ。**問5 (2)** あなたは信じられないほどよく人のことを理解している。他人の長所を見分け，それを活用する方法を教えることができる。僕たちはその証拠だ。僕たちの才能に気づかせてくれた。」とタクヤが言いました。

問5 (1)「皮肉なことに，あなたは自分に同じことができなかった。」とカスミがつけ加えました。

「イシジマ大学ならあなたに理想的だと思うよ。イシジマ大学は，仕事を持っている人向けのカウンセリングの学位プログラムを提供しているんだ。」とタクヤが言いました。

「月に数回通わなければならないけれど，私のところに泊まることができる。また，タクヤがレストランのスタッフ探しを手伝ってくれるよ。」とカスミが言いました。

マキは目を閉じて，カワナカに「マキのキッチン」と「マキのカウンセリング」の両方があることを想像しました。彼女はその考えが気に入りました。

あなたのメモ：

マキのキッチン

物語のあらすじ

マキ，タクヤ，カスミは高校を卒業する。

[30]

[31]

[32]

[33]

マキは第２のキャリアについて考え始める。

マキについて

・年齢：[34]

・職業：レストランオーナー

・友人たちをどのように支えたか：

タクヤを励まし[35]。

カスミを励まし[36]。

重要な瞬間の解釈

・[37]から，カスミとタクヤは電話で居心地の悪い沈黙を経験する。

・最後のシーンで，カスミはマキに「皮肉」という言葉を使う。その皮肉とは，マキが[38]ないことだ。

◆解説◆

問1 30 ❹ 31 ❺ 32 ❶ 33 ❷

「5つの出来事（①～⑤）から4つを選び，起こった順に並べなさい。」

30 → 31 → 32 → 33

❶ **「カスミが自分の会社の副社長になる。」** 32

❷ **「カスミがタクヤと連絡をとる。」** 33

③「マキが大学の学位を取る。」≫**本文にない。**

❹ **「マキが家族の事業で働き始める。」** 30

❺ **「タクヤが自分の事業を始める気になる。」** 31

物語は時系列に沿って書かれていないので，過去（高校卒業後数年以内）に起こった出来事と最近の出来事を区別しながら読もう。本文・全訳の**問1①**より，カスミが副社長になったのは今年のこと。**問1②**より，カスミがタクヤに連絡したのは副社長になったあと。**問1④**（2ヵ所）より，マキが家業を始めたのは高校を卒業した1年後。**問1⑤**より，タクヤが事業を始めたのはマキが家業のレストランで働き始めたあと。したがって❹→❺→❶→❷の順。

問2 34 ❷

「34 に入れるのに最も適当な選択肢を選びなさい。」

①「30代前半」

❷ **「30代後半」**

③「40代前半」

④「40代後半」

本文・全訳の**問2**から，登場人物3人は高校を卒業して20年経つとわかるので，❷が正解。

問3 35 ❶ 36 ❷

「35 と 36 に入れるのに最も適当な選択肢を選びなさい。」

❶ **「その製品を人々に知ってもらった」** 35

❷ **「成功するビジネスアイディアを提案した」** 36

③「事業のための設備を購入した」≫**マキが購入したのではない。**

④「大都市への引越しを提案した」≫**マキは提案していない。**

⑤「成功に必要な技術を教えた」≫**マキは技術を教えていない。**

本文・全訳の**問3①**で，マキはタクヤが焙煎したコーヒー豆を宣伝したので 35 には❶が入る。**問3②**で，マキが提案したワークショップが成功したので 36 には❷が入る。

問4 37 ❸

「37 に入れるのに最も適当な選択肢を選びなさい。」

①「自分たちの成功について話したくない」

②「長い間話をしていない」

❸ **「友人にもっと感謝すればよかったと後悔している」**

④「マキは自分たちの成功をうらやんでいたと思う」

本文・全訳の**問4(1)**から，沈黙の理由は罪悪感からだとわかるのでその理由を探す。**問4(2)**に書かれているカスミの「彼女が予備校をやめなければならない時に支援ができなかった」という自省から，❸が適当。3人が再会したあとのカスミとタクヤの提案も，その裏づけになる。

問5 38 ❷

「38 に入れるのに最も適当な選択肢を選びなさい。」

①「いろいろなことに挑戦するのが好きで」≫**本文にない。**

❷ **「自分の才能を理解してい」**

③「自分に足りない能力を理解してい」≫**本文にない。**

④「自分の夢を追い求めたいと考えてい」≫**「皮肉」の内容に合わない。**

本文・全訳の**問5(1)**から，「皮肉」なのは「自分に同じことができなかった」ことである。「同じこと」の内容は**問5(2)**に書かれている「他人の長所を見分け，それを活用する方法を教えること」である。それが自分にできていないのだから，❷が正解。

【設問・選択肢の語句・表現】

問1 rearrange 他 ～を並べ換える

問1 ❷ get in touch with ～　～と連絡をとる

問1 ❺ inspire ～ to *do*　～を触発して…する気にさせる

問4 ❸ appreciate 他 ～に感謝する

問5 ④ pursue 他 ～を追い求める

第6問 (配点 24)

A Your English teacher has assigned this article to you. You need to prepare notes to give a short talk.

Perceptions of Time

When you hear the word "time," it is probably hours, minutes, and seconds that immediately come to mind. In the late 19th century, however, philosopher Henri Bergson described how people usually do not experience time as it is measured by clocks (**clock time**). Humans do not have a known biological mechanism to measure clock time, so they use mental processes instead. This is called **psychological time**, which everyone perceives differently.

If you were asked how long it had taken to finish your homework, you probably would not know exactly. You would think back and make an estimate. In a 1975 experiment, participants were shown either simple or complex shapes for a fixed amount of time and asked to memorize them. Afterwards, they were asked how long they had looked at the shapes. To answer, they used a mental process called **retrospective timing**, which is estimating time based on the information retrieved from memory. Participants who were shown the complex shapes felt the time was longer, while the people who saw the simple shapes experienced the opposite.

Another process to measure psychological time is called **prospective timing**. It is used when you are actively keeping track of time while doing something. Instead of using the amount of information recalled, the level of attention given to time while doing the activity is used. In several studies, the participants performed tasks while estimating the time needed to complete them. Time seemed shorter for the people doing more challenging mental activities which required them to place more focus on the task than on time. Time felt longer for the participants who did simpler tasks and the longest for those who were waiting or doing nothing.

Your emotional state can influence your awareness of time, too. For example, you can be enjoying a concert so much that you forget about time. Afterwards, you are shocked that hours have passed by in what seemed to be the blink of an eye. To explain this, we often say, "Time flies when you're having fun." The opposite occurs when you are bored. Instead of being focused on an activity, you notice the time. It seems to go very slowly as you

問1(1) 問3 問4 問1(2)

【語句・表現】

l. 3 perception 名 認識
l. 4 second 名 秒
l. 5 philosopher 名 哲学者
l. 8 mental process 精神機能
l.13 a fixed amount of time 一定の時間
l.15 retrospective timing 遡及的時間計測
l.16 retrieve 他 ～を取り出す
l.19 prospective timing 予期時間計測
l.31 the blink of an eye 一瞬

cannot wait for your boredom to end. Fear also affects our perception of time.
35 In a 2006 study, more than 60 people experienced skydiving for the first time. Participants with high levels of unpleasant emotions perceived the time spent skydiving to be much longer than it was in reality.

Psychological time also seems to move differently during life stages. Children constantly encounter new information and have new experiences,
問2(2) 40 which makes each day memorable and seem longer when recalled. Also, time creeps by for them as they anticipate upcoming events such as birthdays and trips. For most adults, unknown information is rarely encountered and new experiences become less frequent, so less mental focus is required and each day becomes less memorable. However, this is not always the case.
問2(1) 45 Daily routines are shaken up when drastic changes occur, such as changing jobs or relocating to a new city. In such cases, the passage of time for those people is similar to that for children. But generally speaking, time seems to accelerate as we mature.

Knowledge of psychological time can be helpful in our daily lives, as it
50 may help us deal with boredom. Because time passes slowly when we are not mentally focused and thinking about time, changing to a more engaging activity, such as reading a book, will help ease our boredom and speed up the time. The next occasion that you hear "Time flies when you're having fun," you will be reminded of this.

Your notes:

Perceptions of Time

Outline by paragraph

1. [39]
2. *Retrospective timing*
3. *Prospective timing*
4. [40]
   - ➤ *Skydiving*
5. *Effects of age*
   - ➤ *Time speeds up as we mature, but a* [41].
6. *Practical tips*

My original examples to help the audience

A. *Retrospective timing*
Example: [42]
B. *Prospective timing*
Example: [43]

l.34 boredom 名 退屈さ
l.41 creep by ゆっくり進む
l.41 anticipate 他 ～を楽しみに待つ
l.41 upcoming 形 もうすぐやってくる
l.45 drastic 形 劇的な
l.46 relocate 自 移動する
l.48 accelerate 自 加速する
l.51 engaging 形 魅力のある
メモ内 practical 形 実用的な

◆全訳◆

A　英語の先生がこの記事をあなたに割り当てました。あなたは短い発表をするためにメモを準備する必要があります。

時間の認識

1.「時間」という言葉を聞くと，すぐに思い浮かぶのはおそらく時，分，秒だろう。しかし19世紀後半に哲学者のアンリ・ベルクソンは，**問1(1)** いかに人々が通常は時計によって計測される時間（**時計時間**）のように時間を体験していないかを説明した。人間には時計時間を計測する既知の生物学的メカニズムがないため，代わりに精神機能を利用するのである。これは**心理的時間**とよばれるもので，人によって認識が異なる。

2.　宿題を終えるまでにかかった時間を聞かれたら，おそらく正確にはわからず，思い返して見積もるだろう。1975年の実験では，被験者は単純な図形か複雑な図形のどちらかを一定時間見せられ，それを記憶するよう求められた。その後，どのくらいの時間その図形を見ていたかを質問された。**問3** 答えるのに，彼らは**遡及的時間計測（レトロスペクティブ・タイミング）**とよばれる精神的プロセスを用いた。これは記憶から取り出した情報に基づいて時間を見積もるものである。複雑な図形を見せられた被験者は時間をより長く感じたが，単純な図形を見た人はその逆を経験した。

3.　**問4** 心理的時間を計測するもう一つの過程は，**予期時間計測（プロスペクティブ・タイミング）**とよばれる。これは何かをしながら積極的に時間経過を追っている時に使われる。思い出した情報量を使う代わりに，活動中の時間に対する注意の度合いが使われる。いくつかの研究では，被験者は完了するのに必要な時間を見積もりながら課題を行った。時間よりも課題に集中が求められる，より困難な精神的活動を行なっている人たちには，時間がより短く感じられた。より単純な課題を行った被験者には時間がもっと長く感じられ，待機しているか何もしていない被験者には時間が最も長く感じられた。

4.　**問1(2)** あなたの感情の状態も時間の認識に影響を与え得る。例えば，コンサートを大いに楽しんで時間を忘れることがあり得る。終わったあと，一瞬と思えるうちに何時間も過ぎていたことに衝撃を受ける。このことを説明するために，私たちはよく「楽しい時は時間が過ぎるのが早い」と言う。退屈している時はその反対のことが生じる。活動に集中する代わりに，時間に気がつく。退屈が終わるのが待ちきれず，時間がとても遅く進むように感じる。恐怖もまた時間の認識に影響を与える。2006年の研究では，60人以上が初めてスカイダイビングを体験した。高レベルの不快な感情を持つ被験者は，スカイダイビングに費やした時間を実際よりもずっと長く感じた。

5.　心理的な時間は人生の段階によっても異なる動きをするようだ。子供たちは常に新しい情報に出会い，新しい経験をし，それが一日一日を忘れがたいものにし，思い出すと長く感じられる。また，誕生日や旅行などもうすぐやってくるイベントを楽しみに待つので，**問2(2)** 子供にとっては時間がゆっくりと過ぎる。ほとんどの大人にとって，未知の情報に出会うことはほとんどなく，新しい経験をすることも少なくなるため，精神的な集中があまり必要とされなくなり，一日一日が記憶に残りにくくなる。しかし，必ずしもそうとは限らない。**問2(1)** 転職や新しい街への引っ越しなど劇的な変化が起きると，日々の日課は揺らぐ。そのような場合，その人たちの時間の経過は子供のものと似る。しかし一般的には，大人になるにつれて時間は加速していくようだ。

6.　心理的な時間の知識は，退屈を解決するのに役立つかもしれないので，私たちの日々の生活で役に立つだろう。精神を集中させず時間について考えている時は，時間がゆっくりと過ぎる。だから，本を読むなど興味をそそる活動に変えることで，退屈を和らげ時間を早めることができる。次に「楽しいことをしていると時間が過ぎるのが早い」という言葉を聞く機会があれば，このことを思い出すだろう。

あなたのメモ：

時間の認識

段落ごとの概要

1. [39]
2. 遡及的時間計測
3. 予期時間計測
4. [40]
   ⇒スカイダイビング
5. 年齢の影響
   ⇒大人になるにつれて時間は加速するが，

41。

6. 実践的なヒント

聴衆に役立つ私の独自の例

A. 遡及的時間計測

例：42

B. 予期時間計測

例：43

◆解説◆

問1 39 ❻ 40 ❷

「39 と 40 に入れるのに最も適当な選択肢を選びなさい。」

① 「生物学的メカニズム」≫**第1段落の内容の一部でしかない。**

❷「感情の影響」40

③「記憶の種類」≫**段落のポイントではない。**

④「人生の段階」≫**第5段落の内容。**

⑤「継続中の研究」≫**本文にない。**

❻「時間の種類」39

本文・全訳の**問1(1)**に書かれているように，第1段落では clock time（時計時間）と psychological time（心理的時間）という2種類の時間を紹介しているので，39 には❻が入る。**問1(2)**に書かれているように，第4段落には「感情の影響」がスカイダイビングの実験などの具体例をあげて書かれている。40 には❷が入る。

問2 41 ❶

「41 に入れるのに最も適当な選択肢を選びなさい。」

❶「何歳でも，大きなライフスタイルの変化は時間の流れを遅くすることがあり得る。」

②「年齢に関係なく，大きなライフスタイルの変化は時間の流れを速くすることがあり得る。」≫**本文に書かれていることと逆である。**

③「大人にとっての小さなライフスタイルの変化は，時間の流れを遅くすることがあり得る。」≫**小さな変化ではなく大きな変化が必要。**

④「子供にとっての小さなライフスタイルの変化は，時間の流れを速くすることがあり得る。」≫**本文にない。**

本文・全訳の**問2(1)**に「(大人でも) 劇的な変化が起きると，日々の日課は揺らぐ。そのような場合，その人たちの時間の経過は子供のものと似る。」とある。「子供のもの」が指す内容は，**問2(2)**に「時間がゆっくりと過ぎる」と書かれている。したがって，❶が正解。

問3 42 ❸

「42 に入れるのに最も適当な選択肢を選びなさい。」

①「クラスメートからのメッセージを楽しみに待つ」≫**すでに行った出来事ではない。**

②「母親の携帯電話番号を覚える」≫**すでに行った出来事ではない。**

❸「今日何時間働いたかを回顧する」

④「明日会議があることを覚えておく」≫**すでに行った出来事ではない。**

「遡及的時間計測」の説明は本文・全訳の**問3**に書かれている。「記憶から取り出した情報に基づいて時間を見積もるもの」とある。選択肢の中でこれにあてはまるのは❸である。

問4 43 ❶

「43 に入れるのに最も適当な選択肢を選びなさい。」

❶「今までのところどれくらいジョギングをし続けているかを推測する」

②「バスケットボール部の夏合宿のスケジュールを立てる」≫**現在継続中のことではない。**

③「駅でテニスコーチに偶然会う」≫**現在継続中のことではない。**

④「この前の温泉への家族旅行のことを考える」≫**現在継続中のことではない。**

「予期時間計測」の説明は本文・全訳の**問4**に書かれている。「何かをしながら積極的に時間経過を追っている時に使われる」とある。選択肢の中で「何かをしながら」にあてはまるのは❶である。

【設問・選択肢の語句・表現】

問1 ⑤ ongoing 形 継続中の

問2 ❶ major 形 大きい

問2 ② regardless of ～　～に関係なく

問3 ❸ reflect on ～　～を回顧する

第6問B

B You are preparing a presentation for your science club, using the following passage from a science website.

Chili Peppers: The Spice of Life

Tiny pieces of red spice in chili chicken add a nice touch of color, but biting into even a small piece can make a person's mouth burn as if it were on fire. While some people love this, others want to avoid the painful sensation. At the same time, though, they can eat sashimi with wasabi. This might lead one to wonder what spiciness actually is and to ask where the difference between chili and wasabi comes from.

Unlike sweetness, saltiness, and sourness, spiciness is not a taste. In fact, we do not actually taste heat, or spiciness, when we eat spicy foods. The bite we feel from eating chili peppers and wasabi is derived from different types of compounds. Chili peppers get their heat from a heavier, oil-like element called capsaicin. Capsaicin leaves a lingering, fire-like sensation in our mouths because it triggers a receptor called TRPV1. TRPV1 induces stress and tells us when something is burning our mouths. Interestingly, there is a wide range of heat across the different varieties of chili peppers, and the level depends on the amount of capsaicin they contain. This is measured using the Scoville Scale, which is also called Scoville Heat Units (SHU). SHUs range from the sweet and mild *shishito* pepper at 50-200 SHUs to the Carolina Reaper pepper, which can reach up to 2.2 million.

Wasabi is considered a root, not a pepper, and does not contain capsaicin. Thus, wasabi is not ranked on the Scoville Scale. However, people have compared the level of spice in it to chilis with around 1,000 SHUs, which is on the lower end of the scale. The reason some people cannot tolerate chili spice but can eat foods flavored with wasabi is that the spice compounds in it are low in density. [問1] The compounds in wasabi vaporize easily, delivering a blast of spiciness to our nose when we eat it.

[問5] Consuming chili peppers can have positive effects on our health, and much research has been conducted into the benefits of capsaicin. [問2-D] When capsaicin activates the TRPV1 receptor in a person's body, it is similar to what happens when they experience stress or pain from an injury. [問2-A] Strangely, capsaicin can also make pain go away. Scientists found that TRPV1 ceases to be turned on after long-term exposure to chili peppers, temporarily easing painful sensations. Thus, skin creams containing capsaicin might be useful for people who experience muscle aches.

[問2-C] Another benefit of eating chili peppers is that they accelerate the metabolism. A group of researchers analyzed 90 studies on capsaicin and body weight and found that people had a reduced appetite when they ate spicy foods. [問2-B] This is because spicy foods increase the heart rate, send more energy to the muscles, and convert fat into energy. Recently, scientists at the University of Wyoming have created a weight-loss drug with capsaicin as a

【語句・表現】

l. 6 sensation 名 感覚
l.12 be derived from ～ ～に由来する
l.14 capsaicin 名 カプサイシン
l.14 lingering 形 （感覚などが）長く続く
l.15 trigger 他 ～の反応を引き起こす
l.15 receptor 名 受容体
l.15 induce 他 ～を誘発する
l.27 vaporize 自 気化する
l.31 activate 他 ～を活性化する
l.33 cease to *do* …するのをやめる，…しなくなる
l.36 muscle 名 筋肉
l.37 accelerate 他 ～（の進行）を速める
l.38 metabolism 名 新陳代謝
l.41 convert ～ into… ～を…に変換する

main ingredient.

It is also believed that chili peppers are connected with food safety, which might lead to a healthier life. When food is left outside of a refrigerated environment, microorganisms multiply on it, which may cause sickness if eaten. 問2-E Studies have shown that capsaicin and other chemicals found in chili peppers have antibacterial properties that can slow down or even stop microorganism growth. As a result, food lasts longer and there are fewer food-borne illnesses. 問4 This may explain why people in hot climates have a tendency to use more chili peppers, and therefore, be more tolerant of spicier foods due to repeated exposure. Also, in the past, before there were refrigerators, they were less likely to have food poisoning than people in cooler climates.

Chili peppers seem to have health benefits, but can they also be bad for our health? Peppers that are high on the Scoville Scale can cause physical discomfort when eaten in large quantities. 問3 People who have eaten several of the world's hottest chilis in a short time have reported experiencing upset stomachs, diarrhea, numb hands, and symptoms similar to a heart attack. Ghost peppers, which contain one million SHUs, can even burn a person's skin if they are touched.

Luckily the discomfort some people feel after eating spicy foods tends to go away soon—usually within a few hours. Despite some negative side effects, spicy foods remain popular around the world and add a flavorful touch to the table. Remember, it is safe to consume spicy foods, but you might want to be careful about the amount of peppers you put in your dishes.

Presentation slides:

Characteristics

chili peppers	wasabi
・oil-like elements	・ 44
・triggering TRPV1	・changing to vapor
・persistent feeling	・spicy rush

2

Positive Effects

Capsaicin can... 45

A. reduce pain.
B. give you more energy.
C. speed up your metabolism.
D. make you feel less stress.
E. decrease food poisoning.

3

Negative Effects

When eating too many strong chili peppers in a short time,

・ 46
・ 47

4

l.45 refrigerated 形 冷蔵保存された
l.46 microorganism 名 微生物
l.46 multiply 自 増殖する
l.51 tolerant 形 耐性がある
l.53 food poisoning 食中毒
l.56 physical 形 体の
l.57 discomfort 名 不快症状
l.59 symptom 名 症状

スライド2
characteristic（通例複数形で）名 特徴
persistent 形 持続する
rush 名 爽快感

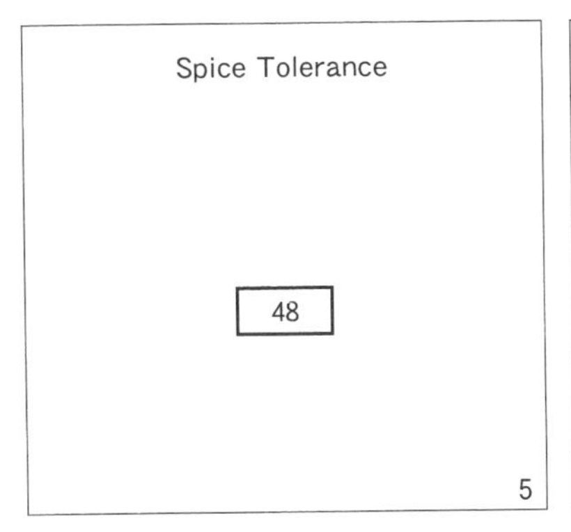

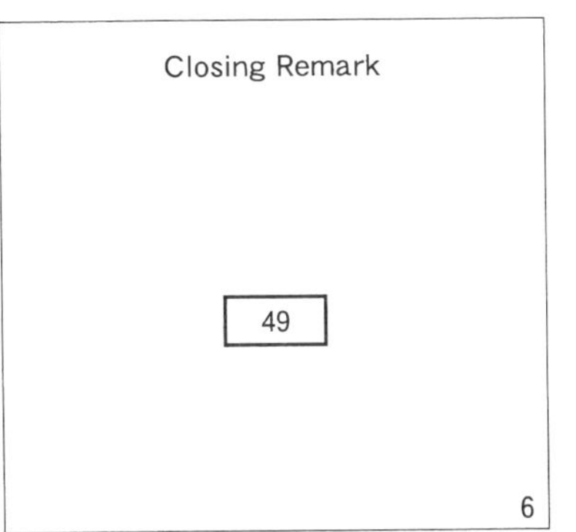

スライド５
tolerance 图 耐性

スライド６
closing remark
締めくくりの所見

◆全訳◆

B　あなたは科学のウェブサイトの以下の文章を使って，科学クラブのプレゼンテーションの準備をしています。

トウガラシ：人生のスパイス

チリチキンに入っている赤いスパイスの小さなかけらはきれいな彩りを添えるが，たとえ小さなかけらでも，かじると口の中に火がついたように熱くなることがある。これが大好きな人もいれば，この痛い感覚を避けたい人もいる。しかし同時に，彼らは刺身にワサビをつけて食べることができる。こうなると，辛さとは実のところ何だろうと不思議に思い，トウガラシとワサビの違いはどこから来るのだろうと問う人が出てくるかもしれない。

甘味，塩味，酸味とは異なり，辛さは味覚ではない。実際，私たちは香辛料の入った食べ物を食べてもヒリヒリ感や辛さを味として感じることはない。私たちがトウガラシやワサビを食べて感じる辛さは，異なる種類の化合物に由来する。トウガラシの辛さはカプサイシンとよばれる比較的重い，油のような成分からくる。カプサイシンは，TRPV1とよばれる受容体の反応を引き起こすため，口の中に長く続く火のような感覚を残す。TRPV1はストレスを引き起こし，何かが口の中でヒリヒリしている時にはそれを教えてくれる。興味深いことに，さまざまな品種のトウガラシの辛さには幅があり，そのレベルは含まれるカプサイシンの量による。これは，スコヴィル・ヒート・ユニット（SHU）ともよばれるスコヴィル・スケールを使って計測される。SHU は，甘くて刺激が少ないシシトウの50～200SHU から，220万 SHU にも達することがあるキャロライナリーパートウガラシまで幅広い。

ワサビはカラシではなく根であるとみなされ，カプサイシンを含まない。したがって，ワサビはスコヴィル・スケールではランクづけされない。しかし，ワサビの辛さの度合いは約1,000SHU のトウガラシと比較されており，これはスケールの下位の方である。トウガラシの辛さには耐えられないが，ワサビ風味の食品なら食べられるという人がいるのは，**問1** ワサビに含まれる香辛料化合物の濃度が低いからである。ワサビに含まれる化合物は気化しやすく，食べた時に鼻に強烈な辛さを一瞬もたらす。

問5 トウガラシを摂取することは健康に良い影響を与える可能性があり，カプサイシンの効能について多くの研究がなされている。**問2-D** カプサイシンが人の体内の TRPV1受容体を活性化する時，それはストレスやケガの痛みを経験する時に起こることと似ている。**問2-A** 奇妙なことに，カプサイシンは痛みを消すこともある。科学者たちは，トウガラシに長期間さらされると TRPV1が活性化されなくなり，一時的に痛みを軽減することを発見した。したがって，カプサイシンを含む皮膚クリームは，筋肉痛を経験する人々に役立つかもしれない。

問2-C トウガラシを食べることのもう一つの利点は，新陳代謝を促進することである。研究者グループがカプサイシンと体重に関する90の研究を分析し，人は辛いものを食べると食欲が減退することがわかった。**問2-B** これは，辛い食べ物が心拍数を上げ，筋肉により多くのエネルギーを送り，脂肪をエネルギーに変えるからである。最近，ワイオミング大学の科学者たちは，カプサイシンを主成分とする減量薬を作った。

また，トウガラシは食品の安全性とも関係があり，より健康的な生活につながるだろうと信じられている。

食品を冷蔵保存されない環境に放置すると微生物が増殖し，食べると病気の原因になる可能性がある。**問 2-E** 研究で，トウガラシに見つかるカプサイシンやその他の化学物質には，微生物の繁殖を遅らせたり，止めたりすることさえできる抗菌作用があるとわかってきた。その結果，食べ物が長持ちし，食中毒が少なくなる。**問 4** このことは，暑い気候の地域の人々がより多くのトウガラシを使い，そのため繰り返しトウガラシにさらされるのでより辛い食べ物に対する耐性が強くなる傾向があることの理由を説明するかもしれない。また，昔冷蔵庫ができる前は，彼らは涼しい気候の地域の人々よりも食中毒になりにくかった。

トウガラシは健康に良い点があるようだが，健康に悪い点もあるのだろうか。スコヴィル・スケールの高いトウガラシは大量に食べると体に不調をきたすことがある。**問 3** 世界一辛いトウガラシのいくつかを短時間に食べた人々は，胃の不調，下痢，手のしびれ，心臓発作に似た症状を経験したと報告している。ゴーストペッパーは，100万 SHU を含むものだが，触れると皮膚が火傷することさえある。

幸いなことに，辛いものを食べたあとに人々が感じる不快感は，すぐに，通常は数時間以内になくなる傾向がある。副作用があるにもかかわらず，辛い食べ物は世界中で人気があり続け，食卓に風味を添えている。辛いものを摂取するのは安全だが，料理に入れるトウガラシの量には注意した方がよいかもしれないことを覚えておこう。

プレゼンテーションスライド：

トウガラシ：

人生のスパイス

1

特徴

トウガラシ	ワサビ
・油のような成分 ・TRPV1の誘因となる ・持続する感覚	・ 44 ・気化する ・突然くる辛さ

2

良い影響

カプサイシンは 45 ことができる

A.　痛みを軽減する。

B.　より多くのエネルギーを与える。

C.　新陳代謝を促進する。

D.　ストレスを感じにくくする。

E.　食中毒の発生を減少させる。

3

悪影響

短時間に強いトウガラシを食べ過ぎた場合，

・ 46

・ 47

4

スパイス耐性

48

5

結びの所見

49

6

◆解説◆

問 1　44　❹

「スライド２のワサビの１つ目の特徴は何か。」

44

①「辛くてヒリヒリする味」≫**トウガラシの特徴。**

②「火のように熱い感覚」≫**トウガラシの特徴。**

③「持続する感覚」≫**気化しやすいので長く続かない。**

❹**「軽い化合物」**

本文・全訳の**問 1**に「香辛料化合物の濃度が低い」とあるので❹が正解。

問 2　45　❹

「スライド３で見つけた誤りはどれか。」 45

①「A」≫**本文に一致する。**

②「B」≫**本文に一致する。**

③「C」≫**本文に一致する。**

❹**「D」**

⑤「E」≫**本文に一致する。**

A・B・C・Eは本文・全訳の**問 2-A**，**問 2-B**，**問 2-C**，**問 2-E** の内容に一致する。**問 2-D** に書かれているように，トウガラシに含まれるカプサイシンが「人の体内の TRPV1受容体を活性化する時，それはストレスやケガの痛みを経験する時に起こることと似ている」ので，❹が正解。

問3 46 47 ❷，❸（順不同）

「スライド4に入れる選択肢を2つ選びなさい。（順不同。）」 46 47

① 「有害な細菌を活性化させる可能性がある。」≫**本文に書かれていることの逆。**

❷「胃痛を感じるかもしれない。」 46

❸「手の感覚がなくなるかもしれない。」 47

④「指に火がついたような感じがするかもしれない。」≫**ゴーストペッパーに触れた時の症状。**

⑤「鼻が痛くなるかもしれない。」≫**ワサビを食べた時の症状。**

強いトウガラシの副作用は本文・全訳の**問3**に列挙されている。本文の upset stomachs（胃の不調）を stomach pain（胃痛）と言い換えた❷と，numb hands（手のしびれ）を lose feeling in your hands（手の感覚がなくなる）と言い換えた❸が正解。

問4 48 ❸

「スライド5で香辛料に対する耐性について推測できることは何か。」 48

①「トウガラシに耐性が高い人は，料理に使う香辛料に注意を払う。」≫**本文にない。**

②「ワサビに対する耐性が高い人は，トウガラシの悪影響を怖れる。」≫**本文にない。**

❸「トウガラシに対する耐性が低い人は，その辛さに慣れることができる。」

④「ワサビに対する耐性が低い人は，SHU レベルが高いものに耐えられない。」≫**本文にない。**

本文・全訳の**問4**に「繰り返しトウガラシにさらされることで辛い食べものに対する耐性が強くなる」とある。つまり，トウガラシを食べていれば慣れてくるので，正解は❸である。

問5 49 ❺

「スライド6に入れるのに最も適当な所見を選びなさい。」 49

①「怖がらないで。辛いものを食べると 自信が高まります。」≫**本文にない。**

②「次にチリチキンを食べる時は，その刺激が一瞬しか残らないことを思い出そう。」≫**刺激がすぐになくなるのはワサビ。**

③「辛さの好みは性格が大いに関わってくるので，気にしないこと。」≫**本文にない。**

④「残念ながら，ワサビ耐性の弱さは治療法がない。」≫**本文にない。**

❺「誰かが辛い食べ物を勧めてくれたら，それには効能があることを思い出そう。」

締めくくりの所見は肯定的で励ましを与えるものにするのがよい。本文・全訳の**問5**に「トウガラシを摂取することは健康に良い影響を与える可能性がある」と書かれており，第4～6段落にはカプサイシンの効能があげられている。したがって「辛い食べ物（＝トウガラシを含む食べ物）には効能がある」という内容の❺が適当である。

【設問・選択肢の語句・表現】

問3 ① bacteria 名 細菌

問4 infer 他 ～を推察する

問5 ① boost 他 ～を強化する

2023 本試　解答

第1問小計	第2問小計	第3問小計	第4問小計	第5問小計	第6問小計	合計点
						/100

問題番号(配点)	設問		解答番号	正解	配点	自己採点
第1問 (10)	A	1	1	①	2	
		2	2	④	2	
	B	1	3	③	2	
		2	4	④	2	
		3	5	③	2	
第2問 (20)	A	1	6	②	2	
		2	7	②	2	
		3	8	②	2	
		4	9	④	2	
		5	10	①	2	
	B	1	11	④	2	
		2	12	①	2	
		3	13	①	2	
		4	14	①	2	
		5	15	②	2	
第3問 (15)	A	1	16	②	3	
		2	17	③	3	
	B	1	18	③	3※	
			19	④		
			20	②		
			21	①		
		2	22	③	3	
		3	23	②	3	

問題番号(配点)	設問		解答番号	正解	配点	自己採点
第4問 (16)	1		24	①	3	
	2		25	①	3	
	3		26	②	2	
			27	⑤	2	
	4		28	①	3	
	5		29	②	3	
第5問 (15)	1		30	④	3	
	2		31	③	3	
	3		32	②	3※	
			33	④		
			34	⑤		
			35	③		
	4		36	③	3	
	5		37 ～ 38	①-⑤	3※	
第6問 (24)	A	1	39	③	3	
		2	40	④	3	
		3	41 ～ 42	④-⑥	3※	
		4	43	①	3	
	B	1	44	④	2	
		2	45 ～ 46	①-⑤	3※	
		3	47	③	2	
		4	48	④	2	
		5	49	④	3	

(注)　1　※は，全部正解の場合のみ点を与える。
　　　2　-(ハイフン)でつながれた正解は，順序を問わない。

問●と囲み枠内…正解の根拠となる箇所

第1問A

第1問 （配点 10）

A You are studying in the US, and as an afternoon activity you need to choose one of two performances to go and see. Your teacher gives you this handout.

Performances for Friday

Palace Theater	Grand Theater
Together Wherever	***The Guitar Queen***
A romantic play that will make you laugh and cry	A rock musical featuring colorful costumes
▸ From 2:00 p.m. (no breaks and a running time of one hour and 45 minutes)	▸ Starts at 1:00 p.m. (three hours long including two 15-minute breaks)
問2(1) ▸ Actors available to talk in the lobby after the performance	問2(2) ▸ Opportunity to greet the cast in their costumes before the show starts
▸ No food or drinks available	▸ Light refreshments (snacks & drinks), original T-shirts, and other goods sold in the lobby
▸ Free T-shirts for five lucky people	

問1 Instructions: Which performance would you like to attend? Fill in the form below and hand it in to your teacher today.

✂- -

Choose (✔) one: *Together Wherever* □ *The Guitar Queen* □

Name: ________________________

【語句・表現】

l. 2 handout 名 プリント

*l.*17 feature 他 ～を呼び物にする

*l.*18 costume 名 衣装

*l.*25 refreshment 名 軽食

*l.*29 hand in ～ ～を提出する（代名詞の場合は hand と in の間に置く）

◆全訳◆

A あなたはアメリカで勉強中で，午後の活動として，2つの公演から見に行く1つを選ぶ必要があります。先生がこのプリントを渡しています。

金曜日の公演

パレスシアター	グランドシアター
『どこでもいっしょ』	『ギター・クイーン』
笑って泣けるロマンチックな劇	カラフルな衣装を呼び物にするロックミュージカル
▶午後2時から（休憩なし，上演時間1時間45分）	▶午後1時開演（15分休憩2回を含む3時間の公演）
問2(1) ▶公演のあと，ロビーにて俳優と話ができます	問2(2) ▶ショーが始まる前，衣装を着たキャストに挨拶する機会があります
▶飲食物は入手できません	▶ロビーにて軽食（スナックと飲み物），オリジナルTシャツとその他のグッズを販売
▶ラッキーな5人にTシャツを無料プレゼント	

問1 指示：どちらの公演に行きたいですか。以下のフォームに記入して，本日，先生に渡してください。

1つ選ぶ（✓）
どこでもいっしょ□　ギター・クイーン□
名前：＿＿＿＿＿＿＿＿

◆解説◆

問1　1　❶

「プリントを読んだあと，何をするように指示されているか。」 1

❶「下部のすべての項目に記入し，提出する。」

②「公演についてもっと調べる。」≫本文にない。

③「自分の決定を先生に話す。」≫話すのではなく用紙で提出する。

④「自分の名前を書いて，自分の選択を説明する。」≫チェックマークを入れるだけで，説明する必要はない。

本文・全訳の**問1**から❶が正解。設問では the form below（以下のフォーム）を the bottom part（下部）と言い換えている。

問2　2　❹

「両公演について，正しいものはどれか。」 2

①「公演前に飲み物を購入できない。」≫「どこでもいっしょ」のみに該当。

②「いくつかのTシャツがプレゼントとしてもらえる。」≫「どこでもいっしょ」のみに該当。

③「同じ時刻に終わる。」≫「どこでもいっしょ」は午後3時45分，「ギター・クイーン」は午後4時に終了する。

❹「劇場で出演者に会うことができる。」

本文・全訳の**問2(1)**，**問2(2)**から❹が正解。どちらの公演も，出演者と会う機会が用意されている。

【設問・選択肢の語句・表現】

問1 ❶ complete 他 ～の全項目に記入する

問2 ① purchase 他 ～を購入する

第1問B

B　You are a senior high school student interested in improving your English during the summer vacation. You find a website for an intensive English summer camp run by an international school.

GIS

Intensive English Summer Camp

Galley International School (GIS) has provided intensive English summer camps for senior high school students in Japan since 1989. Spend two weeks in an all-English environment!

問2(1) **Dates**: August 1-14, 2023

Location: Lake Kawaguchi Youth Lodge, Yamanashi Prefecture

Cost: 120,000 yen, including food and accommodation (additional fees for optional activities such as kayaking and canoeing)

Courses Offered

◆**FOREST**: You'll master basic grammar structures, make short speeches on

【語句・表現】

l. 2 intensive 形 集中的な

l.10 accommodation 名 宿泊（施設）

l.10 additional 形 追加の

l.11 optional 形 任意〔オプション〕の

l.13 structure 名 構造

問1(1) simple topics, and get pronunciation tips. Your instructors have taught
15 English for over 20 years in several countries. On the final day of the camp,
問2(2) you'll take part in a speech contest while all the other campers listen.

◆**MOUNTAIN**: You'll work in a group to write and perform a skit in English.
問1(2) Instructors for this course have worked at theater schools in New York City, London, and Sydney. You'll perform your skit for all the campers to enjoy on
20 August 14. 問2(3)

問1(3)
◆**SKY**: You'll learn debating skills and critical thinking in this course. Your instructors have been to many countries to coach debate teams and some 問2(4) have published best-selling textbooks on the subject. You'll do a short debate in front of all the other campers on the last day. (Note: Only those
25 with an advanced level of English will be accepted.)

▲**Application**

Step 1: Fill in the online application **HERE** by May 20, 2023.

問3 **Step 2**: We'll contact you to set up an interview to assess your English ability and ask about your course preference.

30 **Step 3**: You'll be assigned to a course.

l.16 take part in ～ ～に参加する
l.17 skit 名 寸劇
l.21 debate 自 ディベート〔公開討論〕する
l.21 critical thinking クリティカル・シンキング，批判的思考法
l.28 assess 他 ～を評価する
l.29 preference 名（選択の）好み
l.30 assign 他 ～を割り当てる

◆全訳◆

B あなたは，夏休みの間に英語を上達させることに関心がある高校生です。インターナショナルスクールが運営する集中英語サマーキャンプのウェブサイトを見つけました。

GIS 集中英語サマーキャンプ

ギャリー・インターナショナル・スクール（GIS）は1989年以来，日本の高校生のための集中英語サマーキャンプを提供しています。オールイングリッシュの環境で2週間を過ごしてみましょう！

問2(1) 日程：2023年8月1日～14日
場所：山梨県 河口湖ユースロッジ
費用：12万円，食事・宿泊費用込み（カヤック・カヌーなどのオプションのアクティビティには追加費用が必要）

提供コース

◆**フォレスト**：基本的な文法構造を習得し，簡単なトピックで短いスピーチを行い，発音のコツを学びます。問1(1) 講師たちは，数カ国で20年以上英語を教えた経験があります。問2(2) キャンプの最終日には，他の全キャンプ参加者が聞いている中，スピーチコンテストに参加します。

◆**マウンテン**：英語で寸劇を作り演じるためにグループで学習します。問1(2) このコースの講師たちはニューヨークシティ，ロンドン，シドニーの演劇学校で働いた経験があります。問2(3) 8月14日には，全キャンプ参加者に楽しんでもらえるように寸劇を演じます。

◆**スカイ**：このコースではディベートの技術やクリティカル・シンキングを学びます。問1(3) 講師たちは多くの国へディベートチームの指導に行った経験があり，中にはこの題材のベストセラーの教科書を出版した人もいます。問2(4) 最終日に他の全キャンプ参加者の前で短いディベートを行います。（注：英語力が上級レベルの人のみ入れます。）

▲**申し込み**

ステップ1：2023年5月20日までに，**こちら**のオンライン申し込みに記入してください。

ステップ2：問3 こちらからご連絡し，皆さんの英語能力を評価し，ご希望のコースについて伺うための面接を設定します。

ステップ3：コースに割り当てられます。

◆解説◆

問1 3 ❸

「GISの講師は全員[3]。」

① 「1989年から日本に滞在している」≫GISはキャンプを1989年から行っているが，講師全員が当時からいるとは限らない。

② 「国際的なコンテストで優勝したことがある」≫本文にない。

❸「海外で働いたことがある」

④ 「人気書籍を執筆したことがある」≫スカイコースの一部の講師のみ該当する。

本文・全訳の**問1(1)**，**問1(2)**，**問1(3)**から❸が正解。各コースの講師は海外で英語や演劇，ディベートの指導をした経験がある。

問2 4 ❹

「キャンプ最終日，キャンプ参加者は[4]。」

① 「互いのパフォーマンスを評価し合う」≫発表はするが，評価するとは書いていない。

② 「最優秀賞を得るために競う」≫フォレストコースにはコンテストがあるが，他のコースでは賞のために競わない。

③ 「将来についての発表をする」≫発表するのは，将来についてではない。

❹「キャンプで学んだことを発表する」

本文・全訳の**問2(1)**，**問2(2)**，**問2(3)**，**問2(4)**から❹が正解。最終日（=8月14日）に，それぞれのコースで学習したことを，キャンプ参加者全員の前で発表すると書かれている。

問3 5 ❸

「キャンプの申し込みを提出したあとで，何が起こりますか。」[5]

① 「英語講師に電話連絡する。」≫本文にない。

② 「英語の筆記試験を受ける。」≫筆記試験ではなく面接試験である。

❸「英語レベルがチェックされる。」

④ 「英語スピーチのトピックが送られる。」≫本文にない。

本文・全訳の**問3**から❸が正解。面接による英語の能力テストがある。

【設問・選択肢の語句・表現】

問3 submit 他 ～を提出する

第2問A

第2問 (配点 20)

問2(1)

A You want to buy a good pair of shoes as you walk a long way to school and often get sore feet. You are searching on a UK website and find this advertisement.

Navi 55 presents the new *Smart Support* shoe line

Smart Support shoes are strong, long-lasting, and reasonably priced. They are available in three colours and styles.

Special Features

問1

Smart Support shoes have a nano-chip which analyses the shape of your feet when connected to the *iSupport* application. Download the app onto your

【語句・表現】

l. 2 get sore feet 足が痛くなる

l. 6 reasonably 副 適切に

l. 9 analyse〈英〉他 ～を分析する

smartphone, PC, tablet, and/or smartwatch. Then, while wearing the shoes, let the chip collect the data about your feet. The inside of the shoe will automatically adjust to give correct, personalised foot support. As with other Navi 55 products, the shoes have our popular Route Memory function.

15 **Advantages**

問2(2) **Better Balance**: Adjusting how you stand, the personalised support helps keep feet, legs, and back free from pain.

Promotes Exercise: As they are so comfortable, you will be willing to walk regularly.

20 **Route Memory**: The chip records your daily route, distance, and pace as you walk.

問4(1) **Route Options**: View your live location on your device, have the directions play automatically in your earphones, or use your smartwatch to read directions.

25 **Customers' Comments**

- 問4(2) I like the choices for getting directions, and prefer using audio guidance to visual guidance.
- I lost 2 kg in a month!
- I love my pair now, but 問5 it took me several days to get used to them.
- 30 As they don't slip in the rain, I wear mine all year round.
- They are so light and comfortable I even wear them when cycling.
- Easy to get around! I don't need to worry about getting lost.
- 問3 They look great. The app's basic features are easy to use, but I wouldn't pay for the optional advanced ones.

l.13 automatically 副 自動的に
l.13 adjust 自 調整される（*l*.16では 他 ～を調整する）
l.13 as with ～ ～と同様に
l.14 function 名 機能
l.17 free from ～ ～がない
l.18 promote 他 ～を促進する
l.18 *be* willing to *do* 進んで…する
l.22 device 名 機器
l.26 guidance 名 案内
l.27 visual 形 視覚の
l.29 get used to ～ ～に慣れる

◆全訳◆

A 問2(1) あなたは学校まで長距離を歩くとよく足が痛くなるので，良い靴を買いたいと思っています。英国のウェブサイトで探していて，この広告を見つけました。

ナビ55から新しいスマートサポートシューズの商品を発表

スマートサポートシューズは，丈夫で長持ち，そしてお手頃な価格です。3つの色とスタイルで発売中です。　（イラスト：ナノチップ）

特別な機能

問1 スマートサポートシューズは，*i* サポートアプリケーションに接続されると，あなたの足の形状を分析するナノチップを搭載しています。スマートフォン，パソコン，タブレット，スマートウォッチにアプリをダウンロードしてください。そして，シューズを履いている間にチップに足のデータを収集させます。靴の内部が的確に個人に合った足のサポートをするために自動的に調整されます。ナビ55の他の商品同様に，この靴は我が社の人気があるルートメモリー機能を搭載しています。

長所

問2(2) **より良いバランス**：個人対応のサポートがあなたの立ち方を調整し，足，脚，腰の痛みから解放してくれます。

運動を促進する：とても快適なので，進んで定期的にウォーキングをするようになるでしょう。

ルートメモリー：日常のルート，距離，歩くペースを，あなたが歩く時チップが記録します。

問4(1) **ルートオプション**：機器であなたの現在地を見たり，イヤホンで道案内を自動再生したり，道案内を読むのにスマートウォッチを使ったりしてください。

お客様のコメント

問4(2) ●道案内の選択肢があるのが気に入っています。視覚的な案内よりもオーディオ案内を使う方が好きです。

●1カ月で2kgやせました！

●今は自分の靴をとても気に入っていますが，**問5** 靴に慣れるまで数日かかりました。

●雨でも滑らないので，1年中履いています。

●とても軽くて快適なので，サイクリングをする時でも履いています。

●あちこち移動するのに楽です！迷子になる心配がありません。

●見た目が素晴らしい。**問3** アプリの基本的な機能は使いやすいですが，オプションの高度な機能にはお金を払わないでしょう。

◆解説◆

問1　6　❷

「メーカーの発表によると，新しい靴を最もよく説明しているのはどれか。」［6］

①「安い夏用の靴」≫**「夏用」と書かれていない。**

❷「ハイテクな普段用の靴」

③「軽い快適なスポーツシューズ」≫**「スポーツ用」と書かれていない。**

④「洗練されたカラフルなサイクリングシューズ」≫**メーカーの発表ではサイクリング用と書いていない。**

本文・全訳の**問1**に靴の機能が書かれているが，靴に搭載されたナノチップからアプリにデータを送るハイテクな靴である。したがって❷が正解。

問2　7　❷

「この靴が提供するどの利点があなたには最も魅力がありそうか。」［7］

①「定期的な運動をもっとするようになる」≫**足の痛みという問題の解決にならない。**

❷「個人対応の足のサポートをする」

③「歩く速さを知る」≫**問題の解決にならない。**

④「履いているとかっこよく見える」≫**見た目が素晴らしいというコメントはあるが，問題の解決にならない。**

本文・全訳の**問2(1)**で挙げた「足の痛み」というあなたの問題の解決に役立つ利点は**問2(2)**なので，❷が正解。

問3　8　❷

「顧客が述べた**意見**は［8］である。」

①「アプリが早歩きを促す」≫**コメントにない。**

❷「アプリの無料機能は使いやすい」

③「靴は購入する価値がある」≫**コメントにない。**

④「靴が自転車をこぐスピードを上げる」≫**自転車に乗る時も靴を履くと言っているだけ。**

本文・全訳の**問3**から❷が正解。この顧客は有料機能を使っていないのだから，文中の「基本的な機能」=「無料機能」と言える。

問4　9　❹

「ある顧客のコメントはオーディオ装置の使用について言及している。このコメントはどの利点に基づいているか。」［9］

①「より良いバランス」

②「運動を促進する」

③「ルートメモリー」

❹「ルートオプション」

本文・全訳の**問4(2)**で，顧客が道案内にオーディオ案内を使うのが好きだとコメントしている。これに相当するのは，**問4(1)**のルートオプションの中のイヤホンで聞く道案内なので，❹が正解。

問5　10　❶

「顧客の意見によると，［10］が薦められている。」

❶「靴を履き慣れるのに時間の余裕をみること」

②「体重を減らすのに役立つウォッチを買うこと」≫**体重が減ったコメントはあるが，ウォッチに言及していない。**

③「靴を履く前にアプリに接続すること」≫**コメントにない。**

④「iサポートの高度な機能のためにお金を払うこと」≫「**高度な機能は買わない」と言っている。**

本文・全訳の問5に書いている経験から，❶のアドバイスをしたと考える。get used to ～，get accustomed to ～はいずれも「～に慣れる」の意味。

【設問・選択肢の語句・表現】

問1 statement 名 発表

問2 appeal 自 魅力がある

問3 ❷ user-friendly 形 使いやすい

問3 ③ good value for money 購入する価値がある

問5 ❶ allow time to *do* …する時間の余裕をみる

第2問B

B You are a member of the student council. The members have been discussing a student project helping students to use their time efficiently. To get ideas, you are reading a report about a school challenge. It was written by an exchange student who studied in another school in Japan.

5

Commuting Challenge

Most students come to my school by bus or train. I often see a lot of students playing games on their phones or chatting. However, they could also 問1 use this time for reading or doing homework. We started this activity to help students use their commuting time more effectively. Students had to complete 問2(1) a commuting activity chart from January 17th to February 17th. (10) A total of 300 students participated. More than two thirds of them were second-years; about 問5(1) a quarter were third-years; 問2(2) only 15 first-years participated. How come so few first-years participated? Based on the feedback (given below), there seems to be an answer to this question:

(15) **Feedback from participants**

問3-B HS: Thanks to this project, I got the highest score ever in an English vocabulary test. It was easy to set small goals to complete on my way.

問4 KF: My friend was sad because she couldn't participate. She lives nearby and walks to school. There should have been other ways to take part.

(20) SS: My train is always crowded and I have to stand, so there is no space to open a book or a tablet. I only used audio materials, but there were not nearly enough. 問3-A

JH: I kept a study log, which made me realise how I used my time. For some 問5(2) reason most of my first-year classmates didn't seem to know about this (25) challenge.

MN: I spent most of the time on the bus watching videos, and it helped me to understand classes better. I felt the time went very fast.

【語句・表現】

l. 1 student council 生徒会

l. 2 efficiently 副 効率的に

l. 5 commuting 名 通学

l. 9 effectively 副 有効に

*l.*10 chart 名 表

*l.*11 participate 自 参加する

*l.*12 how come なぜ

*l.*13 feedback 名 フィードバック，意見

*l.*21 not nearly enough 決して十分ではない

*l.*23 log 名 記録，日誌

◆全訳◆

B　あなたは生徒会のメンバーです。メンバーは，生徒が時間を効率的に使えるようにするための学生プロジェクトについて話し合っています。アイデアを得るために，あなたはある学校の挑戦に関するレポートを読んでいます。それは日本の他の学校で学習している交換留学生によって書かれたものです。

通学チャレンジ

私の学校には，ほとんどの生徒がバスや電車で通学します。多くの生徒がスマホでゲームをしたり，おしゃべりしたりしているのをよく見かけます。しかし，この時間を読書や宿題をするのに使うことも可能なはずです。**問1** 私たちは，生徒が通学時間をもっと有効に使うのに役立つように，この活動を始めました。1月17日から2月17日まで，生徒は通学時間の活動表を記入する必要がありました。**問2(1)** 合計300人の生徒が参加しました。3分の2以上が2年生，約4分の1が3年生で，**問2(2)** 1年生は15人だけが参加しました。**問5(1)** なぜ，1年生の参加がそんなに少ないのか？（以下に示した）意見に基づくと，この質問への答えがあるようです。

参加者からのフィードバック

HS：**問3-B** このプロジェクトのおかげで，英単語のテストで過去最高の点数を取りました。小さな目標を立てて，道中で達成するのは簡単でした。

KF：**問4** 友達が参加できなくて悲しんでいました。友達は近くに住んでいて，徒歩通学しています。他の参加方法があるべきだったと思います。

SS：私が乗る電車はいつも混んでいて，立たなければならないので，本やタブレットを開くスペースがありません。オーディオ教材だけを使いましたが，決して十分な量の教材はありませんでした。

JH：**問3-A** 学習記録をつけ，そのことがどのように自分が時間を使っているかを気づかせてくれました。どういうわけか，**問5(2)** ほとんどの1年生のクラスメイトはこのチャレンジについて知らなかったようです。

MN：私はバスの中でほとんどの時間はビデオを見て過ごし，それが授業をより理解するのに役立ちました。時間が経つのがとてもはやく感じました。

◆解説◆

問1　11　❹

「通学チャレンジの目的は，生徒が 11 のを助けることであった。」

①「もっとはやく通学する」≫**本文にない。**

②「テストの点数を上げる」≫**目的ではなく，ある生徒の結果である。**

③「英語の授業をもっとうまく運営する」≫**本文にない。**

❹**「時間をよりよく使う」**

本文・全訳の**問1**から❹が正解。文中の this activity は「通学チャレンジ」を指す。

問2　12　❶

「通学チャレンジに関する1つの<u>事実</u>は 12 ことである。」

❶**「参加者のうち10%未満が1年生だった」**

②「冬の間に2カ月間行われた」≫**実施期間は1カ月。**

③「生徒はバスで携帯機器を使わなければならなかった」≫**本文にない。**

④「参加者の大多数が電車で行った」≫**参加者の交通手段の割合については本文にない。**

本文・全訳の**問2(1)** **問2(2)**によると，参加者300人のうち15人が1年生なので，5%に相当するため，❶が正解。

問3　13　❶

「フィードバックによると， 13 は参加者に報告された活動である。」

A「学習記録をつけること」

B「言語を学習すること」

C「タブレットでメモを取ること」≫**本文にない。**

D「携帯電話で授業の記録を読むこと」≫**本文にない。**

❶**「AとB」**

②「AとC」

③「AとD」

④「BとC」

⑤「BとD」

⑥「CとD」

本文・全訳の**問3-A**はAの内容に一致し，**問3-B**はBの内容に一致する。したがって，❶が正解。

問4 14 ❶

「通学チャレンジについての参加者の意見の１つは 14 である。」

❶「徒歩で通学している生徒も含めることができただろう」

②「電車は本を読むのに良い場所だった」≫ SS が電車で本を読めなかったと書いている。

③「学習のためのオーディオ教材がたくさんあった」≫ SS がオーディオ教材は十分なかったと書いている。

④「娯楽のためのビデオを見ることは時間が速く過ぎるのを助けた」≫ MN が見ていたのは娯楽用ではなく，授業の理解に役立つもの。

本文・全訳の**問4**から❶が正解。本文中の〈should have＋過去分詞〉は「…するべきだったのに」，❶の〈could have＋過去分詞〉は「…できただろう」の意味。

問5 15 ❷

「筆者の質問は 15 に答えられている。」

①「HS」

❷「JH」

③「KF」

④「MN」

⑤「SS」

筆者の質問は，本文・全訳の**問5 (1)**に書かれている。答えは**問5 (2)**にあるので，❷が正解。

【設問・選択肢の語句・表現】

問2 ③ portable 形 携帯用の

問2 ④ majority 名 大多数

第3問A

第3問 （配点 15）

A You are studying at Camberford University, Sydney. You are going on a class camping trip and are reading the camping club's newsletter to prepare.

Going camping? Read me!!!

Hi, I'm Kaitlyn. I want to share two practical camping lessons from my recent club trip. The first thing is to divide your backpack into three main parts and put the heaviest items in the middle section to balance the backpack. Next, more frequently used daily necessities should be placed in the top section. **問1** That means putting your sleeping bag at the bottom; food, cookware and tent in the middle; and your clothes at the top. Most good backpacks come with a "brain" (an additional pouch) for small easy-to-reach items.

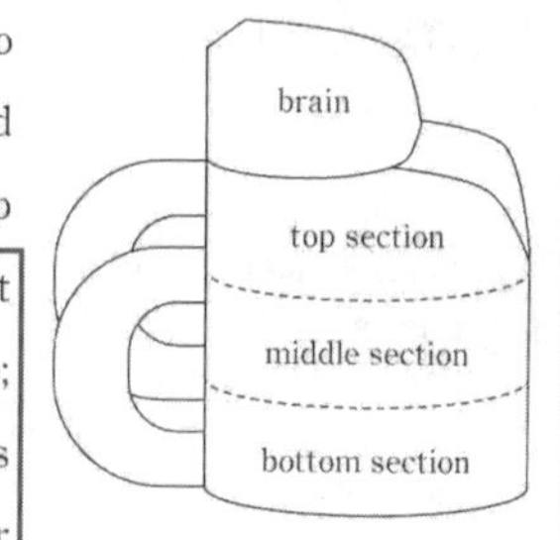

Last year, in the evening, we had fun cooking and eating outdoors. I had been sitting close to our campfire, but by the time I got back to the tent I was freezing. Although I put on extra layers of clothes before going to sleep, I was

【語句・表現】

l. 4 practical 形 実用的な

l. 7 balance 他 ～のバランスをとる

l. 8 necessity 名 必需品

l. 9 that means つまり

l.12 come with ～ ～が付いている

l.12 pouch 名 ポーチ

l.13 easy-to-reach 形 便利な，手が届きやすい

l.16 layer 名 重ね，層

問2 still cold. Then, my friend told me to take off my outer layers and stuff them into my sleeping bag to fill up some of the empty space. This stuffing method was new to me, and surprisingly kept me warm all night!

20 I hope my advice helps you stay warm and comfortable. Enjoy your camping trip!

l.17 outer 形 外側の
l.17 stuff A into B BにAを詰める

◆全訳◆

A　あなたはシドニーにあるキャンバーフォード大学で勉強しています。あなたはクラスのキャンプ旅行に行くことになり，準備のためにキャンプクラブの会報を読んでいます。

キャンプに行く？読んで!!!

こんにちは，ケイトリンです。最近のクラブ旅行から学んだ実用的なキャンプの知識を2つ共有したいと思います。1つ目は，バックパックを3つの主要な部分に分け，バックパックのバランスをとるために，いちばん重いものを真ん中の部分に入れることです。次に，より使用頻度の高い日用必需品は上の部分に置かなければなりません。

ブレイン
上の部分
真ん中の部分
底の部分

問1 つまり寝袋は底に，食料，調理器具，テントは真ん中に，そして衣類は一番上に入れるということです。ほとんどの良いバックパックには，小さな便利な物を入れるための「ブレイン」（追加のポーチ）が付いています。

昨年，夕方に野外で料理や食事を楽しみました。ずっとキャンプファイアの近くに座っていたのですが，テントに戻る時までには凍えていました。寝る前に追加で重ね着をしたけれども，まだ寒かったです。**問2** そこで友人が外側に着ているものを脱いで，寝袋の中に空いた空間をふさぐように詰めるよう教えてくれました。この詰め物をする方法は私にとって初めての体験で，驚くほど一晩中体を暖かくしてくれました！

私のアドバイスが，皆さんが暖かく快適に過ごすのに役に立てばいいなと思います。キャンプ旅行を楽しんでください！

◆解説◆

問1 16 ❷

「ケイトリンのアドバイスを受け入れるなら，バックパックをどのように詰めるべきか。」 16

①
救急セット，地図
食料，皿，カップ，テント
上着，シャツ，ズボン
寝袋

❷
救急セット，地図
上着，シャツ，ズボン
食料，皿，カップ，テント
寝袋

③
食料，皿，カップ，テント
救急セット，地図
上着，シャツ，ズボン
寝袋

④
上着，シャツ，ズボン
救急セット，地図
食料，皿，カップ，テント
寝袋

本文・全訳の**問1**から❷が正解。選択肢では，「調理器具」を「皿，カップ」，「衣類」を「上着，シャツ，ズボン」と具体的に書いている。また，救急セットと地図は，ブレインに入れる「小さな便利な物」と考える。

問2 17 ❸

「ケイトリンによると， 17 が一晩中暖かく過ごす最適な方法だ。」

① 「テントから外に出るのを避けること」 ≫**本文にない。**

② 「キャンプファイアの横で温かい食事をとること」 ≫**この方法を実行したが，凍えたと書いてある。**

❸ **「寝袋の隙間を埋めること」**

④ 「余分な服を全部着ること」 ≫**この方法を実行したが，**

まだ寒かったと書いてある。

本文・全訳の**問2**から❸が正解。本文の empty space を❸では gap と言い換えている。

【設問・選択肢の語句・表現】

問1 first aid kit 救急セット

第3問B

B　Your English club will make an "adventure room" for the school festival. To get some ideas, you are reading a blog about a room a British man created.

Create Your Own "Home Adventure"

問3(1) Last year, I took part in an "adventure room" experience. I really enjoyed it, so I created one for my children. Here are some tips on making your own.

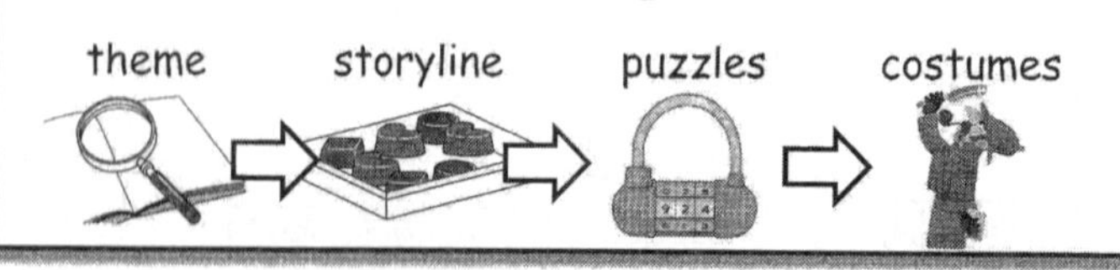

First, pick a theme. My sons are huge Sherlock Holmes fans, so I decided on a detective mystery. **問1③** I rearranged the furniture in our family room, and added some old paintings and lamps I had to set the scene.

Next, create a storyline. Ours was *The Case of the Missing Chocolates*. My children would be "detectives" searching for clues to locate the missing sweets.

The third step is to design puzzles and challenges. A useful idea is to work backwards from the solution. If the task is to open a box locked with a three-digit padlock, think of ways to hide a three-digit code. Old books are fantastic for hiding messages in. I had tremendous fun underlining words on different pages to form mystery sentences. **問1④** Remember that the puzzles should get progressively more difficult near the final goal. **問2** To get into the spirit, I then had the children wear costumes. My eldest son was excited when I handed him a magnifying glass, and immediately began acting like Sherlock Holmes. **問1②** After that, the children started to search for the first clue.

【語句・表現】

l. 5　tip 名 ヒント

図内 key step 重要段階

図内 storyline 名 ストーリー展開，筋

l. 7　detective 形 探偵の

l. 8　set the scene 場所を設定する

*l.*10　clue 名 手がかり

*l.*10　locate 他 ～を見つける

*l.*10　missing 形 行方不明の

*l.*13　backwards from ～ ～からさかのぼって

*l.*13　task 名 課題

*l.*14　digit 名 数字，桁

*l.*14　padlock 名 南京錠

*l.*14　code 名 暗号

*l.*15　tremendous 形 とてつもなく大きい

*l.*17　progressively 副 徐々に

*l.*17　get into the spirit 盛り上がる

*l.*19　magnifying glass 虫眼鏡

問3(2) This "adventure room" was designed specifically for my family, so I made some of the challenges personal. 問1① For the final task, I took a couple of small cups and put a plastic sticker in each one, then filled them with yogurt. The "detectives" had to eat their way to the bottom to reveal the clues. Neither of
25 my kids would eat yogurt, so this truly was tough for them. During the adventure, my children were totally focused, and they enjoyed themselves so much that we will have another one next month.

l.23 sticker 名 シール
l.24 reveal 他 ～を明らかにする
l.25 tough 形 きつい
l.26 *be* focused 集中している

◆全訳◆

B　あなたの所属する英語クラブは，学園祭で「アドベンチャールーム」を作る予定です。アイデアを得るために，英国人の男性が作った部屋についてのブログを読んでいます。

自分の「ホームアドベンチャー 」を作ろう

問3(1) 昨年，私は「アドベンチャールーム」体験に参加しました。とても楽しかったので，自分の子供たちにも作りました。ここに，あなたが自分のアドベンチャールームを作るヒントがあります。

アドベンチャーを作る重要段階
テーマ→ ストーリー展開→ 謎解き→衣装

最初にテーマを決めます。私の息子たちはシャーロック・ホームズの大ファンなので，私は探偵ミステリーに決めました。問1③ 私はファミリールームの家具の配置を変え，場面設定するために，持っていた古い絵画やランプを加えました。

次にストーリー展開を創作します。私たちの場合は「行方不明のチョコレート事件」でした。子供たちは行方不明になったお菓子を見つける手がかりを探している「探偵」になるのです。

３つ目の段階は，謎解きと課題を考案することです。役に立つ考えは，解決策から逆算して取り組むことです。もし課題が３桁の数字の南京錠がかかった箱を開けることなら，３桁の数字の暗号を隠す方法を考えなさい。古い本はメッセージを隠すのに素晴らしいです。ミステリーの文章を構成するために，さまざまなページの単語にアンダーラインを引くのは，とっても楽しかったです。問2 最終目標に近づくにつれて，謎解きが段階的に難しくなるべきなのを覚えておいてください。問1④ それから気分が盛り上がるように，子供たちに衣装を着せました。長男は虫眼鏡を渡すと興奮していて，すぐにシャーロック・ホームズのように振る舞い始めました。問1② その後，子供たちは最初の手がかりを探し始めました。

問3(2) この「アドベンチャールーム」は私の家族用に特別に計画されたものなので，いくつか個人的な課題をつくりました。問1① 最後の課題に，小さなカップを２つ用意し，それぞれの内側にプラスチックのシールを貼って，ヨーグルトで満たしました。「探偵」は手がかりを明らかにするために底まで食べなければなりませんでした。私の子供はどちらもヨーグルトを食べようとしなかったので，これは子供たちにとって本当に難しいことでした。アドベンチャーの間，子供たちは完全に集中し，とても楽しんでいたので，来月も別のアドベンチャールームを開催する予定です。

◆解説◆

問1　18 ❸　19 ❹　20 ❷　21 ❶

「次の出来事（①～④）を起こった順に並べなさい。」
18 → 19 → 20 → 21

❶「子供たちが好きではない食べ物を食べた。」 21

❷「子供たちはお菓子の捜索を始めた。」 20

❸「父親は家のリビングルームを飾り付けた。」 18

❹「父親は息子たちに着る服を与えた。」 19

本文・全訳の 問1① ～ 問1④ を参照。本文の family room を❸では living room，costumes を❹では some clothes to wear と言い換えている。また，問1① の内容を簡潔にまとめると，「課題解決のために，子供たちが好きではないヨーグルトを食べた」ということ。

問2 22 ❸

「あなたが自分の『アドベンチャールーム』をつくるためにこの父親のアドバイスに従うなら， 22 べきだ。」

①「３文字の単語に集中する」≫本文にない。

②「秘密のメッセージをランプの下に置く」≫メッセージを隠すのは古い本の中がよいと言っている。

❸「課題を徐々に難しくする」

④「シャーロック・ホームズのように振る舞う練習をする」≫本文にない。

本文・全訳の 問2 と同じ内容の❸が正解。

問3 23 ❷

「この話から，この父親が 23 と理解できる。」

①「お菓子を探すことに集中するようになった」

≫お菓子探しに集中したのは父ではなく子供たち。

❷「特別に子供たちのために体験を作った」

③「アドベンチャーゲームを準備するのに少し苦労した」≫楽しんだと書いているが，苦労したとはない。

④「部屋を飾りつけるのにたくさんお金をかけた」

≫持っている古い絵画やランプを使ったと書いてある。

本文・全訳の 問3(1)，問3(2) に書いてあるように，自分の子供のために特別なアドベンチャールームを作ったので，❷が正解。

【設問・選択肢の語句・表現】

問2 ❸ gradually 副 徐々に（≒ progressively）

問3 ③ have trouble *doing* …するのに苦労する

第４問

第４問 （配点 16）

Your teacher has asked you to read two articles about effective ways to study. You will discuss what you learned in your next class.

How to Study Effectively: Contextual Learning!

Tim Oxford

Science Teacher, Stone City Junior High School

As a science teacher, I am always concerned about how to help students who struggle to learn. Recently, I found that their main way of learning was to study new information repeatedly until they could recall it all. For example, when they studied for a test, they would use a workbook like the example below and repeatedly say the terms that go in the blanks: "Obsidian is igneous, dark, and glassy. Obsidian is igneous, dark, and glassy. . . ." These students would feel as if they had learned the information, but would quickly forget it and get low scores on the test. 問1 Also, this sort of repetitive learning is dull and demotivating.

問4(1) To help them learn, I tried applying "contextual learning." In this kind of learning, new knowledge is constructed through students' own experiences. For my science class, students learned the properties of different kinds of rocks. Rather than having them memorize the terms from a workbook, I

【語句・表現】

l. 1 effective 形 効果的な

l. 3 contextual 形 文脈的な

l. 7 struggle 自 悪戦苦闘する

l. 8 recall 他 ～を思い出す

l.10 term 名 用語

l.10 obsidian 名 黒曜石

l.10 igneous 形 火成の

l.11 glassy 形 ガラス質の

l.12 feel as if SV（過去完了）S が…したように感じる

l.13 repetitive 形 反復的な

l.14 demotivating 形 やる気を失わせる

l.16 construct 他 ～を構築する

brought a big box of various rocks to the class. Students examined the rocks and identified their names based on the characteristics they observed.

Rock name	Obsidian
Rock type	igneous
Coloring	dark
Texture	glassy
Picture	

Thanks to this experience, I think these students will always be able to describe the properties of the rocks they studied. One issue, however, is that we don't always have the time to do contextual learning, so students will still study by doing drills. I don't think this is the best way. I'm still searching for ways to improve their learning.

How to Make Repetitive Learning Effective

Cheng Lee
Professor, Stone City University

問4(2) 問3(1) 問3(2)

Mr. Oxford's thoughts on contextual learning were insightful. I agree that it can be beneficial. Repetition, though, can also work well. However, the repetitive learning strategy he discussed, which is called "massed learning," is not effective. There is another kind of repetitive learning called "spaced learning," in which students memorize new information and then review it over longer intervals.

The interval between studying is the key difference. In Mr. Oxford's example, his students probably used their workbooks to study over a short period of time. In this case, they might have paid less attention to the content as they continued to review it. The reason for this is that the content was no longer new and could easily be ignored. In contrast, when the intervals are longer, the students' memory of the content is weaker. Therefore, they pay more attention because they have to make a greater effort to recall what they had learned before. For example, if students study with their workbooks, wait three days, and then study again, they are likely to learn the material better.

問5 問2

Previous research has provided evidence for the advantages of spaced learning. In one experiment, students in Groups A and B tried to memorize the names of 50 animals. Both groups studied four times, but Group A studied at one-day intervals while Group B studied at one-week intervals. As the figure to the right shows, 28 days after the last learning session, the average ratio of recalled names on a test was higher for the spaced learning group.

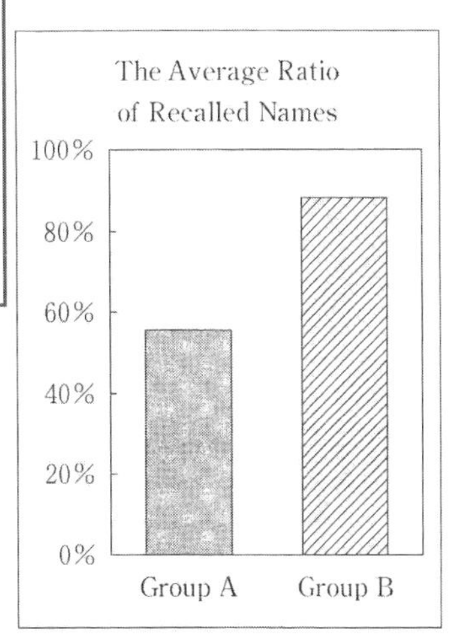

I understand that students often need to learn a lot of information in a short period of time, and long intervals between studying might not be practical. You should understand, though, that massed learning might not be good for long-term recall.

l.19 examine 他 ～を調べる
l.20 identify 他 ～を識別する
l.21 characteristic 名 特徴
l.21 observe 他 ～を観察する
l.24 property 名 性質
図内 texture 名 質感，手触り

l. 4 insightful 形 洞察力に満ちた
l. 5 beneficial 形 有益な
l. 5 repetition 名 反復
l. 6 strategy 名 方法
l. 6 massed learning 集中学習
l. 9 interval 名 間隔
l.12 content 名 内容
l.13 no longer もはや～ない
l.14 ignore 他 ～を無視する
l.14 in contrast 対照的に
l.18 *be* likely to *do* …する可能性が高い
l.19 evidence 名 証拠
l.32 practical 形 実用的な
l.35 recall 名 呼び戻し

◆全訳◆

先生があなたに，効果的な学習法に関する２つの記事を読むように勧めています。次の授業で，学んだことについて話し合うことになります。

効果的に学習する方法：文脈的学習！

ティム・オックスフォード
理科教師，ストーン市立中学校

理科教師として，私は勉強に悪戦苦闘する生徒を助ける方法にいつも関心があります。最近，彼らの主な学習方法は，新しい情報をすべて思い出せるようになるまで繰り返し勉強することだとわかりました。例えば，テスト勉強をする時，下記の例のようにワークブックを使い，空欄に入る用語を繰り返し言うでしょう。「黒曜石は火成岩で，暗くて，ガラス質である。 黒曜石は火成岩で，暗くて，ガラス質で…」このような生徒は，情報を覚えたような気になりますが，すぐに忘れて，テストでは低い点数を取るでしょう。**問１** また，この種の反復学習は退屈で，やる気を失わせます。**問４(1)** 彼らの学習を助けるために，私は「文脈的学習」を適用してみました。この種類の学習では，生徒自身の体験を通して新しい知識は構築されます。私の理科の授業では，生徒はさまざまな種類の岩石の性質を学びました。 ワークブックで用語を覚えさせるのではなく，さまざまな岩石が入った大きな箱を教室に持ち込みました。生徒たちは岩石を調べ，観察した特徴に基づいて名前を識別しました。

この体験のおかげで，生徒たちは，勉強した岩石の性質をいつでも説明できると思います。しかし１つ問題なのは，文脈的学習をする時間がいつもあるわけではないということで，そのため生徒たちはまだドリルで勉強するでしょう。これが最善の方法だとは思いません。彼らの学習を向上させる方法を今も模索中です。

岩石の名前	黒曜石
岩石のタイプ	火成岩
彩色	暗い
質感	ガラス質の
写真	

反復学習を効果的に行うには

チェン・リー
教授，ストーン市立大学

問４(2) オックスフォード氏の文脈的学習についての考え方は洞察に富んでいました。私もそれが有益でありうることに同意します。けれども，反復もうまく機能することがあります。**問３(1)** しかし，彼が考察した反復学習法は，「集中学習」と呼ばれるもので，効果的ではありません。**問３(2)** 「間隔学習」と呼ばれる，もう一種の反復学習があり，この方法では生徒は新しい情報を記憶したあと，比較的長い間隔をあけて復習します。

学習の間隔が重要な違いです。オックスフォード氏の例では，生徒たちは短期間の学習におそらくワークブックを使ったのでしょう。この場合，復習を続けるうちに，内容への注意が薄れてしまったかもしれません。その理由は，内容がもはや新しいものでなく，無視されやすくなったからです。対照的に，間隔が比較的長いと，生徒の内容の記憶は弱くなります。そのため，以前学習した内容を思い出すために，より大きな努力をしなければならないため，より多くの注意を払います。例えば，生徒がワークブックを使って勉強して，３日待ってからもう一度勉強すると，その教材をよりよく学習できる可能性が高いです。

問５ これまでの研究は，間隔学習の長所の証拠を提供しています。ある実験で，グループＡとグループＢの生徒が50匹の動物の名前を覚えようとしました。両グループとも４回学習しましたが，グループＡは１日の間隔をあけて，一方グループＢは１週間の間隔で学習しました。**問２** 右の図が示すように，最後の学習時間から28日後，テストで思い出した名前の平均割合は，間隔学習のグループの方が高かったのです。

生徒は短期間に多くの情報を習得する必要がある場合が多く，長い学習間隔は実用的でないかもしれないということは理解できます。しかし，集中学習は長期的な記憶の呼び戻しには適していないかもしれないことを理解しておく必要があります。

思い出した名前の平均割合
(グラフ)
グループＡ　グループＢ

◆解説◆

問1 24 ❶

「オックスフォード氏は[24]と信じている。」

❶ **「連続した反復練習は退屈だ」**

② 「用語の説明を読むことが役立つ」**≫本文にない。**

③ 「生徒は理科に関心がない」**≫本文にない。**

④ 「ワークブックで学習することが成功につながる」**≫オックスフォード氏の考えと反対の内容である。**

選択肢❶の continuous drilling は本文の repetitive learning を指す。本文・全訳の**問1**を言い換えた❶が正解。

問2 25 ❶

「リー氏が考察した研究では，生徒が最後の学習時間の[25]後にテストを受けた。」

❶ **「4週間」**

② 「直」

③ 「1日」

④ 「1週間」

本文・全訳の**問2**に書かれている 28 days を four weeks と言い換えた❶が正解。

問3 26 ❷ 27 ❺

「リー氏は，[26]間隔をあけた学習を含む，間隔学習を紹介しているが，それはオックスフォード氏が考察した[27]学習のデメリットを克服するためである。(各空欄に選択肢①～⑥から最適なものを選びなさい。)」

① 「文脈的」

❷ **「長期の」**[26]

③ 「固定された」

④ 「不定期の」

❺ **「集中した」**[27]

⑥ 「実用的な」

リー氏は，本文・全訳の**問3(1)**で，オックスフォード氏がとりあげたのは，反復学習法の中でも効果的でない massed learning「集中学習」であると述べているので，[27]には❺の massed が入る。さらにリー氏は本文・全訳の**問3(2)**で，反復学習法には，復習の間隔を長くする「間隔学習」もあると述べている。したがって，[26]には❷の extended が入る。

問4 28 ❶

「両方の筆者は，[28]が新しい情報を覚えるのに役に立つと同意している。」

❶ **「体験学習」**

② 「適切な休憩をとること」**≫本文にない。**

③ 「長期間の注目」**≫本文にない。**

④ 「ワークブックを用いた学習」**≫オックスフォード氏は反対し，リー氏は適切な方法での使用に同意している。**

本文・全訳の**問4(1)**に書かれているように，オックスフォード氏は「文脈的学習」という言葉を使っているが，その内容は「体験に基づいた学習」である。また，**問4(2)**にあるように，リー氏もその効果を認めている。したがって，❶が正解。

問5 29 ❷

「どの追加情報が，リー氏の間隔学習に関する主張をさらに裏付けるのに最適か。」[29]

① 「科学の授業を魅力的にする主な要因」**≫これは体験学習に関するものである。**

❷ **「間隔学習の最も効果的な間隔の長さ」**

③ 「生徒のワークブックが視覚教材を含むかどうか」**≫本文にない。**

④ 「なぜオックスフォード氏の生徒が情報をうまく記憶できなかったか」**≫すでにリー氏の記事に書かれている。**

リー氏はなぜ間隔学習が効果的なのかを説明したあと，本文・全訳の**問5**に，実験で間隔を1週間あけたグループの方が，1日あけたグループよりも，より良い学習結果が出たと紹介している。最も効果的な間隔に関する追加情報は，間隔学習の効果性を述べるリー氏の主張を裏付けることができるので，❷が正解。

【設問・選択肢の語句・表現】

問1 ❶ continuous 形 連続した

問1 ❶ drill 自 何度も練習する，訓練する

問3 overcome 他 ～を克服する

問3 ❷ extended 形 長期の

問5 ① attractive 形 魅力的な

第5問

第5問 (配点 15)

Your English teacher has told everyone in your class to find an inspirational story and present it to a discussion group, using notes. You have found a story written by a high school student in the UK.

Lessons from Table Tennis

Ben Carter

The ball flew at lightning speed to my backhand. It was completely unexpected and I had no time to react. I lost the point and the match. Defeat... Again! This is how it was in the first few months when I started playing table tennis. It was frustrating, but I now know that the sport taught me more than simply how to be a better athlete.

In middle school, I loved football. I was one of the top scorers, but I didn't get along with my teammates. The coach often said that I should be more of a team player. I knew I should work on the problem, but communication was just not my strong point. 問1(1)

I had to leave the football club when my family moved to a new town. I wasn't upset as I had decided to stop playing football anyway. My new school had a table tennis club, coached by the PE teacher, Mr Trent, and I joined that. To be honest, I chose table tennis because I thought it would be easier for me to play individually. 問1(2)

At first, I lost more games than I won. I was frustrated and often went straight home after practice, not speaking to anyone. 問3② One day, however, Mr Trent said to me, "You could be a good player, Ben, but you need to think more about your game. What do you think you need to do?" "I don't know," I replied, "focus on the ball more?" "Yes," Mr Trent continued, "but you also need to study your opponent's moves and adjust your play accordingly. Remember, your opponent is a person, not a ball." 問5①-1 This made a deep impression on me.

I deliberately modified my style of play, paying closer attention to my opponent's moves. 問3④ It was not easy, and took a lot of concentration. My efforts paid off, however, and my play improved. My confidence grew and I started staying behind more after practice. I was turning into a star player and my classmates tried to talk to me more than before. I thought that I was becoming popular, but our conversations seemed to end before they really got started. Although my play might have improved, my communication skills obviously hadn't.

【語句・表現】

l. 1 inspirational 形 心を動かす

l. 6 lightning 名 稲妻

l. 7 react 自 反応する

l. 9 frustrating 形 悔しい，イライラする

l.11 middle school（英国の）中学校

l.11 football 名〈英〉サッカー

l.12 get along with ～ ～と仲良くする

l.14 strong point 名 長所，得意なこと

l.16 upset 形 動揺して，腹を立てて

l.19 individually 副 個々に

l.24 focus on ～ ～に集中する

l.25 opponent 名 対戦相手

l.25 accordingly 副 それに応じて

l.26 make an impression 感銘を与える

l.28 deliberately 副 意図的に

l.28 modify 他 ～を変更する

l.30 pay off 報われる

l.30 confidence 名 自信

l.31 turn into ～ ～に変わる

My older brother Patrick was one of the few people I could communicate with well. One day, I tried to explain my problems with communication to him, but couldn't make him understand. We switched to talking about table tennis. 問 3⑤

問 2(1) 問 5①-2 問 5⑥ "What do you actually enjoy about it?" he asked me curiously. I said I loved (40) analysing my opponent's movements and making instant decisions about the next move. Patrick looked thoughtful. "That sounds like the kind of skill we use when we communicate," he said.

問 3③ At that time, I didn't understand, but soon after our conversation, I won a silver medal in a table tennis tournament. My classmates seemed really (45) pleased. One of them, George, came running over. "Hey, Ben!" he said, "Let's have a party to celebrate!" Without thinking, I replied, "I can't. I've got practice." He looked a bit hurt and walked off without saying anything else.

Why was he upset? I thought about this incident for a long time. Why did he suggest a party? Should I have said something different? A lot of questions 問 4 (50) came to my mind, but then I realised that he was just being kind. If I'd said, "Great idea. Thank you! Let me talk to Mr Trent and see if I can get some time off practice," then maybe the outcome would have been better. 問 2(2) At that moment Patrick's words made sense. Without attempting to grasp someone's intention, I wouldn't know how to respond.

(55) I'm still not the best communicator in the world, but I definitely feel more confident in my communication skills now than before. Next year, my friends and I are going to co-ordinate the table tennis league with other schools.

l.40 analyse（英）他 ～を分析する
l.40 instant 形 即時の
l.41 thoughtful 形 考え込んでいる
l.48 incident 名 出来事
l.51 see if ～ ～かどうか確かめる
l.52 off 前 ～を休んで
l.52 outcome 名 結果
l.53 make sense 意味がわかる
l.53 attempt to *do* …しようと努める
l.53 grasp 他 ～を把握する
l.54 intention 名 意図
l.54 respond 自 答える
l.57 co-ordinate 他 ～をコーディネートする

Your notes:

Lessons from Table Tennis

About the author (Ben Carter)

- Played football at middle school.
- Started playing table tennis at his new school because he [30].

Other important people

- Mr Trent: Ben's table tennis coach, who helped him improve his play.
- Patrick: Ben's brother, who [31].
- George: Ben's classmate, who wanted to celebrate his victory.

Influential events in Ben's journey to becoming a better communicator

Began playing table tennis → [32] → [33] → [34] → [35]

What Ben realised after the conversation with George

He should have [36].

メモ内 victory 名 勝利
メモ内 influential 形 影響力の大きい
メモ内 journey to becoming ～ ～になるための道筋

What we can learn from this story

- 37
- 38

◆全訳◆

あなたの英語の先生は，クラスの全員に，心を動かす話を見つけ，メモを使って討論グループで発表するように言いました。あなたは英国の高校生が書いた話を見つけました。

卓球からの教訓

ベン・カーター

ボールが稲妻のようなスピードで私のバックハンドに飛んできました。全く予想外のことで，反応する時間がありませんでした。私は点を失い，試合に負けました。敗北…またか！ 私が卓球を始めて最初の数カ月は，こんな感じでした。それは悔しかったけれども，そのスポーツは私に，単に強い運動選手になる方法以上のことを教えてくれたと，今は思っています。

中学校で，私はサッカーが大好きでした。問1(1) 私は得点王の1人でしたが，チームメイトとうまくやれませんでした。コーチはよく，私はもっとチームプレーヤーになるべきだと言いました。その問題に取り組むべきだとわかっていましたが，私はコミュニケーションが全く得意でなかったのです。

家族で新しい街に引っ越した時，私はサッカークラブをやめなければなりませんでした。どっちみちサッカーをやめると決めていたので，動揺しませんでした。新しい学校には，体育教師のトレント先生が指導する卓球クラブがあり，私は入部しました。問1(2) 正直なところ，1人でプレーする方が私には簡単だろうと思ったから卓球を選んだのです。

最初は，試合に勝つことよりも負けることの方が多かったです。イライラして，練習後に誰とも口をきかず，まっすぐ家に帰ることが多かったです。問3② 問5①-1 けれどもある日，トレント先生が「ベン，君は良い選手になれるかもしれないが，もっと試合について考える必要があるよ。何をする必要があると思う？」と言いました。「わかりません」と私は答えました。「もっとボールに集中することですか？」「そう」とトレント先生は続けました。「でも，対戦相手の動きを研究して，それに合わせて自分のプレーを調整することも必要だ。覚えていなさい，対戦相手は人間で，ボールではないと。」これは私に深い感銘を与えました。

問3④ 私は，対戦相手の動きに細心の注意を払い，自分のプレースタイルを意図的に変えました。それは簡単なことではないし，かなりの集中力が必要でした。しかし，努力は報われ，私のプレーは上達しました。自信がつき，もっと練習後に残り始めました。私はスター選手に変わっていき，クラスメイトは以前よりも私に話しかけようとしました。私は自分が人気者になっていると思いましたが，私たちの会話は本当に始まる前に終わっているように感じました。私のプレーは上達したかもしれないけれども，コミュニケーション能力は明らかに向上していませんでした。

兄のパトリックは，私がうまくコミュニケーションできる数少ない人の1人でした。ある日，自分のコミュニケーションの問題を兄に説明しようとしましたが，なかなか理解してもらえませんでした。問3⑤ 私たちは卓球の話に切り替えました。問2(1) 問5①-2 問5⑥「実のところ，卓球の何が楽しいの？」と彼は不思議そうにたずねました。私は，対戦相手の動きを分析し，次の動きを即時に決断するのが大好きだと言いました。パトリックは考え込んでいるようでした。「それはコミュニケーションをとる時に使うスキルに似ているようだね」と彼は言いました。

その時私はわからなかったのですが，この会話のあとすぐに，問3③ 私は卓球トーナメントで銀メダルをとりました。クラスメイトはとてもうれしそうでした。そのうちの1人のジョージが駆け寄ってきて，「おい，ベン！お祝いのパーティをしよう！」と言いました。何も考えないで，私は「だめなんだ。練習があるんだ。」と答えました。彼は少し傷ついた様子で，他に何も言わずに立ち去りました。

なぜ，彼は気落ちしたのだろう，私はこの出来事について長い間考えました。なぜ彼はパーティを提案したのだろう。私は何か違うことを言うべきだったのだろうか。たくさんの疑問が心に浮かびましたが，

問4 その時，彼は本当に優しいのだと気づいたのです。「いい考えだね，ありがとう！トレント先生に話して，練習を休めるかどうか確かめるよ。」と言っていたら，たぶん結果はもっとよかったでしょう。
問2(2) その瞬間，パトリックの言葉の意味がわかったのです。相手の意図を把握しようと努めなければ，どう答えていいかわからないでしょう。

まだまだ世界一コミュニケーション能力が高いとは言えませんが，間違いなく，今は以前よりも自分のコミュニケーションスキルに自信が持てるようになりました。来年は友達と私で，他校との卓球リーグをコーディネートする予定です。

あなたのメモ

卓球からの教訓

筆者（ベン・カーター）について
・中学校でサッカーをしていた。
・彼は［30］ので，新しい学校で卓球を始めた。

その他の重要人物
・トレント先生：ベンの卓球のコーチで，彼のプレーを向上させた。
・パトリック：ベンの兄で，［31］。
・ジョージ：ベンのクラスメイトで，彼の勝利を祝いたかった。

ベンがコミュニケーション上手になるための道筋で影響を与えた出来事
卓球を始めた→［32］→［33］→［34］→［35］

ベンがジョージとの会話のあとで気づいたこと
彼は［36］べきであった。

この物語から学べること
・［37］
・［38］

◆解説◆

問1 30 ❹

「［30］に最も適切な選択肢を選びなさい。」

① 「コミュニケーションに役立つだろうと信じた」
≫コミュニケーションが苦手だから卓球クラブに入った。

② 「学校で人気者になりたかった」**≫人気が出たのは，入部の目的ではなく結果である。**

③ 「簡単に試合に勝てると考えた」**≫本文にない。**

❹「チームスポーツをすることを避けたかった」

本文・全訳の**問1(1)**にあるように，ベンはチームスポーツが得意でなかった。だから，**問1(2)**にあるように，個人スポーツを選んだ。したがって，❹が正解。

問2 31 ❸

「［31］に最も適切な選択肢を選びなさい。」

① 「コミュニケーションについて何を楽しんでいるかたずねた」**≫卓球の何が楽しいのかをたずねた。**

② 「もっと自信を持つよう励ました」**≫本文にない。**

❸「彼が必要とする社交術を学ぶよう助けた」

④ 「学校の友達に何と言うべきだったのか教えた」
≫パトリックは教えていない。ベンが自分で考えた。

本文・全訳の**問2(1)**に書かれているように，パトリックは卓球とコミュニケーションの共通点を教えている。ベンはすぐには理解できなかったが**問2(2)**でその意味がわかり，その後コミュニケーションが上達している。communication skills をsocial skills と言い換えた❸が正解。

問3 32 ❷ 33 ❹ 34 ❺ 35 ❸

「5つの選択肢（①～⑤）から**4つ**を選び，起こった順に並べなさい。」［32］→［33］→［34］→［35］

① 「卓球のチャンピオンになった」**≫銀メダルをとったが，チャンピオンにはなっていない。**

❷「先生と上手にプレーする方法を話し合った」 ［32］

❸「彼を祝うパーティを断った」 ［35］

❹「対戦相手を研究し始めた」 ［33］

❺「卓球について兄と話した」 ［34］

ベンの文章では，起こったことが順に書かれている。❷～❺に該当する部分は本文・全訳の**問3②**から**問3⑤**である。

問4 36 ❸

「［36］に最も適切な選択肢を選びなさい。」

① 「友人の動機をもっと知るために質問する」**≫質問するべきだったとは書いていない。**

②「感謝の気持ちを表すために，トレント先生と他のクラスメイトをパーティに招待する」≫**本文にない。**

❸**「適切に行動できるように，友人の考え方を理解しようとする」**

④「上手なコミュニケーションのため，より良いチームプレーヤーになるよう懸命に練習する」≫**本文にない。**

ジョージとの会話のあとでベンが考え，その結果出た答えが本文・全訳の**問4**にある。やるべきことはジョージの気持ちを理解し，適切な行動を取る（練習を休めるか先生にたずねる）ことだったので，❸が正解。

問5 37 38 ❶，❺（順不同）

「37 と 38 に最も適切な選択肢を選びなさい。（順不同）」

❶**「周囲の人からのアドバイスは私たちが変わる助けになることができる。」**

②「上手なコミュニケーションができる人になるには，自信が重要だ。」≫**コミュニケーションができるようになってから自信がついたのであり，上手なコミュニケーションのために自信を持つのではない。**

③「友人に自分の意図を明確に伝えることが重要だ。」≫**自分の意図を明確に伝えることではなく，相手の意図を理解する事が大切だと書かれている。**

④「チームメイトがお互いに提供するサポートは役に立つ。」≫**本文にない。**

❺**「1つのことから学んだことを別のことに当てはめることができる。」**

本文・全訳の**問5①-1**のトレント先生のアドバイスがベンの卓球を上達させ，**問5①-2**＝**問5⑤**のパトリックのアドバイスが，ベンのコミュニケーションスキルを上達させたので，❶が正解。また，パトリックのアドバイスは，相手の動きに合わせて自分のプレーを調整する卓球の技術をコミュニケーションに適用することであり，ベンは実体験を通じてこのことが理解できている。したがって，❺が正解。

【設問・選択肢の語句・表現】

- **問3** ❸ in *one's* honour ～を祝って
- **問4** ① motivation 名 動機
- **問4** ② appreciation 名 感謝の気持ち
- **問4** ❸ point of view 考え方
- **問4** ❸ appropriately 副 適切に
- **問5** ❺ apply 他 ～を適用する

第6問A

第6問 （配点 24）

A You are in a discussion group in school. You have been asked to summarize the following article. You will speak about it, using only notes.

Collecting

Collecting has existed at all levels of society, across cultures and age groups since early times. Museums are proof that things have been collected, saved, and passed down for future generations. There are various reasons for starting a collection. For example, Ms. A enjoys going to yard sales every Saturday morning with her children. At yard sales, people sell unwanted things in front of their houses. One day, while looking for antique dishes, an unusual painting caught her eye and she bought it for only a few dollars. Over

【語句・表現】

- *l*. 1 summarize 他 ～を要約する
- *l*. 5 proof 名 証拠
- *l*. 6 pass down ～ ～を伝える
- *l*.10 catch *one's* eye ～の目に留まる
- *l*.10 over time 徐々に

time, she found similar pieces that left an impression on her, and she now has a modest collection of artwork, some of which may be worth more than she

問1

paid. One person's trash can be another person's treasure. Regardless of how someone's collection was started, it is human nature to collect things.

15 In 1988, researchers Brenda Danet and Tamar Katriel analyzed 80 years of studies on children under the age of 10, and found that about 90% collected something. This shows us that people like to gather things from an early age.

問2

Even after becoming adults, people continue collecting stuff. Researchers in the field generally agree that approximately one third of adults maintain this

20 behavior. Why is this? The primary explanation is related to emotions. Some

問3④

save greeting cards from friends and family, dried flowers from special events, seashells from a day at the beach, old photos, and so on. For others, their collection is a connection to their youth. They may have baseball cards, comic books, dolls, or miniature cars that they have kept since they were small.

25 Others have an attachment to history; they seek and hold onto historical documents, signed letters and autographs from famous people, and so forth.

For some individuals there is a social reason. People collect things such as pins to share, show, and even trade, making new friends this way. Others, like some holders of Guinness World Records, appreciate the fame they achieve for

30 their unique collection. Cards, stickers, stamps, coins, and toys have topped the "usual" collection list, but some collectors lean toward the more unexpected. In September 2014, Guinness World Records recognized Harry Sperl, of Germany, for having the largest hamburger-related collection in the world, with 3,724 items; from T-shirts to pillows to dog toys, Sperl's room is

35 filled with all things "hamburger." Similarly, Liu Fuchang, of China, is a collector of playing cards. He has 11,087 different sets.

Perhaps the easiest motivation to understand is pleasure. Some people start collections for pure enjoyment. They may purchase and put up paintings just to gaze at frequently, or they may collect audio recordings and old-

40 fashioned vinyl records to enjoy listening to their favorite music. This type of collector is unlikely to be very interested in the monetary value of their

問3⑥

treasured music, while others collect objects specifically as an investment. While it is possible to download certain classic games for free, having the same game unopened in its original packaging, in "mint condition," can make

45 the game worth a lot. Owning various valuable "collector's items" could ensure some financial security.

This behavior of collecting things will definitely continue into the distant future. Although the reasons why people keep things will likely remain the

- *l*.11 leave an impression on ～ ～に印象を残す
- *l*.12 modest 形 ささやかな
- *l*.13 trash 名 がらくた
- *l*.13 treasure 名 宝物
- *l*.13 regardless of ～ ～に関係なく
- *l*.17 gather 他 ～を集める
- *l*.18 stuff 名 物
- *l*.19 maintain 他 ～を維持する
- *l*.20 primary 形 一番目の
- *l*.23 youth 名 青春時代
- *l*.25 attachment to ～ ～への愛着
- *l*.25 seek 他 ～を探し求める
- *l*.26 autograph 名 （有名人の）サイン
- *l*.29 appreciate 他 ～の真価を認める
- *l*.29 fame 名 名声
- *l*.35 similarly 副 同様に
- *l*.36 playing cards トランプ
- *l*.38 purchase 他 ～を購入する
- *l*.38 put up ～ ～を飾る
- *l*.39 gaze at ～ ～をじっと見る
- *l*.40 vinyl 名 ビニール
- *l*.41 monetary 形 金銭的な
- *l*.42 treasured 形 貴重な，秘蔵の
- *l*.42 specifically 副 明確に
- *l*.42 investment 名 投資
- *l*.44 in mint condition 新品同様で
- *l*.45 ensure 他 ～を保証する
- *l*.47 distant 形 遠い

問4 same, advances in technology will have an influence on collections. As
50 technology can remove physical constraints, it is now possible for an individual to have vast digital libraries of music and art that would have been unimaginable 30 years ago. It is unclear, though, what other impacts technology will have on collections. Can you even imagine the form and scale that the next generation's collections will take?

l.49 advance 名 進歩
l.49 have an influence on ～ ～に影響を与える
l.50 physical constraint 物理的制約
l.51 vast 形 膨大な

Your notes:

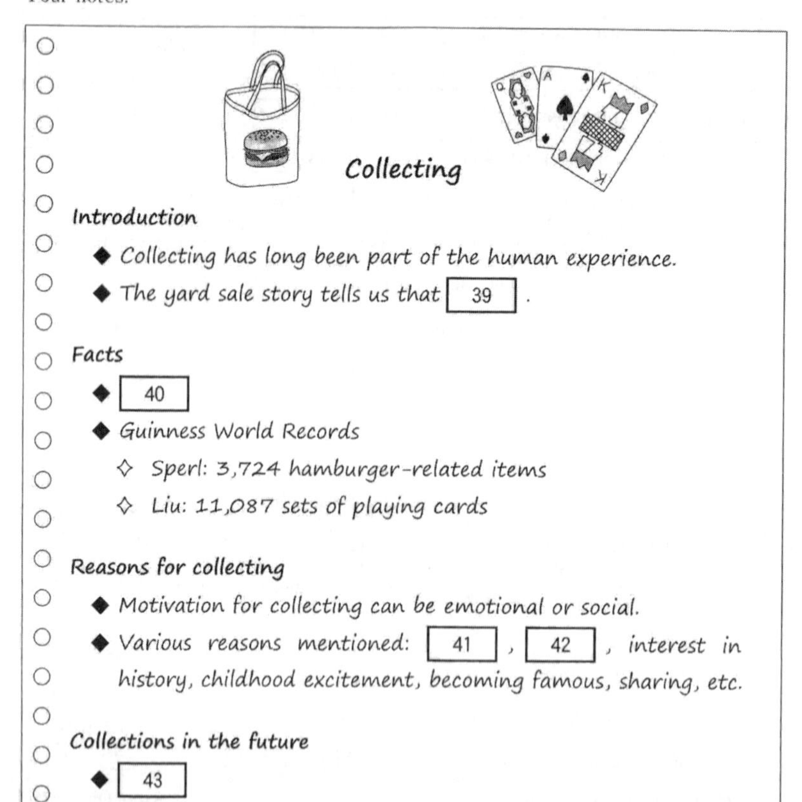

◆全訳◆

A　あなたは学校で討論グループに所属している。次の記事を要約するように頼まれている。あなたはその記事について，メモだけを見て話すことになっている。

収集

　収集は，昔から文化や年齢の層を問わず，社会のあらゆる階層に存在してきた。博物館は，物が集められ，保存され，後世の人々に伝えられてきた証である。コレクションを始めるにはさまざまな理由がある。例えば，Aさんは毎週土曜日の朝，子供たちと一緒にヤードセールに行くのを楽しんでいる。ヤードセールでは，人々が自分の家の前で不要品を売る。ある日，アンティークの皿を探していると，珍しい絵が目に留まり，それをたった数ドルで彼女は購入した。徐々に，彼女は印象に残る似た作品を見つけ，今ではささやかな美術品のコレクションを持ち，そのうちのいくつかは支払った金額以上の価値があるかもしれない。問1 ある人のがらくたが，別の人の宝物になりうる。コレクションを始めたきっかけは関係なく，物を集めるのは人間の本性である。

　1988年，研究者のブレンダ・ダネットとタマル・カトリエルは，10歳以下の子供についての80年間の研究を分析し，約90%が何かを集めていることがわかった。このことから，人は幼い頃から物を集めるのが好きだということがわかる。**問2** 大人になってからでさえも，人は物を集め続ける。この分野の研究者は，成人の約3分の1がこの行動を継続しているということに総じて賛同している。なぜだろうか。その第一の説明は，感情に関連する。**問3④** 友人や家族からのグリーティングカード，特別な出来事のドライフラワー，海辺で過ごした日の貝殻，古い写真などを保存する人もいる。人によっては，コレクションは自分の青春時代とのつながりである。彼らは，小さい頃からとっている野球カード，漫画，人形，ミニチュアカーなどを持っているかもしれない。歴史に対して愛着があり，歴史的な資料や有名人の署名入りの手紙やサインなどを探して持ち続ける人もいる。

一部の人には社会的な理由がある。他の人と共有したり，見せたり，あるいは交換したりするためにピンバッジなどの物を集め，このようにして新しい友人を作る人がいる。また，ギネス世界記録保持者のように，ユニークなコレクションを達成したことへの名声に価値を見出す人もいる。カード，ステッカー，切手，コイン，玩具などが「よくある」コレクションリストの上位にあるが，もっと意外な物に傾倒するコレクターもいる。2014年9月にギネス世界記録は，ドイツのハリー・シュペールさんが，世界最大のハンバーガー関連コレクション3,724点を持っていると認定した。Tシャツから枕，犬のおもちゃまで，シュペールさんの部屋には「ハンバーガー」のあらゆる物があふれている。同様に，中国のリウ・フーチャンさんはトランプのコレクターだ。それぞれ異なる11,087セットを所有している。

最もわかりやすい動機は楽しみだろう。純粋に楽しみのためにコレクションを始める人もいる。単に頻繁に眺めるために絵画を買って飾るかもしれないし，お気に入りの音楽を聞いて楽しむために録音された物や古めかしいビニール盤のレコードを収集するかもしれない。このタイプのコレクターは，秘蔵の音楽の金銭的価値にはあまり興味がないようだが，**問3⑥** 一方で，明確に投資として物を集める人もいる。特定の古典的なゲームを無料でダウンロードできる一方，オリジナルのパッケージが未開封の状態で，つまり「新品同様で」同じゲームを持っていたら，そのゲームは大いに価値が出るかもしれない。様々な価値のある「コレクターズアイテム」を所有することは，ある程度の経済的な安定を保証するかもしれない。

このような物を集めるという行動は，間違いなく遠い未来まで続くだろう。人々が物を保持する理由は同じままであろうが，**問4** 科学技術の進化はコレクションに影響を与えるだろう。科学技術が物理的制約を取り除くことができるので，30年前には想像もできなかったような膨大な音楽や美術のデジタル・ライブラリーを個人で持つことが，今や可能になった。しかし，科学技術がコレクションに与える他の影響については不明だ。次世代のコレクションが持つだろう形態と規模を，そもそも想像することができるだろうか。

あなたのメモ

収集

序論

◆収集は長い間，人間の経験の一部であった。

◆ヤードセールの話は，私たちに［39］ということを教えてくれる。

事実

◆［40］

◆ギネス世界記録

◇シュペール氏：3,724個のハンバーガー関連品

◇リウ氏：11,087セットのトランプ

収集の理由

◆収集の動機には，感情的なものと社会的なものがある。

◆言及された様々な理由：［41］，［42］，歴史への興味，子供時代に興奮したこと，有名になること，共有など。

未来のコレクション

◆［43］

◆解説◆

問1 39 ❸

「［39］に最も適切な選択肢を選びなさい。」

①「人々が物をコレクターに高額で物を売るのに絶好の場所はヤードセールだ」≫**本文にない。**

②「人々は品物を間違って評価し，がらくたに高いお金を払うことになる可能性がある」≫本文にない。

❸「ある人にとっては重要でない物でも，誰か他の人にとっては価値のある物かもしれない」

④「一度は収集して他の人の庭に捨てられた物が，他の人にとっては貴重かもしれない」≫「捨てられた物」ではなく「がらくた」が他人には貴重かもしれない。

本文・全訳の**問1**の trash と treasure を具体的な説明で言い換えた，❸が正解。

問2　40　❹

「40 に最も適切な選択肢を選びなさい。」

①「子供の約 3 分の 2 は普通の物を集めない。」≫10歳以下の子供の90%は何かを集めている。

②「大人の約 3 分の 1 が楽しみのために収集を始める。」≫収集を続ける大人が約 3 分の 1。

③「子供のおよそ10%は友達とよく似たコレクションを持っている。」≫本文にない。

❹「大体30%の人が，大人になっても収集を続ける。」

本文・全訳の**問2**参照。「約3分の1」を「大体30%」と言い換えた❹が正解。

問3　41　42　❹，❻（順不同）

「41 と 42 に最も適切な選択肢を選びなさい。（順不同）」

①「科学技術を進歩させるという願望」≫本文にない。

②「思いがけない機会を逃すことの不安」≫本文にない。

③「むなしさを満たすこと」≫本文にない。

❹「貴重な出来事を思い出させる物」

⑤「将来のための物の再使用」≫本文にない。

❻「ある種の利益追求」

本文・全訳の**問3④**にあげられた収集品は，家族や特別な出来事の思い出にまつわる物であり，これは❹に当てはまる。**問3⑥**には投資として金銭的価値が出そうな物を集めることが書かれており，❻に一致する。

問4　43　❶

「43 に最も適切な選択肢を選びなさい。」

❶「コレクションは規模や形態が変化し続けると思われる。」

②「新品同様のゲームのコレクターは，より多くのデジタルコピーを所有することになるだろう。」≫本文にない。

③「収集への情熱を失った人が再開するだろう。」≫本文にない。

④「科学技術の進歩で，収集の理由が変わるだろう。」≫収集の理由は変わらないだろうと書かれている。

本文・全訳の**問4**参照。科学技術の進化によって，デジタル・ライブラリーのような，30年前は想像もできなかった新しいコレクションが可能になったように，将来のコレクションの「形態と規模」は，科学技術によって想像できないほど変化するだろうと書いてある。したがって❶が正解。

【設問・選択肢の語句・表現】

問1 ② evaluate 他 ～を評価する
問2 ❹ roughly 副 大体
問3 ① desire 名 願望
問3 ❹ reminder 名 思い出させる人・物
問3 ❹ precious 形 貴重な
問3 ❻ profit 名 利益

第6問B

B　You are in a student group preparing for an international science presentation contest. You are using the following passage to create your part of the presentation on extraordinary creatures.

Ask someone to name the world's toughest animal, and they might say the Bactrian camel as it can survive in temperatures as high as 50℃, or the Arctic fox which can survive in temperatures lower than −58℃. However, both

【語句・表現】

l. 2 passage 名（文章の）一節
l. 3 extraordinary 形 驚異的な
l. 5 Bactrian camel フタコブラクダ
l. 5 survive 自 生き延びる

answers would be wrong as it is widely believed that the tardigrade is the toughest creature on earth.

Tardigrades, also known as water bears, are microscopic creatures, which
問4(1) 10 are between 0.1 mm to 1.5 mm in length. They live almost everywhere, from 6,000-meter-high mountains to 4,600 meters below the ocean's surface. They can even be found under thick ice and in hot springs. Most live in water, but some tardigrades can be found in some of the driest places on earth. One researcher reported finding tardigrades living under rocks in a desert without
15 any recorded rainfall for 25 years. All they need are a few drops or a thin
問2① layer of water to live in. When the water dries up, so do they. They lose all but three percent of their body's water and their metabolism slows down to 0.01% of its normal speed. The dried-out tardigrade is now in a state called "tun," a kind of deep sleep. It will continue in this state until it is once again
20 soaked in water. Then, like a sponge, it absorbs the water and springs back to life again as if nothing had happened. Whether the tardigrade is in tun for 1 week or 10 years does not really matter. The moment it is surrounded by
問4(2) water, it comes alive again. When tardigrades are in a state of tun, they are so tough that they can survive in temperatures as low as −272℃ and as high
25 as 151℃. Exactly how they achieve this is still not fully understood.

Perhaps even more amazing than their ability to survive on earth — they have been on earth for some 540 million years — is their ability to survive in
問4(3) space. In 2007, a team of European researchers sent a number of living tardigrades into space on the outside of a rocket for 10 days. On their return
30 to earth, the researchers were surprised to see that 68% were still alive. This
問2⑤ means that for 10 days most were able to survive X-rays and ultraviolet radiation 1,000 times more intense than here on earth. Later, in 2019, an
問5 Israeli spacecraft crashed onto the moon and thousands of tardigrades in a state of tun were spilled onto its surface. Whether these are still alive or not
35 is unknown as no one has gone to collect them — which is a pity.

問1① Tardigrades are shaped like a short cucumber. They have four short legs on each side of their bodies. Some species have sticky pads at the end of each leg, while others have claws. There are 16 known claw variations, which help
問1② identify those species with claws. All tardigrades have a place for eyes, but
40 not all species have eyes. Their eyes are primitive, only having five cells in total — just one of which is light sensitive.

問1③ Basically, tardigrades can be divided into those that eat plant matter, and those that eat other creatures. Those that eat vegetation have a ventral mouth — a mouth located in the lower part of the head, like a shark. The type
問1⑤ 45 that eats other creatures has a terminal mouth, which means the mouth is at
問3(1) the very front of the head, like a tuna. The mouths of tardigrades do not have

l.5 Arctic fox 北極ギツネ
l.7 tardigrade 名 クマムシ
l.9 microscopic 形 微細な
l.16 layer 名 層
l.16 so do S Sもそうである（doは直前の動詞を指す。）
l.16 all but ～を除いてすべて
l.17 metabolism 名 代謝
l.18 state 名 状態
l.20 soaked 形 びしょ濡れの
l.20 absorb 他 ～を吸収する
l.20 spring back to life 復活する，息を吹き返す
l.22 matter 自 大きな違いがある
l.31 ultraviolet radiation 紫外線放射
l.32 intense 形 強烈な
l.36 cucumber 名 キュウリ
l.38 claw 名（鳥・動物などの）爪
l.39 identify 他 ～を識別する
l.40 primitive 形 未発達の
l.40 cell 名 細胞
l.41 sensitive 形 感知できる
l.43 vegetation 名 植物
l.43 ventral 形 腹部の
l.45 terminal 形 末端の

teeth. They do, however, have two sharp needles, called stylets, that they use to pierce plant cells or the bodies of smaller creatures so the contents can be sucked out.

問3(2) 50 Both types of tardigrade have rather simple digestive systems. The mouth leads to the pharynx (throat), where digestive juices and food are mixed. Located above the pharynx is a salivary gland. This produces the juices that flow into the mouth and help with digestion. After the pharynx, there is a tube which transports food toward the gut. This tube is called the esophagus. The 55 middle gut, a simple stomach/intestine type of organ, digests the food and absorbs the nutrients. The leftovers then eventually move through to the anus.

Your presentation slides:

Tardigrades: Earth's Ultimate Survivors

1. Basic Information

- 0.1 mm to 1.5 mm in length
- shaped like a short cucumber
-
- 44
-
-

2. Habitats

- live almost everywhere
- extreme environments such as...
  - ✓ 6 km above sea level
  - ✓ 4.6 km below sea level
  - ✓ in deserts
  - ✓ −272℃ to 151℃
  - ✓ in space (possibly)

3. Secrets to Survival

"tun" ⇔ active

- 45
- 46

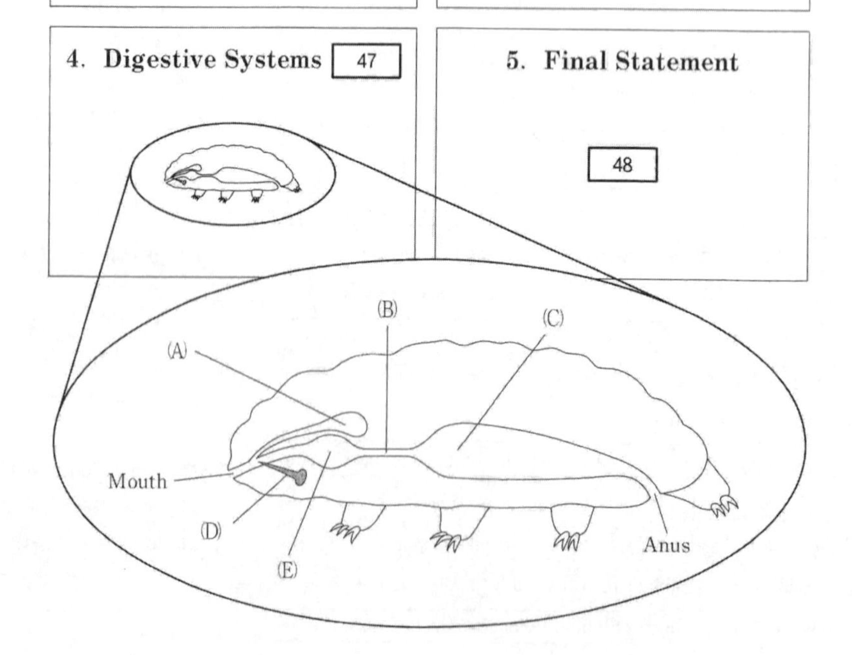

l.47 stylet 图 口針
l.49 suck out ～ ～を吸い出す
l.50 digestive system 消化器官
l.51 pharynx 图 咽頭
l.51 digestive juice 消化液
l.52 salivary gland 唾液腺
l.53 digestion 图 消化
l.54 gut 图 腸
l.54 esophagus 图 食道
l.55 middle gut 图 中腸
l.55 intestine 图 腸
l.55 organ 图 臓器
l.56 nutrient 图 栄養物
l.56 anus 图 肛門

スライド内 ultimate 形 最高の
スライド内 habitat 图 生息環境
スライド内 extreme 形 極端な
スライド内 statement 图 意見

◆全訳◆

B　あなたは，国際科学プレゼンテーションコンテストの準備をしている学生グループに所属している。あなたは，驚異的な〔非凡な〕生物に関するプレゼンテーションの自分の担当部分を作成するのに，次の一節を使用している。

誰かに世界最強の動物の名前を挙げるよう頼んでみなさい。すると50℃もの高温でも生き延びられるフタコブラクダか，－58℃以下の気温でも生き延びられるホッキョクギツネと答えるかもしれない。しかし，どちらの答えも間違っているだろう。クマムシが地球上で最も強い生物であると広く信じられているからだ。

クマムシは水中のクマとも知られているが，体長0.1mmから1.5mmほどの微細な生物だ。**問4(1)** 標高6,000mの山から海面下4,600mまで，ほとんどどこにでも生息している。厚い氷の下や温泉の中でさえ見つけることができる。ほとんどのクマムシは水中に生息しているが，地球上で最も乾燥した場所で見つかるものもある。ある研究者は，25年間一度も降雨記録がない砂漠の岩の下にクマムシが生息しているのを発見したと報告した。クマムシが必要とするのは，生きるための数滴の水，あるいは薄い水の層だけである。**問2①** 水がすっかり乾くとクマムシも乾く。体内の水が3%を除いてすべてなくなると，クマムシの代謝は通常の速さの0.01%まで低下する。干からびたクマムシは今や「乾眠」と呼ばれる，一種の深い眠りの状態になる。再び水で十分濡れるまで，この状態であり続けるだろう。それから，スポンジのように水を吸収し，何事も起こらなかったかのように復活するのだ。クマムシが乾眠だったのが1週間でも10年でも大きな違いはない。水に囲まれた瞬間に生き返るのだ。**問4(2)** 乾眠状態でいる時，クマムシはとても頑強なので，－272℃の低温から151℃の高温まで生き延びることができる。一体どうやってこのようなことを成し遂げるのかは，まだ完全には解明されていない。

おそらく，クマムシの地球で生存する能力（クマムシは約5億4千万年間ずっと地球上に生息し続けている）よりもさらに驚くべきことは，宇宙空間でも生存できるクマムシの能力である。**問4(3)** 2007年，ヨーロッパの研究者チームは，たくさんの生きているクマムシをロケットの外側に搭載して10日間宇宙へ送った。地球に戻ってきた時，研究者たちは68%がまだ生きているのを見て驚いた。**問2⑤** つまり，ここ地球よりも1000倍も強いX線と紫外線放射に，10日間大多数が耐えることができたのだ。**問5** その後，2019年にイスラエルの宇宙船が月に衝突し，数千匹の乾眠状態のクマムシが月面にばらまかれた。これらがまだ生きているかどうかは，誰もまだ採集に行っていないので不明であり，残念なことだ。

クマムシは，短いキュウリのような形をしている。**問1①** 体の両側にそれぞれ4本の短い脚がある。それぞれの脚の先端に粘着性のパッドがある種もあれば，爪がある種もある。知られているもので16種類の爪があり，爪のある種を識別するのに役立つ。**問1②** すべてのクマムシに目のための場所があるが，すべての種に目があるわけではない。クマムシの目は未発達で，合計で5つの細胞しかなく，そのうち1つだけが光を感知できる。

問1③ 基本的にクマムシは，植物を食べる種と，他の生物を食べる種に分類できる。植物を食べる種は，サメのように頭部の下位に位置する口，腹部口を持っている。他の生物を食べる種は末端口を持っている。つまり，マグロのように頭の一番前に口がある。**問1⑤** **問3(1)** クマムシの口には歯がない。しかし実は口針と呼ばれる2本の鋭く尖ったものを持っており，植物細胞や比較的小さな生き物の体に穴を開けるために使うので，その中身を吸い出すことができる。

問3(2) どちらの種のクマムシもかなり単純な消化器官を持つ。口は咽頭（のど）に通じており，そこで消化液と食物が混ぜ合わされる。咽頭の上には，唾液腺がある。これは口の中に流れ込む液体を作り出し，消化を助ける。咽頭の先には，食べ物を腸へ運ぶ管がある。この管は食道と呼ばれる。中腸は，単純な胃と腸のような臓器で，食べ物を消化し栄養を吸収する。それから食べ残しは最終的に肛門へと進んでいく。

あなたの発表スライド

クマムシ：
地球最高の生存者

1. 基本情報
・全長0.1mm～1.5mm
・短いキュウリのような形をしている
・

·

· 44

·

2. 生息環境

・ほとんどどこにでも生息している

・以下のような極端な環境

✓海抜6 km

✓海面下4.6km

✓砂漠

✓ −272℃〜151℃

✓宇宙空間（可能性あり）

3. 生き残るための秘訣

「乾眠」⇔活発

· 45

· 46

4. 消化器官 47

（図中） 口　　肛門

5. 最終意見

48

◆解説◆

問1 44 ❹

「44 に含むべき**でない**のは次のうちどれか。」

①「8本の短い脚」≫**体の両側にそれぞれ4本の短い脚。**

②「目が見えないか見えるかのどちらか」≫**本文に当てはまる。**

③「植物を食べる，または生き物を食べる」≫**本文に当てはまる。**

❹**「16種類の異なる足のタイプ」**

⑤「歯ではなく2本の口針」≫**本文に当てはまる。**

本文・全訳の**問1①，②，③，⑤**によると，❹以外はすべて本文にある。したがって，含むべきでないのは❹。足のタイプは，粘着性パッドのある種と爪のある種の2種類。16種類なのは爪。

問2 45 46 ❶，❺（順不同）

「**生き残るための秘訣**のスライド用に，クマムシが生き残るために最も役立つ特徴を2つ選びなさい。（順不同）」 45 46

❶**「乾燥した環境では，代謝が通常の1%未満に落ちる。」**

②「乾眠状態のクマムシは151℃を超える温度でも生存できる。」≫**151℃まで生きることができると書いてあるが，それ以上についてはわからない。**

③「乾眠状態は，クマムシの体内の水分が0.01%を超えると終わる。」≫**体内の水分が3%以下で乾眠になると書いてある。**

④「サメのような口のおかげで，他の生物を食べやすくなる。」≫**サメのような口をしたクマムシは，植物を食べる。**

❺**「非常に厳しいレベルの放射に耐える能力がある。」**

本文・全訳の**問2①**に代謝は通常の0.01％まで低下するとあり，0.01％は1％未満に含まれるので❶が正解。**問2⑤**に一致するので❺も正解。1,000倍を❺では「非常に厳しい」と言い換えている。

問3 47 ❸

「**消化器官**のスライド用に，クマムシのイラストの抜けている名前を完成させなさい。」 47

①「(A) 食道　(B) 咽頭　(C) 中腸　(D) 口針　(E) 唾液腺」

②「(A) 咽頭　(B) 口針　(C) 唾液腺　(D) 食道　(E) 中腸」

❸**「(A) 唾液腺　(B) 食道　(C) 中腸　(D) 口針 (E) 咽頭」**

④「(A) 唾液腺　(B) 中腸　(C) 口針　(D) 食道　(E) 咽頭」

⑤「(A) 口針　(B) 唾液腺　(C) 咽頭　(D) 中腸　(E) 食道」

本文・全訳の**問3(1)**から，Dの尖ったものが口針だとわかる。**問3(2)**から，口からつながる咽頭はE，咽頭の上のAが唾液腺，咽頭の先の管（B）が食道，さらに食べ物は中腸（＝C）に届き，肛門に行くことがわかる。よって❸が正解。

問4 48 ❹

「最後のスライドに最適な意見はどれか。」

①「クマムシは何千年もの間，地上と宇宙で最も過

酷な環境を生き延びてきた。クマムシは人間よりも長生きするだろう。」≫地球に５億４千万年いる。宇宙に行ったのは2007年以降である。

② 「クマムシは宇宙から来て，ホッキョクギツネやフタコブラクダの限界を超えた気温でも生きられる。だからきっと人類よりも強いだろう。」≫宇宙から来たとは，本文に書かれていない。

③ 「クマムシは，疑いなく地球で最も強い生き物だ。山の頂上，海の底，温泉の湯で生きることができ，月でも繁栄できる。」≫月で繁栄できるかどうかは不明。

❹ 「クマムシは地球上で最も過酷な状況を生き抜いてきて，少なくとも一度は宇宙へ旅した。この注目に値する生物は人類より長生きするだろう。」

本文・全訳の**問４(1)**・**問４(2)**に書かれているように，クマムシは地球の過酷な状況で生きている。また，**問４(3)**にあるように，宇宙にも行っている。この２点に一致する❹が正解。文の後半部分は本文にないが，クマムシの強さから導かれるスライド作成者の意見である。

問５　49　❹

「クマムシを宇宙に送ることについて，何が推察できるか。」 49

① 「クマムシが宇宙で生きていけるかどうかを解明することは，一度も重要だと考えられなかった。」≫宇宙に送り，生存できるか実験をしている。

② 「クマムシは，数百万年間地球上にいる他の生物と同様に，Ｘ線や紫外線に耐えることができる。」≫他の生物ができるかどうかは記述がない。

③ 「イスラエルの研究者は，これほど多くのクマムシが過酷な宇宙の環境を生き抜くとは予期していなかった。」≫クマムシを宇宙に送って生存を確認して驚いたのはヨーロッパの研究者。

❹ 「クマムシが月面で生存できるかどうか誰も調べに行っていない理由が，筆者の関心を引いた。」

最初に，本文と一致している部分を確認する。本文・全訳の**問５**に，クマムシは事故で月に残されたが，誰も生存を調べるために採集に行っていないことが書かれ，筆者は「残念だ」と感じている。ここから筆者の「なぜ誰も調べに行っていないのか」と嘆く気持ちが推察できる。したがって❹が正解。

【設問・選択肢の語句・表現】

問１ ❺ A rather than B　BではなくA〔よりむしろ〕A
問２ feature 名 特徴
問２ ② exceed 他 ～を超える
問２ ③ cease 自 終わる
問２ ❺ withstand 他 ～に耐える
問４ ③ thrive 自 繁栄する
問４ ❹ remarkable 形 注目に値する
問４ ❹ outlive 他 ～より長生きする
問５ infer 他 ～を推察する